MISERANDO ATQUE ELIGENDO

Dear families,
Listen to the Word of God,
meditate on it together,
pray with it,
let the Lord fill your lives
with mercy.

Franciscus

The coat of arms of Pope Francis retains the design used when he was Archbishop of Buenos Aires, with the addition of the papal symbols of a bishop's miter and crossed keys bound by a red cord.

The shield has a blue field. In the center is the emblem of the Pope's religious order, the Society of Jesus: a radiant sun with a cross and the letters IHS (the monogram of Jesus) in red, and three black nails. Below this is a gold star, symbolizing the Virgin Mary, and a cluster of spikenard flowers, symbolizing St Joseph.

The Latin motto beneath the crest is "miserando atque eligendo," meaning approximately "lowly but chosen." Translated literally, it reads, "by having mercy, by choosing him." It is taken from a homily of the Venerable Bede on the call of Saint Matthew the tax collector to be an Apostle. Pope Francis was first called to religious life at age 17 on the Feast of St Matthew.

Archdiocese of Philadelphia
Office of the Archbishop
222 North 17th Street
Philadelphia, PA 19103-1299

September 2015

Dear friends,

All four of the Gospels are rich encounters with the Word of God.
But for many readers, Luke is the Evangelist who speaks most
movingly with the voice of God's mercy. Only in Luke do we find
three of Jesus' greatest expressions of love: the parables of the
Prodigal Son and the Good Samaritan, and his words on the cross to
the "Good Thief."

The Gospel you have in your hands – a wonderful gift from the
American Bible Society – is a reminder of God's tenderness for you
personally; an invitation to walk with Jesus Christ on the pathway
home to heaven. Read it. Pray over it. Treasure it.

May God bless you and those you love during the World Meeting of
Families, and every day thereafter.

Your brother in the Lord,

+ Charles J. Chaput, o.f.m.

Most Reverend Charles J. Chaput, O.F.M. Cap.
Archbishop of Philadelphia

INTRODUCTION

THE GOOD NEWS
of MERCY *in the* FAMILY

Dear families,

I have the great joy of introducing this edition of the Gospel of Luke, a gift from Pope Francis for families around the world on the occasion of the VIII World Meeting in Philadelphia.

Our hope is that this Gospel will accompany the entire Jubilee Year of Mercy that, in accordance with the Holy Father's desire, will begin in a few weeks: Luke is the Gospel, the Good News, of God's mercy for the life of each person and for our families.

THE GOSPEL IN THE FAMILY

Every generation of Christians—including ours—is called to take this little book in hand. For the Gospel is the Church's strength; it is the word from which She was born and by which She lives. In fact, Christianity began when the Word became flesh in Mary's womb. She is the first among believers, and she was immediately designated as such by Elizabeth: "blessed is she who believed that there would be a fulfillment of what was spoken to her by the Lord" (Lk 1:45). Later, after Mary, came the first disciples. When they received Jesus' word, a new fellowship began—we could say a "new family," that of Jesus and his disciples. After Pentecost, the Gospel began to spread through the homes of the Christian families. In short, at the beginning of the first millennium, the path of the Gospel was marked by listening in families.

Dear families, I think we too should do what was done at the beginning of Christianity: take the Gospel in our hands, in our own families, and re-weave a new brotherhood between people, new solidarity between families, in order to transmit the "Good News" of God's love for all. At the opening the Great Jubilee in 2000, St. John Paul II exhorted Christians to enter "into the new millennium with the book of the Gospel!" With the same passion that led him as pilgrim of the Gospel throughout the world, he added: "Let us take up this book! Receive it from the Lord, who continually offers it to us through his Church (cf. Rev 10:8). Let us devour it (cf. Rev 10:9) so that it may become the life of our lives. Let us savor it deeply: it will make demands, but it will also give us joy, because it is sweet as honey (cf. Rev 10:9–10). Filled with hope, we will be able to share it with every man and woman we meet on our way."

Pope Francis exhorts us to go in the same direction: Take the Gospel in hand! He said this to us in the beautiful Letter entitled "The Joy of the Gospel" (*Evangelii Gaudium*). Yes, it is essential to take up the Gospel and listen with renewed attention, if we want a more fraternal and human world, and greater solidarity. The insecurity and fear that are marking the life of our world, the incredible injustices that destroy many people's lives, the violence that seems to spread without restraint even inside our homes, the continuous conflicts and wars that are claiming innocent victims, can be overcome only through the Gospel. For this reason Pope Francis wishes to give a million copies of this book to the families of the world's five major cities: Havana (Cuba), Hanoi (Vietnam), Kinshasa (Congo), Marseille (France), and Sydney (Australia). In places where the urban context and its suburbs seem to make human coexistence even more difficult, the Pope wants Jesus' Word to resonate more strongly.

DAILY EXERCISE

Let us read a small passage of the Gospel each day. We will be compelled to enter into Jesus' heart and days, to follow him on his travels; we will share his compassion for all, and side with him in his tenderness for the small and the weak; we will be moved by his compassion as he accompanies the poor; and we will weep when we see how much he loved us; finally, we will rejoice in his resurrection, which has definitively defeated evil. We will know and love him more.

Remember to do this truly each day. We are daily submerged by words, pictures, messages, invitations... And not all messages are good; only a few help us to live. Then, at home, there is the risk that for various reasons we stop talking with each other or, even if there are no "flying dishes," some words that fly, sometimes doing more harm than dishes. In any case, we all feel the need for good words that touch our hearts. Now, the Gospel is the word that reaches the heart. In the Lord's Prayer, we ask God to give us "our daily bread." Jesus' words are the "living bread from heaven," offered to us daily. This is the best bread. It nourishes the heart and the body.

Dear families, reading the Gospel together in the family is one of the most beautiful and effective ways to pray. The Lord particularly likes it. Do you remember the episode of Martha and Mary? When Martha was annoyed at seeing Mary listening to Jesus, he pointed out that Mary had "chosen the better part," the "only thing necessary." It is easy for all of us to be overwhelmed, like Martha was, by all the things that have to be done, the issues to be resolved, and the difficulties to be overcome. Today as well, Jesus says to us, "Mary has chosen the better part" (Lk 10:42). This little book will help to make listening to the Gospel the "best part" of our day, the "best part" of all the days of the year.

We need to listen. The first step in Christian prayer is listening to Jesus who speaks to us. Yes, dear families, before multiplying our words in prayer to the Lord, let us listen to those He says to us. Every day. Let us listen to them, and we will have the same experience as the two disciples of Emmaus, who felt their hearts warmed and the need to stay with him. Listening turns into prayer, and the encounter with Jesus reilluminates our lives.

Of course, we must gather together and keep silence for a moment in his presence. We know how difficult it has become to find a moment of silence and prayer. However, it is essential. We could say that daily prayer is our way of "praying tirelessly." Yes, praying each day with the Gospel is our way of praying always.

Therefore, we need to find a moment to be together—perhaps before a meal, or at the end of the day, or even at the beginning, or in other moments. What matters is choosing five minutes to pray together briefly but in an effective way.

After the sign of the cross and a short invocation to the Holy Spirit, asking him to enter into our hearts and enlighten our minds, we read a little passage, we offer a simple explanation for the children, and share the thoughts that listening to this text inspires; at this point, we ask each other for whom we want to pray in a special way, and we conclude by reciting the Lord's Prayer together and thanking the Lord for the gift of his Word. Let us, then, not forget to determine together some small and simple way in which this word can mark our lives.

Dear families, while warmly thanking American Bible Society for permitting the creation of this book, I heartily wish you that the first result of these intense days spent together in Philadelphia may be the decision to allow God's Word to live in your houses and in those of your city.

+ Vincenzo Paglia

Archbishop Vincenzo Paglia
President of the Pontifical Council for the Family

THE GOSPEL
ACCORDING TO LUKE

Nihil Obstat

> Stephen J. Hartegen, O.F.M., L.S.S.
> Censor Deputatus

Imprimatur

> +James A. Hickey, S.T.D., J.C.D.
> Archbishop of Washington
> August 27, 1986

INTRODUCTION

The Gospel according to Luke is the first part of a two-volume work that continues the biblical history of God's dealings with humanity found in the Old Testament, showing how God's promises to Israel have been fulfilled in Jesus and how the salvation promised to Israel and accomplished by Jesus has been extended to the Gentiles. The stated purpose of the two volumes is to provide Theophilus and others like him with certainty—assurance—about earlier instruction they have received (Lk 1:4). To accomplish his purpose, Luke shows that the preaching and teaching of the representatives of the early church are grounded in the preaching and teaching of Jesus, who during his historical ministry (Acts 1:21–22) prepared his specially chosen followers and commissioned them to be witnesses to his resurrection and to all else that he did (Acts 10:37–42). This continuity between the historical ministry of Jesus and the ministry of the apostles is Luke's way of guaranteeing the fidelity of the Church's teaching to the teaching of Jesus.

Luke's story of Jesus and the church is dominated by a historical perspective. This history is first of all salvation history. God's divine plan for human salvation was accomplished during the period of Jesus, who through the events of his life (Lk 22:22) fulfilled the Old Testament prophecies (Lk 4:21; 18:31; 22:37; 24:26–27, 44), and this salvation is now extended to all humanity in the period of the church (Acts 4:12). This salvation history, moreover, is a part of human history. Luke relates the story of Jesus and the church to events in contemporary Palestinian (Lk 1:5; 3:1–2; Acts 4:6) and Roman (Lk 2:1–2; 3:1; Acts 11:28; 18:2, 12) history for, as Paul says in Acts 26:26, "this was not done in a corner." Finally, Luke relates the story of Jesus and the church to contemporaneous church history. Luke is concerned with presenting Christianity as a legitimate form of worship in the Roman world, a religion that is capable of meeting the spiritual needs of a world empire like that of Rome. To this end, Luke depicts the Roman governor Pilate declaring Jesus innocent of any wrongdoing three times (Lk 23:4, 14, 22). At the same time Luke argues in Acts that Christianity is the logical development and proper fulfillment of Judaism and is therefore deserving of the same toleration and freedom traditionally accorded Judaism by Rome (Acts 13:16–41; 23:6–9; 24:10–21; 26:2–23).

The prominence given to the period of the church in the story has important consequences for Luke's interpretation of the teachings of Jesus. By presenting the time of the church as a distinct phase of salvation history, Luke accordingly shifts the early Christian emphasis away from the expectation of an imminent parousia to the day-to-day concerns of the Christian community in the world. He does this in the gospel by regularly emphasizing the words "each day" (Lk 9:23; cf. Mk 8:34; Lk 11:3; 16:19; 19:47) in the sayings of Jesus. Although Luke still believes the parousia to be a reality that will come unexpectedly (Lk 12:38, 45–46), he is more concerned with presenting the words and deeds of Jesus as guides for the conduct of Christian disciples in the interim period between the ascension and the parousia and with presenting Jesus himself as the model of Christian life and piety.

Throughout the gospel, Luke calls upon the Christian disciple to identify with the master Jesus, who is caring and tender toward the poor and lowly, the outcast, the sinner, and the afflicted, toward all those who recognize their dependence on God (Lk 4:18; 6:20–23; 7:36–50; 14:12–14; 15:1–32; 16:19–31; 18:9–14; 19:1–10; 21:1–4), but who is severe toward the proud and self-righteous, and particularly toward those who place their material wealth before the service of God and his people (Lk 6:24–26; 12:13–21; 16:13–15, 19–31; 18:9–14, 15–25; cf. Lk 1:50–53). No gospel writer is more concerned than Luke with the mercy and compassion of Jesus (Lk 7:41–43; 10:29–37; 13:6–9; 15:11–32). No gospel writer is more concerned with the role of the Spirit in the life of Jesus and the Christian disciple (Lk 1:35, 41; 2:25–27; 4:1, 14, 18; 10:21; 11:13; 24:49), with the importance of prayer (Lk 3:21; 5:16; 6:12; 9:28; 11:1–13; 18:1–8), or with Jesus' concern for women (Lk 7:11–17, 36–50; 8:2–3; 10:38–42). While Jesus calls all humanity to repent (Lk 5:32; 10:13; 11:32; 13:1–5; 15:7–10; 16:30; 17:3–4; 24:47), he is particularly demanding of those who would be his disciples. Of them he demands absolute and total detachment from family and material possessions (Lk 9:57–62; 12:32–34; 14:25–35). To all who respond in faith and repentance to the word Jesus preaches, he brings salvation (Lk 2:30–32; 3:6; 7:50; 8:48, 50; 17:19; 19:9) and peace (Lk 2:14; 7:50; 8:48; 19:38, 42) and life (Lk 10:25–28; 18:26–30).

Early Christian tradition, from the late second century on, identifies the author of this gospel and of the Acts of the Apostles as Luke, a Syrian from Antioch, who is mentioned in the New Testament in Col 4:14, Phlm 24 and 2 Tm 4:11. The prologue of the gospel makes it clear that Luke is not part of the first generation of Christian disciples but is himself dependent upon the traditions he received from those who were eyewitnesses and ministers of the word (Lk 1:2). His two-volume work marks him as someone who was highly literate both in the Old Testament traditions according to the Greek versions and in Hellenistic Greek writings.

Among the likely sources for the composition of this gospel (Lk 1:3) were the Gospel of Mark, a written collection of sayings of Jesus known also to the author of the Gospel of Matthew (Q; see Introduction to Matthew), and other special traditions that were used by Luke alone among the gospel writers. Some hold that Luke used Mark only as a complementary source for rounding out the material he took from other traditions. Because of its dependence on the Gospel of Mark and because details in Luke's Gospel (Lk 13:35a; 19:43–44; 21:20; 23:28–31) imply that the author was acquainted with the destruction of the city of Jerusalem by the Romans in A.D. 70, the Gospel of Luke is dated by most scholars after that date; many propose A.D. 80–90 as the time of composition.

Luke's consistent substitution of Greek names for the Aramaic or Hebrew names occurring in his sources (e.g., Lk 23:33; Mk 15:22; Lk 18:41; Mk 10:51), his omission from the gospel of specifically Jewish Christian concerns found in his sources (e.g., Mk 7:1–23), his interest in Gentile Christians (Lk 2:30–32; 3:6, 38; 4:16–30; 13:28–30; 14:15–24; 17:11–19; 24:47–48), and his incomplete knowledge of Palestinian geography, customs, and practices are among the characteristics of this gospel that suggest that Luke was a non-Palestinian writing to a non-Palestinian audience that was largely made up of Gentile Christians.

The principal divisions of the Gospel according to Luke are the following:

I. The Prologue (1:1–4)
II. The Infancy Narrative (1:5–2:52)
III. The Preparation for the Public Ministry (3:1–4:13)
IV. The Ministry in Galilee (4:14–9:50)
V. The Journey to Jerusalem. Luke's Travel Narrative (9.51–19.27)
VI. The Teaching Ministry in Jerusalem (19:28–21:38)
VII. The Passion Narrative (22:1–23:56)
VIII. The Resurrection Narrative (24:1–53)

I. THE PROLOGUE*

1 ¹Since many have undertaken to compile a narrative of the events that have been fulfilled among us,ᵃ ²just as those who were eyewitnesses from the beginning and ministers of the word have handed them down to us,ᵇ ³I too have decided, after investigating everything accurately anew, to write it down in an orderly sequence for you, most excellent Theophilus, ⁴so that you may realize the certainty of the teachings you have received.

II. THE INFANCY NARRATIVE†

Announcement of the Birth of John. ⁵In the days of Herod, King of Judea,‡ there was a priest named Zechariah of the priestly division of Abijah; his wife was from the daughters of Aaron, and her name was Elizabeth.ᶜ ⁶Both were righteous in the eyes of God, observing all the commandments and ordinances of the Lord blamelessly. ⁷But they had no child,§ because Elizabeth was barren and both were advanced in years.ᵈ ⁸Once when he was serving as priest in his division's turn before

---

* [1:1–4] The Gospel according to Luke is the only one of the synoptic gospels to begin with a literary prologue. Making use of a formal, literary construction and vocabulary, the author writes the prologue in imitation of Hellenistic Greek writers and, in so doing, relates his story about Jesus to contemporary Greek and Roman literature. Luke is not only interested in the words and deeds of Jesus, but also in the larger context of the birth, ministry, death, and resurrection of Jesus as the fulfillment of the promises of God in the Old Testament. As a second- or third-generation Christian, Luke acknowledges his debt to earlier **eyewitnesses** and **ministers of the word**, but claims that his contribution to this developing tradition is a complete and accurate account, told in an orderly manner, and intended to provide Theophilus ("friend of God," literally) and other readers with certainty about earlier teachings they have received.

† [1:5–2:52] Like the Gospel according to Matthew, this gospel opens with an infancy narrative, a collection of stories about the birth and childhood of Jesus. The narrative uses early Christian traditions about the birth of Jesus, traditions about the birth and circumcision of John the Baptist, and canticles such as the Magnificat (Lk 1:46–55) and Benedictus (Lk 1:67–79), composed of phrases drawn from the Greek Old Testament. It is largely, however, the composition of Luke who writes in imitation of Old Testament birth stories, combining historical and legendary details, literary ornamentation and interpretation of scripture, to answer in advance the question, "Who is Jesus Christ?" The focus of the narrative, therefore, is primarily christological. In this section Luke announces many of the themes that will become prominent in the rest of the gospel: the centrality of Jerusalem and the temple, the journey motif, the universality of salvation, joy and peace, concern for the lowly, the importance of women, the presentation of Jesus as savior, Spirit-guided revelation and prophecy, and the fulfillment of Old Testament promises. The account presents parallel scenes (diptychs) of angelic announcements of the birth of John the Baptist and of Jesus, and of the birth, circumcision, and presentation of John and Jesus. In this parallelism, the ascendency of Jesus over John is stressed: John is prophet of the Most High (Lk 1:76); Jesus is Son of the Most High (Lk 1:32). John is great in the sight of the Lord (Lk 1:15); Jesus will be Great (a LXX attribute, used absolutely, of God) (Lk 1:32). John will go before the Lord (Lk 1:16–17); Jesus will be Lord (Lk 1:43; 2:11).

‡ [1:5] **In the days of Herod, King of Judea:** Luke relates the story of salvation history to events in contemporary world history. Here and in Lk 3:1–2 he connects his narrative with events in Palestinian history; in Lk 2:1–2 and Lk 3:1 he casts the Jesus story in the light of events of Roman history. Herod the Great, the son of the Idumean Antipater, was declared "King of Judea" by the Roman Senate in 40 B.C., but became the undisputed ruler of Palestine only in 37 B.C. He continued as king until his death in 4 B.C. **Priestly division of Abijah:** a reference to the eighth of the twenty-four divisions of priests who, for a week at a time, twice a year, served in the Jerusalem temple.

§ [1:7] **They had no child:** though childlessness was looked upon in contemporary Judaism as a curse or punishment for sin, it is intended here to present Elizabeth in a situation similar to that of some of the great mothers of important Old Testament figures: Sarah (Gn 15:3; 16:1); Rebekah (Gn 25:21); Rachel (Gn 29:31; 30:1); the mother of Samson and wife of Manoah (Jgs 13:2–3); Hannah (1 Sm 1:2).

God, ⁹according to the practice of the priestly service, he was chosen by lot to enter the sanctuary of the Lord to burn incense.ᵉ ¹⁰Then, when the whole assembly of the people was praying outside at the hour of the incense offering, ¹¹the angel of the Lord appeared to him, standing at the right of the altar of incense. ¹²Zechariah was troubled by what he saw, and fear came upon him. ¹³But the angel said to him, "Do not be afraid,* Zechariah, because your prayer has been heard. Your wife Elizabeth will bear you a son, and you shall name him John.ᶠ ¹⁴And you will have joy and gladness, and many will rejoice at his birth, ¹⁵for he will be great in the sight of [the] Lord. He will drink neither wine nor strong drink.† He will be filled with the holy Spirit even from his mother's womb,ᵍ ¹⁶and he will turn many of the children of Israel to the Lord their God. ¹⁷He will go before him in the spirit and power of Elijah‡ to turn the hearts of fathers toward children and the disobedient to the understanding of the righteous, to prepare a people fit for the Lord."ʰ ¹⁸Then Zechariah said to the angel, "How shall I know this? For I am an old man, and my wife is advanced in years." ¹⁹And the angel said to him in reply, "I am Gabriel,§ who stand before God. I was sent to speak to you and to announce to you this good news.ⁱ ²⁰But now you will be speechless and unable to talk¶ until the day these things take place, because you did not believe my words, which will be fulfilled at their proper time."ʲ

²¹Meanwhile the people were waiting for Zechariah and were amazed that he stayed so long in the sanctuary. ²²But when he came out, he was unable to speak to them, and they realized that he had seen a vision in the sanctuary. He was gesturing to them but remained mute. ²³Then, when his days of ministry were completed, he went home. ²⁴After this time his wife Elizabeth conceived, and she went into seclusion for five

---

* [1:13] **Do not be afraid:** a stereotyped Old Testament phrase spoken to reassure the recipient of a heavenly vision (Gn 15:1; Jos 1:9; Dn 10:12, 19 and elsewhere in Lk 1:30; 2:10). **You shall name him John:** the name means "Yahweh has shown favor," an indication of John's role in salvation history.

† [1:15] **He will drink neither wine nor strong drink:** like Samson (Jgs 13:4–5) and Samuel (1 Sm 1:11 LXX and 4QSamᵃ), John is to be consecrated by Nazirite vow and set apart for the Lord's service.

‡ [1:17] **He will go before him in the spirit and power of Elijah:** John is to be the messenger sent before Yahweh, as described in Mal 3:1–2. He is cast, moreover, in the role of the Old Testament fiery reformer, the prophet Elijah, who according to Mal 3:23 (4:5) is sent before "the great and terrible day of the Lord comes."

§ [1:19] **I am Gabriel:** "the angel of the Lord" is identified as Gabriel, the angel who in Dn 9:20–25 announces the seventy weeks of years and the coming of an anointed one, a prince. By alluding to Old Testament themes in Lk 1:17, 19 such as the coming of the day of the Lord and the dawning of the messianic era, Luke is presenting his interpretation of the significance of the births of John and Jesus.

¶ [1:20] **You will be speechless and unable to talk:** Zechariah's becoming mute is the sign given in response to his question in v. 18. When Mary asks a similar question in Lk 1:34, unlike Zechariah who was punished for his doubt, she, in spite of her doubt, is praised and reassured (Lk 1:35–37).

months, saying, [25]"So has the Lord done for me at a time when he has seen fit to take away my disgrace before others."[k]

Announcement of the Birth of Jesus.[*] [26]In the sixth month, the angel Gabriel was sent from God to a town of Galilee called Nazareth, [27]to a virgin betrothed to a man named Joseph, of the house of David, and the virgin's name was Mary.[l] [28]And coming to her, he said, "Hail, favored one! The Lord is with you."[m] [29]But she was greatly troubled at what was said and pondered what sort of greeting this might be. [30]Then the angel said to her, "Do not be afraid, Mary, for you have found favor with God. [31n]Behold, you will conceive in your womb and bear a son, and you shall name him Jesus. [32o]He will be great and will be called Son of the Most High,[†] and the Lord God will give him the throne of David his father, [33]and he will rule over the house of Jacob forever, and of his kingdom there will be no end."[p] [34]But Mary said to the angel, "How can this be, since I have no relations with a man?"[‡] [35]And the angel said to her in reply, "The holy Spirit will come upon you, and the power of the Most High will overshadow you. Therefore the child to be born will be called holy, the Son of God.[q] [36]And behold, Elizabeth, your relative, has also conceived[§] a son in her old age, and this is the sixth month for her who was called barren; [37]for nothing will be impossible for God."[r] [38]Mary said, "Behold, I am the handmaid of the Lord. May it be done to me according to your word." Then the angel departed from her.

Mary Visits Elizabeth. [39]During those days Mary set out and traveled to the hill country in haste to a town of Judah, [40]where she entered the house of Zechariah and greeted Elizabeth. [41]When Elizabeth heard Mary's greeting, the infant leaped in her womb, and Elizabeth, filled with the holy Spirit,[s] [42]cried out in a loud voice and said, "Most blessed

---

[*] [1:26–38] The announcement to Mary of the birth of Jesus is parallel to the announcement to Zechariah of the birth of John. In both the angel Gabriel appears to the parent who is troubled by the vision (Lk 1:11–12, 26–29) and then told by the angel not to fear (Lk 1:13, 30). After the announcement is made (Lk 1:14–17, 31–33) the parent objects (Lk 1:18, 34) and a sign is given to confirm the announcement (Lk 1:20, 36). The particular focus of the announcement of the birth of Jesus is on his identity as Son of David (Lk 1:32–33) and Son of God (Lk 1:32, 35).

[†] [1:32] **Son of the Most High:** cf. Lk 1:76 where John is described as "prophet of the Most High." "Most High" is a title for God commonly used by Luke (Lk 1:35, 76; 6:35; 8:28; Acts 7:48; 16:17).

[‡] [1:34] Mary's questioning response is a denial of sexual relations and is used by Luke to lead to the angel's declaration about the Spirit's role in the conception of this child (Lk 1:35). According to Luke, the virginal conception of Jesus takes place through the holy Spirit, the power of God, and therefore Jesus has a unique relationship to Yahweh: he is Son of God.

[§] [1:36–37] The sign given to Mary in confirmation of the angel's announcement to her is the pregnancy of her aged relative Elizabeth. If a woman past the childbearing age could become pregnant, why, the angel implies, should there be doubt about Mary's pregnancy, for **nothing will be impossible for God**.

are you among women, and blessed is the fruit of your womb.*^t 43And how does this happen to me, that the mother of my Lord* should come to me? 44For at the moment the sound of your greeting reached my ears, the infant in my womb leaped for joy. 45Blessed are you who believed† that what was spoken to you by the Lord would be fulfilled."^u

The Canticle of Mary. 46vAnd Mary said:‡

"My soul proclaims the greatness of the Lord;^w
  47my spirit rejoices in God my savior.^x
48For he has looked upon his handmaid's lowliness;
  behold, from now on will all ages call me blessed.^y
49The Mighty One has done great things for me,
  and holy is his name.^z
50His mercy is from age to age
  to those who fear him.^a
51He has shown might with his arm,
  dispersed the arrogant of mind and heart.^b
52He has thrown down the rulers from their thrones
  but lifted up the lowly.^c
53The hungry he has filled with good things;
  the rich he has sent away empty.^d
54He has helped Israel his servant,
  remembering his mercy,^e
55according to his promise to our fathers,
  to Abraham and to his descendants forever."^f

56Mary remained with her about three months and then returned to her home.

---

* [1:43] Even before his birth, Jesus is identified in Luke as the Lord.
† [1:45] **Blessed are you who believed**: Luke portrays Mary as a believer whose faith stands in contrast to the disbelief of Zechariah (Lk 1:20). Mary's role as believer in the infancy narrative should be seen in connection with the explicit mention of her presence among "those who believed" after the resurrection at the beginning of the Acts of the Apostles (Acts 1:14).
‡ [1:46–55] Although Mary is praised for being the mother of the Lord and because of her belief, she reacts as the servant in a psalm of praise, the Magnificat. Because there is no specific connection of the canticle to the context of Mary's pregnancy and her visit to Elizabeth, the Magnificat (with the possible exception of v 48) may have been a Jewish Christian hymn that Luke found appropriate at this point in his story. Even if not composed by Luke, it fits in well with themes found elsewhere in Luke: joy and exultation in the Lord; the lowly being singled out for God's favor; the reversal of human fortunes; the fulfillment of Old Testament promises. The loose connection between the hymn and the context is further seen in the fact that a few Old Latin manuscripts identify the speaker of the hymn as Elizabeth, even though the overwhelming textual evidence makes Mary the speaker.

The Birth of John.[*] ⁵⁷When the time arrived for Elizabeth to have her child she gave birth to a son. ⁵⁸Her neighbors and relatives heard that the Lord had shown his great mercy toward her, and they rejoiced with her.^g ^{59†} When they came on the eighth day to circumcise^h the child, they were going to call him Zechariah after his father, ⁶⁰but his mother said in reply, "No. He will be called John."ⁱ ⁶¹But they answered her, "There is no one among your relatives who has this name." ⁶²So they made signs, asking his father what he wished him to be called. ⁶³He asked for a tablet and wrote, "John is his name," and all were amazed. ⁶⁴Immediately his mouth was opened, his tongue freed, and he spoke blessing God.^j ⁶⁵Then fear came upon all their neighbors, and all these matters were discussed throughout the hill country of Judea. ⁶⁶All who heard these things took them to heart, saying, "What, then, will this child be?" For surely the hand of the Lord was with him.

The Canticle of Zechariah. ⁶⁷Then Zechariah his father, filled with the holy Spirit, prophesied, saying:

^{68‡} "Blessed be the Lord, the God of Israel,
   for he has visited and brought redemption to his people.^k
^{69§} He has raised up a horn for our salvation
   within the house of David his servant,^l
⁷⁰even as he promised through the mouth of his holy prophets
      from of old:
   ⁷¹salvation from our enemies and from the hand of all who
      hate us,^m

---

* [1:57–66] The birth and circumcision of John above all emphasize John's incorporation into the people of Israel by the sign of the covenant (Gn 17:1–12). The narrative of John's circumcision also prepares the way for the subsequent description of the circumcision of Jesus in Lk 2:21. At the beginning of his two-volume work Luke shows those who play crucial roles in the inauguration of Christianity to be wholly a part of the people of Israel. At the end of the Acts of the Apostles (Acts 21:20; 22:3; 23:6–9; 24:14–16; 26:2–8, 22–23) he will argue that Christianity is the direct descendant of Pharisaic Judaism.

† [1:59] The practice of Palestinian Judaism at this time was to name the child at birth; moreover, though naming a male child after the father is not completely unknown, the usual practice was to name the child after the grandfather (see Lk 1:61). The naming of the child John and Zechariah's recovery from his loss of speech should be understood as fulfilling the angel's announcement to Zechariah in Lk 1:13, 20.

‡ [1:68–79] Like the canticle of Mary (Lk 1:46–55) the canticle of Zechariah is only loosely connected with its context. Apart from Lk 1:76–77, the hymn in speaking of **a horn for our salvation** (Lk 1:69) and **the daybreak from on high** (Lk 1:78) applies more closely to Jesus and his work than to John. Again like Mary's canticle, it is largely composed of phrases taken from the Greek Old Testament and may have been a Jewish Christian hymn of praise that Luke adapted to fit the present context by inserting Lk 1:76–77 to give Zechariah's reply to the question asked in Lk 1:66.

§ [1:69] **A horn for our salvation:** the horn is a common Old Testament figure for strength (Ps 18:3; 75:5–6; 89:18; 112:9; 148:14). This description is applied to God in Ps 18:3 and is here transferred to Jesus. The connection of the phrase with **the house of David** gives the title messianic overtones and may indicate an allusion to a phrase in Hannah's song of praise (1 Sm 2:10), "the horn of his anointed."

⁷²to show mercy to our fathersⁿ
and to be mindful of his holy covenant^o
⁷³and of the oath he swore to Abraham our father,^p
and to grant us that, ⁷⁴rescued from the hand of enemies,
without fear we might worship him ⁷⁵in holiness and
righteousness
before him all our days.^q
⁷⁶And you, child, will be called prophet of the Most High,
for you will go before the Lord* to prepare his ways,^r
⁷⁷to give his people knowledge of salvation
through the forgiveness of their sins,
⁷⁸because of the tender mercy of our God^s
by which the daybreak from on high† will visit us^t
⁷⁹to shine on those who sit in darkness and death's shadow,
to guide our feet into the path of peace."

⁸⁰The child grew and became strong in spirit, and he was in the desert until the day of his manifestation to Israel.^u

---

* [1:76] **You will go before the Lord**: here **the Lord** is most likely a reference to Jesus (contrast Lk 1:15–17 where Yahweh is meant) and John is presented as the precursor of Jesus.

† [1:78] **The daybreak from on high**: three times in the LXX (Jer 23:5; Zec 3:8; 6:12), the Greek word used here for **daybreak** translates the Hebrew word for "scion, branch," an Old Testament messianic title.

a. [1:1–4] Acts 1:1; 1 Cor 15:3.
b. [1:2] 24:48; Jn 15:27; Acts 1:21–22.
c. [1:5] 1 Chr 24:10.
d. [1:7] Gn 18:11, Jgs 13:2–5; 1 Sm 1:5–6.
e. [1:9] Ex 30:7.
f. [1:13] 1:57, 60, 63; Mt 1:20–21.
g. [1:15] 7:33; Nm 6:1–21; Jgs 13:4; 1 Sm 1:11 LXX.
h. [1:17] Sir 48:10; Mal 3:1; 3:23–24; Mt 11:14; 17:11–13.
i. [1:19] Dn 8:16; 9:21.
j. [1:20] 1:45.
k. [1:25] Gn 30:23.
l. [1:27] 2:5; Mt 1:16, 18.
m. [1:28] Jgs 6:12; Ru 2:4; Jdt 13:18.
n. [1:31] Gn 16:11, Jgs 13:3, Is 7:14, Mt 1:21–23.
o. [1:32–33] 2 Sm 7:12, 13, 16; Is 9:7.
p. [1:33] Dn 2:44; 7:14; Mi 4:7; Mt 28:18.
q. [1:35] Mt 1:20.
r [1:37] Gn 18:14; Jer 32:27; Mt 19:26.
s. [1:41] 1:15; Gn 25:22 LXX.
t. [1:42] 11:27–28; Jgs 5:24; Jdt 13:18; Dt 28:4.
u. [1:45] 1:20.
v. [1:46–55] 1 Sm 2:1–10.
w. [1:46] Ps 35:9; Is 61:10; Heb 3:18.
x. [1:47] Ti 3:4; Jude 25.
y. [1:48] 11:27; 1 Sm 1:11; 2 Sm 16:12; 2 Kgs 14:26; Ps 113:7.
z. [1:49] Dt 10:21; Ps 71:19; 111:9; 126:2–3.

a. [1:50] Ps 89:2; 103:13, 17.
b. [1:51] Ps 89:10; 118:15; Jer 32:17 (39:17 LXX).
c. [1:52] 1 Sm 2:7, 2 Sm 22:20, Jb 5:11, 12:19, Ps 147:6; Sir 10:14; Jas 4:6; 1 Pt 5:5.
d. [1:53] 1 Sm 2:5; Ps 107:9.
e. [1:54] Ps 98:3; Is 41:8–9.
f. [1:55] Gn 13:15; 17:7; 18:18; 22:17–18; Mi 7:20.
g. [1:58] 1:14.
h. [1:59] 2:21; Gn 17:10, 12; Lv 12:3.
i. [1:60] 1:13.
j. [1:64] 1:20.
k. [1:68] 7:16; Ps 41:13; 72:18; 106:48; 111:9.
l. [1:69] Ps 18:3.
m. [1:71] Ps 106:10.
n. [1:72–73] Gn 17:7; Lv 26:42; Ps 105:8–9; Mi 7:20.
o. [1:72] Ps 106:45–46.
p. [1:73–74] Gn 22:16–17.
q. [1:75] Ti 2:12.
r. [1:76] Is 40:3; Mal 3:1; Mt 3:3; 11:10.
s. [1:78–79] Is 60:1–2.
t. [1:78] Mal 3:20.
u. [1:80] 2:40; Mt 3:1.

2 The Birth of Jesus.

2 **The Birth of Jesus.** [1]* In those days a decree went out from Caesar Augustus† that the whole world should be enrolled. [2]This was the first enrollment, when Quirinius was governor of Syria. [3]So all went to be enrolled, each to his own town. [4]And Joseph too went up from Galilee from the town of Nazareth to Judea, to the city of David that is called Bethlehem, because he was of the house and family of David,*a* [5]to be enrolled with Mary, his betrothed, who was with child.*b* [6]While they were there, the time came for her to have her child, [7]and she gave birth to her firstborn son.‡ She wrapped him in swaddling clothes and laid him in a manger, because there was no room for them in the inn.*c*

[8]§ Now there were shepherds in that region living in the fields and keeping the night watch over their flock. [9]The angel of the Lord appeared to them and the glory of the Lord shone around them, and they were struck with great fear.*d* [10]The angel said to them, "Do not be afraid; for behold, I proclaim to you good news of great joy that will be for all the people. [11]¶ *e* For today in the city of David a savior has been born for you

---

* [2:1–2] Although universal registrations of Roman citizens are attested in 28 B.C., 8 B.C., and A.D. 14 and enrollments in individual provinces of those who are not Roman citizens are also attested, such a universal census of the Roman world under Caesar Augustus is unknown outside the New Testament. Moreover, there are notorious historical problems connected with Luke's dating the census **when Quirinius was governor of Syria**, and the various attempts to resolve the difficulties have proved unsuccessful. P. Sulpicius Quirinius became legate of the province of Syria in A.D. 6–7 when Judea was annexed to the province of Syria. At that time, a provincial census of Judea was taken up. If Quirinius had been legate of Syria previously, it would have to have been before 10 B.C. because the various legates of Syria from 10 B.C. to 4 B.C. (the death of Herod) are known, and such a dating for an earlier census under Quirinius would create additional problems for dating the beginning of Jesus' ministry (Lk 3:1, 23). A previous legateship after 4 B.C. (and before A.D. 6) would not fit with the dating of Jesus' birth in the days of Herod (Lk 1:5; Mt 2:1). Luke may simply be combining Jesus' birth in Bethlehem with his vague recollection of a census under Quirinius (see also Acts 5:37) to underline the significance of this birth for the whole Roman world: through this child born in Bethlehem peace and salvation come to the empire

† [2:1] **Caesar Augustus**: the reign of the Roman emperor Caesar Augustus is usually dated from 27 B.C. to his death in A.D. 14. According to Greek inscriptions, Augustus was regarded in the Roman Empire as "savior" and "god," and he was credited with establishing a time of peace, the *pax Augusta*, throughout the Roman world during his long reign. It is not by chance that Luke relates the birth of Jesus to the time of Caesar Augustus: the real savior (Lk 2:11) and peace-bearer (Lk 2:14; see also Lk 19:38) is the child born in Bethlehem. The great emperor is simply God's agent (like the Persian king Cyrus in Is 44:28–45:1) who provides the occasion for God's purposes to be accomplished. **The whole world**: that is, the whole Roman world: Rome, Italy, and the Roman provinces.

‡ [2:7] **firstborn son**: the description of Jesus as **firstborn** son does not necessarily mean that Mary had other sons. It is a legal description indicating that Jesus possessed the rights and privileges of the firstborn son (Gn 27; Ex 13:2; Nm 3:12–13; 18:15–16; Dt 21:15–17). See notes on Mt 1:25; Mk 6:3. **Wrapped him in swaddling clothes**: there may be an allusion here to the birth of another descendant of David, his son Solomon, who though a great king was wrapped in swaddling clothes like any other infant (Wis 7:4–6). **Laid him in a manger**: a feeding trough for animals. A possible allusion to Is 1:3 LXX.

§ [2:8–20] The announcement of Jesus' birth to the shepherds is in keeping with Luke's theme that the lowly are singled out as the recipients of God's favors and blessings (see also Lk 1:48, 52).

¶ [2:11] The basic message of the infancy narrative is contained in the angel's announcement: this child is **savior**, **Messiah**, and **Lord**. Luke is the only synoptic gospel writer to use the title **savior** for Jesus (Lk 2:11; Acts 5:31; 13:23; see also Lk 1:69; 19:9; Acts 4:12). As savior, Jesus is looked upon by Luke as the one who rescues humanity from sin and delivers humanity from the condition of alienation from God. The title *christos*, "Christ," is the Greek equivalent of the Hebrew *māšîaḥ*, "Messiah," "anointed one." Among certain groups in first-century Palestinian Judaism, the title was applied to an expected royal leader from the line of David who would restore the kingdom to Israel (see Acts 1:6). The political overtones of the title are played down in Luke and instead the Messiah of the Lord (Lk 2:26) or the Lord's anointed is the one who now brings salvation to all humanity, Jew and Gentile (Lk 2:29–32). Lord is the most

who is Messiah and Lord. [12]And this will be a sign for you: you will find an infant wrapped in swaddling clothes and lying in a manger." [13]And suddenly there was a multitude of the heavenly host with the angel, praising God and saying:

[14]* "Glory to God in the highest[f]
        and on earth peace to those on whom his favor rests."

The Visit of the Shepherds. [15]When the angels went away from them to heaven, the shepherds said to one another, "Let us go, then, to Bethlehem to see this thing that has taken place, which the Lord has made known to us." [16]So they went in haste and found Mary and Joseph, and the infant lying in the manger. [17]When they saw this, they made known the message that had been told them about this child. [18]All who heard it were amazed by what had been told them by the shepherds. [19]And Mary kept all these things, reflecting on them in her heart. [20]Then the shepherds returned, glorifying and praising God for all they had heard and seen, just as it had been told to them.

The Circumcision and Naming of Jesus. [21]When eight days were completed for his circumcision,[†] he was named Jesus, the name given him by the angel before he was conceived in the womb.[g]

The Presentation in the Temple. [22]‡ When the days were completed for their purification[§] according to the law of Moses, they took him up to

---

frequently used title for Jesus in Luke and Acts. In the New Testament it is also applied to Yahweh, as it is in the Old Testament. When used of Jesus it points to his transcendence and dominion over humanity.

* [2:14] **On earth peace to those on whom his favor rests:** the peace that results from the Christ event is for those whom God has favored with his grace. This reading is found in the oldest representatives of the Western and Alexandrian text traditions and is the preferred one; the Byzantine text tradition, on the other hand, reads: "on earth peace, good will toward men." The peace of which Luke's gospel speaks (Lk 2:14; 7:50; 8:48; 10:5–6; 19:38, 42; 24:36) is more than the absence of war of the *pax Augusta*; it also includes the security and well-being characteristic of peace in the Old Testament.

† [2:21] Just as John before him had been incorporated into the people of Israel through his circumcision, so too this child (see note on Lk 1:57–66).

‡ [2:22–40] The presentation of Jesus in the temple depicts the parents of Jesus as devout Jews, faithful observers of the law of the Lord (Lk 2:23–24, 39), i.e., the law of Moses. In this respect, they are described in a fashion similar to the parents of John (Lk 1:6) and Simeon (Lk 2:25) and Anna (Lk 2:36–37).

§ [2:22] **Their purification:** syntactically, **their** must refer to Mary and Joseph, even though the Mosaic law never mentions the purification of the husband. Recognizing the problem, some Western scribes have altered the text to read "his purification," understanding the presentation of Jesus in the temple as a form of purification; the Vulgate version has a Latin form that could be either "his" or "her." According to the Mosaic law (Lv 12:2–8), the woman who gives birth to a boy is unable for forty days to touch anything sacred or to enter the temple area by reason of her legal impurity. At the end of this period she is required to offer a year-old lamb as a burnt offering and a turtledove or young pigeon as an expiation of sin. The woman who could not afford a lamb offered instead two turtledoves or two young pigeons, as Mary does here. **They took him up to Jerusalem to present him to the Lord:** as the firstborn son (Lk 2:7) Jesus was consecrated to the Lord as the law required (Ex 13:2, 12), but there was no requirement that

Jerusalem to present him to the Lord,[h] 23just as it is written in the law of the Lord, "Every male that opens the womb shall be consecrated to the Lord,"[i] 24and to offer the sacrifice of "a pair of turtledoves or two young pigeons," in accordance with the dictate in the law of the Lord.

25Now there was a man in Jerusalem whose name was Simeon. This man was righteous and devout, awaiting the consolation of Israel,* and the holy Spirit was upon him. 26It had been revealed to him by the holy Spirit that he should not see death before he had seen the Messiah of the Lord. 27He came in the Spirit into the temple; and when the parents brought in the child Jesus to perform the custom of the law in regard to him, 28he took him into his arms and blessed God, saying:

> 29"Now, Master, you may let your servant go
>   in peace, according to your word,
> 30for my eyes have seen your salvation,[j]
>   31which you prepared in sight of all the peoples,
> 32a light for revelation to the Gentiles,
> ·   and glory for your people Israel."[k]

33The child's father and mother were amazed at what was said about him; 34and Simeon blessed them and said to Mary his mother, "Behold, this child is destined for the fall and rise of many in Israel, and to be a sign that will be contradicted[l] 35(and you yourself a sword will pierce)† so that the thoughts of many hearts may be revealed." 36There was also a prophetess, Anna, the daughter of Phanuel, of the tribe of Asher. She was advanced in years, having lived seven years with her husband after her marriage, 37and then as a widow until she was eighty-four. She never left the temple, but worshiped night and day with fasting and prayer. 38And coming forward at that very time, she gave thanks to God and spoke about the child to all who were awaiting the redemption of Jerusalem.[m]

---

this be done at the temple. The concept of a presentation at the temple is probably derived from 1 Sm 1:24–28, where Hannah offers the child Samuel for sanctuary services. The law further stipulated (Nm 3:47–48) that the firstborn son should be redeemed by the parents through their payment of five shekels to a member of a priestly family. About this legal requirement Luke is silent.

* [2:25] **Awaiting the consolation of Israel:** Simeon here and later Anna who speak about the child to all who were awaiting the redemption of Jerusalem represent the hopes and expectations of faithful and devout Jews who at this time were looking forward to the restoration of God's rule in Israel. The birth of Jesus brings these hopes to fulfillment.

† [2:35] **(And you yourself a sword will pierce):** Mary herself will not be untouched by the various reactions to the role of Jesus (Lk 2:34). Her blessedness as mother of the Lord will be challenged by her son who describes true blessedness as "hearing the word of God and observing it" (Lk 11:27–28 and Lk 8:20–21).

The Return to Nazareth. [39]When they had fulfilled all the prescriptions of the law of the Lord, they returned to Galilee, to their own town of Nazareth.[n] [40]The child grew and became strong, filled with wisdom; and the favor of God was upon him.[o]

The Boy Jesus in the Temple. [*] [41]Each year his parents went to Jerusalem for the feast of Passover,[p] [42]and when he was twelve years old, they went up according to festival custom. [43]After they had completed its days, as they were returning, the boy Jesus remained behind in Jerusalem, but his parents did not know it. [44]Thinking that he was in the caravan, they journeyed for a day and looked for him among their relatives and acquaintances, [45]but not finding him, they returned to Jerusalem to look for him. [46]After three days they found him in the temple, sitting in the midst of the teachers, listening to them and asking them questions, [47]and all who heard him were astounded at his understanding and his answers. [48]When his parents saw him, they were astonished, and his mother said to him, "Son, why have you done this to us? Your father and I have been looking for you with great anxiety." [49]And he said to them, "Why were you looking for me? Did you not know that I must be in my Father's house?"[†] [50]But they did not understand what he said to them. [51]He went down with them and came to Nazareth, and was obedient to them; and his mother kept all these things in her heart.[q] [52]And Jesus advanced [in] wisdom and age and favor before God and man.[r]

---

* [2:41–52] This story's concern with an incident from Jesus' youth is unique in the canonical gospel tradition. It presents Jesus in the role of the faithful Jewish boy, raised in the traditions of Israel, and fulfilling all that the law requires. With this episode, the infancy narrative ends just as it began, in the setting of the Jerusalem temple.

† [2:49] **I must be in my Father's house:** this phrase can also be translated, "I must be about my Father's work." In either translation, Jesus refers to God as his Father. His divine sonship, and his obedience to his heavenly Father's will, take precedence over his ties to his family.

a. [2:4] Mi 5:2; Mt 2:6.
b. [2:5] 1:27; Mt 1:18.
c. [2:7] Mt 1:25.
d. [2:9] 1:11, 26.
e. [2:11] Mt 1:21; 16:16; Jn 4:42; Acts 2:36; 5:31; Phil 2:11.
f. [2:14] 19:38.
g. [2:21] 1:31; Gn 17:12; Mt 1:21.
h. [2:22–24] Lv 12:2–8.
i. [2:23] Ex 13:2, 12.
j. [2:30–31] 3:6; Is 40:5 LXX; 52:10.
k. [2:32] Is 42:6; 46:13; 49:6; Acts 13:47; 26:23.
l. [2:34] 12:51; Is 8:14; Jn 9:39; Rom 9:33; 1 Cor 1:23; 1 Pt 2:7–8.
m. [2:38] Is 52:9.
n. [2:39] Mt 2:23.
o. [2:40] 1:80; 2:52.

p. [2:41] Ex 12:24–27; 23:15; Dt 16:1–8.
q. [2:51] 2:19.
r. [2:52] 1:80; 2:40; 1 Sm 2:26.

III. THE PREPARATION FOR THE PUBLIC MINISTRY

3 **The Preaching of John the Baptist.*** [1]In the fifteenth year of the reign of Tiberius Caesar,† when Pontius Pilate was governor of Judea,[a] and Herod was tetrarch of Galilee, and his brother Philip tetrarch of the region of Ituraea and Trachonitis, and Lysanias was tetrarch of Abilene, [2]during the high priesthood of Annas and Caiaphas,‡ the word of God came to John[b] the son of Zechariah in the desert. [3]§ He went throughout [the] whole region of the Jordan, proclaiming a baptism of repentance for the forgiveness of sins,[c] [4]¶ as it is written in the book of the words of the prophet Isaiah:[d]

> "A voice of one crying out in the desert:
> 'Prepare the way of the Lord,[e]
>   make straight his paths.
> [5]Every valley shall be filled
>   and every mountain and hill shall be made low.
> The winding roads shall be made straight,

---

* [3:1–20] Although Luke is indebted in this section to his sources, the Gospel of Mark and a collection of sayings of John the Baptist, he has clearly marked this introduction to the ministry of Jesus with his own individual style. Just as the gospel began with a prologue sentence (Lk 1:1–4), so too this section (Lk 3:1–2). He casts the call of John the Baptist in the form of an Old Testament prophetic call (Lk 3:2) and extends the quotation from Isaiah found in Mk 1:3 (Is 40:3) by the addition of Is 40:4–5 in Lk 3:5–6. In doing so, he presents his theme of the universality of salvation, which he has announced earlier in the words of Simeon (Lk 2:30–32). Moreover, in describing the expectation of the people (Lk 3:15), Luke is characterizing the time of John's preaching in the same way as he had earlier described the situation of other devout Israelites in the infancy narrative (Lk 2:25–26, 37–38). In Lk 3:7–18 Luke presents the preaching of John the Baptist who urges the crowds to reform in view of **the coming wrath** (Lk 3:7, 9: eschatological preaching), and who offers the crowds certain standards for reforming social conduct (Lk 3:10–14: ethical preaching), and who announces to the crowds the coming of **one mightier than** he (Lk 3:15–18: messianic preaching).

† [3:1] **Tiberius Caesar**: Tiberius succeeded Augustus as emperor in A.D. 14 and reigned until A.D. 37. The fifteenth year of his reign, depending on the method of calculating his first regnal year, would have fallen between A.D. 27 and 29. **Pontius Pilate**: prefect of Judea from A.D. 26 to 36. The Jewish historian Josephus describes him as a greedy and ruthless prefect who had little regard for the local Jewish population and their religious practices (see Lk 13:1). **Herod**: i.e., Herod Antipas, the son of Herod the Great. He ruled over Galilee and Perea from 4 B.C. to A.D. 39. His official title **tetrarch** means literally, "ruler of a quarter," but came to designate any subordinate prince. **Philip**: also a son of Herod the Great, tetrarch of the territory to the north and east of the Sea of Galilee from 4 B.C. to A.D. 34. Only two small areas of this territory are mentioned by Luke. **Lysanias**: nothing is known about this Lysanias who is said here to have been tetrarch of Abilene, a territory northwest of Damascus.

‡ [3:2] **During the high priesthood of Annas and Caiaphas**: after situating the call of John the Baptist in terms of the civil rulers of the period, Luke now mentions the religious leadership of Palestine (see note on Lk 1:5). Annas had been high priest A.D. 6–15. After being deposed by the Romans in A.D. 15 he was succeeded by various members of his family and eventually by his son-in-law, Caiaphas, who was high priest A.D. 18–36. Luke refers to Annas as high priest at this time (but see Jn 18:13, 19), possibly because of the continuing influence of Annas or because the title continued to be used for the ex-high priest. **The word of God came to John**: Luke is alone among the New Testament writers in associating the preaching of John with a call from God. Luke is thereby identifying John with the prophets whose ministries began with similar calls. In Lk 7:26 John will be described as "more than a prophet"; he is also the precursor of Jesus (Lk 7:27), a transitional figure inaugurating the period of the fulfillment of prophecy and promise.

§ [3:3] See note on Mt 3:2.

¶ [3:4] The Essenes from Qumran used the same passage to explain why their community was in the desert studying and observing the law and the prophets (1QS 8:12–15).

and the rough ways made smooth,
⁶and all flesh shall see the salvation of God.'"*f*

⁷He said to the crowds who came out to be baptized by him, "You brood of vipers! Who warned you to flee from the coming wrath?*g* ⁸Produce good fruits as evidence of your repentance; and do not begin to say to yourselves, 'We have Abraham as our father,' for I tell you, God can raise up children to Abraham from these stones.*h* ⁹Even now the ax lies at the root of the trees. Therefore every tree that does not produce good fruit will be cut down and thrown into the fire."*i*

¹⁰And the crowds asked him, "What then should we do?" ¹¹He said to them in reply, "Whoever has two tunics should share with the person who has none. And whoever has food should do likewise." ¹²Even tax collectors came to be baptized and they said to him, "Teacher, what should we do?"*j* ¹³He answered them, "Stop collecting more than what is prescribed." ¹⁴Soldiers also asked him, "And what is it that we should do?" He told them, "Do not practice extortion, do not falsely accuse anyone, and be satisfied with your wages."

¹⁵*k* Now the people were filled with expectation, and all were asking in their hearts whether John might be the Messiah. ¹⁶* John answered them all, saying,*l* "I am baptizing you with water, but one mightier than I is coming. I am not worthy to loosen the thongs of his sandals. He will baptize you with the holy Spirit and fire. ¹⁷His winnowing fan† is in his hand to clear his threshing floor and to gather the wheat into his barn, but the chaff he will burn with unquenchable fire."*m* ¹⁸Exhorting them in many other ways, he preached good news to the people. ¹⁹‡ Now Herod the tetrarch,*n* who had been censured by him because of Herodias, his brother's wife, and because of all the evil deeds Herod had committed, ²⁰added still another to these by [also] putting John in prison.

---

* [3:16] **He will baptize you with the holy Spirit and fire**: in contrast to John's baptism with water, Jesus is said to baptize with the holy Spirit and with fire. From the point of view of the early Christian community, the Spirit and fire must have been understood in the light of the fire symbolism of the pouring out of the Spirit at Pentecost (Acts 2:1–4); but as part of John's preaching, the Spirit and fire should be related to their purifying and refining characteristics (Ez 36:25–27; Mal 3:2–3). See note on Mt 3:11.

† [3:17] **Winnowing fan**: see note on Mt 3:12.

‡ [3:19–20] Luke separates the ministry of John the Baptist from that of Jesus by reporting the imprisonment of John before the baptism of Jesus (Lk 3:21–22). Luke uses this literary device to serve his understanding of the periods of salvation history. With John the Baptist, the time of promise, the period of Israel, comes to an end; with the baptism of Jesus and the descent of the Spirit upon him, the time of fulfillment, the period of Jesus, begins. In his second volume, the Acts of the Apostles, Luke will introduce the third epoch in salvation history, the period of the church.

The Baptism of Jesus.[*] [21o]After all the people had been baptized and Jesus also had been baptized and was praying,[†] heaven was opened [22‡p] and the holy Spirit descended upon him in bodily form like a dove. And a voice came from heaven, "You are my beloved Son; with you I am well pleased."

The Genealogy of Jesus.[§] [23q] When Jesus began his ministry he was about thirty years of age. He was the son, as was thought, of Joseph, the son of Heli,[r] [24]the son of Matthat, the son of Levi, the son of Melchi, the son of Jannai, the son of Joseph, [25]the son of Mattathias, the son of Amos, the son of Nahum, the son of Esli, the son of Naggai, [26]the son of Maath, the son of Mattathias, the son of Semein, the son of Josech, the son of Joda, [27]the son of Joanan, the son of Rhesa, the son of Zerubbabel, the son of Shealtiel, the son of Neri,[s] [28]the son of Melchi, the son of Addi, the son of Cosam, the son of Elmadam, the son of Er, [29]the son of Joshua, the son of Eliezer, the son of Jorim, the son of Matthat, the son of Levi, [30]the son of Simeon, the son of Judah, the son of Joseph, the son of Jonam, the son of Eliakim, [31t] the son of Melea, the son of Menna, the son of Mattatha, the son of Nathan, the son of David,[ˢ] [32]the son of Jesse,[u] the son of Obed, the son of Boaz, the son of Sala, the son of Nahshon, [33]the son of Amminadab, the son of Admin, the son of Arni, the son of Hezron, the son of Perez,[v] the son of Judah,[w] [34]the son of Jacob, the son of Isaac, the son of Abraham,[x] the son of Terah, the son of Nahor, [35]the son of Serug, the son of Reu, the son of Peleg, the son of Eber, the son of Shelah, [36]the son of Cainan, the son of Arphaxad, the son of Shem,[y] the son of Noah, the son of Lamech, [37]the son of Methuselah, the son of Enoch, the son of Jared, the son of Mahalaleel, the son of Cainan, [38]the son of Enos, the son of Seth, the son of Adam,[z] the son of God.

---

[*] [3:21–22] This episode in Luke focuses on the heavenly message identifying Jesus as Son and, through the allusion to Is 42:1, as Servant of Yahweh. The relationship of Jesus to the Father has already been announced in the infancy narrative (Lk 1:32, 35; 2:49); it occurs here at the beginning of Jesus' Galilean ministry and will reappear in Lk 9:35 before another major section of Luke's gospel, the travel narrative (Lk 9:51–19:27). Elsewhere in Luke's writings (Lk 4:18; Acts 10:38), this incident will be interpreted as a type of anointing of Jesus.

[†] [3:21] **Was praying**: Luke regularly presents Jesus at prayer at important points in his ministry: here at his baptism; at the choice of the Twelve (Lk 6:12); before Peter's confession (Lk 9:18); at the transfiguration (Lk 9:28); when he teaches his disciples to pray (Lk 11:1); at the Last Supper (Lk 22:32); on the Mount of Olives (Lk 22:41); on the cross (Lk 23:46).

[‡] [3:22] **You are my beloved Son; with you I am well pleased**: this is the best attested reading in the Greek manuscripts. The Western reading, "You are my Son, this day I have begotten you," is derived from Ps 2:7.

[§] [3:23–38] Whereas Mt 1:2 begins the genealogy of Jesus with Abraham to emphasize Jesus' bonds with the people of Israel, Luke's universalism leads him to trace the descent of Jesus beyond Israel to Adam and beyond that to God (Lk 3:38) to stress again Jesus' divine sonship.

[¶] [3:31] **The son of Nathan, the son of David**: in keeping with Jesus' prophetic role in Luke and Acts (e.g., Lk 7:16, 39; 9:8; 13:33; 24:19; Acts 3:22–23; 7:37) Luke traces Jesus' Davidic ancestry through the prophet Nathan (see 2 Sm 7:2) rather than through King Solomon, as Mt 1:6–7.

a. [3:1–20] Mt 3:1–12; Mk 1:1–8; Jn 1:19–28.
b. [3:2] 1:80.
c. [3:3] Acts 13:24; 19:4.
d. [3:4–6] Is 40:3–5.
e. [3:4] Jn 1:23.
f. [3:6] 2:30–31.
g. [3:7] Mt 12:34.
h. [3:8] Jn 8:39.
i. [3:9] Mt 7:19; Jn 15:6.
j. [3:12] 7:29.
k. [3:15–16] Acts 13:25.
l. [3:16] 7:19–20; Jn 1:27; Acts 1:5; 11:16.
m. [3:17] Mt 3:12.
n. [3:19–20] Mt 14:3–4; Mk 6:17–18.

o. [3:21–22] Mt 3:13–17; Mk 1:9–11.
p. [3:22] 9:35; Ps 2:7; Is 42:1; Mt 12:18; 17:5; Mk 9:7; Jn 1:32; 2 Pt 1:17.
q. [3:23–38] Mt 1:1–17.
r. [3:23] 4:22; Jn 6:42.
s. [3:27] 1 Chr 3:17; Ez 3:2.
t. [3:31] 2 Sm 5:14.
u. [3:31–32] 1 Sm 16:1, 18.
v. [3:31–33] Ru 4:17–22; 1 Chr 2:1–15.
w. [3:33] Gn 29:35; 38:29.
x. [3:34] Gn 21:3; 25:26; 1 Chr 1:34; 28:34.
y. [3:34–36] Gn 11:10–26; 1 Chr 1:24–27.
z. [3:36–38] Gn 4:25–5:32; 1 Chr 1:1–4.

4 **The Temptation of Jesus.** [*] [1a] Filled with the holy Spirit, [†] Jesus returned from the Jordan and was led by the Spirit into the desert [2]for forty days, [‡] to be tempted by the devil. He ate nothing during those days, and when they were over he was hungry. [b] [3]The devil said to him, "If you are the Son of God, command this stone to become bread." [4]Jesus answered him, "It is written, 'One does not live by bread alone.'" [c] [5]Then he took him up and showed him all the kingdoms of the world in a single instant. [6]The devil said to him, "I shall give to you all this power and their glory; for it has been handed over to me, and I may give it to whomever I wish. [d] [7]All this will be yours, if you worship me." [8]Jesus said to him in reply, "It is written:

> 'You shall worship the Lord, your God,
>   and him alone shall you serve.'" [e]

[9][§] Then he led him to Jerusalem, made him stand on the parapet of the temple, and said to him, "If you are the Son of God, throw yourself down from here, [10]for it is written:

> 'He will command his angels concerning you,
>   to guard you,' [f]

[11]and:

> 'With their hands they will support you,
>   lest you dash your foot against a stone.'" [g]

---

* [4:1–13] See note on Mt 4:1–11.
† [4:1] **Filled with the holy Spirit**: as a result of the descent of the Spirit upon him at his baptism (Lk 3:21–22), Jesus is now equipped to overcome the devil. Just as the Spirit is prominent at this early stage of Jesus' ministry (Lk 4:1, 14, 18), so too it will be at the beginning of the period of the church in Acts (Acts 1:4; 2:4, 17).
‡ [4:2] **For forty days**: the mention of forty days recalls the forty years of the wilderness wanderings of the Israelites during the Exodus (Dt 8:2).
§ [4:9] **To Jerusalem**: the Lucan order of the temptations concludes on the parapet of the temple in Jerusalem, the city of destiny in Luke-Acts. It is in Jerusalem that Jesus will ultimately face his destiny (Lk 9:51; 13:33).

¹²Jesus said to him in reply, "It also says, 'You shall not put the Lord, your God, to the test.'"ʰ ¹³* When the devil had finished every temptation,ⁱ he departed from him for a time.

IV. THE MINISTRY IN GALILEE

The Beginning of the Galilean Ministry. ¹⁴ʲ Jesus returned to Galilee in the power of the Spirit, and news of him spread† throughout the whole region.ᵏ ¹⁵He taught in their synagogues and was praised by all.

The Rejection at Nazareth.‡ ˡ ¹⁶He came to Nazareth, where he had grown up, and went according to his custom§ into the synagogue on the sabbath day. He stood up to read ¹⁷and was handed a scroll of the prophet Isaiah. He unrolled the scroll and found the passage where it was written:

¹⁸"The Spirit of the Lord is upon me,⁵
　　because he has anointed me
　　　　to bring glad tidings to the poor.ᵐ
He has sent me to proclaim liberty to captives
　　and recovery of sight to the blind,
　　　　to let the oppressed go free,
¹⁹and to proclaim a year acceptable to the Lord."

²⁰Rolling up the scroll, he handed it back to the attendant and sat down, and the eyes of all in the synagogue looked intently at him. ²¹He said to them, "Today this scripture passage is fulfilled in your hearing."** ²²And

---

* [4:13] **For a time**: the devil's opportune time will occur before the passion and death of Jesus (Lk 22:3, 31–32, 53).

† [4:14] **News of him spread**: a Lucan theme; see Lk 4:37; 5:15; 7:17.

‡ [4:16–30] Luke has transposed to the beginning of Jesus' ministry an incident from his Marcan source, which situated it near the end of the Galilean ministry (Mk 6:1–6a). In doing so, Luke turns the initial admiration (Lk 4:22) and subsequent rejection of Jesus (Lk 4:28–29) into a foreshadowing of the whole future ministry of Jesus. Moreover, the rejection of Jesus in his own hometown hints at the greater rejection of him by Israel (Acts 13:46).

§ [4:16] **According to his custom**: Jesus' practice of regularly attending synagogue is carried on by the early Christians' practice of meeting in the temple (Acts 2:46; 3:1; 5:12).

⁵ [4:18] **The Spirit of the Lord is upon me, because he has anointed me**: see note on Lk 3:21–22. As this incident develops, Jesus is portrayed as a prophet whose ministry is compared to that of the prophets Elijah and Elisha. Prophetic anointings are known in first-century Palestinian Judaism from the Qumran literature that speaks of prophets as God's anointed ones. **To bring glad tidings to the poor**: more than any other gospel writer Luke is concerned with Jesus' attitude toward the economically and socially poor (see Lk 6:20, 24; 12:16–21; 14:12–14; 16:19–26; 19:8). At times, the poor in Luke's gospel are associated with the downtrodden, the oppressed and afflicted, the forgotten and the neglected (Lk 4:18; 6:20–22; 7:22; 14:12–14), and it is they who accept Jesus' message of salvation.

** [4:21] **Today this scripture passage is fulfilled in your hearing**: this sermon inaugurates the time of fulfillment of Old Testament prophecy. Luke presents the ministry of Jesus as fulfilling Old Testament hopes and expectations (Lk 7:22); for Luke, even Jesus' suffering, death, and resurrection are done in fulfillment of the scriptures (Lk 24:25–27, 44–46; Acts 3:18).

all spoke highly of him and were amazed at the gracious words that came from his mouth. They also asked, "Isn't this the son of Joseph?"*n* ²³He said to them, "Surely you will quote me this proverb, 'Physician, cure yourself,' and say, 'Do here in your native place the things that we heard were done in Capernaum.'"*** ²⁴And he said, "Amen, I say to you, no prophet is accepted in his own native place. ^{25†} Indeed, I tell you, there were many widows in Israel in the days of Elijah when the sky was closed for three and a half years and a severe famine spread over the entire land.*o* ^{26‡} It was to none of these that Elijah was sent, but only to a widow in Zarephath*p* in the land of Sidon. ²⁷Again, there were many lepers in Israel during the time of Elisha the prophet; yet not one of them was cleansed, but only Naaman the Syrian."*q* ²⁸When the people in the synagogue heard this, they were all filled with fury. ²⁹They rose up, drove him out of the town, and led him to the brow of the hill on which their town had been built, to hurl him down headlong. ³⁰But he passed through the midst of them and went away.

The Cure of a Demoniac.

^{31§} Jesus then went down to Capernaum,*r* a town of Galilee.*s* He taught them on the sabbath, ³²and they were astonished at his teaching because he spoke with authority.*t* ³³In the synagogue there was a man with the spirit of an unclean demon,*u* and he cried out in a loud voice, ³⁴"Ha! What have you to do with us, Jesus of Nazareth? Have you come to destroy us? I know who you are—the Holy One of God!"*v* ³⁵Jesus rebuked him and said, "Be quiet! Come out of him!" Then the demon threw the man down in front of them and came out of him without doing him any harm. ³⁶They were all amazed and said to one another, "What is there about his word? For with authority

---

* [4:23] **The things that we heard were done in Capernaum:** Luke's source for this incident reveals an awareness of an earlier ministry of Jesus in Capernaum that Luke has not yet made use of because of his transposition of this Nazareth episode to the beginning of Jesus' Galilean ministry. It is possible that by use of the future tense **you will quote me…,** Jesus is being portrayed as a prophet.

† [4:25–26] The references to Elijah and Elisha serve several purposes in this episode: they emphasize Luke's portrait of Jesus as a prophet like Elijah and Elisha; they help to explain why the initial admiration of the people turns to rejection; and they provide the scriptural justification for the future Christian mission to the Gentiles.

‡ [4:26] **A widow in Zarephath in the land of Sidon:** like Naaman the Syrian in Lk 4:27, a non-Israelite becomes the object of the prophet's ministry.

§ [4:31–44] The next several incidents in Jesus' ministry take place in Capernaum and are based on Luke's source, Mk 1:21–39. To the previous portrait of Jesus as prophet (Lk 4:16–30) they now add a presentation of him as teacher (Lk 4:31–32), exorcist (Lk 4:32–37, 41), healer (Lk 4:38–40), and proclaimer of God's kingdom (Lk 4:43).

¶ [4:34] **What have you to do with us?:** see note on Jn 2:4. **Have you come to destroy us?:** the question reflects the current belief that before the day of the Lord control over humanity would be wrested from the evil spirits, evil destroyed, and God's authority over humanity reestablished. The synoptic gospel tradition presents Jesus carrying out this task.

and power he commands the unclean spirits, and they come out." [37]And news of him spread everywhere in the surrounding region.

The Cure of Simon's Mother-in-Law. [38w] After he left the synagogue, he entered the house of Simon.[*] Simon's mother-in-law was afflicted with a severe fever, and they interceded with him about her. [39]He stood over her, rebuked the fever, and it left her. She got up immediately and waited on them.

Other Healings.[x] [40]At sunset, all who had people sick with various diseases brought them to him. He laid his hands on each of them and cured them. [41†] And demons also came out from many, shouting, "You are the Son of God."[y] But he rebuked them and did not allow them to speak because they knew that he was the Messiah.

Jesus Leaves Capernaum.[z] [42‡] At daybreak, Jesus left and went to a deserted place. The crowds went looking for him, and when they came to him, they tried to prevent him from leaving them. [43]But he said to them, "To the other towns also I must proclaim the good news of the kingdom of God, because for this purpose I have been sent."[a] [44]And he was preaching in the synagogues of Judea.[§]

---

[*] [4:38] **The house of Simon:** because of Luke's arrangement of material, the reader has not yet been introduced to Simon (cf. Mk 1:16–18, 29–31). Situated as it is before the call of Simon (Lk 5:1–11), it helps the reader to understand Simon's eagerness to do what Jesus says (Lk 5:5) and to follow him (Lk 5:11).

[†] [4:41] **They knew that he was the Messiah:** that is, the Christ (see note on Lk 2:11).

[‡] [4:42] **They tried to prevent him from leaving them:** the reaction of these strangers in Capernaum is presented in contrast to the reactions of those in his hometown who rejected him (Lk 4:28–30).

[§] [4:44] **In the synagogues of Judea:** instead of **Judea**, which is the best reading of the manuscript tradition, the Byzantine text tradition and other manuscripts read "Galilee," a reading that harmonizes Luke with Mt 4:23 and Mk 1:39. Up to this point Luke has spoken only of a ministry of Jesus in Galilee. Luke may be using **Judea** to refer to the land of Israel, the territory of the Jews, and not to a specific portion of it.

a. [4:1–13] Mt 4:1–11; Mk 1:12–13.
b. [4:2] Heb 4:15.
c. [4:4] Dt 8:3.
d. [4:6] Jer 27:5; Mt 28:18.
e. [4:8] Dt 6:13.
f. [4:10] Ps 91:11.
g. [4:11] Ps 91:12.
h. [4:12] Dt 6:16; 1 Cor 10:9.
i. [4:13] 22:3; Jn 13:2, 27; Heb 4:15.
j. [4:14–15] Mt 4:12–17; Mk 1:14–15.
k. [4:14] 5:15; Mt 3:16.
l. [4:16–30] Mt 13:53–58; Mk 6:1–6.
m. [4:18–19] Is 61:1–2; 58:6.
n. [4:22] 3:23; Jn 6:42.
o. [4:25] 1 Kgs 17:1–7; 18:1; Jas 5:17.
p. [4:26] 1 Kgs 17:9.
q. [4:27] 2 Kgs 5:1–14.

r. [4:31–37] Mk 1:21–28.
s. [4:31] Mt 4:13; Jn 2:12.
t. [4:32] Mt 7:28–29.
u. [4:33–34] 8:28; Mt 8:29; Mk 1:23–24; 5:7.
v. [4:34] 4:41; Jn 6:69.
w. [4:38–39] Mt 8:14–15; Mk 1:29–31.
x. [4:40–41] Mt 8:16; Mk 1:32–34.
y. [4:41] 4:34; Mt 8:29; Mk 3:11–12.
z. [4:42–44] Mk 1:35–39.
a. [4:43] 8:1; Mk 1:14–15.

5

The Call of Simon the Fisherman.*a 1b While the crowd was pressing in on Jesus and listening to the word of God, he was standing by the Lake of Gennesaret. 2He saw two boats there alongside the lake; the fishermen had disembarked and were washing their nets. 3Getting into one of the boats, the one belonging to Simon, he asked him to put out a short distance from the shore. Then he sat down and taught the crowds from the boat. 4c After he had finished speaking, he said to Simon, "Put out into deep water and lower your nets for a catch." 5Simon said in reply, "Master, we have worked hard all night and have caught nothing, but at your command I will lower the nets." 6When they had done this, they caught a great number of fish and their nets were tearing. 7They signaled to their partners in the other boat to come to help them. They came and filled both boats so that they were in danger of sinking. 8When Simon Peter saw this, he fell at the knees of Jesus and said, "Depart from me, Lord, for I am a sinful man." 9For astonishment at the catch of fish they had made seized him and all those with him, 10and likewise James and John, the sons of Zebedee, who were partners of Simon. Jesus said to Simon, "Do not be afraid; from now on you will be catching men."d 11When they brought their boats to the shore, they left everything† and followed him.e

The Cleansing of a Leper.f 12Now there was a man full of leprosy‡ in one of the towns where he was; and when he saw Jesus, he fell prostrate, pleaded with him, and said, "Lord, if you wish, you can make me clean." 13Jesus stretched out his hand, touched him, and said, "I do will it. Be made clean." And the leprosy left him immediately. 14Then he ordered him not to tell anyone, but "Go, show yourself to the priest and offer for

---

* [5:1–11] This incident has been transposed from his source, Mk 1:16–20, which places it immediately after Jesus makes his appearance in Galilee. By this transposition Luke uses this example of Simon's acceptance of Jesus to counter the earlier rejection of him by his hometown people, and since several incidents dealing with Jesus' power and authority have already been narrated, Luke creates a plausible context for the acceptance of Jesus by Simon and his partners. Many commentators have noted the similarity between the wondrous catch of fish reported here (Lk 4:4–9) and the post-resurrectional appearance of Jesus in Jn 21:1–11. There are traces in Luke's story that the post-resurrectional context is the original one: in Lk 4:8 Simon addresses Jesus as **Lord** (a post-resurrectional title for Jesus—see Lk 24:34; Acts 2:36—that has been read back into the historical ministry of Jesus) and recognizes himself as a sinner (an appropriate recognition for one who has denied knowing Jesus—Lk 22:54–62). As used by Luke, the incident looks forward to Peter's leadership in Luke-Acts (Lk 6:14; 9:20; 22:31–32; 24:34; Acts 1:15; 2:14–40; 10:11–18; 15:7–12) and symbolizes the future success of Peter as fisherman (Acts 2:41).

† [5:11] **They left everything**: in Mk 1:16–20 and Mt 4:18–22 the fishermen who follow Jesus leave their nets and their father; in Luke, they leave **everything** (see also Lk 5:28; 12:33; 14:33; 18:22), an indication of Luke's theme of complete detachment from material possessions.

‡ [5:12] **Full of leprosy**: see note on Mk 1:40.

your cleansing what Moses prescribed;* that will be proof for them."g
15The report about him spread all the more, and great crowds assembled
to listen to him and to be cured of their ailments, 16but he would
withdraw to deserted places to pray.h

The Healing of a Paralytic.i 17† One day as Jesus was teaching, Pharisees‡
and teachers of the law were sitting there who had come from every
village of Galilee and Judea and Jerusalem, and the power of the Lord
was with him for healing. 18And some men brought on a stretcher a man
who was paralyzed; they were trying to bring him in and set [him] in his
presence. 19But not finding a way to bring him in because of the crowd,
they went up on the roof and lowered him on the stretcher through the
tiles§ into the middle in front of Jesus. 20When he saw their faith, he said,
"As for you, your sins are forgiven."¶ 21Then the scribes** and Pharisees
began to ask themselves, "Who is this who speaks blasphemies? Who
but God alone can forgive sins?"j 22Jesus knew their thoughts and said to
them in reply, "What are you thinking in your hearts?k 23Which is easier,
to say, 'Your sins are forgiven,' or to say, 'Rise and walk'? 24†† l But that you
may know that the Son of Man has authority on earth to forgive sins"—
he said to the man who was paralyzed, "I say to you, rise, pick up your
stretcher, and go home." 25He stood up immediately before them, picked
up what he had been lying on, and went home, glorifying God. 26Then
astonishment seized them all and they glorified God, and, struck with
awe, they said, "We have seen incredible things today."

The Call of Levi.m 27After this he went out and saw a tax collector
named Levi sitting at the customs post. He said to him, "Follow me."

---

* [5:14] **Show yourself to the priest. . .what Moses prescribed:** this is a reference to Lv 14:2–9 that gives detailed
instructions for the purification of one who had been a victim of leprosy and thereby excluded from contact with
others (see Lv 13:45–46, 49; Nm 5:2–3). **That will be proof for them:** see note on Mt 8:4.
† [5:17–6:11] From his Marcan source, Luke now introduces a series of controversies with Pharisees: controversy over
Jesus' power to forgive sins (Mk 2:4, a reference to Palestinian straw and eating and drinking with tax collectors and sinners (Lk
5:27–32); controversy over not fasting (Lk 5:33–36); and finally two episodes narrating controversies over observance
of the sabbath (Lk 5:1–11).
‡ [5:17] **Pharisees:** see note on Mt 3:7.
§ [5:19] **Through the tiles:** Luke has adapted the story found in Mark to his non-Palestinian audience by changing
"opened up the roof" (Mk 2:4, a reference to Palestinian straw and clay roofs) to **through the tiles,** a detail that
reflects the Hellenistic Greco-Roman house with tiled roof.
¶ [5:20] **As for you, your sins are forgiven:** literally, "O man, your sins are forgiven you." The connection between
the forgiveness of sins and the cure of the paralytic reflects the belief of first-century Palestine (based on the Old
Testament: Ex 20:5; Dt 5:9) that sickness and infirmity are the result of sin, one's own or that of one's ancestors (see
also Lk 13:2; Jn 5:14; 9:2).
** [5:21] **The scribes:** see note on Mk 2:6.
†† [5:24] See notes on Mt 9:6 and Mk 2:10.

²⁸And leaving everything behind,* he got up and followed him. ²⁹ⁿ Then Levi gave a great banquet for him in his house, and a large crowd of tax collectors and others were at table with them. ³⁰The Pharisees and their scribes complained to his disciples, saying, "Why do you eat and drink with tax collectors and sinners?" ³¹Jesus said to them in reply, "Those who are healthy do not need a physician, but the sick do. ³²I have not come to call the righteous to repentance but sinners."

The Question About Fasting.ᵒ ³³And they said to him, "The disciples of John fast often and offer prayers, and the disciples of the Pharisees do the same; but yours eat and drink." ³⁴† Jesus answered them, "Can you make the wedding guests‡ fast while the bridegroom is with them? ³⁵But the days will come, and when the bridegroom is taken away from them, then they will fast in those days." ³⁶§ And he also told them a parable. "No one tears a piece from a new cloak to patch an old one. Otherwise, he will tear the new and the piece from it will not match the old cloak. ³⁷Likewise, no one pours new wine into old wineskins. Otherwise, the new wine will burst the skins, and it will be spilled, and the skins will be ruined. ³⁸Rather, new wine must be poured into fresh wineskins. ³⁹[And] no one who has been drinking old wine desires new, for he says, 'The old is good.'"¶

---

* [5:28] **Leaving everything behind**: see note on Lk 5:11.
† [5:34–35] See notes on Mt 9:15 and Mk 2:19.
‡ [5:34] **Wedding guests**: literally, "sons of the bridal chamber"
§ [5:36–39] See notes on Mt 9:16–17 and Mk 2:19.
¶ [5:39] **The old is good**: this saying is meant to be ironic and offers an explanation for the rejection by some of the new wine that Jesus offers: satisfaction with old forms will prevent one from sampling the new

a. [5:1–11] Mt 4:18–20; Mk 1:16–20.
b. [5:1–3] Mt 13:1–2; Mk 2:13; 3:9–10; 4:1–2.
c. [5:4–9] Jn 21:1–11.
d. [5:10] Jer 16:16.
e. [5:11] Mt 19:27.
f. [5:12–16] Mt 8:2–4; Mk 1:40–45.
g. [5:14] 8:56; Lv 14:2–32; Mk 7:36.
h. [5:16] Mk 1:35.
i. [5:17–26] Mt 9:1–8; Mk 2:1–12.
j. [5:21] 7:49; Is 43:25.
k. [5:22] 6:8; 9:47.
l. [5:24–25] Jn 5:8–9, 27.
m. [5:27–32] Mt 9:9–13; Mk 2:13–17.
n. [5:29–30] 15:1–2.
o. [5:33–39] Mt 9:14–17; Mk 2:18–22.

6

Debates About the Sabbath.** ¹ᵃ While he was going through a field of grain on a sabbath, his disciples were picking the heads of grain, rubbing them in their hands, and eating them.ᵇ ²Some Pharisees said,

---

** [6:1–11] The two episodes recounted here deal with gathering grain and healing, both of which were forbidden on the sabbath. In his defense of his disciples' conduct and his own charitable deed, Jesus argues that satisfying human needs such as hunger and performing works of mercy take precedence even over the sacred sabbath rest. See also notes on Mt 12:1–14 and Mk 2:25–26.

"Why are you doing what is unlawful on the sabbath?" ³ᶜ Jesus said to them in reply, "Have you not read what David did when he and those [who were] with him were hungry? ⁴[How] he went into the house of God, took the bread of offering,* which only the priests could lawfully eat, ate of it, and shared it with his companions."ᵈ ⁵Then he said to them, "The Son of Man is lord of the sabbath."

⁶ᵉ On another sabbath he went into the synagogue and taught, and there was a man there whose right hand was withered. ⁷The scribes and the Pharisees watched him closely to see if he would cure on the sabbath so that they might discover a reason to accuse him.ᶠ ⁸But he realized their intentions and said to the man with the withered hand, "Come up and stand before us." And he rose and stood there.ᵍ ⁹Then Jesus said to them, "I ask you, is it lawful to do good on the sabbath rather than to do evil, to save life rather than to destroy it?" ¹⁰Looking around at them all, he then said to him, "Stretch out your hand." He did so and his hand was restored. ¹¹But they became enraged and discussed together what they might do to Jesus.

The Mission of the Twelve.† ¹²ʰ In those days he departed to the mountain to pray, and he spent the night in prayer‡ to God. ¹³When day came, he called his disciples to himself, and from them he chose Twelve,§ whom he also named apostles: ¹⁴ⁱ Simon, whom he named Peter,¶ and his brother Andrew, James, John, Philip, Bartholomew, ¹⁵Matthew, Thomas, James the son of Alphaeus, Simon who was called a Zealot,** ¹⁶and Judas the son of James, and Judas Iscariot,†† who became a traitor.

---

* [6:4] **The bread of offering**: see note on Mt 12:5–6.

† [6:12–16] See notes on Mt 10:1–11:1 and Mk 3:14–15.

‡ [6:12] **Spent the night in prayer**: see note on Lk 3:21.

§ [6:13] **He chose Twelve**: the identification of this group as the **Twelve** is a part of early Christian tradition (see 1 Cor 15:5), and in Matthew and Luke, the **Twelve** are associated with the twelve tribes of Israel (Lk 22:29–30; Mt 19:28). After the fall of Judas from his position among the Twelve, the need is felt on the part of the early community to reconstitute this group before the Christian mission begins at Pentecost (Acts 1:15–26). From Luke's perspective, they are an important group who because of their association with Jesus from the time of his baptism to his ascension (Acts 1:21–22) provide the continuity between the historical Jesus and the church of Luke's day and who as the original eyewitnesses guarantee the fidelity of the church's beliefs and practices to the teachings of Jesus (Lk 1:1–4). **Whom he also named apostles**: only Luke among the gospel writers attributes to Jesus the bestowal of the name **apostles** upon the Twelve. See note on Mt 10:2–4. "Apostle" becomes a technical term in early Christianity for a missionary sent out to preach the word of God. Although Luke seems to want to restrict the title to the Twelve (only in Acts 4:4, 14 are Paul and Barnabas termed apostles), other places in the New Testament show an awareness that the term was more widely applied (1 Cor 15:5–7; Gal 1:19; 1 Cor 1:1; 9:1; Rom 16:7).

¶ [6:14] **Simon, whom he named Peter**: see note on Mk 3:16.

** [6:15] **Simon who was called a Zealot**: the Zealots were the instigators of the First Revolt of Palestinian Jews against Rome in A.D. 66–70. Because the existence of the Zealots as a distinct group during the lifetime of Jesus is the subject of debate, the meaning of the identification of Simon as a Zealot is unclear.

†† [6:16] **Judas Iscariot**: the name **Iscariot** may mean "man from Kerioth."

Ministering to a Great Multitude.[j] [17]* And he came down with them and stood on a stretch of level ground. A great crowd of his disciples and a large number of the people from all Judea and Jerusalem and the coastal region of Tyre and Sidon [18]came to hear him and to be healed of their diseases; and even those who were tormented by unclean spirits were cured. [19]Everyone in the crowd sought to touch him because power came forth from him and healed them all.

Sermon on the Plain.[k] [20]† And raising his eyes toward his disciples he said:

> "Blessed are you who are poor,[l]
> for the kingdom of God is yours.
> [21]Blessed are you who are now hungry,
> for you will be satisfied.
> Blessed are you who are now weeping,
> for you will laugh.[l]
> [22]Blessed are you when people hate you,
> and when they exclude and insult you,
> and denounce your name as evil
> on account of the Son of Man.["m]

[23]Rejoice and leap for joy on that day! Behold, your reward will be great in heaven. For their ancestors treated the prophets in the same way."

---

* [6:17] **The coastal region of Tyre and Sidon:** not only Jews from Judea and Jerusalem, but even Gentiles from outside Palestine come to hear Jesus (see Lk 2:31–32; 3:6; 4:24–27).

† [6:20–49] Luke's "Sermon on the Plain" is the counterpart to Matthew's "Sermon on the Mount" (Mt 5:1–7:27). It is addressed to the disciples of Jesus, and, like the sermon in Matthew, it begins with beatitudes (Lk 6:20–22) and ends with the parable of the two houses (Lk 6:46–49). Almost all the words of Jesus reported by Luke are found in Matthew's version, but because Matthew includes sayings that were related to specifically Jewish Christian problems (e.g., Mt 5:17–20; 6:1–8, 16–18) that Luke did not find appropriate for his predominantly Gentile Christian audience, the "Sermon on the Mount" is considerably longer. Luke's sermon may be outlined as follows: an introduction consisting of blessings and woes (Lk 6:20–26); the love of one's enemies (Lk 6:27–36); the demands of loving one's neighbor (Lk 6:37–42); good deeds as proof of one's goodness (Lk 6:43–45); a parable illustrating the result of listening to and acting on the words of Jesus (Lk 6:46–49). At the core of the sermon is Jesus' teaching on the love of one's enemies (Lk 6:27–36) that has as its source of motivation God's graciousness and compassion for all humanity (Lk 6:35–36) and Jesus' teaching on the love of one's neighbor (Lk 6:37–42) that is characterized by forgiveness and generosity.

‡ [6:20–26] The introductory portion of the sermon consists of blessings and woes that address the real economic and social conditions of humanity (the poor—the rich; the hungry—the satisfied; those grieving—those laughing; the outcast—the socially acceptable). By contrast, Matthew emphasizes the religious and spiritual values of disciples in the kingdom inaugurated by Jesus ("poor in spirit," Mt 5:3; "hunger and thirst for righteousness," Mt 5:6). In the sermon, **blessed** extols the fortunate condition of persons who are favored with the blessings of God; the woes, addressed as they are to the disciples of Jesus, threaten God's profound displeasure on those so blinded by their present fortunate situation that they do not recognize and appreciate the real values of God's kingdom. In all the blessings and woes, the present condition of the persons addressed will be reversed in the future.

²⁴But woe to you who are rich,
>   for you have received your consolation.^o
²⁵But woe to you who are filled now,
>   for you will be hungry.
Woe to you who laugh now,
>   for you will grieve and weep.^p
²⁶Woe to you when all speak well of you,
>   for their ancestors treated the false prophets in this way.^q

Love of Enemies.[*] ^{27r}"But to you who hear I say, love your enemies, do good to those who hate you,^s ²⁸bless those who curse you, pray for those who mistreat you.^t ²⁹To the person who strikes you on one cheek, offer the other one as well, and from the person who takes your cloak, do not withhold even your tunic. ³⁰Give to everyone who asks of you, and from the one who takes what is yours do not demand it back. ³¹Do to others as you would have them do to you.^u ³²For if you love those who love you, what credit is that to you? Even sinners love those who love them. ³³And if you do good to those who do good to you, what credit is that to you? Even sinners do the same. ³⁴If you lend money to those from whom you expect repayment, what credit [is] that to you? Even sinners lend to sinners, and get back the same amount.^v ³⁵But rather, love your enemies and do good to them, and lend expecting nothing back; then your reward will be great and you will be children of the Most High, for he himself is kind to the ungrateful and the wicked.^w ³⁶Be merciful, just as [also] your Father is merciful.

Judging Others.[†] ^{37x}"Stop judging and you will not be judged. Stop condemning and you will not be condemned. Forgive and you will be forgiven.^y ³⁸Give and gifts will be given to you; a good measure, packed together, shaken down, and overflowing, will be poured into your lap. For the measure with which you measure will in return be measured out to you."^z ³⁹And he told them a parable, "Can a blind person guide a blind person? Will not both fall into a pit?^a ⁴⁰No disciple is superior to the teacher; but when fully trained, every disciple will be like his teacher.^b ⁴¹Why do you notice the splinter in your brother's eye, but do

---

* [6:27–36] See notes on Mt 5:43–48 and Mt 5:48.
† [6:37–42] See notes on Mt 7:1–12; 7:1; 7:5.

not perceive the wooden beam in your own? [42]How can you say to your brother, 'Brother, let me remove that splinter in your eye,' when you do not even notice the wooden beam in your own eye? You hypocrite! Remove the wooden beam from your eye first; then you will see clearly to remove the splinter in your brother's eye.

A Tree Known by Its Fruit.[c] [43]* "A good tree does not bear rotten fruit, nor does a rotten tree bear good fruit. [44]For every tree is known by its own fruit. For people do not pick figs from thornbushes, nor do they gather grapes from brambles. [45]A good person out of the store of goodness in his heart produces good, but an evil person out of a store of evil produces evil; for from the fullness of the heart the mouth speaks.

The Two Foundations. [46]d "Why do you call me, 'Lord, Lord,' but not do what I command? [47]† I will show you what someone is like who comes to me, listens to my words, and acts on them.[e] [48]That one is like a person building a house, who dug deeply and laid the foundation on rock; when the flood came, the river burst against that house but could not shake it because it had been well built. [49]But the one who listens and does not act is like a person who built a house on the ground without a foundation. When the river burst against it, it collapsed at once and was completely destroyed."

---

* [6:43–46] See notes on Mt 7:15–20 and 12:33.
† [6:47–49] See note on Mt 7:24–27.

a. [6:1–5] Mt 12:1–8; Mk 2:23–28.
b. [6:1] Dt 23:26.
c. [6:3–4] 1 Sm 21:1–6.
d. [6:4] Lv 24:5–9.
e. [6:6–11] Mt 12:9–14; Mk 3:1–6.
f. [6:7] 14:1.
g. [6:8] 5:22; 9:47.
h. [6:12–16] Mt 10:1–4; Mk 3:13–19.
i. [6:14–16] Acts 1:13.
j. [6:17–19] Mt 4:23–25; Mk 3:7–10.
k. [6:20–26] Mt 5:1–12.
l. [6:21] Ps 126:5–6; Is 61:3; Jer 31:25; Rev 7:16–17.
m. [6:22] Jn 15:19; 16:2; 1 Pt 4:14.
n. [6:23] 11:47–48; 2 Chr 36:16; Mt 23:30–31.
o. [6:24] Jas 5:1.
p. [6:25] Is 65:13–14.
q. [6:26] Jas 4:4.
r. [6:27–36] Mt 5:38–48.
s. [6:27] Prv 25:21; Rom 12:20–21.
t. [6:28] Rom 12:14; 1 Pt 3:9.
u. [6:31] Mt 7:12.
v. [6:34] Dt 15:7–8.
w. [6:35] Lv 25:35–36.
x. [6:37–42] Mt 7:1–5.
y. [6:37] Mt 6:14; Jas 2:13.
z. [6:38] Mk 4:24.
a. [6:39] Mt 15:14; 23:16–17, 24.
b. [6:40] Mt 10:24–25; Jn 13:16; 15:20.
c. [6:43–45] Mt 7:16–20; 12:33, 35.
d. [6:46] Mt 7:21; Rom 2:13; Jas 1:22.
e. [6:47–49] Mt 7:24–27.

7 The Healing of a Centurion's Slave.[a] [1]* When he had finished all his words to the people, he entered Capernaum.[†] [2]A centurion[‡] there had a slave who was ill and about to die, and he was valuable to him. [3]When he heard about Jesus, he sent elders of the Jews to him, asking him to come and save the life of his slave. [4]They approached Jesus and strongly urged him to come, saying, "He deserves to have you do this for him, [5]for he loves our nation and he built the synagogue for us." [6]And Jesus went with them, but when he was only a short distance from the house, the centurion sent friends to tell him, "Lord, do not trouble yourself, for I am not worthy to have you enter under my roof.[§] [7]Therefore, I did not consider myself worthy to come to you; but say the word and let my servant be healed. [8]For I too am a person subject to authority, with soldiers subject to me. And I say to one, 'Go,' and he goes; and to another, 'Come here,' and he comes; and to my slave, 'Do this,' and he does it." [9]When Jesus heard this he was amazed at him and, turning, said to the crowd following him, "I tell you, not even in Israel have I found such faith." [10]When the messengers returned to the house, they found the slave in good health.

Raising of the Widow's Son.[¶] [11b] Soon afterward he journeyed to a city called Nain, and his disciples and a large crowd accompanied him. [12]As he drew near to the gate of the city, a man who had died was being carried out, the only son of his mother, and she was a widow. A large crowd from the city was with her.[c] [13]When the Lord saw her, he was moved with pity for her and said to her, "Do not weep." [14]He stepped forward and touched the coffin; at this the bearers halted, and he said, "Young man, I tell you, arise!" [15]The dead man sat up and began to

---

* [7:1–8:3] The episodes in this section present a series of reactions to the Galilean ministry of Jesus and reflect some of Luke's particular interests: the faith of a Gentile (Lk 7:1–10); the prophet Jesus' concern for a widowed mother (Lk 7:11–17); the ministry of Jesus directed to the afflicted and unfortunate of Is 61:1 (Lk 7:18–23); the relation between John and Jesus and their role in God's plan for salvation (Lk 7:24–35); a forgiven sinner's manifestation of love (Lk 7:36–50); the association of women with the ministry of Jesus (Lk 8:1–3).

† [7:1–10] This story about the faith of the centurion, a Gentile who cherishes the Jewish nation (Lk 7:5), prepares for the story in Acts of the conversion by Peter of the Roman centurion Cornelius who is similarly described as one who is generous to the Jewish nation (Acts 10:2). See also Acts 10:34–35 in the speech of Peter: "God shows no partiality. . .whoever fears him and acts righteously is acceptable to him." See also notes on Mt 8:5–13 and Jn 4:43–54.

‡ [7:2] **A centurion:** see note on Mt 8:5.

§ [7:6] **I am not worthy to have you enter under my roof:** to enter the house of a Gentile was considered unclean for a Jew; cf. Acts 10:28.

¶ [7:11–17] In the previous incident Jesus' power was displayed for a Gentile whose servant was dying; in this episode it is displayed toward a widowed mother whose only son has already died. Jesus' power over death prepares for his reply to John's disciples in Lk 7:22: "the dead are raised." This resuscitation in alluding to the prophet Elijah's resurrection of the only son of a widow of Zarephath (1 Kgs 17:17–24) leads to the reaction of the crowd: "A great prophet has arisen in our midst" (Lk 7:16).

speak, and Jesus gave him to his mother.[d] [16]Fear seized them all, and they glorified God, exclaiming, "A great prophet has arisen in our midst," and "God has visited his people."[e] [17]This report about him spread through the whole of Judea and in all the surrounding region.

The Messengers from John the Baptist.[*] [18f] The disciples of John told him about all these things. John summoned two of his disciples [19]and sent them to the Lord to ask, "Are you the one who is to come, or should we look for another?"[g] [20]When the men came to him, they said, "John the Baptist has sent us to you to ask, 'Are you the one who is to come, or should we look for another?'" [21]At that time he cured many of their diseases, sufferings, and evil spirits; he also granted sight to many who were blind. [22]And he said to them in reply, "Go and tell John what you have seen and heard: the blind regain their sight, the lame walk, lepers are cleansed, the deaf hear, the dead are raised, the poor have the good news proclaimed to them.[h] [23]And blessed is the one who takes no offense at me."[†]

Jesus' Testimony to John. [24‡] When the messengers of John had left, Jesus began to speak to the crowds about John.[i] "What did you go out to the desert to see—a reed swayed by the wind? [25]Then what did you go out to see? Someone dressed in fine garments? Those who dress luxuriously and live sumptuously are found in royal palaces. [26]Then what did you go out to see? A prophet? Yes, I tell you, and more than a prophet.[j] [27]This is the one about whom scripture says:

'Behold, I am sending my messenger ahead of you,
    he will prepare your way before you.'[k]

[28]I tell you, among those born of women, no one is greater than John; yet the least in the kingdom of God is greater than he." [29l] (All the people who listened, including the tax collectors, and who were baptized with the baptism of John, acknowledged the righteousness of God; [30]but

---

* [7:18–23] In answer to John's question, **Are you the one who is to come?**—a probable reference to the return of the fiery prophet of reform, Elijah, "before the day of the Lord comes, the great and terrible day" (Mal 3:23)—Jesus responds that his role is rather to bring the blessings spoken of in Is 61:1 to the oppressed and neglected of society (Lk 7:22; cf. Lk 4:18).

† [7:23] **Blessed is the one who takes no offense at me**: this beatitude is pronounced on the person who recognizes Jesus' true identity in spite of previous expectations of what "the one who is to come" would be like.

‡ [7:24–30] In his testimony to John, Jesus reveals his understanding of the relationship between them: John is the precursor of Jesus (Lk 7:27); John is the messenger spoken of in Mal 3:1 who in Mal 3:23 is identified as Elijah. Taken with the previous episode, it can be seen that Jesus identifies John as precisely the person John envisioned Jesus to be: the Elijah who prepares the way for the coming of the day of the Lord.

the Pharisees and scholars of the law, who were not baptized by him, rejected the plan of God for themselves.)

[31*] "Then to what shall I compare the people of this generation? What are they like?[m] [32]They are like children who sit in the marketplace and call to one another,

> 'We played the flute for you, but you did not dance.
> We sang a dirge, but you did not weep.'

[33]For John the Baptist came neither eating food nor drinking wine, and you said, 'He is possessed by a demon.' [34]The Son of Man came eating and drinking and you said, 'Look, he is a glutton and a drunkard, a friend of tax collectors and sinners.'[n] [35]But wisdom is vindicated by all her children."

The Pardon of the Sinful Woman.[†] [36o] A Pharisee invited him to dine with him, and he entered the Pharisee's house and reclined at table.[‡] [37]Now there was a sinful woman in the city who learned that he was at table in the house of the Pharisee.[p] Bringing an alabaster flask of ointment,[q] [38]she stood behind him at his feet weeping and began to bathe his feet with her tears. Then she wiped them with her hair, kissed them, and anointed them with the ointment. [39]When the Pharisee who had invited him saw this he said to himself, "If this man were a prophet, he would know who and what sort of woman this is who is touching him, that she is a sinner." [40]Jesus said to him in reply, "Simon, I have something to say to you." "Tell me, teacher," he said. [41]"Two people were in debt to a certain creditor; one owed five hundred days' wages[§] and the other owed fifty. [42]Since they were unable to repay the debt, he forgave it for both. Which of them will love him more?" [43]Simon said in reply, "The one, I suppose, whose larger debt was forgiven." He said to him, "You have judged rightly." [44]Then he turned to the woman and said to Simon, "Do you see this woman? When

---

[*] [7:31–35] See note on Mt 11:16–19.

[†] [7:36–50] In this story of the pardoning of the sinful woman Luke presents two different reactions to the ministry of Jesus. A Pharisee, suspecting Jesus to be a prophet, invites Jesus to a festive banquet in his house, but the Pharisee's self-righteousness leads to little love shown toward Jesus. The sinful woman, on the other hand, manifests a faith in God (Lk 7:50) that has led her to seek forgiveness for her sins, and because so much was forgiven, she now overwhelms Jesus with her display of love; cf. the similar contrast in attitudes in Lk 18:9–14. The whole episode is a powerful lesson on the relation between forgiveness and love.

[‡] [7:36] **Reclined at table**: the normal posture of guests at a banquet. Other oriental banquet customs alluded to in this story include the reception by the host with a kiss (Lk 7:45), washing the feet of the guests (Lk 7:44), and the anointing of the guests' heads (Lk 7:46).

[§] [7:41] **Days' wages**: one denarius is the normal daily wage of a laborer.

I entered your house, you did not give me water for my feet, but she has bathed them with her tears and wiped them with her hair. ⁴⁵You did not give me a kiss, but she has not ceased kissing my feet since the time I entered. ⁴⁶You did not anoint my head with oil, but she anointed my feet with ointment. ⁴⁷So I tell you, her many sins have been forgiven; hence, she has shown great love.* But the one to whom little is forgiven, loves little." ⁴⁸He said to her, "Your sins are forgiven."ʳ ⁴⁹The others at table said to themselves, "Who is this who even forgives sins?"ˢ ⁵⁰But he said to the woman, "Your faith has saved you; go in peace."

---

* [7:47] **Her many sins have been forgiven; hence, she has shown great love**: literally, "her many sins have been forgiven, seeing that she has loved much." That the woman's sins have been forgiven is attested by the great love she shows toward Jesus. Her love is the consequence of her forgiveness. This is also the meaning demanded by the parable in Lk 7:41–43.

a. [7:1–10] Mt 8:5–13; Jn 4:43–54.
b. [7:11–17] 4:25–26; 1 Kgs 17:17–24.
c. [7:12] 8:42; 1 Kgs 17:17.
d. [7:15] 1 Kgs 17:23; 2 Kgs 4:36.
e. [7:16] 1:68; 19:44.
f. [7:18–23] Mt 11:2–6.
g. [7:19] Mal 3:1; Rev 1:4, 8; 4:8.
h. [7:22] 4:18; Is 35:5–6; 61:1.
i. [7:24–30] Mt 11:7–15.
j. [7:26] 1:76.

k. [7:27] Mal 3:1 / Is 40:3.
l. [7:29–30] 3:7, 12; Mt 21:32.
m. [7:31–35] Mt 11:16–19.
n. [7:34] 15:2.
o. [7:36] 11:37; 14:1.
p. [7:37] Mt 26:7; Mk 14:3.
q. [7:37–38] Jn 12:3.
r. [7:48] 5:20; Mt 9:20; Mk 2:5.
s. [7:49] 5:21.

---

8 Galilean Women Follow Jesus.†

¹Afterward he journeyed from one town and village to another, preaching and proclaiming the good news of the kingdom of God.ᵃ Accompanying him were the Twelve ²ᵇ and some women who had been cured of evil spirits and infirmities, Mary, called Magdalene, from whom seven demons had gone out, ³Joanna, the wife of Herod's steward Chuza, Susanna, and many others who provided for them out of their resources.

The Parable of the Sower.ᶜ ⁴‡ When a large crowd gathered, with people from one town after another journeying to him, he spoke in a parable.§ ⁵"A sower went out to sow his seed. And as he sowed, some seed fell on

---

† [8:1–3] Luke presents Jesus as an itinerant preacher traveling in the company of the Twelve and of the Galilean women who are sustaining them out of their means. These Galilean women will later accompany Jesus on his journey to Jerusalem and become witnesses to his death (Lk 23:49) and resurrection (Lk 24:9–11, where Mary Magdalene and Joanna are specifically mentioned; cf. also Acts 1:14). The association of women with the ministry of Jesus is most unusual in the light of the attitude of first-century Palestinian Judaism toward women. The more common attitude is expressed in Jn 4:27, and early rabbinic documents caution against speaking with women in public.

‡ [8:4–21] The focus in this section is on how one should hear the word of God and act on it. It includes the parable of the sower and its explanation (Lk 8:4–15), a collection of sayings on how one should act on the word that is heard (Lk 8:16–18), and the identification of the mother and brothers of Jesus as the ones who hear the word and act on it (Lk 8:19–21). See also notes on Mt 13:1–53 and Mk 4:1–34.

§ [8:4–8] See note on Mt 13:3–8.

the path and was trampled, and the birds of the sky ate it up. ⁶Some seed fell on rocky ground, and when it grew, it withered for lack of moisture. ⁷Some seed fell among thorns, and the thorns grew with it and choked it. ⁸And some seed fell on good soil, and when it grew, it produced fruit a hundredfold." After saying this, he called out, "Whoever has ears to hear ought to hear."*d*

The Purpose of the Parables.*e* ⁹Then his disciples asked him what the meaning of this parable might be. ¹⁰He answered, "Knowledge of the mysteries of the kingdom of God has been granted to you; but to the rest, they are made known through parables so that 'they may look but not see, and hear but not understand.'*f*

The Parable of the Sower Explained.* ¹¹*g* "This is the meaning of the parable. The seed is the word of God.*h* ¹²Those on the path are the ones who have heard, but the devil comes and takes away the word from their hearts that they may not believe and be saved. ¹³Those on rocky ground are the ones who, when they hear, receive the word with joy, but they have no root; they believe only for a time and fall away in time of trial. ¹⁴As for the seed that fell among thorns, they are the ones who have heard, but as they go along, they are choked by the anxieties and riches and pleasures of life, and they fail to produce mature fruit. ¹⁵But as for the seed that fell on rich soil, they are the ones who, when they have heard the word, embrace it with a generous and good heart, and bear fruit through perseverance.

The Parable of the Lamp.† ¹⁶*i* "No one who lights a lamp conceals it with a vessel or sets it under a bed; rather, he places it on a lampstand so that those who enter may see the light.*j* ¹⁷For there is nothing hidden that will not become visible, and nothing secret that will not be known and come to light.*k* ¹⁸Take care, then, how you hear. To anyone who has, more will be given, and from the one who has not, even what he seems to have will be taken away."*l*

---

* [8:11–15] On the interpretation of the parable of the sower, see note on Mt 13:18–23.
† [8:16–18] These sayings continue the theme of responding to the word of God. Those who hear the word must become a light to others (Lk 8:16); even the mysteries of the kingdom that have been made known to the disciples (Lk 8:9–10) must come to light (Lk 8:17); a generous and persevering response to the word of God leads to a still more perfect response to the word.

Jesus and His Family.[m] 19Then his mother and his brothers* came to him but were unable to join him because of the crowd. 20n He was told, "Your mother and your brothers are standing outside and they wish to see you." 21He said to them in reply, "My mother and my brothers are those who hear the word of God and act on it."†

The Calming of a Storm at Sea.[o] 22‡ One day he got into a boat with his disciples and said to them, "Let us cross to the other side of the lake." So they set sail, 23and while they were sailing he fell asleep. A squall blew over the lake, and they were taking in water and were in danger. 24They came and woke him saying, "Master, master, we are perishing!" He awakened, rebuked the wind and the waves, and they subsided and there was a calm. 25Then he asked them, "Where is your faith?" But they were filled with awe and amazed and said to one another, "Who then is this, who commands even the winds and the sea, and they obey him?"

The Healing of the Gerasene Demoniac.[p] 26Then they sailed to the territory of the Gerasenes,§ which is opposite Galilee. 27When he came ashore a man from the town who was possessed by demons met him. For a long time he had not worn clothes; he did not live in a house, but lived among the tombs. 28q When he saw Jesus, he cried out and fell down before him; in a loud voice he shouted, "What have you to do with me, Jesus, son of the Most High God? I beg you, do not torment me!" 29For he had ordered the unclean spirit to come out of the man. (It had taken hold of him many times, and he used to be bound with chains and shackles as a restraint, but he would break his bonds and be driven by the demon into deserted places.) 30Then Jesus asked him, "What is your name?"§ He replied, "Legion," because many demons

* [8:19] **His brothers:** see note on Mk 6:3.

† [8:21] The family of Jesus is not constituted by physical relationship with him but by obedience to the word of God. In this, Luke agrees with the Marcan parallel (Mk 3:31–35), although by omitting Mk 3:33 and especially Mk 3:20–21 Luke has softened the Marcan picture of Jesus' natural family. Probably he did this because Mary has already been presented in Lk 1:38 as the obedient handmaid of the Lord who fulfills the requirement for belonging to the eschatological family of Jesus; cf. also Lk 11:27–28.

‡ [8:22–56] This section records four miracles of Jesus that manifest his power and authority: (1) the calming of a storm on the lake (Lk 8:22–25); (2) the exorcism of a demoniac (Lk 8:26–39); (3) the cure of a hemorrhaging woman (Lk 8:40–48); (4) the raising of Jairus's daughter to life (Lk 8:49–56). They parallel the same sequence of stories at Mk 4:35–5:43.

§ [8:26] **Gerasenes:** other manuscripts read Gadarenes or Gergesenes. See also note on Mt 8:28. **Opposite Galilee:** probably Gentile territory (note the presence in the area of pigs—unclean animals to Jews) and an indication that the person who receives salvation (Lk 8:36) is a Gentile.

§ [8:30] **What is your name?:** the question reflects the popular belief that knowledge of the spirit's name brought control over the spirit. **Legion:** to Jesus' question the demon replies with a Latin word transliterated into Greek. The Roman legion at this period consisted of 5,000 to 6,000 foot soldiers; hence the name implies a very large number of demons.

had entered him. [31]And they pleaded with him not to order them to depart to the abyss.[*]

[32]A herd of many swine was feeding there on the hillside, and they pleaded with him to allow them to enter those swine; and he let them. [33]The demons came out of the man and entered the swine, and the herd rushed down the steep bank into the lake and was drowned. [34]When the swineherds saw what had happened, they ran away and reported the incident in the town and throughout the countryside. [35]People came out to see what had happened and, when they approached Jesus, they discovered the man from whom the demons had come out sitting at his feet.[†] He was clothed and in his right mind, and they were seized with fear. [36]Those who witnessed it told them how the possessed man had been saved. [37]The entire population of the region of the Gerasenes asked Jesus to leave them because they were seized with great fear. So he got into a boat and returned. [38]The man from whom the demons had come out begged to remain with him, but he sent him away, saying, [39]"Return home and recount what God has done for you." The man went off and proclaimed throughout the whole town what Jesus had done for him.

Jairus's Daughter and the Woman with a Hemorrhage.[‡] [40r] When Jesus returned, the crowd welcomed him, for they were all waiting for him. [41]And a man named Jairus, an official of the synagogue, came forward. He fell at the feet of Jesus and begged him to come to his house, [42]because he had an only daughter,[§] about twelve years old, and she was dying. As he went, the crowds almost crushed him. [43]And a woman afflicted with hemorrhages for twelve years,[¶] who [had spent her whole livelihood on doctors and] was unable to be cured by anyone, [44]came up behind him and touched the tassel on his cloak. Immediately her bleeding stopped. [45]Jesus then asked, "Who touched me?" While all were denying it, Peter said, "Master, the crowds are pushing and pressing in upon you." [46]But

---

[*] [8:31] **Abyss**: the place of the dead (Rom 10:7) or the prison of Satan (Rev 20:3) or the subterranean "watery deep" that symbolizes the chaos before the order imposed by creation (Gn 1:2).

[†] [8:35] **Sitting at his feet**: the former demoniac takes the position of a disciple before the master (Lk 10:39; Acts 22:3).

[‡] [8:40–56] Two interwoven miracle stories, one a healing and the other a resuscitation, present Jesus as master over sickness and death. In the Lucan account, faith in Jesus is responsible for the cure (Lk 8:48) and for the raising to life (Lk 8:50).

[§] [8:42] **An only daughter**: cf. the son of the widow of Nain whom Luke describes as an "only" son (Lk 7:12; see also Lk 9:38).

[¶] [8:43] **Afflicted with hemorrhages for twelve years**: according to the Mosaic law (Lv 15:25–30) this condition would render the woman unclean and unfit for contact with other people.

Jesus said, "Someone has touched me; for I know that power has gone out from me."[s] [47]When the woman realized that she had not escaped notice, she came forward trembling. Falling down before him, she explained in the presence of all the people why she had touched him and how she had been healed immediately. [48]He said to her, "Daughter, your faith has saved you; go in peace."[t]

[49]While he was still speaking, someone from the synagogue official's house arrived and said, "Your daughter is dead; do not trouble the teacher any longer." [50]On hearing this, Jesus answered him, "Do not be afraid; just have faith and she will be saved." [51]When he arrived at the house he allowed no one to enter with him except Peter and John and James, and the child's father and mother. [52]* [u] All were weeping and mourning for her, when he said, "Do not weep any longer, for she is not dead, but sleeping." [53]And they ridiculed him, because they knew that she was dead. [54]But he took her by the hand and called to her, "Child, arise!" [55]Her breath returned and she immediately arose. He then directed that she should be given something to eat. [56]Her parents were astounded, and he instructed them to tell no one what had happened.

---

* [8:52] **Sleeping**: her death is a temporary condition; cf. Jn 11:11–14.

a. [8:1] 4:43.
b. [8:2–3] 23:49; 24:10; Mt 27:55–56; Mk 15:40–41; Jn 19:5.
c. [8:4–8] Mt 13:1–9; Mk 4:1–9.
d. [8:8] 14:35; Mt 11:15; 13:43; Mk 4:23.
e. [8:9–10] Mt 13:10–13; Mk 4:10–12.
f. [0.10] Is 6.9.
g. [8:11–15] Mt 13:18–23; Mk 4.13–20.
h. [8:11] 1 Pt 1:23.
i. [8:16–18] Mk 4:21–25.
j. [8:16] 11:33; Mt 5:15.
k. [8:17] 12:2; Mt 10:26.

l. [8:18] 19:26; Mt 13:12; 25:29.
m. [8:19–21] Mt 12:46 50; Mk 3:31–35.
n. [8:20–21] 11:27–28.
o. [8:22–25] Mt 8:18, 23–27; Mk 4:35–41.
p. [8:26–39] Mt 8:28–34; Mk 5:1–20.
q. [8:28–29] 4:33–35; Mt 8:29; Mk 1:23–24.
r. [8:40–56] Mt 9:18–26; Mk 5:21–43.
s. [8:46] 6:19.
t. [8:48] 7:50; 17:19; 18:42.
u. [8:52] 7:13.

---

9 **The Mission of the Twelve.**[†] [1a] He summoned the Twelve and gave them power and authority over all demons and to cure diseases, [2]and he sent them to proclaim the kingdom of God and to heal [the sick]. [3]He said to them, "Take nothing for the journey,[‡] neither walking stick, nor sack, nor food, nor money, and let no one take a second tunic.

---

† [9:1–6] Armed with the power and authority that Jesus himself has been displaying in the previous episodes, the Twelve are now sent out to continue the work that Jesus has been performing throughout his Galilean ministry: (1) proclaiming the kingdom (Lk 4:43; 8:1); (2) exorcising demons (Lk 4:33–37, 41; 8:26–39) and (3) healing the sick (Lk 4:38–40; 5:12–16, 17–26; 6:6–10; 7:1–10, 17, 22; 8:40–56).
‡ [9:3] **Take nothing for the journey**: the absolute detachment required of the disciple (Lk 14:33) leads to complete reliance on God (Lk 12:22–31).

⁴Whatever house you enter, stay there and leave from there.ᵇ ⁵And as for those who do not welcome you, when you leave that town, shake the dust from your feet* in testimony against them."ᶜ ⁶Then they set out and went from village to village proclaiming the good news and curing diseases everywhere.

Herod's Opinion of Jesus.ᵈ ⁷† Herod the tetrarch‡ heard about all that was happening, and he was greatly perplexed because some were saying, "John has been raised from the dead";ᵉ ⁸others were saying, "Elijah has appeared"; still others, "One of the ancient prophets has arisen." ⁹§ ᶠ But Herod said, "John I beheaded. Who then is this about whom I hear such things?" And he kept trying to see him.

The Return of the Twelve and the Feeding of the Five Thousand.ᵍ ¹⁰When the apostles returned, they explained to him what they had done. He took them and withdrew in private to a town called Bethsaida. ¹¹The crowds, meanwhile, learned of this and followed him. He received them and spoke to them about the kingdom of God, and he healed those who needed to be cured. ¹²As the day was drawing to a close, the Twelve approached him and said, "Dismiss the crowd so that they can go to the surrounding villages and farms and find lodging and provisions; for we are in a deserted place here." ¹³ʰ He said to them, "Give them some food yourselves." They replied, "Five loaves and two fish are all we have, unless we ourselves go and buy food for all these people." ¹⁴Now the men there numbered about five thousand. Then he said to his disciples, "Have them sit down in groups of [about] fifty." ¹⁵They did so and made them all sit down. ¹⁶Then taking⁵ the five loaves and the two fish, and looking up to heaven, he said the blessing over them, broke them, and gave them to the disciples to set before the crowd.ⁱ

---

* [9:5] **Shake the dust from your feet**: see note on Mt 10:14.

† [9:7–56] This section in which Luke gathers together incidents that focus on the identity of Jesus is introduced by a question that Herod is made to ask in this gospel: "Who then is this about whom I hear such things?"(Lk 9:9) In subsequent episodes, Luke reveals to the reader various answers to Herod's question: Jesus is one in whom God's power is present and who provides for the needs of God's people (Lk 9:10–17); Peter declares Jesus to be "the Messiah of God" (Lk 9:18–21); Jesus says he is the suffering Son of Man (Lk 9:22, 43–45); Jesus is the Master to be followed, even to death (Lk 9:23–27); Jesus is God's son, his Chosen One (Lk 9:28–36).

‡ [9:7] **Herod the tetrarch**: see note on Lk 3:1.

§ [9:9] **And he kept trying to see him**: this indication of Herod's interest in Jesus prepares for Lk 13:31–33 and for Lk 23:8–12 where Herod's curiosity about Jesus' power to perform miracles remains unsatisfied.

⁵ [9:16] **Then taking…**: the actions of Jesus recall the institution of the Eucharist in Lk 22:19; see also note on Mt 14:19.

[17]They all ate and were satisfied. And when the leftover fragments were picked up, they filled twelve wicker baskets.

Peter's Confession About Jesus.[*] [18][j] Once when Jesus was praying in solitude,[†] and the disciples were with him, he asked them, "Who do the crowds say that I am?" [19]They said in reply, "John the Baptist; others, Elijah; still others, 'One of the ancient prophets has arisen.'"[k] [20]Then he said to them, "But who do you say that I am?" Peter said in reply, "The Messiah of God."[‡] [21]He rebuked them and directed them not to tell this to anyone.

The First Prediction of the Passion. [22]He said, "The Son of Man must suffer greatly and be rejected by the elders, the chief priests, and the scribes, and be killed and on the third day be raised."[l]

The Conditions of Discipleship.[m] [23]Then he said to all, "If anyone wishes to come after me, he must deny himself and take up his cross daily[§] and follow me.[n] [24]For whoever wishes to save his life will lose it, but whoever loses his life for my sake will save it.[o] [25]What profit is there for one to gain the whole world yet lose or forfeit himself? [26]Whoever is ashamed of me and of my words, the Son of Man will be ashamed of when he comes in his glory and in the glory of the Father and of the holy angels.[p] [27]Truly I say to you, there are some standing here who will not taste death until they see the kingdom of God."

The Transfiguration of Jesus.[¶] [28][q] About eight days after he said this, he took Peter, John, and James and went up the mountain to pray.[**] [29]While he was praying his face changed in appearance and his clothing became dazzling white. [30]And behold, two men were conversing with

---

[*] [9:18–22] This incident is based on Mk 8:27–33, but Luke has eliminated Peter's refusal to accept Jesus as suffering Son of Man (Mk 8:32) and the rebuke of Peter by Jesus (Mk 8:33). Elsewhere in the gospel, Luke softens the harsh portrait of Peter and the other apostles found in his Marcan source (cf. Lk 22:39–46, which similarly lacks a rebuke of Peter that occurs in the source, Mk 14:37–38).

[†] [9:18] **When Jesus was praying in solitude:** see note on Lk 3:21.

[‡] [9:20] **The Messiah of God:** on the meaning of this title in first-century Palestinian Judaism, see notes on Lk 2:11 and on Mt 8:27–30.

[§] [9:23] **Daily:** this is a Lucan addition to a saying of Jesus, removing the saying from a context that envisioned the imminent suffering and death of the disciple of Jesus (as does the saying in Mk 8:34–35) to one that focuses on the demands of daily Christian existence.

[¶] [9:28–36] Situated shortly after the first announcement of the passion, death, and resurrection, this scene of Jesus' transfiguration provides the heavenly confirmation to Jesus' declaration that his suffering will end in glory (Lk 9:32); see also notes on Mt 17:1–8 and Mk 9:2–8.

[**] [9:28] **Up the mountain to pray:** the "mountain" is the regular place of prayer in Luke (see Lk 6:12; 22:39–41).

him, Moses and Elijah,* ^{31†} ^r who appeared in glory and spoke of his exodus that he was going to accomplish in Jerusalem. ³²Peter and his companions had been overcome by sleep, but becoming fully awake, they saw his glory‡ and the two men standing with him.^s ³³As they were about to part from him, Peter said to Jesus, "Master, it is good that we are here; let us make three tents,[§] one for you, one for Moses, and one for Elijah." But he did not know what he was saying. ³⁴¶ While he was still speaking, a cloud came and cast a shadow over them, and they became frightened when** they entered the cloud. ³⁵** ^t Then from the cloud came a voice that said, "This is my chosen Son; listen to him." ³⁶After the voice had spoken, Jesus was found alone. They fell silent and did not at that time†† tell anyone what they had seen.

The Healing of a Boy with a Demon.‡‡ ^{37u} On the next day, when they came down from the mountain, a large crowd met him. ³⁸There was a man in the crowd who cried out, "Teacher, I beg you, look at my son; he is my only child. ³⁹For a spirit seizes him and he suddenly screams and it convulses him until he foams at the mouth; it releases him only with difficulty, wearing him out. ⁴⁰I begged your disciples to cast it out but they could not." ⁴¹Jesus said in reply, "O faithless and perverse generation, how long will I be with you and endure you? Bring your son here." ⁴²As he was coming forward, the demon threw him to the ground in a convulsion; but Jesus rebuked the unclean spirit, healed the boy, and returned him to his father. ⁴³And all were astonished by the majesty of God.

The Second Prediction of the Passion.^v While they were all amazed at his every deed, he said to his disciples, ⁴⁴"Pay attention to what I am

---

* [9:30] **Moses and Elijah:** the two figures represent the Old Testament law and the prophets. At the end of this episode, the heavenly voice will identify Jesus as the one to be listened to now (Lk 9:35). See also note on Mk 9:5.

† [9:31] **His exodus that he was going to accomplish in Jerusalem:** Luke identifies the subject of the conversation as the *exodus* of Jesus, a reference to the death, resurrection, and ascension of Jesus that will take place in Jerusalem, the city of destiny (see Lk 9:51). The mention of exodus, however, also calls to mind the Israelite Exodus from Egypt to the promised land.

‡ [9:32] **They saw his glory:** the **glory** that is proper to God is here attributed to Jesus (see Lk 24:26).

§ [9:33] **Let us make three tents:** in a possible allusion to the feast of Tabernacles, Peter may be likening his joy on the occasion of the transfiguration to the joyful celebration of this harvest festival.

¶ [9:34] **Over them:** it is not clear whether **them** refers to Jesus, Moses, and Elijah, or to the disciples. For the cloud casting its shadow, see note on Mk 9:7.

** [9:35] Like the heavenly voice that identified Jesus at his baptism prior to his undertaking the Galilean ministry (Lk 3:22), so too here before the journey to the city of destiny is begun (Lk 9:51) the heavenly voice again identifies Jesus as Son. **Listen to him:** the two representatives of Israel of old depart (Lk 9:33) and Jesus is left alone (Lk 9:36) as the teacher whose words must be heeded (see also Acts 3:22).

†† [9:36] **At that time:** i.e., before the resurrection.

‡‡ [9:37–43a] See note on Mk 9:14–29.

telling you. The Son of Man is to be handed over to men." [45]But they did not understand this saying; its meaning was hidden from them so that they should not understand it, and they were afraid to ask him about this saying.

The Greatest in the Kingdom.[w] [46]* An argument arose among the disciples about which of them was the greatest.[x] [47]Jesus realized the intention of their hearts and took a child and placed it by his side [48]and said to them, "Whoever receives this child in my name receives me, and whoever receives me receives the one who sent me. For the one who is least among all of you is the one who is the greatest."[y]

Another Exorcist.[z] [49]Then John said in reply, "Master, we saw someone casting out demons in your name and we tried to prevent him because he does not follow in our company." [50]Jesus said to him, "Do not prevent him, for whoever is not against you is for you."

V. THE JOURNEY TO JERUSALEM: LUKE'S TRAVEL NARRATIVE[†]

Departure for Jerusalem; Samaritan Inhospitality. [51]‡ When the days for his being taken up[§] were fulfilled, he resolutely determined to journey to Jerusalem,[a] [52]¶ and he sent messengers ahead of him.[b] On the way they entered a Samaritan village to prepare for his reception there, [53]but they would not welcome him because the destination of

---

* [9:46–50] These two incidents focus on attitudes that are opposed to Christian discipleship: rivalry and intolerance of outsiders.

† [9:51–18:14] The Galilean ministry of Jesus finishes with the previous episode and a new section of Luke's gospel begins, the journey to Jerusalem. This journey is based on Mk 10:1–52 but Luke uses his Marcan source only in Lk 18:15–19:27. Before that point he has inserted into his gospel a distinctive collection of sayings of Jesus and stories about him that he has drawn from Q, a collection of sayings of Jesus used also by Matthew, and from his own special traditions. All of the material collected in this section is loosely organized within the framework of a journey of Jesus to Jerusalem, the city of destiny, where his exodus (suffering, death, resurrection, ascension) is to take place (Lk 9:31), where salvation is accomplished, and from where the proclamation of God's saving word is to go forth (Lk 24:47; Acts 1:8). Much of the material in the Lucan travel narrative is teaching for the disciples. During the course of this journey Jesus is preparing his chosen Galilean witnesses for the role they will play after his exodus (Lk 9:31): they are to be his witnesses to the people (Acts 10:39; 13:31) and thereby provide certainty to the readers of Luke's gospel that the teachings they have received are rooted in the teachings of Jesus (Lk 1:1–4).

‡ [9:51–55] Just as the Galilean ministry began with a rejection of Jesus in his hometown, so too the travel narrative begins with the rejection of Jesus by Samaritans. In this episode Jesus disassociates himself from the attitude expressed by his disciples that those who reject him are to be punished severely. The story alludes to 2 Kgs 1:10, 12 where the prophet Elijah takes the course of action Jesus rejects, and Jesus thereby rejects the identification of himself with Elijah.

§ [9:51] **Days for his being taken up**: like the reference to his exodus in Lk 9:31 this is probably a reference to all the events (suffering, death, resurrection, ascension) of his last days in Jerusalem. **He resolutely determined**: literally, "he set his face."

¶ [9:52] **Samaritan**: Samaria was the territory between Judea and Galilee west of the Jordan river. For ethnic and religious reasons, the Samaritans and the Jews were bitterly opposed to one another (see Jn 4:9).

his journey was Jerusalem. [54]When the disciples James and John saw this they asked, "Lord, do you want us to call down fire from heaven to consume them?"[c] [55]Jesus turned and rebuked them, [56]and they journeyed to another village.

The Would-be Followers of Jesus. [*] [57d] As they were proceeding on their journey someone said to him, "I will follow you wherever you go." [58]Jesus answered him, "Foxes have dens and birds of the sky have nests, but the Son of Man has nowhere to rest his head." [59]And to another he said, "Follow me." But he replied, "[Lord,] let me go first and bury my father." [60]But he answered him, "Let the dead bury their dead.[†] But you, go and proclaim the kingdom of God." [61e] And another said, "I will follow you, Lord, but first let me say farewell to my family at home." [62][To him] Jesus said, "No one who sets a hand to the plow and looks to what was left behind is fit for the kingdom of God."

---

[*] [9:57–62] In these sayings Jesus speaks of the severity and the unconditional nature of Christian discipleship. Even family ties and filial obligations, such as burying one's parents, cannot distract one no matter how briefly from proclaiming the kingdom of God. The first two sayings are paralleled in Mt 8:19–22; see also notes there.

[†] [9:60] **Let the dead bury their dead**: i.e., let the spiritually dead (those who do not follow) bury their physically dead. See also note on Mt 8:22.

a. [9:1–6] Mt 10:1, 5–15; Mk 6:7–13.
b. [9:4] 10:5–7.
c. [9:5] 10:10–11; Acts 13:51.
d. [9:7–9] Mt 14:1–12; Mk 6:14–29.
e. [9:7–8] 9:19; Mt 16:14; Mk 8:28.
f. [9:9] 23:8.
g. [9:10–17] Mt 14:13–21; Mk 6:30–44; Jn 6:1–14.
h. [9:13–17] 2 Kgs 4:42–44.
i. [9:16] 22:19; 24:30–31; Acts 2:42; 20:11; 27:35.
j. [9:18–21] Mt 16:13–20; Mk 8:27–30.
k. [9:19] 9:7–8.
l. [9:22] 24:7, 26; Mt 16:21; 20:18–19; Mk 8:31; 10:33–34.
m. [9:23–27] Mt 16:24–28; Mk 8:34–9:1.
n. [9:23] 14:27; Mt 10:38.
o. [9:24] 17:33; Mt 10:39; Jn 12:25.
p. [9:26] 12:9; Mt 10:33; 2 Tm 2:12.
q. [9:28–36] Mt 17:1–8; Mk 9:2–8.

r. [9:31] 9:22; 13:33.
s. [9:32] Jn 1:14; 2 Pt 1:16.
t. [9:35] 3:22; Dt 18:15; Ps 2:7; Is 42:1; Mt 3:17; 12:18; Mk 1:11; 2 Pt 1:17–18.
u. [9:37–43] Mt 17:14–18; Mk 9:14–27.
v. [9:43–45] 18:32–34; Mt 17:22–23; Mk 9:30–32.
w. [9:46–48] Mt 18:1–5; Mk 9:33–37.
x. [9:46] 22:24.
y. [9:48] 10:16; Mt 10:40; Jn 13:20.
z. [9:49–50] Mk 9:38–40.
a. [9:51] 9:53; 13:22, 33; 17:11; 18:31; 19:28; 24:51; Acts 1:2, 9–11, 22.
b. [9:52] Mal 3:1.
c. [9:54] 2 Kgs 1:10, 12.
d. [9:57–60] Mt 8:19–22.
e. [9:61–62] 1 Kgs 19:20.

---

10   **The Mission of the Seventy-two.**[‡] [1]After this the Lord appointed seventy[-two][§] others whom he sent ahead of him in pairs

---

[‡] [10:1–12] Only the Gospel of Luke contains two episodes in which Jesus sends out his followers on a mission: the first (Lk 9:1–6) is based on the mission in Mk 6:6b–13 and recounts the sending out of the Twelve; here in Lk 10:1–12 a similar report based on Q becomes the sending out of seventy-two in this gospel. The episode continues the theme of Jesus preparing witnesses to himself and his ministry. These witnesses include not only the Twelve but also the seventy-two who may represent the Christian mission in Luke's own day. Note that the instructions given to the Twelve and to the seventy-two are similar and that what is said to the seventy-two in Lk 10:4 is directed to the Twelve in Lk 22:35.

[§] [10:1] **Seventy[-two]**: important representatives of the Alexandrian and Caesarean text types read "seventy," while other important Alexandrian texts and Western readings have "seventy-two."

to every town and place he intended to visit.*a* ²He said to them, "The harvest is abundant but the laborers are few; so ask the master of the harvest to send out laborers for his harvest.*b* ³Go on your way; behold, I am sending you like lambs among wolves.*c* ⁴* Carry no money bag,*d* no sack, no sandals;*e* and greet no one along the way. ⁵Into whatever house you enter, first say, 'Peace to this household.'*† ⁶If a peaceful person‡ lives there, your peace will rest on him; but if not, it will return to you. ⁷Stay in the same house and eat and drink what is offered to you, for the laborer deserves his payment. Do not move about from one house to another.*f* ⁸Whatever town you enter and they welcome you, eat what is set before you,*g* ⁹cure the sick in it and say to them, 'The kingdom of God is at hand for you.'*h* ¹⁰Whatever town you enter and they do not receive you, go out into the streets and say,*i* ¹¹'The dust of your town that clings to our feet, even that we shake off against you.' Yet know this: the kingdom of God is at hand.'*j* ¹²I tell you, it will be more tolerable for Sodom on that day than for that town.*k*

Reproaches to Unrepentant Towns.§ ¹³*l* "Woe to you, Chorazin! Woe to you, Bethsaida!*m* For if the mighty deeds done in your midst had been done in Tyre and Sidon, they would long ago have repented, sitting in sackcloth and ashes. ¹⁴But it will be more tolerable for Tyre and Sidon at the judgment than for you. ¹⁵*n* And as for you, Capernaum, 'Will you be exalted to heaven? You will go down to the netherworld.'¶ ¹⁶Whoever listens to you listens to me. Whoever rejects you rejects me. And whoever rejects me rejects the one who sent me."*o*

Return of the Seventy-two. ¹⁷The seventy[-two] returned rejoicing, and said, "Lord, even the demons are subject to us because of your name." ¹⁸Jesus said, "I have observed Satan fall like lightning** from the sky.*p* ¹⁹Behold, I have given you the power 'to tread upon serpents' and

* [10:4] **Carry no money bag … greet no one along the way**: because of the urgency of the mission and the single-mindedness required of missionaries, attachment to material possessions should be avoided and even customary greetings should not distract from the fulfillment of the task.

† [10:5] First say, **'Peace to this household'**: see notes on Lk 2:14 and Mt 10:13.

‡ [10:6] **A peaceful person**: literally, "a son of peace."

§ [10:13–16] The call to repentance that is a part of the proclamation of the kingdom brings with it a severe judgment for those who hear it and reject it.

¶ [10:15] **The netherworld**: the underworld, the place of the dead (Acts 2:27, 31) here contrasted with heaven; see also note on Mt 11:23.

** [10:18] **I have observed Satan fall like lightning**: the effect of the mission of the seventy-two is characterized by the Lucan Jesus as a symbolic fall of Satan. As the kingdom of God is gradually being established, evil in all its forms is being defeated; the dominion of Satan over humanity is at an end.

scorpions and upon the full force of the enemy and nothing will harm you.[q] [20]Nevertheless, do not rejoice because the spirits are subject to you, but rejoice because your names are written in heaven."[r]

Praise of the Father.[s] [21]At that very moment he rejoiced [in] the holy Spirit and said, "I give you praise, Father, Lord of heaven and earth, for although you have hidden these things from the wise and the learned you have revealed them to the childlike.* Yes, Father, such has been your gracious will.[t] [22]All things have been handed over to me by my Father. No one knows who the Son is except the Father, and who the Father is except the Son and anyone to whom the Son wishes to reveal him."[u]

The Privileges of Discipleship.[v] [23]Turning to the disciples in private he said, "Blessed are the eyes that see what you see. [24]For I say to you, many prophets and kings desired to see what you see, but did not see it, and to hear what you hear, but did not hear it."

The Greatest Commandment.[w] [25]† There was a scholar of the law‡ who stood up to test him and said, "Teacher, what must I do to inherit eternal life?"[x] [26]Jesus said to him, "What is written in the law? How do you read it?" [27]He said in reply, "You shall love the Lord, your God, with all your heart, with all your being, with all your strength, and with all your mind, and your neighbor as yourself."[y] [28]He replied to him, "You have answered correctly; do this and you will live."[z]

The Parable of the Good Samaritan. [29]But because he wished to justify himself, he said to Jesus, "And who is my neighbor?" [30]Jesus replied, "A man fell victim to robbers as he went down from Jerusalem to Jericho. They stripped and beat him and went off leaving him half-dead. [31]§ A priest happened to be going down that road, but when he saw him, he passed by on the opposite side. [32]Likewise a Levite came to the

---

* [10:21] **Revealed them to the childlike**: a restatement of the theme announced in Lk 8:10: the mysteries of the kingdom are revealed to the disciples. See also note on Mt 11:25–27.

† [10:25–37] In response to a question from a Jewish legal expert about inheriting eternal life, Jesus illustrates the superiority of love over legalism through the story of the good Samaritan. The law of love proclaimed in the "Sermon on the Plain" (Lk 6:27–36) is exemplified by one whom the legal expert would have considered ritually impure (see Jn 4:9). Moreover, the identity of the "neighbor" requested by the legal expert (Lk 10:29) turns out to be a Samaritan, the enemy of the Jew (see note on Lk 9:52).

‡ [10:25] **Scholar of the law**: an expert in the Mosaic law, and probably a member of the group elsewhere identified as the scribes (Lk 5:21).

§ [10:31–32] **Priest … Levite**: those religious representatives of Judaism who would have been expected to be models of "neighbor" to the victim pass him by.

place, and when he saw him, he passed by on the opposite side. [33]But a Samaritan traveler who came upon him was moved with compassion at the sight. [34]He approached the victim, poured oil and wine over his wounds and bandaged them. Then he lifted him up on his own animal, took him to an inn and cared for him. [35]The next day he took out two silver coins and gave them to the innkeeper with the instruction, 'Take care of him. If you spend more than what I have given you, I shall repay you on my way back.' [36]Which of these three, in your opinion, was neighbor to the robbers' victim?" [37]He answered, "The one who treated him with mercy." Jesus said to him, "Go and do likewise."

Martha and Mary. [*] [38a] As they continued their journey he entered a village where a woman whose name was Martha welcomed him. [39†] She had a sister named Mary [who] sat beside the Lord at his feet listening to him speak. [40]Martha, burdened with much serving, came to him and said, "Lord, do you not care that my sister has left me by myself to do the serving? Tell her to help me." [41]The Lord said to her in reply, "Martha, Martha, you are anxious and worried about many things. [42‡] There is need of only one thing. Mary has chosen the better part and it will not be taken from her."

---

* [10:38–42] The story of Martha and Mary further illustrates the importance of hearing the words of the teacher and the concern with women in Luke.

† [10:39] **Sat beside the Lord at his feet:** it is remarkable for first-century Palestinian Judaism that a woman would assume the posture of a disciple at the master's feet (see also Lk 8:35; Acts 22:3), and it reveals a characteristic attitude of Jesus toward women in this gospel (see Lk 8:2–3).

‡ [10:42] **There is need of only one thing:** some ancient versions read, "there is need of few things"; another important, although probably inferior, reading found in some manuscripts is, "there is need of few things, or of one."

a. [10:1] Mk 6:7.
b. [10:2] Mt 9:37–38; Jn 4:35.
c. [10:3] Mt 10:16.
d. [10:4–11] Mt 10:7–14.
e. [10:4] Mk 2 Kgs 4:29.
f. [10:7] 9:4; Mt 10:10; 1 Cor 9:6–14; 1 Tm 5:18.
g. [10:8] 1 Cor 10:27.
h. [10:9] Mt 3:2; 4:17; Mk 1:15.
i. [10:10–11] 9:5.
j. [10:11] Acts 13:51; 18:6.
k. [10:12] Mt 10:15; 11:24.
l. [10:13–15] Mt 11:20–24.
m. [10:13–14] Is 23; Ez 26–28; Jl 3:4–8; Am 1:1–10; Zec 9:2–4.
n. [10:15] Is 14:13–15.
o. [10:16] Mt 10:40; Jn 5:23; 13:20; 15:23.
p. [10:18] Is 14:12; Jn 12:31; Rev 12:7–12.
q. [10:19] Ps 91:13; Mk 16:18.
r. [10:20] Ex 32:32; Dn 12:1; Mt 7:22; Phil 4:3; Heb 12:23; Rev 3:5; 21:27.
s. [10:21–22] Mt 11:25–27.

t. [10:21] 1 Cor 1:26–28.
u. [10:22] Jn 3:35; 10:15.
v. [10:23–24] Mt 13:16–17.
w. [10:25–28] Mt 22:34–40; Mk 12:28–34.
x. [10:25] 18:18; Mt 19:16; Mk 10:17.
y. [10:27] Lv 19:18; Dt 6:5; 10:12; Jos 22:5; Mt 19:19; 22:37–39; Rom 13:9; Gal 5:14; Jas 2:8.
z. [10:28] Lv 18:5; Prv 19:16; Rom 10:5; Gal 3:12.
u. [10:30–39] Jn 11:1; 12:1–3.

11 The Lord's Prayer.[a] [1*] He was praying in a certain place, and when he had finished, one of his disciples said to him, "Lord, teach us to pray just as John taught his disciples."[†] [2†] He said to them, "When you pray, say:

> Father, hallowed be your name,
>> your kingdom come.
> [3] Give us each day our daily bread[§]
> [4] and forgive us our sins
> for we ourselves forgive everyone in debt to us,
> and do not subject us to the final test."

Further Teachings on Prayer.[b] [5] And he said to them, "Suppose one of you has a friend to whom he goes at midnight and says, 'Friend, lend me three loaves of bread, [6] for a friend of mine has arrived at my house from a journey and I have nothing to offer him,' [7] and he says in reply from within, 'Do not bother me; the door has already been locked and my children and I are already in bed. I cannot get up to give you anything.' [8] I tell you, if he does not get up to give him the loaves because of their friendship, he will get up to give him whatever he needs because of his persistence.

The Answer to Prayer.[c] [9] "And I tell you, ask and you will receive; seek and you will find; knock and the door will be opened to you.[d] [10] For everyone who asks, receives; and the one who seeks, finds; and to the one who knocks, the door will be opened. [11] What father among you would hand his son a snake when he asks for a fish? [12] Or hand him a scorpion when he asks for an egg? [13] If you then, who are wicked, know

---

* [11:1–13] Luke presents three episodes concerned with prayer. The first (Lk 11:1–4) recounts Jesus teaching his disciples the Christian communal prayer, the "Our Father"; the second (Lk 11:5–8), the importance of persistence in prayer; the third (Lk 11:9–13), the effectiveness of prayer.

† [11:1–4] The Matthean form of the "Our Father" occurs in the "Sermon on the Mount" (Mt 6:9–15); the shorter Lucan version is presented while Jesus is at prayer (see note on Lk 3:21) and his disciples ask him to teach them to pray just as John taught his disciples to pray. In answer to their question, Jesus presents them with an example of a Christian communal prayer that stresses the fatherhood of God and acknowledges him as the one to whom the Christian disciple owes daily sustenance (Lk 11:3), forgiveness (Lk 11:4), and deliverance from the final trial (Lk 11:4). See also notes on Mt 6:9–13.

‡ [11:2] **Your kingdom come:** in place of this petition, some early church Fathers record: "May your holy Spirit come upon us and cleanse us," a petition that may reflect the use of the "Our Father" in a baptismal liturgy.

§ [11:3–4] **Daily bread:** see note on Mt 6:11. **The final test:** see note on Mt 6:13.

how to give good gifts to your children, how much more will the Father in heaven give the holy Spirit* to those who ask him?"

Jesus and Beelzebul.[e] [14]He was driving out a demon [that was] mute, and when the demon had gone out, the mute person spoke and the crowds were amazed. [15]Some of them said, "By the power of Beelzebul, the prince of demons, he drives out demons."[f] [16]Others, to test him, asked him for a sign from heaven.[g] [17]But he knew their thoughts and said to them, "Every kingdom divided against itself will be laid waste and house will fall against house. [18]And if Satan is divided against himself, how will his kingdom stand? For you say that it is by Beelzebul that I drive out demons. [19]If I, then, drive out demons by Beelzebul, by whom do your own people[†] drive them out? Therefore they will be your judges. [20]But if it is by the finger of God that [I] drive out demons, then the kingdom of God has come upon you.[h] [21]When a strong man fully armed guards his palace, his possessions are safe. [22]But when one stronger[‡] than he attacks and overcomes him, he takes away the armor on which he relied and distributes the spoils. [23]Whoever is not with me is against me, and whoever does not gather with me scatters.[i]

The Return of the Unclean Spirit.[j] [24]"When an unclean spirit goes out of someone, it roams through arid regions searching for rest but, finding none, it says, 'I shall return to my home from which I came.' [25]But upon returning, it finds it swept clean and put in order. [26]Then it goes and brings back seven other spirits more wicked than itself who move in and dwell there, and the last condition of that person is worse than the first."[k]

True Blessedness.[§] [27]While he was speaking, a woman from the crowd called out and said to him, "Blessed is the womb that carried you and the breasts at which you nursed."[l] [28]He replied, "Rather, blessed are those who hear the word of God and observe it."

---

* [11:13] **The holy Spirit**: this is a Lucan editorial alteration of a traditional saying of Jesus (see Mt 7:11). Luke presents the gift of the holy Spirit as the response of the Father to the prayer of the Christian disciple.

† [11:19] **Your own people**: the Greek reads "your sons." Other Jewish exorcists (see Acts 19:13–20), who recognize that the power of God is active in the exorcism, would themselves convict the accusers of Jesus. See also note on Mt 12:27.

‡ [11:22] **One stronger**: i.e., Jesus. Cf. Lk 3:16 where John the Baptist identifies Jesus as "mightier than I."

§ [11:27–28] The beatitude in Lk 11:28 should not be interpreted as a rebuke of the mother of Jesus; see note on Lk 8:21. Rather, it emphasizes (like Lk 2:35) that attentiveness to God's word is more important than biological relationship to Jesus.

The Demand for a Sign.[*] ²⁹While still more people gathered in the crowd, he said to them,[m] "This generation is an evil generation; it seeks a sign, but no sign will be given it, except the sign of Jonah.[n] ³⁰Just as Jonah became a sign to the Ninevites, so will the Son of Man be to this generation. ³¹At the judgment the queen of the south will rise with the men of this generation and she will condemn them, because she came from the ends of the earth to hear the wisdom of Solomon, and there is something greater than Solomon here.[o] ³²At the judgment the men of Nineveh will arise with this generation and condemn it, because at the preaching of Jonah they repented, and there is something greater than Jonah here.[p]

The Simile of Light. ³³"No one who lights a lamp hides it away or places it [under a bushel basket], but on a lampstand so that those who enter might see the light.[q] ³⁴The lamp of the body is your eye.[r] When your eye is sound, then your whole body is filled with light, but when it is bad, then your body is in darkness. ³⁵Take care, then, that the light in you not become darkness. ³⁶If your whole body is full of light, and no part of it is in darkness, then it will be as full of light as a lamp illuminating you with its brightness."

Denunciation of the Pharisees and Scholars of the Law.[†] ³⁷ˢ After he had spoken, a Pharisee invited him to dine at his home. He entered and reclined at table to eat.[t] ³⁸The Pharisee was amazed to see that he did not observe the prescribed washing before the meal.[u] ³⁹The Lord said to him, "Oh you Pharisees![v] Although you cleanse the outside of the cup and the dish, inside you are filled with plunder and evil. ⁴⁰You fools! Did not the maker of the outside also make the inside? ⁴¹But as to what is within, give alms, and behold, everything will be clean for you. ⁴²Woe to you Pharisees! You pay tithes of mint and of rue and of every garden herb, but you pay no attention to judgment and to love for God. These you should have done, without overlooking the others.[w] ⁴³Woe to you

---

* [11:29–32] The "sign of Jonah" in Luke is the preaching of the need for repentance by a prophet who comes from afar. Cf. Mt 12:38–42 (and see notes there) where the "sign of Jonah" is interpreted by Jesus as his death and resurrection.

† [11:37–54] This denunciation of the Pharisees (Lk 11:39–44) and the scholars of the law (Lk 11:45–52) is set by Luke in the context of Jesus' dining at the home of a Pharisee. Controversies with or reprimands of Pharisees are regularly set by Luke within the context of Jesus' eating with Pharisees (see Lk 5:29–39; 7:36–50; 14:1–24). A different compilation of similar sayings is found in Mt 23 (see also notes there).

Pharisees! You love the seat of honor in synagogues and greetings in marketplaces.[x] [44]Woe to you! You are like unseen graves[*] over which people unknowingly walk."[y]

[45]Then one of the scholars of the law[†] said to him in reply, "Teacher, by saying this you are insulting us too."[z] [46]And he said, "Woe also to you scholars of the law! You impose on people burdens hard to carry, but you yourselves do not lift one finger to touch them. [47a] Woe to you! You build the memorials of the prophets whom your ancestors killed. [48]Consequently, you bear witness and give consent to the deeds of your ancestors, for they killed them and you do the building. [49b] Therefore, the wisdom of God said, 'I will send to them prophets and apostles;[‡] some of them they will kill and persecute' [50]in order that this generation might be charged with the blood of all the prophets shed since the foundation of the world, [51]from the blood of Abel to the blood of Zechariah[§] who died between the altar and the temple building. Yes, I tell you, this generation will be charged with their blood![c] [52]Woe to you, scholars of the law! You have taken away the key of knowledge. You yourselves did not enter and you stopped those trying to enter."[d] [53]When he left, the scribes and Pharisees began to act with hostility toward him and to interrogate him about many things,[e] [54]for they were plotting to catch him at something he might say.[f]

---

* [11:44] **Unseen graves**: contact with the dead or with human bones or graves (see Nm 19:16) brought ritual impurity. Jesus presents the Pharisees as those who insidiously lead others astray through their seeming attention to the law.
† [11:45] **Scholars of the law**: see note on Lk 10:25.
‡ [11:49] **I will send to them prophets and apostles**: Jesus connects the mission of the church (apostles) with the mission of the Old Testament prophets who often suffered the rebuke of their contemporaries.
§ [11:51] **From the blood of Abel to the blood of Zechariah**: the murder of Abel is the first murder recounted in the Old Testament (Gn 4:8). The Zechariah mentioned here may be the Zechariah whose murder is recounted in 2 Chr 24:20–22, the last murder presented in the Hebrew canon of the Old Testament.

a. [11:1–4] Mt 6:9–15.
b. [11:5–8] 18:1–5.
c. [11:9–13] Mt 7:7–11.
d. [11:9] Mt 21:22; Mk 11:24; Jn 14:13; 15:7; 1 Jn 5:14–15.
e. [11:14–23] Mt 12:22–30; Mk 3:20–27.
f. [11:15] Mt 9:34.
g. [11:16] Mt 12:38; 16:1; Mk 8:11; 1 Cor 1:22.
h. [11:20] Ex 8:19.
i. [11:23] 9:50; Mk 9:40.
j. [11:24–26] Mt 12:43–45.
k. [11:26] Jn 5:14.
l. [11:27] 1:28, 42, 48.
m. [11:29–32] Mt 12:38–42; Mk 8:12.
n. [11:29] Mt 16:1, 4; Jn 6:30; 1 Cor 1:22.
o. [11:31] 1 Kgs 10:1–10; 2 Chr 9:1–12.
p. [11:32] Jon 3:8, 10.
q. [11:33] 8:16; Mt 5:15; Mk 4:21.
r. [11:34–36] Mt 6:22–23.

s. [11:37–54] 20:45–47; Mt 23:1–36; Mk 12:38–40.
t. [11:37] 7:36; 14:1.
u. [11:38] Mt 15:2; Mk 7:2–5.
v. [11:39–41] Mt 23:25–26.
w. [11:42] 1 v 27:30; Mt 23:23.
x. [11:43] 20:46; Mt 23:6; Mk 12:38–39.
y. [11:44] Mt 23:27.
z. [11:45] Mt 23:4.
a. [11:47–48] Mt 23:29–32.
b. [11:49–51] Mt 23:34–36.
c. [11:51] Gn 4:8; 2 Chr 24:20–22.
d. [11:52] Mt 23:13.
e. [11:53] 6:11; Mt 22:15–22.
f. [11:54] 20:20.

12 **The Leaven of the Pharisees.**[*] [1]Meanwhile, so many people were crowding together that they were trampling one another underfoot.[a] He began to speak, first to his disciples, "Beware of the leaven—that is, the hypocrisy—of the Pharisees.

Courage Under Persecution.[†] [2b] "There is nothing concealed that will not be revealed, nor secret that will not be known.[c] [3]Therefore whatever you have said in the darkness will be heard in the light, and what you have whispered behind closed doors will be proclaimed on the housetops. [4]I tell you, my friends, do not be afraid of those who kill the body but after that can do no more. [5]I shall show you whom to fear. Be afraid of the one who after killing has the power to cast into Gehenna;[‡] yes, I tell you, be afraid of that one. [6]Are not five sparrows sold for two small coins?[§] Yet not one of them has escaped the notice of God. [7]Even the hairs of your head have all been counted. Do not be afraid. You are worth more than many sparrows.[d] [8]I tell you, everyone who acknowledges me before others the Son of Man will acknowledge before the angels of God. [9]But whoever denies me before others will be denied before the angels of God.[e]

Sayings About the Holy Spirit.[¶] [10]"Everyone who speaks a word against the Son of Man will be forgiven, but the one who blasphemes against the holy Spirit will not be forgiven.[f] [11]When they take you before synagogues and before rulers and authorities,[g] do not worry about how or what your defense will be or about what you are to say. [12]For the holy Spirit will teach you at that moment what you should say."

Saying Against Greed.[**] [13]Someone in the crowd said to him, "Teacher, tell my brother to share the inheritance with me." [14]He replied to him, "Friend, who appointed me as your judge and arbitrator?"[h] [15]Then he

---

* [12:1] See notes on Mk 8:15 and Mt 16:5–12.

† [12:2–9] Luke presents a collection of sayings of Jesus exhorting his followers to acknowledge him and his mission fearlessly and assuring them of God's protection even in times of persecution. They are paralleled in Mt 10:26–33.

‡ [12:5] **Gehenna**: see note on Mt 5:22.

§ [12:6] **Two small coins**: the Roman copper coin, the assarion (Latin *as*), was worth about one-sixteenth of a denarius (see note on Lk 7:41).

¶ [12:10–12] The sayings about the holy Spirit are set in the context of fearlessness in the face of persecution (Lk 12:2–9; cf. Mt 12:31–32). The holy Spirit will be presented in Luke's second volume, the Acts of the Apostles, as the power responsible for the guidance of the Christian mission and the source of courage in the face of persecution.

** [12:13–34] Luke has joined together sayings contrasting those whose focus and trust in life is on material possessions, symbolized here by the rich fool of the parable (Lk 12:16–21), with those who recognize their complete dependence on God (Lk 12:21), those whose radical detachment from material possessions symbolizes their heavenly treasure (Lk 12:33–34).

said to the crowd, "Take care to guard against all greed, for though one may be rich, one's life does not consist of possessions."[i]

Parable of the Rich Fool. [16]Then he told them a parable. "There was a rich man whose land produced a bountiful harvest. [17]He asked himself, 'What shall I do, for I do not have space to store my harvest?' [18]And he said, 'This is what I shall do: I shall tear down my barns and build larger ones. There I shall store all my grain and other goods [19][j] and I shall say to myself, "Now as for you, you have so many good things stored up for many years, rest, eat, drink, be merry!"'[k] [20]But God said to him, 'You fool, this night your life will be demanded of you; and the things you have prepared, to whom will they belong?' [21]Thus will it be for the one who stores up treasure for himself but is not rich in what matters to God.'"[*]

Dependence on God. [22][l] He said to [his] disciples, "Therefore I tell you, do not worry about your life and what you will eat, or about your body and what you will wear. [23]For life is more than food and the body more than clothing. [24]Notice the ravens: they do not sow or reap; they have neither storehouse nor barn, yet God feeds them. How much more important are you than birds![m] [25]Can any of you by worrying add a moment to your life-span? [26]If even the smallest things are beyond your control, why are you anxious about the rest? [27]Notice how the flowers grow. They do not toil or spin. But I tell you, not even Solomon in all his splendor was dressed like one of them.[n] [28]If God so clothes the grass in the field that grows today and is thrown into the oven tomorrow, will he not much more provide for you, O you of little faith? [29]As for you, do not seek what you are to eat and what you are to drink, and do not worry anymore. [30]All the nations of the world seek for these things, and your Father knows that you need them. [31]Instead, seek his kingdom, and these other things will be given you besides. [32]Do not be afraid any longer, little flock, for your Father is pleased to give you the kingdom.[o] [33]Sell your belongings and give alms. Provide money bags for yourselves that do not wear out, an inexhaustible treasure in heaven that no thief can reach nor moth destroy.[p] [34]For where your treasure is, there also will your heart be.

---

[*] [12:21] **Rich in what matters to God:** literally, "rich for God."

Vigilant and Faithful Servants.[*] [35q] "Gird your loins and light your lamps [36]and be like servants who await their master's return from a wedding, ready to open immediately when he comes and knocks.[r] [37]Blessed are those servants whom the master finds vigilant on his arrival. Amen, I say to you, he will gird himself, have them recline at table, and proceed to wait on them. [38]And should he come in the second or third watch and find them prepared in this way, blessed are those servants. [39s] Be sure of this: if the master of the house had known the hour when the thief was coming, he would not have let his house be broken into. [40]You also must be prepared, for at an hour you do not expect, the Son of Man will come."

[41]Then Peter said, "Lord, is this parable meant for us or for everyone?" [42]And the Lord replied, "Who, then, is the faithful and prudent steward whom the master will put in charge of his servants to distribute [the] food allowance at the proper time? [43]Blessed is that servant whom his master on arrival finds doing so. [44]Truly, I say to you, he will put him in charge of all his property. [45]But if that servant says to himself, 'My master is delayed in coming,'[†] and begins to beat the menservants and the maidservants, to eat and drink and get drunk, [46]then that servant's master will come on an unexpected day and at an unknown hour and will punish him severely and assign him a place with the unfaithful. [47]That servant who knew his master's will but did not make preparations nor act in accord with his will shall be beaten severely;[t] [48]and the servant who was ignorant of his master's will but acted in a way deserving of a severe beating shall be beaten only lightly. Much will be required of the person entrusted with much, and still more will be demanded of the person entrusted with more.

Jesus: A Cause of Division.[‡] [49]"I have come to set the earth on fire, and how I wish it were already blazing! [50s] There is a baptism with which I must be baptized, and how great is my anguish until it is accomplished![u]

---

[*] [12:35–48] This collection of sayings relates to Luke's understanding of the end time and the return of Jesus. Luke emphasizes for his readers the importance of being faithful to the instructions of Jesus in the period before the parousia.

[†] [12:45] **My master is delayed in coming:** this statement indicates that early Christian expectations for the imminent return of Jesus had undergone some modification. Luke cautions his readers against counting on such a delay and acting irresponsibly. Cf. the similar warning in Mt 24:48.

[‡] [12:49–53] Jesus' proclamation of the kingdom is a refining and purifying fire. His message that meets with acceptance or rejection will be a source of conflict and dissension even within families.

[§] [12:50] **Baptism:** i.e., his death.

[51]Do you think that I have come to establish peace on the earth?[v] No, I tell you, but rather division.[w] [52]From now on a household of five will be divided, three against two and two against three; [53]a father will be divided against his son and a son against his father, a mother against her daughter and a daughter against her mother, a mother-in-law against her daughter-in-law and a daughter-in-law against her mother-in-law."[x]

Signs of the Times.[y] [54]He also said to the crowds, "When you see [a] cloud rising in the west you say immediately that it is going to rain—and so it does; [55]and when you notice that the wind is blowing from the south you say that it is going to be hot and so it is. [56]You hypocrites! You know how to interpret the appearance of the earth and the sky; why do you not know how to interpret the present time?

Settlement with an Opponent.[z] [57]"Why do you not judge for yourselves what is right? [58]If you are to go with your opponent before a magistrate, make an effort to settle the matter on the way; otherwise your opponent will turn you over to the judge, and the judge hand you over to the constable, and the constable throw you into prison. [59]I say to you, you will not be released until you have paid the last penny."

* [12:59] **The last penny:** Greek, **lepton,** a very small amount. Mt 5:26 has for "the last penny" the Greek word *kodrantēs* (Latin *quadrans,* "farthing").

a. [12:1] Mt 16:6; Mk 8:15.
b. [12:2–9] Mt 10:26–33.
c. [12:2] 0.17, Mk 4:22.
d. [12:7] 12:24; 21:18; Acts 27:34.
e. [12:9] 9:26; Mk 8:38; 2 Tm 2:12.
f. [12:10] Mt 12:31–32; Mk 3:28–29.
g. [12:11–12] 21:12–15; Mt 10:17–20; Mk 13:11.
h. [12:14] Ex 2:14; Acts 7:27.
i. [12:15] 1 Tm 6:9–10.
j. [12:19–21] Mt 6:19–21; 1 Tm 6:17.
k. [12:19–20] Sir 11:19.
l. [12:22–32] Mt 6:25–34.
m. [12:24] 12:7.

n. [12:27] 1 Kgs 10:4–7; 2 Chr 9:3–6.
o. [12:32] 22:29; Rev 1:6.
p. [12:33] 18:22; Mt 6:20–21; Mk 10:21.
q. [12:35–46] Mt 24:45–51.
r. [12:36] Mt 25:1–13; Mk 13:35–37.
s. [12:39–40] Mt 24:43–44; 1 Thes 5:2.
t. [12:47] Jas 4:17.
u. [12:50] Mk 10:38–39.
v. [12:51–53] Mt 10:34–35.
w. [12:51] 2:14.
x. [12:53] Mi 7:6.
y. [12:54–56] Mt 16:2–3.
z. [12:57–59] Mt 5:25–26.

13 **A Call to Repentance.**[†] [1]At that time some people who were present there told him about the Galileans whose blood Pilate[‡]

† [13:1–5] The death of the Galileans at the hands of Pilate (Lk 13:1) and the accidental death of those on whom the tower fell (Lk 13:4) are presented by the Lucan Jesus as timely reminders of the need for all to repent, for the victims of these tragedies should not be considered outstanding sinners who were singled out for punishment.

‡ [13:1] The slaughter of the Galileans by Pilate is unknown outside Luke; but from what is known about Pilate from the Jewish historian Josephus, such a slaughter would be in keeping with the character of Pilate. Josephus reports that Pilate had disrupted a religious gathering of the Samaritans on Mount Gerizim with a slaughter of the participants (*Antiquities* 18:86–87), and that on another occasion Pilate had killed many Jews who had opposed him when he

had mingled with the blood of their sacrifices. [2]He said to them in reply, "Do you think that because these Galileans suffered in this way they were greater sinners than all other Galileans?[a] [3]By no means! But I tell you, if you do not repent,[b] you will all perish as they did! [4]Or those eighteen people who were killed when the tower at Siloam fell on them*—do you think they were more guilty than everyone else who lived in Jerusalem? [5]By no means! But I tell you, if you do not repent, you will all perish as they did!"

The Parable of the Barren Fig Tree.[†] [6c] And he told them this parable: "There once was a person who had a fig tree planted in his orchard, and when he came in search of fruit on it but found none, [7]he said to the gardener, 'For three years now I have come in search of fruit on this fig tree but have found none. [So] cut it down. Why should it exhaust the soil?' [8]He said to him in reply, 'Sir, leave it for this year also, and I shall cultivate the ground around it and fertilize it; [9]it may bear fruit in the future. If not you can cut it down.'"

Cure of a Crippled Woman on the Sabbath.[‡] [10]He was teaching in a synagogue on the sabbath. [11]And a woman was there who for eighteen years had been crippled by a spirit; she was bent over, completely incapable of standing erect. [12]When Jesus saw her, he called to her and said, "Woman, you are set free of your infirmity." [13]He laid his hands on her, and she at once stood up straight and glorified God. [14d] But the leader of the synagogue, indignant that Jesus had cured on the sabbath, said to the crowd in reply, "There are six days when work should be done. Come on those days to be cured, not on the sabbath day." [15§] The Lord said to him in reply, "Hypocrites! Does not each one of you on the sabbath untie his ox or his ass from the manger and lead it out for

---

appropriated money from the temple treasury to build an aqueduct in Jerusalem (*Jewish War* 2:175–77; *Antiquities* 18:60–62).

* [13:4] Like the incident mentioned in Lk 13:1 nothing of this accident in Jerusalem is known outside Luke and the New Testament.

† [13:6–9] Following on the call to repentance in Lk 13:1–5, the parable of the barren fig tree presents a story about the continuing patience of God with those who have not yet given evidence of their repentance (see Lk 3:8). The parable may also be alluding to the delay of the end time, when punishment will be meted out, and the importance of preparing for the end of the age because the delay will not be permanent (Lk 13:8–9).

‡ [13:10–17] The cure of the crippled woman on the sabbath and the controversy that results furnishes a parallel to an incident that will be reported by Luke in 14:1–6, the cure of the man with dropsy on the sabbath. A characteristic of Luke's style is the juxtaposition of an incident that reveals Jesus' concern for a man with an incident that reveals his concern for a woman; cf., e.g., Lk 7:11–17 and Lk 8:49–56.

§ [13:15–16] If the law as interpreted by Jewish tradition allowed for the untying of bound animals on the sabbath, how much more should this woman who has been bound by Satan's power be freed on the sabbath from her affliction.

watering?[e] [16*] This daughter of Abraham, whom Satan has bound for eighteen years now, ought she not to have been set free on the sabbath day from this bondage?"[f] [17]When he said this, all his adversaries were humiliated; and the whole crowd rejoiced at all the splendid deeds done by him.

The Parable of the Mustard Seed.[g] [18†] Then he said, "What is the kingdom of God like? To what can I compare it? [19]It is like a mustard seed that a person took and planted in the garden. When it was fully grown, it became a large bush and 'the birds of the sky dwelt in its branches.'"[h]

The Parable of the Yeast.[i] [20]Again he said, "To what shall I compare the kingdom of God? [21]It is like yeast that a woman took and mixed [in] with three measures of wheat flour until the whole batch of dough was leavened."

The Narrow Door; Salvation and Rejection.[‡] [22]He passed through towns and villages, teaching as he went and making his way to Jerusalem. [23]Someone asked him, "Lord, will only a few people be saved?" He answered them, [24j] "Strive to enter through the narrow door, for many, I tell you, will attempt to enter but will not be strong enough.[k] [25]After the master of the house has arisen and locked the door, then will you stand outside knocking and saying, 'Lord, open the door for us.' He will say to you in reply, 'I do not know where you are from.'[l] [26]And you will say, 'We ate and drank in your company and you taught in our streets.' [27m] Then he will say to you, 'I do not know where [you] are from. Depart from me, all you evildoers!' [28n] And there will be wailing and grinding of teeth when you see Abraham, Isaac, and Jacob and all the prophets in the kingdom of God and you yourselves cast out. [29]And people will come from the east and the west and from the north and the south and

---

* [13:16] **Whom Satan has bound**: affliction and infirmity are taken as evidence of Satan's hold on humanity. The healing ministry of Jesus reveals the gradual wresting from Satan of control over humanity and the establishment of God's kingdom.

† [13:18–21] Two parables are used to illustrate the future proportions of the kingdom of God that will result from its deceptively small beginning in the preaching and healing ministry of Jesus. They are paralleled in Mt 13:31–33 and Mk 4:30–32.

‡ [13:22–30] These sayings of Jesus follow in Luke upon the parables of the kingdom (Lk 13:18–21) and stress that great effort is required for entrance into the kingdom (Lk 13:24) and that there is an urgency to accept the present opportunity to enter because the narrow door will not remain open indefinitely (Lk 13:25). Lying behind the sayings is the rejection of Jesus and his message by his Jewish contemporaries (Lk 13:26) whose places at table in the kingdom will be taken by Gentiles from the four corners of the world (Lk 13:29). Those called last (the Gentiles) will precede those to whom the invitation to enter was first extended (the Jews). See also Lk 14:15–24.

will recline at table in the kingdom of God.^{o} ^{30}For behold, some are last who will be first, and some are first who will be last."^{p}

Herod's Desire to Kill Jesus. ^{31}At that time some Pharisees came to him and said, "Go away, leave this area because Herod wants to kill you." ^{32}He replied, "Go and tell that fox, 'Behold, I cast out demons and I perform healings today and tomorrow, and on the third day I accomplish my purpose.' ^{33†} Yet I must continue on my way today,^{q} tomorrow, and the following day, for it is impossible that a prophet should die outside of Jerusalem.'

The Lament over Jerusalem.^{r} ^{34}"Jerusalem, Jerusalem, you who kill the prophets and stone those sent to you, how many times I yearned to gather your children together as a hen gathers her brood under her wings, but you were unwilling! ^{35}Behold, your house will be abandoned. [But] I tell you, you will not see me until [the time comes when] you say, 'Blessed is he who comes in the name of the Lord.'"^{s}

---

* [13:32] Nothing, not even Herod's desire to kill Jesus, stands in the way of Jesus' role in fulfilling God's will and in establishing the kingdom through his exorcisms and healings.
† [13:33] **It is impossible that a prophet should die outside of Jerusalem**: Jerusalem is the city of destiny and the goal of the journey of the prophet Jesus. Only when he reaches the holy city will his work be accomplished.

a. [13:2] Jn 9:2.
b. [13:3–5] Jn 8:24.
c. [13:6–9] Jer 8:13; Heb 3:17; Mt 21:19; Mk 11:13.
d. [13:14] 6:7; 14:3; Ex 20:8–11; Dt 5:12–15; Mt 12:10; Mk 3:2–4; Jn 5:16; 7:23; 9:14, 16.
e. [13:15] 14:5; Dt 22:4; Mt 12:11.
f. [13:16] 19:9.
g. [13:18–19] Mt 13:31–32; Mk 4:30–32.
h. [13:19] Ez 17:23–24; 31:6.
i. [13:20–21] Mt 13:33.
j. [13:24–30] Mt 7:13–14, 21–23.
k. [13:24] Mk 10:25.
l. [13:25] Mt 25:10–12.
m. [13:27] Ps 6:9; Mt 7:23; 25:41.
n. [13:28–29] Mt 8:11–12.
o. [13:29] Ps 107:2–3.
p. [13:30] Mt 19:20; 20:16; Mk 10:31.
q. [13:33] 2:38; Jn 6:30; 8:20.
r. [13:34–35] 19:41–44; Mt 23:37–39.
s. [13:35] 19:38; 1 Kgs 9:7–8; Ps 118:26; Jer 7:4–7, 13–15; 12:7; 22:5.

---

14 **Healing of the Man with Dropsy on the Sabbath.**‡ ^{1a}On a sabbath he went to dine at the home of one of the leading Pharisees, and the people there were observing him carefully.^{b} ^{2}In front of him there was a man suffering from dropsy.§ ^{3}Jesus spoke to the scholars of the law and Pharisees in reply, asking, "Is it lawful to cure on the sabbath or not?"^{c} ^{4}But they kept silent; so he took the man and, after he had healed him, dismissed him. ^{5}Then he said to them, "Who among you, if your son

---

‡ [14:1–6] See note on Lk 13:10–17.
§ [14:2] **Dropsy**: an abnormal swelling of the body because of the retention and accumulation of fluid.

or ox* falls into a cistern, would not immediately pull him out on the sabbath day?"*d* 6But they were unable to answer his question.*e*

Conduct of Invited Guests and Hosts.† 7*f* He told a parable to those who had been invited, noticing how they were choosing the places of honor at the table. 8*g* "When you are invited by someone to a wedding banquet, do not recline at table in the place of honor. A more distinguished guest than you may have been invited by him, 9and the host who invited both of you may approach you and say, 'Give your place to this man,' and then you would proceed with embarrassment to take the lowest place. 10Rather, when you are invited, go and take the lowest place so that when the host comes to you he may say, 'My friend, move up to a higher position.' Then you will enjoy the esteem of your companions at the table. 11For everyone who exalts himself will be humbled, but the one who humbles himself will be exalted."*h* 12Then he said to the host who invited him, "When you hold a lunch or a dinner, do not invite your friends or your brothers or your relatives or your wealthy neighbors, in case they may invite you back and you have repayment.*i* 13Rather, when you hold a banquet, invite the poor, the crippled, the lame, the blind; 14blessed indeed will you be because of their inability to repay you. For you will be repaid at the resurrection of the righteous."*j*

The Parable of the Great Feast.‡ 15One of his fellow guests on hearing this said to him, "Blessed is the one who will dine in the kingdom of God." 16*k* He replied to him, "A man gave a great dinner to which he invited many. 17When the time for the dinner came, he dispatched his servant to say to those invited, 'Come, everything is now ready.' 18But one by one, they all began to excuse themselves. The first said to him, 'I have purchased a field and must go to examine it; I ask you, consider me excused.' 19And another said, 'I have purchased five yoke of oxen and am on my way to evaluate them; I ask you, consider me excused.'

" [14:5] **Your son or ox**: this is the reading of many of the oldest and most important New Testament manuscripts. Because of the strange collocation of **son** and **ox**, some copyists have altered it to "your ass or ox," on the model of the saying in Lk 13:15.

† [14:7–14] The banquet scene found only in Luke provides the opportunity for these teachings of Jesus on humility and presents a setting to display Luke's interest in Jesus' attitude toward the rich and the poor (see notes on Lk 4:18; 6:20–26; 12:13–34).

‡ [14:15–24] The parable of the great dinner is a further illustration of the rejection by Israel, God's chosen people, of Jesus' invitation to share in the banquet in the kingdom and the extension of the invitation to other Jews whose identification as the poor, crippled, blind, and lame (Lk 14:21) classifies them among those who recognize their need for salvation, and to Gentiles (Lk 14:23). A similar parable is found in Mt 22:1–10.

²⁰And another said, 'I have just married a woman, and therefore I cannot come.' ²¹The servant went and reported this to his master. Then the master of the house in a rage commanded his servant, 'Go out quickly into the streets and alleys of the town and bring in here the poor and the crippled, the blind and the lame.' ²²The servant reported, 'Sir, your orders have been carried out and still there is room.' ²³The master then ordered the servant, 'Go out to the highways and hedgerows and make people come in that my home may be filled. ²⁴For, I tell you, none of those men who were invited will taste my dinner.'"

Sayings on Discipleship.* ²⁵Great crowds were traveling with him, and he turned and addressed them, ²⁶*l* "If any one comes to me without hating his father† and mother, wife and children, brothers and sisters, and even his own life, he cannot be my disciple.*m* ²⁷Whoever does not carry his own cross and come after me cannot be my disciple.*n* ²⁸Which of you wishing to construct a tower does not first sit down and calculate the cost to see if there is enough for its completion? ²⁹Otherwise, after laying the foundation and finding himself unable to finish the work the onlookers should laugh at him ³⁰and say, 'This one began to build but did not have the resources to finish.' ³¹Or what king marching into battle would not first sit down and decide whether with ten thousand troops he can successfully oppose another king advancing upon him with twenty thousand troops? ³²But if not, while he is still far away, he will send a delegation to ask for peace terms. ³³In the same way, everyone of you who does not renounce all his possessions cannot be my disciple.*o*

The Simile of Salt.‡ ³⁴"Salt is good, but if salt itself loses its taste, with what can its flavor be restored?*p* ³⁵It is fit neither for the soil nor for the manure pile; it is thrown out. Whoever has ears to hear ought to hear."*q*

---

* [14:25–33] This collection of sayings, most of which are peculiar to Luke, focuses on the total dedication necessary for the disciple of Jesus. No attachment to family (Lk 14:26) or possessions (Lk 14:33) can stand in the way of the total commitment demanded of the disciple. Also, acceptance of the call to be a disciple demands readiness to accept persecution and suffering (Lk 14:27) and a realistic assessment of the hardships and costs (Lk 14:28–32).

† [14:26] **Hating his father. . .:** cf. the similar saying in Mt 10:37. The disciple's family must take second place to the absolute dedication involved in following Jesus (see also Lk 9:59–62).

‡ [14:34–35] The simile of salt follows the sayings of Jesus that demanded of the disciple total dedication and detachment from family and possessions and illustrates the condition of one who does not display this total commitment. The halfhearted disciple is like salt that cannot serve its intended purpose. See the simile of salt in Mt 5:13 and the note there.

a. [14:1–6] 6:6–11; 13:10–17.   b. [14:1] 11:37.

c. [14:3] 6:9; Mk 3:4.
d. [14:5] 13:15; Dt 22:4; Mt 12:11.
e. [14:6] Mt 22:46.
f. [14:7] 11:43; Mt 23:6; Mk 12:38–39.
g. [14:8–10] Prv 25:6–7.
h. [14:11] 18:14.
i. [14:12] 6:32–35.
j. [14:14] Jn 5:29.

k. [14:16–24] Mt 22:2–10.
l. [14:26–27] Mt 10:37–38.
m. [14:26] 9:57–62; 18:29; Jn 12:25.
n. [14:27] 9:23; Mt 16:24; Mk 8:34.
o. [14:33] 5:11.
p. [14:34] Mt 5:13; Mk 9:50.
q. [14:35] 8:8; Mt 11:15; 13:9; Mk 4:9, 23.

15

The Parable of the Lost Sheep.[a] [1] The tax collectors and sinners were all drawing near to listen to him, [2]but the Pharisees and scribes began to complain, saying, "This man welcomes sinners and eats with them."[b] [3]So to them he addressed this parable. [4c]"What man among you having a hundred sheep and losing one of them would not leave the ninety-nine in the desert and go after the lost one[d] until he finds it?[e] [5]And when he does find it, he sets it on his shoulders with great joy [6]and, upon his arrival home, he calls together his friends and neighbors and says to them, 'Rejoice with me because I have found my lost sheep.' [7]I tell you, in just the same way there will be more joy in heaven over one sinner who repents than over ninety-nine righteous people who have no need of repentance.[f]

The Parable of the Lost Coin. [8]"Or what woman having ten coins[†] and losing one would not light a lamp and sweep the house, searching carefully until she finds it? [9]And when she does find it, she calls together her friends and neighbors and says to them, 'Rejoice with me because I have found the coin that I lost.' [10]In just the same way, I tell you, there will be rejoicing among the angels of God over one sinner who repents."

The Parable of the Lost Son. [11]Then he said, "A man had two sons, [12]and the younger son said to his father, 'Father, give me the share of your estate that should come to me.' So the father divided the property between them. [13]After a few days, the younger son collected all his belongings and set off to a distant country where he squandered his inheritance on a life of dissipation.[g] [14]When he had freely spent everything, a severe famine struck that country, and he found himself in dire need. [15]So he hired himself out to one of the local citizens who sent him to his farm to tend

---

* [15:1–32] To the parable of the lost sheep (Lk 15:1–7) that Luke shares with Matthew (Mt 18:12–14), Luke adds two parables (the lost coin, Lk 15:8–10; the prodigal son, Lk 15:11–32) from his own special tradition to illustrate Jesus' particular concern for the lost and God's love for the repentant sinner.

† [15:8] **Ten coins:** literally, "ten drachmas." A drachma was a Greek silver coin.

the swine. [16]And he longed to eat his fill of the pods on which the swine fed, but nobody gave him any. [17]Coming to his senses he thought, 'How many of my father's hired workers have more than enough food to eat, but here am I, dying from hunger. [18]I shall get up and go to my father and I shall say to him, "Father, I have sinned against heaven and against you. [19]I no longer deserve to be called your son; treat me as you would treat one of your hired workers."' [20]So he got up and went back to his father. While he was still a long way off, his father caught sight of him, and was filled with compassion. He ran to his son, embraced him and kissed him. [21]His son said to him, 'Father, I have sinned against heaven and against you; I no longer deserve to be called your son.' [22]But his father ordered his servants, 'Quickly bring the finest robe and put it on him; put a ring on his finger and sandals on his feet. [23]Take the fattened calf and slaughter it. Then let us celebrate with a feast, [24]because this son of mine was dead, and has come to life again; he was lost, and has been found.' Then the celebration began. [25]Now the older son had been out in the field and, on his way back, as he neared the house, he heard the sound of music and dancing. [26]He called one of the servants and asked what this might mean. [27]The servant said to him, 'Your brother has returned and your father has slaughtered the fattened calf because he has him back safe and sound.' [28]He became angry, and when he refused to enter the house, his father came out and pleaded with him. [29]He said to his father in reply, 'Look, all these years I served you and not once did I disobey your orders; yet you never gave me even a young goat to feast on with my friends. [30]But when your son returns who swallowed up your property with prostitutes, for him you slaughter the fattened calf.' [31]He said to him, 'My son, you are here with me always; everything I have is yours. [32]But now we must celebrate and rejoice, because your brother was dead and has come to life again; he was lost and has been found.'"

a. [15:1–7] Mt 9:10–13.
b. [15:2] 5:30; 19:7.
c. [15:4–7] Mt 18:12–14.
d. [15:4–6] 19:10.

e. [15:4] Ez 34:11–12, 16.
f. [15:7] Ez 18:23.
g. [15:13] Prv 29:3.

16 The Parable of the Dishonest Steward.[*] [1]Then he also said to his disciples, "A rich man had a steward who was reported to

---

[*] [16:1–8a] The parable of the dishonest steward has to be understood in the light of the Palestinian custom of agents

him for squandering his property. [2]He summoned him and said, 'What is this I hear about you? Prepare a full account of your stewardship, because you can no longer be my steward.' [3]The steward said to himself, 'What shall I do, now that my master is taking the position of steward away from me? I am not strong enough to dig and I am ashamed to beg. [4]I know what I shall do so that, when I am removed from the stewardship, they may welcome me into their homes.' [5]He called in his master's debtors one by one. To the first he said, 'How much do you owe my master?' [6*] He replied, 'One hundred measures of olive oil.' He said to him, 'Here is your promissory note. Sit down and quickly write one for fifty.' [7]Then to another he said, 'And you, how much do you owe?' He replied, 'One hundred kors[†] of wheat.' He said to him, 'Here is your promissory note; write one for eighty.' [8]And the master commended that dishonest steward for acting prudently.

Application of the Parable.[‡] "For the children of this world are more prudent in dealing with their own generation than are the children of light.[§a] [9]I tell you, make friends for yourselves with dishonest wealth,[¶] so that when it fails, you will be welcomed into eternal dwellings.[b] [10**]The person who is trustworthy in very small matters is also trustworthy in great ones; and the person who is dishonest in very small matters is also dishonest in great ones.[c] [11]If, therefore, you are not trustworthy with dishonest wealth, who will trust you with true wealth? [12]If you are not trustworthy with what belongs to another, who will give you what is yours? [13]No servant can serve two masters.[††] He will either hate one and

---

acting on behalf of their masters and the usurious practices common to such agents. The dishonesty of the steward consisted in the squandering of his master's property (Lk 16:1) and not in any subsequent graft. The master commends the dishonest steward who has forgone his own usurious commission on the business transaction by having the debtors write new notes that reflected only the real amount owed the master (i.e., minus the steward's profit). The dishonest steward acts in this way in order to ingratiate himself with the debtors because he knows he is being dismissed from his position (Lk 16:3). The parable, then, teaches the prudent use of one's material goods in light of an imminent crisis.

* [16:6] **One hundred measures**: literally, "one hundred baths." A bath is a Hebrew unit of liquid measurement equivalent to eight or nine gallons.

† [16:7] **One hundred kors**: a **kor** is a Hebrew unit of dry measure for grain or wheat equivalent to ten or twelve bushels.

‡ [16:8b–13] Several originally independent sayings of Jesus are gathered here by Luke to form the concluding application of the parable of the dishonest steward.

§ [16:8b–9] The first conclusion recommends the prudent use of one's wealth (in the light of the coming of the end of the age) after the manner of the children of this world, represented in the parable by the dishonest steward.

¶ [16:9] **Dishonest wealth**: literally, "mammon of iniquity." Mammon is the Greek transliteration of a Hebrew or Aramaic word that is usually explained as meaning "that in which one trusts." The characterization of this wealth as **dishonest** expresses a tendency of wealth to lead one to dishonesty. **Eternal dwellings**: or, "eternal tents," i.e., heaven.

** [16:10–12] The second conclusion recommends constant fidelity to those in positions of responsibility.

†† [16:13] The third conclusion is a general statement about the incompatibility of serving God and being a slave to riches. To be dependent upon wealth is opposed to the teachings of Jesus who counseled complete dependence on the

love the other, or be devoted to one and despise the other. You cannot serve God and mammon."*d*

A Saying Against the Pharisees. [14*] The Pharisees, who loved money,[†] heard all these things and sneered at him. [15]And he said to them, "You justify yourselves in the sight of others, but God knows your hearts; for what is of human esteem is an abomination in the sight of God.*e*

Sayings About the Law. [16]"The law and the prophets lasted until John;[‡] but from then on the kingdom of God is proclaimed, and everyone who enters does so with violence.*f* [17]It is easier for heaven and earth to pass away than for the smallest part of a letter of the law to become invalid.*g*

Sayings About Divorce. [18]"Everyone who divorces his wife and marries another commits adultery, and the one who marries a woman divorced from her husband commits adultery.*h*

The Parable of the Rich Man and Lazarus.[§] [19]"There was a rich man[¶] who dressed in purple garments and fine linen and dined sumptuously each day. [20]And lying at his door was a poor man named Lazarus, covered with sores,*i* [21]who would gladly have eaten his fill of the scraps that fell from the rich man's table. Dogs even used to come and lick his sores. [22]When the poor man died, he was carried away by angels to the bosom of Abraham. The rich man also died and was buried, [23]and from the netherworld,** where he was in torment, he raised his eyes and saw Abraham far off and Lazarus at his side. [24]And he cried out, 'Father Abraham, have pity on me. Send Lazarus to dip the tip of his finger in water and cool my tongue, for I am suffering torment in these flames.'

Father as one of the characteristics of the Christian disciple (Lk 12:22–39). **God and mammon:** see note on Lk 16:9. Mammon is used here as if it were itself a god.

* [16:14–18] The two parables about the use of riches in chap. 16 are separated by several isolated sayings of Jesus on the hypocrisy of the Pharisees (Lk 16:14–15), on the law (Lk 16:16–17), and on divorce (Lk 16:18).

† [16:14–15] The Pharisees are here presented as examples of those who are slaves to wealth (see Lk 16:13) and, consequently, they are unable to serve God.

‡ [16:16] John the Baptist is presented in Luke's gospel as a transitional figure between the period of Israel, the time of promise, and the period of Jesus, the time of fulfillment. With John, the fulfillment of the Old Testament promises has begun.

§ [16:19–31] The parable of the rich man and Lazarus again illustrates Luke's concern with Jesus' attitude toward the rich and the poor. The reversal of the fates of the rich man and Lazarus (Lk 16:22–23) illustrates the teachings of Jesus in Luke's "Sermon on the Plain" (Lk 6:20–21, 24–25).

¶ [16:19] The oldest Greek manuscript of Luke dating from ca. A.D. 175–225 records the name of the rich man as an abbreviated form of "Nineveh," but there is very little textual support in other manuscripts for this reading. "Dives" of popular tradition is the Latin Vulgate's translation for "rich man" (Lk 16:19–31).

** [16:23] **The netherworld:** see note on Lk 10:15.

²⁵Abraham replied, 'My child, remember that you received what was good during your lifetime while Lazarus likewise received what was bad; but now he is comforted here, whereas you are tormented.ʲ ²⁶Moreover, between us and you a great chasm is established to prevent anyone from crossing who might wish to go from our side to yours or from your side to ours.' ²⁷He said, 'Then I beg you, father, send him to my father's house, ²⁸for I have five brothers, so that he may warn them, lest they too come to this place of torment.' ²⁹But Abraham replied, 'They have Moses and the prophets. Let them listen to them.' ³⁰* He said, 'Oh no, father Abraham, but if someone from the dead goes to them, they will repent.' ³¹Then Abraham said, 'If they will not listen to Moses and the prophets, neither will they be persuaded if someone should rise from the dead.'"ᵏ

* [16:30–31] A foreshadowing in Luke's gospel of the rejection of the call to repentance even after Jesus' resurrection.

a. [16:8] Eph 5:8; 1 Thes 5:5.
b. [16:9] 12:33.
c. [16:10] 19:17; Mt 25:20–23.
d. [16:13] Mt 6:24.
e. [16:15] 18:9–14.
f. [16:16] Mt 11:12–13.
g. [16:17] Mt 5:18.
h. [16:18] Mt 5:32; 19:9; Mk 10:11–12; 1 Cor 7:10–11.
i. [16:20] Mt 15:27; Mk 7:28.
j. [16:25] 6:24–25.
k. [16:31] Jn 5:46–47; 11:44–48.

17

Temptations to Sin. ¹ᵃ He said to his disciples, "Things that cause sin will inevitably occur, but woe to the person through whom they occur. ²It would be better for him if a millstone were put around his neck and he be thrown into the sea than for him to cause one of these little ones to sin. ³Be on your guard!† If your brother sins, rebuke him; and if he repents, forgive him.ᵇ ⁴And if he wrongs you seven times in one day and returns to you seven times saying, 'I am sorry,' you should forgive him."ᶜ

Saying of Faith. ⁵And the apostles said to the Lord, "Increase our faith." ⁶The Lord replied, "If you have faith the size of a mustard seed, you would say to [this] mulberry tree, 'Be uprooted and planted in the sea,' and it would obey you.ᵈ

Attitude of a Servant.‡ ⁷"Who among you would say to your servant who has just come in from plowing or tending sheep in the field, 'Come

† [17:3] **Be on your guard**: the translation takes Lk 17:3a as the conclusion to the saying on scandal in Lk 17:1–2. It is not impossible that it should be taken as the beginning of the saying on forgiveness in Lk 17:3b–4.
‡ [17:7–10] These sayings of Jesus, peculiar to Luke, which continue his response to the apostles' request to increase their faith (Lk 17:5–6), remind them that Christian disciples can make no claim on God's graciousness; in fulfilling

here immediately and take your place at table'? [8]Would he not rather say to him, 'Prepare something for me to eat. Put on your apron and wait on me while I eat and drink. You may eat and drink when I am finished'? [9]Is he grateful to that servant because he did what was commanded? [10]So should it be with you. When you have done all you have been commanded, say, 'We are unprofitable servants; we have done what we were obliged to do.'"

The Cleansing of Ten Lepers.[*] [11]As he continued his journey to Jerusalem,[e] he traveled through Samaria and Galilee.[†] [12]As he was entering a village, ten lepers met [him]. They stood at a distance from him [13]and raised their voice, saying, "Jesus, Master! Have pity on us!"[f] [14]And when he saw them, he said, "Go show yourselves to the priests."[‡] As they were going they were cleansed.[g] [15]And one of them, realizing he had been healed, returned, glorifying God in a loud voice; [16]and he fell at the feet of Jesus and thanked him. He was a Samaritan. [17]Jesus said in reply, "Ten were cleansed, were they not? Where are the other nine? [18]Has none but this foreigner returned to give thanks to God?" [19]Then he said to him, "Stand up and go; your faith has saved you."[h]

The Coming of the Kingdom of God. [20][§] Asked by the Pharisees when the kingdom of God would come, he said in reply, "The coming of the kingdom of God cannot be observed,[i] [21][¶] and no one will announce, 'Look, here it is,' or, 'There it is.'[j] For behold, the kingdom of God is among you."

---

the exacting demands of discipleship, they are only doing their duty.
* [17:11–19] This incident recounting the thankfulness of the cleansed Samaritan leper is narrated only in Luke's gospel and provides an instance of Jesus holding up a non-Jew (Lk 17:18) as an example to his Jewish contemporaries (cf. Lk 10:33 where a similar purpose is achieved in the story of the good Samaritan). Moreover, it is the faith in Jesus manifested by the foreigner that has brought him salvation (Lk 17:19; cf. the similar relationship between faith and salvation in Lk 7:50; 8:48, 50).
† [17:11] **Through Samaria and Galilee**: or, "between Samaria and Galilee."
‡ [17:14] See note on Lk 5:14.
§ [17:20–37] To the question of the Pharisees about the time of the coming of God's kingdom, Jesus replies that the kingdom is **among you** (Lk 17:20–21). The emphasis has thus been shifted from an imminent observable coming of the kingdom to something that is already present in Jesus' preaching and healing ministry. Luke has also appended further traditional sayings of Jesus about the unpredictable suddenness of the day of the Son of Man, and assures his readers that in spite of the delay of that day (Lk 12:45), it will bring judgment unexpectedly on those who do not continue to be vigilant.
¶ [17:21] **Among you**: the Greek preposition translated as **among** can also be translated as "within." In the light of other statements in Luke's gospel about the presence of the kingdom (see Lk 10:9, 11; 11:20) "among" is to be preferred.

The Day of the Son of Man. [22]Then he said to his disciples, "The days will come when you will long to see one of the days of the Son of Man, but you will not see it. [23]There will be those who will say to you, 'Look, there he is,' [or] 'Look, here he is.' Do not go off, do not run in pursuit.[k] [24]For just as lightning flashes and lights up the sky from one side to the other, so will the Son of Man be [in his day].[l] [25]But first he must suffer greatly and be rejected by this generation.[m] [26]As it was in the days of Noah,[n] so it will be in the days of the Son of Man; [27]they were eating and drinking, marrying and giving in marriage up to the day that Noah entered the ark, and the flood came and destroyed them all. [28][o] Similarly, as it was in the days of Lot: they were eating, drinking, buying, selling, planting, building; [29]on the day when Lot left Sodom, fire and brimstone rained from the sky to destroy them all. [30]So it will be on the day the Son of Man is revealed. [31][p] On that day, a person who is on the housetop and whose belongings are in the house must not go down to get them, and likewise a person in the field must not return to what was left behind.[q] [32]Remember the wife of Lot. [33]Whoever seeks to preserve his life will lose it, but whoever loses it will save it.[r] [34]I tell you, on that night there will be two people in one bed; one will be taken, the other left. [35][s] And there will be two women grinding meal together; one will be taken, the other left." [36]* [37]They said to him in reply, "Where, Lord?" He said to them, "Where the body is, there also the vultures will gather."[t]

* [17:36] The inclusion of Lk 17:36, "There will be two men in the field; one will be taken, the other left behind," in some Western manuscripts appears to be a scribal assimilation to Mt 24:40.

a. [17:1–2] Mt 18:6–7.
b. [17:3] Mt 18:15.
c. [17:4] Mt 6:14; 18:21–22, 35; Mk 11:25.
d. [17:6] Mt 17:20; 21:21; Mk 11:23.
e. [17:11] 9:51–53; 13:22, 33; 18:31; 19:28; Jn 4:4.
f. [17:13] 18:38; Mt 9:27; 15:22.
g. [17:14] 5:14; Lv 14:2–32; Mt 8:4; Mk 1:44.
h. [17:19] 7:50; 18:42.
i. [17:20] Jn 3:3.
j. [17:21] 17:23; Mt 24:23; Mk 13:21.
k. [17:23] 17:21; Mt 24:23, 26; Mk 13:21.
l. [17:24] Mt 24:27.
m. [17:25] 9:22; 18:32–33; Mt 16:21; 17:22–23; 20:18–19; Mk 8:31; 9:31; 10:33–34.
n. [17:26–27] Gn 6–8; Mt 24:37–39.
o. [17:28–29] Gn 18:20–21; 19:1–29.
p. [17:31–32] Gn 19:17, 26.
q. [17:31] Mt 24:17–18; Mk 13:15–16.
r. [17:33] 9:24; Mt 10:39; 16:25; Mk 8:35; Jn 12:25.
s. [17:35] Mt 24:40–41.
t. [17:37] Jb 39:30; Mt 24:28.

18

The Parable of the Persistent Widow. [1]† Then he told them a parable about the necessity for them to pray always without

† [18:1–14] The particularly Lucan material in the travel narrative concludes with two parables on prayer. The first (Lk 18:1–8) teaches the disciples the need of persistent prayer so that they not fall victims to apostasy (Lk 18:8). The second (Lk 18:9–14) condemns the self-righteous, critical attitude of the Pharisee and teaches that the fundamental attitude of the Christian disciple must be the recognition of sinfulness and complete dependence on God's gracious-

becoming weary.[a] He said, [2]"There was a judge in a certain town who neither feared God nor respected any human being. [3]And a widow in that town used to come to him and say, 'Render a just decision for me against my adversary.' [4]For a long time the judge was unwilling, but eventually he thought, 'While it is true that I neither fear God nor respect any human being, [5][b] because this widow keeps bothering me I shall deliver a just decision for her lest she finally come and strike me.'" [6]The Lord said, "Pay attention to what the dishonest judge says. [7]Will not God then secure the rights of his chosen ones who call out to him day and night? Will he be slow to answer them? [8]I tell you, he will see to it that justice is done for them speedily. But when the Son of Man comes, will he find faith on earth?"

The Parable of the Pharisee and the Tax Collector. [9]He then addressed this parable to those who were convinced of their own righteousness and despised everyone else.[c] [10]"Two people went up to the temple area to pray; one was a Pharisee and the other was a tax collector. [11]The Pharisee took up his position and spoke this prayer to himself, 'O God, I thank you that I am not like the rest of humanity—greedy, dishonest, adulterous—or even like this tax collector. [12]I fast twice a week, and I pay tithes on my whole income.'[d] [13]But the tax collector stood off at a distance and would not even raise his eyes to heaven but beat his breast and prayed, 'O God, be merciful to me a sinner.'[e] [14]I tell you, the latter went home justified, not the former; for everyone who exalts himself will be humbled, and the one who humbles himself will be exalted."[f]

Saying on Children and the Kingdom. [15][†] People were bringing even infants to him that he might touch them,[‡] and when the disciples saw this, they rebuked them.[g] [16]Jesus, however, called the children to himself and said, "Let the children come to me and do not prevent them; for the

---

ness. The second parable recalls the story of the pardoning of the sinful woman (Lk 7:36–50) where a similar contrast is presented between the critical attitude of the Pharisee Simon and the love shown by the pardoned sinner.

* [18:5] **Strike me:** the Greek verb translated as strike means "to strike under the eye" and suggests the extreme situation to which the persistence of the widow might lead. It may, however, be used here in the much weaker sense of "to wear one out."

† [18:15–19:27] Luke here includes much of the material about the journey to Jerusalem found in his Marcan source (Lk 10:1–52) and adds to it the story of Zacchaeus (Lk 19:1–10) from his own particular tradition and the parable of the gold coins (minas) (Lk 19:11–27) from Q, the source common to Luke and Matthew.

‡ [18:15–17] The sayings on children furnish a contrast to the attitude of the Pharisee in the preceding episode (Lk 18:9–14) and that of the wealthy official in the following one (Lk 18:18–23) who think that they can lay claim to God's favor by their own merit. The attitude of the disciple should be marked by the receptivity and trustful dependence characteristic of the child.

kingdom of God belongs to such as these. [17]Amen, I say to you, whoever does not accept the kingdom of God like a child will not enter it."[h]

The Rich Official. [18i] An official asked him this question, "Good teacher, what must I do to inherit eternal life?"[j] [19]Jesus answered him, "Why do you call me good? No one is good but God alone. [20]You know the commandments, 'You shall not commit adultery; you shall not kill; you shall not steal; you shall not bear false witness; honor your father and your mother.'"[k] [21]And he replied, "All of these I have observed from my youth." [22* l] When Jesus heard this he said to him, "There is still one thing left for you: sell all that you have and distribute it to the poor, and you will have a treasure in heaven. Then come, follow me." [23]But when he heard this he became quite sad, for he was very rich.

On Riches and Renunciation. [24]Jesus looked at him [now sad] and said, "How hard it is for those who have wealth to enter the kingdom of God! [25]For it is easier for a camel to pass through the eye of a needle than for a rich person to enter the kingdom of God." [26]Those who heard this said, "Then who can be saved?" [27]And he said, "What is impossible for human beings is possible for God."[m] [28]Then Peter said, "We have given up our possessions and followed you." [29n] He said to them, "Amen, I say to you, there is no one who has given up house or wife or brothers or parents or children for the sake of the kingdom of God [30]who will not receive [back] an overabundant return in this present age and eternal life in the age to come."

The Third Prediction of the Passion. [o] [31†] Then he took the Twelve aside and said to them, "Behold, we are going up to Jerusalem and everything written by the prophets about the Son of Man will be fulfilled.[‡] [32p] He will be handed over to the Gentiles and he will be mocked and insulted and spat upon; [33]and after they have scourged him they will kill him, but on the third day he will rise." [34]But they understood nothing of this; the

---

* [18:22] Detachment from material possessions results in the total dependence on God demanded of one who would inherit eternal life. **Sell all that you have:** the original saying (cf. Mk 10:21) has characteristically been made more demanding by Luke's addition of "all."

† [18:31–33] The details included in this third announcement of Jesus' suffering and death suggest that the literary formulation of the announcement has been directed by the knowledge of the historical passion and death of Jesus.

‡ [18:31] **Everything written by the prophets … will be fulfilled:** this is a Lucan addition to the words of Jesus found in the Marcan source (Mk 10:32–34). Luke understands the events of Jesus' last days in Jerusalem to be the fulfillment of Old Testament prophecy, but, as is usually the case in Luke-Acts, the author does not specify which Old Testament prophets he has in mind; cf. Lk 24:25, 27, 44; Acts 3:8; 13:27; 26:22–23.

word remained hidden from them and they failed to comprehend what he said.*q*

The Healing of the Blind Beggar.*r* ³⁵Now as he approached Jericho a blind man was sitting by the roadside begging, ³⁶and hearing a crowd going by, he inquired what was happening. ³⁷They told him, "Jesus of Nazareth is passing by." ³⁸*s* He shouted, "Jesus, Son of David,* have pity on me!" ³⁹The people walking in front rebuked him, telling him to be silent, but he kept calling out all the more, "Son of David, have pity on me!" ⁴⁰Then Jesus stopped and ordered that he be brought to him; and when he came near, Jesus asked him, ⁴¹"What do you want me to do for you?" He replied, "Lord, please let me see."*t* ⁴²Jesus told him, "Have sight; your faith has saved you."*u* ⁴³He immediately received his sight and followed him, giving glory to God. When they saw this, all the people gave praise to God.

---

* [18:38] **Son of David**: the blind beggar identifies Jesus with a title that is related to Jesus' role as Messiah (see note on Lk 2:11). Through this Son of David, salvation comes to the blind man. Note the connection between salvation and house of David mentioned earlier in Zechariah's canticle (Lk 1:69). See also note on Mt 9:27.

a. [18:1] Rom 12:12; Col 4:2; 1 Thes 5:17.
b. [18:5] 11:8.
c. [18:9] 16:5; Mt 23:25–28.
d. [18:12] Mt 23:23.
e. [18:13] Ps 51:3.
f. [18:14] 14:11; Mt 23:12.
g. [18:15–17] Mt 19:13–15; Mk 10:13–16.
h. [18:17] Mt 18:3.
i. [18:18–30] Mt 19:16–30; Mk 10:17–31.
j. [18:18] 10:25.
k. [18:20] Ex 20:12–16; Dt 5:16–20.
l. [18:22] 12:33; Sir 29:11; Mt 6:20.
m. [18:27] Mk 14:36.
n. [18:29–30] 14:26.
o. [18:31–34] 24:25–27, 44; Mt 20:17–19; Mk 10:32–34; Acts 3:18.
p. [18:32–33] 9:22, 44.
q. [18:34] Mk 9:32.
r. [18:35–43] Mt 20:29–34; Mk 10:46–52.
s. [18:38–39] 17:13; Mt 9:27; 15:22.
t. [18:41] Mk 10:36.
u. [18:42] 7:50; 17:19.

19

Zacchaeus the Tax Collector.† ¹He came to Jericho and intended to pass through the town. ²Now a man there named Zacchaeus, who was a chief tax collector and also a wealthy man, ³was seeking to see who Jesus was; but he could not see him because of the crowd, for he was short in stature. ⁴So he ran ahead and climbed a sycamore tree in order to see Jesus, who was about to pass that way. ⁵When he reached the place, Jesus looked up and said to him, "Zacchaeus, come down quickly, for today I must stay at your house." ⁶And he came down quickly and received him with joy. ⁷When they all saw this, they began to grumble,

---

† [19:1–10] The story of the tax collector Zacchaeus is unique to this gospel. While a rich man (Lk 19:2), Zacchaeus provides a contrast to the rich man of Lk 18:18–23 who cannot detach himself from his material possessions to become a follower of Jesus. Zacchaeus, according to Luke, exemplifies the proper attitude toward wealth: he promises to give half of his possessions to the poor (Lk 19:8) and consequently is the recipient of salvation (Lk 19:9–10).

saying, "He has gone to stay at the house of a sinner."*a* 8But Zacchaeus stood there and said to the Lord, "Behold, half of my possessions, Lord, I shall give to the poor, and if I have extorted anything from anyone I shall repay it four times over."*b* 9*And Jesus said to him, "Today salvation*c* has come to this house because this man too is a descendant of Abraham. 10†*d* For the Son of Man has come to seek and to save what was lost."

The Parable of the Ten Gold Coins.‡ 11*e* While they were listening to him speak, he proceeded to tell a parable because he was near Jerusalem and they thought that the kingdom of God would appear there immediately. 12So he said, "A nobleman went off to a distant country to obtain the kingship for himself and then to return.*f* 13He called ten of his servants and gave them ten gold coins§ and told them, 'Engage in trade with these until I return.' 14His fellow citizens, however, despised him and sent a delegation after him to announce, 'We do not want this man to be our king.' 15But when he returned after obtaining the kingship, he had the servants called, to whom he had given the money, to learn what they had gained by trading. 16The first came forward and said, 'Sir, your gold coin has earned ten additional ones.' 17He replied, 'Well done, good servant! You have been faithful in this very small matter; take charge of ten cities.'*g* 18Then the second came and reported, 'Your gold coin, sir, has earned five more.' 19And to this servant too he said, 'You, take charge of five cities.' 20Then the other servant came and said, 'Sir, here is your gold coin; I kept it stored away in a handkerchief, 21for I was afraid of you, because you are a demanding person; you take up what you did not lay down and you harvest what you did not plant.' 22He said to him,

---

* [19:9] A descendant of Abraham: literally, "a son of Abraham." The tax collector Zacchaeus, whose repentance is attested by his determination to amend his former ways, shows himself to be a true descendant of Abraham, the true heir to the promises of God in the Old Testament. Underlying Luke's depiction of Zacchaeus as a descendant of Abraham, the father of the Jews (Lk 1:73; 16:22–31), is his recognition of the central place occupied by Israel in the plan of salvation.

† [19:10] This verse sums up for Luke his depiction of the role of Jesus as savior in this gospel.

‡ [19:11–27] In this parable Luke has combined two originally distinct parables: (1) a parable about the conduct of faithful and productive servants (Lk 19:13, 15b–26) and (2) a parable about a rejected king (Lk 19:12, 14–15a, 27). The story about the conduct of servants occurs in another form in Mt 25:14–20. The story about the rejected king may have originated with a contemporary historical event. After the death of Herod the Great, his son Archelaus traveled to Rome to receive the title of king. A delegation of Jews appeared in Rome before Caesar Augustus to oppose the request of Archelaus. Although not given the title of king, Archelaus was made ruler over Judea and Samaria. As the story is used by Luke, however, it furnishes a correction to the expectation of the imminent end of the age and of the establishment of the kingdom in Jerusalem (Lk 19:11). Jesus is not on his way to Jerusalem to receive the kingly power; for that, he must go away and only after returning from the distant country (a reference to the parousia) will reward and judgment take place.

§ [19:13] Ten gold coins: literally, "ten minas." A mina was a monetary unit that in ancient Greece was the equivalent of one hundred drachmas.

'With your own words I shall condemn you, you wicked servant. You knew I was a demanding person, taking up what I did not lay down and harvesting what I did not plant; ²³why did you not put my money in a bank? Then on my return I would have collected it with interest.' ²⁴And to those standing by he said, 'Take the gold coin from him and give it to the servant who has ten.' ²⁵But they said to him, 'Sir, he has ten gold coins.' ²⁶'I tell you, to everyone who has, more will be given, but from the one who has not, even what he has will be taken away.'ʰ ²⁷Now as for those enemies of mine who did not want me as their king, bring them here and slay them before me.'"

VI. THE TEACHING MINISTRY IN JERUSALEM*

The Entry into Jerusalem.ⁱ ²⁸After he had said this, he proceeded on his journey up to Jerusalem. ²⁹As he drew near to Bethphage and Bethany at the place called the Mount of Olives, he sent two of his disciples.ʲ ³⁰He said, "Go into the village opposite you, and as you enter it you will find a colt tethered on which no one has ever sat. Untie it and bring it here.ᵏ ³¹And if anyone should ask you, 'Why are you untying it?' you will answer, 'The Master has need of it.'" ³²So those who had been sent went off and found everything just as he had told them.ˡ ³³And as they were untying the colt, its owners said to them, "Why are you untying this colt?" ³⁴They answered, "The Master has need of it." ³⁵ᵐ So they brought it to Jesus, threw their cloaks over the colt, and helped Jesus to mount. ³⁶As he rode along, the people were spreading their cloaks on the road; ³⁷and now as he was approaching the slope of the Mount of Olives, the whole multitude of his disciples began to praise God aloud with joy for all the mighty deeds they had seen. ³⁸They proclaimed:

"Blessed is the king who comes
in the name of the Lord.†

---

* [19:28–21:38] With the royal entry of Jesus into Jerusalem, a new section of Luke's gospel begins, the ministry of Jesus in Jerusalem before his death and resurrection. Luke suggests that this was a lengthy ministry in Jerusalem (Lk 19:47; 20:1; 21:37–38; 22:53) and it is characterized by Jesus' daily teaching in the temple (Lk 21:37–38). For the story of the entry of Jesus into Jerusalem, see also Mt 21:1–11; Mk 11:1–10; Jn 12:12–19 and the notes there.

† [19:38] **Blessed is the king who comes in the name of the Lord:** only in Luke is Jesus explicitly given the title **king** when he enters Jerusalem in triumph. Luke has inserted this title into the words of Ps 118:26 that heralded the arrival of the pilgrims coming to the holy city and to the temple. Jesus is thereby acclaimed as **king** (see Lk 1:32) and as the one **who comes** (see Mal 3:1; Lk 7:19). **Peace in heaven. . .:** the acclamation of the disciples of Jesus in Luke echoes the announcement of the angels at the birth of Jesus (Lk 2:14). The peace Jesus brings is associated with the salvation to be accomplished here in Jerusalem.

> Peace in heaven
> and glory in the highest.'"[n]

³⁹Some of the Pharisees in the crowd said to him, "Teacher, rebuke your disciples."* ⁴⁰He said in reply, "I tell you, if they keep silent, the stones will cry out!"

The Lament for Jerusalem.† ⁴¹ᵒ As he drew near, he saw the city and wept over it,[p] ⁴²saying, "If this day you only knew what makes for peace—but now it is hidden from your eyes.[q] ⁴³†For the days are coming upon you when your enemies will raise a palisade against you; they will encircle you and hem you in on all sides.[r] ⁴⁴They will smash you to the ground and your children within you, and they will not leave one stone upon another within you because you did not recognize the time of your visitation."[s]

The Cleansing of the Temple. ⁴⁵†Then Jesus entered the temple area§ and proceeded to drive out those who were selling things,[u] ⁴⁶saying to them, "It is written, 'My house shall be a house of prayer, but you have made it a den of thieves.'"[v] ⁴⁷And every day he was teaching in the temple area.[w] The chief priests, the scribes, and the leaders of the people, meanwhile, were seeking to put him to death,[x] ⁴⁸but they could find no way to accomplish their purpose because all the people were hanging on his words.

---

* [19:39] **Rebuke your disciples**: this command, found only in Luke, was given so that the Roman authorities would not interpret the acclamation of Jesus as king as an uprising against them; cf. Lk 23:2–3.

† [19:41–44] The lament for Jerusalem is found only in Luke. By not accepting Jesus (the one who mediates peace), Jerusalem will not find peace but will become the victim of devastation.

‡ [19:43–44] Luke may be describing the actual disaster that befell Jerusalem in A.D. 70 when it was destroyed by the Romans during the First Revolt.

§ [19:45–46] Immediately upon entering the holy city, Jesus in a display of his authority enters the temple (see Mal 3:1–3) and lays claim to it after cleansing it that it might become a proper place for his teaching ministry in Jerusalem (Lk 19:47; 20:1; 21:37; 22:53). See Mt 21:12–17; Mk 11:15–19; Jn 2:13–17 and the notes there.

a. [19:7] 5:30; 15:2.
b. [19:8] Ex 21:37; Nm 5:6–7; 2 Sm 12:6.
c. [19:9] 13:16; Mt 21:31.
d. [19:10] 15:4–10; Ez 34:16.
e. [19:11–27] Mt 25:14–30.
f. [19:12] Mk 13:34.
g. [19:17] 16:10.
h. [19:26] 8:18; Mt 13:12; Mk 4:25.
i. [19:28–40] Mt 21:1–11; Mk 11:1–11; Jn 12:12–19.
j. [19:29] Zec 14:4.
k. [19:30] Nm 19:2; Dt 21:3; 1 Sm 6:7; Zec 9:9.
l. [19:32] 22:13.
m. [19:35–36] 2 Kgs 9:13.
n. [19:38] 2:14; Ps 118:26.

o. [19:41–44] 13:34–35.
p. [19:41] 2 Kgs 8:11–12; Jer 14:17; 15:5.
q. [19:42] 8:10; Is 6:9–10; Mt 13:14; Mk 4:12; Acts 28:26–27; Rom 11:8, 10.
r. [19:43] Is 29:3.
s. [19:44] 1:68; 21:6; Ps 137:9; Mt 24:2; Mk 13:2.
t. [19:45–46] Mt 21:12–13; Mk 11:15–17; Jn 2:13–17.
u. [19:45] 3:1 / Hos 9:15.
v. [19:46] Is 56:7; Jer 7:11.
w. [19:47–48] 20:19; 22:2; Mt 21:46; Mk 11:18; 12:12; 14:1–2; Jn 5:18; 7:30.
x. [19:47] 21:37; 22:53; Jn 18:20.

20

The Authority of Jesus Questioned.[a] [1]One day as he was teaching the people in the temple area and proclaiming the good news, the chief priests and scribes, together with the elders, approached him [2]and said to him, "Tell us, by what authority are you doing these things? Or who is the one who gave you this authority?"[b] [3]He said to them in reply, "I shall ask you a question. Tell me, [4]was John's baptism of heavenly or of human origin?"[c] [5]They discussed this among themselves, and said, "If we say, 'Of heavenly origin,' he will say, 'Why did you not believe him?'[d] [6]But if we say, 'Of human origin,' then all the people will stone us, for they are convinced that John was a prophet." [7]So they answered that they did not know from where it came. [8]Then Jesus said to them, "Neither shall I tell you by what authority I do these things."

The Parable of the Tenant Farmers.[†] [9e]Then he proceeded to tell the people this parable. "[A] man planted a vineyard, leased it to tenant farmers, and then went on a journey for a long time.[f] [10]At harvest time he sent a servant[g] to the tenant farmers to receive some of the produce of the vineyard. But they beat the servant and sent him away empty-handed. [11]So he proceeded to send another servant, but him also they beat and insulted and sent away empty-handed. [12]Then he proceeded to send a third, but this one too they wounded and threw out. [13]The owner of the vineyard said, 'What shall I do? I shall send my beloved son; maybe they will respect him.'[h] [14]But when the tenant farmers saw him they said to one another, 'This is the heir. Let us kill him that the inheritance may become ours.' [15]So they threw him out of the vineyard and killed him.[‡] What will the owner of the vineyard do to them? [16]He will come and put those tenant farmers to death and turn over the vineyard to others." When the people heard this, they exclaimed, "Let it not be so!" [17]But he looked at them and asked, "What then does this scripture passage mean:

---

* [20:1–47] The Jerusalem religious leaders or their representatives, in an attempt to incriminate Jesus with the Romans and to discredit him with the people, pose a number of questions to him (about his authority, Lk 20:2; about payment of taxes, Lk 20:22; about the resurrection, Lk 20:28–33).

† [20:9–19] This parable about an absentee landlord and a tenant farmers' revolt reflects the social and economic conditions of rural Palestine in the first century. The synoptic gospel writers use the parable to describe how the rejection of the landlord's son becomes the occasion for the vineyard to be taken away from those to whom it was entrusted (the religious leadership of Judaism that rejects the teaching and preaching of Jesus; Lk 20:19).

‡ [20:15] **They threw him out of the vineyard and killed him**: cf. Mk 12:8. Luke has altered his Marcan source and reports that the murder of the son takes place outside the vineyard to reflect the tradition of Jesus' death outside the walls of the city of Jerusalem (see Heb 13:12).

> 'The stone which the builders rejected
> has become the cornerstone'?[i]

[18]Everyone who falls on that stone will be dashed to pieces; and it will crush anyone on whom it falls." [19]The scribes and chief priests sought to lay their hands on him at that very hour, but they feared the people, for they knew that he had addressed this parable to them.[j]

Paying Taxes to the Emperor.[k] [20] They watched him closely and sent agents pretending to be righteous who were to trap him in speech,[l] in order to hand him over to the authority and power of the governor.* [21]They posed this question to him, "Teacher, we know that what you say and teach is correct, and you show no partiality, but teach the way of God in accordance with the truth.[m] [22]Is it lawful for us to pay tribute to Caesar or not?"[†] [23]Recognizing their craftiness he said to them, [24]"Show me a denarius;[‡] whose image and name does it bear?" They replied, "Caesar's." [25]So he said to them, "Then repay to Caesar what belongs to Caesar and to God what belongs to God."[n] [26]They were unable to trap him by something he might say before the people, and so amazed were they at his reply that they fell silent.

The Question About the Resurrection.[o] [27]Some Sadducees,[§] those who deny that there is a resurrection, came forward and put this question to him,[p] [28]¶ saying, "Teacher, Moses wrote for us, 'If someone's brother dies leaving a wife but no child, his brother must take the wife and raise up descendants for his brother.'[q] [29]Now there were seven brothers; the first married a woman but died childless. [30]Then the second [31]and the third married her, and likewise all the seven died childless. [32]Finally the woman also died. [33]Now at the resurrection whose wife will that woman be? For all seven had been married to her." [34]Jesus said to them, "The

---

* [20:20] **The governor:** i.e., Pontius Pilate, the Roman administrator responsible for the collection of taxes and maintenance of order in Palestine.

† [20:22] Through their question the agents of the Jerusalem religious leadership hope to force Jesus to take sides on one of the sensitive political issues of first-century Palestine. The issue of nonpayment of taxes to Rome becomes one of the focal points of the First Jewish Revolt (A.D. 66–70) that resulted in the Roman destruction of Jerusalem and the temple. See also note on Mt 22:15–22.

‡ [20:24] **Denarius:** a Roman silver coin (see note on Lk 7:41).

§ [20:27] **Sadducees:** see note on Mt 3:7.

¶ [20:28–33] The Sadducees' question, based on the law of levirate marriage recorded in Dt 25:5–10, ridicules the idea of the resurrection. Jesus rejects their naive understanding of the resurrection (Lk 20:35–36) and then argues on behalf of the resurrection of the dead on the basis of the written law (Lk 20:37–38) that the Sadducees accept. See also notes on Mt 22:23–33.

children of this age marry and are given in marriage; [35]but those who are deemed worthy to attain to the coming age and to the resurrection of the dead neither marry nor are given in marriage. [36]They can no longer die, for they are like angels; and they are the children of God because they are the ones who will rise.* [37]That the dead will rise even Moses made known in the passage about the bush, when he called 'Lord' the God of Abraham, the God of Isaac, and the God of Jacob;[r] [38]and he is not God of the dead, but of the living, for to him all are alive."[s] [39]Some of the scribes said in reply, "Teacher, you have answered well." [40]And they no longer dared to ask him anything.[t]

The Question About David's Son.[†] [41u] Then he said to them, "How do they claim that the Messiah is the Son of David? [42]For David himself in the Book of Psalms says:[v]

> "The Lord said to my lord,
>> "Sit at my right hand
>>> [43]till I make your enemies your footstool."'

[44]Now if David calls him 'lord,' how can he be his son?"

Denunciation of the Scribes.[w] [45]Then, within the hearing of all the people, he said to [his] disciples, [46]"Be on guard against the scribes, who like to go around in long robes and love greetings in marketplaces, seats of honor in synagogues, and places of honor at banquets.[x] [47]They devour the houses of widows and, as a pretext, recite lengthy prayers. They will receive a very severe condemnation."

---

* [20:36] **Because they are the ones who will rise**: literally, "being sons of the resurrection."
† [20:41–44] After successfully answering the three questions of his opponents, Jesus now asks them a question. Their inability to respond implies that they have forfeited their position and authority as the religious leaders of the people because they do not understand the scriptures. This series of controversies between the religious leadership of Jerusalem and Jesus reveals Jesus as the authoritative teacher whose words are to be listened to (see Lk 9:35). See also notes on Mt 22:41–46.

a. [20:1–8] Mt 21:23–27; Mk 11:27–33.
b. [20:2] Acts 4:7.
c. [20:4] 3:3, 16.
d. [20:5] Mt 21:32.
e. [20:9–19] Mt 21:33–46; Mk 12:1–12.
f. [20:9] Is 5:1–7.
g. [20:10–12] 2 Chr 36:15–16.
h. [20:13] 3:22.
i. [20:17] Ps 118:22; Is 28:16.
j. [20:19] 19:47–48; 22:2; Mt 21:46; Mk 11:18; 12:12; 14:1–2; Jn 5:18; 7:30.
k. [20:20–26] Mt 22:15–22; Mk 12:13–17.
l. [20:20] 11:54.

m. [20:21] Jn 3:2.
n. [20:25] Rom 13:6–7.
o. [20:27–40] Mt 22:23–33; Mk 12:18–27.
p. [20:27] Acts 23:8.
q. [20:28] Gn 38:8; Dt 25:5.
r. [20:37] Ex 3:2, 6, 15–16.
s. [20:38] Rom 14:8–9.
t. [20:40] Mt 22:46; Mk 12:34.
u. [20:41–44] Mt 22:41–45; Mk 12:35–37.
v. [20:42–43] Ps 110:1.
w. [20:45–47] 11:37–54; Mt 23:1–36; Mk 12:38–40.
x. [20:46] 14:7–11.

21 The Poor Widow's Contribution.[*] [1a] When he looked up he saw some wealthy people putting their offerings into the treasury [2]and he noticed a poor widow putting in two small coins. [3]He said, "I tell you truly, this poor widow put in more than all the rest; [4]for those others have all made offerings from their surplus wealth, but she, from her poverty, has offered her whole livelihood."

The Destruction of the Temple Foretold.[b] [5†] While some people were speaking about how the temple was adorned with costly stones and votive offerings, he said, [6]"All that you see here—the days will come when there will not be left a stone upon another stone that will not be thrown down."[c]

The Signs of the End. [7d] Then they asked him, "'Teacher, when will this happen? And what sign will there be when all these things are about to happen?" [8]He answered, "See that you not be deceived, for many will come in my name, saying, 'I am he,' and 'The time has come.'[‡] Do not follow them! [e] [9]When you hear of wars and insurrections, do not be terrified; for such things must happen first, but it will not immediately be the end." [10]Then he said to them, "Nation will rise against nation, and kingdom against kingdom.[f] [11]There will be powerful earthquakes, famines, and plagues from place to place; and awesome sights and mighty signs will come from the sky.

The Coming Persecution. [12g] "Before all this happens,[§] however, they will seize and persecute you, they will hand you over to the synagogues and to prisons, and they will have you led before kings and governors

---

* [21:1–4] The widow is another example of the poor ones in this gospel whose detachment from material possessions and dependence on God leads to their blessedness (Lk 6:20). Her simple offering provides a striking contrast to the pride and pretentiousness of the scribes denounced in the preceding section (Lk 20:45–47). The story is taken from Mk 12:41–44.

† [21:5–36] Jesus' eschatological discourse in Luke is inspired by Mk 13 but Luke has made some significant alterations to the words of Jesus found there. Luke maintains, though in a modified form, the belief in the early expectation of the end of the age (see Lk 21:27, 28, 31, 32, 36), but, by focusing attention throughout the gospel on the importance of the day-to-day following of Jesus and by reinterpreting the meaning of some of the signs of the end from Mk 13 he has come to terms with what seemed to the early Christian community to be a delay of the parousia. Mark, for example, described the desecration of the Jerusalem temple by the Romans (Mk 13:14) as the apocalyptic symbol (see Dn 9:27; 12:11) accompanying the end of the age and the coming of the Son of Man. Luke (Lk 21:20–24), however, removes the apocalyptic setting and separates the historical destruction of Jerusalem from the signs of the coming of the Son of Man by a period that he refers to as "the times of the Gentiles" (Lk 21:24). See also notes on Mt 24:1–36 and Mk 13:1–37.

‡ [21:8] The time has come: in Luke, the proclamation of the imminent end of the age has itself become a false teaching.

§ [21:12] Before all this happens. . .: to Luke and his community, some of the signs of the end just described (Lk 21:10–11) still lie in the future. Now in dealing with the persecution of the disciples (Lk 21:12–19) and the destruction of Jerusalem (Lk 21:20–24) Luke is pointing to eschatological signs that have already been fulfilled.

because of my name.[h] [13]It will lead to your giving testimony. [14]Remember, you are not to prepare your defense beforehand, [15i] for I myself shall give you a wisdom in speaking* that all your adversaries will be powerless to resist or refute. [16j] You will even be handed over by parents, brothers, relatives, and friends, and they will put some of you to death.[k] [17]You will be hated by all because of my name, [18]but not a hair on your head will be destroyed.[l] [19]By your perseverance you will secure your lives.[m]

The Great Tribulation.[†] [20n] "When you see Jerusalem surrounded by armies, know that its desolation is at hand.[o] [21]Then those in Judea must flee to the mountains. Let those within the city escape from it, and let those in the countryside not enter the city,[p] [22]for these days are the time of punishment when all the scriptures are fulfilled. [23]Woe to pregnant women and nursing mothers in those days, for a terrible calamity will come upon the earth and a wrathful judgment upon this people.[q] [24]They will fall by the edge of the sword and be taken as captives to all the Gentiles; and Jerusalem will be trampled underfoot by the Gentiles until the times of the Gentiles[‡] are fulfilled.[r]

The Coming of the Son of Man.[s] [25]"There will be signs in the sun, the moon, and the stars, and on earth nations will be in dismay, perplexed by the roaring of the sea and the waves.[t] [26]People will die of fright in anticipation of what is coming upon the world, for the powers of the heavens[§] will be shaken.[u] [27]And then they will see the Son of Man coming in a cloud with power and great glory.[v] [28]But when these signs begin to happen, stand erect and raise your heads because your redemption is at hand."[w]

The Lesson of the Fig Tree.[x] [29]He taught them a lesson. "Consider the fig tree and all the other trees. [30]When their buds burst open, you see for yourselves and know that summer is now near; [31]in the same way, when you see these things happening, know that the kingdom of God is near. [32]Amen, I say to you, this generation will not pass away until all

---

* [21:15] **A wisdom in speaking**: literally, "a mouth and wisdom."
† [21:20–24] The actual destruction of Jerusalem by Rome in A.D. 70 upon which Luke and his community look back provides the assurance that, just as Jesus' prediction of Jerusalem's destruction was fulfilled, so too will be his announcement of their final redemption (Lk 21:27–28).
‡ [21:24] **The times of the Gentiles**: a period of indeterminate length separating the destruction of Jerusalem from the cosmic signs accompanying the coming of the Son of Man.
§ [21:26] **The powers of the heavens**: the heavenly bodies mentioned in Lk 21:25 and thought of as cosmic armies.

these things have taken place.*y* 33Heaven and earth will pass away, but my words will not pass away.*z*

Exhortation to Be Vigilant. 34"Beware that your hearts do not become drowsy from carousing and drunkenness and the anxieties of daily life, and that day catch you by surprise*a* 35like a trap. For that day will assault everyone who lives on the face of the earth. 36Be vigilant at all times and pray that you have the strength to escape the tribulations that are imminent and to stand before the Son of Man."*b*

Ministry in Jerusalem. 37During the day, Jesus was teaching in the temple area, but at night he would leave and stay at the place called the Mount of Olives.*c* 38And all the people would get up early each morning to listen to him in the temple area.

a. [21:1–4] Mk 12:41–44.
b. [21:5–6] Mt 24:1–2; Mk 13:1–2.
c. [21:6] 19:44.
d. [21:7–19] Mt 24:3–14; Mk 13:3–13.
e. [21:8] 17:23; Mk 13:5, 6, 21; 1 Jn 2:18.
f. [21:10] 2 Chr 15:6; Is 19:2.
g. [21:12–15] 12:11–12; Mt 10:17–20; Mk 13:9–11.
h. [21:12] Jn 16:2; Acts 25:24.
i. [21:15] Acts 6:10.
j. [21:16–18] Mt 10:21–22.
k. [21:16] 12:52–53.
l. [21:18] 12:7; 1 Sm 14:45; Mt 10:30; Acts 27:34.
m. [21:19] 8:15.
n. [21:20–24] Mt 24:15–21; Mk 13:14–19.
o. [21:20–22] 19:41–44.
p. [21:21] 17:31.

q. [21:23] 1 Cor 7:26.
r. [21:24] Tb 14:5; Ps 79:1; Is 63:18; Jer 21:7; Rom 11:25; Rev 11:2.
s. [21:25–28] Mt 24:29–31; Mk 13:24–27.
t. [21:25] Wis 5:22; Is 13:10; Ez 32:7; Jl 2:10; 3:3–4; 4:15; Rev 6:12–14.
u. [21:26] Hg 2:6, 21.
v. [21:27] Dn 7:13–14; Mt 26:64; Rev 1:7.
w. [21:28] 2:38.
x. [21:29–33] Mt 24:32–35; Mk 13:28–31.
y. [21:32] 9:27; Mt 16:28.
z. [21:33] 16:17.
a. [21:34] 12:45–46; Mt 24:48–50; 1 Thes 5:3, 6–7.
b. [21:36] Mk 13:33.
c. [21:37] 19:47; 22:39.

VII. THE PASSION NARRATIVE*

22 **The Conspiracy Against Jesus.** 1a Now the feast of Unleavened Bread, called the Passover,† was drawing near. 2b and the chief priests and the scribes were seeking a way to put him to death, for they were afraid of the people. 3c Then Satan entered into Judas,‡ the one

---

* [22:1–23:56a] The passion narrative. Luke is still dependent upon Mark for the composition of the passion narrative but has incorporated much of his own special tradition into the narrative. Among the distinctive sections in Luke are: (1) the tradition of the institution of the Eucharist (Lk 22:15–20); (2) Jesus' farewell discourse (Lk 22:21–38); (3) the mistreatment and interrogation of Jesus (Lk 22:63–71); (4) Jesus before Herod and his second appearance before Pilate (Lk 23:6–16); (5) words addressed to the women followers on the way to the crucifixion (Lk 23:27–32); (6) words to the penitent thief (Lk 23:39–41); (7) the death of Jesus (Lk 23:46, 47b–49). Luke stresses the innocence of Jesus (Lk 23:4, 14–15, 22) who is the victim of the powers of evil (Lk 22:3, 31, 53) and who goes to his death in fulfillment of his Father's will (Lk 22:42, 46). Throughout the narrative Luke emphasizes the mercy, compassion, and healing power of Jesus (Lk 22:51; 23:43) who does not go to death lonely and deserted, but is accompanied by others who follow him on the way of the cross (Lk 23:26–31, 49).

† [22:1] **Feast of Unleavened Bread, called the Passover:** see note on Mk 14:1.

‡ [22:3] **Satan entered into Judas:** see note on Lk 4:13.

surnamed Iscariot, who was counted among the Twelve,^d ⁴and he went to the chief priests and temple guards to discuss a plan for handing him over to them. ⁵They were pleased and agreed to pay him money. ⁶He accepted their offer and sought a favorable opportunity to hand him over to them in the absence of a crowd.

Preparations for the Passover.^e ⁷When the day of the feast of Unleavened Bread arrived, the day for sacrificing the Passover lamb,^f ⁸he sent out Peter and John, instructing them, "Go and make preparations for us to eat the Passover." ⁹They asked him, "Where do you want us to make the preparations?" ¹⁰And he answered them, "When you go into the city, a man will meet you carrying a jar of water.[*] Follow him into the house that he enters ¹¹and say to the master of the house, 'The teacher says to you, "Where is the guest room where I may eat the Passover with my disciples?"' ¹²He will show you a large upper room that is furnished. Make the preparations there." ¹³Then they went off and found everything exactly as he had told them, and there they prepared the Passover.^g

The Last Supper.^h ¹⁴When the hour came, he took his place at table with the apostles. ¹⁵He said to them, "I have eagerly desired to eat this Passover[†] with you before I suffer, ¹⁶for, I tell you, I shall not eat it [again] until there is fulfillment in the kingdom of God."ⁱ ¹⁷Then he took a cup,[‡] gave thanks, and said, "Take this and share it among yourselves; ¹⁸for I tell you [that] from this time on I shall not drink of the fruit of the vine until the kingdom of God comes." ^{19§ j} Then he took the bread, said the blessing, broke it, and gave it to them, saying, "This is my body, which will be given for you; do this in memory of me." ²⁰And likewise the cup after they had eaten, saying, "This cup is the new covenant in my blood, which will be shed for you.^k

---

* [22:10] **A man will meet you carrying a jar of water:** see note on Mk 14:13.

† [22:15] **This Passover:** Luke clearly identifies this last supper of Jesus with the apostles as a Passover meal that commemorated the deliverance of the Israelites from slavery in Egypt. Jesus reinterprets the significance of the Passover by setting it in the context of the kingdom of God (Lk 22:16). The "deliverance" associated with the Passover finds its new meaning in the blood that will be shed (Lk 22:20).

‡ [22:17] Because of a textual problem in Lk 22:19–20 some commentators interpret this cup as the eucharistic cup.

§ [22:19c–20] **Which will be given … do this in memory of me:** these words are omitted in some important Western text manuscripts and a few Syriac manuscripts. Other ancient text types, including the oldest papyrus manuscript of Luke dating from the late second or early third century, contain the longer reading presented here. The Lucan account of the words of institution of the Eucharist bears a close resemblance to the words of institution in the Pauline tradition (see 1 Cor 11:23–26). See also notes on Mt 26:26–29; 26:27–28; and Mk 14:22–24.

The Betrayal Foretold. [21l] "And yet behold, the hand of the one who is to betray me is with me on the table; [22]for the Son of Man indeed goes as it has been determined; but woe to that man by whom he is betrayed." [23]And they began to debate among themselves who among them would do such a deed.

The Role of the Disciples. [24*] Then an argument broke out among them[m] about which of them should be regarded as the greatest. [25† n] He said to them, "The kings of the Gentiles lord it over them and those in authority over them are addressed as 'Benefactors'; [26]but among you it shall not be so. Rather, let the greatest among you be as the youngest, and the leader as the servant.[o] [27]For who is greater: the one seated at table or the one who serves? Is it not the one seated at table? I am among you as the one who serves. [28]It is you who have stood by me in my trials; [29]and I confer a kingdom on you, just as my Father has conferred one on me,[p] [30]that you may eat and drink at my table in my kingdom; and you will sit on thrones judging the twelve tribes of Israel.[q]

Peter's Denial Foretold.[r] [31‡] "Simon, Simon, behold Satan has demanded to sift all of you[s] like wheat,[s] [32]but I have prayed that your own faith may not fail; and once you have turned back, you must strengthen your brothers." [33]He said to him, "Lord, I am prepared to go to prison and to die with you."[t] [34]But he replied, "I tell you, Peter, before the cock crows this day, you will deny three times that you know me."[u]

Instructions for the Time of Crisis. [35v] He said to them, "When I sent you forth without a money bag or a sack or sandals, were you in need of anything?" "No, nothing," they replied. [36w] He said to them,⁵ "But now one who has a money bag should take it, and likewise a sack, and one who does not have a sword should sell his cloak and buy one. [37]For I tell you that this scripture must be fulfilled in me, namely, 'He was counted

---

* [22:24–38] The Gospel of Luke presents a brief farewell discourse of Jesus; compare the lengthy farewell discourses and prayer in Jn 13–17.

† [22:25] **'Benefactors':** this word occurs as a title of rulers in the Hellenistic world.

‡ [22:31–32] Jesus' prayer for Simon's faith and the commission to strengthen his brothers anticipates the post-resurrectional prominence of Peter in the first half of Acts, where he appears as the spokesman for the Christian community and the one who begins the mission to the Gentiles (Acts 10–11).

§ [22:31] **All of you:** literally, "you." The translation reflects the meaning of the Greek text that uses a second person plural pronoun here.

¶ [22:36] In contrast to the ministry of the Twelve and of the seventy-two during the period of Jesus (Lk 9:3; 10:4), in the future period of the church the missionaries must be prepared for the opposition they will face in a world hostile to their preaching.

among the wicked'; and indeed what is written about me is coming to fulfillment."[x] [38]Then they said, "Lord, look, there are two swords here." But he replied, "It is enough!'"

The Agony in the Garden.[y] [39]Then going out he went, as was his custom, to the Mount of Olives, and the disciples followed him. [40]When he arrived at the place he said to them, "Pray that you may not undergo the test."[z] [41]After withdrawing about a stone's throw from them and kneeling, he prayed,[a] [42]saying, "Father, if you are willing, take this cup away from me; still, not my will but yours be done."[b] †[[43]And to strengthen him an angel from heaven appeared to him. [44]He was in such agony and he prayed so fervently that his sweat became like drops of blood falling on the ground.] [45]When he rose from prayer and returned to his disciples, he found them sleeping from grief. [46]He said to them, "Why are you sleeping? Get up and pray that you may not undergo the test."[c]

The Betrayal and Arrest of Jesus.[d] [47]While he was still speaking, a crowd approached and in front was one of the Twelve, a man named Judas. He went up to Jesus to kiss him. [48]Jesus said to him, "Judas, are you betraying the Son of Man with a kiss?" [49]His disciples realized what was about to happen, and they asked, "Lord, shall we strike with a sword?"[e] [50]And one of them struck the high priest's servant and cut off his right ear.[f] [51]‡ But Jesus said in reply, "Stop, no more of this!" Then he touched the servant's ear and healed him. [52]And Jesus said to the chief priests and temple guards and elders who had come for him, "Have you come out as against a robber, with swords and clubs?[g] [53]Day after day I was with you in the temple area, and you did not seize me; but this is your hour, the time for the power of darkness."[h]

Peter's Denial of Jesus. [54]i After arresting him they led him away and took him into the house of the high priest; Peter was following at a distance.[j] [55]They lit a fire in the middle of the courtyard and sat around it, and Peter sat down with them. [56]When a maid saw him seated in the light, she looked intently at him and said, "This man too was with him."

---

* [22:38] **It is enough!**: the farewell discourse ends abruptly with these words of Jesus spoken to the disciples when they take literally what was intended as figurative language about being prepared to face the world's hostility.

† [22:43–44] These verses, though very ancient, were probably not part of the original text of Luke. They are absent from the oldest papyrus manuscripts of Luke and from manuscripts of wide geographical distribution.

‡ [22:51] **And healed him**: only Luke recounts this healing of the injured servant.

⁵⁷But he denied it saying, "Woman, I do not know him." ⁵⁸A short while later someone else saw him and said, "You too are one of them"; but Peter answered, "My friend, I am not." ⁵⁹About an hour later, still another insisted, "Assuredly, this man too was with him, for he also is a Galilean." ⁶⁰But Peter said, "My friend, I do not know what you are talking about." Just as he was saying this, the cock crowed, ⁶¹and the Lord turned and looked at Peter;* and Peter remembered the word of the Lord, how he had said to him, "Before the cock crows today, you will deny me three times."ᵏ ⁶²He went out and began to weep bitterly. ⁶³ˡ The men who held Jesus in custody were ridiculing and beating him. ⁶⁴They blindfolded him and questioned him, saying, "Prophesy! Who is it that struck you?" ⁶⁵And they reviled him in saying many other things against him.

Jesus Before the Sanhedrin.† ⁶⁶ᵐ When day came the council of elders of the people met, both chief priests and scribes,ⁿ and they brought him before their Sanhedrin.‡ ⁶⁷They said, "If you are the Messiah, tell us," but he replied to them, "If I tell you, you will not believe,ᵒ ⁶⁸and if I question, you will not respond. ⁶⁹But from this time on the Son of Man will be seated at the right hand of the power of God."ᵖ ⁷⁰They all asked, "Are you then the Son of God?" He replied to them, "You say that I am." ⁷¹Then they said, "What further need have we for testimony? We have heard it from his own mouth."

---

* [22:61] Only Luke recounts that **the Lord turned and looked at Peter**. This look of Jesus leads to Peter's weeping bitterly over his denial (Lk 22:62).

† [22:66–71] Luke recounts one daytime trial of Jesus (Lk 22:66–71) and hints at some type of preliminary nighttime investigation (Lk 22:54–65). Mark (and Matthew who follows Mark) has transferred incidents of this day into the nighttime interrogation with the result that there appear to be two Sanhedrin trials of Jesus in Mark (and Matthew); see note on Mk 14:53.

‡ [22:66] **Sanhedrin**: the word is a Hebraized form of a Greek word meaning a "council," and refers to the elders, chief priests, and scribes who met under the high priest's leadership to decide religious and legal questions that did not pertain to Rome's interests. Jewish sources are not clear on the competence of the Sanhedrin to sentence and to execute during this period.

a. [22:1–2] Mt 26:1–5; Mk 14:1–2; Jn 11:47–53.
b. [22:2] 19:47–48; 20:19; Mt 21:46; Mk 12:12; Jn 5:18; 7:30.
c. [22:3–6] Mt 26:14–16; Mk 14:10–11; Jn 13:2, 27.
d. [22:3] Acts 1:17.
e. [22:7–13] Mt 26:17–19; Mk 14:12–16.
f. [22:7] Ex 12:6, 14–20.
g. [22:13] 19:32.
h. [22:14–20] Mt 26:20, 26–30; Mk 14:17, 22–26; 1 Cor 11:23–25.
i. [22:16] 13:29.
j. [22:19] 24:30; Acts 27:35.
k. [22:20] Ex 24:8; Jer 31:31; 32:40; Zec 9:11.
l. [22:21–23] Ps 41:10; Mt 26:21–25; Mk 14:18–21; Jn 13:21–30.

m. [22:24] 9:46; Mt 18:1; Mk 9:34.
n. [22:25–27] Mt 20:25–27; Mk 10:42–44; Jn 13:3–16.
o. [22:26] Mt 23:11; Mk 9:35.
p. [22:29] 12:32.
q. [22:30] Mt 19:28.
r. [22:31–34] Mt 26:33–35; Mk 14:29–31; Jn 13:37–38.
s. [22:31] Jb 1:6–12; Am 9:9.
t. [22:33] 22:54.
u. [22:34] 22:54–62.
v. [22:35] 9:3; 10:4; Mt 10:9–10; Mk 6:7–9.
w. [22:36] 22:49.
x. [22:37] Is 53:12.
y. [22:39–46] Mt 26:30, 36–46; Mk 14:26, 32–42; Jn 18:1–2.
z. [22:40] 22:46.
a. [22:41] Heb 5:7–8.

b. [22:42] Mt 6:10.
c. [22:46] 22:40.
d. [22:47–53] Mt 26:47–56; Mk 14:43–50; Jn 18:3–4.
e. [22:49] 22:36.
f. [22:50] Jn 18:26.
g. [22:52] 22:37.
h. [22:53] 19:47; 21:37; Jn 7:30; 8:20; Col 1:13.
i. [22:54–62] Mt 26:57–58, 69–75; Mk 14:53–54, 66–72;

Jn 18:12–18, 25–27.
j. [22:54] 22:33.
k. [22:61] 22:34.
l. [22:63–65] Mt 26:67–68; Mk 14:65.
m. [22:66–71] Mt 26:59–66; Mk 14:55–64.
n. [22:66] Mt 27:1; Mk 15:1.
o. [22:67] Jn 3:12; 8:45; 10:24.
p. [22:69] Ps 110:1; Dn 7:13–14; Acts 7:56.

23

Jesus Before Pilate.[a] [1*] Then the whole assembly of them arose and brought him before Pilate. [2]They brought charges against him, saying, "We found this man misleading our people; he opposes the payment of taxes to Caesar and maintains that he is the Messiah, a king."[b] [3]Pilate asked him, "Are you the king of the Jews?" He said to him in reply, "You say so."[c] [4]Pilate then addressed the chief priests and the crowds, "I find this man not guilty." [5]But they were adamant and said, "He is inciting the people with his teaching throughout all Judea, from Galilee where he began even to here."[d]

Jesus Before Herod. [6†] On hearing this Pilate asked if the man was a Galilean; [7]and upon learning that he was under Herod's jurisdiction, he sent him to Herod who was in Jerusalem at that time.[e] [8]Herod was very glad to see Jesus; he had been wanting to see him for a long time, for he had heard about him and had been hoping to see him perform some sign.[f] [9]He questioned him at length, but he gave him no answer.[g] [10]The chief priests and scribes, meanwhile, stood by accusing him harshly.[h] [11][Even] Herod and his soldiers treated him contemptuously and mocked him, and after clothing him in resplendent garb, he sent him back to Pilate.[i] [12]Herod and Pilate became friends that very day, even though they had been enemies formerly. [13]Pilate then summoned the chief priests, the rulers, and the people [14]and said to them, "You brought this man to me and accused him of inciting the people to revolt. I have conducted my investigation in your presence and have not found this man guilty of the charges you have brought against him,[j] [15]nor did Herod, for he sent him back to us. So no capital crime has

---

* [23:1–5, 13–25] Twice Jesus is brought before Pilate in Luke's account, and each time Pilate explicitly declares Jesus innocent of any wrongdoing (Lk 23:4, 14, 22). This stress on the innocence of Jesus before the Roman authorities is also characteristic of John's gospel (Jn 18:38; 19:4, 6). Luke presents the Jerusalem Jewish leaders as the ones who force the hand of the Roman authorities (Lk 23:1–2, 5, 10, 13, 18, 21, 23–25).

† [23:6–12] The appearance of Jesus before Herod is found only in this gospel. Herod has been an important figure in Luke (Lk 9:7–9; 13:31–33) and has been presented as someone who has been curious about Jesus for a long time. His curiosity goes unrewarded. It is faith in Jesus, not curiosity, that is rewarded (Lk 7:50; 8:48, 50; 17:19).

been committed by him. [16k] Therefore I shall have him flogged and then release him." [[17]]*

The Sentence of Death.[l] [18]But all together they shouted out, "Away with this man! Release Barabbas to us." [19](Now Barabbas had been imprisoned for a rebellion that had taken place in the city and for murder.) [20]Again Pilate addressed them, still wishing to release Jesus, [21]but they continued their shouting, "Crucify him! Crucify him!" [22]Pilate addressed them a third time, "What evil has this man done? I found him guilty of no capital crime. Therefore I shall have him flogged and then release him." [23]With loud shouts, however, they persisted in calling for his crucifixion, and their voices prevailed. [24]The verdict of Pilate was that their demand should be granted. [25]So he released the man who had been imprisoned for rebellion and murder, for whom they asked, and he handed Jesus over to them to deal with as they wished.

The Way of the Cross.† [26m] As they led him away they took hold of a certain Simon, a Cyrenian, who was coming in from the country; and after laying the cross on him, they made him carry it behind Jesus. [27]A large crowd of people followed Jesus, including many women who mourned and lamented him. [28n] Jesus turned to them and said, "Daughters of Jerusalem, do not weep for me; weep instead for yourselves and for your children, [29]for indeed, the days are coming when people will say, 'Blessed are the barren, the wombs that never bore and the breasts that never nursed.' [30]At that time people will say to the mountains, 'Fall upon us!' and to the hills, 'Cover us!'[o] [31]for if these things are done when the wood is green what will happen when it is dry?" [32]Now two others, both criminals, were led away with him to be executed.

The Crucifixion.[p] [33]When they came to the place called the Skull, they crucified him and the criminals there, one on his right, the other on his left.[q] [34][Then Jesus said, "Father, forgive them, they know not what they

---

* [23:17] This verse, "He was obliged to release one prisoner for them at the festival," is not part of the original text of Luke. It is an explanatory gloss from Mk 15:6 (also Mt 27:15) and is not found in many early and important Greek manuscripts. On its historical background, see notes on Mt 27:15–26.

† [23:26–32] An important Lucan theme throughout the gospel has been the need for the Christian disciple to follow in the footsteps of Jesus. Here this theme comes to the fore with the story of Simon of Cyrene who takes up the cross and follows Jesus (see Lk 9:23; 14:27) and with the large crowd who likewise follow Jesus on the way of the cross. See also note on Mk 15:21.

do."]* They divided his garments by casting lots.^{r} ^{35}The people stood by and watched; the rulers, meanwhile, sneered at him and said,^{s} "He saved others, let him save himself if he is the chosen one, the Messiah of God."^{t} ^{36}Even the soldiers jeered at him. As they approached to offer him wine^u ^{37}they called out, "If you are King of the Jews, save yourself." ^{38}Above him there was an inscription that read, "This is the King of the Jews."

^{39†} Now one of the criminals hanging there reviled Jesus, saying, "Are you not the Messiah? Save yourself and us." ^{40}The other, however, rebuking him, said in reply, "Have you no fear of God, for you are subject to the same condemnation? ^{41}And indeed, we have been condemned justly, for the sentence we received corresponds to our crimes, but this man has done nothing criminal."^{v} ^{42}Then he said, "Jesus, remember me when you come into your kingdom."^{w} ^{43}He replied to him, "Amen, I say to you, today you will be with me in Paradise."^{x}

The Death of Jesus.^{y} ^{44‡} It was now about noon^z and darkness came over the whole land until three in the afternoon ^{45}because of an eclipse of the sun. Then the veil of the temple was torn down the middle.^{a} ^{46}Jesus cried out in a loud voice, "Father, into your hands I commend my spirit"; and when he had said this he breathed his last.^{b} ^{47}The centurion who witnessed what had happened glorified God and said, "This man was innocent§ beyond doubt." ^{48}When all the people who had gathered for this spectacle saw what had happened, they returned home beating their breasts;^{c} ^{49}but all his acquaintances stood at a distance, including the women who had followed him from Galilee and saw these events.^{d}

The Burial of Jesus.^{e} ^{50}Now there was a virtuous and righteous man named Joseph who, though he was a member of the council, ^{51}had not consented to their plan of action. He came from the Jewish town of Arimathea and was awaiting the kingdom of God.^{f} ^{52}He went to Pilate and asked for the body of Jesus. ^{53}After he had taken the body down, he wrapped it in a linen cloth and laid him in a rock-hewn tomb in which

---

* [23:34] [Then Jesus said, "Father, forgive them, they know not what they do."]: this portion of Lk 23:34 does not occur in the oldest papyrus manuscript of Luke and in other early Greek manuscripts and ancient versions of wide geographical distribution.

† [23:39–43] This episode is recounted only in this gospel. The penitent sinner receives salvation through the crucified Jesus. Jesus' words to the penitent thief reveal Luke's understanding that the destiny of the Christian is "to be with Jesus."

‡ [23:44] Noon … three in the afternoon: literally, the sixth and ninth hours. See note on Mk 15:25.

§ [23:47] This man was innocent: or, "This man was righteous."

no one had yet been buried.*g* *54*It was the day of preparation, and the sabbath was about to begin. *55*The women who had come from Galilee with him followed behind, and when they had seen the tomb and the way in which his body was laid in it,*h* *56*they returned and prepared spices and perfumed oils. Then they rested on the sabbath according to the commandment.*i*

a. [23:1–5] Mt 27:1–2, 11–14; Mk 15:1–5; Jn 18:28–38.
b. [23:2] 20:22–25; Acts 17:7; 24:5.
c. [23:3] 22:70; 1 Tm 6:13.
d. [23:5] 23:14, 22, 41; Mt 27:24; Jn 19:4, 6; Acts 13:28.
e. [23:7] 3:1; 9:7.
f. [23:8] 9:9; Acts 4:27–28.
g. [23:9] Mk 15:5.
h. [23:10] Mt 27:12; Mk 15:3.
i. [23:11] Mt 27:28–30, Mk 15:17–19; Jn 19:2–3.
j. [23:14] 23:4, 22, 41.
k. [23:16] 23:22; Jn 19:12–14.
l. [23:18–25] Mt 27:20–26; Mk 15:6–7, 11–15; Jn 18:38b–40; 19:14–16; Acts 3:13–14.
m. [23:26–32] Mt 27:32, 38; Mk 15:21, 27; Jn 19:17.
n. [23:28–31] 19:41–44; 21:23–24.
o. [23:30] Hos 10:8; Rev 6:16.
p. [23:33–43] Mt 27:33–44; Mk 15:22–32; Jn 19:17–24.
q. [23:33] 22:37; Is 53:12.
r. [23:34] Nm 15:27–31; Ps 22:19; Mt 5:44; Acts 7:60.

s. [23:35–36] Ps 22:8–9.
t. [23:35] 4:23.
u. [23:36] Ps 69:22; Mt 27:48; Mk 15:36.
v. [23:41] 23:4, 14, 22.
w. [23:42] 9:27; 23:2, 3, 38.
x. [23:43] 2 Cor 12:3; Rev 2:7.
y. [23:44–49] Mt 27:45–56; Mk 15:33–41; Jn 19:25–30.
z. [23:44–45] Am 8:9.
a. [23:45] Ex 26:31–33; 36:35.
b. [23:45] Ps 31:6; Acts 7:59.
c. [23:48] 18:13; Zec 12:10.
d. [23:49] 8:1–3; 23:55–56; 24:10; Ps 38:12.
e. [23:50–56] Mt 27:57–61; Mk 15:42–47; Jn 19:38–42; Acts 13:29.
f. [23:51] 2:25, 38.
g. [23:53] 19:30; Acts 13:29.
h. [23:55] 8:2; 23:49; 24:10.
i. [23:56] Ex 12:16; 20:10; Dt 5:14.

VIII. THE RESURRECTION NARRATIVE*

24 **The Resurrection of Jesus.** *1a* But at daybreak on the first day of the week they took the spices they had prepared and went to the tomb. *2*They found the stone rolled away from the tomb; *3*but when they entered, they did not find the body of the Lord Jesus. *4*While they were puzzling over this, behold, two men in dazzling garments appeared to them.*b* *5*They were terrified and bowed their faces to the ground. They said to them, "Why do you seek the living one among the dead?*c* *6*He is not here, but he has been raised.† Remember what he said to you while he was still in Galilee, *7*that the Son of Man must be handed over to sinners and be crucified, and rise on the third day."*d* *8*And they

---

* [24:1–53] The resurrection narrative in Luke consists of five sections: (1) the women at the empty tomb (Lk 23:56b–24:12); (2) the appearance to the two disciples on the way to Emmaus (Lk 24:13–35); (3) the appearance to the disciples in Jerusalem (Lk 24:36–43); (4) Jesus' final instructions (Lk 24:44–49); (5) the ascension (Lk 24:50–53). In Luke, all the resurrection appearances take place in and around Jerusalem; moreover, they are all recounted as having taken place on Easter Sunday. A consistent theme throughout the narrative is that the suffering, death, and resurrection of Jesus were accomplished in fulfillment of Old Testament promises and Jewish hopes (Lk 24:19a, 21, 26–27, 44, 46). In his second volume, Acts, Luke will argue that Christianity is the fulfillment of the hopes of Pharisaic Judaism and its logical development (see Acts 24:10–21).

† [24:6] **He is not here, but he has been raised**: this part of the verse is omitted in important representatives of the Western text tradition, but its presence in other text types and the slight difference in wording from Mt 28:6 and Mk 16:6 argue for its retention.

remembered his words.*e* *9** *f* Then they returned from the tomb and announced all these things to the eleven and to all the others. [10]The women were Mary Magdalene, Joanna, and Mary the mother of James; the others who accompanied them also told this to the apostles,*g* [11]but their story seemed like nonsense and they did not believe them. [12† h] But Peter got up and ran to the tomb, bent down, and saw the burial cloths alone; then he went home amazed at what had happened.

The Appearance on the Road to Emmaus. ‡ [13]Now that very day two of them were going to a village seven miles§ from Jerusalem called Emmaus,*i* [14]and they were conversing about all the things that had occurred. [15]And it happened that while they were conversing and debating, Jesus himself drew near and walked with them, [16¶ j] but their eyes were prevented from recognizing him. [17]He asked them, "What are you discussing as you walk along?" They stopped, looking downcast. [18]One of them, named Cleopas, said to him in reply, "Are you the only visitor to Jerusalem who does not know of the things that have taken place there in these days?" [19]And he replied to them, "What sort of things?" They said to him, "The things that happened to Jesus the Nazarene, who was a prophet mighty in deed and word before God and all the people,*k* [20]how our chief priests and rulers both handed him over to a sentence of death and crucified him. [21l] But we were hoping that he would be the one to redeem Israel; and besides all this, it is now the third day since this took place. [22m] Some women from our group, however, have astounded us: they were at the tomb early in the morning [23]and did not find his body; they came back and reported that they had indeed seen a vision of angels who announced that he was alive. [24n] Then some of those with us went to the tomb and found things just as the women had described, but him they did not see." [25o] And he said to them, "Oh, how foolish

---

* [24:9] The women in this gospel do not flee from the tomb and tell no one, as in Mk 16:8 but return and tell the disciples about their experience. The initial reaction to the testimony of the women is disbelief (Lk 24:11).

† [24:12] This verse is missing from the Western textual tradition but is found in the best and oldest manuscripts of other text types.

‡ [24:13–35] This episode focuses on the interpretation of scripture by the risen Jesus and the recognition of him in the breaking of the bread. The references to the quotations of scripture and explanation of it (Lk 24:25–27), the kerygmatic proclamation (Lk 24:34), and the liturgical gesture (Lk 24:30) suggest that the episode is primarily catechetical and liturgical rather than apologetic.

§ [24:13] **Seven miles:** literally, "sixty stades." A stade was 607 feet. Some manuscripts read "160 stades" or more than eighteen miles. The exact location of Emmaus is disputed.

¶ [24:16] A consistent feature of the resurrection stories is that the risen Jesus was different and initially unrecognizable (Lk 24:37; Mk 16:12; Jn 20:14; 21:4).

you are! How slow of heart to believe all that the prophets spoke! 26 Was
it not necessary that the Messiah should suffer* these things and enter
into his glory?" 27 Then beginning with Moses and all the prophets, he
interpreted to them what referred to him in all the scriptures.[p] 28 As they
approached the village to which they were going, he gave the impression
that he was going on farther. 29 But they urged him, "Stay with us, for
it is nearly evening and the day is almost over." So he went in to stay
with them. 30 And it happened that, while he was with them at table, he
took bread, said the blessing, broke it, and gave it to them. 31 With that
their eyes were opened and they recognized him, but he vanished from
their sight. 32 Then they said to each other, "Were not our hearts burning
[within us] while he spoke to us on the way and opened the scriptures
to us?" 33 So they set out at once and returned to Jerusalem where they
found gathered together the eleven and those with them 34 who were
saying, "The Lord has truly been raised and has appeared to Simon!"[q]
35 Then the two recounted what had taken place on the way and how he
was made known to them in the breaking of the bread.

The Appearance to the Disciples in Jerusalem. 36† While they were still
speaking about this,[r] he stood in their midst and said to them, "Peace be
with you."[s] 37 But they were startled and terrified and thought that they
were seeing a ghost.[t] 38 Then he said to them, "Why are you troubled?
And why do questions arise in your hearts? 39‡ Look at my hands and
my feet, that it is I myself. Touch me and see, because a ghost does not
have flesh and bones as you can see I have." 40[u] And as he said this, he
showed them his hands and his feet. 41 While they were still incredulous
for joy and were amazed, he asked them, "Have you anything here to
eat?" 42 They gave him a piece of baked fish;[v] 43 he took it and ate it in
front of them.

44 He said to them, "These are my words that I spoke to you while I
was still with you, that everything written about me in the law of Moses

---

* [24:26] **That the Messiah should suffer. . .**: Luke is the only New Testament writer to speak explicitly of a suffering Messiah (Lk 24:26, 46; Acts 3:18; 17:3; 26:23). The idea of a suffering Messiah is not found in the Old Testament or in other Jewish literature prior to the New Testament period, although the idea is hinted at in Mk 8:31–33. See notes on Mt 26:63 and 26:67–68.

† [24:36–43, 44–49] The Gospel of Luke, like each of the other gospels (Mt 28:16–20; Mk 16:14–15; Jn 20:19–23), focuses on an important appearance of Jesus to the Twelve in which they are commissioned for their future ministry. As in Lk 24:6, 12, so in Lk 24:36, 40 there are omissions in the Western text.

‡ [24:39–42] The apologetic purpose of this story is evident in the concern with the physical details and the report that Jesus ate food.

and in the prophets and psalms must be fulfilled."[w] [45]Then he opened their minds to understand the scriptures.[x] [46*] And he said to them,[y] "Thus it is written that the Messiah would suffer and rise from the dead on the third day [47]and that repentance, for the forgiveness of sins, would be preached in his name to all the nations, beginning from Jerusalem.[z] [48]You are witnesses of these things.[a] [49]And [behold] I am sending the promise of my Father[†] upon you; but stay in the city until you are clothed with power from on high."[b]

The Ascension.[‡] [50c] Then he led them [out] as far as Bethany, raised his hands, and blessed them. [51]As he blessed them he parted from them and was taken up to heaven. [52]They did him homage and then returned to Jerusalem with great joy,[d] [53]and they were continually in the temple praising God.[§]

---

* [24:46] See note on Lk 24:26.
† [24:49] **The promise of my Father**: i.e., the gift of the holy Spirit.
‡ [24:50–53] Luke brings his story about the time of Jesus to a close with the report of the ascension. He will also begin the story of the time of the church with a recounting of the ascension. In the gospel, Luke recounts the ascension of Jesus on Easter Sunday night, thereby closely associating it with the resurrection. In Acts 1:3, 9–11; 13:31 he historicizes the ascension by speaking of a forty-day period between the resurrection and the ascension. The Western text omits some phrases in Lk 24:51, 52 perhaps to avoid any chronological conflict with Acts 1 about the time of the ascension.
§ [24:53] The Gospel of Luke ends as it began (Lk 1:9), in the Jerusalem temple.

a. [24:1–8] Mt 28:1–8; Mk 16:1–8; Jn 20:1–17.
b. [24:4] 2 Mc 3:26; Acts 1:10.
c. [24:5] Acts 2:9.
d. [24:7] 9:22, 44; 17:25; 18:32–33; Mt 16:21; 17:22–23; Mk 9:31; Acts 17:3.
e. [24:8] Jn 2:22.
f. [24:9–11] Mk 16:10–11; Jn 20:18.
g. [24:10] 8:2–3; Mk 16:9.
h. [24:12] Jn 20:3–7.
i. [24:13] Mk 16:12–13.
j. [24:16] Jn 20:14; 21:4.
k. [24:19] Mt 2:23; 21:11; Acts 2:22.
l. [24:21] 1:54, 68; 2:38.
m. [24:22–23] 24:1–11; Mt 28:1–8; Mk 16:1–8.
n. [24:24] Jn 20:3–10.
o. [24:25–26] 9:22; 18:31; 24:44; 3:24; 17:3.

p. [24:27] 24:44; Dt 18:15; Ps 22:1–18; Is 53; 1 Pt 1:10–11.
q. [24:34] 1 Cor 15:4–5.
r. [24:36–53] Mk 16:14–19; Jn 20:19–20.
s. [24:36] 1 Cor 15:5.
t. [24:37] Mt 14:26.
u. [24:40–41] Jn 21:5, 9–10, 13.
v. [24:42] Acts 10:41.
w. [24:44] 18:31; 24:27; Mt 16:21; Jn 5:39, 46.
x. [24:45] Jn 20:9.
y. [24:46] 9:22; Is 53; Hos 6:2.
z. [24:47] Mt 3:2; 28:19–20; Mk 16:15–16; Acts 10:41.
a. [24:48] Acts 1:8.
b. [24:49] Jn 14:26; Acts 1:4; 2:3–4.
c. [24:50–51] Mk 16:19; Acts 1:9–11.
d. [24:52] Acts 1:12.

How can you celebrate your family—a sanctuary of love and life—after you leave World Meeting of Families? **Sign up** for a 21-day Lectio Divina devotional and journey through the Gospel of Luke with your family or community. As you listen to God's Word, and meditate on stories of hope and healing, allow the Sacred Scripture to transform your understanding of God's unconditional love.

MEDITATIONS
ON THE GOSPEL
OF LUKE FOR THE FAMILY

Sign up for this 21-day Lectio Divina devotional in one of three ways.

📱 SMS: Text **families** to 72717

✉️ Email: Visit www.abs.us/families

🌐 Mobile application: Visit app.bible.com/wmf to download

Familias,
escuchad la Palabra de Dios,
meditadla juntos,
orad con ella,
dejad que el Señor colme de misericordia
vuestra vida.

Franciscus

El escudo de armas del Papa Francisco conserva el diseño que había usado como arzobispo de Buenos Aires, al que se le añaden los símbolos papales de la mitra entre llaves de oro entrelazadas por un cordón rojo.

El escudo es de color azul. En el centro se refleja el emblema de la Orden de procedencia del Papa, la Compañía de Jesús: un sol radiante y llameante con las letras, en rojo, IHS, monograma de Cristo. Encima de la letra h se halla una cruz; en la punta, los tres clavos en negro. En la parte inferior se contempla la estrella, que simboliza a la Virgen María, y la flor de nardo que simboliza a San José.

El lema que se lee debajo del escudo "miserando atque eligendo," que significa más o menos "sígueme". Una traducción literal sería, "lo miró con misericordia y lo eligió". El lema procede de las Homilías de san Beda el Venerable, comentando el episodio evangélico de la vocación de san Mateo, el recaudador de impuestos que se convirtió en apóstol. El Papa Francisco fue llamado a la vida religiosa a la edad de 17 años en la fiesta de san Mateo.

Archdiocese of Philadelphia
Office of the Archbishop
222 North 17th Street
Philadelphia, PA 19103-1299

Septiembre de 2015

Queridos amigos:

Los cuatro evangelios constituyen en sí un rico encuentro con la Palabra de Dios. Para muchos lectores, sin embargo, es Lucas el Evangelista quien nos llega más adentro con la voz misericordiosa de Dios. Solo en Lucas encontramos tres de las más grandes expresiones de amor de Jesús: las parábolas del hijo pródigo y el buen samaritano, y las palabras de Jesús en la cruz al "Buen Ladrón".

El Evangelio que tiene en sus manos —un regalo hermoso de la Sociedad Bíblica Americana- es un recordatorio de la bondad de Dios hacia usted a nivel personal; una invitación a andar con Jesucristo en el camino que nos devuelve al cielo. Léalo. Rece con él. Cuídelo.

Que Dios le bendiga a usted y a todos los que ama durante este Encuentro Mundial de las Familias, y cada día de su vida.

Su hermano en el Señor,

+ Charles J. Chaput, o.f.m. cap.

Reverendísimo Charles J. Chaput, O.F.M. Cap.
Arzobispo de Filadelfia

INTRODUCCIÓN

LA BUENA NOTICIA *de la* MISERICORDIA *en* FAMILIA

Queridas familias,

Con gran alegría os presento esta edición del Evangelio de Lucas, un regalo del Papa Francisco para las familias de todo el mundo con motivo del VIII Encuentro Mundial en Filadelfia.

Espero que la lectura de este Evangelio acompañe el Año Santo de la Misericordia que el Santo Padre quiere comenzar dentro de algunas semanas: Lucas es el Evangelio, la Buena Nueva de la misericordia de Dios para la vida de cada uno de nosotros y de nuestras familias.

EL EVANGELIO EN FAMILIA

Cada generación de cristianos — también la nuestra — está llamada a tomar este pequeño libro. El Evangelio es la fuerza de la Iglesia, es la Palabra por la cual nació y por la cual vive. El cristianismo comienza, precisamente, cuando el Verbo (la Palabra) se hace carne en el seno de María. Ella es la primera entre los creyentes y así fue designada por Isabel: "Feliz la que ha creído en el cumplimiento de la palabra del Señor" (Lc 1,45). Y, después de ella, llegaron los primeros discípulos. Cuando recibieron la palabra de Jesús comenzó una nueva fraternidad, podríamos decir una "nueva familia": la de Jesús y sus discípulos. Después de Pentecostés el Evangelio comenzó a difundirse a través las casas, las familias de los cristianos. En resumen, el camino del Evangelio a principios del primer milenio ha estado marcado por la acogida y la escucha en las familias.

Queridas familias, creo que también nosotros deberíamos recorrer el mismo camino del inicio del cristianismo: tomar el Evangelio en nuestras manos, en nuestras propias familias, y volver a tejer una nueva fraternidad entre las personas, una nueva solidaridad entre las familias, para poder comunicar la "buena noticia" del amor de Dios para todos. San Juan Pablo II, en la apertura del Gran Jubileo del 2000, exhortó a los cristianos a entrar "¡en el nuevo milenio con el libro del Evangelio!". Con esa pasión que lo condujo como a un peregrino del Evangelio por todo el mundo, añadía: "¡Tomemos este Libro! ¡Aceptémoslo del Señor que continuamente nos lo ofrece a través de su Iglesia (cfr. Ap 10,8). Devorémoslo (cfr. Ap 10,9) para que llegue a ser vida de nuestra vida. Saboreémoslo hasta el final: nos producirá amargura, pero nos dará la alegría porque es dulce como la miel (cfr Ap 10,9-10). Seremos colmados de esperanza, nos hará capaces de compartir esta esperanza con todo hombre y mujer que encontremos en nuestro camino".

El Papa Francisco nos exhorta en la misma dirección: ¡volved a tomar el Evangelio! Nos lo dice en la hermosa Carta titulada "La alegría del Evangelio" *(Evangelii gaudium)*. Sí, es indispensable volver a tomar el Evangelio y escucharlo con una atención renovada para tener un mundo más fraterno, más solidario, más humano. La inseguridad y el miedo que están marcando la vida de nuestro mundo, las injusticias increíbles que desgarran la vida de muchas personas, la violencia que parece expandirse sin restricciones incluso dentro de nuestros hogares, los conflictos y las guerras que continúan cobrándose víctimas inocentes, sólo pueden ser superadas a través del Evangelio. Por esta razón el Papa Francisco quiso regalar un millón de copias de este libro a las familias de cinco grandes ciudades del mundo: La Habana (Cuba), Hanói (Vietnam), Kinshasa (Congo), Marsella (Francia), Sídney (Australia). Allí donde el contexto urbano y sus suburbios parecen hacer aún más difícil la convivencia humana, el Papa deseó que la Palabra de Jesús resonara aún con más fuerza.

UN EJERCICIO COTIDIANO

Leamos todos los días un pequeño pasaje del Evangelio. Estaremos como obligados a entrar en el corazón y en los días de Jesús: lo seguiremos en sus viajes, participaremos de su compasión por todos, compartiremos su ternura por los pequeños y los débiles, nos conmoveremos con su compasión cuando está con los pobres, lloraremos al ver cuánto nos ha amado, nos alegraremos por su resurrección que finalmente derrotó el mal. Lo conoceremos y lo amaremos más.

Recordemos hacerlo realmente todos los días. Todos los días nos inundan de palabras, de imágenes, mensajes, invitaciones ... Y no todos son buenos mensajes, y sólo unos pocos ayudan a vivir. En casa, también existe el riesgo de que, por diversas razones no lleguemos ni a hablar, o, si no "vuelan los platos", vuelan palabras que hacen más daño que los platos. En cualquier caso, todos sentimos la necesidad de buenas palabras que lleguen al corazón: el Evangelio es la palabra que llega hasta el corazón. En el Padrenuestro pedimos a Dios que nos dé el "pan de cada día". Las palabras de Jesús son el "pan vivo bajado del cielo" que se da a nosotros cada día. Es el mejor pan. Alimenta el corazón y el cuerpo.

Queridas familias, leer juntos el Evangelio en familia es una de las formas más bellas y eficaces de rezar. Al Señor le gusta particularmente. ¿Recordáis el episodio de Marta y María? Jesús, a Marta, que estaba molesta al ver que María escuchaba a Jesús, le dice: "María ha elegido la mejor parte", "la necesaria". Es fácil para todos nosotros dejarnos abrumar, al igual que Marta, por todas las cosas que hemos de hacer, las cuestiones que deben resolverse, los problemas, las dificultades que hay que superar. "María — Jesús nos dice hoy también a nosotros — ha elegido la mejor parte"(Lc 10,42). Este pequeño libro ayudará a que la escucha del Evangelio sea "la mejor parte" de nuestros días, la "mejor parte" de todos los días del año.

Tenemos que escuchar. El primer paso de la oración cristiana es escuchar a Jesús que nos habla. Sí, queridas familias, antes de multiplicar nuestras palabras para rezar al Señor, escuchemos lo que Él nos dice. Cada día. Intentemos escucharlo y haremos la misma experiencia que los dos discípulos de Emaús, que sintieron que su corazón ardía y necesitaban quedarse con Jesús. La escucha se convierte en oración y el encuentro con Jesús ilumina sus vidas de nuevo.

Por supuesto, hay que recogerse y hacer un poco de silencio a su alrededor. Sabemos lo difícil que es encontrar un momento de silencio y oración. Pero es indispensable. Podríamos decir que la oración cotidiana es nuestra manera de "orar siempre, sin descanso". Sí, orar cada día con el Evangelio es nuestra manera de orar siempre.

Así que hay que encontrar un tiempo para estar juntos, tal vez antes de una comida, o al final del día, o incluso al principio. O, en otros momentos. Lo que importa es la elección de cinco minutos para rezar juntos de manera breve pero eficaz.

Después de la señal de la cruz y de una breve invocación al Espíritu Santo, para que venga a nuestros corazones e ilumine nuestra mente, leemos un pequeño pasaje, hagamos una explicación simple para los más pequeños y comuniquémonos algo de lo esta escucha suscita; en este momento preguntémonos por quién queremos rezar de una manera especial y acabemos recitando el Padrenuestro juntos y dando gracias al Señor por el don de su Palabra. No olvidemos de decidir juntos un pequeño y sencillo propósito con el que esta palabra puede marcar nuestras vidas.

Queridas familias, al mismo tiempo que agradezco profundamente a la American Bible Society, el haber hecho posible la edición de este libro, deseo con todo mi corazón que el primer fruto de estos intensos días que pasamos juntos en Filadelfia sea la decisión de permitir que la Palabra de Dios habite en vuestras casas y en todas las casas de vuestra ciudad.

+ Vincenzo Paglia

Arzobispo Vincenzo Paglia
Presidente del Pontificio Consejo para la Familia

el Evangelio
según San Lucas

Introducción al Evangelio de Lucas

Este evangelio se diferencia de los otros (de Mateo, Marcos y Juan) contenidos en el Nuevo Testamento de la Biblia por una serie de características particulares. En este evangelio más que en ningún otro se le reserva una posición especial a Jerusalén, pues es esta ciudad el escenario central de la actividad de Jesús. En torno a Jesús se desarrollan los acontecimientos decisivos de la «historia de la salvación». Aquellos acontecimientos son los actos del Dios que rescata a la raza humana del pecado. Ahora llega a su fin la larga premisa constituida por la historia del antiguo Israel (Antiguo Testamento), y se abre la nueva época de los creyentes en todo el mundo. Comienza la espera del cumplimiento final. La salvación en Cristo se entrelaza con los avatares de la historia terrena (2,1; 3,1-4) y afecta a todos los hombres (3,6). Jesús se dirige sobre todo a los «pobres» – es decir, a personas poco importantes, enfermas o despreciadas –, y es precisamente entre ellas donde el mensaje del evangelio es acogido mejor y se manifiesta más visiblemente el comienzo del reino de Dios.

Primeros lectores

Este evangelio nace cuando la generación de los apóstoles está a punto de desaparecer. Ahora no es ya posible escuchar de viva voz la experiencia de aquellos que conocieron directamente a Jesús, escucharon su enseñanza y vieron sus gestos, aquellos que vivieron los días de su pasión, muerte y resurrección. Entretanto surgen otros predicadores, quizá se difunden nuevas doctrinas. Por eso Lucas comprende que los creyentes necesitan una sólida documentación sobre los acontecimientos centrales de la fe. Entonces él hace cuidadosas investigaciones entre las memorias más seguras – escritas y orales – y las ofrece como apoyo a la enseñanza cristiana de su tiempo (1,1-4). No sabemos nada del destinatario «Teófilo», pero sin duda representa a los lectores para quienes Lucas ha escrito.

Autor

De un cierto «Lucas» hablan algunas cartas del Nuevo Testamento (Filemón 24; Colosenses 4,14; 2 Timoteo 4,11). Este Lucas es un discípulo del apóstol Pablo, médico de profesión, de cultura y lengua griega. ¿Es la misma persona que escribió este evangelio y el libro de los Hechos? Tradiciones antiguas así lo afirman. Muchos eruditos modernos son del mismo parecer; otros estudiosos hacen notar, sin embargo, que ninguna idea característica de Pablo figura significativamente en este evangelio. En todo caso el autor refleja el ambiente de comunidades cristianas no palestinenses, de finales del siglo primero. El libro de los Hechos nos lo muestra muy interesado en la primera difusión misionera en el mundo griego. La fecha de composición de este evangelio es cercana al año 80 d.C.

Esquema

EL EVANGELIO SEGÚN SAN LUCAS

Prólogo

1 Muchos han emprendido la tarea de escribir la historia de los hechos sucedidos entre nosotros, [2] tal y como nos los enseñaron quienes, habiendo sido testigos presenciales desde el principio, recibieron el encargo de anunciar el mensaje. [3] Yo también, excelentísimo Teófilo, lo he investigado todo con cuidado desde sus comienzos, y me ha parecido oportuno escribirte estas cosas ordenadamente [4] para que compruebes la verdad de cuanto te han enseñado.

Un ángel anuncia el nacimiento de Juan el Bautista

[5] En el tiempo en que Herodes era rey de Judea, vivía un sacerdote llamado Zacarías, perteneciente al grupo de Abías. Su esposa, llamada Isabel, descendía de Aarón. [6] Ambos eran justos delante de Dios y cumplían los mandatos y leyes del Señor, de tal manera que nadie los podía tachar de nada. [7] Pero no tenían hijos, porque Isabel no había podido tenerlos. Ahora eran ya los dos muy ancianos.

[8] Un día en que al grupo sacerdotal de Zacarías le correspondía el turno de oficiar delante de Dios, [9] según era costumbre entre los sacerdotes, le tocó en suerte a Zacarías entrar en el santuario del templo del Señor para quemar incienso. [10] Y mientras se quemaba el incienso, todo el pueblo estaba orando fuera. [11] En esto se le apareció un ángel del Señor, de pie al lado derecho del altar del incienso. [12] Al ver al ángel, Zacarías se echó a temblar lleno de miedo. [13] Pero el ángel le dijo:

«Zacarías, no tengas miedo, porque Dios ha oído tu oración, y tu esposa Isabel te va a dar un hijo, al que pondrás por nombre Juan. [14] Tú te llenarás de gozo y muchos se alegrarán de su nacimiento, [15] porque tu hijo va a ser grande delante del Señor. No beberá vino ni licor, y estará lleno del Espíritu Santo desde antes de nacer. [16] Hará que muchos de la nación de Israel se vuelvan al Señor su Dios. [17] Irá Juan delante del Señor con el espíritu y el poder del profeta Elías, para reconciliar a los padres con los hijos y para que los rebeldes aprendan a obedecer. De este modo preparará al pueblo para recibir al Señor.»

[18] Zacarías preguntó al ángel:

«¿Cómo puedo estar seguro de esto? Porque yo soy muy anciano, y mi esposa también.»

[19] El ángel le contestó:

«Yo soy Gabriel, y estoy al servicio de Dios. Él me ha enviado a hablar contigo y a darte estas buenas noticias. [20] Pero ahora, como no has creído lo que te he dicho, vas a quedarte mudo; y no volverás a hablar hasta que, a su debido tiempo, suceda todo esto.»

[21] Mientras tanto, la gente estaba fuera esperando a Zacarías y preguntándose por qué tardaba tanto en salir del santuario. [22] Cuando por fin salió, no les podía hablar. Entonces se dieron cuenta de que había tenido una visión en el santuario, pues les hablaba por señas. Y así siguió, sin poder hablar.

[23] Cumplido el tiempo de su servicio en el templo, Zacarías se fue a su casa. [24] Después de esto, su esposa Isabel quedó encinta, y durante cinco meses no salió de casa, pensando: [25] «Esto me ha hecho ahora el Señor para librarme de mi vergüenza ante la gente.»

Un ángel anuncia el nacimiento de Jesús

[26] A los seis meses envió Dios al ángel Gabriel a un pueblo de Galilea llamado Nazaret, [27] a visitar a una joven virgen llamada María que estaba comprometida para casarse con un hombre llamado José, descendiente del rey David. [28] El ángel entró donde ella estaba, y le dijo:

«¡Te saludo, favorecida de Dios! El Señor está contigo.»

[29] Cuando vio al ángel, se sorprendió de sus palabras, y se preguntaba qué significaría aquel saludo. [30] El ángel le dijo:

«María, no tengas miedo, pues tú gozas del favor de Dios. [31] Ahora vas a quedar encinta: tendrás un hijo y le pondrás por nombre Jesús. [32] Será un gran hombre, al que llamarán Hijo del Dios altísimo; y Dios el Señor lo hará rey, como a su antepasado David, [33] para que reine por siempre en la nación de Israel. Su reinado no tendrá fin.»

[34] María preguntó al ángel:

«¿Cómo podrá suceder esto, si no vivo con ningún hombre?»

[35] El ángel le contestó:

«El Espíritu Santo se posará sobre ti y el poder del Dios altísimo te cubrirá como una nube. Por eso, el niño que va a nacer será llamado Santo e Hijo de Dios. [36] También tu parienta Isabel, a pesar de ser anciana, va a tener un hijo; la que decían que no podía tener hijos está encinta desde hace seis meses. [37] Para Dios no hay nada imposible.»

[38] Entonces María dijo:

«Soy la esclava del Señor. ¡Que Dios haga conmigo como me has dicho!»

Con esto, el ángel se fue.

María visita a Isabel

[39] Por aquellos días, María se dirigió de prisa a un pueblo de la región montañosa de Judea, [40] y entró en casa de Zacarías y saludó a Isabel. [41] Cuando Isabel oyó el saludo de María, la criatura se movió en su vientre, y ella quedó llena del Espíritu Santo. [42] Entonces, con voz muy fuerte, dijo:

«¡Dios te ha bendecido más que a todas las mujeres, y ha bendecido a tu hijo! [43] ¿Quién soy yo para que venga a visitarme la madre de mi Señor? [44] Tan pronto como he oído tu saludo, mi hijo se ha movido de alegría en mi vientre. [45] ¡Dichosa tú por haber creído que han de cumplirse las cosas que el Señor te ha dicho!»

El cántico de María

[46] María dijo:

«Mi alma alaba la grandeza del Señor.

[47] Mi espíritu se alegra en Dios mi Salvador,

[48] porque Dios ha puesto sus ojos en mí, su humilde esclava,
y desde ahora me llamarán dichosa;

[49] porque el Todopoderoso ha hecho en mí grandes cosas.
¡Santo es su nombre!

[50] Dios tiene siempre misericordia de quienes le honran.

[51] Actuó con todo su poder:
deshizo los planes de los orgullosos,

[52] derribó a los reyes de sus tronos
y puso en alto a los humildes.

⁵³ Llenó de bienes a los hambrientos
    y despidió a los ricos con las manos vacías.
⁵⁴ Ayudó al pueblo de Israel, su siervo,
    y no se olvidó de tratarlo con misericordia.
⁵⁵ Así lo había prometido a nuestros antepasados,
    a Abraham y a sus futuros descendientes.»

⁵⁶ María se quedó con Isabel unos tres meses, y después regresó a su casa.

Nacimiento de Juan el Bautista

⁵⁷ Al cumplirse el tiempo en que Isabel había de dar a luz, tuvo un hijo. ⁵⁸ Sus vecinos y parientes fueron a felicitarla cuando supieron que el Señor había sido tan bueno con ella. ⁵⁹ A los ocho días llevaron a circuncidar al niño, y querían ponerle el nombre de su padre, Zacarías. ⁶⁰ Pero la madre dijo:

«No. Tiene que llamarse Juan.»

⁶¹ Le contestaron:

«No hay nadie en tu familia con ese nombre.»

⁶² Entonces preguntaron por señas al padre del niño, para saber qué nombre quería ponerle. ⁶³ El padre pidió una tabla para escribir, y escribió: «Su nombre es Juan.» Y todos se quedaron admirados. ⁶⁴ En aquel mismo momento, Zacarías recobró el habla y comenzó a alabar a Dios. ⁶⁵ Todos los vecinos estaban asombrados, y en toda la región montañosa de Judea se contaba lo sucedido. ⁶⁶ Cuantos lo oían se preguntaban a sí mismos: «¿Qué llegará a ser este niño?» Porque ciertamente el Señor mostraba su poder en favor de él.

El cántico de Zacarías

⁶⁷ Zacarías, el padre del niño, lleno del Espíritu Santo y hablando en profecía, dijo:

⁶⁸ «¡Bendito sea el Señor, Dios de Israel,
    porque ha venido a rescatar a su pueblo!
⁶⁹ Nos ha enviado un poderoso salvador,
    un descendiente de David, su siervo.
⁷⁰ Esto es lo que había prometido en el pasado por medio
    de sus santos profetas:

⁷¹ que nos salvaría de nuestros enemigos y de todos los que nos odian,
⁷² que tendría compasión de nuestros antepasados
y que no se olvidaría de su santo pacto.
⁷³ Y este es el juramento que había hecho a nuestro padre Abraham:
⁷⁴ que nos libraría de nuestros enemigos,
para servirle sin temor
⁷⁵ con santidad y justicia, y estar en su presencia todos los días
de nuestra vida.
⁷⁶ En cuanto a ti, hijito mío, serás llamado profeta del Dios altísimo,
porque irás delante del Señor preparando sus caminos,
⁷⁷ para hacer saber a su pueblo que Dios les perdona sus pecados
y les da la salvación.
⁷⁸ Porque nuestro Dios, en su gran misericordia,
nos trae de lo alto el sol de un nuevo día,
⁷⁹ para iluminar a los que viven en la más profunda oscuridad,
para dirigir nuestros pasos por un camino de paz.»
⁸⁰ El niño crecía y se hacía fuerte espiritualmente, y vivió en lugares desiertos hasta el día en que se dio a conocer a los israelitas.

Nacimiento de Jesús

2 Por aquel tiempo, el emperador Augusto ordenó que se hiciera un censo de todo el mundo. ² Este primer censo fue hecho siendo Quirinio gobernador de Siria. ³ Todos tenían que ir a inscribirse a su propia ciudad.

⁴ Por esto salió José del pueblo de Nazaret, de la región de Galilea, y se fue a Belén, en Judea, donde había nacido el rey David, porque José era descendiente de David. ⁵ Fue allá a inscribirse, junto con María, su esposa, que se encontraba encinta. ⁶ Y sucedió mientras estaban en Belén, que a María le llegó el tiempo de dar a luz. ⁷ Allí nació su hijo primogénito, y lo envolvió en pañales y lo acostó en el pesebre, porque no había alojamiento para ellos en el mesón.

Los ángeles y los pastores

⁸ Cerca de Belén había unos pastores que pasaban la noche en el campo cuidando sus ovejas. ⁹ De pronto se les apareció un ángel del Señor, la gloria del Señor brilló alrededor de ellos y tuvieron mucho

miedo. [10] Pero el ángel les dijo: «No tengáis miedo, porque os traigo una buena noticia que será motivo de gran alegría para todos: [11] Hoy os ha nacido en el pueblo de David un salvador, que es el Mesías, el Señor. [12] Como señal, encontraréis al niño envuelto en pañales y acostado en un pesebre.»

[13] En aquel momento, junto al ángel, aparecieron muchos otros ángeles del cielo que alababan a Dios y decían:

[14] «¡Gloria a Dios en las alturas! ¡Paz en la tierra entre los hombres que gozan de su favor!»

[15] Cuando los ángeles se volvieron al cielo, los pastores comenzaron a decirse unos a otros:

«Vamos, pues, a Belén, a ver lo que ha sucedido y que el Señor nos ha anunciado.»

[16] Fueron corriendo y encontraron a María, a José y al niño acostado en el pesebre. [17] Al verlo se pusieron a contar lo que el ángel les había dicho acerca del niño, [18] y todos los que lo oían se admiraban de lo que decían los pastores. [19] María guardaba todo esto en su corazón, y lo tenía muy presente. [20] Los pastores, por su parte, regresaron dando gloria y alabanza a Dios por todo lo que habían visto y oído, pues todo sucedió como se les había dicho.

Presentación del niño Jesús en el templo

[21] A los ocho días circuncidaron al niño y le pusieron por nombre Jesús, el mismo nombre que el ángel había dicho a María antes de que estuviera encinta.

[22] Cuando se cumplieron los días en que debían purificarse según las ceremonias de la ley de Moisés, llevaron al niño a Jerusalén para presentarlo al Señor. [23] Lo hicieron así porque en la ley del Señor está escrito: «Todo primer hijo varón será consagrado al Señor.» [24] Fueron, pues, a ofrecer en sacrificio lo que manda la ley del Señor: un par de tórtolas o dos pichones.

[25] En aquel tiempo vivía en Jerusalén un hombre llamado Simeón. Era un hombre justo, que adoraba a Dios y esperaba la restauración de Israel. El Espíritu Santo estaba con él [26] y le había hecho saber que no moriría sin ver antes al Mesías, a quien el Señor había de enviar. [27] Guiado por el Espíritu Santo, Simeón fue al templo. Y cuando los

padres del niño Jesús entraban para cumplir con lo dispuesto por la ley, [28] Simeón lo tomó en brazos, y alabó a Dios diciendo:

[29] «Ahora, Señor, tu promesa está cumplida:
ya puedes dejar que tu siervo muera en paz.
[30] Porque he visto la salvación
[31] que has comenzado a realizar ante los ojos de todas las naciones,
[32] la luz que alumbrará a los paganos
y que será la honra de tu pueblo Israel.»

[33] El padre y la madre de Jesús estaban admirados de lo que Simeón decía acerca del niño. [34] Simeón les dio su bendición, y dijo a María, la madre de Jesús:

«Mira, este niño está destinado a hacer que muchos en Israel caigan y muchos se levanten. Será un signo de contradicción [35] que pondrá al descubierto las intenciones de muchos corazones. Pero todo esto va a ser para ti como una espada que te atraviese el alma.»

[36] También estaba allí una profetisa llamada Ana, hija de Penuel, de la tribu de Aser. Era muy anciana. Se había casado siendo muy joven y vivió con su marido siete años; [37] pero hacía ya ochenta y cuatro que había quedado viuda. Nunca salía del templo, sino que servía día y noche al Señor, con ayunos y oraciones. [38] Ana se presentó en aquel mismo momento, y comenzó a dar gracias a Dios y a hablar del niño Jesús a todos los que esperaban la liberación de Jerusalén.

El regreso a Nazaret

[39] Cuando ya habían cumplido con todo lo que dispone la ley del Señor, regresaron a Galilea, a su pueblo de Nazaret. [40] Y el niño crecía y se hacía más fuerte y más sabio, y gozaba del favor de Dios.

El niño Jesús en el templo

[41] Los padres de Jesús iban cada año a Jerusalén para la fiesta de la Pascua. [42] Y así, cuando Jesús cumplió doce años, fueron todos allá, como era costumbre en esa fiesta. [43] Pero pasados aquellos días, cuando volvían a casa, el niño Jesús se quedó en Jerusalén sin que sus padres se dieran cuenta. [44] Pensando que Jesús iba entre la gente hicieron un día de camino; pero luego, al buscarlo entre los parientes y conocidos, [45] no lo encontraron. Así que regresaron a Jerusalén para buscarlo allí.

⁴⁶ Al cabo de tres días lo encontraron en el templo, sentado entre los maestros de la ley, escuchándolos y haciéndoles preguntas. ⁴⁷ Y todos los que le oían se admiraban de su inteligencia y de sus respuestas. ⁴⁸ Cuando sus padres le vieron, se sorprendieron. Y su madre le dijo:

«Hijo mío, ¿por qué nos has hecho esto? Tu padre y yo te hemos estado buscando llenos de angustia.»

⁴⁹ Jesús les contestó:

«¿Por qué me buscabais? ¿No sabéis que tengo que estar en la casa de mi Padre?»

⁵⁰ Pero ellos no entendieron lo que les decía.

⁵¹ Jesús volvió con ellos a Nazaret, donde vivió obedeciéndolos en todo. Su madre guardaba todo esto en el corazón. ⁵² Y Jesús seguía creciendo en cuerpo y mente, y gozaba del favor de Dios y de los hombres.

Juan el Bautista en el desierto

3 En el año quince del gobierno del emperador Tiberio, Poncio Pilato era gobernador de Judea, Herodes gobernaba en Galilea, su hermano Filipo gobernaba en Iturea y Traconítide, y Lisanias gobernaba en Abilene. ² Anás y Caifás eran los sumos sacerdotes. Por aquel tiempo habló Dios en el desierto a Juan, el hijo de Zacarías, ³ y Juan pasó por toda la región del río Jordán diciendo a la gente que debían volverse a Dios y ser bautizados, para que Dios les perdonara sus pecados. ⁴ Esto sucedió como el profeta Isaías había escrito:

«Se oye la voz de alguien que grita en el desierto:
"¡Preparad el camino del Señor;
abridle un camino recto!

⁵   Todo valle será rellenado,
todo monte y colina será nivelado,
los caminos torcidos serán enderezados
y allanados los caminos escabrosos.

⁶   Todo el mundo verá la salvación que Dios envía."»

⁷ Y decía Juan a la gente que acudía a él para recibir el bautismo: «¡Raza de víboras!, ¿quién os ha dicho que vais a libraros del terrible castigo que se acerca? ⁸ Demostrad con vuestros actos que os habéis vuelto a Dios y no os digáis a vosotros mismos: "Nosotros somos

descendientes de Abraham", porque os aseguro que incluso de estas piedras puede Dios sacar descendientes a Abraham. [9] Además, el hacha ya está lista para cortar de raíz los árboles. Todo árbol que no dé buen fruto será cortado y arrojado al fuego.»

[10] La gente le preguntaba:

«¿Qué debemos hacer?»

[11] Y Juan les contestaba:

«El que tiene dos vestidos dé uno al que no tiene ninguno, y el que tiene comida compártala con el que no la tiene.»

[12] Se acercaron también para ser bautizados algunos de los que cobraban impuestos para Roma, y preguntaron a Juan:

«Maestro, ¿qué debemos hacer nosotros?»

[13] «No cobréis más de lo que está ordenado» les dijo Juan.

[14] También algunos soldados le preguntaron:

«Y nosotros, ¿qué debemos hacer?»

Les contestó:

«No quitéis nada a nadie con amenazas o falsas acusaciones. Y conformaos con vuestra paga.»

[15] La gente se encontraba en gran expectación y se preguntaba si tal vez Juan sería el Mesías. [16] Pero Juan les dijo a todos: «Yo, ciertamente, os bautizo con agua; pero viene uno que os bautizará con el Espíritu Santo y con fuego. Él es más poderoso que yo, que ni siquiera merezco desatar la correa de sus sandalias. [17] Trae la pala en la mano para limpiar el trigo y separarlo de la paja. Guardará el trigo en su granero, pero quemará la paja en un fuego que nunca se apagará.»

[18] De este modo y con otros muchos consejos anunciaba Juan la buena noticia a la gente. [19] Además reprendió a Herodes, el gobernante, porque tenía por mujer a Herodías, la esposa de su hermano Felipe, y también por todo lo malo que había hecho. [20] Pero Herodes, a todas sus malas acciones añadió una más: metió a Juan en la cárcel.

Jesús es bautizado

[21] Sucedió que cuando Juan estaba bautizando a todos, también Jesús fue bautizado. Y mientras oraba, el cielo se abrió, [22] y el Espíritu Santo bajó sobre él en forma visible, como una paloma, y se oyó una voz del cielo, que decía: «Tú eres mi Hijo amado, a quien he elegido.»

Los antepasados de Jesús

²³ Jesús tenía unos treinta años cuando comenzó su actividad. Fue hijo, según se creía, de José. José fue hijo de Elí, ²⁴ que a su vez fue hijo de Matat, que fue hijo de Leví, que fue hijo de Melquí, que fue hijo de Janai, que fue hijo de José, ²⁵ que fue hijo de Matatías, que fue hijo de Amós, que fue hijo de Nahúm, que fue hijo de Eslí, que fue hijo de Nagai, ²⁶ que fue hijo de Máhat, que fue hijo de Matatías, que fue hijo de Semeí, que fue hijo de Josec, que fue hijo de Joiadá, ²⁷ que fue hijo de Johanán, que fue hijo de Resá, que fue hijo de Zorobabel, que fue hijo de Salatiel, que fue hijo de Nerí, ²⁸ que fue hijo de Melquí, que fue hijo de Adí, que fue hijo de Cosam, que fue hijo de Elmadam, que fue hijo de Er, ²⁹ que fue hijo de Jesús, que fue hijo de Eliézer, que fue hijo de Jorim, que fue hijo de Matat, que fue hijo de Leví, ³⁰ que fue hijo de Simeón, que fue hijo de Judá, que fue hijo de José, que fue hijo de Jonam, que fue hijo de Eliaquim, ³¹ que fue hijo de Meleá, que fue hijo de Mená, que fue hijo de Matatá, que fue hijo de Natán, que fue hijo de David, ³² que fue hijo de Jesé, que fue hijo de Obed, que fue hijo de Booz, que fue hijo de Sélah, que fue hijo de Nahasón, ³³ que fue hijo de Aminadab, que fue hijo de Admín, que fue hijo de Arní, que fue hijo de Hesrón, que fue hijo de Fares, que fue hijo de Judá, ³⁴ que fue hijo de Jacob, que fue hijo de Isaac, que fue hijo de Abraham, que fue hijo de Térah, que fue hijo de Nahor, ³⁵ que fue hijo de Serug, que fue hijo de Ragau, que fue hijo de Péleg, que fue hijo de Éber, que fue hijo de Sélah, ³⁶ que fue hijo de Cainán, que fue hijo de Arfaxad, que fue hijo de Sem, que fue hijo de Noé, que fue hijo de Lámec, ³⁷ que fue hijo de Matusalén, que fue hijo de Henoc, que fue hijo de Jéred, que fue hijo de Mahalaleel, que fue hijo de Cainán, ³⁸ que fue hijo de Enós, que fue hijo de Set, que fue hijo de Adán, que fue hijo de Dios.

El diablo pone a prueba a Jesús

4 Jesús, lleno del Espíritu Santo, volvió del río Jordán, y el Espíritu lo llevó al desierto. ² Allí estuvo cuarenta días, y el diablo le puso a prueba. No comió nada durante aquellos días, y después sintió hambre. ³ El diablo le dijo:

«Si de veras eres Hijo de Dios, ordena a esta piedra que se convierta en pan.»

⁴ Jesús le contestó:

«La Escritura dice: "No solo de pan vivirá el hombre."»

⁵ Luego el diablo lo llevó a un lugar alto, y mostrándole en un momento todos los países del mundo ⁶ le dijo:

«Yo te daré todo este poder y la grandeza de estos países, porque yo lo he recibido y se lo daré a quien quiera dárselo. ⁷ Si te arrodillas y me adoras, todo será tuyo.»

⁸ Jesús le contestó:

«La Escritura dice: "Adora al Señor tu Dios y sírvele solo a él."»

⁹ Después el diablo lo llevó a la ciudad de Jerusalén, lo subió al alero del templo y le dijo:

«Si de veras eres Hijo de Dios, tírate abajo, ¹⁰ porque la Escritura dice:

"Dios mandará a sus ángeles para que cuiden de ti y te protejan.

¹¹ Te levantarán con sus manos

para que no tropieces con piedra alguna."

¹² Jesús le contestó:

«También dice la Escritura: "No pongas a prueba al Señor tu Dios."»

¹³ Cuando ya el diablo no encontró otra forma de poner a prueba a Jesús, se alejó de él por algún tiempo.

Jesús comienza su trabajo en Galilea

¹⁴ Jesús volvió a Galilea lleno del poder del Espíritu Santo, y su fama se extendía por toda la tierra de alrededor. ¹⁵ Enseñaba en la sinagoga de cada lugar, y todos le alababan.

Jesús en Nazaret

¹⁶ Jesús fue a Nazaret, al pueblo donde se había criado. Un sábado entró en la sinagoga, como era su costumbre, y se puso en pie para leer las Escrituras. ¹⁷ Le dieron a leer el libro del profeta Isaías, y al abrirlo encontró el lugar donde estaba escrito:

¹⁸ «El Espíritu del Señor está sobre mí,

porque me ha consagrado para llevar la buena noticia a los pobres;

me ha enviado a anunciar libertad a los presos

y a dar vista a los ciegos;

a poner en libertad a los oprimidos;

¹⁹ a anunciar el año favorable del Señor.»

²⁰ Luego Jesús cerró el libro, lo dio al ayudante de la sinagoga y se sentó. Todos los presentes le miraban atentamente. ²¹ Él comenzó a hablar, diciendo:

«Hoy mismo se ha cumplido esta Escritura delante de vosotros.»

²² Todos hablaban bien de Jesús y estaban admirados de la belleza de su palabra. Se preguntaban:

«¿No es este el hijo de José?»

²³ Jesús les respondió:

«Seguramente me aplicaréis el refrán: "Médico, cúrate a ti mismo", y me diréis: "Lo que oímos que hiciste en Cafarnaum, hazlo también aquí, en tu propia tierra."»

²⁴ Y siguió diciendo:

«Os aseguro que ningún profeta es bien recibido en su propia tierra. ²⁵ Verdaderamente había muchas viudas en Israel en tiempos del profeta Elías, cuando no llovió durante tres años y medio y hubo mucha hambre en todo el país. ²⁶ Sin embargo, Elías no fue enviado a ninguna de las viudas israelitas, sino a una de Sarepta, cerca de la ciudad de Sidón. ²⁷ También había en Israel muchos enfermos de lepra en tiempos del profeta Eliseo, pero ninguno de ellos fue sanado, sino Naamán, que era de Siria.»

²⁸ Al oír esto, todos los que estaban en la sinagoga se llenaron de ira. ²⁹ Se levantaron y echaron del pueblo a Jesús. Lo llevaron a lo alto del monte sobre el que se alzaba el pueblo, para arrojarle abajo. ³⁰ Pero Jesús pasó por en medio de ellos y se fue.

Un hombre que tenía un espíritu impuro

³¹ Llegó Jesús a Cafarnaum, un pueblo de Galilea, y los sábados enseñaba a la gente; ³² y se admiraban de cómo les enseñaba, porque hablaba con plena autoridad.

³³ En la sinagoga había un hombre que tenía un demonio o espíritu impuro que gritaba con fuerza:

³⁴ «¡Déjanos! ¿Por qué te metes con nosotros, Jesús de Nazaret? ¿Has venido a destruirnos? Yo te conozco: ¡sé que eres el Santo de Dios!»

³⁵ Jesús reprendió a aquel demonio diciéndole:

«¡Cállate y deja a ese hombre!»

Entonces el demonio arrojó al hombre al suelo delante de todos y salió de él sin hacerle ningún daño. [36] Todos se asustaron y se decían unos a otros:

«¿Qué palabras son esas? ¡Este hombre da órdenes con plena autoridad y poder a los espíritus impuros y los hace salir!»

[37] La fama de Jesús se extendía por todos los lugares de la región.

Jesús sana a la suegra de Simón

[38] Jesús salió de la sinagoga y entró en casa de Simón. La suegra de Simón estaba enferma, con mucha fiebre, y rogaron a Jesús que la sanase. [39] Jesús se inclinó sobre ella y reprendió a la fiebre, y la fiebre la dejó. Al momento, ella se levantó y se puso a atenderlos.

Jesús sana a muchos enfermos

[40] Al ponerse el sol, todos los que tenían enfermos de diferentes enfermedades los llevaron a Jesús; él puso las manos sobre cada uno de ellos y los sanó. [41] De muchos enfermos salieron también demonios que gritaban:

«¡Tú eres el Hijo de Dios!»

Pero Jesús reprendía a los demonios y no los dejaba hablar, porque sabían que él era el Mesías.

Jesús anuncia el mensaje en las sinagogas

[42] Al amanecer, Jesús salió de la ciudad y se dirigió a un lugar apartado. Pero la gente le buscó hasta encontrarle. Querían retenerlo para que no se marchase, [43] pero Jesús les dijo:

«También tengo que anunciar las buenas noticias del reino de Dios a los otros pueblos, porque para esto he sido enviado.»

[44] Así iba Jesús anunciando el mensaje en las sinagogas de Judea.

La pesca abundante

5 En una ocasión se encontraba Jesús a orillas del lago de Genesaret, y se sentía apretujado por la multitud que quería oir el mensaje de Dios. [2] Vio Jesús dos barcas en la playa. Estaban vacías, porque los pescadores habían bajado de ellas a lavar sus redes. [3] Jesús subió a una de las barcas, que era de Simón, y le pidió que la alejara un poco de la orilla. Luego se sentó en la barca y comenzó a enseñar a la gente. [4] Cuando terminó de hablar dijo a Simón:

«Lleva la barca lago adentro, y echad allí vuestras redes, para pescar.»

[5] Simón le contestó:

«Maestro, hemos estado trabajando toda la noche sin pescar nada; pero, puesto que tú lo mandas, echaré las redes.»

[6] Cuando lo hicieron, recogieron tal cantidad de peces que las redes se rompían. [7] Entonces hicieron señas a sus compañeros de la otra barca, para que fueran a ayudarlos. Ellos fueron, y llenaron tanto las dos barcas que les faltaba poco para hundirse. [8] Al ver esto, Simón Pedro se puso de rodillas delante de Jesús y le dijo:

«¡Apártate de mí, Señor, porque soy un pecador!»

[9] Porque Simón y todos los demás estaban asustados por aquella gran pesca que habían hecho. [10] También lo estaban Santiago y Juan, hijos de Zebedeo, que eran compañeros de Simón. Pero Jesús dijo a Simón:

«No tengas miedo. Desde ahora vas a pescar hombres.»

[11] Entonces llevaron las barcas a tierra, lo dejaron todo y se fueron con Jesús.

Jesús sana a un leproso

[12] Un día estaba Jesús en un pueblo donde había un hombre enfermo de lepra. Al ver a Jesús se inclinó hasta el suelo y le rogó:

«Señor, si quieres, puedes limpiarme de mi enfermedad.» [13] Jesús le tocó con la mano, diciendo:

«Quiero. ¡Queda limpio!»

Al momento se le quitó la lepra al enfermo, [14] y Jesús le ordenó:

«No lo digas a nadie. Solamente ve, preséntate al sacerdote y lleva por tu purificación la ofrenda que ordenó Moisés, para que todos sepan que ya estás limpio de tu enfermedad.»

[15] Sin embargo, la fama de Jesús se extendía cada vez más, y mucha gente se juntaba para oírle y para que sanase sus enfermedades. [16] Pero Jesús se retiraba a orar a lugares apartados.

Jesús sana a un paralítico

[17] Un día estaba Jesús enseñando, y se habían sentado por allí algunos fariseos y maestros de la ley venidos de todas las aldeas de Galilea,

y de Judea y Jerusalén. El poder de Dios se manifestaba en Jesús cuando curaba a los enfermos. [18] En esto llegaron unos hombres que llevaban en una camilla a un paralítico. Querían meterlo en la casa y ponerlo delante de Jesús, [19] pero no encontraban por dónde entrar porque había mucha gente; así que subieron al techo, y haciendo un hueco entre las tejas bajaron al enfermo en la camilla, allí en medio de todos, delante de Jesús. [20] Cuando Jesús vio la fe que tenían, le dijo al enfermo:

«Amigo, tus pecados quedan perdonados.»

[21] Entonces los maestros de la ley y los fariseos comenzaron a pensar: «¿Quién es este, que se atreve a decir palabras ofensivas contra Dios? Tan sólo Dios puede perdonar pecados.»

[22] Pero Jesús, dándose cuenta de lo que estaban pensando, les preguntó:

«¿Por qué pensáis así? [23] ¿Qué es más fácil, decir: "Tus pecados quedan perdonados" o decir: "Levántate y anda"? [24] Pues voy a demostraros que el Hijo del hombre tiene poder en la tierra para perdonar pecados.»

Entonces dijo al paralítico:

«A ti te digo: levántate, toma tu camilla y vete a tu casa.»

[25] Al momento, el paralítico se levantó delante de todos, tomó la camilla en que estaba acostado y se fue a su casa alabando a Dios. [26] Todos se quedaron asombrados y alabaron a Dios, y llenos de miedo dijeron:

«Hoy hemos visto cosas maravillosas.»

Jesús llama a Leví

[27] Después de esto, Jesús salió y se fijó en uno de los que cobraban impuestos para Roma. Se llamaba Leví y estaba sentado en el lugar donde cobraba los impuestos. Jesús le dijo:

«Sígueme.»

[28] Entonces Leví se levantó, y dejándolo todo siguió a Jesús.

[29] Más tarde, Leví hizo en su casa una gran fiesta en honor de Jesús; y muchos de los que cobraban impuestos para Roma, junto con otras personas, estaban sentados con ellos a la mesa. [30] Pero los fariseos y los maestros de la ley pertenecientes a este partido comenzaron a criticar a los discípulos de Jesús. Les decían:

«¿Por qué coméis y bebéis con los cobradores de impuestos y los pecadores?»

[31] Jesús les contestó:

«Los que gozan de buena salud no necesitan médico, sino los enfermos. [32] Yo no he venido a llamar a los justos, sino a los pecadores, para que se conviertan a Dios.»

La cuestión del ayuno

[33] Le dijeron a Jesús:

«Los seguidores de Juan y los de los fariseos ayunan mucho y hacen muchas oraciones, pero tus discípulos no dejan de comer y beber.»

[34] Jesús les contestó:

«¿Acaso podéis hacer que ayunen los invitados a una boda mientras el novio está con ellos? [35] Ya llegará el momento en que se lleven al novio; cuando llegue ese día, ayunarán.»

[36] También les contó esta parábola:

«Nadie corta un trozo de un vestido nuevo para arreglar un vestido viejo. De hacerlo así, echará a perder el vestido nuevo; además el trozo nuevo no quedará bien en el vestido viejo. [37] Ni tampoco se echa vino nuevo en odres viejos, porque el vino nuevo hace que los odres revienten, y tanto el vino como los odres se pierden. [38] Por eso hay que echar el vino nuevo en odres nuevos. [39] Y nadie que beba vino añejo querrá después beber el nuevo, porque dirá que el añejo es mejor.»

Los discípulos arrancan espigas en sábado

6 Un sábado pasaba Jesús entre los sembrados. Sus discípulos arrancaban espigas de trigo, las desgranaban entre las manos y se comían los granos. [2] Entonces algunos fariseos les preguntaron:

«¿Por qué hacéis algo que no está permitido en sábado?»

[3] Jesús les contestó:

«¿No habéis leído lo que hizo David en una ocasión en que él y sus compañeros tuvieron hambre? [4] Entró en la casa de Dios y tomó los panes consagrados, comió de ellos y dio también a sus compañeros, a pesar de que solamente a los sacerdotes les estaba permitido comer de aquel pan.»

⁵ Y añadió:

«El Hijo del hombre tiene autoridad sobre el sábado.»

Jesús sana en sábado a un enferemo

⁶ Sucedió que otro sábado entró Jesús en la sinagoga y comenzó a enseñar. Había en ella un hombre que tenía la mano derecha tullida; ⁷ y los maestros de la ley y los fariseos espiaban a Jesús, por ver si lo sanaría en sábado y tener así algún pretexto para acusarle. ⁸ Pero él, sabiendo lo que estaban pensando, dijo al hombre de la mano tullida:

«Levántate y ponte ahí en medio.»

El hombre se levantó y se puso de pie, ⁹ y Jesús dijo a los demás:

«Os voy a hacer una pregunta: ¿Qué está permitido hacer en sábado, el bien o el mal? ¿Salvar una vida o destruirla?»

¹⁰ Luego miró a todos los que le rodeaban y dijo a aquel hombre:

«Extiende la mano.»

El hombre la extendió y su mano quedó sana. ¹¹ Pero los demás se llenaron de ira y comenzaron a discutir lo que podrían hacer contra Jesús.

Jesús escoge a los doce apóstoles

¹² Por aquellos días, Jesús se fue a un cerro a orar, y pasó toda la noche orando a Dios. ¹³ Cuando se hizo de día, reunió a sus discípulos y escogió a doce de ellos, a los cuales llamó apóstoles. ¹⁴ Estos fueron: Simón, a quien puso también el nombre de Pedro; Andrés, hermano de Simón; Santiago, Juan, Felipe, Bartolomé, ¹⁵ Mateo, Tomás, Santiago hijo de Alfeo; Simón el celote, ¹⁶ Judas, hijo de Santiago, y Judas Iscariote, que traicionó a Jesús.

Jesús enseña a mucha gente

¹⁷ Jesús bajó del cerro con ellos, y se detuvo en un llano. Se habían reunido allí muchos de sus seguidores y mucha gente de toda la región de Judea, y de Jerusalén y de la costa de Tiro y Sidón. Habían venido para oír a Jesús y para que los curase de sus enfermedades. ¹⁸ Los que sufrían a causa de espíritus impuros, también quedaban sanados. ¹⁹ Así que toda la gente quería tocar a Jesús, porque los sanaba a todos con el poder que de él salía.

Lo que realmente cuenta ante Dios

²⁰ Jesús miró a sus discípulos y les dijo:

«Dichosos vosotros los pobres, porque el reino de Dios os pertenece.

²¹ «Dichosos los que ahora tenéis hambre, porque quedaréis satisfechos.

«Dichosos los que ahora lloráis, porque después reiréis.

²² «Dichosos vosotros cuando la gente os odie, cuando os expulsen, cuando os insulten y cuando desprecien vuestro nombre como cosa mala, por causa del Hijo del hombre. ²³ Alegraos mucho, llenaos de gozo en aquel día, porque recibiréis un gran premio en el cielo; pues también maltrataron así sus antepasados a los profetas.

²⁴ «Pero ¡ay de vosotros los ricos, porque ya habéis tenido vuestra alegría!

²⁵ «¡Ay de vosotros los que ahora estáis satisfechos, porque tendréis hambre!

«¡Ay de vosotros los que ahora reís, porque vais a llorar de tristeza!

²⁶ «¡Ay de vosotros cuando todos os alaben, porque así hacían los antepasados de esta gente con los falsos profetas!

El amor a los enemigos

²⁷ «Pero a vosotros que me escucháis os digo: Amad a vuestros enemigos, haced bien a los que os odian, ²⁸ bendecid a los que os maldicen, orad por los que os insultan. ²⁹ Al que te pegue en una mejilla ofrécele también la otra, y al que te quite la capa déjale que se lleve también tu túnica. ³⁰ Al que te pida algo dáselo, y al que te quite lo que es tuyo, no se lo reclames. ³¹ Haced con los demás como queréis que los demás hagan con vosotros. ³² Si amáis solamente a quienes os aman, ¿qué hacéis de extraordinario? ¡Hasta los pecadores se portan así! ³³ Y si hacéis bien solamente a quienes os hacen bien a vosotros, ¿qué tiene de extraordinario? ¡También los pecadores se portan así! ³⁴ Y si dais prestado sólo a aquellos de quienes pensáis recibir algo, ¿qué hacéis de extraordinario? ¡También los pecadores se prestan entre sí esperando recibir unos de otros! ³⁵ Amad a vuestros enemigos, haced el bien y dad prestado sin esperar nada a cambio. Así será grande vuestra recompensa y seréis hijos del Dios altísimo, que es

también bondadoso con los desagradecidos y los malos. [36] Sed compasivos, como también vuestro Padre es compasivo.

No juzgar a otros

[37] «No juzguéis a nadie y Dios no os juzgará a vosotros. No condenéis a nadie y Dios no os condenará. Perdonad y Dios os perdonará. [38] Dad a otros y Dios os dará a vosotros: llenará vuestra bolsa con una medida buena, apretada, sacudida y repleta. Dios os medirá con la misma medida con que vosotros midáis a los demás.»

[39] Jesús les puso esta comparación: «¿Acaso puede un ciego servir de guía a otro ciego? ¿No caerán los dos en algún hoyo? [40] El discípulo no es más que su maestro: solo cuando termine su aprendizaje llegará a ser como su maestro.

[41] «¿Por qué miras la paja que tiene tu hermano en el ojo y no te fijas en el tronco que tú tienes en el tuyo? [42] Y si no te das cuenta del tronco que tienes en tu ojo, ¿cómo te atreves a decirle a tu hermano: "Hermano, déjame sacarte la paja que tienes en el ojo?" ¡Hipócrita!, saca primero el tronco de tu ojo y así podrás ver bien para sacar la paja del ojo de tu hermano.

El árbol se conoce por su fruto

[43] «No hay árbol bueno que dé mal fruto ni árbol malo que dé fruto bueno. [44] Cada árbol se conoce por su fruto: no se recogen higos de los espinos ni se vendimian uvas de las zarzas. [45] El hombre bueno dice cosas buenas porque el bien está en su corazón, y el hombre malo dice cosas malas porque el mal está en su corazón. Pues de lo que rebosa su corazón, habla su boca.

Parábola de los dos cimientos

[46] «¿Por qué me llamáis "Señor, Señor" y no hacéis lo que yo os digo? [47] Voy a deciros a quién se parece aquel que viene a mí, y me oye y hace lo que digo: [48] se parece a un hombre que para construir una casa cavó profundamente y puso los cimientos sobre la roca. Cuando creció el río, el agua dio con fuerza contra la casa, pero no pudo moverla porque estaba bien construida. [49] Pero el que me oye y no hace lo que yo digo se parece a un hombre que construyó su casa sobre la tie-

rra, sin cimientos; y cuando el río creció y dio con fuerza contra ella, se derrumbó y quedó completamente destruida.»

Jesús sana al criado de un oficial romano

7 Cuando Jesús terminó de hablar a la gente, se fue a Cafarnaum. ² Vivía allí un centurión romano, cuyo criado, al que quería mucho, se encontraba a punto de morir. ³ Habiendo oído hablar de Jesús, el capitán envió a unos ancianos de los judíos a rogarle que fuera a sanar a su criado. ⁴ Ellos se presentaron a Jesús y le rogaron mucho, diciendo:

«Este centurión merece que le ayudes, ⁵ porque ama a nuestra nación. Él mismo hizo construir nuestra sinagoga.»

⁶ Jesús fue con ellos, pero cuando ya estaban cerca de la casa el centurión le envió unos amigos a decirle:

«Señor, no te molestes, porque yo no merezco que entres en mi casa. ⁷ Por eso, ni siquiera me atreví a ir en persona a buscarte. Solamente da la orden y mi criado se curará. ⁸ Porque yo mismo estoy bajo órdenes superiores, y a la vez tengo soldados bajo mi mando. Cuando a uno de ellos le digo que vaya, va; cuando a otro le digo que venga, viene; y cuando ordeno a mi criado que haga algo, lo hace.»

⁹ Al oir esto, Jesús se quedó admirado, y mirando a la gente que le seguía dijo:

«Os aseguro que ni aun en Israel he encontrado tanta fe como en este hombre.»

¹⁰ Al regresar a la casa, los enviados encontraron sanado ya al criado.

Jesús resucita al hijo de una viuda

¹¹ Después de esto se dirigió Jesús a un pueblo llamado Naín. Iba acompañado de sus discípulos y de mucha otra gente. ¹² Al acercarse al pueblo vio que llevaban a enterrar a un muerto, hijo único de su madre, que era viuda. Mucha gente del pueblo la acompañaba. ¹³ Al verla, el Señor tuvo compasión de ella y le dijo:

«No llores.»

¹⁴ En seguida se acercó y tocó la camilla, y los que la llevaban se detuvieron. Jesús dijo al muerto:

«Muchacho, a ti te digo, ¡levántate!»

¹⁵ Entonces el muerto se sentó y comenzó a hablar, y Jesús se lo entregó a la madre. ¹⁶ Al ver esto, todos tuvieron miedo y comenzaron a alabar a Dios diciendo:

«Un gran profeta ha aparecido entre nosotros.»

También decían:

«Dios ha venido a ayudar a su pueblo.»

¹⁷ Y por toda Judea y sus alrededores corrió la noticia de lo que había hecho Jesús.

Los enviados de Juan el Bautista

¹⁸ Juan se enteró de todas estas cosas, porque sus seguidores se las contaron. Llamó a dos de ellos ¹⁹ y los envió a Jesús, a preguntarle si él era el que había de venir o si debían esperar a otro. ²⁰ Los enviados de Juan se acercaron, pues, a Jesús y le dijeron:

«Juan el Bautista nos ha mandado a preguntarte si tú eres el que había de venir o si debemos esperar a otro.»

²¹ En aquel mismo momento sanó Jesús a muchas personas de sus enfermedades y sufrimientos, y de los espíritus malignos, y dio la vista a muchos ciegos. ²² Luego les contestó:

«Id y contad a Juan lo que habéis visto y oído: que los ciegos ven, los cojos andan, los leprosos quedan limpios de su enfermedad, los sordos oyen, los muertos resucitan y a los pobres se les anuncia la buena noticia. ²³ ¡Y dichoso el que no pierde su confianza en mí!»

²⁴ Cuando los enviados de Juan se fueron, Jesús comenzó a hablar a la gente acerca de Juan, diciendo:

«¿Qué salisteis a ver al desierto? ¿Una caña sacudida por el viento? ²⁵ Y si no, ¿qué salisteis a ver? ¿Un hombre lujosamente vestido? Los que se visten con lujo y viven entre placeres están en los palacios de los reyes. ²⁶ En fin, ¿qué salisteis a ver? ¿Un profeta? Sí, verdaderamente: y a uno que es mucho más que profeta. ²⁷ Juan es aquel de quien dice la Escritura:

"Yo envío mi mensajero delante de ti,

para que te prepare el camino."

²⁸ Os digo que ninguno entre todos los hombres ha sido más grande que Juan; sin embargo, el más pequeño en el reino de Dios es más grande que él.»

²⁹ Todos los que oyeron a Juan, incluso los que cobraban impuestos para Roma, se hicieron bautizar por él, reconociendo así que Dios es justo; ³⁰ pero los fariseos y los maestros de la ley no se hicieron bautizar por Juan, y de ese modo despreciaron lo que Dios había querido hacer en favor de ellos.

³¹ «¿A qué compararé la gente de este tiempo? ¿A qué se parece? ³² Se parece a los niños que se sientan a jugar en la plaza y gritan a sus compañeros: "Tocamos la flauta y no bailasteis; cantamos canciones tristes y no llorasteis." ³³ Porque vino Juan el Bautista, que ni come pan ni bebe vino, y decís que tiene un demonio. ³⁴ Luego ha venido el Hijo del hombre, que come y bebe, y decís que es un glotón y bebedor, amigo de gente de mala fama y de los que cobran los impuestos para Roma. ³⁵ Pero la sabiduría de Dios se demuestra por todos sus resultados.»

Jesús en casa de Simón el fariseo

³⁶ Un fariseo invitó a Jesús a comer, y Jesús fue a su casa. Estaba sentado a la mesa, ³⁷ cuando una mujer de mala fama que vivía en el mismo pueblo y que supo que Jesús había ido a comer a casa del fariseo, llegó con un frasco de alabastro lleno de perfume. ³⁸ Llorando, se puso junto a los pies de Jesús y comenzó a bañarlos con sus lágrimas. Luego los secó con sus cabellos, los besó y derramó sobre ellos el perfume. ³⁹ Al ver esto, el fariseo que había invitado a Jesús pensó: «Si este hombre fuera verdaderamente un profeta se daría cuenta de quién y qué clase de mujer es esta pecadora que le está tocando.» ⁴⁰ Entonces Jesús dijo al fariseo:

«Simón, tengo algo que decirte.»

«Dímelo, Maestro» contestó el fariseo.

⁴¹ Jesús siguió:

«Dos hombres debían dinero a un prestamista. Uno le debía quinientos denarios, y el otro cincuenta: ⁴² pero, como no le podían pagar, el prestamista perdonó la deuda a los dos. Ahora dime: ¿cuál de ellos le amará más?»

⁴³ Simón le contestó:

«Me parece que aquel a quien más perdonó.»

Jesús le dijo:

«Tienes razón.»

⁴⁴ Y volviéndose a la mujer, dijo a Simón:

«¿Ves esta mujer? Entré en tu casa y no me diste agua para los pies; en cambio, esta mujer me ha bañado los pies con lágrimas y los ha secado con sus cabellos. ⁴⁵ No me besaste, pero ella, desde que entré, no ha dejado de besarme los pies. ⁴⁶ No derramaste aceite sobre mi cabeza, pero ella ha derramado perfume sobre mis pies. ⁴⁷ Por esto te digo que sus muchos pecados le son perdonados, porque amó mucho; pero aquel a quien poco se perdona, poco amor manifiesta.»

⁴⁸ Luego dijo a la mujer:

«Tus pecados te son perdonados.»

⁴⁹ Los otros invitados que estaban allí comenzaron a preguntarse:

«¿Quién es este que hasta perdona pecados?»

⁵⁰ Pero Jesús añadió, dirigiéndose a la mujer:

«Por tu fe has sido salvada. Vete tranquila.»

Mujeres que ayudaban a Jesús

8 Después de esto, Jesús anduvo por muchos pueblos y aldeas proclamando y anunciando el reino de Dios. Le acompañaban los doce apóstoles ² y algunas mujeres que él había librado de espíritus malignos y enfermedades. Entre ellas estaba María, la llamada Magdalena, de la que habían salido siete demonios; ³ también Juana, esposa de Cuza, el administrador de Herodes; y Susana, y otras muchas que les ayudaban con lo que tenían.

Parábola del sembrador

⁴ Mucha gente que estaba allí, más otra llegada de los pueblos, se reunió junto a Jesús, y él les contó esta parábola: ⁵ «Un sembrador salió a sembrar su semilla. Y al sembrar, una parte de ella cayó en el camino, y fue pisoteada y las aves se la comieron. ⁶ Otra parte cayó entre las piedras, y brotó, pero se secó por falta de humedad. ⁷ Otra parte cayó entre espinos, y al nacer juntamente los espinos, la ahogaron. ⁸ Pero otra parte cayó en buena tierra, y creció y dio una buena cosecha, hasta de cien granos por semilla.»

Esto dijo Jesús, y añadió con voz fuerte: «¡Los que tienen oídos, oigan!»

El porqué de las parábolas

[9] Los discípulos preguntaron a Jesús qué significaba aquella parábola. [10] Él les dijo: «A vosotros, Dios os da a conocer los secretos de su reino; pero a los otros les hablo por medio de parábolas, para que por mucho que miren no vean y por mucho que oigan no entiendan.

Jesús explica la parábola del sembrador

[11] «Esto significa la parábola: La semilla representa el mensaje de Dios. [12] La parte que cayó por el camino representa a los que oyen el mensaje, pero viene el diablo y se lo quita del corazón para que no crean y se salven. [13] La semilla que cayó entre las piedras representa a los que oyen el mensaje y lo reciben con gusto, pero luego, a la hora de la prueba, fallan. [14] La semilla que cayó entre espinos representa a los que oyen, pero poco a poco se dejan ahogar por las preocupaciones, las riquezas y los placeres, de modo que no llegan a dar fruto. [15] Pero la semilla que cayó en buena tierra representa a las personas que con corazón bueno y dispuesto oyen el mensaje y lo guardan, y permaneciendo firmes dan una buena cosecha.

El símil de la lámpara

[16] «Nadie enciende una lámpara para taparla con una olla o ponerla debajo de la cama, sino que la pone en alto para que tengan luz los que entran. [17] De la misma manera, no hay nada escondido que no llegue a descubrirse, ni nada secreto que no llegue a conocerse y ponerse en claro.

[18] «Así que oíd bien, pues al que tiene se le dará más; pero al que no tiene, hasta lo poco que cree tener se le quitará.»

La madre y los hermanos de Jesús

[19] La madre y los hermanos de Jesús acudieron a donde él estaba, pero no pudieron acercársele porque había mucha gente. [20] Alguien avisó a Jesús:

«Tu madre y tus hermanos están ahí fuera y quieren verte.»

[21] Él contestó:

«Los que oyen el mensaje de Dios y lo ponen en práctica, esos son mi madre y mis hermanos.»

La tempestad apaciguada

[22] Un día, Jesús entró en una barca con sus discípulos y les dijo:

«Pasemos a la otra orilla del lago.»

Partieron, pues, [23] y mientras cruzaban el lago, Jesús se quedó dormido. De pronto se desató una fuerte tormenta de viento sobre el lago; la barca se llenaba de agua y corrían peligro de hundirse. [24] Fueron a despertar a Jesús, diciéndole:

«¡Maestro, Maestro, nos estamos hundiendo!»

Jesús se levantó, dio una orden al viento y a las olas y todo se calmó y quedó tranquilo. [25] Después dijo a sus discípulos:

«¿Qué pasa con vuestra fe?»

Pero ellos, asustados y asombrados, se preguntaban unos a otros:

«¿Quién es este, que da órdenes al viento y al agua y le obedecen?»

El endemoniado de Gerasa

[26] Por fin llegaron a la tierra de Gerasa, que está al otro lado del lago, frente a Galilea. [27] Al bajar Jesús a tierra, un hombre que estaba endemoniado salió del pueblo y se le acercó. Hacía mucho tiempo que andaba sin ropas y que no vivía en una casa, sino entre las tumbas. [28] Cuando vio a Jesús, cayó de rodillas delante de él gritando:

«¡No te metas conmigo, Jesús, Hijo del Dios altísimo! ¡Te ruego que no me atormentes!»

[29] Dijo esto porque Jesús había ordenado al espíritu impuro que saliese de aquel hombre. Muchas veces el demonio se había apoderado de él, y aunque la gente le sujetaba las manos y los pies con cadenas para tenerle seguro, él las rompía y el demonio le hacía huir a lugares desiertos. [30] Jesús le preguntó:

«¿Cómo te llamas?»

«Me llamo Legión» contestó, porque eran muchos los demonios que habían entrado en él, [31] los cuales pidieron a Jesús que no los mandara al abismo. [32] Como allí, en el monte, estaba paciendo una gran piara de cerdos, los espíritus le rogaron que los dejara entrar en ellos. Jesús les dio permiso. [33] Los demonios salieron entonces del hombre y entraron en los cerdos, y estos echaron a correr pendiente abajo hasta el lago, y se ahogaron.

³⁴ Al ver lo sucedido, los que cuidaban los cerdos salieron huyendo y fueron a contarlo en el pueblo y por los campos. ³⁵ La gente salió a ver lo que había pasado. Y cuando llegaron a donde estaba Jesús, encontraron sentado a sus pies al hombre de quien habían salido los demonios, vestido y en su cabal juicio, y tuvieron miedo. ³⁶ Los que habían visto lo sucedido, les contaron cómo había sido curado aquel endemoniado. ³⁷ Toda la gente de la región de Gerasa comenzó entonces a rogar a Jesús que se marchara de allí, porque tenían mucho miedo. Así que Jesús entró en la barca y se fue. ³⁸ El hombre de quien habían salido los demonios le rogó que le permitiera ir con él, pero Jesús le ordenó que se quedase. Le dijo:

³⁹ «Vuelve a tu casa y cuenta todo lo que Dios ha hecho por ti.»

El hombre se fue y contó por todo el pueblo lo que Jesús había hecho por él.

La hija de Jairo y la mujer enferma

⁴⁰ Cuando Jesús regresó al otro lado del lago, la gente le recibió con alegría, porque todos le estaban esperando. ⁴¹ En esto llegó uno llamado Jairo, que era jefe de la sinagoga. Este hombre se echó a los pies de Jesús suplicándole que fuera a su casa, ⁴² porque su única hija, que tenía unos doce años, estaba a punto de morir.

Mientras Jesús iba, se sentía oprimido por la multitud. ⁴³ Entre la gente había una mujer que desde hacía doce años estaba enferma, con hemorragias. Había gastado en médicos todo lo que tenía, pero ninguno la había podido sanar. ⁴⁴ Esta mujer se acercó a Jesús por detrás y tocó el borde de su capa, y en el acto se detuvo su hemorragia.
⁴⁵ Entonces Jesús preguntó:

«¿Quién me ha tocado?»

Como todos negaban haberlo hecho, Pedro dijo:

«Maestro, la gente te oprime y empuja por todos los lados.»
⁴⁶ Pero Jesús insistió:

«Alguien me ha tocado, porque he notado que de mí ha salido poder para sanar.»
⁴⁷ La mujer, al ver que no podía ocultarse, fue temblando a arrodillarse a los pies de Jesús. Le confesó delante de todos por qué razón le había tocado y cómo había sido sanada en el acto. ⁴⁸ Jesús le dijo:

«Hija, por tu fe has sido sanada. Vete tranquila.»

[49] Todavía estaba hablando Jesús, cuando llegó un mensajero que dijo al jefe de la sinagoga:

«Tu hija ha muerto. No molestes más al Maestro.»

[50] Pero Jesús lo oyó y le dijo:

«No tengas miedo. Solamente cree y tu hija se salvará.»

[51] Al llegar a la casa, no dejó entrar con él a nadie más que a Pedro, Santiago y Juan, junto con el padre y la madre de la niña. [52] Todos lloraban y se lamentaban por ella, pero Jesús les dijo:

«No lloréis. La niña no está muerta, sino dormida.»

[53] La gente se burlaba de él, viendo que estaba muerta. [54] Entonces Jesús tomó de la mano a la niña y dijo con voz fuerte:

«¡Muchacha, levántate!»

[55] Ella volvió a la vida, y al punto se levantó; y Jesús mandó que le dieran de comer. [56] Sus padres estaban impresionados, pero Jesús les ordenó que no contaran a nadie lo que había sucedido.

Jesús instruye y envía a los apóstoles

9 Reunió Jesús a sus doce discípulos y les dio poder y autoridad para expulsar toda clase de demonios y sanar enfermedades. [2] Los envió a anunciar el reino de Dios y a sanar a los enfermos. [3] Les dijo:

«No llevéis nada para el camino: ni bastón ni bolsa ni pan ni dinero ni ropa de repuesto. [4] En cualquier casa donde entréis, quedaos hasta que os vayáis del lugar. [5] Y si en algún pueblo no os quieren recibir, salid de él y sacudíos el polvo de los pies, para que les sirva de advertencia.»

[6] Salieron, pues, y fueron por todas las aldeas anunciando la buena noticia y sanando enfermos.

La incertidumbre de Herodes

[7] El rey Herodes oyó hablar de Jesús y de todo lo que hacía. Y no sabía qué pensar, porque unos decían que era Juan, que había resucitado; [8] otros, que había aparecido el profeta Elías, y otros, que era alguno de los antiguos profetas que había resucitado. [9] Pero Herodes dijo:

«Yo mismo mandé que cortaran la cabeza a Juan. ¿Quién, pues, será este de quien oigo contar tantas cosas?»

Por eso Herodes tenía ganas de ver a Jesús.

Jesús da de comer a una multitud

[10] Cuando los apóstoles regresaron, contaron a Jesús lo que habían hecho. Él, tomándolos aparte, los llevó a un pueblo llamado Betsaida. [11] Pero cuando la gente lo supo, le siguieron; y Jesús los recibió, les habló del reino de Dios y sanó a los enfermos.

[12] Cuando ya comenzaba a hacerse tarde, se acercaron a Jesús los doce discípulos y le dijeron:

«Despide a la gente, para que vayan a descansar y a buscar comida por las aldeas y los campos cercanos, porque en este lugar no hay nada.»

[13] Jesús les dijo:

«Dadles vosotros de comer.»

Contestaron:

«No tenemos más que cinco panes y dos peces, a menos que vayamos a comprar comida para toda esta gente.»

[14] Eran unos cinco mil hombres. Pero Jesús dijo a sus discípulos:

«Haced que se sienten en grupos, como de cincuenta en cincuenta.»

[15] Así lo hicieron, y se sentaron todos. [16] Luego Jesús tomó en sus manos los cinco panes y los dos peces, y mirando al cielo dio gracias a Dios, los partió y los dio a sus discípulos para que los repartieran entre la gente. [17] La gente comió hasta quedar satisfecha, y todavía llenaron doce canastas con los trozos que sobraron.

Pedro declara que Jesús es el Mesías

[18] Un día estaba Jesús orando, él solo. Luego sus discípulos se le reunieron, y él les preguntó:

«¿Quién dice la gente que soy yo?»

[19] Ellos contestaron:

«Unos dicen que eres Juan el Bautista; otros dicen que Elías, y otros, que uno de los antiguos profetas, que ha resucitado.»

[20] «Y vosotros, ¿quién decís que soy?» les preguntó.

Pedro le respondió:

«El Mesías de Dios.»

[21] Pero Jesús les encargó mucho que no se lo dijeran a nadie.

Jesús anuncia su muerte

²² Les decía Jesús:

«El Hijo del hombre tendrá que sufrir mucho, y será rechazado por los ancianos, por los jefes de los sacerdotes y por los maestros de la ley. Lo van a matar, pero al tercer día resucitará.»

²³ Después dijo a todos:

«El que quiera ser mi discípulo, olvídese de sí mismo, cargue con su cruz cada día y sígame. ²⁴ Porque el que quiera salvar su vida la perderá; pero el que pierda su vida por causa mía, la salvará. ²⁵ ¿De qué le sirve al hombre ganar el mundo entero, si se pierde o se destruye a sí mismo? ²⁶ Pues si alguno se avergüenza de mí y de mi mensaje, también el Hijo del hombre se avergonzará de él cuando venga con su gloria y con la gloria de su Padre y de los santos ángeles. ²⁷ Os aseguro que algunos de los que están aquí no morirán sin haber visto el reino de Dios.»

Transfiguración de Jesús

²⁸ Unos ocho días después de esta conversación, Jesús subió a un monte a orar, acompañado de Pedro, Santiago y Juan. ²⁹ Mientras oraba, cambió el aspecto de su rostro y sus ropas se volvieron muy blancas y brillantes. ³⁰ Y aparecieron dos hombres conversando con él: eran Moisés y Elías, ³¹ que estaban rodeados de un resplandor glorioso y hablaban de la muerte que Jesús iba a sufrir en Jerusalén. ³² Aunque Pedro y sus compañeros tenían mucho sueño, permanecieron despiertos y vieron la gloria de Jesús y a los dos hombres que estaban con él. ³³ Cuando aquellos hombres se separaban ya de Jesús, Pedro le dijo:

«Maestro, ¡qué bien que estemos aquí! Vamos a hacer tres chozas: una para ti, otra para Moisés y otra para Elías.»

Pero Pedro no sabía lo que decía. ³⁴ Mientras hablaba, una nube los envolvió en sombra; y al verse dentro de la nube, tuvieron miedo. ³⁵ Entonces de la nube salió una voz que dijo: «Este es mi Hijo, mi elegido. Escuchadle.»

³⁶ Después que calló la voz, vieron que Jesús estaba solo. Ellos guardaron esto en secreto, y por entonces no contaron a nadie lo que habían visto.

Jesús sana a un muchacho que tenía un espíritu impuro

[37] Al día siguiente, cuando bajaron del monte, una gran multitud salió al encuentro de Jesús. [38] En esto, un hombre de en medio de la gente gritó con voz fuerte:

«¡Maestro, por favor, mira a mi hijo, el único que tengo! [39] Un espíritu se apodera de él, y de repente le hace gritar, retorcerse violentamente y echar espuma por la boca. Lo está destrozando, porque apenas se separa de él. [40] He rogado a tus discípulos que expulsen ese espíritu, pero no han podido.»

[41] Jesús contestó:

«¡Oh gente sin fe y perversa! ¿Hasta cuándo tendré que estar con vosotros y soportaros? Trae aquí a tu hijo.»

[42] Cuando el muchacho se acercaba, el demonio lo arrojó al suelo y le hizo retorcerse con violencia; pero Jesús reprendió al espíritu impuro, sanó al muchacho y lo devolvió a su padre. [43] Todos se quedaron admirados de la grandeza de Dios.

Jesús anuncia por segunda vez su muerte

Mientras todos seguían asombrados por lo que Jesús había hecho, dijo él a sus discípulos:

[44] «Oíd bien esto y no lo olvidéis: el Hijo del hombre va a ser entregado en manos de los hombres.»

[45] Pero ellos no entendían estas palabras, pues Dios no les había permitido entenderlo. Además tenían miedo de pedirle a Jesús que se las explicase.

¿Quién es el más importante?

[46] Por aquel entonces, los discípulos se pusieron a discutir quién de ellos sería el más importante.

[47] Jesús, al darse cuenta de lo que estaban pensando, tomó a un niño, lo puso junto a él [48] y les dijo:

«El que recibe a este niño en mi nombre, me recibe a mí; y el que me recibe a mí, recibe también al que me envió. Por eso, el más insignificante entre todos vosotros, ese será el más importante.»

Contra nosotros o a nuestro favor

[49] Juan le dijo:

«Maestro, hemos visto a uno que expulsaba demonios en tu nombre, pero como no es de los nuestros se lo hemos prohibido.»

[50] Jesús le contestó:

«No se lo prohibáis, porque el que no está contra nosotros está a nuestro favor.»

Jesús reprende a Santiago y Juan

[51] Cuando ya se acercaba el tiempo en que Jesús había de subir al cielo, emprendió con valor su viaje a Jerusalén. [52] Envió por delante mensajeros, que fueron a una aldea de Samaria para prepararle alojamiento; [53] pero los samaritanos no quisieron recibirle, porque se daban cuenta de que se dirigía a Jerusalén. [54] Cuando sus discípulos Santiago y Juan vieron esto le dijeron:

«Señor, si quieres, diremos que baje fuego del cielo para que acabe con ellos.»

[55] Pero Jesús se volvió y los reprendió. [56] Luego se fueron a otra aldea.

Los que querían seguir a Jesús

[57] Mientras iban de camino, un hombre dijo a Jesús:

«Señor, deseo seguirte adondequiera que vayas.»

[58] Jesús le contestó:

«Las zorras tienen cuevas y las aves nidos, pero el Hijo del hombre no tiene donde recostar la cabeza.»

[59] Jesús dijo a otro:

«Sígueme.»

Pero él respondió:

«Señor, déjame ir primero a enterrar a mi padre.»

[60] Jesús le contestó:

«Deja que los muertos entierren a sus muertos. Tú ve y anuncia el reino de Dios.»

[61] Otro le dijo:

«Señor, quiero seguirte, pero deja que primero me despida de los míos.»

[62] Jesús le contestó:

«El que pone la mano en el arado y vuelve la vista atrás, no sirve para el reino de Dios.»

Los setenta y dos enviados

10 Después de esto escogió también el Señor a otros setenta y dos, y los mandó delante de él, de dos en dos, a todos los pueblos y lugares a donde tenía que ir.

[2] Les dijo: «Ciertamente la mies es mucha, pero los obreros son pocos. Por eso, pedidle al Dueño de la mies que mande obreros a recogerla. [3] Andad y ved que os envío como a corderos en medio de lobos. [4] No llevéis bolsa ni monedero ni sandalias, y no os detengáis a saludar a nadie en el camino. [5] Cuando entréis en una casa, saludad primero diciendo: "Paz a esta casa." [6] Si en ella hay gente de paz, vuestro deseo de paz se cumplirá; si no, no se cumplirá. [7] Y quedaos en la misma casa, comiendo y bebiendo lo que tengan, pues el obrero tiene derecho a su salario. No andéis de casa en casa. [8] Al llegar a un pueblo donde os reciban bien, comed lo que os ofrezcan; [9] y sanad a los enfermos del lugar y decidles: "El reino de Dios ya está cerca de vosotros." [10] Pero si llegáis a un pueblo y no os reciben, salid a las calles diciendo: [11] "¡Hasta el polvo de vuestro pueblo que se ha pegado a nuestros pies nos lo sacudimos en protesta contra vosotros! Pero sabed que el reino de Dios está cerca." [12] Os digo que, en aquel día, el castigo de ese pueblo será más duro que el de los habitantes de Sodoma.»

Reproches contra las ciudades incrédulas

[13] «¡Ay de ti, Corazín! ¡Ay de ti, Betsaida! Porque si en Tiro y Sidón se hubieran hecho los milagros que se han hecho entre vosotras, ya hace tiempo que su gente se habría vuelto a Dios y lo habría demostrado poniéndose ropas ásperas y sentándose en ceniza. [14] Pero en el día del juicio el castigo para vosotras será peor que para la gente de Tiro y Sidón. [15] Y tú, Cafarnaum, ¿crees que serás levantada hasta el cielo? ¡Hasta lo más hondo del abismo serás arrojada!

[16] «El que os escucha a vosotros me escucha a mí, y el que os rechaza a vosotros me rechaza a mí; y el que a mí me rechaza, rechaza al que me envió.»

El regreso de los setenta y dos

[17] Los setenta y dos regresaron muy contentos, diciendo:

«¡Señor, hasta los demonios nos obedecen en tu nombre!»

[18] Jesús les dijo:

«Sí, pues yo veía a Satanás caer del cielo como un rayo. [19] Os he dado poder para que pisoteéis serpientes y alacranes, y para que triunféis sobre toda la fuerza del enemigo sin sufrir ningún daño. [20] Pero no os alegréis de que los espíritus os obedezcan, sino de que vuestros nombres ya estén escritos en el cielo.»

Solo el Hijo sabe quién es el Padre

[21] En aquel momento, Jesús, lleno de alegría por el Espíritu Santo, dijo: «Te alabo, Padre, Señor del cielo y de la tierra, porque has mostrado a los sencillos las cosas que ocultaste a los sabios y entendidos. Sí, Padre, porque así lo has querido.

[22] «Mi Padre me ha entregado todas las cosas. Nadie sabe quién es el Hijo, sino el Padre; y nadie sabe quién es el Padre, sino el Hijo y aquellos a quienes el Hijo quiera darlo a conocer.»

[23] Volviéndose a los discípulos les dijo aparte: «Dichosos quienes vean lo que estáis viendo vosotros, [24] porque os digo que muchos profetas y reyes desearon ver lo que vosotros veis, y no lo vieron; desearon oír lo que vosotros oís, y no lo oyeron.»

Parábola del buen samaritano

[25] Un maestro de la ley fue a hablar con Jesús, y para ponerle a prueba le preguntó:

«Maestro, ¿qué debo hacer para alcanzar la vida eterna?»

[26] Jesús le contestó:

«¿Qué está escrito en la ley? ¿Qué lees en ella?»

[27] El maestro de la ley respondió:

«"Ama al Señor tu Dios con todo tu corazón, con toda tu alma, con todas tus fuerzas y con toda tu mente; y ama a tu prójimo como a ti mismo."»

[28] Jesús le dijo:

«Bien contestado. Haz eso y tendrás la vida.»

²⁹ Pero el maestro de la ley, queriendo justificar su pregunta, dijo a Jesús:

«¿Y quién es mi prójimo?»

³⁰ Jesús le respondió:

«Un hombre que bajaba por el camino de Jerusalén a Jericó fue asaltado por unos bandidos. Le quitaron hasta la ropa que llevaba puesta, le golpearon y se fueron dejándolo medio muerto. ³¹ Casualmente pasó un sacerdote por aquel mismo camino, pero al ver al herido dio un rodeo y siguió adelante. ³² Luego pasó por allí un levita, que al verlo dio también un rodeo y siguió adelante. ³³ Finalmente, un hombre de Samaria que viajaba por el mismo camino, le vio y sintió compasión de él. ³⁴ Se le acercó, le curó las heridas con aceite y vino, y se las vendó. Luego lo montó en su propia cabalgadura, lo llevó a una posada y cuidó de él. ³⁵ Al día siguiente, el samaritano sacó dos denarios, se los dio al posadero y le dijo: "Cuida a este hombre. Si gastas más, te lo pagaré a mi regreso." ³⁶ Pues bien, ¿cuál de aquellos tres te parece que fue el prójimo del hombre asaltado por los bandidos?»

³⁷ El maestro de la ley contestó:

«El que tuvo compasión de él.»

Jesús le dijo:

«Ve, pues, y haz tú lo mismo.»

Jesús en casa de Marta y María

³⁸ Seguían ellos su camino. Jesús entró en una aldea, donde una mujer llamada Marta le recibió en su casa. ³⁹ Marta tenía una hermana llamada María, la cual, sentada a los pies de Jesús, escuchaba sus palabras. ⁴⁰ Pero Marta, atareada con sus muchos quehaceres, se acercó a Jesús y le dijo:

«Señor, ¿no te importa que mi hermana me deje sola con todo el trabajo? Dile que me ayude.»

⁴¹ Jesús le contestó:

«Marta, Marta, estás preocupada e inquieta por muchas cosas; ⁴² sin embargo, solo una es necesaria. María ha escogido la mejor parte, y nadie se la quitará.»

Jesús y la oración

11 Estaba Jesús una vez orando en cierto lugar. Cuando terminó, uno de sus discípulos le rogó:

«Señor, enséñanos a orar, lo mismo que Juan enseñaba a sus discípulos.»

² Jesús les contestó:

«Cuando oréis, decid:

"Padre, santificado sea tu nombre.

Venga tu reino.

³ Danos cada día el pan que necesitamos.

⁴ Perdónanos nuestros pecados, porque también nosotros perdonamos a todos los que nos han ofendido.

Y no nos expongas a la tentación."»

⁵ También les dijo Jesús:

«Supongamos que uno de vosotros tiene un amigo, y que a medianoche va a su casa y le dice: "Amigo, préstame tres panes, ⁶ porque otro amigo mío acaba de llegar de viaje a mi casa y no tengo nada que ofrecerle." ⁷ Sin duda, aquel le contestará desde dentro: "¡No me molestes! La puerta está cerrada y mis hijos y yo estamos acostados. No puedo levantarme a darte nada." ⁸ Pues bien, os digo que aunque no se levante a dárselo por ser su amigo, se levantará por serle importuno y le dará cuanto necesite. ⁹ Por esto os digo: Pedid y Dios os dará, buscad y encontraréis, llamad a la puerta y se os abrirá. ¹⁰ Porque el que pide recibe, el que busca encuentra y al que llama a la puerta se le abre.

¹¹ «¿Acaso algún padre entre vosotros sería capaz de darle a su hijo una culebra cuando le pide pescado? ¹² ¿O de darle un alacrán cuando le pide un huevo? ¹³ Pues si vosotros, que sois malos, sabéis dar cosas buenas a vuestros hijos, ¡cuánto más el Padre que está en el cielo dará el Espíritu Santo a quienes se lo pidan!»

Acusación contra Jesús

¹⁴ Jesús estaba expulsando un demonio que había dejado mudo a un hombre. Cuando el demonio salió, el mudo comenzó a hablar. La gente se quedó asombrada, ¹⁵ aunque algunos dijeron:

«Beelzebú, el jefe de los demonios, es quien ha dado a este hombre poder para expulsarlos.»

¹⁶ Otros, para tenderle una trampa, le pidieron una señal milagrosa del cielo. ¹⁷ Pero él, que sabía lo que estaban pensando, les dijo:

«Todo país dividido en bandos enemigos se destruye a sí mismo, y sus casas se derrumban una tras otra. ¹⁸ Así también, si Satanás se divide contra sí mismo, ¿cómo mantendrá su poder? Digo esto porque afirmáis que yo expulso a los demonios por el poder de Beelzebú. ¹⁹ Pues si yo expulso a los demonios por el poder de Beelzebú, ¿quién da a vuestros seguidores el poder para expulsarlos? Por eso, ellos mismos demuestran que estáis equivocados. ²⁰ Pero si yo expulso a los demonios por el poder de Dios, es que el reino de Dios ya ha llegado a vosotros.

²¹ «Cuando un hombre fuerte y bien armado cuida de su casa, lo que guarda en ella está seguro. ²² Pero si otro más fuerte que él llega y le vence, le quita las armas en las que confiaba y reparte sus bienes como botín.

²³ «El que no está conmigo está contra mí; y el que conmigo no recoge, desparrama.

El regreso de un espíritu impuro

²⁴ «Cuando un espíritu impuro sale de un hombre, anda por lugares desiertos en busca de descanso; pero, no encontrándolo, piensa: "Regresaré a mi casa, de donde salí." ²⁵ Al llegar, encuentra la casa barrida y arreglada. ²⁶ Entonces va y reúne otros siete espíritus peores que él y todos juntos se meten a vivir en aquel hombre, que al final queda peor que al principio.»

Lo que realmente cuenta

²⁷ Mientras Jesús decía estas cosas, una mujer gritó de en medio de la gente:

«¡Dichosa la mujer que te dio a luz y te crió!»

²⁸ El contestó:

«¡Dichosos más bien los que escuchan el mensaje de Dios y le obedecen!»

Algunos piden una señal milagrosa

²⁹ La multitud seguía juntándose alrededor de Jesús, y él comenzó a decirles:

«La gente de este tiempo es malvada. Pide una señal milagrosa, pero no se le dará otra señal que la de Jonás. [30] Porque así como Jonás fue señal para la gente de Nínive, así también el Hijo del hombre será señal para la gente de este tiempo. [31] En el día del juicio, cuando se juzgue a la gente de este tiempo, la reina del Sur se levantará y la condenará; porque ella vino de lo más lejano de la tierra para escuchar la sabiduría de Salomón, y lo que hay aquí es más que Salomón. [32] También los habitantes de Nínive se levantarán en el día del juicio, cuando se juzgue a la gente de este tiempo, y la condenarán; porque los de Nínive se convirtieron a Dios cuando oyeron el mensaje de Jonás, y lo que hay aquí es más que Jonás.

La lámpara del cuerpo

[33] «Nadie enciende una lámpara y la pone en un lugar escondido o debajo de una vasija, sino en alto, para que los que entran tengan luz. [34] Tus ojos son como la lámpara del cuerpo. Si tus ojos son buenos, todo tu cuerpo será luminoso; pero si son malos, tu cuerpo será oscuridad. [35] Ten cuidado de que la luz que hay en ti no resulte oscuridad. [36] Pues si todo tu cuerpo es luminoso y no hay oscuridad en él, todo en ti será tan claro como cuando una lámpara te alumbra con su luz.»

Jesús denuncia a los fariseos y a los maestros de la ley

[37] Cuando Jesús dejó de hablar, un fariseo le invitó a comer en su casa. Jesús entró y se sentó a la mesa. [38] Y como el fariseo se extrañase al ver que no había cumplido con el rito de lavarse las manos antes de comer, [39] el Señor le dijo:

«Vosotros los fariseos limpiáis por fuera el vaso y el plato, pero por dentro estáis llenos de lo que habéis obtenido mediante el robo y la maldad. [40] ¡Necios!, ¿no sabéis que el que hizo lo de fuera hizo también lo de dentro? [41] Dad vuestras limosnas de lo que está dentro y así todo quedará limpio.

[42] «¡Ay de vosotros, fariseos!, que separáis para Dios la décima parte de la menta, de la ruda y de toda clase de legumbres, pero no hacéis caso de la justicia y el amor a Dios. Esto es lo que se debe hacer, sin dejar de hacer lo otro.

[43] «¡Ay de vosotros, fariseos!, que deseáis los asientos de honor en las sinagogas y ser saludados con todo respeto en la calle.

[44] «¡Ay de vosotros, que sois como esas tumbas ocultas a la vista, que la gente pisotea sin darse cuenta!»

[45] Uno de los maestros de la ley le contestó entonces:

«Maestro, al decir esto nos ofendes también a nosotros.»

[46] Pero Jesús dijo:

«¡Ay también de vosotros, maestros de la ley!, que cargáis a los demás con cargas insoportables y vosotros ni siquiera con un dedo queréis tocarlas.

[47] «¡Ay de vosotros!, que construís los sepulcros de los profetas que mataron vuestros antepasados. [48] Con eso dais a entender que estáis de acuerdo con lo que vuestros antepasados hicieron, pues ellos los mataron y vosotros construís sus sepulcros.

[49] «Por eso, Dios dijo en su sabiduría: "Les mandaré profetas y apóstoles; a unos los matarán y a otros los perseguirán." [50] Dios pedirá cuentas a la gente de hoy de la sangre de todos los profetas que fueron asesinados desde la creación del mundo, [51] desde la sangre de Abel hasta la de Zacarías, a quien mataron entre el altar y el santuario. Sí, os digo que Dios pedirá cuentas de la muerte de ellos a la gente de hoy.

[52] «¡Ay de vosotros, maestros de la ley!, que os habéis apoderado de la llave de la ciencia, y ni vosotros entráis ni dejáis entrar a los que quieren hacerlo.»

[53] Cuando Jesús les dijo estas cosas, los maestros de la ley y los fariseos se llenaron de ira y comenzaron a molestarle con muchas preguntas, [54] tendiéndole trampas para cazarlo en alguna palabra.

Jesús instruye contra la hipocresía

12 Se juntaron entre tanto miles de personas, que se atropellaban unas a otras. Jesús comenzó a hablar, dirigiéndose primero a sus discípulos: «Guardaos de la levadura de los fariseos, es decir, de su hipocresía. [2] Porque no hay nada secreto que no llegue a descubrirse, ni nada oculto que no llegue a conocerse. [3] Por tanto, todo lo que habéis dicho en la oscuridad se oirá a la luz del día; y lo que habéis dicho en secreto y a puerta cerrada será pregonado desde las azoteas de las casas.

A quién se debe tener miedo

⁴ «A vosotros, amigos míos, os digo que no debéis tener miedo a quienes pueden matar el cuerpo, pero después no pueden hacer más. ⁵ Os voy a decir a quién debéis tener miedo: tened miedo a aquel que, además de quitar la vida, tiene poder para arrojar en el infierno. Sí, tenedle miedo a él.

⁶ «¿No se venden cinco pajarillos por dos pequeñas monedas? Sin embargo, Dios no se olvida de ninguno de ellos. ⁷ En cuanto a vosotros mismos, hasta los cabellos de la cabeza los tenéis contados uno por uno. Así que no tengáis miedo: vosotros valéis más que muchos pajarillos.

Reconocer a Jesucristo delante de los hombres

⁸ «Os digo que si alguien se declara a favor mío delante de los hombres, también el Hijo del hombre se declarará a favor suyo delante de los ángeles de Dios; ⁹ pero el que me niegue delante de los hombres, será negado delante de los ángeles de Dios.

¹⁰ «Dios perdonará incluso a aquel que diga algo contra el Hijo del hombre, pero no perdonará al que con sus palabras ofenda al Espíritu Santo.

¹¹ «Cuando os lleven a las sinagogas o ante los jueces y las autoridades, no os preocupéis por cómo tenéis que defenderos o qué tenéis que decir; ¹² porque en el momento en que hayáis de hablar, el Espíritu Santo os enseñará lo que habéis de decir.»

El peligro de las riquezas

¹³ Uno de entre la gente dijo a Jesús.

«Maestro, dile a mi hermano que reparta conmigo la herencia.»
¹⁴ Jesús le contestó:

«Amigo, ¿quién me ha puesto sobre vosotros como juez o partidor?»
¹⁵ También dijo:

«Guardaos de toda avaricia, porque la vida no depende del poseer muchas cosas.»

¹⁶ Entonces les contó esta parábola: «Había un hombre rico, cuyas tierras dieron una gran cosecha. ¹⁷ El rico se puso a pensar: "¿Qué haré? ¡No tengo donde guardar mi cosecha!" ¹⁸ Y se dijo: "Ya sé qué voy

a hacer: derribaré mis graneros y construiré otros más grandes en los que guardar toda mi cosecha y mis bienes. ¹⁹ Luego me diré: Amigo, ya tienes muchos bienes guardados para muchos años; descansa, come, bebe y goza de la vida." ²⁰ Pero Dios le dijo: "Necio, vas a morir esta misma noche: ¿para quién será lo que tienes guardado?" ²¹ Eso le pasa al hombre que acumula riquezas para sí mismo, pero no es rico delante de Dios.»

Dios cuida de sus hijos

²² Después dijo Jesús a sus discípulos: «Por tanto os digo: No estéis preocupados por lo que habéis de comer para vivir, ni por la ropa con que habéis de cubrir vuestro cuerpo. ²³ La vida vale más que la comida, y el cuerpo, más que la ropa. ²⁴ Fijaos en los cuervos: no siembran, ni siegan, ni tienen almacén ni granero. Sin embargo, Dios les da de comer. ¡Cuánto más valéis vosotros que las aves! ²⁵ De todos modos, por mucho que uno se preocupe, ¿cómo podrá prolongar su vida ni siquiera una hora? ²⁶ Pues si no podéis hacer ni aun lo más pequeño, ¿por qué preocuparos por las demás cosas?

²⁷ «Fijaos cómo crecen los lirios: no trabajan ni hilan. Sin embargo, os digo que ni aun el rey Salomón, con todo su lujo, se vestía como uno de ellos. ²⁸ Pues si Dios viste así a la hierba, que hoy está en el campo y mañana se quema en el horno, ¡cuánto más habrá de vestiros a vosotros, gente falta de fe! ²⁹ Por tanto, no andéis afligidos buscando qué comer y qué beber. ³⁰ Porque todas esas cosas preocupan a la gente del mundo, pero vosotros tenéis un Padre que ya sabe que las necesitáis. ³¹ Buscad el reino de Dios y esas cosas se os darán por añadidura.

Riquezas en el cielo

³² «No tengáis miedo, pequeño rebaño, que el Padre, en su bondad, ha decidido daros el reino. ³³ Vended lo que tenéis y dad a los necesitados; procuraos bolsas que no envejezcan, riquezas sin fin en el cielo, donde el ladrón no puede entrar ni la polilla destruye. ³⁴ Pues donde esté vuestra riqueza, allí estará también vuestro corazón.

Hay que estar preparados

³⁵ «Estad preparados y mantened vuestras lámparas encendidas. ³⁶ Sed como criados que esperan que su amo regrese de una boda, para

abrirle la puerta tan pronto como llegue y llame. [37] ¡Dichosos los cria
dos a quienes su amo, al llegar, encuentre despiertos! Os aseguro que
los hará sentar a la mesa y se dispondrá a servirles la comida. [38] Dichosos ellos, si los encuentra despiertos aunque llegue a medianoche
o de madrugada. [39] Y pensad que si el dueño de la casa supiera a qué
hora va a llegar el ladrón, no dejaría que se la abrieran para robarle.
[40] Estad también vosotros preparados, porque el Hijo del hombre
vendrá cuando menos lo esperéis.»

La fidelidad y la infidelidad en el servicio

[41] Pedro le preguntó:

«Señor, ¿has contado esta parábola solo para nosotros, o para todos?»

[42] Dijo el Señor: «¿Quién es el mayordomo fiel y atento, a quien su
amo deja al cargo de la servidumbre para repartirles la comida a su
debido tiempo? [43] ¡Dichoso el criado a quien su amo, al llegar, encuentra cumpliendo con su deber! [44] De verdad os digo que el amo le
pondrá al cargo de todos sus bienes. [45] Pero si ese criado, pensando
que su amo va a tardar en volver, comienza a maltratar a los demás
criados y a las criadas, y se pone a comer, beber y emborracharse, [46] el
día que menos lo espera y a una hora que no sabe llegará su amo y lo
castigará. Le condenará a correr la misma suerte que los infieles.

[47] «El criado que sabe lo que quiere su amo, pero no está preparado ni le obedece, será castigado con muchos golpes. [48] Pero el criado
que por ignorancia hace cosas que merecen castigo, será castigado
con menos golpes. A quien mucho se le da, también se le pedirá mucho; a quien mucho se le confía, se le exigirá mucho más.

Jesús, causa de división

[49] «He venido a encender fuego en el mundo, ¡y cómo querría que
ya estuviera ardiendo! [50] Tengo que pasar por una terrible prueba, ¡y
cómo he de sufrir hasta que haya terminado! [51] ¿Creéis que he venido
a traer paz a la tierra? Pues os digo que no, sino división. [52] Porque, de
ahora en adelante, cinco en una familia estarán divididos, tres contra
dos y dos contra tres. [53] El padre estará contra su hijo y el hijo contra
su padre; la madre contra su hija y la hija contra su madre; la suegra
contra su nuera y la nuera contra su suegra.»

Las señales de los tiempos

[54] Jesús dijo también a la gente: «Cuando veis que las nubes aparecen por occidente, decís que va a llover, y así sucede. [55] Y cuando el viento sopla del sur, decís que va a hacer calor, y lo hace. [56] ¡Hipócritas!, si sabéis interpretar tan bien el aspecto del cielo y de la tierra, ¿cómo no sabéis interpretar el tiempo en que vivís?

Ponerse en paz con el enemigo

[57] «¿Por qué no juzgas por ti mismo lo que es justo? [58] Si alguien te demanda ante las autoridades, procura llegar a un acuerdo con él mientras aún estés a tiempo, para que no te lleve ante el juez; porque si no, el juez te entregará a los guardias y los guardias te meterán en la cárcel. [59] Te digo que no saldrás de allí hasta que pagues el último céntimo.»

Importancia de la conversión

13 Por aquel mismo tiempo fueron unos a ver a Jesús, y le contaron que Pilato había matado a ciertos hombres de Galilea y había mezclado su sangre con la de los animales ofrecidos por ellos en sacrificio.

[2] Jesús les dijo: «¿Pensáis que aquellos galileos murieron así por ser más pecadores que los demás galileos? [3] Os digo que no, y que si vosotros no os volvéis a Dios, también moriréis. [4] ¿O creéis que aquellos dieciocho que murieron cuando la torre de Siloé les cayó encima, eran más culpables que los demás que vivían en Jerusalén? [5] Os digo que no, y que si vosotros no os volvéis a Dios, también moriréis.»

Parábola de la higuera sin fruto

[6] Jesús les contó esta parábola: «Un hombre había plantado una higuera en su viña, pero cuando fue a ver si tenía higos no encontró ninguno. [7] Así que dijo al hombre que cuidaba la viña: "Mira, hace tres años que vengo a esta higuera en busca de fruto, pero nunca lo encuentro. Córtala. ¿Para qué ha de ocupar terreno inútilmente?" [8] Pero el que cuidaba la viña le contestó: "Señor, déjala todavía este año. Cavaré la tierra a su alrededor y le echaré abono. [9] Con eso, tal vez dé fruto; y si no, ya la cortarás."»

Jesús sana en sábado a una mujer enferma

[10] Un sábado se puso Jesús a enseñar en una sinagoga. [11] Había allí una mujer que estaba enferma desde hacía dieciocho años. Un espíritu maligno la había dejado encorvada, y no podía enderezarse para nada. [12] Cuando Jesús la vio, la llamó y le dijo:

«Mujer, ya estás libre de tu enfermedad.»

[13] Puso las manos sobre ella, y al momento la mujer se enderezó y comenzó a alabar a Dios. [14] Pero el jefe de la sinagoga, enojado porque Jesús la había sanado en sábado, dijo a la gente:

«Hay seis días para trabajar: venid cualquiera de ellos a ser sanados, y no el sábado.»

[15] El Señor le contestó:

«Hipócritas, ¿no desata cualquiera de vosotros su buey o su asno en sábado, para llevarlo a beber? [16] Pues a esta mujer, que es descendiente de Abraham y que Satanás tenía atada con esa enfermedad desde hace dieciocho años, ¿acaso no se la debía desatar aunque sea en sábado?»

[17] Cuando Jesús dijo esto, sus enemigos quedaron avergonzados; pero toda la gente se alegraba viendo las grandes cosas que él hacía.

Parábola de la semilla de mostaza

[18] Jesús decía: «¿A qué se parece el reino de Dios y a qué podré compararlo? [19] Es como una semilla de mostaza que un hombre siembra en su campo, y que crece hasta llegar a ser como un árbol tan grande que las aves anidan entre sus ramas.»

Parábola de la levadura

[20] También dijo Jesús: «¿A qué podré comparar el reino de Dios? [21] Es como la levadura que una mujer mezcla con tres medidas de harina para que toda la masa fermente.»

La puerta angosta

[22] En su camino a Jerusalén, Jesús enseñaba en los pueblos y aldeas por donde pasaba. [23] Alguien le preguntó:

«Señor, ¿son pocos los que se salvan?»

Él contestó:

²⁴ «Procurad entrar por la puerta estrecha, porque os digo que muchos querrán entrar y no podrán. ²⁵ Después que el dueño de la casa se levante y cierre la puerta, vosotros, los que estáis fuera, llamaréis y diréis: "¡Señor, ábrenos!" Pero él os contestará: "No sé de dónde sois." ²⁶ Entonces comenzaréis a decir: "Hemos comido y bebido contigo, y tú enseñaste en nuestras calles." ²⁷ Pero él os contestará: "Ya os digo que no sé de dónde sois. ¡Apartaos de mí, malhechores!" ²⁸ Allí lloraréis y os rechinarán los dientes al ver que Abraham, Isaac, Jacob y todos los profetas están en el reino de Dios, y que vosotros sois echados fuera. ²⁹ Porque vendrá gente del norte, del sur, del este y del oeste, y se sentará a la mesa en el reino de Dios. ³⁰ Y mira d, algunos de los que ahora son los últimos serán los primeros; y algunos que ahora son los primeros serán los últimos.»

Jesús llora por Jerusalén

³¹ También entonces llegaron algunos fariseos, a decirle a Jesús:

«Vete de aquí, porque Herodes te quiere matar.»

³² Él les contestó:

«Id y decidle a ese zorro: "Mira, hoy y mañana expulso a los demonios y sano a los enfermos, y pasado mañana termino." ³³ Pero tengo que seguir mi camino hoy, mañana y al día siguiente, porque no es posible que un profeta muera fuera de Jerusalén.

³⁴ «¡Jerusalén, Jerusalén, que matas a los profetas y apedreas a los mensajeros que Dios te envía! ¡Cuántas veces quise reunir a tus hijos como la gallina reúne a sus polluelos bajo las alas, pero no quisisteis! ³⁵ Pues mirad, vuestro hogar va a quedar desierto. Y os digo que no volveréis a verme hasta que llegue el tiempo en que digáis:

"¡Bendito el que viene en el nombre del Señor!"»

Jesús sana a un enfermo de hidropesía

14 Sucedió que un sábado fue Jesús a comer a casa de un jefe fariseo, y otros fariseos le estaban espiando. ² Había allí, delante de él, un hombre enfermo de hidropesía. ³ Jesús preguntó a los maestros de la ley y a los fariseos:

«¿Está permitido sanar a un enfermo en sábado, o no?»

⁴ Pero ellos se quedaron callados. Entonces Jesús tomó al enfermo, lo sanó y lo despidió. ⁵ Y dijo a los fariseos:

« ¿Quién de vosotros, si su hijo o su buey cae a un pozo, no lo saca en seguida aunque sea sábado?»

[6] Y no pudieron contestarle nada.

Normas de comportamiento

[7] Al ver Jesús que los invitados escogían los asientos de honor en la mesa, les dio este consejo:

[8] «Cuando alguien te invite a una fiesta de bodas, no te sientes en el lugar principal, no sea que llegue otro invitado más importante que tú, [9] y el que os invitó a los dos venga a decirte: "Deja tu sitio a este otro." Entonces tendrás que ir con vergüenza a ocupar el último asiento. [10] Al contrario, cuando te inviten, siéntate en el último lugar, para que cuando venga el que te invitó te diga: "Amigo, pásate a este sitio de más categoría." Así quedarás muy bien delante de los que están sentados contigo a la mesa. [11] Porque el que a sí mismo se engrandece será humillado, y el que se humilla será engrandecido.»

[12] Dijo también al hombre que le había invitado:

«Cuando des una comida o una cena, no invites a tus amigos, a tus hermanos, a tus parientes o a tus vecinos ricos; porque ellos a su vez te invitarán, y quedarás así recompensado.

[13] «Al contrario, cuando des una fiesta, invita a los pobres, a los inválidos, a los cojos y a los ciegos; [14] así serás feliz, porque ellos no te pueden pagar, pero tú recibirás tu recompensa cuando los justos resuciten.»

Parábola de la gran cena

[15] Al oir esto, uno de los que estaban sentados a la mesa dijo a Jesús:

«¡Dichoso el que tenga parte en el banquete del reino de Dios!»

[16] Jesús le dijo:

«Un hombre dio una gran cena e invitó a muchos. [17] A la hora de la cena envió a su criado a decir a los invitados: "Venid, que ya está todo preparado." [18] Pero ellos comenzaron a una a excusarse. El primero dijo: "Acabo de comprar un campo y tengo que ir a verlo. Te ruego que me disculpes." [19] Otro dijo: "He comprado cinco yuntas de bueyes y he de probarlas. Te ruego que me disculpes." [20] Y otro dijo: "No puedo ir, porque acabo de casarme." [21] El criado regresó y se lo contó todo a su amo. Entonces el amo, indignado, dijo a su criado: "Sal en seguida a las calles y callejas de la ciudad, y trae acá a los pobres, a los inválidos, a los ciegos y a los cojos." ²² Volvió el criado, diciendo: "Señor, he hecho lo que me mandaste y aún queda sitio." ²³ Y el amo le contestó: "Ve por los caminos y cercados y obliga a otros a entrar, para que se llene mi casa. ²⁴ Porque os digo que ninguno de aquellos primeros invitados comerá de mi cena." »

Lo que cuesta seguir a Cristo

²⁵ Jesús iba de camino acompañado por mucha gente. En esto se volvió y dijo: ²⁶ «Si alguno no me ama más que a su padre, a su madre, a su esposa, a sus hijos, a sus hermanos y a sus hermanas, y aun más que a sí mismo, no puede ser mi discípulo. ²⁷ Y el que no toma su propia cruz y me sigue, no puede ser mi discípulo. ²⁸ Si alguno de vosotros quiere construir una torre, ¿acaso no se sentará primero a calcular los gastos y ver si tiene dinero para terminarla? ²⁹ No sea que, una vez puestos los cimientos, si no puede terminarla, todos los que lo vean comiencen a burlarse de él, ³⁰ diciendo: "Este hombre empezó a construir, pero no pudo terminar." ³¹ O si un rey tiene que ir a la guerra contra otro rey, ¿no se sentará primero a calcular si con diez mil soldados podrá hacer frente a quien va a atacarle con veinte mil? ³² Y si no puede hacerle frente, cuando el otro rey esté todavía lejos le enviará mensajeros a pedirle la paz. ³³ Así pues, cualquiera de vosotros que no renuncie a todo lo que tiene no puede ser mi discípulo.

Cuando la sal deja de ser salada

³⁴ «La sal es buena; pero si deja de ser salada, ¿cómo volverá a ser útil? ³⁵ No sirve ya ni para la tierra ni como abono. Simplemente se la tira. Los que tienen oídos, oigan.»

Parábola del pastor que encuentra a su oveja

15 Todos los que cobraban impuestos para Roma, y otras gentes de mala fama, se acercaban a escuchar a Jesús. ² Y los fariseos y maestros de la ley le criticaban diciendo:

«Este recibe a los pecadores y come con ellos.»

³ Entonces Jesús les contó esta parábola: ⁴ «¿Quién de vosotros, si tiene cien ovejas y pierde una de ellas, no deja las otras noventa y nue-

ve en el campo y va en busca de la oveja perdida, hasta encontrarla?
[5] Y cuando la encuentra la pone contento sobre sus hombros, [6] y al llegar a casa junta a sus amigos y vecinos y les dice: "¡Felicitadme, porque ya he encontrado la oveja que se me había perdido!" [7] Os digo que hay también más alegría en el cielo por un pecador que se convierte, que por noventa y nueve justos que no necesitan convertirse.

Parábola de la mujer que encuentra su moneda

[8] «O bien, ¿qué mujer que tiene diez monedas y pierde una, no enciende una lámpara y barre la casa y busca con cuidado hasta encontrarla? [9] Y cuando la encuentra reúne a sus amigas y vecinas y les dice: "¡Felicitadme, porque ya he encontrado la moneda que había perdido!" [10] Os digo que así también hay alegría entre los ángeles de Dios por un pecador que se convierte.»

Parábola del padre que recobra a su hijo

[11] Contó Jesús esta otra parábola: «Un hombre tenía dos hijos. [12] El más joven le dijo: "Padre, dame la parte de la herencia que me corresponde." Y el padre repartió los bienes entre ellos. [13] Pocos días después, el hijo menor vendió su parte y se marchó lejos, a otro país, donde todo lo derrochó viviendo de manera desenfrenada. [14] Cuando ya no le quedaba nada, vino sobre aquella tierra una época de hambre terrible y él comenzó a pasar necesidad. [15] Fue a pedirle trabajo a uno del lugar, que le mandó a sus campos a cuidar cerdos. [16] Y él deseaba llenar el estómago de las algarrobas que comían los cerdos, pero nadie se las daba. [17] Al fin se puso a pensar: "¡Cuántos trabajadores en la casa de mi padre tienen comida de sobra, mientras que aquí yo me muero de hambre! [18] Volveré a la casa de mi padre y le diré: Padre, he pecado contra Dios y contra ti, [19] y ya no merezco llamarme tu hijo: trátame como a uno de tus trabajadores." [20] Así que se puso en camino y regresó a casa de su padre.

«Todavía estaba lejos, cuando su padre le vio; y sintiendo compasión de él corrió a su encuentro y le recibió con abrazos y besos. [21] El hijo le dijo: "Padre, he pecado contra Dios y contra ti, y ya no merezco llamarme tu hijo." [22] Pero el padre ordenó a sus criados: "Sacad en seguida las mejores ropas y vestidlo; ponedle también un anillo en el dedo y sandalias en los pies. ²³ Traed el becerro cebado y matadlo. ¡Vamos a comer y a hacer fiesta, ²⁴ porque este hijo mío estaba muerto y ha vuelto a vivir; se había perdido y le hemos encontrado!" Y comenzaron, pues, a hacer fiesta.

²⁵ «Entre tanto, el hijo mayor se hallaba en el campo. Al regresar, llegando ya cerca de la casa, oyó la música y el baile. ²⁶ Llamó a uno de los criados y le preguntó qué pasaba, ²⁷ y el criado le contestó: "Tu hermano ha vuelto, y tu padre ha mandado matar el becerro cebado, porque ha venido sano y salvo." ²⁸ Tanto irritó esto al hermano mayor, que no quería entrar; así que su padre tuvo que salir a rogarle que lo hiciese. ²⁹ Él respondió a su padre: "Tú sabes cuántos años te he servido, sin desobedecerte nunca, y jamás me has dado ni siquiera un cabrito para hacer fiesta con mis amigos. ³⁰ En cambio, llega ahora este hijo tuyo, que ha malgastado tu dinero con prostitutas, y matas para él el becerro cebado."

³¹ «El padre le contestó: "Hijo, tú siempre estás conmigo y todo lo mío es tuyo. ³² Pero ahora debemos hacer fiesta y alegrarnos, porque tu hermano, que estaba muerto, ha vuelto a vivir; se había perdido y lo hemos encontrado."»

Parábola del mayordomo astuto

16 Jesús contó también esto a sus discípulos: «Un hombre rico tenía un administrador que fue acusado de malversación de bienes. ² El amo le llamó y le dijo: "¿Qué es eso que me dicen de ti? Dame cuenta de tu trabajo porque no puedes seguir siendo mi administrador." ³ El administrador se puso a pensar: "¿Qué haré ahora que el amo me deja sin empleo? No tengo fuerzas para cavar la tierra, y me da vergüenza pedir limosna... ⁴ Ah, ya sé qué hacer para que haya quienes me reciban en sus casas cuando me quede sin trabajo." ⁵ Llamó entonces uno por uno a los que tenían alguna deuda con el amo, y preguntó al primero: "¿Cuánto debes a mi amo?" ⁶ Le contestó: "Cien barriles de aceite." El administrador le dijo: "Aquí está tu recibo. Siéntate en seguida y apunta solo cincuenta." ⁷ Después preguntó a otro: "Y tú, ¿cuánto le debes?" Este le contestó: "Cien medidas de trigo." Le dijo: "Aquí está tu recibo. Apunta solo ochenta." ⁸ El amo reconoció que aquel administrador deshonesto había actuado con astucia. Y es que, tratándose de sus propios negocios, los que pertenecen al mundo son más listos que los que pertenecen a la luz.

⁹ «Os aconsejo que uséis las riquezas de este mundo malo para ganaros amigos, para que cuando esas riquezas se acaben haya quien os reciba en las moradas eternas.

¹⁰ «El que se porta honradamente en lo poco, también se porta honradamente en lo mucho; y el que es deshonesto en lo poco, también es deshonesto en lo mucho. ¹¹ De manera que, si con las riquezas de este mundo malo no os portáis honradamente, ¿quién os confiará las verdaderas riquezas? ¹² Y si no os portáis honradamente con lo ajeno, ¿quién os dará lo que os pertenece?

¹³ «Ningún criado puede servir a dos amos, porque odiará a uno y querrá al otro, o será fiel a uno y despreciará al otro. No se puede servir a Dios y al dinero.»

¹⁴ Los fariseos, que eran amigos del dinero, al oir estas cosas se burlaban de Jesús. ¹⁵ Él les dijo: «Vosotros pasáis por buenos delante de la gente, pero Dios conoce vuestros corazones; y lo que los hombres tienen por más elevado, Dios lo aborrece.»

La ley y el reino de Dios

¹⁶ «La ley de Moisés y los escritos de los profetas llegan hasta Juan. Desde entonces se anuncia la buena noticia del reino de Dios, y a todos se les fuerza a entrar.

¹⁷ «Más fácil es que pasen el cielo y la tierra, que pierda su valor una sola letra de la ley.

La enseñanza de Jesús acerca del divorcio

¹⁸ «Si un hombre se separa de su esposa y se casa con otra, comete adulterio; y el que se casa con una mujer separada, también comete adulterio.

Parábola del rico y Lázaro

¹⁹ «Había una vez un hombre rico, que vestía ropas espléndidas y todos los días celebraba brillantes fiestas. ²⁰ Había también un mendigo llamado Lázaro, el cual, lleno de llagas, se sentaba en el suelo a la puerta del rico. ²¹ Este mendigo deseaba llenar su estómago de lo que

caía de la mesa del rico; y los perros se acercaban a lamerle las llagas.
²² Un día murió el mendigo, y los ángeles lo llevaron junto a Abraham, al paraíso. Y el rico también murió, y lo enterraron.

²³ «El rico, padeciendo en el lugar al que van los muertos, levantó los ojos y vio de lejos a Abraham, y a Lázaro con él. ²⁴ Entonces gritó: "¡Padre Abraham, ten compasión de mí! Envía a Lázaro, a que moje la punta de su dedo en agua y venga a refrescar mi lengua, porque estoy sufriendo mucho entre estas llamas." ²⁵ Pero Abraham le contestó: "Hijo, recuerda que a ti te fue muy bien en la vida y que a Lázaro le fue muy mal. Ahora él recibe consuelo aquí, y tú en cambio estás sufriendo. ²⁶ Pero además hay un gran abismo abierto entre nosotros y vosotros; de modo que los que quieren pasar de aquí ahí, no pueden, ni los de ahí tampoco pueden pasar aquí."

²⁷ «El rico dijo: "Te suplico entonces, padre Abraham, que envíes a Lázaro a casa de mi padre, ²⁸ donde tengo cinco hermanos. Que les hable, para que no vengan también ellos a este lugar de tormento." ²⁹ Abraham respondió: "Ellos ya tienen lo que escribieron Moisés y los profetas: ¡que les hagan caso!" ³⁰ El rico contestó: "No se lo harán, padre Abraham. En cambio, sí que se convertirán si se les aparece alguno de los que ya han muerto." ³¹ Pero Abraham le dijo: "Si no quieren hacer caso a Moisés y a los profetas, tampoco creerán aunque algún muerto resucite."»

El peligro de caer en pecado

17 Jesús dijo a sus discípulos: «Siempre habrá incitaciones al pecado, pero ¡ay de aquel que haga pecar a los demás! ² Mejor le sería que lo arrojasen al mar con una piedra de molino atada al cuello, que hacer caer en pecado a uno de estos pequeños. ³ ¡Tened cuidado!

«Si tu hermano te ofende, repréndele; pero si cambia de actitud, perdónale. ⁴ Aunque te ofenda siete veces en un día, si siete veces viene a decirte: "No volveré a hacerlo", debes perdonarle.»

El poder de la fe

⁵ Los apóstoles pidieron al Señor:
«Danos más fe.»
⁶ El Señor les contestó:

«Si tuvierais fe, aunque fuera tan pequeña como una semilla de mostaza, podríais decirle a esta morera: "Desarráigate de aquí y plántate en el mar", y el árbol os obedecería.

El deber del que sirve

[7] «Si uno de vosotros tiene un criado que regresa del campo después de haber estado arando o cuidando el ganado, ¿acaso le dice: "Pasa y siéntate a comer"? [8] No, sino que le dice: "Prepárame la cena y estáte atento a servirme mientras como y bebo. Después podrás tú comer y beber." [9] Y tampoco da las gracias al criado por haber hecho lo que le mandó. [10] Igualmente vosotros, cuando ya hayáis hecho todo lo que Dios os manda deberéis decir: "Somos servidores inútiles; no hicimos más que cumplir con nuestra obligación."»

Jesús sana a diez leprosos

[11] En su camino a Jerusalén, pasó Jesús entre las regiones de Samaria y Galilea. [12] Al llegar a cierta aldea le salieron al encuentro diez hombres enfermos de lepra, que desde lejos [13] gritaban:

«¡Jesús, Maestro, ten compasión de nosotros!»

[14] Al verlos, Jesús les dijo:

«Id a presentaros a los sacerdotes.»

Mientras iban, quedaron limpios de su enfermedad. [15] Uno de ellos, al verse sanado, regresó alabando a Dios a grandes voces, [16] y se inclinó hasta el suelo ante Jesús para darle las gracias. Este hombre era de Samaria. [17] Jesús dijo:

«¿Acaso no son diez los que quedaron limpios de su enfermedad? ¿Dónde están los otros nueve? [18] ¿Únicamente este extranjero ha vuelto para alabar a Dios?»

[19] Y dijo al hombre:

«Levántate y vete. Por tu fe has sido sanado.»

Cómo llegará el reino de Dios

[20] Los fariseos preguntaron a Jesús cuándo había de llegar el reino de Dios, y él les contestó:

«El reino de Dios no vendrá en forma visible. [21] No se dirá: "Aquí está" o "Allí está", porque el reino de Dios ya está entre vosotros.»

²² Y dijo a sus discípulos:

«Vendrán tiempos en que querréis ver siquiera uno de los días del Hijo del hombre, pero no lo veréis. ²³ Algunos dirán: "Aquí está", o "Allí está", pero no vayáis ni los sigáis. ²⁴ Porque así como el relámpago, con su resplandor, ilumina el cielo de uno a otro lado, así será el Hijo del hombre el día de su venida. ²⁵ Pero primero tiene que sufrir mucho y ser rechazado por la gente de este tiempo. ²⁶ Como sucedió en tiempos de Noé, sucederá también en los días en que venga el Hijo del hombre. ²⁷ La gente comía y bebía y se casaba, hasta el día en que Noé entró en el arca, cuando llegó el diluvio y todos murieron. ²⁸ Y lo mismo pasó en los tiempos de Lot: la gente comía y bebía, compraba y vendía, sembraba y construía casas; ²⁹ pero cuando Lot salió de la ciudad de Sodoma, llovió del cielo fuego y azufre y todos murieron. ³⁰ Así será el día en que se manifieste el Hijo del hombre.

³¹ «Aquel día, el que se encuentre en la azotea y tenga sus cosas dentro de la casa, que no baje a sacarlas; y el que esté en el campo, que no regrese a su casa. ³² ¡Acordaos de la mujer de Lot! ³³ El que trate de salvar su vida la perderá, pero el que la pierda, vivirá.

³⁴ «Os digo que aquella noche estarán dos en una misma cama: a uno se lo llevarán y al otro lo dejarán. ³⁵ Dos mujeres estarán moliendo juntas: a una se la llevarán y a la otra la dejarán.» [³⁶ Dos hombres estarán en el campo: a uno se lo llevarán y al otro lo dejarán.]

³⁷ Le preguntaron entonces:

«¿Dónde ocurrirá eso, Señor?»

Y él les contestó:

«Donde esté el cadáver, allí se juntarán los buitres.»

Parábola de la viuda y el juez

18 Jesús les contó una parábola para enseñarles que debían orar siempre y no desanimarse. ² Les dijo: «Había en un pueblo un juez que no temía a Dios ni respetaba a los hombres. ³ Y en el mismo pueblo vivía también una viuda, que tenía planteado un pleito y que fue al juez a pedirle justicia contra su adversario. ⁴ Durante mucho tiempo el juez no quiso atenderla, pero finalmente pensó: "Yo no temo a Dios ni respeto a los hombres. ⁵ Sin embargo, como esta viuda no deja de molestarme, le haré justicia, para que no siga viniendo y acabe con mi paciencia."»

⁶ El Señor añadió: «Pues bien, si esto es lo que dijo aquel mal juez, ⁷ ¿cómo Dios no va a hacer justicia a sus escogidos, que claman a él día y noche? ¿Los hará esperar? ⁸ Os digo que les hará justicia sin demora. Pero cuando el Hijo del hombre venga, ¿encontrará todavía fe en la tierra?»

Parábola del fariseo y el cobrador de impuestos

⁹ Jesús contó esta otra parábola para algunos que se consideraban a sí mismos justos y despreciaban a los demás: ¹⁰ «Dos hombres fueron al templo a orar: el uno era fariseo, y el otro era uno de esos que cobran impuestos para Roma. ¹¹ El fariseo, de pie, oraba así: "Oh Dios, te doy gracias porque no soy como los demás: ladrones, malvados y adúlteros. Ni tampoco soy como ese cobrador de impuestos. ¹² Ayuno dos veces por semana y te doy la décima parte de todo lo que gano." ¹³ A cierta distancia, el cobrador de impuestos ni siquiera se atrevía a levantar los ojos al cielo, sino que se golpeaba el pecho y decía: "¡Oh Dios, ten compasión de mí que soy pecador!" ¹⁴ Os digo que este cobrador de impuestos volvió a su casa justificado por Dios; pero no el fariseo. Porque el que a sí mismo se engrandece será humillado, y el que se humilla será engrandecido.»

Jesús bendice a los niños

¹⁵ También llevaban niños a Jesús, para que los tocara; pero los discípulos, al verlo, reprendían a quienes los llevaban. ¹⁶ Entonces Jesús los llamó y dijo:

«Dejad que los niños vengan a mí y no se lo impidáis, porque el reino de Dios es de quienes son como ellos. ¹⁷ Os aseguro que el que no acepta el reino de Dios como un niño, no entrará en él.»

El hombre rico

¹⁸ Uno de los jefes preguntó a Jesús:

«Maestro bueno, ¿qué debo hacer para alcanzar la vida eterna?»
¹⁹ Jesús le contestó:

«¿Por qué me llamas bueno? Bueno solamente hay uno: Dios. ²⁰ Ya sabes los mandamientos: "No cometas adulterio, no mates, no robes, no mientas en perjuicio de nadie y honra a tu padre y a tu madre."»

²¹ El hombre le dijo:

«Todo eso lo he cumplido desde joven.»

²² Al oírlo, Jesús le contestó:

«Todavía te falta una cosa: vende todo lo que tienes y dáselo a los pobres. Así tendrás riquezas en el cielo. Luego ven y sígueme.»

²³ Pero cuando el hombre oyó esto se puso muy triste, porque era muy rico. ²⁴ Jesús, viéndole tan triste, dijo:

«¡Qué difícil les va a ser a los ricos entrar en el reino de Dios! ²⁵ Más fácil es para un camello pasar por el ojo de una aguja que para un rico entrar en el reino de Dios.»

²⁶ Los que lo oyeron preguntaron:

«Entonces, ¿quién podrá salvarse?»

²⁷ Jesús les contestó:

«Lo que es imposible para los hombres es posible para Dios.»

²⁸ Pedro le dijo:

«Señor, nosotros hemos dejado todo lo nuestro y te hemos seguido.»

²⁹ Él les respondió:

«Os aseguro que todo el que por causa del reino de Dios haya dejado casa, esposa, hermanos, padres o hijos, ³⁰ recibirá mucho más en este mundo, y en el mundo venidero recibirá la vida eterna.»

Jesús anuncia por tercera vez su muerte

³¹ Jesús llamó aparte a los doce discípulos y les dijo: «Ahora vamos a Jerusalén, donde se ha de cumplir todo lo que los profetas escribieron acerca del Hijo del hombre. ³² Pues lo entregarán a los extranjeros, se burlarán de él, lo insultarán y le escupirán. ³³ Le golpearán y lo matarán; pero al tercer día resucitará.»

³⁴ Ellos no entendieron nada de esto ni sabían de qué les hablaba, pues eran cosas que no podían comprender.

Jesús sana a un ciego en Jericó

³⁵ Se encontraba Jesús ya cerca de Jericó. Un ciego que estaba sentado junto al camino, pidiendo limosna, ³⁶ al oír que pasaba mucha

gente preguntó qué sucedía. [37] Le dijeron que Jesús de Nazaret pasaba por allí, [38] y él gritó:

«¡Jesús, Hijo de David, ten compasión de mí!»

[39] Los que iban delante le reprendían para que se callase, pero él gritaba todavía más:

«¡Hijo de David, ten compasión de mí!»

[40] Jesús se detuvo y mandó que se lo trajeran. Cuando lo tuvo cerca le preguntó:

[41] «¿Qué quieres que haga por ti?»

El ciego contestó:

«Señor, quiero recobrar la vista.»

[42] Jesús le dijo:

«¡Recóbrala! Por tu fe has sido sanado.»

[43] En aquel mismo momento recobró el ciego la vista, y siguió a Jesús alabando a Dios. Y toda la gente que vio esto alababa también a Dios.

Jesús y Zaqueo

19 Jesús entró en Jericó e iba atravesando la ciudad. [2] Vivía en ella un hombre rico llamado Zaqueo, jefe de los que cobraban impuestos para Roma. [3] Quería conocer a Jesús, pero no conseguía verle, porque había mucha gente y Zaqueo era de baja estatura. [4] Así que, echando a correr, se adelantó, y para alcanzar a verle se subió a un árbol junto al cual tenía que pasar Jesús. [5] Al llegar allí, Jesús miró hacia arriba y le dijo:

«Zaqueo, baja en seguida porque hoy he de quedarme en tu casa.»

[6] Zaqueo bajó aprisa, y con alegría recibió a Jesús. [7] Al ver esto comenzaron todos a criticar a Jesús, diciendo que había ido a quedarse en casa de un pecador. [8] Pero Zaqueo, levantándose entonces, dijo al Señor:

«Mira, Señor, voy a dar a los pobres la mitad de mis bienes; y si he robado algo a alguien, le devolveré cuatro veces más.»

[9] Jesús le dijo:

«Hoy ha llegado la salvación a esta casa, porque este hombre también es descendiente de Abraham. [10] Pues el Hijo del hombre ha venido a buscar y salvar lo que se había perdido.»

Parábola del dinero

¹¹ La gente escuchaba estas cosas que decía Jesús. Y él les contó una parábola, porque ya se encontraba cerca de Jerusalén y ellos pensaban que el reino de Dios estaba a punto de manifestarse. ¹² Les dijo: «Un hombre de la nobleza se fue lejos, a otro país, para ser hecho rey y regresar. ¹³ Antes de partir llamó a diez de sus criados, entregó a cada uno una gran suma de dinero y les dijo: "Negociad con este dinero hasta que yo vuelva." ¹⁴ Pero las gentes de su país le odiaban, y enviaron tras él una comisión con el encargo de decir: "No queremos que este hombre sea nuestro rey."

¹⁵ «Pero él fue hecho rey. A su vuelta, mandó llamar a aquellos criados a quienes había entregado el dinero, para saber cuánto había ganado cada uno. ¹⁶ El primero se presentó y dijo: "Señor, tu dinero ha producido diez veces más." ¹⁷ El rey le contestó: "Muy bien, eres un buen administrador. Y como has sido fiel en lo poco, te hago gobernador de diez ciudades." ¹⁸ Se presentó otro y dijo: "Señor, tu dinero ha producido cinco veces más." ¹⁹ También a este le contestó: "Tú serás gobernador de cinco ciudades."

²⁰ «Pero se presentó otro, que dijo: "Señor, aquí está tu dinero. Lo guardé en un pañuelo, ²¹ pues tuve miedo de ti, porque eres un hombre duro que recoges lo que no pusiste y cosechas donde no sembraste." ²² Entonces le dijo el rey: "Tú eres un mal administrador, y por tus propias palabras te juzgo. Puesto que sabías que yo soy un hombre duro, que recojo lo que no puse y cosecho donde no sembré, ²³ ¿por qué no llevaste mi dinero al banco para, a mi regreso, devolvérmelo junto con los intereses?" ²⁴ Y ordenó a los que estaban allí: "Quitadle el dinero y dádselo al que ganó diez veces más." ²⁵ Ellos le dijeron: "Señor, ¡pero si este ya tiene diez veces más!" ²⁶ El rey contestó: "Os digo que al que tiene se le dará más; pero al que no tiene, hasta lo poco que tiene se le quitará. ²⁷ Y en cuanto a mis enemigos, a esos que no querían tenerme por rey, traedlos acá y matadlos en mi presencia."»

Jesús entra en Jerusalén

²⁸ Dicho esto, Jesús siguió su viaje a Jerusalén. ²⁹ Cuando ya estaba cerca de Betfagé y Betania, junto al monte llamado de los Olivos, envió a dos de sus discípulos ³⁰ diciéndoles:

«Id a la aldea de enfrente, y al llegar encontraréis un asno atado que nadie ha montado todavía. Desatadlo y traedlo. [31] Si alguien os pregunta por qué lo desatáis, respondedle que el Señor lo necesita.»

[32] Los discípulos fueron y lo encontraron todo como Jesús se lo había dicho. [33] Mientras desataban el asno, los dueños les preguntaron:

«¿Por qué lo desatáis?»

[34] Ellos contestaron:

«Porque el Señor lo necesita.»

[35] Se lo llevaron a Jesús, cubrieron el asno con sus capas e hicieron que Jesús montara en él. [36] Conforme Jesús avanzaba, la gente tendía sus capas por el camino. [37] Y al acercarse a la bajada del monte de los Olivos, todos sus seguidores comenzaron a gritar de alegría y a alabar a Dios por todos los milagros que habían visto. [38] Decían:

«¡Bendito el Rey que viene en el nombre del Señor! ¡Paz en el cielo y gloria en las alturas!»

[39] Entonces algunos fariseos que se hallaban entre la gente le dijeron:

«Maestro, reprende a tus seguidores.»

[40] Pero Jesús les contestó:

«Os digo que si estos callan, las piedras gritarán.»

[41] Cuando llegó cerca de Jerusalén, al ver la ciudad, lloró por ella [42] y dijo: «¡Si entendieras siquiera en este día lo que puede darte paz!... Pero ahora eso te está oculto y no puedes verlo. [43] Pues van a venir días malos para ti, en los que tus enemigos te cercarán con barricadas, te sitiarán, te atacarán por todas partes [44] y te destruirán por completo. Matarán a tus habitantes y no dejarán en ti piedra sobre piedra, porque no reconociste el momento en que Dios vino a salvarte.»

Jesús purifica el templo

[45] Después de esto, Jesús entró en el templo y comenzó a expulsar a los que allí estaban vendiendo. [46] Les dijo:

«En las Escrituras se dice: "Mi casa será casa de oración", pero vosotros la habéis convertido en una cueva de ladrones.»

[47] Todos los días enseñaba Jesús en el templo, y los jefes de los sacerdotes, los maestros de la ley y también los jefes del pueblo andaban buscando cómo matarlo. [48] Pero no encontraban la manera de hacerlo, porque toda la gente le escuchaba con gran atención.

La autoridad de Jesús

20 Un día, mientras Jesús estaba en el templo enseñando a la gente y anunciando la buena noticia, llegaron los jefes de los sacerdotes y los maestros de la ley, junto con los ancianos, ² y le preguntaron:

«¿Con qué autoridad haces estas cosas? ¿Quién te ha dado esa autoridad?»

³ Jesús les contestó:

«Yo también os voy a hacer una pregunta. Respondedme: ⁴ ¿Quién envió a Juan a bautizar: Dios o los hombres?»

⁵ Empezaron a discutir unos con otros: «Si respondemos que Dios lo envió, él nos dirá: "¿Por qué no le creísteis?" ⁶ Y si decimos que fueron los hombres, la gente nos matará a pedradas, porque todos están convencidos de que Juan era un profeta.» ⁷ Así pues, respondieron que no sabían quién había enviado a Juan a bautizar. ⁸ Jesús les contestó:

«Entonces tampoco yo os digo con qué autoridad hago estas cosas.»

Parábola de los labradores malvados

⁹ Luego comenzó Jesús a hablar a la gente contando esta parábola: «Un hombre plantó una viña, la arrendó a unos labradores y emprendió un largo viaje. ¹⁰ A su debido tiempo, mandó un criado a pedir a los labradores la parte de cosecha que le correspondía; pero ellos le golpearon y lo enviaron con las manos vacías. ¹¹ Entonces el dueño mandó otro criado; pero también a este lo insultaron, le golpearon y lo enviaron con las manos vacías. ¹² Volvió a mandar otro, pero los labradores también le hirieron y lo echaron fuera.

¹³ «Finalmente, el dueño de la viña dijo: "¿Qué haré? Mandaré a mi hijo, que me es tan querido. Seguramente lo respetarán." ¹⁴ Pero cuando los labradores le vieron, se dijeron unos a otros: "Este es el heredero: matémoslo y la viña será para nosotros." ¹⁵ Así que lo sacaron de la viña y lo mataron.

«¿Qué, pues, creéis que hará con ellos el dueño de la viña? ¹⁶ Irá y matará a aquellos labradores, y dará la viña a otros.»

Al oírlo, dijeron:

«¡Eso, jamás!»

¹⁷ Pero Jesús los miró y dijo:

«Entonces ¿qué significa esto que dicen las Escrituras:

"La piedra que despreciaron los constructores
 es ahora la piedra principal"?

¹⁸ «Cualquiera que caiga sobre esa piedra se hará pedazos, y si la piedra cae sobre alguien, lo aplastará.»

¹⁹ Los jefes de los sacerdotes y los maestros de la ley quisieron apresar a Jesús en aquel mismo momento, porque sabían que al contar esta parábola se refería a ellos. Pero tenían miedo de la gente.

La cuestión de los impuestos

²⁰ Enviaron unos espías que, aparentando ser hombres de bien, hicieran decir a Jesús algo que les diera pretexto para entregarle al gobernador. ²¹ Le preguntaron:

«Maestro, sabemos que lo que dices y enseñas es correcto, y que no juzgas por las apariencias. Tú enseñas de veras a vivir como Dios ordena. ²² ¿Estamos nosotros obligados a pagar impuestos al césar, o no?»

²³ Jesús, dándose cuenta de la mala intención que llevaban, les dijo:

²⁴ «Enseñadme un denario. ¿De quién es la imagen y el nombre aquí escrito?»

Le contestaron:

«Del césar.»

²⁵ Jesús les dijo:

«Pues dad al césar lo que es del césar, y a Dios lo que es de Dios.»

²⁶ Y no pudieron sorprenderle en ninguna palabra delante de la gente. Al contrario, admirados de su respuesta, se callaron.

La pregunta sobre la resurrección

²⁷ Después acudieron algunos saduceos a ver a Jesús. Los saduceos niegan que haya resurrección de los muertos, y por eso le plantearon este caso:

²⁸ «Maestro, Moisés nos dejó escrito que si un hombre casado muere sin haber tenido hijos con su mujer, el hermano del difunto deberá tomar por esposa a la viuda para darle hijos al hermano que murió. ²⁹ Pues bien, había una vez siete hermanos, el primero de los

cuales se casó, pero murió sin dejar hijos. ³⁰ El segundo ³¹ y luego el tercero se casaron con la viuda, y lo mismo hicieron los demás, pero los siete murieron sin dejar hijos. ³² Finalmente murió también la mujer. ³³ Así pues, en la resurrección, ¿cuál de ellos la tendrá por esposa, si los siete estuvieron casados con ella?»

³⁴ Jesús les contestó:

«En este mundo, los hombres y las mujeres se casan; ³⁵ pero los que merezcan llegar a aquel otro mundo y resucitar, sean hombres o mujeres, ya no se casarán, ³⁶ puesto que ya tampoco podrán morir. Serán como los ángeles, y serán hijos de Dios por haber resucitado. ³⁷ Hasta el mismo Moisés, en el pasaje de la zarza ardiendo, nos hace saber que los muertos resucitan. Allí dice que el Señor es el Dios de Abraham, de Isaac y de Jacob. ³⁸ ¡Y Dios no es Dios de muertos, sino de vivos, pues para él todos están vivos!»

³⁹ Algunos maestros de la ley dijeron entonces:

«Bien dicho, Maestro.»

⁴⁰ Y ya no se atrevieron a hacerle más preguntas.

¿De quién desciende el Mesías?

⁴¹ Jesús les preguntó:

«¿Por qué se dice que el Mesías desciende de David? ⁴² Pues David mismo, en el libro de los Salmos, dice:

"El Señor dijo a mi Señor:
Siéntate a mi derecha
⁴³ hasta que yo haga de tus enemigos
el estrado de tus pies."

⁴⁴ ¿Cómo puede entonces el Mesías descender de David, si David mismo le llama Señor?»

Jesús acusa a los maestros de la ley

⁴⁵ Toda la gente estaba escuchando, y Jesús dijo a sus discípulos: ⁴⁶ «Guardaos de los maestros de la ley, pues les gusta andar con ropas largas y que los saluden con todo respeto en la calle. Buscan los asientos de honor en las sinagogas y los mejores puestos en los banquetes, ⁴⁷ y so pretexto de hacer largas oraciones devoran las casas de las viudas. ¡Esos recibirán mayor castigo!»

La ofrenda de la viuda pobre

21 Jesús estaba viendo cómo los ricos echaban dinero en las arcas de las ofrendas, [2] y vio también a una viuda pobre que echaba dos monedas de cobre. [3] Entonces dijo:

«Verdaderamente os digo que esta viuda pobre ha dado más que nadie, [4] pues todos dan sus ofrendas de lo que les sobra, pero ella, en su pobreza, ha dado todo lo que tenía para su sustento.»

Jesús anuncia la destrucción del templo

[5] Algunos estaban hablando del templo, de la belleza de sus piedras y de las ofrendas que lo adornaban. Jesús dijo:

[6] «Vienen días en que de todo esto que estáis viendo no quedará piedra sobre piedra. ¡Todo será destruido!»

Señales antes del fin

[7] Preguntaron a Jesús:

«Maestro, ¿cuándo ocurrirán esas cosas? ¿Cuál será la señal de que ya están a punto de suceder?»

[8] Jesús contestó: «Tened cuidado y no os dejéis engañar. Porque vendrán muchos haciéndose pasar por mí y diciendo: "Yo soy" y "Ahora es el momento", pero no los sigáis. [9] Y cuando oigáis alarmas de guerras y revoluciones no os asustéis, pues aunque todo eso tiene que ocurrir primero, aún no habrá llegado el fin.»

[10] Siguió diciéndoles: «Una nación peleará contra otra y un país hará guerra contra otro; [11] en diferentes lugares habrá grandes terremotos, hambres y enfermedades, y en el cielo se verán cosas espantosas y grandes señales.

[12] «Pero antes de eso os echarán mano y os perseguirán: os llevarán a juicio en las sinagogas, os meterán en la cárcel y os conducirán ante reyes y gobernadores por causa mía. [13] Así tendréis oportunidad de dar testimonio de mí. [14] Haceos el propósito de no preparar de antemano vuestra defensa, [15] porque yo os daré palabras tan llenas de sabiduría que ninguno de vuestros enemigos podrá resistiros ni contradeciros en nada. [16] Pero seréis traicionados incluso por vuestros padres, hermanos, parientes y amigos. Matarán a algunos de vosotros [17] y todo el mundo os odiará por causa mía, [18] pero no se

perderá ni solo un cabello de vuestra cabeza. ¹⁹ ¡Permaneced firmes y salvaréis vuestra vida!

²⁰ «Cuando veáis a Jerusalén rodeada de ejércitos, sabed que pronto será destruida. ²¹ Entonces los que estén en Judea, que huyan a las montañas; los que estén en Jerusalén, que salgan de la ciudad; y los que estén en el campo, que no regresen a ella. ²² Porque serán días de castigo en los que se cumplirá cuanto dicen las Escrituras. ²³ ¡Pobres de las mujeres que en aquellos días estén embarazadas o tengan niños de pecho!, porque habrá mucho dolor en el país y un castigo terrible contra este pueblo. ²⁴ A unos los matarán a filo de espada, a otros los llevarán prisioneros por todas las naciones, y los paganos pisotearán Jerusalén hasta que se cumpla el tiempo que les ha sido señalado.

El regreso del Hijo del hombre

²⁵ «Habrá señales en el sol, la luna y las estrellas. En la tierra, las naciones estarán confusas y angustiadas por el ruido terrible del mar y de las olas. ²⁶ La gente se desmayará de espanto pensando en lo que ha de sucederle al mundo, pues hasta las fuerzas celestiales se tambalearán. ²⁷ Entonces verán al Hijo del hombre venir en una nube con gran poder y gloria. ²⁸ Cuando empiecen a suceder estas cosas, animaos y levantad la cabeza, porque muy pronto seréis liberados.»

²⁹ También les propuso Jesús esta comparación: «Mirad la higuera, o cualquier otro árbol: ³⁰ cuando veis que ya brotan sus hojas, comprendéis que el verano está cerca. ³¹ De la misma manera, cuando veáis que suceden esas cosas, sabed que el reino de Dios ya está cerca.

³² «Os aseguro que todo ello sucederá antes que haya muerto la gente de este tiempo. ³³ El cielo y la tierra pasarán, pero mis palabras no pasarán.

³⁴ «Tened cuidado y no dejéis que vuestro corazón se endurezca por los vicios, las borracheras y las preocupaciones de esta vida, para que aquel día no caiga de pronto sobre vosotros ³⁵ como una trampa; porque así vendrá sobre todos los habitantes de la tierra. ³⁶ Permaneced vigilantes, orando en todo tiempo para que podáis escapar de todas esas cosas que van a suceder, y para que podáis presentaros delante del Hijo del hombre.»

[37] Jesús enseñaba de día en el templo, pero de noche se quedaba en el monte llamado de los Olivos. [38] Y toda la gente madrugaba para ir al templo a escucharle.

Conspiración para arrestar y matar a Jesús

22 Estaba ya cerca la fiesta en que se come el pan sin levadura, o sea, la fiesta de la Pascua. [2] Los jefes de los sacerdotes y los maestros de la ley, que tenían miedo de la gente, buscaban la manera de matar a Jesús.

[3] Entonces Satanás entró en Judas, uno de los doce discípulos, al que llamaban Iscariote. [4] Este fue a ver a los jefes de los sacerdotes y a los oficiales del templo, y habló con ellos sobre cómo entregarles a Jesús. [5] Ellos se alegraron y prometieron dinero a Judas. [6] Este aceptó, y empezó a buscar un momento oportuno, cuando no hubiera gente, para entregarles a Jesús.

La Cena del Señor

[7] Llegó el día de la fiesta en que se comía el pan sin levadura, cuando se sacrificaba el cordero de Pascua. [8] Jesús envió a Pedro y a Juan, diciendo:

«Id a prepararnos la cena de Pascua.»

[9] Ellos le preguntaron:

«¿Dónde quieres que la preparemos?»

[10] Jesús les contestó:

«Al entrar en la ciudad encontraréis a un hombre que lleva un cántaro de agua; seguidle hasta la casa donde entre [11] y decidle al dueño de la casa: "El Maestro pregunta: ¿Cuál es la sala donde he de comer con mis discípulos la cena de Pascua?" [12] Él os mostrará en el piso alto una habitación grande y arreglada: preparad allí la cena.»

[13] Fueron, pues, y lo encontraron todo como Jesús les había dicho, y prepararon la cena de Pascua.

[14] Cuando llegó la hora, Jesús y los apóstoles se sentaron a la mesa. [15] Él les dijo:

«¡Cuánto he deseado celebrar con vosotros esta cena de Pascua antes de mi muerte! [16] Porque os digo que no volveré a celebrarla hasta que se cumpla en el reino de Dios.»

¹⁷ Entonces tomó en sus manos una copa, y habiendo dado gracias a Dios dijo:

«Tomad esto y repartidlo entre vosotros; ¹⁸ porque os digo que no volveré a beber del fruto de la vid hasta que venga el reino de Dios.»

¹⁹ Después tomó el pan en sus manos, y habiendo dado gracias a Dios lo partió y se lo dio a ellos, diciendo:

«Esto es mi cuerpo, entregado a muerte en favor vuestro. Haced esto en memoria de mí.»

²⁰ Lo mismo hizo con la copa después de la cena, diciendo:

«Esta copa es el nuevo pacto confirmado con mi sangre, la cual es derramada en favor vuestro. ²¹ Pero mirad, la mano del que me va a traicionar está aquí, con la mía, sobre la mesa. ²² Pues el Hijo del hombre ha de recorrer el camino que se le ha señalado, pero ¡ay de aquel que le traiciona!»

²³ Entonces comenzaron a preguntarse unos a otros quién sería el traidor.

Quién es el más importante

²⁴ Los discípulos tuvieron una discusión sobre cuál de ellos debía ser considerado el más importante. ²⁵ Jesús les dijo: «Entre los paganos, los reyes gobiernan con tiranía a sus súbditos, y a los jefes se les llama benefactores. ²⁶ Pero vosotros no debéis ser así. Al contrario, el más importante entre vosotros tiene que hacerse como el más joven, y el que manda tiene que hacerse como el que sirve. ²⁷ Pues ¿quién es más importante, el que se sienta a la mesa a comer o el que sirve? ¿No es acaso el que se sienta a la mesa? En cambio yo estoy entre vosotros como el que sirve.

²⁸ «Vosotros habéis estado siempre conmigo en mis pruebas. ²⁹ Por eso yo os asigno un reino, como mi Padre me lo asignó a mí, ³⁰ y comeréis y beberéis a mi mesa en mi reino, y os sentaréis en tronos para juzgar a las doce tribus de Israel.»

Jesús anuncia la negación de Pedro

³¹ Dijo también el Señor:

«Simón, Simón, mira que Satanás os ha reclamado para zarandearos como a trigo; ³² pero yo he rogado por ti, para que no te falte la fe. Y tú, cuando te hayas vuelto a mí, ayuda a tus hermanos a permanecer firmes.»

³³ Simón le dijo:

«Señor, estoy dispuesto a ir contigo a la cárcel y hasta a morir contigo.»

³⁴ Jesús le contestó:

«Pedro, te digo que hoy mismo, antes que cante el gallo, negarás tres veces que me conoces.»

Se acerca la hora de la prueba

³⁵ Luego Jesús les preguntó:

«Cuando os envié sin bolsa ni provisiones ni sandalias, ¿acaso os faltó algo?»

Ellos contestaron:

«Nada.»

³⁶ Entonces les dijo:

«Ahora, en cambio, el que tenga bolsa, que la traiga, y también provisiones; y el que no tenga espada, que venda su abrigo y se compre una. ³⁷ Porque os digo que ha de cumplirse en mí lo que dicen las Escrituras: "Y fue contado entre los malvados". Porque todo lo que de mí está escrito ha de cumplirse.»

³⁸ Ellos dijeron:

«Señor, aquí hay dos espadas.»

Y él contestó:

«Ya basta.»

Jesús ora en Getsemaní

³⁹ Luego salió Jesús y, según su costumbre, se fue al monte de los Olivos. Los discípulos le siguieron. ⁴⁰ Al llegar al lugar, les dijo:

«Orad, para que no caigáis en tentación.»

⁴¹ Se alejó de ellos como a distancia de un tiro de piedra, y se puso a orar de rodillas, ⁴² diciendo:

«Padre, si quieres, líbrame de esta copa amarga; pero no se haga mi voluntad, sino la tuya.»

[⁴³ En esto se le apareció un ángel del cielo, que le daba fuerzas. ⁴⁴ En medio de un gran sufrimiento, Jesús oraba aún más intensa-

mente, y el sudor le caía al suelo como grandes gotas de sangre.]
⁴⁵ Cuando se levantó de la oración fue a donde estaban los discípulos, y los encontró dormidos, vencidos por la tristeza. ⁴⁶ Les dijo:

«¿Por qué dormís? Levantaos y orad, para que no caigáis en tentación.»

Jesús es arrestado

⁴⁷ Todavía estaba hablando Jesús, cuando llegó un grupo de gente. El que se llamaba Judas, que era uno de los doce discípulos, iba a la cabeza, y se acercó a besar a Jesús. ⁴⁸ Jesús le dijo:

«Judas, ¿con un beso traicionas al Hijo del hombre?»

⁴⁹ Los que estaban con Jesús, al ver lo que pasaba, le preguntaron:

«Señor, ¿atacamos con espada?»

⁵⁰ Y uno de ellos hirió al criado del sumo sacerdote cortándole la oreja derecha. ⁵¹ Jesús dijo:

«Dejadlo. Ya basta.»

Y tocando la oreja al criado, se la curó. ⁵² Luego dijo a los jefes de los sacerdotes, a los oficiales del templo y a los ancianos que habían ido a apresarle:

«¿Por qué venís con espadas y palos como si yo fuera un bandido? ⁵³ Todos los días he estado con vosotros en el templo, y ni siquiera me tocasteis. Pero esta es vuestra hora, la del poder de las tinieblas.»

Pedro niega conocer a Jesús

⁵⁴ Arrestaron entonces a Jesús y lo llevaron a la casa del sumo sacerdote. Pedro le seguía de lejos. ⁵⁵ Allí, en medio del patio, habían hecho fuego, y se sentaron alrededor. Pedro también se sentó entre ellos. ⁵⁶ En esto, una sirvienta, al verle sentado junto al fuego, se quedó mirándole y dijo:

«También este estaba con él.»

⁵⁷ Pero Pedro lo negó, diciendo:

«Mujer, yo no le conozco.»

⁵⁸ Poco después le vio otro y dijo:

«Tú también eres de ellos.»

Pedro contestó:

«No, hombre, no lo soy.»

⁵⁹ Como una hora más tarde, otro insistió:

«Seguro que este estaba con él. Además es de Galilea.»

⁶⁰ Pedro dijo:

«¡Hombre, no sé de qué hablas!»

En el mismo instante, mientras Pedro aún estaba hablando, cantó un gallo. ⁶¹ Entonces el Señor se volvió y miró a Pedro, y Pedro se acordó de que el Señor le había dicho: «Hoy, antes que cante el gallo, me negarás tres veces.» ⁶² Y salió Pedro de allí y lloró amargamente.

Se burlan de Jesús

⁶³ Los hombres que estaban vigilando a Jesús se burlaban de él y le golpeaban. ⁶⁴ Le taparon los ojos y le decían:

«¡Adivina quién te ha pegado!»

⁶⁵ Y le insultaban de otras muchas maneras.

Jesús ante la Junta Suprema

⁶⁶ Al hacerse de día se reunieron los ancianos de los judíos, los jefes de los sacerdotes y los maestros de la ley. Condujeron a Jesús ante la Junta Suprema, y allí le preguntaron:

⁶⁷ «Dinos, ¿eres tú el Mesías?»

«Si os digo que sí» les contestó, «no me vais a creer; ⁶⁸ y si os hago preguntas, no me vais a responder. ⁶⁹ Pero desde ahora el Hijo del hombre estará sentado a la derecha del Dios todopoderoso.»

⁷⁰ Todos le preguntaron:

«¿Así que tú eres el Hijo de Dios?»

«Vosotros decís que lo soy» contestó Jesús.

⁷¹ Entonces dijeron ellos:

«¿Qué necesidad tenemos de más testigos? ¡Nosotros mismos lo hemos oído de sus propios labios!»

Jesús ante Pilato

23 Se levantaron todos y condujeron a Jesús ante Pilato. ² En presencia de este comenzaron a acusarle, diciendo:

«Hemos encontrado a este hombre alborotando a nuestra nación. Dice que no debemos pagar impuestos al césar y afirma que él es el Mesías, el Rey.»

[3] Pilato le preguntó:

«¿Eres tú el Rey de los judíos?»

«Tú lo dices» contestó Jesús.

[4] Entonces Pilato dijo a los jefes de los sacerdotes y a la gente:

«No encuentro culpa alguna en este hombre.»

[5] Pero ellos insistían aún más:

«Con sus enseñanzas está alborotando a todo el pueblo. Empezó en Galilea y ahora sigue haciéndolo aquí, en Judea.»

Jesús ante Herodes

[6] Al oir esto, Pilato preguntó si Jesús era de Galilea. [7] Y al saber que, en efecto, lo era, se lo envió a Herodes, el gobernador de Galilea, que por aquellos días se encontraba también en Jerusalén. [8] Al ver a Jesús, Herodes se alegró mucho, porque ya hacía bastante tiempo que quería conocerle, pues había oído hablar de él y esperaba verle hacer algún milagro. [9] Le preguntó muchas cosas, pero Jesús no le contestó nada. [10] También estaban allí los jefes de los sacerdotes y los maestros de la ley, que le acusaban con gran insistencia. [11] Entonces Herodes y sus soldados le trataron con desprecio, y para burlarse de él le pusieron un espléndido manto real. Luego Herodes se lo envió nuevamente a Pilato. [12] Aquel día se hicieron amigos Pilato y Herodes, que hasta entonces habían sido enemigos.

Jesús, sentenciado a muerte

[13] Pilato reunió a los jefes de los sacerdotes, a las autoridades y al pueblo, [14] y les dijo:

«Aquí me habéis traído a este hombre, diciendo que alborota al pueblo, pero le he interrogado delante de vosotros y no le he encontrado culpable de nada de lo que le acusáis. [15] Ni tampoco Herodes, puesto que nos lo ha devuelto. Ya veis que no ha hecho nada que merezca la pena de muerte. [16] Le voy a castigar y luego lo pondré en libertad.» [[17] Durante la fiesta, Pilato tenía que agradar a la gente poniendo en libertad a un preso.]

[18] Pero todos a una comenzaron a gritar:

«¡Fuera con ese! ¡Suéltanos a Barrabás!»

¹⁹ Barrabás era uno que estaba en la cárcel por una rebelión en la ciudad, y por un asesinato. ²⁰ Pilato, que quería poner en libertad a Jesús, les habló otra vez; ²¹ pero ellos gritaron más aún:

«¡Crucifícalo! ¡Crucifícalo!»

²² Por tercera vez les dijo Pilato:

«Pues ¿qué mal ha hecho? Yo no encuentro en él nada que merezca la pena de muerte. Le voy a castigar y luego lo pondré en libertad.»

²³ Pero ellos insistían a grandes voces, pidiendo que lo crucificase. Y como sus gritos crecían más y más, ²⁴ Pilato decidió hacer lo que le pedían: ²⁵ puso en libertad al que habían escogido, el que estaba en la cárcel por rebelión y asesinato, y entregó a Jesús a la voluntad de ellos.

Crucifixión de Jesús

²⁶ Cuando llevaban a crucificar a Jesús, echaron mano de un hombre de Cirene llamado Simón, que venía del campo, y le hicieron cargar con la cruz y llevarla detrás de Jesús.

²⁷ Mucha gente y muchas mujeres que lloraban y gritaban de dolor por él, le seguían. ²⁸ Jesús las miró, y les dijo:

«Mujeres de Jerusalén, no lloréis por mí, sino por vosotras mismas y por vuestros hijos. ²⁹ Porque vendrán días en que se dirá: "¡Dichosas las que no pueden tener hijos, los vientres que nunca concibieron y los pechos que no dieron de mamar!" ³⁰ Y entonces comenzará la gente a decir a los montes: "¡Caed sobre nosotros!", y a las colinas: "¡Escondednos!" ³¹ Porque si con el árbol verde hacen todo esto, ¿qué no harán con el seco?»

³² También llevaban a dos malhechores, para matarlos junto con Jesús. ³³ Cuando llegaron al sitio llamado de la Calavera, crucificaron a Jesús y a los dos malhechores, uno a su derecha y otro a su izquierda. [³⁴ Jesús dijo: «Padre, perdónalos porque no saben lo que hacen.»]

Los soldados echaron suertes para repartirse entre sí la ropa de Jesús. ³⁵ La gente estaba allí mirando; y hasta las autoridades se burlaban de él diciendo:

«Salvó a otros: ¡que se salve a sí mismo ahora, si de veras es el Mesías de Dios y su escogido!»

³⁶ Los soldados también se burlaban de Jesús. Se acercaban a él y le daban a beber vino agrio, ³⁷ diciéndole:

«¡Si eres el Rey de los judíos, sálvate a ti mismo!»

[38] Y sobre su cabeza había un letrero que decía: «Este es el Rey de los judíos.»

[39] Uno de los malhechores allí colgados le insultaba, diciéndole:

«¡Si tú eres el Mesías, sálvate a ti mismo y sálvanos a nosotros!»

[40] Pero el otro reprendió a su compañero diciendo:

«¿No temes a Dios, tú que estás sufriendo el mismo castigo? [41] Nosotros padecemos con toda razón, pues recibimos el justo pago de nuestros actos; pero este no ha hecho nada malo.»

[42] Luego añadió:

«Jesús, acuérdate de mí cuando comiences a reinar.»

[43] Jesús le contestó:

«Te aseguro que hoy estarás conmigo en el paraíso.»

Muerte de Jesús

[44] Desde el mediodía y hasta las tres de la tarde, toda aquella tierra quedó en oscuridad. [45] El sol dejó de brillar y el velo del templo se rasgó por la mitad. [46] Jesús, gritando con fuerza, dijo:

«¡Padre, en tus manos encomiendo mi espíritu!»

Dicho esto, murió.

[47] Cuando el centurión vio lo que había sucedido, alabó a Dios diciendo:

«¡No hay duda de que este hombre era inocente!»

[48] Toda la multitud que estaba presente y que vio lo ocurrido regresó a la ciudad golpeándose el pecho. [49] Pero todos los amigos de Jesús, y también las mujeres que le habían seguido desde Galilea, se quedaron allí, mirando de lejos aquellas cosas.

Jesús es sepultado

[50-51] Un hombre bueno y justo llamado José, que era miembro de la Junta Suprema de los judíos y que esperaba el reino de Dios, no estuvo de acuerdo con la actuación de la Junta. Este José, natural de Arimatea, un pueblo de Judea, [52] fue a ver a Pilato y le pidió el cuerpo de Jesús. [53] Después de bajarlo de la cruz, lo envolvió en una sábana de lino y lo puso en un sepulcro excavado en una peña, donde todavía no habían sepultado a nadie. [54] Era el día de la preparación para el sábado, que estaba a punto de comenzar.

⁵⁵ Las mujeres que habían acompañado a Jesús desde Galilea fueron y vieron el sepulcro, y se fijaron en cómo sepultaban el cuerpo. ⁵⁶ Cuando volvieron a casa, prepararon perfumes y ungüentos.

El anuncio de la resurrección de Jesús

24 Las mujeres descansaron el sábado, conforme al mandamiento, pero el primer día de la semana volvieron al sepulcro muy temprano, llevando los perfumes que habían preparado. ² Al llegar, encontraron que la piedra que tapaba el sepulcro no se hallaba en su lugar; ³ y entraron, pero no encontraron el cuerpo del Señor Jesús. ⁴ Estaban asustadas, sin saber qué hacer, cuando de pronto vieron a dos hombres de pie junto a ellas, vestidos con ropas brillantes. ⁵ Llenas de miedo se inclinaron hasta el suelo, pero aquellos hombres les dijeron:

«¿Por qué buscáis entre los muertos al que está vivo? ⁶ No está aquí. Ha resucitado. Acordaos de lo que os dijo cuando aún se hallaba en Galilea: ⁷ que el Hijo del hombre había de ser entregado en manos de pecadores, que lo crucificarían y que al tercer día resucitaría.»

⁸ Entonces recordaron ellas las palabras de Jesús, ⁹ y al regresar del sepulcro contaron todo esto a los once apóstoles y a los demás. ¹⁰ Las que llevaron la noticia a los apóstoles fueron María Magdalena, Juana, María madre de Santiago, y las otras mujeres. ¹¹ Pero a los apóstoles les parecía una locura lo que ellas contaban, y no las creían.

¹² Sin embargo, Pedro fue corriendo al sepulcro. Miró dentro, pero no vio más que las sábanas. Entonces volvió a casa admirado de lo que había sucedido.

En el camino de Emaús

¹³ Dos de los discípulos se dirigían aquel mismo día a un pueblo llamado Emaús, a unos once kilómetros de Jerusalén. ¹⁴ Iban hablando de todo lo que había pasado. ¹⁵ Mientras conversaban y discutían, Jesús mismo se les acercó y se puso a caminar a su lado. ¹⁶ Pero, aunque le veían, algo les impedía reconocerle. ¹⁷ Jesús les preguntó:

«¿De qué venís hablando por el camino?»

Se detuvieron tristes, ¹⁸ y uno de ellos llamado Cleofás contestó:

«Seguramente tú eres el único que, habiendo estado en Jerusalén, no sabe lo que allí ha sucedido estos días.»

[19] Les preguntó:

«¿Qué ha sucedido?»

Le dijeron:

«Lo de Jesús de Nazaret, que era un profeta poderoso en hechos y palabras delante de Dios y de todo el pueblo. [20] Los jefes de los sacerdotes y nuestras autoridades lo entregaron para que lo condenaran a muerte y lo crucificaran. [21] Nosotros teníamos la esperanza de que él fuese el libertador de la nación de Israel, pero ya han pasado tres días desde entonces. [22] Sin embargo, algunas de las mujeres que están con nosotros nos han asustado, pues fueron de madrugada al sepulcro [23] y no encontraron el cuerpo; y volvieron a casa contando que unos ángeles se les habían aparecido y les habían dicho que Jesús está vivo. [24] Algunos de nuestros compañeros fueron después al sepulcro y lo encontraron todo como las mujeres habían dicho, pero no vieron a Jesús.»

[25] Jesús les dijo entonces:

«¡Qué faltos de comprensión sois y cuánto os cuesta creer todo lo que dijeron los profetas! [26] ¿Acaso no tenía que sufrir el Mesías estas cosas antes de ser glorificado?»

[27] Luego se puso a explicarles todos los pasajes de las Escrituras que hablaban de él, comenzando por los libros de Moisés y siguiendo por todos los libros de los profetas.

[28] Al llegar al pueblo adonde se dirigían, Jesús hizo como si fuera a seguir adelante; [29] pero ellos le obligaron a quedarse, diciendo:

«Quédate con nosotros, porque ya es tarde y se está haciendo de noche.»

Entró, pues, Jesús, y se quedó con ellos. [30] Cuando estaban sentados a la mesa, tomó en sus manos el pan, y habiendo dado gracias a Dios, lo partió y se lo dio. [31] En ese momento se les abrieron los ojos y reconocieron a Jesús; pero él desapareció. [32] Se dijeron el uno al otro:

«¿No es cierto que el corazón nos ardía en el pecho mientras nos venía hablando por el camino y nos explicaba las Escrituras?»

[33] Sin esperar a más, se pusieron en camino y regresaron a Jerusalén, donde encontraron reunidos a los once apóstoles y a los que estaban con ellos. [34] Estos les dijeron:

«Verdaderamente ha resucitado el Señor y se ha aparecido a Simón.»

[35] Entonces ellos contaron lo que les había pasado en el camino, y cómo reconocieron a Jesús al partir el pan.

Jesús se aparece a los discípulos

[36] Todavía estaban hablando de estas cosas, cuando Jesús se puso en medio de ellos y los saludó diciendo:

«Paz a vosotros.»

[37] Ellos, sobresaltados y muy asustados, pensaron que estaban viendo un espíritu. [38] Pero Jesús les dijo:

«¿Por qué estáis tan asustados y por qué tenéis esas dudas en vuestro corazón? [39] Ved mis manos y mis pies: ¡soy yo mismo! Tocadme y mirad: un espíritu no tiene carne ni huesos como veis que yo tengo.»

[40] Al decirles esto, les mostró las manos y los pies. [41] Pero como ellos no acababan de creerlo, a causa de la alegría y el asombro que sentían, Jesús les preguntó:

«¿Tenéis aquí algo de comer?»

[42] Le dieron un trozo de pescado asado, [43] y él lo tomó y lo comió en su presencia. [44] Luego les dijo:

«Lo que me ha sucedido es lo mismo que os anuncié cuando aún me hallaba entre vosotros: que había de cumplirse todo lo que está escrito de mí en la ley de Moisés, en los libros de los profetas y en los salmos.»

[45] Entonces les abrió la mente para que comprendieran las Escrituras, [46] y les dijo:

«Está escrito que el Mesías tenía que morir y que resucitaría al tercer día; [47] y que en su nombre, y comenzando desde Jerusalén, hay que anunciar a todas las naciones que se vuelvan a Dios, para que él les perdone sus pecados. [48] Vosotros sois testigos de estas cosas. [49] Y yo enviaré sobre vosotros lo que mi Padre prometió. Pero vosotros quedaos aquí, en Jerusalén, hasta que recibáis el poder que viene de Dios.»

Ascensión de Jesús

[50] Luego Jesús los llevó fuera de la ciudad, hasta Betania, y alzando las manos los bendijo. [51] Y mientras los bendecía se apartó de ellos y fue llevado al cielo. [52] Ellos, después de adorarle, volvieron muy contentos a Jerusalén. [53] Y estaban siempre en el templo, alabando a Dios.

Notes * *Notas* * *Note* * *Ghi chú*

¿Cómo celebrar a su familia —santuario de amor y vida— luego que concluya su asistencia a la Reunión Mundial de las Familias? Subscríbase para obtener un devocionario de 21 días de la Lectio Divina y recorrer el evangelio de Lucas con miembros de su familia o comunidad. A medida que escucha la palabra de Dios y medita en los relatos de esperanza y curación, permita que las Sagradas Escrituras transformen su comprensión del amor incondicional de Dios.

MEDITACIONES SOBRE
EL EVANGELIO
DE LUCAS PARA LA FAMILIA

Subscríbase para obtener este devocionario de 21 días de la Lectio Divina en cualquiera de las siguientes tres maneras.

- **Mensaje de texto:** Enviar texto **familia** al 72717

- **Correo electrónico:** Visite www.abs.us/familia

- **Aplicación móvil:** Visite app.bible.com/wmf para descargarla

 WORLD MEETING OF FAMILIES 2015 Philadelphia

 AMERICAN BIBLE SOCIETY

 **You**Version®

Famiglie,
ascoltate la Parola di Dio,
meditatela insieme,
pregate con essa,
lasciate che il Signore colmi di misericordia
la vostra vita.

Franciscus

Lo stemma di Papa Francesco ritiene il disegno usato quando era ancora Arcivescovo di Buenos Aires, con l'aggiunta dei simboli papali della mitra vescovile e le chiavi incrociate legate da uno spago rosso.

Lo scudo è di color azzurro. Nel centro c'è l'emblema dell'ordine religioso del papa, la Società di Gesù: un sole risplendente con la croce e le lettere IHS (la monogramma di Gesù) in rosso, e tre chiodi neri. Di sotto c'è una stella dorata, simbolo della Vergine Maria, e un grappolo di fiori, simbolo di San Giuseppe.

Il motto latino al di sotto dello stemma è: "miserando atque eligendo," signifciando approssimativamente "modesto ma scelto." Tradotto letteralmente, significa: "avendo pietà, scegliendo lui." Questa frase viene dall'omelia di Beda il Venerabile sulla vocazione di San Matteo, esattore delle tasse, a diventare apostolo. Papa Francesco fu chiamata alla vita religiosa all'età di 17 anni, il giorno della festa di San Matteo.

Archdiocese of Philadelphia
Office of the Archbishop
222 North 17th Street
Philadelphia, PA 19103-1299

Settembre 2015

Cari amici,

Tutti e quattro i Vangeli sono ricchi incontri con la Parola di Dio.
Ma per molti lettori, Luca è l'evangelista che parla in modo più
commovente con la voce della misericordia di Dio. Solo in Luca
troviamo tre delle più grandi espressioni dell'amore di Gesù: la
parabola del figlio prodigo, la parabola del buon samaritano, e le sue
parole sulla croce al "buon ladrone."

Il Vangelo che tenete nelle vostre mani- un regalo meraviglioso da
parte del *American Bible Society* – è un ricordo della tenerezza di Dio
per voi personalmente; un invito di camminare con Gesù Cristo sul
cammino verso il paradiso. Leggetelo. Pregate su di esso. Amatelo.

Che Dio benedica voi e i vostri cari durante l'Incontro Mondiale delle
Famiglie, e ogni giorno in seguito.

Il vostro fratello nel Signore,

+ Charles J. Chaput, ofm. cap.

Il Reverendissimo Charles J. Chaput, O.F.M. Cap.
Arcivescovo di Philadelphia

INTRODUZIONE

LA BUONA NOTIZIA *della* MISERICORDIA *in* FAMIGLIA

Care famiglie,

Con grande gioia introduco questa edizione del Vangelo di Luca, dono di Papa Francesco alle famiglie di tutto il mondo in occasione dell'VIII Incontro Mondiale di Philadelphia.

L'augurio è che la lettura di questo Vangelo accompagni l'Anno Santo della Misericordia che il Santo Padre ha voluto inizi fra poche settimane: Luca è il vangelo, la Buona Notizia della misericordia di Dio per la vita di ognuno e delle nostre famiglie.

IL VANGELO IN FAMIGLIA

Ogni generazione cristiana – anche la nostra – è chiamata a prendere in mano questo piccolo libro. Il Vangelo infatti è la forza della Chiesa, è la Parola da cui essa è nata e per cui essa vive. Il cristiancsimo inizia, appunto, quando il Verbo (la Parola) si è fatta carne nel seno di Maria. Lei è la prima dei credenti e subito è stata indicata come tale da Elisabetta: «Beata colei che ha creduto all'adempimento della parola del Signore» (Lc 1,45). E, dopo di lei, sono venuti i primi discepoli. Quando essi accolsero la parola di Gesù iniziò una nuova fraternità, potremmo dire una "nuova famiglia": quella di Gesù con i suoi discepoli. Dopo la Pentecoste il Vangelo ha iniziato a espandersi attraverso le case, le famiglie dei cristiani. Insomma, il cammino del Vangelo all'inizio del primo millennio è stato segnato dall'ascolto nelle famiglie.

Care famiglie, credo che anche noi dobbiamo ripercorrere quel che avvenne all'inizio del cristianesimo: riprendere il Vangelo nelle nostre mani, anche nelle nostre famiglie, e ritessere una nuova fraternità tra le persone, una nuova solidarietà tra le famiglie, per poter dare la "buona notizia" dell'amore di Dio per tutti. San Giovanni Paolo II, aprendo il grande Giubileo del 2000, esortava i cristiani a entrare «nel nuovo millennio con il libro del Vangelo!». Con quella passione che lo ha portato pellegrino del Vangelo ovunque nel mondo, aggiungeva: «Prendiamo nelle nostre mani questo Libro! Accettiamolo dal Signore che continuamente ce lo offre tramite la sua Chiesa (cfr. Ap 10,8). Divoriamolo (cfr. Ap 10,9), perché diventi vita della nostra vita. Gustiamolo fino in fondo: ci riserverà fatiche, ma ci darà gioia perché è dolce come il miele (cfr. Ap 10,9-10). Saremo ricolmi di speranza e capaci di comunicarla a ogni uomo e donna che incontriamo sul nostro cammino».

Papa Francesco ci esorta nella stessa direzione: riprendete in mano il Vangelo! Ce lo dice nella splendida Lettera intitolata "La gioia del Vangelo" (Evangelii gaudium). Sì, è indispensabile riprendere in mano il Vangelo e ascoltarlo con rinnovata attenzione per avere un mondo più fraterno, più solidale, più umano. L'insicurezza e la paura che stanno segnando la vita di questo nostro mondo, le incredibili ingiustizie che lacerano la vita di tanti popoli, la violenza che sembra espandersi senza freno anche dentro le nostre case, i conflitti e le guerre che ancora continuano a mietere vittime innocenti, possono essere superate solo grazie al Vangelo. Per questo motivo Papa Francesco ha voluto regalare un milione di copie di questo libro alle famiglie di cinque grandi città del mondo: L'Avana (Cuba), Hanoi (Vietnam), Kinshasa (Congo), Marsiglia (Francia), Sidney (Australia). Laddove il contesto urbano e le sue periferie sembrano rendere ancor più faticosa la convivenza umana, il Papa ha voluto che la Parola di Gesù risuoni con più forza.

UN ESERCIZIO QUOTIDIANO

Leggiamo ogni giorno un piccolo brano di Vangelo. Saremo come costretti a entrare nel cuore e nei giorni di Gesù: lo seguiremo nei suoi viaggi, parteciperemo alla sua compassione per tutti, prenderemo parte alla sua tenerezza per i piccoli e i deboli, ci commuoveremo per la sua compassione nello stare accanto ai poveri, piangeremo al vedere quanto ci ha voluto bene, gioiremo per la sua risurrezione che ha sconfitto definitivamente il male. Lo conosceremo di più e lo ameremo di più.

Ricordiamoci di farlo realmente ogni giorno. Quotidianamente noi siamo invasi da parole, da immagini, da messaggi, da inviti... E non tutti sono buoni messaggi, e solo pochi aiutano a vivere. A casa poi c'è il rischio che per motivi vari neppure ci parliamo, oppure, se non "volano i piatti", volano parole che talora fanno male più dei piatti. In ogni caso, tutti sentiamo il bisogno di parole buone che giungano sino al cuore: il Vangelo è la parola che giunge sino al cuore. Nella preghiera del *Padre nostro* chiediamo a Dio che ci dia il «pane quotidiano». Le parole di Gesù sono il «pane vivo disceso dal cielo» offerto a noi quotidianamente. È il pane migliore. Nutre il cuore e il corpo.

Care famiglie, leggere assieme il Vangelo in famiglia è uno dei modi più belli ed efficaci per pregare. Il Signore lo gradisce in maniera particolare. Vi ricordate l'episodio di Marta e Maria? Gesù, a Marta che si era indispettita nel vedere Maria che ascoltava Gesù, fa notare che Maria si è scelta «la parte migliore», quella di cui «c'è bisogno». È facile per tutti noi essere travolti, come lo fu Marta, dalle cose da fare, dalle questioni da risolvere, dai problemi da affrontare, dalle difficoltà da superare. «Maria – dice anche a noi Gesù, oggi – si è scelta la parte migliore» (Lc 10,42). Questo piccolo libro vuole aiutare a rendere l'ascolto del Vangelo la "parte migliore" delle nostre giornate, la "parte migliore" di tutte le giornate dell'anno.

Abbiamo bisogno di ascoltare. Il primo passo della preghiera cristiana è ascoltare Gesù che ci parla. Sì, care famiglie, prima di moltiplicare le nostre parole da rivolgere al Signore, ascoltiamo quelle che Egli ci rivolge. Ogni giorno. Proviamo ad ascoltarle e faremo la stessa esperienza dei due discepoli di Emmaus, i quali sentirono il cuore riscaldarsi e il bisogno di restare con lui. L'ascolto si trasforma in preghiera e l'incontro con Gesù illumina di nuovo la loro vita.

Certo, bisogna radunarsi assieme e fare un po' di silenzio attorno a sé. Sappiamo quanto sia diventato difficile trovare un momento di silenzio e di preghiera. Ma è indispensabile. Potremmo dire che la preghiera quotidiana è il nostro modo di «pregare sempre, senza stancarci mai». Sì, pregare ogni giorno con il Vangelo è il nostro modo di pregare sempre.

Quindi si deve trovare un momento per stare assieme, magari prima di un pasto, oppure alla fine della giornata, o anche all'inizio. O in altri momenti. Quel che conta è scegliere cinque minuti per pregare assieme in maniera breve ma efficace.

Dopo il segno della croce e una breve invocazione allo Spirito santo perché scenda nei nostri cuori e illumini la nostra mente, leggiamo un piccolo passo, offriamo qualche semplice spiegazione ai più piccoli e comunichiamoci reciprocamente qualche pensiero che questo ascolto suscita; a questo punto chiediamoci per chi vogliamo pregare in modo particolare e concludiamo recitando insieme il *Padre nostro* e ringraziando il Signore per il dono della sua Parola. Non dimentichiamo di decidere insieme un piccolo e semplice proposto con cui questa parola può segnare le nostre vite.

Care famiglie, mentre ringrazio vivamente l'American Bible Society che ha permesso la realizzazione di questo volume, vi auguro di tutto cuore che il primo frutto di questi giorni intensi vissuti insieme a Philadelphia sia la decisione di lasciare che la Parola di Dio abiti le vostre case e quelle della vostra città.

+ Vincenzo Paglia

Arcivescovo Vincenzo Paglia
Presidente del Pontificio Consiglio per la Famiglia

IL VANGELO
SECONDO LUCA

The Gospel according to Luke / Il Vangelo secondo Luca
Italian text from / Testo italiano da «Parola del Signore, la Bibbia. Traduzione interconfessionale in lingua corrente»

© 2000
Editrice Elle Di Ci, Leumann ~ Alleanza Biblica Universale/United Bible Societies, Società Biblica Britannica & Forestiera, Roma.

Il testo finale di questa traduzione è stato approvato dall'Alleanza Biblica Universale (United Bible Societies) e, da parte cattolica, dall'autorità ecclesiastica (Conferenza Episcopale Italiana).

INTRODUZIONE

CARATTERISTICHE PRINCIPALI

Le caratteristiche particolari di questo Vangelo sono diverse da quelle degli altri Vangeli (di Matteo, di Marco, di Giovanni) contenuti nel Nuovo Testamento della Bibbia cristiana. Una posizione speciale è riservata a Gerusalemme: qui più che altrove essa è il centro e il vertice dell'attività di Gesù. Attorno a Gesù si svolgono gli avvenimenti decisivi della «storia della salvezza», quelle azioni di Dio che riscattano la condizione umana dal male. Ora giunge a conclusione la lunga premessa costituita dalla storia dell'antico Israele (Antico Testamento). Si apre l'epoca nuova dei credenti in tutto il mondo. Incomincia l'attesa del compimento finale.

La salvezza cristiana si intreccia con le vicende della storia terrena (2,1; 3,1-4) e riguarda tutti gli uomini (3,6). Gesù si rivolge soprattutto ai «poveri» (cioè a persone poco importanti, malate o disprezzate) e proprio tra loro il messaggio del Vangelo è più accolto e più visibilmente si manifesta l'inizio del regno di Dio.

PRIMI LETTORI

Al tempo di questo Vangelo la generazione degli apostoli sta per scomparire. Ormai non è più possibile ascoltare dalla loro viva voce l'esperienza di coloro che hanno conosciuto direttamente Gesù, hanno udito il suo insegnamento e visto i suoi gesti, hanno vissuto i giorni della sua passione, morte e risurrezione. Intanto sorgono altri predicatori, forse nuove dottrine si diffondono.

Perciò Luca comprende che i credenti hanno bisogno di una solida documentazione sugli avvenimenti centrali che riguardano la fede. Egli fa allora accurate ricerche tra le memorie più sicure, scritte e orali, e le offre come sostegno all'insegnamento cristiano del suo tempo (1,1-4). Non sappiamo nulla del destinatario Teofilo, ma sicuramente egli rappresenta i lettori per i quali Luca ha scritto.

AUTORE

Di un certo Luca parlano alcune lettere del Nuovo Testamento (Filemone 24; Colossesi 4,14; 2 Timoteo 4,11). Questo Luca è un discepolo dell'apostolo Paolo, medico di professione, di cultura e di lingua greca. È la medesima persona che ha scritto questo Vangelo e il libro degli Atti? Antichissime tradizioni lo affermano. Molti moderni sono dello stesso parere; altri studiosi invece fanno notare che nessuna idea caratteristica di Paolo è molto evidente in questo Vangelo. In ogni caso l'autore rispecchia l'ambiente di comunità cristiane non palestinesi, verso la fine del primo secolo. Dal libro degli Atti egli risulta molto interessato alla prima diffusione missionaria nel mondo greco. La data di composizione di questo vangelo è vicina all'anno 80 d.C.

SCHEMA

Introduzione-dedica	*1,1-4*
Giovanni e Gesù: nascita e infanzia	*1,5–2,52*
Giovanni il Battezzatore	*3,1-20*
Battesimo e tentazioni di Gesù	*3,21–4,13*
Gesù in Galilea	*4,14–9,50*
Viaggio verso Gerusalemme	*9,51–19,27*
Gesù a Gerusalemme	*19,28–21,37*
Passione, morte, risurrezione,	
apparizioni, ascensione	*22,1–24,53*

IL VANGELO SECONDO LUCA

Introduzione

1 Caro Teòfilo, molti prima di me hanno tentato di narrare con ordine i fatti che sono accaduti tra noi. [2] I primi a raccontarli sono stati i testimoni di quei fatti che avevano visto e udito: essi hanno ricevuto da Gesù l'incarico di annunziare la parola di Dio. [3] Anch'io perciò mi sono deciso di fare ricerche accurate su tutto, risalendo fino alle origini. Ora, o illustre Teòfilo, ti scrivo tutto con ordine, [4] e così potrai renderti conto di quanto sono solidi gli insegnamenti che hai ricevuto.

Annunzio della nascita di Giovanni

[5] Al tempo di Erode, re della Giudea, c'era un sacerdote che si chiamava Zaccaria e apparteneva all'ordine sacerdotale di Abia. Anche sua moglie, Elisabetta, era di famiglia sacerdotale: discendeva infatti dalla famiglia di Aronne. [6] Essi vivevano rettamente di fronte a Dio, e nessuno poteva dir niente contro di loro perché ubbidivano ai comandamenti e alle leggi del Signore. [7] Erano senza figli perché Elisabetta non poteva averne, e tutti e due ormai erano troppo vecchi.

[8] Un giorno Zaccaria era di turno al Tempio per le funzioni sacerdotali. [9] Secondo l'uso dei sacerdoti, quella volta a lui toccò in sorte di entrare nel santuario del Signore per offrire l'incenso. [10] Nell'ora in cui si bruciava l'incenso egli si trovava all'interno del santuario e tutta la folla dei fedeli stava fuori a pregare. [11] In quell'istante un angelo del Signore apparve a Zaccaria al lato destro dell'altare sul quale si offriva l'incenso. [12] Appena lo vide, Zaccaria rimase molto sconvolto. [13] Ma l'angelo gli disse:

«Non temere, Zaccaria! Dio ha ascoltato la tua preghiera. Tua moglie Elisabetta ti darà un figlio e tu lo chiamerai Giovanni. [14] La sua nascita ti darà una grande gioia, e molti si rallegreranno. [15] Egli infatti sarà grande nei progetti di Dio. Egli non berrà mai vino né bevande inebrianti ma Dio lo colmerà di Spirito Santo fin dalla nascita. [16] Questo tuo figlio riporterà molti Israeliti al Signore loro Dio: [17] forte e potente come il profeta Elia, verrà prima del Signore, per riconciliare i padri con i figli, per ricondurre i ribelli a pensare come i giusti. Così egli preparerà al Signore un popolo ben disposto».

[18] Ma Zaccaria disse all'angelo:

«Come potrò essere sicuro di quel che mi dici? Io sono ormai vecchio, e anche mia moglie è avanti negli anni».

[19] L'angelo gli rispose:

«Io sono Gabriele e sto davanti a Dio sempre pronto a servirlo. Lui mi ha mandato da te a parlarti e a portarti questa bella notizia. [20] Tu non hai creduto alle mie parole che al momento giusto si avvereranno. Per questo diventerai muto e non potrai parlare fino al giorno in cui si compirà la promessa che ti ho fatto».

[21] Intanto, fuori del santuario, il popolo aspettava Zaccaria e si meravigliava che restasse là dentro tanto tempo. [22] Quando poi Zaccaria uscì e si accorsero che non poteva parlare con loro, capirono che nel santuario egli aveva avuto una visione. Faceva loro dei segni con le mani, ma non riusciva a dire neppure una parola.

[23] Passati i giorni del suo servizio al Tempio, Zaccaria tornò a casa sua. [24] Dopo un po' di tempo, sua moglie Elisabetta si accorse di aspettare un figlio, e non uscì di casa per cinque mesi [25] e diceva: «Ecco che cosa ha fatto per me il Signore! Finalmente ha voluto liberarmi da una condizione che mi faceva vergognare di fronte a tutti».

Annunzio della nascita di Gesù

[26] Quando Elisabetta fu al sesto mese Dio mandò l'angelo Gabriele a Nàzaret, un villaggio della Galilea. [27] L'angelo andò da una fanciulla che era fidanzata con un certo Giuseppe, discendente del re Davide. La fanciulla si chiamava Maria. [28] L'angelo entrò in casa e le disse:

«Ti saluto, Maria! Il Signore è con te: egli ti ha colmata di grazia».

[29] A queste parole Maria rimase sconvolta e si domandava che significato poteva avere quel saluto. [30] Ma l'angelo le disse:

«Non temere, Maria! Tu hai trovato grazia presso Dio. [31] Avrai un figlio, lo darai alla luce e gli metterai nome Gesù. [32] Egli sarà grande e Dio, l'Onnipotente, lo chiamerà suo Figlio. Il Signore lo farà re, lo porrà sul trono di Davide, suo padre, ³³ ed egli regnerà per sempre sul popolo d'Israele. Il suo regno non finirà mai».

³⁴ Allora Maria disse all'angelo:

«Com'è possibile questo, dal momento che io sono vergine?».

³⁵ L'angelo rispose:

«Lo Spirito Santo verrà su di te, e l'Onnipotente Dio, come una nube, ti avvolgerà. Per questo il bambino che avrai sarà santo, Figlio di Dio. ³⁶ Vedi: anche Elisabetta, tua parente, alla sua età aspetta un figlio. Tutti pensavano che non potesse avere bambini, eppure è già al sesto mese. ³⁷ Nulla è impossibile a Dio!».

³⁸ Allora Maria disse:

«Eccomi, sono la serva del Signore. Dio faccia con me come tu hai detto».

Poi l'angelo la lasciò.

Maria va a trovare Elisabetta

³⁹ In quei giorni Maria si mise in viaggio e raggiunse in fretta un villaggio che si trovava nella parte montagnosa della Giudea. ⁴⁰ Entrò in casa di Zaccaria e salutò Elisabetta. ⁴¹ Appena Elisabetta udì il saluto di Maria, il bambino dentro di lei ebbe un fremito, ed essa fu colmata di Spirito Santo ⁴² e a gran voce esclamò: «Dio ti ha benedetta più di tutte le altre donne, e benedetto è il bambino che avrai! ⁴³ Che grande cosa per me! Perché mai la madre del mio Signore viene a farmi visita? ⁴⁴ Appena ho sentito il tuo saluto, il bambino si è mosso dentro di me per la gioia. ⁴⁵ Beata te che hai avuto fiducia nel Signore e hai creduto che egli può compiere ciò che ti ha annunziato».

⁴⁶ Allora Maria disse:

«Grande è il Signore: lo voglio lodare.

⁴⁷ Dio è mio salvatore: sono piena di gioia.

⁴⁸ Ha guardato a me, alla sua povera serva:
tutti, d'ora in poi, mi diranno beata.

⁴⁹ Dio è potente:
ha fatto in me grandi cose,
santo è il suo nome.

⁵⁰ La sua misericordia resta per sempre
con tutti quelli che lo servono.

⁵¹ Ha dato prova della sua potenza,
　ha distrutto i superbi e i loro progetti.
⁵² Ha rovesciato dal trono i potenti,
　ha rialzato da terra gli oppressi.
⁵³ Ha colmato i poveri di beni,
　ha rimandato i ricchi a mani vuote.
⁵⁴ Fedele nella sua misericordia,
　ha risollevato il suo popolo, Israele.
⁵⁵ Così aveva promesso ai nostri padri:
　a favore di Abramo e dei suoi discendenti per sempre».

⁵⁶ Maria rimase con Elisabetta circa tre mesi. Poi ritornò a casa sua.

La nascita di Giovanni

⁵⁷ Giunse intanto per Elisabetta il tempo di partorire e diede alla luce un bambino. ⁵⁸ I suoi parenti e i vicini si rallegravano con lei perché avevano sentito dire che il Signore le aveva dato una grande prova della sua bontà. ⁵⁹ Quando il bambino ebbe otto giorni vennero per il rito della circoncisione. Lo volevano chiamare Zaccaria, che era anche il nome di suo padre. ⁶⁰ Ma intervenne la madre: «No!» disse. «Il suo nome sarà Giovanni».

⁶¹ Gli altri le dissero: «Nessuno tra i tuoi parenti ha questo nome!».

⁶² Si rivolsero allora con i gesti al padre, per sapere quale doveva essere, secondo lui, il nome del bambino. ⁶³ Zaccaria chiese allora una tavoletta e scrisse: «Il suo nome è Giovanni».

Tutti rimasero meravigliati. ⁶⁴ In quel medesimo istante Zaccaria aprì la bocca e riuscì di nuovo a parlare, e subito si mise a lodare Dio. ⁶⁵ Tutti i loro vicini furono presi da un senso di paura, e dappertutto in quella regione montagnosa della Giudea la gente parlava di questi fatti. ⁶⁶ Coloro che li sentivano raccontare si facevano pensierosi e tra le altre cose dicevano: «Che cosa diventerà mai questo bambino?». Davvero la potenza del Signore era con lui.

Il canto profetico di Zaccaria

⁶⁷ Allora Zaccaria, suo padre, fu riempito di Spirito Santo e si mise a profetare:

68 «Benedetto il Signore, il Dio d'Israele:
   è venuto incontro al suo popolo,
   lo ha liberato.
69 Per noi ha fatto sorgere
   un Salvatore potente
   tra i discendenti di Davide, suo servo.
70 Da molto tempo lo aveva promesso
   per bocca dei suoi santi profeti.
71 Ci ha liberato dai nostri nemici
   e dalle mani di tutti quelli che ci odiano.
72 Ha avuto misericordia dei nostri padri,
   è rimasto fedele alla sua alleanza.
73 Ha giurato ad Abramo, nostro padre,
74 di strapparci dalle mani dei nemici.
   Ora possiamo servirlo senza timore,
75 santi e fedeli a lui per tutta la vita.
76 E tu, figlio mio,
   diventerai profeta del Dio Altissimo:
   andrai dinanzi al Signore
   a preparargli la via.
77 E dirai al suo popolo
   che Dio lo salva e perdona i suoi peccati.
78 Il nostro Dio è bontà e misericordia:
   ci verrà incontro dall'alto,
   come luce che sorge.
79 Splenderà nelle tenebre per chi vive
   all'ombra della morte
   e guiderà i nostri passi sulla via della pace».

80 Il bambino intanto cresceva fisicamente e spiritualmente. Per molto tempo visse in regioni deserte fino a quando pubblicamente si manifestò al popolo d'Israele.

La nascita di Gesù

2 In quel tempo l'imperatore Augusto con un decreto ordinò il censimento di tutti gli abitanti dell'impero romano. ² Questo primo censimento fu fatto quando Quirinio era governatore della Siria. ³ Tut-

ti andavano a far scrivere il loro nome nei registri, ciascuno nel proprio luogo d'origine.

[4] Anche Giuseppe partì da Nàzaret, in Galilea, e salì a Betlemme, la città del re Davide, in Giudea. Andò là perché era un discendente diretto del re Davide, [5] e Maria sua sposa, che era incinta, andò con lui.

[6] Mentre si trovavano a Betlemme, giunse per Maria il tempo di partorire, [7] ed essa diede alla luce un figlio, il suo primogenito. Lo avvolse in fasce e lo mise a dormire nella mangiatoia di una stalla, perché per loro non c'era posto nell'alloggio.

Gli angeli portano l'annunzio ai pastori

[8] In quella stessa regione c'erano anche alcuni pastori. Essi passavano la notte all'aperto per fare la guardia al loro gregge. [9] Un angelo del Signore si presentò a loro e la gloria del Signore li avvolse di luce, così che essi ebbero una grande paura. [10] L'angelo disse: «Non temete! Io vi porto una bella notizia che procurerà una grande gioia a tutto il popolo: [11] oggi per voi, nella città di Davide è nato il Salvatore, il Cristo, il Signore. [12] Lo riconoscerete così: troverete un bambino avvolto in fasce che giace in una mangiatoia».

[13] Subito apparvero e si unirono a lui molti altri angeli. Essi lodavano Dio con questo canto:
[14] «Gloria a Dio in cielo
e sulla terra pace per quelli che egli ama».

Poi gli angeli si allontanarono dai pastori e se ne tornarono in cielo.

[15] Intanto i pastori dicevano gli uni agli altri: «Andiamo fino a Betlemme per vedere quel che è accaduto e che il Signore ci ha fatto sapere». [16] Giunsero in fretta a Betlemme e là trovarono Maria, Giuseppe e il bambino che giaceva nella mangiatoia. [17] Dopo averlo visto, fecero sapere ciò che avevano sentito di questo bambino. [18] Tutti quelli che ascoltarono i pastori si meravigliarono di quello che essi raccontavano. [19] Maria, da parte sua, custodiva il ricordo di tutti questi fatti e li meditava dentro di sé. [20] I pastori, sulla via del ritorno, lodavano Dio e lo ringraziavano per quel che avevano sentito e visto, perché tutto era avvenuto come l'angelo aveva loro detto.

[21] Passati otto giorni, venne il tempo di compiere il rito della circoncisione del bambino. Gli fu messo nome Gesù, come aveva detto l'angelo ancor prima che fosse concepito nel grembo di sua madre.

Gesù è presentato al Tempio

[22] Venne poi per la madre e per il bambino il momento della loro purificazione, com'è stabilito dalla legge di Mosè. I genitori allora portarono il bambino a Gerusalemme per presentarlo al Signore. [23] Sta scritto infatti nella legge del Signore: *Ogni maschio primogenito appartiene al Signore.*

[24] Essi offrirono anche il sacrificio stabilito dalla legge del Signore: *un paio di tortore o due giovani colombi.*

[25] Viveva allora a Gerusalemme un uomo chiamato Simeone: un uomo retto e pieno di fede in Dio, che aspettava con fiducia la liberazione d'Israele. Lo Spirito Santo era con lui [26] e gli aveva rivelato che non sarebbe morto prima di aver veduto il Messia mandato dal Signore. [27] Mosso dallo Spirito Santo, Simeone andò nel Tempio dove s'incontrò con i genitori di Gesù, proprio mentre essi stavano portando il loro bambino per compiere quel che ordina la legge del Signore. [28] Simeone allora prese il bambino tra le braccia e ringraziò Dio così:

[29] «Ormai, Signore, puoi lasciare
    che il tuo servo se ne vada in pace:
    la tua promessa si è compiuta.
[30] Con i miei occhi ho visto il Salvatore.
[31] Tu l'hai messo davanti a tutti i popoli:
[32] luce per illuminare le nazioni
    e gloria del tuo popolo, Israele».

[33] Il padre e la madre di Gesù rimasero meravigliati per le cose che Simeone aveva detto del bambino. [34] Simeone poi li benedisse e parlò a Maria, la madre di Gesù: «Dio ha deciso che questo bambino sarà occasione di rovina o di risurrezione per molti in Israele. Sarà un segno di Dio che molti rifiuteranno: [35] così egli metterà in chiaro le intenzioni nascoste nel cuore di molti. Quanto a te, Maria, il dolore ti colpirà come fa una spada».

[36] In Gerusalemme viveva anche una profetessa, Anna, figlia di Fanuèle e apparteneva alla tribù di Aser. Era molto anziana: si era sposata giovane e aveva vissuto solo sette anni con suo marito, [37] poi era rimasta vedova. Ora aveva ottantaquattro anni. Essa non abbandonava mai il Tempio, e serviva Dio giorno e notte con digiuni e preghiere. [38] Arrivò anche lei in quello stesso momento e si mise a ringraziare il Signore, e parlava del bambino a tutti quelli che aspettavano la liberazione di Gerusalemme.

Ritornano a Nàzaret

[39] Quando i genitori di Gesù ebbero fatto tutto quello che è stabilito dalla legge del Signore, ritornarono con Gesù in Galilea, nel loro villaggio di Nàzaret. [40] Intanto il bambino cresceva e diventava sempre più robusto. Era pieno di sapienza e la benedizione di Dio era su di lui.

Gesù dodicenne a Gerusalemme

[41] I genitori di Gesù ogni anno andavano in pellegrinaggio a Gerusalemme per la festa di Pasqua. [42] Quando Gesù ebbe dodici anni, lo portarono per la prima volta con loro secondo l'usanza. [43] Finita la festa, ripresero il viaggio di ritorno. Ma Gesù rimase in Gerusalemme senza che i genitori se ne accorgessero. [44] Credevano che anche lui fosse in viaggio con la comitiva. Dopo un giorno di cammino, si misero a cercarlo tra parenti e conoscenti. [45] Non riuscendo a trovarlo, ritornarono a cercarlo in Gerusalemme. [46] Dopo tre giorni lo trovarono nel Tempio: era là, seduto in mezzo ai maestri della Legge: li ascoltava e discuteva con loro. [47] Tutti quelli che lo udivano erano meravigliati per l'intelligenza che dimostrava con le sue risposte. [48] Anche i suoi genitori, appena lo videro, rimasero stupiti, e sua madre gli disse:

«Figlio, che cosa ci hai combinato? Vedi, tuo padre e io ti abbiamo tanto cercato e siamo stati molto preoccupati per causa tua».

[49] Egli rispose loro:

«Perché cercarmi tanto? Non sapevate che io devo stare nella casa del Padre mio?».

[50] Ma essi non capirono il significato di quelle parole.

⁵¹ Gesù poi ritornò a Nàzaret con i genitori e ubbidiva loro volentieri. Sua madre custodiva dentro di sé il ricordo di tutti questi fatti.

⁵² Gesù intanto cresceva, progrediva in sapienza e godeva il favore di Dio e degli uomini.

Giovanni il Battezzatore predica nel deserto

3 Era l'anno quindicesimo del regno dell'imperatore Tiberio. Ponzio Pilato era governatore nella provincia della Giudea. Erode regnava sulla Galilea, suo fratello Filippo sull'Iturèa e sulla Traconìtide, e Lisània governava la provincia dell'Abilène, ² mentre Anna e Caifa erano sommi sacerdoti. In quel tempo Giovanni, il figlio di Zaccaria, era ancora nel deserto. Là Dio lo chiamò.

³ Allora Giovanni cominciò a percorrere tutta la regione del Giordano e a dire: «Cambiate vita e fatevi battezzare, e Dio perdonerà i vostri peccati». ⁴ Si realizzava così quel che sta scritto nel libro delle profezie di Isaia:

Una voce grida nel deserto:
Preparate la via del Signore,
spianate i suoi sentieri.
⁵ *Le valli siano tutte riempite,*
le montagne e le colline abbassate.
Raddrizzate le curve delle strade,
togliete tutti gli ostacoli.
⁶ *Allora tutti vedranno che Dio è il salvatore.*

⁷ Una gran folla andava da Giovanni per farsi battezzare, ed egli diceva loro: «Razza di vipere! Chi vi ha fatto credere che potete sfuggire al castigo ormai vicino? ⁸ Fate vedere con i fatti che avete cambiato vita e non mettetevi a dire: "Noi siamo discendenti di Abramo". Vi assicuro infatti che Dio è capace di far sorgere veri figli di Abramo anche da queste pietre. ⁹ La scure è già alla radice degli alberi, pronta per tagliare: ogni albero che non fa frutti buoni sarà tagliato e gettato nel fuoco».

¹⁰ Tra la folla qualcuno lo interrogava così:
«In fin dei conti che cosa dobbiamo fare?».

¹¹ Giovanni rispondeva:
«Chi possiede due abiti ne dia uno a chi non ne ha, e chi ha dei viveri li distribuisca agli altri».

[12] Anche alcuni agenti delle tasse vennero da Giovanni per farsi battezzare. Gli domandarono:
«Maestro, noi che cosa dobbiamo fare?».

[13] Giovanni rispose:
«Non prendete niente di più di quanto è stabilito dalla legge».

[14] Lo interrogavano infine anche alcuni soldati:
«E noi che cosa dobbiamo fare?».

Giovanni rispose:
«Non portate via soldi a nessuno, né con la violenza né con false accuse, ma accontentatevi della vostra paga».

[15] Intanto le speranze del popolo crescevano e tutti si chiedevano:
«Chissà, forse Giovanni è il Messia!».

[16] Ma Giovanni disse a tutti:
«Io vi battezzo con acqua, ma sta per venire uno che è più potente di me. Io non sono degno neppure di slacciargli i sandali. Lui vi battezzerà con lo Spirito Santo e il fuoco. [17] Egli tiene in mano la pala per separare il grano dalla paglia. Raccoglierà il grano nel suo granaio, ma brucerà la paglia con un fuoco senza fine».

[18] Con queste e molte altre parole Giovanni esortava il popolo e gli annunziava la salvezza.

[19] Inoltre Giovanni aveva rimproverato il governatore Erode perché si era preso Erodìade, moglie di suo fratello, e per tutte le altre cose cattive che aveva fatto. [20] Allora Erode aggiunse un altro delitto a quelli che già aveva fatto: fece imprigionare anche Giovanni.

Il battesimo di Gesù

[21] Intanto tutto il popolo si faceva battezzare. Anche Gesù si fece battezzare e mentre pregava, il cielo si aprì. [22] Lo Spirito Santo discese sopra di lui in modo visibile come una colomba, e una voce venne dal cielo: «Tu sei il Figlio mio, che io amo. Io ti ho mandato».

Gli antenati di Gesù

[23] Gesù aveva circa trent'anni quando diede inizio alla sua opera. Secondo l'opinione comune egli era figlio di Giuseppe, il quale a sua volta era figlio di Eli [24] e questi era figlio di Mattàt, figlio di Levi, figlio di Melchi, figlio di Innài, figlio di Giuseppe, [25] figlio di Mattatìa, figlio

di Amos, figlio di Naum, figlio di Esli, figlio di Naggài, [26] figlio di Maat, figlio di Mattatìa, figlio di Semèin, figlio di Iosech, figlio di Ioda, [27] figlio di Ioanan, figlio di Resa, figlio di Zorobabèle, figlio di Salatiel, figlio di Neri, [28] figlio di Melchi, figlio di Addi, figlio di Cosam, figlio di Elmadàm, figlio di Er, [29] figlio di Gesù, figlio di Eliezer, figlio di Iorim, figlio di Mattàt, figlio di Levi, [30] figlio di Simeone, figlio di Giuda, figlio di Giuseppe, figlio di Ionam, figlio di Eliacim, [31] figlio di Melèa, figlio di Menna, figlio di Mattatà, figlio di Natàm, figlio di Davide, [32] figlio di Iesse, figlio di Obed, figlio di Booz, figlio di Sala, figlio di Naassòn, [33] figlio di Aminadàb, figlio di Admin, figlio di Arni, figlio di Esrom, figlio di Fares, figlio di Giuda, [34] figlio di Giacobbe, figlio di Isacco, figlio di Abramo, figlio di Tare, figlio di Nacor, [35] figlio di Seruch, figlio di Ragau, figlio di Falek, figlio di Eber, figlio di Sala, [36] figlio di Cainam, figlio di Arfàcsad, figlio di Sem, figlio di Noè, figlio di Lamech, [37] figlio di Matusalemme, figlio di Enoc, figlio di Iaret, figlio di Mallèel, figlio di Cainam, [38] figlio di Enos, figlio di Set, figlio di Adamo, figlio di Dio.

Le tentazioni di Gesù

4 Gesù, pieno di Spirito Santo, si allontanò dalla regione del Giordano. Poi, sempre sotto l'azione dello Spirito, andò nel deserto [2] e rimase là quaranta giorni, mentre Satana lo assaliva con le sue tentazioni. Per tutti quei giorni non mangiò nulla e alla fine ebbe fame. [3] Allora il diavolo gli disse:

«Se tu sei il Figlio di Dio comanda a questa pietra di diventare pane».

[4] Ma Gesù gli rispose:

«No, perché nella Bibbia è scritto:

Non di solo pane vive l'uomo».

[5] Il diavolo allora condusse Gesù sopra un monte e in un solo istante gli fece vedere tutti i regni della terra. [6-7] Gli disse:

«Vedi, tutti questi regni, ricchi e potenti, sono miei: a me sono stati dati e io li do a chi voglio. Ebbene, se ti inginocchierai davanti a me saranno tutti tuoi».

[8] Gesù rispose di nuovo:

«No, perché nella Bibbia è scritto:

Adora il Signore, che è il tuo Dio:
a lui solo rivolgi la tua preghiera!».

⁹ Alla fine il diavolo condusse Gesù a Gerusalemme, lo mise sulla punta più alta del Tempio e gli disse: «Se tu sei il Figlio di Dio buttati giù di qui. ¹⁰ Perché nella Bibbia è scritto:

Dio comanderà ai suoi angeli di proteggerti.
¹¹ *Essi ti sosterranno con le loro mani*
perché tu non inciampi contro alcuna pietra».

¹² Gesù gli rispose per l'ultima volta: «Ma la Bibbia dice anche:

Non sfidare il Signore, tuo Dio».

¹³ Il diavolo allora, avendo esaurito ogni genere di tentazione, si allontanò da Gesù, ma aspettando un altro momento propizio.

Gesù inizia la sua attività in Galilea

¹⁴ Poi Gesù ritornò in Galilea e la potenza dello Spirito Santo era con lui. In tutta quella regione si parlava di lui. ¹⁵ Egli insegnava nelle sinagoghe degli Ebrei, e tutti lo lodavano.

Gesù viene respinto dalla gente di Nàzaret

¹⁶ Poi Gesù andò a Nàzaret, il villaggio nel quale era cresciuto. Era sabato, il giorno del riposo. Come al solito Gesù entrò nella sinagoga e si alzò per fare la lettura della Bibbia. ¹⁷ Gli diedero il libro del profeta Isaia ed egli, aprendolo, trovò questa profezia:

¹⁸ *Il Signore ha mandato*
il suo Spirito su di me.
Egli mi ha scelto
per portare il lieto messaggio ai poveri.
Mi ha mandato per proclamare
la liberazione ai prigionieri
e il dono della vista ai ciechi,
per liberare gli oppressi,
¹⁹ *per annunziare il tempo*
nel quale il Signore sarà favorevole.

²⁰ Quando ebbe finito di leggere, Gesù chiuse il libro, lo restituì all'inserviente e si sedette. La gente che era nella sinagoga teneva gli occhi fissi su Gesù. ²¹ Allora egli cominciò a dire: «Oggi per voi che

mi ascoltate si realizza questa profezia». [22] La gente, sorpresa per le cose meravigliose che diceva, gli dava ragione ma si chiedeva: «Non è lui il figlio di Giuseppe?». [23] Allora Gesù aggiunse: «Sono sicuro che voi mi ricorderete il famoso proverbio: "Medico, cura te stesso" e mi direte: "Fa' anche qui, nel tuo villaggio, quelle cose che, a quanto si sente dire, hai fatto a Cafàrnao". [24] Ma io vi dico: nessun profeta ha fortuna in patria. [25] Anzi, vi voglio dire un'altra cosa: al tempo del profeta Elia vi erano molte vedove in Israele, quando per tre anni e mezzo non cadde neppure una goccia di pioggia e ci fu una grande carestia in tutta quella regione; [26] eppure Dio non ha mandato il profeta Elia a nessuna di loro, ma soltanto a una povera vedova straniera che viveva a Sarepta, nella regione di Sidone. [27] Così pure ai tempi del profeta Eliseo, vi erano molti lebbrosi in Israele; eppure Dio non ha guarito nessuno di loro, ma soltanto Naaman, uno straniero della Siria».

[28] Sentendo queste cose i presenti nella sinagoga si adirarono [29] e, alzatisi, spinsero Gesù fuori del villaggio. Lo trascinarono fino in cima al monte di Nàzaret per farlo precipitare giù. [30] Ma Gesù passò in mezzo a loro e se ne andò.

Gesù insegna e agisce con autorità

[31] Allora Gesù andò a Cafàrnao, un'altra città della Galilea. Anche qui, in giorno di sabato, insegnava alla gente che si era radunata nella sinagoga. [32] Chi lo ascoltava si meravigliava del suo insegnamento perché parlava con autorità. [33] In quella sinagoga c'era un uomo posseduto da uno spirito maligno e si mise a urlare: [34] «Che vuoi da noi, Gesù di Nàzaret? Sei forse venuto a rovinarci? Io so chi sei: tu sei il Santo mandato da Dio».

[35] Ma Gesù gli ordinò severamente: «Taci ed esci da quest'uomo».

Allora lo spirito maligno gettò a terra quel povr'uomo davanti a tutti e alla fine uscì da lui senza fargli più alcun male.

[36] Tutti i presenti rimasero sbalorditi e dicevano tra loro: «Che modo di parlare è questo? Egli comanda perfino agli spiriti maligni con irresistibile autorità ed essi se ne vanno».

[37] Ormai si parlava di Gesù in tutta quella regione.

Gesù guarisce la suocera di Pietro e molti altri

[38] Gesù poi uscì dalla sinagoga e andò nella casa di Simone. La suocera di Simone era a letto malata con la febbre alta, e chiesero perciò a Gesù di far qualcosa per lei. [39] Gesù allora si chinò sopra di lei, comandò alla febbre di lasciarla e la febbre sparì. La donna si alzò subito e si mise a servirli.

[40] Dopo il tramonto del sole, quelli che avevano in casa malati di ogni genere li portavano da Gesù, ed egli li guariva posando le mani sopra ciascuno di loro. [41] Molti spiriti maligni uscivano dagli ammalati e gridavano: «Tu sei il Figlio di Dio». Ma Gesù li rimproverava severamente e non li lasciava parlare perché essi sapevano che egli era il Messia.

Gesù predica nelle sinagoghe della Giudea

[42] Fattosi giorno, Gesù uscì e si ritirò in un luogo isolato, ma la folla andò in cerca di lui. Quando lo raggiunsero, volevano trattenerlo con loro e non lasciarlo più partire. [43] Ma Gesù disse loro: «Anche agli altri villaggi io devo annunziare il regno di Dio. Per questo Dio mi ha mandato».

[44] E Gesù andò ad annunziare il suo messaggio nelle sinagoghe della Giudea.

Gesù chiama i primi discepoli

5 Un giorno Gesù si trovava sulla riva del lago di Genèsaret. Egli stava in piedi e la folla si stringeva attorno a lui per poter ascoltare la parola di Dio. [2] Vide allora sulla riva due barche vuote: i pescatori erano scesi e stavano lavando le reti. [3] Gesù salì su una di quelle barche, quella che apparteneva a Simone, e lo pregò di riprendere i remi e di allontanarsi un po' dalla riva. Poi si sedette sulla barca e si mise a insegnare alla folla.

[4] Quando ebbe finito di parlare, Gesù disse a Simone: «Prendi il largo e gettate le reti per pescare».

[5] Ma Simone gli rispose: «Maestro, abbiamo lavorato tutta la notte senza prendere nulla; però, se lo dici tu, getterò le reti».

⁶ Le gettarono e subito presero una quantità così grande di pesci che le loro reti cominciarono a rompersi. ⁷ Allora chiamarono i loro compagni che stavano sull'altra barca perché venissero ad aiutarli. Essi vennero e riempirono di pesci le due barche a tal punto che quasi affondavano.

⁸ Appena si rese conto di quel che stava accadendo, Simon Pietro si gettò ai piedi di Gesù dicendo:

«Allontanati da me, Signore, perché io sono un peccatore».

⁹⁻¹⁰ In effetti Pietro e i suoi compagni, Giacomo e Giovanni, figli di Zebedèo, e tutti quelli che erano con lui erano rimasti sconvolti per la straordinaria quantità di pesci che avevano preso. Ma Gesù disse a Simone:

«Non temere, d'ora in poi tu sarai pescatore di uomini».

¹¹ Essi allora riportarono le barche verso riva, abbandonarono tutto e seguirono Gesù.

Gesù guarisce un lebbroso

¹² Mentre Gesù si trovava in un villaggio, un uomo tutto coperto di lebbra gli venne incontro. Appena vide Gesù si gettò ai suoi piedi e lo supplicò:

«Signore, se vuoi, tu puoi guarirmi».

¹³ Gesù lo toccò con la mano e gli disse:

«Sì, lo voglio: guarisci!».

E subito la lebbra sparì.

¹⁴ Ma Gesù gli diede quest'ordine:

«Non dire a nessuno quel che ti è capitato. Presentati invece dal sacerdote e fatti vedere da lui. Poi offri per la tua guarigione quel che Mosè ha stabilito nella Legge. Così avranno una prova».

¹⁵ Tuttavia la gente parlava sempre più spesso di Gesù, e molta folla si radunava per ascoltarlo e per essere guarita dalle malattie. ¹⁶ Ma Gesù si ritirava in luoghi isolati per pregare.

Gesù guarisce e può perdonare i peccati

¹⁷ Un giorno Gesù stava insegnando. Da molti villaggi della Galilea e della Giudea e da Gerusalemme erano venuti alcuni farisei e maestri

della Legge i quali si erano messi a sedere attorno a Gesù: Dio gli aveva dato il potere di guarire i malati.

[18] Mentre parlava, alcune persone portarono verso Gesù un uomo: era paralitico e giaceva sopra un letto. Volevano farlo passare e metterlo davanti a Gesù, [19] ma non riuscivano a causa della folla. Allora salirono sul tetto di quella casa, levarono delle tegole e fecero scendere il letto con dentro il paralitico proprio nel mezzo dove si trovava Gesù.

[20] Vedendo la fede di quelle persone, Gesù disse a quell'uomo: «I tuoi peccati ti sono perdonati».

[21] I maestri della Legge e i farisei cominciarono a domandarsi: «Perché quest'uomo bestemmia? Chi può perdonare i peccati? Dio solo può farlo!».

[22] Ma Gesù indovinò i loro pensieri e disse: «Perché ragionate così dentro di voi? [23] È più facile dire: "I tuoi peccati ti sono perdonati", oppure dire: "Alzati e cammina!"? [24] Ebbene, io vi farò vedere che il Figlio dell'uomo ha il potere sulla terra di perdonare i peccati».

E disse al paralitico: «Alzati, prendi la tua barella e torna a casa tua».

[25] Immediatamente quell'uomo si alzò davanti a tutti, prese la barella sulla quale era sdraiato e se ne andò a casa sua ringraziando Dio.

[26] Tutti furono pieni di stupore e lodavano Dio. Pieni di timore dicevano: «Oggi abbiamo visto cose straordinarie».

Gesù chiama Levi

[27] Più tardi Gesù uscì lungo la strada e vide un certo Levi seduto dietro il banco dove si pagavano le tasse. Era infatti un esattore. Gesù gli disse: «Seguimi».

[28] Allora Levi abbandonò tutto, si alzò e cominciò a seguirlo.

[29] Poi Levi preparò un grande banchetto in casa sua. C'era molta gente: agenti delle tasse e altre persone sedute a tavola con loro.

[30] I farisei e i maestri della Legge mormoravano e dicevano ai discepoli di Gesù:
«Perché mangiate e bevete con quelli delle tasse e con persone di cattiva reputazione?».

[31] Gesù rispose:
«Quelli che stanno bene non hanno bisogno del medico; ne hanno

invece bisogno i malati. [32] Io non sono venuto a chiamare quelli che si credono giusti, ma quelli che si sentono peccatori, perché cambino vita».

La questione del digiuno. Il nuovo e il vecchio

[33] I farisei e i maestri della legge insistettero ancora con Gesù: «I discepoli di Giovanni il Battezzatore fanno spesso digiuno e ripetono preghiere; così fanno anche i nostri discepoli. I tuoi discepoli invece mangiano e bevono!».

[34] Gesù rispose:
«Vi pare possibile che gli invitati a un banchetto di nozze se ne stiano senza mangiare mentre lo sposo è con loro? [35] Verrà il tempo in cui lo sposo gli sarà portato via, allora faranno digiuno».

[36] Gesù disse loro anche questa parabola: «Nessuno strappa un pezzo di stoffa da un vestito nuovo per metterlo su un vestito vecchio, altrimenti si trova con il vestito nuovo rovinato, mentre il pezzo preso dal vestito nuovo non si adatta al vestito vecchio. [37] E nessuno mette del vino nuovo in otri vecchi, altrimenti il vino li fa scoppiare: così il vino esce fuori e gli otri vanno perduti. [38] Invece, per vino nuovo ci vogliono otri nuovi. [39] Chi beve vino vecchio non vuole vino nuovo. Dice infatti: quello vecchio è migliore».

La questione del sabato

6 Un sabato Gesù stava passando attraverso i campi di grano. I suoi discepoli strapparono qualche spiga, la sgranavano con le mani e ne mangiavano i chicchi.

[2] Allora alcuni farisei dissero:
«Perché fate ciò che la nostra Legge non permette di fare nel giorno del riposo?».

[3] Gesù rispose:
«E voi non avete mai letto nella Bibbia quel che fece il re Davide un giorno nel quale lui e i suoi compagni avevano fame? [4] Come sapete, Davide entrò nel santuario del Tempio e prese quei pani che erano offerti a Dio. Ne mangiò lui e ne diede anche a quelli che erano con lui. Eppure la Legge dice che i soli sacerdoti possono mangiarli».

⁵ Gesù concluse:
«Il Figlio dell'uomo è padrone del sabato».

Gesù guarisce un uomo in giorno di sabato

⁶ Un altro sabato Gesù entrò nella sinagoga e si mise a insegnare. C'era là un uomo che aveva la mano destra paralizzata.

⁷ I farisei e i maestri della Legge stavano a vedere se Gesù lo guariva in giorno di sabato, per avere così un pretesto di accusa contro di lui.

⁸ Ma Gesù conosceva bene le loro trame e disse all'uomo che aveva la mano paralizzata: «Alzati e vieni in mezzo a tutti». Quell'uomo si alzò e vi andò.

⁹ Poi Gesù chiese agli altri: «Ho una domanda da farvi: che cosa è permesso fare in giorno di sabato? Fare del bene o fare del male? Salvare la vita di un uomo o lasciarlo morire?».

¹⁰ Poi li guardò tutti e disse al malato: «Dammi la tua mano!».
Egli lo fece e la sua mano ritornò perfettamente sana.

¹¹ Ma i maestri della Legge e i farisei si adirarono e discutevano tra loro su quel che potevano fare contro Gesù.

Gesù sceglie i dodici apostoli

¹² In quei giorni Gesù andò sul monte a pregare e passò tutta la notte pregando Dio. ¹³ Quando fu giorno, radunò i suoi discepoli: ne scelse dodici e diede loro il nome di apostoli: ¹⁴ Simone, che Gesù chiamò Pietro, e suo fratello Andrea; Giacomo e Giovanni; Filippo e Bartolomeo; ¹⁵ Matteo e Tommaso; Giacomo, figlio di Alfeo, e Simone, che era del partito degli zeloti; ¹⁶ Giuda, figlio di Giacomo, e Giuda Iscariota che poi fu il traditore di Gesù.

Gesù insegna alla folla

¹⁷ Gesù, disceso dal monte, si fermò in un luogo di pianura con i suoi discepoli. Ne aveva attorno molti, e per di più c'era una gran folla di gente venuta da tutta la Giudea, da Gerusalemme e dalla zona costiera di Tiro e Sidone: ¹⁸ erano venuti per ascoltarlo e per farsi guarire dalle loro malattie. Anche quelli che erano tormentati da spiriti maligni venivano guariti. ¹⁹ Tutti cercavano di toccarlo, perché da lui usciva una forza che guariva ogni genere di mali.

Benedizioni e maledizioni

[20] Allora Gesù alzò gli occhi verso i suoi discepoli e disse:
«Beati voi, poveri:
Dio vi darà il suo regno.
[21] Beati voi che ora avete fame:
Dio vi sazierà.
Beati voi che ora piangete:
Dio vi darà gioia.

[22] «Beati voi quando gli altri vi odieranno, quando parleranno male di voi e vi disprezzeranno come gente malvagia perché avete creduto nel Figlio dell'uomo. [23] Quando vi accadranno queste cose siate lieti e gioite, perché Dio vi ha preparato in cielo una grande ricompensa: infatti i padri di questa gente hanno trattato allo stesso modo gli antichi profeti.

[24] «Ma, guai a voi, ricchi,
perché avete già la vostra consolazione.
[25] Guai a voi che ora siete sazi,
perché un giorno avrete fame.
Guai a voi che ora ridete,
perché sarete tristi e piangerete.

[26] «Guai a voi quando tutti parleranno bene di voi: infatti i padri di questa gente hanno trattato allo stesso modo i falsi profeti.

L'amore verso i nemici

[27] «Ma a voi che mi ascoltate io dico: Amate i vostri nemici, fate del bene a quelli che vi odiano. [28] Benedite quelli che vi maledicono, pregate per quelli che vi fanno del male. [29] Se qualcuno ti percuote su una guancia, tu presentagli anche l'altra. Se qualcuno ti strappa il mantello, tu lasciati prendere anche la camicia. [30] Da' a tutti quelli che ti chiedono qualcosa e, se qualcuno ti prende ciò che ti appartiene, tu lasciaglielo. [31] Fate agli altri quel che volete che essi facciano a voi.

[32] «Se voi amate soltanto quelli che vi amano, come potrà Dio essere contento di voi? Anche quelli che non pensano a Dio fanno così. [33] E se voi fate del bene soltanto a quelli che vi fanno del bene, come potrà Dio essere contento di voi? Anche quelli che non pensano a Dio fanno così. [34] E se voi prestate denaro soltanto a quelli dai qua-

li sperate di riaverne, come potrà Dio essere contento di voi? Anche quelli che non pensano a Dio concedono prestiti ai loro amici per riceverne altrettanto!

³⁵ «Voi invece amate i vostri nemici, fate del bene e prestate senza sperare di ricevere in cambio: allora la vostra ricompensa sarà grande: sarete veramente figli di Dio che è buono anche verso gli ingrati e i cattivi. ³⁶ Siate anche voi pieni di bontà, così come Dio, vostro Padre, è pieno di bontà.

Non giudicare

³⁷ «Non giudicate e Dio non vi giudicherà. Non condannate gli altri e Dio non vi condannerà. Perdonate e Dio vi perdonerà. ³⁸ Date agli altri e Dio darà a voi: riceverete da lui una misura buona, pigiata, scossa e traboccante. Con la stessa misura con cui voi trattate gli altri Dio tratterà voi».

³⁹ Gesù disse loro anche questa parabola:

«Un cieco può forse pretendere di fare da guida a un altro cieco? Se lo facesse, cadrebbero tutti e due in una buca! ⁴⁰ Nessun discepolo è più grande del suo maestro; tutt'al più, se si lascia istruire bene, sarà come il suo maestro.

⁴¹ «E tu perché stai a guardare la pagliuzza che è nell'occhio di un tuo fratello e non ti accorgi della trave che è nel tuo occhio? ⁴² Come osi dirgli: "Fratello, lascia che tolga la pagliuzza dal tuo occhio", mentre tu non vedi la trave che è nel tuo? Ipocrita, togli prima la trave dal tuo occhio, allora vedrai chiaramente e potrai togliere la pagliuzza dall'occhio di tuo fratello.

L'albero e i suoi frutti

⁴³ «Un albero buono non dà frutti cattivi e un albero cattivo non dà frutti buoni. ⁴⁴ La qualità di un albero la si conosce dai suoi frutti: difatti non si raccolgono fichi dalle spine e non si vendemmia uva da un cespuglio selvatico. ⁴⁵ L'uomo buono prende il bene dal prezioso tesoro del suo cuore; l'uomo cattivo invece prende il male dal cattivo tesoro del suo cuore. Ciascuno infatti esprime con la sua bocca quel che ha nel cuore.

Le due case

⁴⁶ «Perché mi chiamate: "Signore, Signore" e non fate quel che vi dico? ⁴⁷ Se uno mi segue, ascolta le mie parole e le mette in pratica, vi dirò a chi assomiglia: ⁴⁸ egli è come quell'uomo che si è messo a costruire una casa: ha scavato molto profondamente ed ha appoggiato le fondamenta della sua casa sopra la roccia. Poi è venuta un'alluvione e le acque del fiume hanno investito quella casa, ma non sono riuscite a scuoterla perché era stata costruita bene. ⁴⁹ Al contrario, chi ascolta le mie parole e non le mette in pratica somiglia a quell'uomo che si è messo a costruire una casa direttamente sul terreno senza fare le fondamenta. Quando le acque del fiume hanno investito quella casa essa è crollata subito. E il disastro fu grande».

Gesù guarisce il servo di un ufficiale romano

7 Quando ebbe terminato di parlare al popolo che lo ascoltava, Gesù entrò nella città di Cafàrnao. ² Là, si trovava un ufficiale dell'esercito romano il quale aveva un servo. Egli era molto affezionato a quel servo, che ora era malato ed era in punto di morte. ³ Quando l'ufficiale sentì parlare di Gesù, mandò alcuni Ebrei autorevoli a pregarlo di venire e di guarire il suo servo. ⁴ Questi Ebrei andarono da Gesù e lo pregavano con insistenza così: «L'ufficiale che ci manda merita il tuo aiuto. ⁵ È amico del nostro popolo. È stato lui a far costruire la nostra sinagoga».

⁶ Allora Gesù andò con loro. Non era molto distante dalla casa, quando l'ufficiale gli mandò incontro alcuni amici per dirgli: «Signore, non disturbarti! Io non sono degno che tu entri in casa mia, ⁷ per questo non ho osato venire personalmente da te, ma di' anche una sola parola e il mio servo certamente guarirà. ⁸ Perché anch'io ho i miei superiori e ai miei ordini ho dei soldati sotto di me. Se dico a uno: Va', egli va; se dico a un altro: Vieni, costui viene; e se dico al mio servo: Fa' questo, egli lo fa».

⁹ Quando Gesù sentì queste parole, lo ammirò. Si rivolse alla folla che lo seguiva e disse: «Vi assicuro che non ho mai trovato una fede così grande tra quelli che appartengono al popolo d'Israele». ¹⁰ E quando gli amici dell'ufficiale tornarono a casa trovarono il servo guarito.

Gesù fa risorgere il figlio di una vedova

¹¹ In seguito Gesù andò in un villaggio chiamato Nain: lo accompagnavano i suoi discepoli insieme a una gran folla. ¹² Quando fu vicino all'entrata di quel villaggio, Gesù incontrò un funerale: veniva portato alla sepoltura l'unico figlio di una vedova, e molti abitanti di quel villaggio erano con lei.

¹³ Appena la vide, il Signore ne ebbe compassione e le disse: «Non piangere!».

¹⁴ Poi si avvicinò alla bara e la toccò: quelli che la portavano si fermarono. Allora Gesù disse: «Ragazzo, te lo dico io: alzati!».

¹⁵ Il morto si alzò e cominciò a parlare. Gesù allora lo restituì a sua madre.

¹⁶ Tutti furono presi da stupore e ringraziavano Dio con queste parole: «Tra noi è apparso un grande profeta!». Altri dicevano: «Dio è venuto a salvare il suo popolo». ¹⁷ E la notizia di questi fatti si diffuse in quella regione e in tutta la Giudea.

Giovanni manda due discepoli a interrogare Gesù

¹⁸ Anche Giovanni venne a sapere queste cose dai suoi discepoli. Chiamò allora due di loro ¹⁹ e li mandò dal Signore a chiedergli: «Sei tu quello che deve venire oppure dobbiamo aspettare un altro?». ²⁰ Quando arrivarono da Gesù quegli uomini dissero: «Giovanni il Battezzatore ci ha mandati da te per domandarti se sei tu quello che deve venire o se dobbiamo aspettare un altro».

²¹ In quello stesso momento Gesù guarì molta gente dalle loro malattie e dalle loro sofferenze; alcuni li liberò dagli spiriti maligni e a molti ciechi restituì la vista. ²² Poi rispose così ai discepoli di Giovanni: «Andate a raccontargli quello che avete visto e udito: i ciechi vedono, gli zoppi camminano, i lebbrosi sono risanati, i sordi odono, i morti risorgono, la salvezza viene annunziata ai poveri. ²³ Beato chi non perderà la fede in me».

Gesù parla di Giovanni il Battezzatore

²⁴ I messaggeri di Giovanni partirono e Gesù cominciò a parlare alla folla. Diceva: «Che cosa siete andati a vedere nel deserto? Una canna agitata dal vento? No! ²⁵ Che cosa allora? Un uomo vestito con

abiti di lusso? Ma quelli che portano abiti preziosi e vivono nel lusso stanno nei palazzi dei re. [26] Che cosa siete andati a vedere? Un profeta? Sì, ve lo dico io, qualcosa di più che un profeta! [27] Nella Bibbia Dio dice di lui:

> *Io mando il mio messaggero davanti a te:*
> *egli ti preparerà la strada.*

[28] «E vi assicuro che tra gli uomini nessuno è più grande di Giovanni. Eppure, il più piccolo nel regno di Dio è più grande di lui.

[29] «Tutto il popolo ha ascoltato Giovanni; perfino gli agenti delle tasse hanno ricevuto il suo battesimo e così hanno mostrato di ubbidire alla volontà di Dio. [30] I farisei e i maestri della Legge invece hanno respinto la volontà di Dio e non hanno voluto farsi battezzare da Giovanni».

Gesù giudica la gente del suo tempo

[31] Gesù disse ancora: «A chi posso paragonare gli uomini di questo tempo? A chi sono simili? [32] Essi sono come quei bambini seduti in piazza che gridano gli uni contro gli altri:

> "Vi abbiamo suonato con il flauto una musica allegra,
> e non avete ballato,
> vi abbiamo cantato un canto di dolore,
> e non avete pianto!".

[33] «Così fate anche voi: è venuto Giovanni il Battezzatore, che non mangia pane e non beve vino, e voi dite: "È un indemoniato!". [34] Poi è venuto il Figlio dell'uomo, che mangia e beve, e voi dite: "Ecco un mangione e un beone, amico degli agenti delle tasse e di altre persone di cattiva reputazione".

[35] «Eppure la sapienza di Dio è riconosciuta da tutti i suoi figli».

Gesù, il fariseo e la peccatrice

[36] Un giorno un fariseo invitò Gesù a pranzo a casa sua. Gesù entrò e si mise a tavola. [37] In quel villaggio vi era una prostituta. Quando ella seppe che Gesù si trovava a casa di quel fariseo, venne con un vasetto di olio profumato, [38] si fermò dietro a Gesù, si rannicchiò ai suoi piedi piangendo e cominciò a bagnarli con le sue lacrime; poi li asciugava con i suoi capelli e li baciava e li cospargeva di profumo.

[39] Il fariseo che aveva invitato Gesù, vedendo quella scena, pensò tra sé: «Se costui fosse proprio un profeta saprebbe che donna è questa che lo tocca: è una prostituta!».

[40] Gesù allora si voltò verso di lui e gli disse:

«Simone, ho una cosa da dirti!».

Ed egli rispose:

«Di' pure, Maestro!».

[41] Gesù riprese:

«Un tale aveva due debitori: uno doveva restituirgli cinquecento denari, l'altro solo cinquanta, [42] ma nessuno dei due aveva la possibilità di restituire i soldi. Allora quell'uomo condonò il debito a tutti e due. Dei due chi gli sarà più riconoscente?».

[43] Simone rispose subito:

«Penso, quello che ha ricevuto un favore più grande».

E Gesù gli disse:

«Hai ragione!».

[44] Poi rivolgendosi verso quella donna Gesù disse a Simone: «Vedi questa donna? Sono venuto in casa tua e tu non mi hai dato dell'acqua per lavarmi i piedi; lei invece, con le sue lacrime, mi ha bagnato i piedi e con i suoi capelli me li ha asciugati. [45] Tu non mi hai salutato con il bacio; lei invece da quando sono qui non ha ancora smesso di baciarmi i piedi. [46] Tu non mi hai versato il profumo sul capo; lei invece mi ha cosparso di profumo i piedi. [47] Per questo ti dico: i suoi peccati sono molti, ma le sono perdonati perché ha mostrato un amore riconoscente. Invece quelli ai quali si perdona poco sono meno riconoscenti».

[48] Poi Gesù disse alla donna: «Io ti perdono i tuoi peccati».

[49] Allora quelli che erano a tavola con lui cominciarono a dire tra loro: «Chi è costui che perdona anche i peccati?».

[50] Ma Gesù disse alla donna: «La tua fede ti ha salvata. Va' in pace!».

Le donne che accompagnavano Gesù

8 Qualche tempo dopo Gesù se ne andava per città e villaggi, predicando e annunziando il lieto messaggio del regno di Dio. Con lui c'erano i dodici discepoli [2] e alcune donne che egli aveva guarito da malattie e liberato da spiriti maligni. Le donne erano Maria di

Màgdala, dalla quale Gesù aveva scacciato sette dèmoni, [3] Giovanna, moglie di Cusa, amministratore di Erode, Susanna e molte altre. Con i loro beni esse aiutavano Gesù e i suoi discepoli.

La parabola del seminatore

[4] Un giorno si radunò attorno a Gesù una gran folla di persone che accorrevano a lui da ogni città. Gesù raccontò loro una parabola: [5] «Un contadino andò a seminare e, mentre seminava, una parte dei semi andò a cadere sulla strada: fu calpestata e gli uccelli la mangiarono. [6] Un po' di semente andò a finire su un terreno pietroso: appena germogliata seccò perché non aveva umidità. [7] Parte della semente cadde in mezzo alle spine: e le spine crescendo insieme con essa la soffocarono. [8] Ma una parte cadde in terreno buono: i semi germogliarono e produssero il cento per uno». Detto questo Gesù esclamò: «Chi ha orecchi cerchi di capire!».

Perché Gesù usa le parabole

[9] I discepoli poi domandarono a Gesù il senso della parabola. [10] Egli disse: «A voi Dio fa conoscere apertamente i misteri del suo regno; agli altri invece li fa conoscere solo in parabole, perché come dice la Bibbia:

guardano, ma non vedono,
ascoltano, ma non capiscono.

Gesù spiega la parabola del seminatore

[11] «Ora vi spiego la parabola. La semente è la parola di Dio. [12] I semi caduti sulla strada indicano certe persone che ascoltano la parola di Dio, ma poi viene il diavolo e porta via la parola dai loro cuori e così impedisce loro di credere e di salvarsi. [13] I semi caduti sul terreno pietroso indicano quelle persone che quando ascoltano la parola di Dio l'accolgono con entusiasmo, ma non hanno radici: credono per un certo tempo, ma quando si tratta di affrontare qualche prova abbandonano la fede. [14] Il seme caduto tra le spine indica quelle persone che ascoltano, ma poi, cammin facendo, si lasciano prendere dalle preoccupazioni materiali, dalle ricchezze e dai piaceri della vita, e così rimangono senza frutto. [15] Infine, il seme caduto nel buon

terreno indica quelle persone che ascoltano la parola di Dio con cuore buono e sincero, la custodiscono, sono perseveranti e producono frutto.

La parabola della lampada

[16] «Nessuno accende una lampada per nasconderla sotto un vaso o metterla sotto il letto, ma piuttosto per metterla in alto perché chi entra in casa veda la luce. [17] Così, tutto quello che ora è nascosto sarà portato alla luce, tutto ciò che è segreto sarà conosciuto e diventerà chiaro.

[18] «Fate bene attenzione, dunque, a come ascoltate: perché chi ha molto riceverà ancor di più; ma a chi ha poco sarà portato via anche quel poco che pensa di avere».

I veri parenti di Gesù

[19] Un giorno la madre e i fratelli di Gesù andarono a trovarlo, ma non potevano avvicinarlo perché era circondato dalla folla. [20] Qualcuno gli disse:

«Qui fuori ci sono tua madre e i tuoi fratelli che desiderano vederti».

[21] Ma Gesù rispose loro:

«Mia madre e i miei fratelli sono quelli che ascoltano la parola di Dio e la mettono in pratica!».

Gesù calma una tempesta

[22] Un giorno Gesù salì su una barca con i suoi discepoli e disse loro: «Andiamo all'altra riva del lago». E partirono. [23] Mentre navigavano Gesù si addormentò. Sul lago il vento si mise a soffiare tanto forte che la barca si riempiva di acqua ed essi erano in pericolo. [24] Allora i discepoli svegliarono Gesù e gli dissero:

«Maestro, maestro, affondiamo!».

Gesù si svegliò, sgridò il vento e le onde. Essi cessarono, e ci fu una grande calma.

[25] Poi Gesù disse ai suoi discepoli:

«Dov'è la vostra fede?».

Essi però erano intimoriti e meravigliati. Dicevano tra loro: «Ma chi è costui? Egli comanda al vento e alle acque, e gli ubbidiscono!».

Gesù guarisce l'indemoniato di Gerasa

²⁶ Poi approdarono nella regione dei Gerasèni, che sta di fronte alla Galilea. ²⁷ Gesù era appena sceso a terra, quando dalla città gli venne incontro un uomo: era indemoniato e da molto tempo non portava vestiti; non abitava in una casa ma stava sempre tra le tombe.

²⁸ Egli vide Gesù, gli si gettò ai piedi urlando, poi disse a gran voce: «Che cosa vuoi da me, Gesù, Figlio del Dio Onnipotente? Ti prego, non tormentarmi».

²⁹ Parlava così perché Gesù stava comandando allo spirito maligno di uscire da quell'uomo. Molte volte infatti quello spirito si era impossessato di lui. Quando ciò accadeva, legavano quell'uomo con catene e lo immobilizzavano, ma egli riusciva a spezzare i legami, e il demonio lo spingeva in luoghi deserti.

³⁰ Gesù domandò allo spirito maligno:

«Come ti chiami?».

Quello rispose:

«Il mio nome è "Moltitudine"»: in quell'uomo infatti erano entrati molti demòni. ³¹ Essi chiedevano a Gesù di non mandarli nell'abisso.

³² Lì vicino vi erano molti maiali che pascolavano sulla montagna. Allora gli spiriti maligni chiesero con insistenza a Gesù che permettesse loro di entrare nei maiali ed egli lo permise. ³³ I demòni allora uscirono da quell'uomo ed entrarono nei maiali. Tutti quegli animali si misero a correre giù per la discesa, si precipitarono nel lago e affogarono.

³⁴ I guardiani dei maiali, quando videro quel che era accaduto, fuggirono e andarono a raccontare il fatto in città e in campagna. ³⁵ Perciò la gente venne a vedere quel che era accaduto.

Quando arrivarono vicino a Gesù trovarono anche quell'uomo che Gesù aveva liberato dai demòni: se ne stava seduto ai piedi di Gesù, era vestito e ragionava bene. Ed essi si spaventarono. ³⁶ Quelli che avevano visto il fatto raccontarono agli altri come l'indemoniato era stato guarito.

³⁷ Allora tutta la popolazione del territorio dei Gerasèni pregò Gesù di andarsene via, lontano da loro, perché avevano molta paura.

Gesù salì su una barca per tornare indietro. [38] Intanto l'uomo liberato dai demòni chiedeva a Gesù di poter stare con lui, ma Gesù lo mandò indietro dicendogli: [39] «Torna a casa tua e racconta quel che Dio ha fatto per te».

Quello se ne andò e raccontò in tutta la città quel che Gesù aveva fatto per lui.

La figlia di Giàiro e la donna che toccò il mantello di Gesù

[40] Quando Gesù tornò all'altra riva del lago, la gente gli andò incontro perché tutti lo aspettavano. [41] Venne allora un uomo, un certo Giàiro, che era capo della sinagoga. Si gettò ai piedi di Gesù e gli chiese con insistenza di andare a casa sua, [42] perché la sua unica figlia, di circa dodici anni, stava per morire.

Lungo la strada la folla lo premeva da ogni parte. [43] C'era anche una donna che già da dodici anni aveva continue perdite di sangue. Aveva speso tutto il suo denaro con i medici, ma nessuno era riuscito a guarirla. [44] Essa si avvicinò dietro a Gesù e arrivò a toccare l'orlo del suo mantello. E subito la perdita di sangue si fermò.

[45] Gesù disse:

«Chi mi ha toccato?».

Tutti dicevano che non lo avevano toccato, e Pietro esclamò: «Maestro, vedi che la folla ti circonda e ti schiaccia da tutte le parti!».

[46] Ma Gesù insisté:

«Qualcuno mi ha toccato: mi sono accorto che una forza è uscita da me».

[47] Allora la donna si rese conto che non poteva più rimanere nascosta. Si fece avanti tutta tremante, si gettò ai piedi di Gesù e disse davanti a tutti per quale motivo aveva toccato Gesù e come era stata subito guarita.

[48] Gesù le disse:

«Figlia mia, la tua fede ti ha salvata. Va' in pace!».

[49] Mentre Gesù parlava, arrivò uno dalla casa del caposinagoga e gli disse: «Tua figlia è morta, non disturbare più il Maestro!».

[50] Ma Gesù, che aveva sentito, disse a Giàiro: «Non temere, abbi solo fiducia e tua figlia sarà salva».

⁵¹ Quando giunse alla casa di Giàiro, Gesù non lasciò entrare nessuno con lui, eccetto Pietro, Giovanni e Giacomo, il padre e la madre della bambina. ⁵² Tutti piangevano e facevano lamenti per la fanciulla morta.

Gesù disse: «Non piangete! Non è morta, dorme».

⁵³ Ma quelli ridevano di lui, sapendo bene che era morta.

⁵⁴ Gesù allora prese la fanciulla per mano e disse ad alta voce: «Bambina, alzati!». ⁵⁵ La bambina ritornò in vita e subito si alzò. Gesù allora ordinò ai suoi genitori di darle da mangiare.

⁵⁶ Essi rimasero sbalorditi, ma Gesù raccomandò loro di non far sapere a nessuno quel che era accaduto.

Gesù manda i discepoli in missione

9 Gesù riunì i Dodici e diede loro autorità sugli spiriti maligni e il potere di guarire le malattie. ² Poi li mandò ad annunziare il regno di Dio e a guarire i malati. ³ Disse loro: «Quando vi mettete in viaggio non prendete nulla: né bastone, né borsa, né pane, né denaro e non portate un vestito di ricambio. ⁴ E quando entrate in una casa fermatevi là finché non è ora di andarvene da quella città. ⁵ Se gli abitanti di un villaggio non vi accolgono, lasciate quel villaggio e scuotete via la polvere dai piedi: sarà un gesto di minaccia contro di loro».

⁶ Allora i discepoli partirono e passavano di villaggio in villaggio. In ogni luogo annunziavano il messaggio del vangelo e guarivano i malati.

Opinioni su Gesù

⁷ Intanto Erode, re della Galilea, venne a conoscere tutte queste cose e non sapeva che cosa pensare. Alcuni infatti dicevano: «Giovanni il Battezzatore è tornato dal mondo dei morti». ⁸ Altri invece dicevano: «Il profeta Elia è riapparso tra noi». Altri ancora: «È uno degli antichi profeti ritornato in vita».

⁹ Ma Erode disse: «A Giovanni gli ho fatto tagliare la testa io. Chi è dunque costui del quale sento dire queste cose?». E faceva di tutto per vedere Gesù.

Gesù dà da mangiare a cinquemila uomini

¹⁰ Gli apostoli tornarono da Gesù e gli raccontarono tutto quel che avevano fatto. Allora Gesù li prese con sé e si ritirarono presso un villaggio chiamato Betsàida. ¹¹ Ma la gente se ne accorse e seguì Gesù. Egli li accolse volentieri, parlava loro del regno di Dio e guariva quelli che avevano bisogno di cure.

¹² Quando ormai era quasi sera, i Dodici si avvicinarono a Gesù e gli dissero:
«Lascia andare la gente, in modo che possa trovare da mangiare e da dormire nei villaggi e nelle campagne qui intorno: perché questo è un luogo isolato».

¹³ Ma Gesù rispose:
«Date voi qualcosa da mangiare a questa gente!».

I discepoli dissero:
«Noi abbiamo soltanto cinque pani e due pesci. A meno che non andiamo noi a comprare cibo per tutta questa gente!».

¹⁴ Gli uomini presenti erano circa cinquemila.

Gesù disse ai suoi discepoli:
«Fateli sedere a gruppi di cinquanta circa!».

¹⁵ Così fecero e invitarono tutti a sedersi per terra.

¹⁶ Poi Gesù prese i cinque pani e i due pesci, alzò gli occhi al cielo e disse la preghiera di benedizione. Poi cominciò a spezzare i pani e a darli ai discepoli perché li distribuissero alla folla.

¹⁷ Tutti mangiarono e ne ebbero abbastanza. Alla fine raccolsero i pezzi avanzati e ne riempirono dodici ceste.

Pietro dichiara che Gesù è il Messia

¹⁸ Un giorno Gesù si trovava in un luogo isolato per pregare. I suoi discepoli lo raggiunsero ed egli chiese loro:
«Chi sono io secondo la gente?».

¹⁹ Essi risposero:
«Alcuni dicono che tu sei Giovanni il Battezzatore; altri invece dicono che sei il profeta Elia; altri ancora dicono che tu sei uno degli antichi profeti tornati in vita».

²⁰ Gesù riprese:
«E voi, che dite? Chi sono io?».

Pietro rispose:
«Tu sei il Messia, il Cristo promesso da Dio».

Gesù annunzia la sua morte e risurrezione

[21] Allora Gesù ordinò severamente ai discepoli di non dir niente a nessuno, [22] e aggiunse: «Il Figlio dell'uomo dovrà soffrire molto: è necessario. Gli anziani del popolo, i capi dei sacerdoti e i maestri della Legge lo rifiuteranno. Egli sarà ucciso, ma al terzo giorno risusciterà».

Condizioni per seguire Gesù

[23] Poi a tutti diceva: «Se qualcuno vuol venire con me, smetta di pensare a se stesso, prenda ogni giorno la sua croce e mi segua. [24] Chi pensa soltanto a salvare la propria vita la perderà; chi invece è pronto a sacrificare la propria vita per me la salverà. [25] Se un uomo riesce a guadagnare anche il mondo intero, ma perde la sua vita o rovina se stesso, che vantaggio ne ricava? [26] Se uno si vergognerà di me o delle mie parole, il Figlio dell'uomo si vergognerà di lui quando ritornerà glorioso come Dio Padre, circondato dagli angeli santi. [27] Vi assicuro che certamente alcuni tra quelli che sono qui presenti non moriranno prima di aver visto il regno di Dio».

La trasfigurazione: Gesù manifesta la sua gloria a tre discepoli

[28] Circa otto giorni dopo questi discorsi, Gesù prese con sé tre discepoli, Pietro, Giovanni e Giacomo e salì su un monte a pregare. [29] Mentre pregava, il suo volto cambiò d'aspetto e il suo vestito diventò candido e sfolgorante. [30-31] Poi si videro due uomini avvolti di uno splendore celeste: erano Mosè ed Elia. Parlavano con Gesù del suo destino che doveva compiersi a Gerusalemme. [32] Pietro e i suoi compagni erano oppressi dal sonno, ma riuscirono a restare svegli e videro la gloria di Gesù e i due uomini che stavano con lui. [33] Mentre questi si separavano da Gesù, Pietro gli disse: «Maestro, è bello per noi stare qui. Prepareremo tre tende: una per te, una per Mosè e una per Elia». Egli non sapeva quel che diceva.

[34] Mentre diceva queste cose venne una nube e li avvolse con la sua ombra. Vedendosi avvolti dalla nube, i discepoli ebbero paura. [35] Al-

lora dalla nube si fece sentire una voce: «Questi è il mio Figlio, che io ho scelto: ascoltatelo!». [36] Appena la voce risuonò, i discepoli si accorsero che Gesù era solo. Essi rimasero senza parola e in quei giorni non raccontarono a nessuno quello che avevano visto.

Gesù guarisce un ragazzo tormentato da uno spirito maligno

[37] Il giorno seguente, Gesù e i suoi discepoli discesero dal monte, e molta gente andò incontro a Gesù. [38] All'improvviso in mezzo alla gente un uomo si mise a gridare:
«Maestro, ti scongiuro, vieni a vedere mio figlio: è l'unico che ho! [39] Talvolta uno spirito maligno lo assale, e improvvisamente egli si mette a gridare. Poi gli fa venire le convulsioni e la bava alla bocca. Alla fine lo lascia, ma a fatica, dopo averlo straziato. [40] Ho chiesto ai tuoi discepoli di scacciare questo spirito maligno, ma non ci sono riusciti».
[41] Gesù disse:
«Gente malvagia e senza fede! Fino a quando dovrò restare con voi e dovrò sopportarvi? Portami qui tuo figlio!».
[42] Mentre il ragazzo si avvicinava, lo spirito maligno lo buttò a terra e gli fece venire le convulsioni. Ma Gesù gridò contro lo spirito maligno e guarì il ragazzo. Poi lo riconsegnò a suo padre.
[43] Tutti i presenti rimasero stupiti nel vedere la potenza di Dio. Erano infatti sbalorditi di ciò che Gesù aveva fatto.

Gesù annunzia di nuovo la sua passione

Gesù disse ai suoi discepoli: [44] «Mettetevi bene in mente queste parole: il Figlio dell'uomo sta per essere consegnato nelle mani degli uomini». [45] Ma i discepoli non capivano queste parole: erano così misteriose per loro che non potevano intenderle. Inoltre, avevano paura di interrogare Gesù su questo argomento.

Chi è il più importante?

[46] Poi i discepoli di Gesù si misero a discutere per sapere chi tra loro era il più importante. [47] Gesù si accorse dei loro ragionamenti: allora prese un bambino, se lo pose accanto [48] e disse loro: «Chi accoglie questo bambino per amor mio accoglie me, e chi accoglie me

accoglie il Padre che mi ha mandato. Infatti, chi è il più piccolo tra tutti voi, quello è il più importante!».

Chi non è contro di voi è con voi

⁴⁹ Giovanni allora disse:
«Maestro, abbiamo visto uno che usava il tuo nome per scacciare i demòni e noi abbiamo cercato di farlo smettere perché non è uno che ti segue insieme a noi».

⁵⁰ Ma Gesù gli disse:
«Lasciatelo fare, perché chi non è contro di voi è per voi».

I Samaritani respingono Gesù

⁵¹ Si avvicinava il tempo nel quale Gesù doveva lasciare questo mondo, perciò decise fermamente di andare verso Gerusalemme ⁵² e mandò avanti alcuni messaggeri. Questi partirono ed entrarono in un villaggio di Samaritani per preparare quel che era necessario all'arrivo di Gesù. ⁵³ Ma gli abitanti di quel villaggio non vollero accogliere Gesù perché stava andando a Gerusalemme. ⁵⁴ Due discepoli, Giacomo e Giovanni, se ne accorsero e dissero a Gesù: «Signore, vuoi che diciamo al fuoco di scendere dal cielo e di distruggerli?». ⁵⁵ Ma Gesù si voltò verso di loro e li rimproverò. ⁵⁶ Poi si avviarono verso un altro villaggio.

Gesù risponde a chi vuole seguirlo

⁵⁷ Mentre camminavano, un tale disse a Gesù:
«Io verrò con te dovunque andrai».

⁵⁸ Ma Gesù gli rispose:
«Le volpi hanno una tana e gli uccelli hanno un nido, ma il Figlio dell'uomo non ha un posto dove poter riposare».

⁵⁹ Poi disse a un altro:
«Vieni con me!».

Ma quello rispose:
«Signore, permettimi di andare prima a seppellire mio padre».

⁶⁰ Gesù gli rispose:
«Lascia che i morti seppelliscano i loro morti. Tu invece va' ad annunziare il regno di Dio!».

⁶¹ Un altro disse a Gesù:

«Signore, io verrò con te, prima però lasciami andare a salutare i miei parenti».

⁶² Gesù gli rispose:

«Chi si mette all'aratro e poi si volta indietro non è adatto per il regno di Dio».

Gesù manda altri discepoli in missione

10 ¹⁻² Dopo questi fatti il Signore scelse altri settantadue discepoli. Essi dovevano entrare prima di Gesù nei villaggi o nelle borgate che egli stava per visitare. Li mandò a due a due dicendo loro: «La messe da raccogliere è molta ma gli operai sono pochi. Pregate perciò il padrone del campo perché mandi operai a raccogliere la sua messe.

³ «Andate! Io vi mando come agnelli in mezzo ai lupi. ⁴ Non portate né borsa, né sacco, né sandali. Lungo il cammino non fermatevi a salutare nessuno. ⁵ Quando entrate in una casa, dite subito a quelli che vi abitano: Pace a voi! ⁶ Se tra loro vi è qualcuno che ama la pace riceverà quella pace che gli avete augurato, altrimenti il vostro augurio resterà senza effetto. ⁷ Restate in quella casa, mangiate e bevete quel che vi daranno, perché l'operaio ha diritto al suo salario. Non passate di casa in casa.

⁸ «Quando andate in una città, se qualcuno vi accoglie, mangiate quel che vi offre. ⁹ Guarite i malati che trovate e dite loro: il regno di Dio ora è vicino a voi!

¹⁰ «Se invece entrate in una città e nessuno vi accoglie, allora uscite sulle piazze e dite: ¹¹ Contro di voi noi scuotiamo anche la polvere della vostra città che si è attaccata ai nostri piedi. Sappiate però che il regno di Dio è vicino.

¹² «Vi assicuro che nel giorno del giudizio gli abitanti di Sòdoma saranno trattati meno severamente degli abitanti di quella città.

Gesù minaccia alcune città della Galilea

¹³ «Guai a voi, abitanti di Corazin! Guai a voi, abitanti di Betsàida! Perché se i miracoli compiuti in mezzo a voi fossero stati fatti nelle città pagane di Tiro e di Sidone, già da tempo i loro abitanti si sareb-

bero vestiti di sacco e seduti nella cenere per mostrare che volevano cambiar vita. [14] Perciò, nel giorno del giudizio gli abitanti di Tiro e di Sidone saranno trattati meno severamente di voi. [15] E tu, città di Cafàrnao,

credi forse che Dio ti innalzerà fino al cielo?

No, tu precipiterai nell'abisso!

[16] «Chi ascolta voi ascolta me. Chi disprezza voi disprezza me, ma chi disprezza me disprezza il Padre che mi ha mandato».

Ritornano i settantadue discepoli

[17] I settantadue discepoli tornarono dalla loro missione molto lieti dicendo:

«Signore, anche i demòni ci ubbidiscono quando noi invochiamo il tuo nome».

[18] Gesù disse loro:

«Ho visto Satana precipitare dal cielo come un fulmine. [19] Io vi ho dato il potere di calpestare serpenti e scorpioni e di annientare ogni resistenza del nemico. Niente vi potrà fare del male. [20] Non rallegratevi però perché gli spiriti maligni si sottomettono a voi, ma piuttosto rallegratevi perché i vostri nomi sono scritti in cielo».

Gesù ringrazia il Padre

[21] In quella stessa ora Gesù fu pieno di gioia per opera dello Spirito Santo e disse:

«Ti ringrazio, o Padre,

Signore del cielo e della terra:

perché tu hai nascosto queste cose

ai grandi e ai sapienti

e le hai fatte conoscere ai piccoli.

Sì, Padre, così tu hai voluto».

[22] E disse ancora: «Il Padre mio ha messo tutto nelle mie mani. Nessuno sa chi è il Figlio se non il Padre; così pure nessuno sa chi è il Padre se non il Figlio e quelli ai quali il Figlio lo vuol rivelare».

[23] Poi Gesù si voltò verso i discepoli, in disparte, e disse loro: «Beati voi che potete vedere queste cose [24] perché vi assicuro che molti profeti e molti re avrebbero voluto vedere quel che voi vedete ma non

l'hanno visto. Molti avrebbero voluto udire quel che voi udite ma non l'hanno udito».

La parabola del buon Samaritano

²⁵ Un maestro della Legge voleva tendere un tranello a Gesù. Si alzò e disse:

«Maestro, che cosa devo fare per avere la vita eterna?».

²⁶ Gesù gli disse:

«Che cosa c'è scritto nella legge di Mosè? Che cosa vi leggi?».

²⁷ Quell'uomo rispose:

«C'è scritto: *Ama il Signore Dio tuo con tutto il tuo cuore, con tutta la tua anima, con tutte le tue forze* e con tutta la tua mente, *e ama il prossimo tuo come te stesso*».

²⁸ Gesù gli disse:

«Hai risposto bene! Fa' questo e vivrai!».

²⁹ Ma quel maestro della Legge per giustificare la sua domanda chiese ancora a Gesù:

«Ma chi è il mio prossimo?».

³⁰ Gesù rispose: «Un uomo scendeva da Gerusalemme verso Gèrico, quando incontrò i briganti. Gli portarono via tutto, lo presero a bastonate e poi se ne andarono lasciandolo mezzo morto. ³¹ Per caso passò di là un sacerdote; vide l'uomo ferito, passò dall'altra parte della strada e proseguì. ³² Anche un levita del Tempio passò per quella strada; lo vide, lo scansò e proseguì. ³³ Invece un uomo della Samaria, che era in viaggio, gli passò accanto, lo vide e ne ebbe compassione. ³⁴ Gli andò vicino, versò olio e vino sulle sue ferite e gliele fasciò. Poi lo caricò sul suo asino e lo portò a una locanda e fece tutto il possibile per aiutarlo. ³⁵ Il giorno dopo tirò fuori due monete d'argento, le diede al padrone dell'albergo e gli disse: "Abbi cura di lui e se spenderai di più pagherò io quando ritorno"».

³⁶ A questo punto Gesù domandò:

«Secondo te, chi di questi tre si è comportato come prossimo per quell'uomo che aveva incontrato i briganti?».

³⁷ Il maestro della Legge rispose:

«Quello che ha avuto compassione di lui».

Gesù allora gli disse:

«Va' e comportati allo stesso modo».

Marta e Maria

³⁸ Mentre era in cammino con i suoi discepoli Gesù entrò in un villaggio e una donna, che si chiamava Marta, lo ospitò in casa sua. ³⁹⁻⁴⁰ Marta si mise subito a preparare per loro, ed era molto affaccendata. Sua sorella invece, che si chiamava Maria, si era seduta ai piedi del Signore e stava ad ascoltare quel che diceva.

Allora Marta si fece avanti e disse:

«Signore, non vedi che mia sorella mi ha lasciata sola a servire? Dille di aiutarmi!».

⁴¹ Ma il Signore le rispose:

«Marta, Marta, tu ti affanni e ti preoccupi di troppe cose! ⁴² Una sola cosa è necessaria. Maria ha scelto la parte migliore e nessuno gliela porterà via».

Gesù insegna a pregare

11 Un giorno Gesù andò in un luogo a pregare. Quando ebbe finito, uno dei suoi discepoli gli disse: «Signore, insegnaci a pregare. Anche Giovanni lo ha insegnato ai suoi discepoli».

² Allora Gesù disse:

«Quando pregate, dite così:

Padre,

fa' che tutti ti riconoscano come Dio,

fa' che il tuo regno venga.

³ Dacci ogni giorno il pane necessario,

⁴ perdonaci i nostri peccati

perché anche noi perdoniamo

a chi ci ha offeso,

e fa' che non cadiamo nella tentazione».

⁵ Poi disse loro: «Supponiamo che uno di voi abbia un amico e che a mezzanotte vada da lui e gli dica: "Amico, prestami tre pani ⁶ perché è arrivato da me un amico di passaggio e in casa non ho nulla da dargli". ⁷ Supponiamo pure che quello dall'interno della sua casa gli risponda: "Non darmi fastidio: la porta di casa è già chiusa; io e i miei bambini stiamo già a letto. Non posso alzarmi per darti quello che vuoi". ⁸ Ebbene, io vi dico: se quel tale non si alzerà a dargli il pane perché gli è amico, lo farà dandogli tutto quel che gli occorre perché l'altro insiste.

⁹ «Perciò io vi dico: Chiedete e riceverete! Cercate e troverete! Bussate e la porta vi sarà aperta. ¹⁰ Perché, chiunque chiede riceve, chi cerca trova, a chi bussa sarà aperto.

¹¹ «Se vostro figlio vi chiede un pesce, voi gli dareste un serpente? ¹² Oppure se vi chiede un uovo, voi gli dareste uno scorpione? ¹³ Dunque, voi che siete cattivi sapete dare cose buone ai vostri figli. A maggior ragione il Padre, che è in cielo, darà lo Spirito Santo a quelli che glielo chiedono».

Gesù ha potere sui demòni

¹⁴ Gesù stava scacciando uno spirito maligno che aveva reso muto un uomo. Appena quel tale fu guarito, si mise a parlare e la meraviglia delle folle fu grande. ¹⁵ Alcuni dei presenti dissero: «È con l'aiuto di Beelzebùl, il capo dei demòni, che egli ha il potere di scacciare gli spiriti!». ¹⁶ Altri invece volevano metterlo in difficoltà e gli chiesero di fare un segno miracoloso come prova che veniva da Dio.

¹⁷ Ma Gesù, conoscendo le loro intenzioni, disse: «Se gli abitanti di una nazione si dividono e combattono tra loro, quella nazione va in rovina e le sue case crollano una sull'altra. ¹⁸ Se perfino Satana è in lotta contro se stesso, come potrà durare il suo regno?

«Voi dite che io scaccio i demòni con l'aiuto di Beelzebùl, il capo dei demòni. ¹⁹ Ma se io scaccio i demòni con l'aiuto di Beelzebùl, con l'aiuto di chi li scacciano i vostri discepoli? Perciò saranno proprio loro a mostrare che avete torto! ²⁰ Se invece è con l'aiuto di Dio che io scaccio i demòni, allora vuol dire che è giunto per voi il regno di Dio.

²¹ «Quando un uomo forte e ben armato fa la guardia alla sua casa, allora tutti i suoi beni sono al sicuro. ²² Ma se arriva un altro più forte di lui e lo vince, gli strappa le armi che gli davano sicurezza e ne distribuisce il bottino.

²³ «Chi non è con me è contro di me, e chi non raccoglie insieme con me spreca il raccolto.

Quando lo spirito maligno ritorna

²⁴ «Quando uno spirito maligno è uscito da un uomo, se ne va per luoghi deserti in cerca di riposo. Se però non lo trova, dice: "Ritornerò nella mia casa, quella che ho lasciato". ²⁵ Egli ci va e la trova pulita e

bene ordinata. [26] Allora va a chiamare altri sette spiriti più maligni di lui; poi, entrano in quella persona e vi rimangono come a casa loro. Così, alla fine, quell'uomo si trova in condizioni peggiori di prima».

La vera beatitudine

[27] Mentre Gesù parlava in tal modo, una donna alzò la voce in mezzo alla folla e gli disse:
«Beata la donna che ti ha generato e allattato!».
[28] Ma Gesù rispose:
«Beati piuttosto quelli che ascoltano la parola di Dio e la mettono in pratica».

Alcuni chiedono a Gesù un miracolo

[29] Mentre la gente si affollava attorno a Gesù, egli cominciò a dire: «Questa gente è davvero gente malvagia, vuol vedere un segno miracoloso. Ma non riceverà nessun segno; eccetto il segno del profeta Giona. [30] Infatti, come Giona fu un segno miracoloso per gli abitanti di Nìnive, così anche il Figlio dell'uomo sarà un segno per gli uomini d'oggi. [31] Nel giorno del giudizio, la regina del sud si alzerà a condannare questa gente: essa infatti venne da molto lontano per ascoltare le sagge parole del re Salomone. Eppure, di fronte a voi c'è uno che è più grande di Salomone!

[32] «Nel giorno del giudizio gli abitanti di Nìnive si alzeranno a condannare questa gente: essi infatti cambiarono vita quando ascoltarono la predicazione di Giona. Eppure, di fronte a voi c'è uno che è più grande di Giona.

La luce del corpo

[33] «Non si accende una lampada per nasconderla o metterla sotto un secchio. Piuttosto si mette in alto perché faccia luce a quelli che entrano nella casa. [34] I tuoi occhi sono come una lampada per il corpo: se i tuoi occhi sono buoni, tu sei totalmente nella luce; se invece sono cattivi, tu sei nelle tenebre. [35] Perciò, stai attento che la tua luce non diventi tenebra. [36] Se dunque tu sei totalmente nella luce, senza alcuna parte nelle tenebre, allora tutto sarà splendente, come quando una lampada ti illumina con il suo splendore».

Gesù accusa i farisei e i maestri della Legge

37 Quando Gesù ebbe finito di parlare, un fariseo lo invitò a pranzo a casa sua. Gesù andò e si mise a tavola. 38 Quel fariseo vide che Gesù non aveva fatto la purificazione delle mani che era d'uso e se ne meravigliò.

39 Allora il Signore gli disse: «Voi farisei vi preoccupate di pulire la parte esterna del bicchiere e del piatto, ma all'interno siete pieni di furti e di cattiverie.

40 «Stolti! Dio non ha forse creato l'esterno e l'interno dell'uomo? 41 Ebbene, se volete che tutto sia puro per voi, date in elemosina ai poveri quel che si trova nei vostri piatti.

42 «Guai a voi, farisei, che offrite al Tempio la decima parte delle piante aromatiche, come la menta e la ruta, e perfino di tutti gli ortaggi, ma poi trascurate la giustizia e l'amore di Dio. Queste sono le cose da fare, senza trascurare le altre.

43 «Guai a voi, farisei, che desiderate occupare i posti d'onore nelle sinagoghe ed essere salutati sulle piazze. 44 Guai a voi, perché siete come quei sepolcri che non si vedono e la gente vi passa sopra senza accorgersene!».

45 Allora un maestro della Legge disse a Gesù: «Maestro, parlando così tu offendi anche noi».

46 Gesù rispose:
«Sì, parlo anche a voi, maestri della Legge!
Guai a voi, perché mettete sulle spalle della gente dei pesi troppo faticosi da portare, ma voi neppure con un dito aiutate a portarli. 47 Guai a voi, che costruite sepolcri per quei profeti che i vostri antichi padri hanno ucciso! 48 Così facendo, voi dimostrate di approvare ciò che i vostri padri hanno fatto: essi hanno ucciso i profeti e voi costruite le tombe per loro. 49 Per questo, Dio nella sua sapienza ha detto: "Manderò loro profeti e apostoli, ma essi li uccideranno o li perseguiteranno". 50 Ma Dio chiederà conto a questa gente dell'uccisione di tutti i profeti, dalle origini del mondo in poi: 51 dall'uccisione di Abele fino a quella di Zaccaria che è stato assassinato tra l'altare e il santuario. Ve lo ripeto: Dio chiederà conto a questa gente di tutti questi misfatti!

⁵² Guai a voi, maestri della Legge, perché avete portato via la chiave della vera scienza: voi non ci siete entrati e non avete lasciato entrare quelli che avrebbero voluto».

⁵³ Quando Gesù fu uscito da quella casa, i maestri della Legge e i farisei cominciarono a trattarlo con ostilità e a fargli domande di ogni genere: ⁵⁴ gli tendevano tranelli per coglierlo in fallo in qualche suo discorso.

Contro l'ipocrisia

12 Nel frattempo si erano radunate alcune migliaia di persone e si accalcavano gli uni sugli altri. Allora Gesù disse ai suoi discepoli: «Tenetevi lontani dal lievito dei farisei, dalla loro ipocrisia! ² Perché non c'è nulla di nascosto che non sarà svelato, nulla di segreto che non sarà conosciuto. ³ Quel che avete detto nel buio sarà udito alla luce del giorno, e quel che avete detto sottovoce all'interno della casa sarà proclamato dalle terrazze.

Chi dobbiamo temere?

⁴ «A voi, che siete miei amici, dico: Non abbiate paura di quelli che possono togliervi la vita, ma non possono fare niente di più. ⁵ Ve lo dirò io chi dovete temere! Temete Dio, il quale, dopo la morte, ha il potere di gettare uno nell'inferno. Ve lo ripeto: è lui che dovete temere! ⁶ Cinque passeri non si vendono per due soldi? Eppure, Dio non ne dimentica neanche uno. ⁷ Dio conosce anche il numero dei capelli del vostro capo. Dunque, non abbiate paura: voi valete più di molti passeri.

È necessario riconoscere Gesù

⁸ «Inoltre vi dico: Tutti quelli che pubblicamente dichiareranno di essere miei discepoli, anche il Figlio dell'uomo dichiarerà che sono suoi davanti agli angeli di Dio. ⁹ Ma quelli che pubblicamente diranno di non essere miei discepoli, non saranno riconosciuti miei davanti agli angeli di Dio.

¹⁰ «Chiunque avrà detto una parola contro il Figlio dell'uomo potrà essere perdonato; ma chi avrà bestemmiato lo Spirito Santo non otterrà perdono.

[11] «Quando vi porteranno nelle sinagoghe per essere giudicati davanti ai magistrati e alle autorità, non preoccupatevi di quel che dovrete dire per difendervi. [12] Sarà lo Spirito Santo a insegnarvi quel che dovrete dire in quel momento».

Gesù narra la parabola del ricco stolto

[13] Un tale che stava in mezzo alla folla disse a Gesù: «Maestro, di' a mio fratello di spartire con me l'eredità».

[14] Ma Gesù gli rispose:
«Amico, non sono qui per fare da giudice nei vostri affari o da mediatore nella spartizione dei vostri beni».

[15] Poi disse agli altri:
«Badate di tenervi lontani dall'ansia per la ricchezza, perché la vita di un uomo non dipende dai suoi beni, anche se è molto ricco».

[16] Poi raccontò loro questa parabola: «Un ricco aveva terreni che gli davano abbondanti raccolti. [17] Tra sé e sé faceva questi ragionamenti: "Ora che non ho più posto dove mettere i nuovi raccolti cosa farò?". [18] E disse: "Ecco, farò così: demolirò i vecchi magazzini e ne costruirò altri più grandi. Così potrò metterci tutto il mio grano e i miei beni. [19] Poi finalmente potrò dire a me stesso: Bene! Ora hai fatto molte provviste per molti anni. Riposati, mangia, bevi e divertiti!". [20] Ma Dio gli disse: "Stolto! Proprio questa notte dovrai morire, e a chi andranno le ricchezze che hai accumulato?"».

[21] Alla fine Gesù disse: «Questa è la situazione di quelli che accumulano ricchezze solo per se stessi e non si preoccupano di arricchire davanti a Dio».

La vita e le vere preoccupazioni

[22] Poi Gesù disse ai suoi discepoli: «Per questo io vi dico: Non preoccupatevi troppo del cibo che vi serve per vivere o del vestito che vi serve per coprirvi. [23] La vita infatti è più importante del cibo e il corpo è più importante del vestito. [24] Osservate i corvi: non seminano e non raccolgono, non hanno né dispensa né granaio, eppure Dio li nutre. Ebbene, voi valete molto più degli uccelli! [25] E chi di voi con tutte le sue preoccupazioni può vivere un giorno in più di quello che

è stabilito? ²⁶ Se dunque voi non potete fare neppure così poco, perché vi preoccupate per il resto?

²⁷ «Osservate come crescono i fiori dei campi: non lavorano e non si fanno vestiti, eppure io vi assicuro che nemmeno il re Salomone, con tutta la sua ricchezza, ha mai avuto un vestito così bello. ²⁸ Se dunque Dio rende così belli i fiori dei campi, che oggi ci sono e il giorno dopo vengono bruciati, a maggior ragione procurerà un vestito a voi, gente di poca fede! ²⁹ Perciò, non state sempre in ansia nel cercare che cosa mangerete o che cosa berrete: ³⁰ sono gli altri, quelli che non conoscono Dio, a cercare sempre tutte queste cose. Voi invece avete un Padre che sa bene quello di cui avete bisogno. ³¹ Cercate piuttosto il regno di Dio, e tutto il resto Dio ve lo darà in più.

³² «Non aver paura, piccolo gregge, perché il Padre vostro ha voluto darvi il suo regno. ³³ Vendete quel che possedete e il denaro datelo ai poveri: procuratevi ricchezze che non si consumano, un tesoro sicuro in cielo. Là i ladri non possono arrivare e la ruggine non lo può distruggere. ³⁴ Perché, dove sono le vostre ricchezze là c'è anche il vostro cuore.

I servi pronti e vigilanti

³⁵ «Siate sempre pronti, con la cintura ai fianchi e le lampade accese. ³⁶ Siate anche voi come quel servi che aspettano il loro padrone che sta per tornare da una festa di nozze, per essere pronti ad aprire subito appena arriva e bussa. ³⁷ Beati quei servi che il padrone al suo ritorno troverà ancora svegli. Io vi assicuro che egli si metterà un grembiule, li farà sedere a tavola e comincerà a servirli. ³⁸ E se il padrone tornerà a mezzanotte oppure alle tre del mattino e troverà i suoi servi ancora svegli, beati loro!

³⁹ «Cercate di capire: se il capofamiglia sapesse a che ora viene il ladro, non si lascerebbe scassinare la casa. ⁴⁰ Anche voi tenetevi pronti, perché il Figlio dell'uomo verrà quando voi non ve lo aspettate».

⁴¹ Allora Pietro disse: «Signore, questa parabola vale solo per noi oppure per tutti?».

⁴² Il Signore rispose: «Chi è dunque l'amministratore fedele e saggio che il padrone metterà a capo dei suoi servi, perché al momento

giusto dia a ciascuno il suo cibo? [43] Se il padrone, quando ritorna, lo troverà occupato a fare così, beato quel servo! [44] Io vi assicuro che gli affiderà l'amministrazione di tutti i suoi beni. [45] Se invece quel servo pensa: "Il mio padrone tarda a venire", e comincia a maltrattare i servi e le serve, per di più si mette a mangiare, a bere e a ubriacarsi, [46] in un momento che lui non sa, quando meno se l'aspetta il padrone arriverà. Lo separerà dagli altri e lo punirà come si fa con i servi infedeli.

[47] «Se un servo sa quel che il suo padrone vuole, ma non lo esegue con prontezza, sarà punito severamente. [48] Se invece un servo si comporta in modo da meritare un castigo, ma non sa quel che il suo padrone vuole, sarà punito meno severamente. In effetti, chi ha ricevuto molto dovrà rendere conto di molto. Quanto più ciascuno ha ricevuto, tanto più gli sarà richiesto.

Gesù è causa di divisione tra gli uomini

[49] «Io sono venuto ad accendere un fuoco sulla terra e vorrei davvero che fosse già acceso. [50] Ho un battesimo da ricevere, ed è grande la mia angoscia fino a quando non l'avrò ricevuto. [51] Pensate che io sia venuto a portare pace nel mondo? No, ve lo assicuro, non la pace ma la divisione. [52] D'ora in poi, se in famiglia ci sono cinque persone, si divideranno fino a mettersi tre contro gli altri due e due contro gli altri tre.

[53] Il padre contro il figlio
e il figlio contro il padre,
la madre contro la figlia
e la figlia contro la madre,
la suocera contro la nuora
e la nuora contro la suocera».

Come comprendere i segni dei tempi

[54] Gesù diceva ancora alla gente: «Quando vedete una nuvola che sale da ponente, voi dite subito: "Presto pioverà", e così avviene. [55] Quando invece sentite lo scirocco, dite: "Farà caldo", e così accade. [56] Ipocriti! Siete capaci di capire l'aspetto della terra e del cielo, come mai non sapete capire quel che accade in questo tempo?

Mettiti d'accordo con il tuo avversario

[57] «Perché non giudicate da soli ciò che è giusto fare? [58] Quando vai con il tuo avversario dal giudice, cerca di trovare un accordo con lui mentre siete ancora tutti e due per strada, perché il tuo avversario può trascinarti davanti al giudice, il giudice può consegnarti alle guardie e le guardie possono gettarti in prigione. [59] Ti assicuro che non uscirai fino a quando non avrai pagato anche l'ultimo spicciolo».

Gesù riflette su fatti di cronaca

13 In quel momento si presentarono a Gesù alcuni uomini per riferirgli il fatto di quei Galilei che Pilato aveva fatto uccidere mentre stavano offrendo i loro sacrifici. [2] Gesù disse loro: «Pensate voi che quei Galilei siano stati massacrati in questa maniera perché erano più peccatori di tutti gli altri Galilei? [3] Vi assicuro che non è vero: anzi, se non cambierete vita, finirete tutti allo stesso modo. [4] E quei diciotto che morirono schiacciati sotto la torre di Siloe, pensate voi che fossero più colpevoli di tutti gli altri abitanti di Gerusalemme? [5] Vi assicuro che non è vero: anzi, se non cambierete vita, finirete tutti allo stesso modo».

Gesù narra la parabola del fico che non dà frutti

[6] Poi Gesù raccontò questa parabola: «Un tale aveva piantato un albero di fico nella sua vigna. Un giorno andò nella vigna per cogliere alcuni fichi ma non ne trovò. [7] Allora disse al contadino: "Sono già tre anni che vengo a cercare frutti su questo albero e non ne trovo. Taglialo! Perché deve occupare inutilmente il terreno?".

[8] Ma il contadino rispose:

"Padrone, lascialo ancora per quest'anno! Voglio zappare bene la terra attorno a questa pianta e metterci il concime. [9] Può darsi che il prossimo anno faccia frutti; se no, la farai tagliare"».

Gesù guarisce una donna di sabato

[10] Una volta Gesù stava insegnando in una sinagoga ed era sabato. [11] C'era anche una donna malata: da diciotto anni uno spirito maligno la teneva ricurva e non poteva in nessun modo stare dritta. [12] Quando

Gesù la vide, la chiamò e le disse: «Donna, ormai sei guarita dalla tua malattia». [13] Posò le sue mani su di lei ed essa subito si raddrizzò e si mise a lodare Dio.

[14] Ma il capo della sinagoga era indignato perché Gesù aveva fatto quella guarigione di sabato. Si rivolse alla folla e disse: «In una settimana ci sono sei giorni per lavorare: venite dunque a farvi guarire in un giorno di lavoro e non di sabato!».

[15] Ma il Signore gli rispose: «Siete ipocriti! Anche di sabato voi slegate il bue o l'asino dalla mangiatoia per portarli a bere, non è così? [16] Ebbene, questa donna è discendente di Abramo; Satana la teneva legata da diciotto anni: non doveva dunque essere liberata dalla sua malattia, anche se oggi è sabato?».

[17] Mentre Gesù diceva queste cose, tutti i suoi avversari erano pieni di vergogna. La gente invece si rallegrava per tutte le cose meravigliose che Gesù faceva.

La parabola del granello di senape e del lievito

[18] Gesù diceva: «A che cosa somiglia il regno di Dio? A che cosa lo posso paragonare? [19] Esso è simile a un piccolo granello di senape che un uomo prese e seminò nel suo orto. Quel granello crebbe e diventò un albero, e gli uccelli vennero a fare il nido tra i suoi rami».

[20] Gesù disse ancora: «A che cosa posso paragonare il regno di Dio? [21] Esso è simile a un po' di lievito che una donna ha preso e messo in una grande quantità di farina: a un certo punto tutta la pasta è lievitata».

La porta stretta

[22] Gesù attraversava città e villaggi e insegnava; intanto andava verso Gerusalemme. [23] Un tale gli domandò: «Signore, sono pochi quelli che si salvano?».

Gesù rispose:
[24] «Sforzatevi di entrare per la porta stretta, perché vi assicuro che molti cercheranno di entrare, ma non ci riusciranno. [25] Quando il padrone di casa si alzerà e chiuderà la porta della sua casa, voi vi troverete chiusi fuori. Allora comincerete a picchiare alla porta dicendo:

"Signore, aprici!", ma egli vi risponderà: "Non vi conosco. Di dove venite?". [26] Allora voi direte: "Noi abbiamo mangiato e bevuto con te, e tu hai insegnato nelle nostre piazze". [27] Alla fine egli vi dirà: "Non vi conosco. Di dove venite? Andate via da me, gente malvagia!". [28] Piangerete e soffrirete molto, perché sarete cacciati via dal regno di Dio, ove ci sono Abramo, Isacco, Giacobbe e tutti i profeti. [29] Verranno invece in molti dal nord e dal sud, dall'est e dall'ovest: parteciperanno tutti al banchetto nel regno di Dio. [30] Ed ecco: alcuni di quelli che ora sono gli ultimi saranno i primi, mentre altri che ora sono i primi saranno gli ultimi».

Gesù rimprovera la città di Gerusalemme

[31] In quel momento si avvicinarono a Gesù alcuni farisei e gli dissero:
«Lascia questi luoghi e vattene altrove, perché Erode vuol farti uccidere».
[32] Ma Gesù rispose:
«Andate da quel volpone e diritegli: Ecco, io scaccio gli spiriti maligni e guarisco i malati oggi e domani, e il terzo giorno raggiungerò la mia mèta. [33] Però oggi, domani e il giorno seguente io devo continuare il mio cammino, perché nessun profeta può morire fuori di Gerusalemme. [34] Gerusalemme, Gerusalemme! tu che metti a morte i profeti e uccidi a colpi di pietra quelli che Dio ti manda! Quante volte ho voluto riunire i tuoi abitanti attorno a me, come una gallina raccoglie i suoi pulcini sotto le sue ali. Ma voi non avete voluto! [35] Ebbene, la vostra casa sarà abbandonata! Perciò io vi dico che non mi vedrete più fino a quando esclamerete:
Benedetto colui che viene
nel nome del Signore!».

Gesù guarisce un malato in giorno di sabato

14 Un giorno Gesù era a pranzo in casa di un capo dei farisei. I presenti lo osservavano attentamente perché era sabato. [2] Di fronte a lui c'era un uomo malato di idropisia. [3] Rivolgendosi ai maestri della Legge e ai farisei Gesù chiese: «È permesso o no, in giorno di sabato, guarire un malato?».

⁴ Ma quelli tacevano. Allora Gesù prese per mano il malato e lo guarì. Poi lo lasciò andare. ⁵ E disse loro: «Se a uno di voi cade nel pozzo un figlio o un bue, voi lo tirate fuori subito, anche se è sabato, non è vero?». ⁶ Ma essi non sapevano rispondere.

Contro l'ambizione dei primi posti

⁷ Gesù osservava che alcuni invitati sceglievano volentieri i primi posti. Per loro raccontò questa parabola: ⁸ «Quando sei invitato a nozze, non occupare i primi posti, perché potrebbe esserci un invitato più importante di te: ⁹ in questo caso lo sposo sarà costretto a venire da te e dirti: "Cedigli il posto". Allora tu, pieno di vergogna, dovrai prendere l'ultimo posto. ¹⁰ Invece, quando sei invitato a nozze, va' a sederti all'ultimo posto. Quando arriverà lo sposo, ti dirà: "Vieni, amico! Prendi un posto migliore". E questo sarà per te motivo di onore di fronte a tutti gli invitati. ¹¹ Ricordate: chi si esalta sarà abbassato; chi invece si abbassa sarà innalzato!».

¹² Poi Gesù disse a colui che lo aveva invitato:

«Quando offri un pranzo o una cena, non invitare i tuoi amici e fratelli, i tuoi parenti e i ricchi che abitano vicino a te: essi infatti hanno la possibilità di invitarti a loro volta a casa loro e tu, in questo modo, hai già ricevuto la tua ricompensa.

¹³ «Invece, quando offri un banchetto, chiama i poveri, gli storpi, gli zoppi e i ciechi. ¹⁴ Allora avrai motivo di rallegrarti, perché questi non hanno la possibilità di ricambiarti l'invito. Dio stesso ti darà la ricompensa alla fine, quando i giusti risorgeranno».

La parabola degli invitati scortesi

¹⁵ Uno degli invitati, appena udì queste parole di Gesù, esclamò: «Beato chi potrà partecipare al banchetto nel regno di Dio!».

¹⁶ Gesù allora gli raccontò un'altra parabola:

«Un uomo fece una volta un grande banchetto e invitò molta gente. ¹⁷ All'ora del pranzo mandò uno dei suoi servi a dire agli invitati: Tutto è pronto, venite! ¹⁸ Ma, uno dopo l'altro, gli invitati cominciarono a scusarsi. Uno gli disse: "Ho comprato un terreno e devo andare a vederlo. Ti prego di scusarmi". ¹⁹ Un altro gli disse: "Ho comprato

cinque paia di buoi e sto andando a provarli. Ti prego di scusarmi".
[20] Un terzo invitato gli disse: "Mi sono sposato da poco e perciò non posso venire".

[21] «Quel servo tornò dal suo padrone e gli riferì tutto. Il padrone di casa allora, pieno di sdegno, ordinò al suo servo: Esci subito e va' per le piazze e per le vie della città e fa' venire qui, al mio banchetto, i poveri e gli storpi, i ciechi e gli zoppi.

[22] «Più tardi il servo tornò dal padrone per dirgli: "Signore, ho eseguito il tuo ordine, ma c'è ancora posto".

[23] «Il padrone allora disse al servo: Esci di nuovo e va' per i sentieri di campagna e lungo le siepi e spingi la gente a venire. Voglio che la mia casa sia piena di gente. [24] Nessuno di quelli che ho invitato per primi parteciperà al mio banchetto: ve lo assicuro!».

Le condizioni per seguire Gesù

[25] Molta gente accompagnava Gesù durante il suo viaggio. Egli si rivolse a loro e disse: [26] «Se qualcuno viene con me e non ama me prima di suo padre, sua madre, sua moglie, i suoi figli, i fratelli e le sorelle, anzi, se non mi ama più di se stesso, non può essere mio discepolo. [27] Chi mi segue senza portare la sua croce non può essere mio discepolo.

[28] «Se uno di voi decide di costruire una casa, che cosa fa prima di tutto? Si mette a calcolare la spesa per vedere se ha soldi abbastanza per portare a termine i lavori. [29] Altrimenti, se getta le fondamenta e non è in grado di portare a termine i lavori, la gente vedrà e comincerà a ridere di lui [30] e dirà: "Quest'uomo ha cominciato a costruire e non è stato capace di portare a termine i lavori".

[31] «Facciamo un altro caso: se un re va in guerra contro un altro re, che cosa fa prima di tutto? Si mette a calcolare se con diecimila soldati può affrontare il nemico che avanza con ventimila, non vi pare? [32] Se vede che non è possibile, allora manda dei messaggeri incontro al nemico; e mentre il nemico si trova ancora lontano gli fa chiedere quali sono le condizioni per la pace.

[33] «La stessa cosa vale anche per voi: chi non rinunzia a tutto quel che possiede non può essere mio discepolo.

Il sale che non serve a nulla

³⁴ «Il sale è una cosa utile, ma anche il sale se perde il suo sapore come si fa a ridarglielo? ³⁵ Non serve più a niente, neppure come concime per i campi: perciò lo si getta via. Chi ha orecchi cerchi di capire!».

La parabola della pecora smarrita

15 Gli agenti delle tasse e altre persone di cattiva reputazione si avvicinarono a Gesù per ascoltarlo. ² Ma i farisei e i maestri della Legge lo criticavano per questo. Dicevano: «Quest'uomo tratta bene la gente di cattiva reputazione e va a mangiare con loro».

³ Allora Gesù raccontò questa parabola:

⁴ «Se uno di voi ha cento pecore e ne perde una, che cosa fa? Lascia le altre novantanove al sicuro per andare a cercare quella che si è smarrita e la cerca finché non l'ha ritrovata. ⁵ Quando la trova, se la mette sulle spalle pieno di gioia, ⁶ e ritorna a casa sua. Poi chiama gli amici e i vicini e dice loro: "Fate festa con me, perché ho ritrovato la mia pecora, quella che si era smarrita".

⁷ «Così è anche per il regno di Dio: vi assicuro che in cielo si fa più festa per un peccatore che si converte che per novantanove giusti che non hanno bisogno di conversione.

La parabola della moneta d'argento

⁸ «Se una donna possiede dieci monete d'argento e ne perde una, che cosa fa? Accende la luce, spazza bene la casa e si mette a cercare accuratamente la sua moneta finché non la trova. ⁹ Quando l'ha trovata, chiama le amiche e le vicine di casa e dice loro: "Fate festa con me, perché ho ritrovato la moneta d'argento che avevo perduta".

¹⁰ «Così, vi dico, anche gli angeli di Dio fanno grande festa per un solo peccatore che cambia vita».

La parabola del padre misericordioso

¹¹ Gesù raccontò anche questa parabola: «Un uomo aveva due figli. ¹² Il più giovane disse a suo padre: "Padre, dammi la mia parte d'eredità". Allora il padre divise il patrimonio tra i due figli.

[13] «Pochi giorni dopo, il figlio più giovane vendette tutti i suoi beni e con i soldi ricavati se ne andò in un paese lontano. Là, si abbandonò a una vita disordinata e così spese tutti i suoi soldi.

[14] «Ci fu poi in quella regione una grande carestia, e quel giovane non avendo più nulla si trovò in grave difficoltà. [15] Andò da uno degli abitanti di quel paese e si mise alle sue dipendenze. Costui lo mandò nei campi a fare il guardiano dei maiali. [16] Era talmente affamato che avrebbe voluto sfamarsi con le ghiande che si davano ai maiali, ma nessuno gliene dava.

[17] «Allora si mise a riflettere sulla sua condizione e disse: "Tutti i dipendenti di mio padre hanno cibo in abbondanza. Io, invece, sto qui a morire di fame. [18] Ritornerò da mio padre e gli dirò: Padre ho peccato contro Dio e contro di te. [19] Non sono più degno di essere considerato tuo figlio. Trattami come uno dei tuoi dipendenti".

[20] «Si mise subito in cammino e ritornò da suo padre.

«Era ancora lontano dalla casa paterna, quando suo padre lo vide e, commosso, gli corse incontro. Lo abbracciò e lo baciò. [21] Ma il figlio gli disse: "Padre, ho peccato contro Dio e contro di te. Non sono più degno di essere considerato tuo figlio".

[22] «Ma il padre ordinò subito ai suoi servi: "Presto, andate a prendere il vestito più bello e fateglielo indossare. Mettetegli l'anello al dito e dategli un paio di sandali. [23] Poi prendete il vitello, quello che abbiamo ingrassato, e ammazzatelo. Dobbiamo festeggiare con un banchetto il suo ritorno, [24] perché questo mio figlio era per me come morto e ora è tornato in vita, era perduto e ora l'ho ritrovato". E cominciarono a far festa.

[25] «Il figlio maggiore, intanto, si trovava nei campi. Al suo ritorno, quando fu vicino alla casa, sentì un suono di musiche e di danze. [26] Chiamò uno dei servi e gli domandò che cosa stava succedendo. [27] Il servo gli rispose: "È ritornato tuo fratello, e tuo padre ha fatto ammazzare il vitello, quello che abbiamo ingrassato, perché ha potuto riavere suo figlio sano e salvo".

[28] «Allora il fratello maggiore si sentì offeso e non voleva neppure entrare in casa. Suo padre uscì e cercò di convincerlo a entrare.

[29] «Ma il figlio maggiore gli disse: "Da tanti anni io lavoro con te e non ho mai disubbidito a un tuo comando. Ma tu non mi hai dato

neppure un capretto per far festa con i miei amici. [30] Adesso, invece, torna a casa questo tuo figlio che ha sprecato i tuoi beni con le prostitute, e per lui tu fai ammazzare il vitello grasso".

[31] «Il padre gli rispose: "Figlio mio, tu stai sempre con me e tutto ciò che è mio è anche tuo. [32] Non potevo non essere contento e non far festa, perché questo tuo fratello era per me come morto e ora è tornato in vita, era perduto e ora l'ho ritrovato"».

La parabola dell'amministratore astuto

16 Gesù disse ai suoi discepoli: «C'era una volta un uomo ricco che aveva un amministratore. Un giorno alcuni andarono dal padrone e accusarono l'amministratore di aver sperperato i suoi beni. [2] Il padrone chiamò l'amministratore e gli disse: "È vero quel che sento dire di te? Presentami i conti della tua amministrazione, perché da questo momento tu sei licenziato".

[3] «Allora l'amministratore pensò: "Che cosa farò ora che il mio padrone mi licenzia? Di lavorare la terra non me la sento e di chiedere l'elemosina mi vergogno. [4] So io quel che farò! Farò in modo che ci sia sempre qualcuno che mi accoglie in casa sua, anche se mi viene tolta l'amministrazione".

[5] «Poi, a uno a uno, chiamò tutti quelli che avevano dei debiti con il suo padrone. Disse al primo:
"Tu, quanto devi al mio padrone?".

[6] «Quello rispose:
"Gli devo cento barili d'olio".

«Ma l'amministratore gli disse:
"Prendi il tuo foglio, mettiti qui e scrivi in fretta cinquanta".

[7] «Poi disse al secondo debitore:
"E tu, quanto devi al mio padrone?".

«Quello rispose:
"Io gli devo cento sacchi di grano".

«Ma l'amministratore gli disse:
"Prendi il tuo foglio e scrivi ottanta".

[8] «Ebbene, il padrone ammirò l'amministratore disonesto, perché aveva agito con molta furbizia. Così, gli uomini di questo mondo, nei loro rapporti con gli altri, sono più astuti dei figli della luce.

Parole sulla ricchezza e sulla fedeltà

⁹ «Io vi dico: ogni ricchezza puzza d'ingiustizia: voi usatela per farvi degli amici; così, quando non avrete più ricchezze, i vostri amici vi accoglieranno presso Dio.

¹⁰ «Chi è fedele in cose di poco conto è fedele anche nelle cose importanti. Al contrario, chi è disonesto nelle piccole cose è disonesto anche nelle cose importanti.

¹¹ «Perciò, se voi non siete stati fedeli nel modo di usare le ricchezze di questo mondo, chi vi affiderà le vere ricchezze? ¹² E se non siete stati fedeli nell'amministrare i beni degli altri, chi vi darà il bene che vi spetta?

¹³ «Nessun servitore può servire due padroni: perché, o amerà l'uno e odierà l'altro; oppure preferirà il primo e disprezzerà il secondo. Non potete servire Dio e il denaro».

¹⁴ I farisei stavano ad ascoltare tutto quel che Gesù diceva. Essi erano molto attaccati al denaro e perciò ridevano delle sue parole.

¹⁵ Gesù allora disse: «Davanti agli uomini voi fate la figura di persone giuste, ma Dio conosce molto bene i vostri cuori. Infatti ci sono cose che gli uomini considerano molto, mentre Dio le considera senza valore.

Legge e volontà di Dio

¹⁶ «La legge di Mosè e gli scritti dei profeti arrivarono fino al tempo di Giovanni il Battezzatore. Dopo di lui viene annunziato il regno di Dio e molti si sforzano per entrarvi.

¹⁷ «È più facile che finiscano il cielo e la terra, piuttosto che cada anche la più piccola parola della legge di Dio.

¹⁸ «Chiunque divorzia da sua moglie e ne sposa un'altra commette adulterio. E chi sposa una donna divorziata dal marito commette adulterio anche lui.

Parabola dell'uomo ricco e del povero Lazzaro

¹⁹ «C'era una volta un uomo ricco. Portava sempre vestiti di lusso e costosi e faceva festa ogni giorno con grandi banchetti. ²⁰ C'era anche un povero, un certo Lazzaro, che si metteva vicino alla porta del suo palazzo. Era tutto coperto di piaghe e chiedeva l'elemosina. ²¹ Aveva

una gran voglia di sfamarsi con gli avanzi dei pasti di quel ricco. Perfino i cani venivano a leccargli le piaghe.

²² «Un giorno, il povero Lazzaro morì, e gli angeli lo portarono accanto ad Abramo nella pace. Poi morì anche l'uomo ricco e fu sepolto. ²³ Andò a finire all'inferno e soffriva terribilmente.

«Alzando lo sguardo verso l'alto, da lontano vide Abramo e Lazzaro che era con lui. ²⁴ Allora gridò:

"Padre Abramo, abbi pietà di me! Di' a Lazzaro che vada a mettere la punta di un dito nell'acqua e mi rinfreschi la lingua. Io soffro terribilmente in queste fiamme!".

²⁵ «Ma Abramo gli rispose:

"Figlio mio, ricordati che durante la tua vita hai già ricevuto molti beni, e Lazzaro ha avuto soltanto sofferenze. Ora invece, lui si trova nella gioia e tu soffri terribilmente. ²⁶ Per di più, tra noi e voi c'è un grande abisso: se qualcuno di noi vuole venire da voi non può farlo; così pure, nessuno di voi può venire da noi".

²⁷ «Ma il ricco disse ancora:

"Ti supplico, padre Abramo, almeno manda Lazzaro nella casa di mio padre. ²⁸ Ho cinque fratelli e vorrei che Lazzaro li convincesse a non venire anche loro in questo luogo di tormenti".

²⁹ «Abramo gli rispose:

"I tuoi fratelli hanno la legge di Mosè e gli scritti dei profeti. Li ascoltino!".

³⁰ «Ma il ricco replicò:

"No, ti supplico, padre Abramo! Se qualcuno dei morti andrà da loro cambieranno modo di vivere".

³¹ «Alla fine Abramo gli disse:

"Se non ascoltano le parole di Mosè e dei profeti non si lasceranno convincere neppure se uno risorge dai morti"».

Gli scandali e la fede

17 Un giorno Gesù disse ai suoi discepoli: «Certo, gli scandali non mancheranno mai! Però, guai a quelli che li provocano. ² Se qualcuno fa perdere la fede a una di queste persone semplici, sarebbe meglio per lui che fosse gettato in mare con una grossa pietra al collo! ³ State bene attenti!

«Se un tuo fratello ti fa del male, tu rimproveralo! Se poi si pente di quel che ha fatto, tu perdonalo! [4] E se anche ti fa del male sette volte al giorno e sette volte al giorno torna da te a chiederti scusa, tu perdonalo».

[5] Poi gli apostoli dissero al Signore:
«Accresci la nostra fede!».

[6] Il Signore rispose:
«Se aveste una fede piccola come un granello di senape, voi potreste dire a questa pianta di gelso: Togliti via da questo terreno e vai a piantarti nel mare! Ebbene, se aveste fede, quell'albero farebbe come avete detto voi.

Servizio senza pretesa

[7] «Uno di voi ha un servo, e questo servo si trova nei campi ad arare oppure a pascolare il gregge. Come si comporterà quando il servo torna dai campi? Gli dirà forse: Vieni subito qui e mettiti a tavola con me? [8] No certamente, ma gli dirà: Cambiati il vestito, preparami la cena e servi in tavola. Quando io avrò finito di mangiare, allora ti metterai a tavola anche tu. [9] Quando un servo ha fatto quel che gli è stato comandato, il padrone non ha obblighi speciali verso di lui. [10] Questo vale anche per voi! Quando avete fatto tutto quel che vi è stato comandato, dite: "Siamo soltanto servitori. Abbiamo fatto quel che dovevamo fare"».

Gesù guarisce dieci lebbrosi

[11] Mentre andava verso Gerusalemme, Gesù passò attraverso la Galilea e la Samaria. [12] Entrò in un villaggio e gli vennero incontro dieci lebbrosi. Questi si fermarono a una certa distanza [13] e ad alta voce dissero a Gesù:
«Gesù, Signore, abbi pietà di noi!».

[14] Appena li vide, Gesù disse:
«Andate dai sacerdoti e presentatevi a loro!».

Quelli andarono, e mentre camminavano, improvvisamente furono guariti.

[15] Uno di loro, appena si accorse di essere guarito, tornò indietro e lodava Dio con tutta la voce che aveva. [16] Poi si gettò ai piedi di Gesù per ringraziarlo. Era un abitante della Samaria. [17] Gesù allora osservò:
«Quei dieci lebbrosi sono stati guariti tutti! Dove sono gli altri nove?

¹⁸ Perché non sono tornati indietro a ringraziare Dio? Nessuno lo ha fatto, eccetto quest'uomo che è straniero».

¹⁹ Poi Gesù gli disse: «Alzati e va'! la tua fede ti ha salvato!».

Gesù ritornerà glorioso nel suo regno

²⁰ Alcuni farisei rivolsero a Gesù questa domanda: «Quando verrà il regno di Dio?».

Gesù rispose:

«Il regno di Dio non viene in modo spettacolare. ²¹ Nessuno potrà dire: "Eccolo qua", perché il regno di Dio è già in mezzo a voi».

²² Poi disse ai suoi discepoli: «Verranno tempi nei quali voi desidererete vedere anche solo per poco il Figlio dell'uomo che viene, ma non lo vedrete. ²³ Allora molti vi diranno: "Eccolo là", oppure: "Eccolo qua", ma voi non muovetevi! Non seguiteli! ²⁴ Perché come il lampo improvvisamente splende e illumina tutto il cielo, così verrà il Figlio dell'uomo nel suo giorno. ²⁵ Prima, però, egli deve soffrire molto. Sarà rifiutato dagli uomini di questo tempo.

²⁶ «Come accadde ai tempi di Noè, così avverrà anche quando tornerà il Figlio dell'uomo. ²⁷ Si mangiava e si beveva anche allora. C'era chi prendeva moglie e chi prendeva marito, fino al giorno nel quale Noè entrò nell'arca. Poi venne il diluvio e li spazzò via tutti. ²⁸ Lo stesso avvenne al tempo di Lot: la gente mangiava e beveva, comprava e vendeva, piantava alberi e costruiva case, ²⁹ fino al giorno in cui Lot uscì da Sòdoma: allora dal cielo venne fuoco e zolfo, e tutti furono distrutti.

³⁰ «Così succederà anche nel giorno in cui il Figlio dell'uomo si manifesterà. ³¹ In quel momento, se qualcuno si troverà sulla terrazza di casa sua non scenda a pianterreno a prendere le sue cose. Se uno si troverà nei campi a lavorare non torni indietro. ³² Ricordatevi come finì la moglie di Lot! ³³ Se uno farà di tutto per mettere in salvo la propria vita la perderà. Chi invece è pronto a sacrificare la propria vita la riavrà di nuovo.

³⁴ «Io vi dico: Quella notte quando tornerà il Figlio dell'uomo, se due persone si troveranno nello stesso letto, una sarà presa e l'altra lasciata. ³⁵ Se due donne si troveranno insieme a macinare il grano, una sarà presa e l'altra sarà lasciata». [³⁶ Se due uomini si troveranno insieme a lavorare nello stesso campo uno sarà preso e l'altro lasciato.]

³⁷ I discepoli allora gli chiesero:
«Signore, queste cose dove accadranno?».

Gesù rispose loro:
«Dove c'è un cadavere, là si radunano anche gli avvoltoi».

La parabola del giudice e della vedova

18 Gesù raccontò una parabola per insegnare ai discepoli che bisogna pregare sempre, senza stancarsi mai. ² Disse: «C'era in una città un giudice che non rispettava nessuno: né Dio né gli uomini. ³ Nella stessa città viveva anche una vedova. Essa andava sempre da quel giudice e gli chiedeva: Fammi giustizia contro il mio avversario.

⁴ «Per un po' di tempo il giudice non volle intervenire, ma alla fine pensò: "Di Dio non me ne importa niente e degli uomini non me ne curo: ⁵ tuttavia farò giustizia a questa vedova perché mi dà ai nervi. Così non verrà più a stancarmi con le sue richieste"».

⁶ Poi il Signore continuò: «Fate bene attenzione a ciò che ha detto quel giudice ingiusto. ⁷ Se fa così lui, volete che Dio non faccia giustizia ai suoi figli che lo invocano giorno e notte? Tarderà ad aiutarli? ⁸ Vi assicuro che Dio farà loro giustizia, e molto presto! Ma quando il Figlio dell'uomo tornerà troverà ancora fede sulla terra?».

Parabola del fariseo e del pubblicano

⁹ Poi Gesù raccontò un'altra parabola per alcuni che si ritenevano giusti e disprezzavano gli altri. ¹⁰ Disse: «Una volta c'erano due uomini: uno era fariseo e l'altro era un agente delle tasse. Un giorno salirono al Tempio per pregare.

¹¹ «Il fariseo se ne stava in piedi e pregava così tra sé: "O Dio, ti ringrazio perché io non sono come gli altri uomini: ladri, imbroglioni, adùlteri. Io sono diverso anche da quell'agente delle tasse. ¹² Io digiuno due volte alla settimana e offro al Tempio la decima parte di quello che guadagno".

¹³ «L'agente delle tasse invece si fermò indietro e non voleva neppure alzare lo sguardo al cielo. Anzi si batteva il petto dicendo: "O Dio, abbi pietà di me che sono un povero peccatore!".

¹⁴ «Vi assicuro che l'agente delle tasse tornò a casa perdonato; l'altro invece no. Perché, chi si esalta sarà abbassato; chi invece si abbassa sarà innalzato».

Gesù benedice i bambini

¹⁵ Alcune persone portavano i loro bambini a Gesù e volevano farglieli benedire, ma i discepoli li sgridavano. ¹⁶ Allora Gesù chiamò vicino a sé i bambini e disse ai suoi discepoli: «Lasciate che i bambini vengano a me e non impediteglielo, perché Dio dà il suo regno a quelli che sono come loro. ¹⁷ Io vi assicuro: chi non l'accoglie come farebbe un bambino non vi entrerà».

Gesù incontra un uomo ricco

¹⁸ Uno dei capi domandò un giorno a Gesù:
«Maestro buono, che cosa devo fare per ottenere la vita eterna?».
¹⁹ Gesù gli rispose:
«Perché mi chiami buono? Nessuno è buono, tranne Dio! ²⁰ I comandamenti li conosci:
Non commettere adulterio,
non uccidere,
non rubare,
non dire il falso contro nessuno,
rispetta tuo padre e tua madre!».
²¹ Ma quell'uomo disse:
«Fin da giovane io ho ubbidito a tutti questi comandamenti».
²² Gesù lo ascoltò, poi gli disse:
«Ancora una cosa ti manca: vendi tutto quel che possiedi e i soldi che ricavi distribuiscili ai poveri. Allora avrai un tesoro in cielo. Poi vieni e seguimi!».
²³ Ma quell'uomo, udita la proposta di Gesù, diventò molto triste. Era troppo ricco.
²⁴ Gesù notò la sua tristezza e disse: «Com'è difficile per quelli che sono ricchi entrare nel regno di Dio! ²⁵ Se è difficile che un cammello passi attraverso la cruna di un ago, è ancor più difficile che un ricco possa entrare nel regno di Dio».

²⁶ Quelli che lo ascoltavano domandarono a Gesù: «Ma allora chi potrà mai salvarsi?».

²⁷ Gesù rispose: «Ciò che è impossibile agli uomini è possibile a Dio».

²⁸ Allora Pietro gli disse: «E noi? Noi abbiamo abbandonato tutto quel che avevamo per venire con te».

²⁹ Gesù si volse ai discepoli e rispose: «Io vi assicuro che se qualcuno ha abbandonato casa, moglie, fratelli, genitori e figli... per il regno di Dio, ³⁰ costui riceverà molto di più già in questa vita, e nel mondo futuro riceverà la vita eterna».

Gesù annunzia ancora la sua morte e risurrezione

³¹ Poi Gesù prese da parte i dodici discepoli e disse loro: «Ecco, noi stiamo salendo verso Gerusalemme. Là si realizzerà tutto quel che i profeti hanno scritto riguardo al Figlio dell'uomo. ³² Egli sarà consegnato ai pagani ed essi gli rideranno in faccia, lo copriranno di offese e di sputi, ³³ lo prenderanno a frustate e lo uccideranno. Ma il terzo giorno risorgerà».

³⁴ I discepoli però non capirono nulla di tutto questo. Il significato di ciò che Gesù diceva rimase per loro misterioso e non riuscivano affatto a capire.

Gesù guarisce un cieco

³⁵ Gesù stava avvicinandosi alla città di Gèrico; un cieco seduto sul bordo della strada chiedeva l'elemosina. ³⁶ Il cieco sentì passare la gente e domandò che cosa c'era. ³⁷ Gli risposero: «Passa Gesù di Nàzaret!».

³⁸ Allora quel cieco gridò: «Gesù, Figlio di Davide, abbi pietà di me!».

³⁹ Quelli che passavano lo sgridavano per farlo stare zitto. Ma egli gridava ancor più forte: «Figlio di Davide, abbi pietà di me!».

⁴⁰ Gesù si fermò e ordinò che gli portassero il cieco. Quando fu vicino Gesù gli chiese:

⁴¹ «Che cosa vuoi che io faccia per te?».

Il cieco disse: «Signore, fa' che io possa vederci di nuovo!».

⁴² Allora Gesù gli disse:
«Apri i tuoi occhi! La tua fede ti ha salvato».

⁴³ In un attimo il cieco ricuperò la vista. Poi si mise a seguire Gesù, ringraziando Dio. Anche la gente che era presente ed aveva visto il fatto si mise a lodare Dio.

Gesù entra nella casa di Zaccheo

19 Gesù entrò nella città di Gèrico e la stava attraversando. ² Qui viveva un certo Zaccheo. Era un capo degli agenti delle tasse ed era molto ricco. ³ Desiderava però vedere chi fosse Gesù, ma non ci riusciva: c'era molta gente attorno a Gesù e lui era troppo piccolo. ⁴ Allora corse un po' avanti e si arrampicò sopra un albero in un punto dove Gesù doveva passare: sperava così di poterlo vedere.

⁵ Quando arrivò in quel punto, Gesù guardò in alto e gli disse: «Zaccheo, scendi in fretta, perché oggi devo fermarmi a casa tua!». ⁶ Zaccheo scese subito dall'albero e con grande gioia accolse Gesù in casa sua.

⁷ I presenti vedendo queste cose si misero a mormorare contro Gesù. Dicevano: «È andato ad alloggiare da uno strozzino». ⁸ Zaccheo invece, stando davanti al Signore, gli disse:
«Signore, la metà dei miei beni la do ai poveri e se ho rubato a qualcuno gli restituisco quattro volte tanto».

⁹ Allora Gesù disse a Zaccheo:
«Oggi la salvezza è entrata in questa casa. Anche tu sei un discendente di Abramo. ¹⁰ Ora il Figlio dell'uomo è venuto proprio a cercare e a salvare quelli che erano perduti».

La parabola dei dieci servi

¹¹ Gesù era ormai vicino a Gerusalemme, e perciò molti pensavano che il regno di Dio si manifestasse da un momento all'altro. ¹² Allora Gesù raccontò quest'altra parabola: «C'era una volta un uomo di famiglia nobile. Egli doveva andare in un paese lontano per ricevere il titolo di re, poi sarebbe tornato. ¹³ Prima di partire chiamò dieci dei suoi servi; consegnò a ciascuno una medesima somma di denaro e disse: "Cercate di far fruttare questo denaro fino a quando non sarò tornato".

[14] «Ma i suoi cittadini odiavano quell'uomo e gli mandarono dietro alcuni rappresentanti per far sapere che non lo volevano come re.

[15] «E invece quell'uomo diventò re e ritornò al suo paese. Fece chiamare i servi ai quali aveva consegnato il suo denaro per sapere quanto guadagno ne avevano ricavato.

[16] «Si fece avanti il primo servo e disse: "Signore, con quello che tu mi hai dato io ho guadagnato dieci volte tanto".

[17] «Il padrone gli rispose: "Bene, sei un servo bravo. Sei stato fedele in cose da poco: ora io ti faccio governatore di dieci città".

[18] «Poi venne il secondo servo e disse: "Signore, con quello che tu mi hai dato ho guadagnato cinque volte tanto".

[19] «Il padrone rispose: "Anche tu avrai l'amministrazione di cinque città".

[20] «Infine si fece avanti un altro servo e disse: "Signore, ecco il tuo denaro! L'ho nascosto in un fazzoletto. [21] Avevo paura di te, perché sapevo che sei un padrone esigente: tu pretendi anche quel che non hai depositato e raccogli anche quel che non hai seminato".

[22] «Allora il padrone gli rispose: "Tu sei stato un servo cattivo e io ti giudico secondo quel che hai detto. Tu sapevi che sono un padrone esigente, che pretendo anche quel che non ho depositato e raccolgo anche quel che non ho seminato. [23] Perché allora non hai depositato il mio denaro alla banca? Al mio ritorno l'avrei ritirato con gli interessi!".

[24] «Poi il padrone disse ai presenti: "Via, toglietegli il denaro che ha e datelo a quello che lo ha fatto fruttare di più".

[25] «Gli fecero osservare: "Signore, ma lui ne ha già fin troppo".

[26] «Il padrone allora rispose: "Chi ha molto riceverà ancora di più; ma a chi ha poco sarà portato via anche quel poco che ha. [27] Ed ora i miei nemici, quelli che non mi volevano come loro re: portateli qui, uccideteli alla mia presenza"».

Gesù si avvicina a Gerusalemme

[28] Dopo questi discorsi Gesù continuò la sua strada verso Gerusalemme: camminava davanti a tutti. [29] Quando fu vicino ai villaggi di Bètfage e di Betània, presso il monte degli Ulivi, Gesù mandò avanti due discepoli. [30] Disse loro: «Andate nel villaggio che sta qui di fronte. Appena entrati, troverete un piccolo asino sul quale nessuno è mai salito. Lo troverete legato: voi slegatelo e portatelo qui. [31] Se qualcuno vi domanda: "Perché slegate quell'asinello?", voi rispondete: "Perché il Signore ne ha bisogno"».

[32] I due discepoli andarono e trovarono tutto come aveva detto Gesù. [33] Mentre slegavano il puledro, i proprietari chiesero ai due discepoli:

«Perché lo prendete?».

[34] Essi risposero:

«Perché il Signore ne ha bisogno».

[35] Allora portarono il puledro da Gesù. Poi lo coprirono con i loro mantelli e vi fecero salire Gesù. [36] Man mano che Gesù avanzava, stendevano i mantelli sulla strada davanti a lui.

[37] Gesù scendeva dal monte degli Ulivi ed era ormai vicino alla città. Tutti i suoi discepoli, pieni di gioia e a gran voce, si misero a lodare Dio per tutti i miracoli che avevano visto. [38] Gridavano:

«*Benedetto colui che viene*
nel nome del Signore: egli è il re!
In cielo sia la pace,
e gloria nell'alto dei cieli!».

[39] Alcuni farisei che si trovavano tra la folla dissero a Gesù:

«Maestro, fa' tacere i tuoi discepoli!».

[40] Ma Gesù rispose:

«Vi assicuro che se tacciono loro si metteranno a gridare le pietre».

Gesù piange per Gerusalemme

[41] Quando fu vicino alla città, Gesù la guardò e si mise a piangere per lei. [42] Diceva: «Gerusalemme, se tu sapessi, almeno oggi, quel che occorre alla tua pace! Ma non riesci a vederlo! [43] Per te verrà un tempo nel quale i tuoi nemici ti circonderanno di trincee. Ti assedieran-

no e premeranno su di te da ogni parte. ⁴⁴ Distruggeranno te e i tuoi abitanti e sarai rasa al suolo, perché tu non hai saputo riconoscere il tempo nel quale Dio è venuto a salvarti».

Gesù scaccia i mercanti dal Tempio

⁴⁵ Poi Gesù entrò nel cortile del Tempio e cominciò a cacciar via quelli che stavano là a vendere. ⁴⁶ Diceva loro: «Nella Bibbia sta scritto:
La mia casa sarà casa di preghiera,
voi invece ne avete fatto un covo di briganti».

⁴⁷ Gesù insegnava ogni giorno nel Tempio. I capi dei sacerdoti, i maestri della Legge e le altre autorità del popolo cercavano di farlo morire. ⁴⁸ Ma non sapevano come fare, perché la gente era sempre attorno a Gesù ad ascoltare le sue parole.

Discussione sull'autorità di Gesù

20 Un giorno Gesù stava insegnando nel Tempio e annunziava al popolo il suo messaggio. I capi dei sacerdoti, i maestri della Legge, insieme con le altre autorità, andarono da lui e gli dissero: ² «Tu devi dirci una cosa: che diritto hai di fare quel che fai? Chi ti ha dato l'autorità di agire così?».

³ Gesù rispose loro:
«Voglio farvi anch'io una domanda. ⁴ Ditemi: Giovanni, chi lo ha mandato a battezzare? Dio o gli uomini?».

⁵ Quelli allora si consultarono tra loro: «Se diciamo che Giovanni è stato mandato da Dio, ci chiederà: "Perché dunque non avete creduto in lui?". ⁶ Se invece diciamo che Giovanni è stato mandato dagli uomini, allora il popolo ci ucciderà, perché tutti sono convinti che Giovanni era un profeta».

⁷ Perciò risposero di non saperlo.

⁸ E Gesù disse loro: «Ebbene, allora neanch'io vi dirò con quale autorità faccio queste cose».

Parabola della vigna e dei contadini omicidi

⁹ Poi Gesù si rivolse al popolo e raccontò loro questa parabola: «Un uomo piantò una vigna. Poi l'affittò ad alcuni contadini e se ne andò lontano per lungo tempo.

¹⁰ «Venne il tempo della vendemmia, e quell'uomo mandò un servo dai contadini per farsi dare la sua parte di raccolto. Ma i contadini bastonarono quel servo e lo mandarono via senza dargli niente. ¹¹ Allora il padrone mandò ancora un altro servo, ma i contadini lo accolsero a parolacce, bastonarono anche lui e lo rimandarono indietro senza dargli niente. ¹² Il padrone volle mandare ancora un terzo servo, ma quei contadini ferirono gravemente anche lui e lo buttarono fuori.

¹³ «Allora il padrone della vigna pensò: Che cosa posso fare ancora? Manderò mio figlio, il mio carissimo figlio. Spero che avranno rispetto almeno di lui.

¹⁴ «Ma i contadini, appena videro arrivare il figlio del padrone, dissero tra loro: "Ecco, un giorno costui sarà il padrone della vigna. Uccidiamolo e l'eredità diventerà nostra!". ¹⁵ Perciò lo gettarono fuori della vigna e l'uccisero».

A questo punto Gesù domandò loro:
«Che cosa farà dunque il padrone della vigna con quei contadini? ¹⁶ Certamente egli verrà e ucciderà quei contadini e darà la vigna ad altre persone».

Sentendo queste parole i presenti dissero:
«Questo no! Non accadrà mai!».

¹⁷ Ma Gesù fissò lo sguardo su di loro e disse:
«Eppure nella Bibbia sta scritto:
    La pietra che i costruttori hanno rifiutato
    è diventata la pietra più importante.
¹⁸ Chiunque cadrà su quella pietra si sfracellerà; e colui sul quale essa cadrà rimarrà schiacciato».

¹⁹ I maestri della Legge e i capi dei sacerdoti avevano capito che Gesù con quella parabola si riferiva a loro, cercarono di catturarlo, ma avevano paura del popolo.

Le tasse da pagare all'imperatore romano

²⁰ I capi dei sacerdoti e i maestri della Legge si misero a spiare Gesù. Mandarono alcuni per spiarlo e consigliarono loro di fingersi brave persone. Dovevano cogliere Gesù in fallo su qualche punto dei suoi discorsi, in modo da poterlo consegnare al governatore romano e farlo condannare. ²¹ Essi domandarono a Gesù:

«Maestro, sappiamo che quel che tu dici e insegni è giusto. Tu non guardi in faccia a nessuno e insegni veramente la volontà di Dio. ²² Una domanda: la nostra Legge permette o non permette che noi paghiamo le tasse all'imperatore romano?».

²³ Gesù si rese conto che lo volevano ingannare e quindi disse loro: ²⁴ «Fatemi vedere una moneta d'argento: Questo volto e questo nome di chi sono?».

²⁵ Risposero:
«Dell'imperatore».

E Gesù concluse:
«Date dunque all'imperatore quel che è dell'imperatore, ma quel che è di Dio datelo a Dio».

²⁶ Così non poterono cogliere in fallo Gesù su quel che egli diceva al popolo. Anzi si meravigliarono della sua risposta e non avevano più il coraggio di fare domande.

Discussione a proposito della risurrezione

²⁷ I sadducei dicevano che nessuno può risorgere dopo la morte. Alcuni di loro si fecero avanti e domandarono a Gesù: ²⁸ «Maestro, Mosè ci ha lasciato questo comandamento scritto: *Se uno muore* e lascia la moglie *senza figli, suo fratello deve sposare la vedova e cercare di avere dei figli per quello che è morto.* ²⁹ Dunque: c'era-no una volta sette fratelli. Il primo si sposò e morì senza lasciare figli. ³⁰ Anche il secondo ³¹ e il terzo sposarono quella vedova senza avere figli, e così via tutti e sette: tutti morirono senza lasciare figli. ³² Poi morì anche quella donna. ³³ Ora, nel giorno della risurrezione, di chi sarà moglie quella donna? Perché tutti e sette i fratelli l'hanno avuta come moglie».

³⁴ Gesù rispose loro:
«Solo in questa vita gli uomini e le donne sposano e sono sposati. ³⁵ Ma quelli che risorgeranno dai morti e saranno giudicati degni della vita futura non prenderanno più né moglie né marito. ³⁶ Essi non possono più morire perché sono uguali agli angeli e sono figli di Dio perché sono risorti. ³⁷ È certo che i morti risorgono: lo afferma anche Mosè quando parla del cespuglio in fiamme. In quel punto Mosè dice che *il Signore è il Dio di Abramo, il Dio di Isacco, il Dio di*

Giacobbe. [38] Quindi Dio è il Dio dei vivi e non dei morti, perché tutti da lui ricevono la vita».

[39] Intervennero allora alcuni maestri della Legge e dissero: «Maestro, hai risposto molto bene».

[40] Da quel momento nessuno aveva più il coraggio di far domande a Gesù.

Il Messia e il re Davide

[41] Ma Gesù domandò ai maestri della Legge: «Si dice che il Messia deve essere discendente del re Davide; com'è possibile? [42] Nel libro dei Salmi lo stesso Davide dice:

Il Signore ha detto al mio Signore:
siedi alla mia destra,
[43] *finché io metterò i tuoi nemici*
come sgabello sotto i tuoi piedi.
[44] Se Davide lo chiama Signore, come può il Messia essere discendente di Davide?».

Gesù parla contro i maestri della Legge

[45] Tutto il popolo stava ad ascoltare Gesù. Allora egli disse ai suoi discepoli: [46] «State attenti a non lasciarvi corrompere dai maestri della Legge. A loro piace passeggiare con vesti di lusso, desiderano essere salutati in piazza, avere i posti d'onore nelle sinagoghe e i primi posti nei banchetti. [47] Con avidità cercano di portar via alle vedove tutto quello che hanno, e intanto, per farsi vedere, fanno lunghe preghiere. Queste persone saranno giudicate con estrema severità».

L'offerta di una povera vedova

21 Poi Gesù, guardandosi attorno, vide alcune persone ricche che gettavano le loro offerte nelle cassette del Tempio. [2] Vide anche una povera vedova, che vi metteva due monetine di rame. [3] Allora disse: «Vi assicuro che questa vedova, povera com'è, ha dato un'offerta più grande di quella di tutti gli altri. [4] Quelli infatti hanno offerto, come dono, quello che avevano d'avanzo, mentre questa donna, povera com'è, ha dato tutto ciò che le rimaneva per vivere».

Gesù annunzia che il Tempio sarà distrutto

[5] Alcuni stavano parlando del Tempio e dicevano che era molto bello per le pietre che lo formavano e per i doni offerti dai fedeli. Allora Gesù disse: [6] «Verrà un tempo in cui tutto quello che ora vedete sarà distrutto. Non rimarrà una sola pietra sull'altra».

Gesù annunzia dolori e persecuzioni

[7] Allora rivolsero a Gesù questa domanda: «Maestro, quando avverranno queste cose? E quale sarà il segno che queste cose stanno per accadere?».

[8] Gesù rispose: «Fate attenzione a non lasciarvi ingannare! Perché molti verranno, si presenteranno con il mio nome e diranno: "Sono io il Messia!", oppure vi diranno: "Il tempo è giunto!". Voi però non ascoltateli e non seguiteli! [9] Quando sentirete parlare di guerre e di rivoluzioni, non abbiate paura! Fatti del genere devono avvenire prima, ma non sarà subito la fine».

[10] Poi Gesù disse loro: «I popoli combatteranno l'uno contro l'altro, e un regno contro un altro regno. [11] Ci saranno grandi terremoti, pestilenze e carestie in molte regioni. Si vedranno fenomeni spaventosi, e dal cielo verranno segni grandiosi.

[12] «Però, prima di queste cose, vi prenderanno con violenza e vi perseguiteranno. Vi porteranno nelle loro sinagoghe e nelle loro prigioni, vi trascineranno davanti a re e governatori a causa del mio nome. [13] Avrete allora occasione per dare testimonianza di me. [14] Siate decisi! Non preoccupatevi di quel che dovrete dire per difendervi. [15] Sarò io a suggerirvi le parole giuste, e vi darò una sapienza tale che tutti i vostri avversari non potranno resistere e tanto meno combattere.

[16] «In quel tempo, perfino i genitori, i fratelli, i parenti e gli amici vi tradiranno e faranno morire alcuni di voi. [17] Sarete odiati da tutti per causa mia. [18] Eppure, neanche un capello del vostro capo andrà perduto. [19] Se saprete resistere sino alla fine salverete voi stessi.

Gesù annunzia la distruzione di Gerusalemme

[20] «Un giorno vedrete Gerusalemme assediata da eserciti nemici: allora ricordate che è vicina la sua rovina.

²¹ «In quel tempo, quelli che si troveranno in Gerusalemme si allontanino da essa; e quelli che si troveranno in aperta campagna non ritornino in città.

²² «Quello sarà il tempo del giudizio: tutto ciò che è stato scritto nella Bibbia dovrà accadere. ²³ Saranno giorni tristi per le donne incinte e per quelle che allattano! Tutto il paese sarà colpito da una grande tribolazione, e l'ira di Dio si scatenerà contro questo popolo. ²⁴ Alcuni cadranno sotto i colpi della spada, altri saranno portati via come schiavi in paesi stranieri, e Gerusalemme sarà calpestata dai pagani e distrutta, fino a quando non sarà finito il tempo che Dio ha stabilito per loro.

Gesù annunzia il ritorno del Figlio dell'uomo

²⁵ «Ci saranno anche strani fenomeni nel sole, nella luna e nelle stelle. Sulla terra i popoli saranno presi dall'angoscia e dallo spavento per il fragore del mare in tempesta. ²⁶ Gli abitanti della terra moriranno per la paura e per il presentimento di ciò che dovrà accadere. Infatti le forze del cielo saranno sconvolte. ²⁷ Allora vedranno il *Figlio dell'uomo venire sopra una nube*, con grande potenza e splendore! ²⁸ Quando queste cose cominceranno a succedere, alzatevi e state sicuri, perché è vicino il tempo della vostra liberazione».

Parabola del fico

²⁹ Poi Gesù disse questa parabola: «Osservate bene l'albero del fico e anche tutte le altre piante. ³⁰ Quando vedete che mettono le prime foglioline, voi capite che l'estate è vicina. ³¹ Allo stesso modo, quando vedrete accadere queste cose, sappiate che il regno di Do è vicino. ³² Vi assicuro che non passerà questa generazione prima che tutte queste cose siano accadute. ³³ Il cielo e la terra passeranno, ma le mie parole non passeranno!

Gesù esorta a essere vigilanti

³⁴ «Badate bene! Non lasciatevi intontire da orge e ubriachezze! Non abbiate troppe preoccupazioni materiali! Altrimenti diventerete pigri, vi dimenticherete del giorno del giudizio, e quel giorno vi pioverà addosso improvvisamente. ³⁵ Infatti esso verrà su tutti gli abitan-

ti della terra come una trappola. [36] Voi invece state svegli e pregate in ogni momento. Avrete così la forza di superare tutti i mali che stanno per accadere e potrete presentarvi davanti al Figlio dell'uomo».

[37] Durante il giorno Gesù continuava a insegnare nel Tempio. Di notte invece usciva dalla città di Gerusalemme e se ne stava all'aperto, sul monte degli Ulivi. [38] Ma già di buon mattino la gente andava nel Tempio per ascoltarlo.

Giuda tradisce Gesù

22 Si avvicinava intanto la festa dei Pani non lievitati, detta anche la festa di Pasqua. [2] Intanto i capi dei sacerdoti e i maestri della Legge stavano cercando il modo di eliminare Gesù. Però avevano paura del popolo.

[3] Ma Satana entrò in Giuda, quello che era chiamato anche Iscariota, e apparteneva al gruppo dei dodici discepoli. [4] Giuda andò dai capi dei sacerdoti e dalle guardie del Tempio, e con loro si mise d'accordo sul modo di aiutarli ad arrestare Gesù. [5] Quelli furono molto contenti e furono d'accordo di dargli del denaro. [6] Giuda accettò e si mise a cercare un'occasione per fare arrestare Gesù, lontano dalla folla.

Gesù fa preparare la cena pasquale

[7] Venne poi il giorno della festa dei Pani non lievitati, nel quale si doveva uccidere l'agnello pasquale. [8] Gesù mandò avanti Pietro e Giovanni con questo incarico:
«Andate a preparare per noi la cena di Pasqua».

[9] Essi risposero:
«Dove vuoi che la prepariamo?».

[10] Gesù disse:
«Quando entrerete in città incontrerete un uomo che porta una brocca d'acqua. Seguitelo fino alla casa dove entrerà. [11] Poi direte al padrone di quella casa: Il Maestro desidera fare la cena pasquale con i suoi discepoli e ti chiede la sala. [12] Egli vi mostrerà al piano superiore una sala grande con i tappeti. In quella sala preparate la cena».

[13] Pietro e Giovanni andarono, trovarono come aveva detto Gesù e prepararono la cena pasquale.

La Cena del Signore

[14] Quando venne l'ora per la cena pasquale, Gesù si mise a tavola con i suoi apostoli. [15] Poi disse loro: «Ho tanto desiderato fare questa cena pasquale con voi prima di soffrire. [16] Vi assicuro che non celebrerò più la Pasqua, fino a quando non si realizzerà nel regno di Dio».

[17] Poi Gesù prese un calice, ringraziò Dio e disse: «Prendete questo calice e fatelo passare tra di voi. [18] Vi assicuro che da questo momento non berrò più vino fino a quando non verrà il regno di Dio». [19] Poi prese il pane, fece la preghiera di ringraziamento, spezzò il pane, lo diede ai suoi discepoli e disse: «Questo è il mio corpo, che viene offerto per voi. Fate questo in memoria di me». [20] Allo stesso modo, alla fine della cena, offrì loro il calice, dicendo: «Questo calice è la nuova alleanza che Dio stabilisce per mezzo del mio sangue, offerto per voi.

[21] «Ma ecco: il mio traditore è qui a tavola con me. [22] Il Figlio dell'uomo va incontro alla morte, come è stato stabilito per lui; ma guai a quell'uomo per mezzo del quale egli è tradito».

[23] Allora i discepoli di Gesù cominciarono a domandarsi gli uni con gli altri chi di loro stava per fare una cosa simile.

Chi è il più importante

[24] Tra i discepoli sorse una discussione per stabilire chi tra essi doveva essere considerato il più importante. [25] Ma Gesù disse loro: «I re comandano sui loro popoli e quelli che hanno il potere si fanno chiamare benefattori del popolo. [26] Voi però non dovete agire così! Anzi, chi tra voi è il più importante diventi come il più piccolo; chi comanda diventi come quello che serve. [27] Secondo voi, chi è più importante: chi siede a tavola oppure chi sta a servire? Quello che siede a tavola, non vi pare? Eppure io sto in mezzo a voi come un servo. [28] Voi siete quelli rimasti sempre con me, anche nelle mie prove. [29] Ora, io vi faccio eredi di quel regno che Dio, mio Padre, ha dato a me. [30] Quando comincerò a regnare, voi mangerete e berrete con me, alla mia tavola. E sederete su dodici troni per giudicare le dodici tribù del popolo d'Israele.

Gesù annunzia che Pietro lo rinnegherà

[31] «Simone, Simone, ascolta! Satana ha preteso di passarvi al vaglio, come si fa con il grano per pulirlo. [32] Ma io ho pregato per te, perché la tua fede non venga meno. E tu, quando sarai tornato a me, da' forza ai tuoi fratelli».

[33] Allora Pietro gli disse:

«Signore, con te sono pronto ad andare anche in prigione e persino alla morte».

[34] Ma Gesù rispose:

«Pietro, ascolta quel che ti dico: oggi, prima che il gallo canti, avrai dichiarato tre volte che non mi conosci».

La borsa, il sacco e la spada

[35] Poi Gesù disse ai suoi discepoli:

«Quando vi mandai senza soldi, senza bagagli e senza sandali, vi è mancato qualcosa?».

Essi risposero:

«Niente!».

[36] Allora Gesù disse:

«Ora però è diverso: chi ha dei soldi li prenda; così anche chi ha una borsa. E chi non ha una spada venda il suo mantello e se ne procuri una. [37] Vi dico infatti che deve avverarsi per me quel che dice la Bibbia:

È stato messo tra i malfattori.

Ecco, quel che mi riguarda sta ormai per compiersi».

[38] Allora i discepoli dissero a Gesù:

«Signore, ecco qui due spade!».

Ma Gesù rispose:

«Basta!».

Gesù va verso il monte degli Ulivi a pregare

[39] Come faceva di solito, Gesù uscì e andò verso il monte degli Ulivi, e i suoi discepoli lo seguirono. [40] Quando giunse sul posto disse loro: «Pregate per resistere nel momento della prova».

[41] Poi si allontanò da loro alcuni passi, si mise in ginocchio [42] e pregò così: «Padre, se vuoi, allontana da me questo calice di dolore.

Però non sia fatta la mia volontà, ma la tua». [43] Allora dal cielo venne un angelo a Gesù per confortarlo; [44] e in quel momento di grande tensione pregava più intensamente. Il suo sudore cadeva a terra come gocce di sangue.

[45] Quindi, dopo aver pregato, Gesù si alzò e andò verso i suoi discepoli. Li trovò addormentati, sfiniti per la tristezza [46] e disse loro: «Perché dormite? Alzatevi e pregate per resistere nel momento della prova».

Gesù è arrestato

[47] Mentre Gesù ancora parlava con i discepoli, arrivò molta gente. Giuda, uno dei Dodici, faceva loro da guida. Si avvicinò a Gesù per baciarlo. [48] Allora Gesù disse: «Giuda, con un bacio tu tradisci il Figlio dell'uomo?».

[49] Quelli che erano con Gesù, appena si accorsero di ciò che stava per accadere, dissero: «Signore, usiamo la spada?».

[50] E in quel momento uno di loro colpì il servo del sommo sacerdote e gli tagliò l'orecchio destro.

[51] Ma Gesù intervenne e disse: «Lasciate, basta così».

Toccò l'orecchio di quel servo e lo guarì.

[52] Poi Gesù si rivolse ai capi dei sacerdoti, ai capi delle guardie del Tempio e alle altre autorità del popolo che erano venuti contro di lui e disse: «Siete venuti con spade e bastoni, come per arrestare un delinquente. [53] Eppure io stavo ogni giorno con voi, nel Tempio, e non mi avete mai arrestato. Ma questa è l'ora vostra: ora si scatena il potere delle tenebre».

Pietro nega di conoscere Gesù

[54] Le guardie del Tempio arrestarono Gesù e lo portarono nella casa del sommo sacerdote. Pietro lo seguiva da lontano. [55] Alcuni accesero un fuoco in mezzo al cortile e si sedettero. Pietro si mise insieme a loro.

[56] Una serva lo vide là, seduto presso il fuoco, lo guardò bene e poi disse:

«Anche quest'uomo era con Gesù!».

[57] Ma Pietro negò e disse:

«Donna, non so chi è!».

[58] Poco dopo, un altro vedendo Pietro disse:
«Anche tu sei uno di quelli».

Ma Pietro dichiarò:
«Uomo, non sono io!».

[59] Dopo circa un'ora, un altro affermò con insistenza:
«Sono sicuro: anche quest'uomo era con Gesù: infatti viene dalla Galilea».

[60] Ma Pietro protestò:
«Io non so quello che tu dici».

In quel momento, mentre Pietro ancora parlava, un gallo cantò.

[61] Il Signore si voltò verso Pietro e lo guardò. Pietro allora si ricordò di quel che il Signore gli aveva detto: «Oggi, prima che il gallo canti, avrai dichiarato tre volte che non mi conosci».

[62] Poi uscì fuori e pianse amaramente.

Gesù viene insultato e picchiato

[63] Intanto gli uomini che facevano la guardia a Gesù lo deridevano e lo maltrattavano. [64] Gli bendarono gli occhi e gli domandavano: «Indovina! Chi ti ha picchiato?». [65] E lanciavano contro di lui molti altri insulti.

Gesù davanti al tribunale ebraico

[66] Appena fu giorno, si riunirono le autorità del popolo, i capi dei sacerdoti e i maestri della Legge. Fecero condurre Gesù davanti al loro tribunale [67] e gli dissero:
«Se tu sei il Messia, dillo apertamente a noi».

Ma Gesù rispose:
«Anche se lo dico voi non mi credete. [68] Se invece vi faccio domande voi non mi rispondete. [69] Ma d'ora in avanti *il Figlio dell'uomo starà accanto a Dio Onnipotente*».

[70] Tutti allora domandarono:
«Dunque, tu sei proprio il Figlio di Dio?».

Gesù rispose loro:
«Voi stessi lo dite! Io lo sono!».

[71] I capi allora conclusero: «Ormai non abbiamo più bisogno di prove! Noi stessi lo abbiamo udito direttamente dalla sua bocca».

Gesù davanti a Pilato, governatore romano

23 Tutta quell'assemblea si alzò e condussero Gesù da Pilato. [2] Là, cominciarono ad accusarlo: «Quest'uomo noi lo abbiamo trovato mentre metteva in agitazione la nostra gente: non vuole che si paghino le tasse all'imperatore romano e pretende di essere il Messia-re promesso da Dio».

[3] Allora Pilato lo interrogò:

«Sei tu il re dei Giudei?».

Gesù gli rispose:

«Tu lo dici!».

[4] Pilato quindi si rivolse ai capi dei sacerdoti e alla folla e disse: «Io non trovo alcun motivo per condannare quest'uomo».

[5] Ma quelli insistevano dicendo: «Egli crea disordine tra il popolo. Ha cominciato a diffondere le sue idee in Galilea; ora è arrivato fin qui e va predicando per tutta la Giudea».

Gesù davanti a Erode

[6] Quando Pilato udì questa accusa domandò se quell'uomo era galileo. [7] Venne così a sapere che Gesù apparteneva al territorio governato da Erode. In quei giorni anche Erode si trovava a Gerusalemme: perciò Pilato ordinò che Gesù fosse portato da lui.

[8] Da molto tempo Erode desiderava vedere Gesù. Di lui aveva sentito dire molte cose e sperava di vederlo fare qualche miracolo. Perciò, quando vide Gesù davanti a sé, Erode fu molto contento. [9] Lo interrogò con insistenza, ma Gesù non gli rispose nulla. [10] Intanto i capi dei sacerdoti e i maestri della Legge che erano presenti lo accusavano con rabbia. [11] Anche Erode, insieme con i suoi soldati, insultò Gesù. Per scherzo gli mise addosso una veste d'effetto e lo rimandò da Pilato. [12] Erode e Pilato erano sempre stati nemici tra di loro: quel giorno invece diventarono amici.

Gesù condannato a morte

[13] Pilato riunì i capi dei sacerdoti, altre autorità e il popolo, [14] e disse loro:

«Voi mi avete portato qui quest'uomo come uno che mette disordine fra il popolo. Ebbene, ho esaminato il suo caso pubblicamente davanti a voi. Voi lo accusate di molte colpe, ma io non lo trovo colpevole di nulla. [15] Anche Erode è dello stesso parere: tant'è vero che lo ha rimandato da noi senza condannarlo. Dunque, quest'uomo non ha fatto nulla che meriti la morte. [16] Perciò lo farò flagellare e poi lo lascerò libero». [[17] Ora egli doveva consegnare loro qualcuno ad ogni festa.]

[18] Ma tutti insieme si misero a gridare: «A morte quest'uomo! Vogliamo libero Barabba!».

[19] Barabba era stato messo in prigione perché aveva preso parte a una sommossa del popolo in città e aveva ucciso un uomo.

[20] Pilato parlò di nuovo ai presenti, perché voleva liberare Gesù. [21] Ma essi gridavano ancor più forte: «In croce! In croce!».

[22] Per la terza volta Pilato dichiarò: «Ma che male ha fatto quest'uomo? Io non ho trovato in lui nessuna colpa che meriti la morte. Perciò lo farò frustare e poi lo lascerò libero».

[23] Essi però insistevano a gran voce nel chiedere che Gesù venisse crocifisso. Le loro grida diventarono sempre più forti.

[24] Alla fine Pilato decise di lasciar fare come volevano. [25] Avevano chiesto la liberazione di Barabba, quello che era stato messo in prigione per sommossa e omicidio, e Pilato lo liberò. Invece consegnò loro Gesù perché ne facessero quel che volevano.

Gesù sulla via del Calvario

[26] Presero Gesù e lo portarono via. Lungo la strada, fermarono un certo Simone, originario di Cirene, che tornava dai campi. Gli caricarono sulle spalle la croce e lo costrinsero a portarla dietro a Gesù.

[27] Erano in molti a seguire Gesù: una gran folla di popolo e un gruppo di donne che si battevano il petto e manifestavano il loro dolore per lui.

[28] Gesù si voltò verso di loro e disse: «Donne di Gerusalemme, non piangete per me. Piangete piuttosto per voi e per i vostri figli. [29] Ecco, verranno giorni nei quali si dirà: Beate le donne che non possono avere bambini, quelle che non hanno mai avuto figli e quelle che non ne hanno mai allattato.

[30] «Allora la gente comincerà a *dire ai monti:*
"Franate su di noi"
e alle colline: *"Nascondeteci".*
[31] Perché se si tratta così il legno verde, che ne sarà di quello secco?».

Gesù è inchiodato a una croce

[32] Insieme con Gesù venivano condotti a morte anche due malfattori.

[33] Quando furono arrivati sul posto detto «luogo del Cranio», prima crocifissero Gesù e poi i due malfattori: uno alla sua destra e l'altro alla sua sinistra.

[34] Gesù diceva: «Padre, perdona loro perché non sanno quel che fanno». I soldati intanto si divisero le vesti di Gesù, tirandole a sorte.

[35] La gente stava a guardare. I capi del popolo invece si facevano beffe di Gesù e gli dicevano: «Ha salvato tanti altri, ora salvi se stesso, se egli è veramente il Messia scelto da Dio». [36] Anche i soldati lo insultavano: si avvicinavano a Gesù, gli davano da bere aceto [37] e gli dicevano: «Se tu sei davvero il re dei Giudei salva te stesso!».

[38] Sopra il capo di Gesù avevano messo un cartello con queste parole: «Quest'uomo è il re dei Giudei».

La preghiera di un malfattore

[39] I due malfattori intanto erano stati crocifissi con Gesù. Uno di loro, insultandolo, diceva:
«Non sei tu il Messia? Salva te stesso e noi».

[40] L'altro invece si mise a rimproverare il suo compagno e disse: «Tu che stai subendo la stessa condanna non hai proprio nessun timore di Dio? [41] Per noi due è giusto scontare il castigo per ciò che abbiamo fatto, lui invece non ha fatto nulla di male».

[42] Poi aggiunse:
«Gesù, ricordati di me quando sarai nel tuo regno».

[43] Gesù gli rispose:
«Ti assicuro che oggi sarai con me in paradiso».

Gesù muore

[44] Verso mezzogiorno si fece buio per tutta la regione fino alle tre del pomeriggio. [45] Il sole si oscurò e il grande velo appeso nel Tempio

si squarciò a metà. [46] Allora Gesù gridò a gran voce: «Padre, *nelle tue mani affido la mia vita*». Dopo queste parole spirò.

[47] L'ufficiale romano, vedendo quel che accadeva, rese gloria a Dio dicendo: «Egli era veramente un uomo giusto!». [48] Anche quelli che erano venuti per vedere lo spettacolo, davanti a questi fatti se ne tornavano a casa battendosi il petto. [49] Invece gli amici di Gesù e le donne che lo avevano seguito fin dalla Galilea se ne stavano ad una certa distanza e osservavano tutto quel che accadeva.

Il corpo di Gesù è messo nella tomba

[50-51] Vi era un certo Giuseppe originario di Arimatèa. Faceva parte anche del tribunale ebraico; ma non aveva approvato quel che gli altri consiglieri avevano deciso e fatto contro Gesù. Era uomo buono e giusto, e aspettava con fiducia il regno di Dio. [52] Giuseppe dunque andò da Pilato e gli chiese il corpo di Gesù. Lo depose dalla croce e lo avvolse in un lenzuolo. [53] Infine lo mise in un sepolcro scavato nella roccia, dove nessuno era stato ancora deposto.

[54] Era la vigilia del giorno di festa, già stava per cominciare il sabato. [55] Le donne, che erano venute con Gesù fin dalla Galilea, avevano seguito Giuseppe. Videro la tomba e osservarono come veniva deposto il corpo di Gesù. [56] Poi se ne tornarono a casa per preparare aromi e unguenti. Il giorno festivo lo trascorsero nel riposo, come prescrive la legge ebraica.

Gesù è vivo

24 Il primo giorno della settimana, di buon mattino le donne andarono al sepolcro di Gesù, portando gli aromi che avevano preparato per la sepoltura. [2] Videro che la pietra che chiudeva il sepolcro era stata spostata. [3] Entrarono nel sepolcro, ma non trovarono il corpo del Signore Gesù.

[4] Le donne stavano ancora lì senza sapere che cosa fare, quando apparvero loro due uomini con vesti splendenti. [5] Impaurite, tennero la faccia abbassata verso terra. Ma quegli uomini dissero loro: «Perché cercate tra i morti colui che è vivo? [6] Egli non si trova qui ma è risuscitato! Ricordatevi che ve lo disse quando era ancora in Galilea. [7] Allora vi diceva: "È necessario che il Figlio dell'uomo sia consegna-

to nelle mani di persone malvage e queste lo crocifiggeranno. Ma il terzo giorno risusciterà"».

[8] Allora le donne si ricordarono che Gesù aveva detto quelle parole. [9] Lasciarono il sepolcro e andarono a raccontare agli undici discepoli e a tutti gli altri quello che avevano visto e udito. [10] Erano Maria, nativa di Màgdala, Giovanna e Maria, madre di Giacomo. Anche le altre donne che erano con loro riferirono agli apostoli le stesse cose.

[11] Ma gli apostoli non vollero credere a queste parole. Pensavano che le donne avevano perso la testa.

[12] Pietro però si alzò e corse al sepolcro. Guardò dentro, e vide solo le bende usate per la sepoltura. Poi tornò a casa pieno di stupore per quello che era accaduto.

Gesù risorto appare ai discepoli di Emmaus

[13] Quello stesso giorno due discepoli stavano andando verso Emmaus, un villaggio lontano circa undici chilometri da Gerusalemme. [14] Lungo la via parlavano tra loro di quel che era accaduto in Gerusalemme in quei giorni.

[15] Mentre parlavano e discutevano, Gesù si avvicinò e si mise a camminare con loro. [16] Essi però non lo riconobbero, perché i loro occhi erano come accecati.

[17] Gesù domandò loro:

«Di che cosa state discutendo tra voi mentre camminate?».

Essi allora si fermarono, tristi. [18] Uno di loro, un certo Clèopa, disse a Gesù:

«Sei tu l'unico a Gerusalemme a non sapere quel che è successo in questi ultimi giorni?».

[19] Gesù domandò:

«Che cosa?».

Quelli risposero:

«Il caso di Gesù, il Nazareno! Era un profeta potente davanti a Dio e agli uomini, sia per quel che faceva sia per quel che diceva. [20] Ma i capi dei sacerdoti e il popolo l'hanno condannato a morte e l'hanno fatto crocifiggere. [21] Noi speravamo che fosse lui a liberare il popolo d'Israele! Ma siamo già al terzo giorno da quando sono accaduti questi fatti. [22] Una cosa però ci ha sconvolto: alcune donne del nostro gruppo sono andate di buon mattino al sepolcro di Gesù [23] ma non hanno trovato il suo corpo. Allora sono tornate indietro e ci hanno detto di aver avuto una visione: alcuni angeli le hanno assicurate che Gesù è vivo. [24] Poi sono andati al sepolcro altri del nostro gruppo e hanno trovato tutto come avevano detto le donne, ma lui, Gesù, non l'hanno visto».

[25] Allora Gesù disse:

«Voi capite poco davvero; come siete lenti a credere quel che i profeti hanno scritto! [26] Il Messia non doveva forse soffrire queste cose prima di entrare nella sua gloria?».

[27] Quindi Gesù spiegò ai due discepoli i passi della Bibbia che lo riguardavano. Cominciò dai libri di Mosè fino agli scritti di tutti i profeti.

[28] Intanto arrivarono al villaggio dove erano diretti, e Gesù fece finta di continuare il viaggio. [29] Ma quei due discepoli lo trattennero dicendo: «Resta con noi perché il sole ormai tramonta». Perciò Gesù entrò nel villaggio per rimanere con loro. [30] Poi si mise a tavola con loro, prese il pane e pronunziò la preghiera di benedizione; lo spezzò e cominciò a distribuirlo.

[31] In quel momento gli occhi dei due discepoli si aprirono e riconobbero Gesù, ma lui sparì dalla loro vista. [32] Si dissero l'un l'altro: «Non ci sentivamo come un fuoco nel cuore, quando egli lungo la via ci parlava e ci spiegava la Bibbia?».

[33] Quindi si alzarono e ritornarono subito a Gerusalemme. Là, trovarono gli undici discepoli riuniti con i loro compagni.

[34] Questi dicevano: «Il Signore è veramente risorto ed è apparso a Simone». [35] A loro volta i due discepoli raccontarono quel che era loro accaduto lungo il cammino, e dicevano che lo avevano riconosciuto mentre spezzava il pane.

Gesù appare ai discepoli

[36] Gli undici apostoli e i loro compagni stavano parlando di queste cose. Gesù apparve in mezzo a loro e disse: «La pace sia con voi!».

[37] Sconvolti e pieni di paura, essi pensavano di vedere un fantasma. [38] Ma Gesù disse loro: «Perché avete tanti dubbi dentro di voi? [39] Guardate le mie mani e i miei piedi! Sono proprio io! Toccatemi e verificate: un fantasma non ha carne e ossa come vedete che io ho».

⁴⁰ Gesù diceva queste cose ai suoi discepoli, e intanto mostrava loro le mani e i piedi. ⁴¹ Essi però, pieni di stupore e di gioia, non riuscivano a crederci: era troppo grande la loro gioia!

Allora Gesù disse: «Avete qualcosa da mangiare?». ⁴² Essi gli diedero un po' di pesce arrostito. ⁴³ Gesù lo prese e lo mangiò davanti a tutti.

⁴⁴ Poi disse loro: «Era questo il senso dei discorsi che vi facevo quando ero ancora con voi! Vi dissi chiaramente che doveva accadere tutto quel che di me era stato scritto nella legge di Mosè, negli scritti dei profeti e nei salmi!».

⁴⁵ Allora Gesù li aiutò a capire le profezie della Bibbia. ⁴⁶ Poi aggiunse: «Così sta scritto: il Messia doveva morire, ma il terzo giorno doveva risuscitare dai morti. ⁴⁷⁻⁴⁸ Per suo incarico ora deve essere portato a tutti i popoli l'invito a cambiare vita e a ricevere il perdono dei peccati. Voi sarete testimoni di tutto ciò cominciando da Gerusalemme. ⁴⁹ Perciò io manderò su di voi lo Spirito Santo, che Dio, mio Padre, ha promesso. Voi però restate nella città di Gerusalemme fino a quando Dio non vi riempirà con la sua forza».

Gesù sale verso il cielo

⁵⁰ Poi Gesù condusse i suoi discepoli verso il villaggio di Betània. Alzò le mani sopra di loro e li benedisse. ⁵¹ Mentre li benediceva si separò da loro e fu portato verso il cielo. ⁵² I suoi discepoli lo adorarono.

Poi tornarono verso Gerusalemme, pieni di gioia. ⁵³ E stavano sempre nel Tempio lodando e ringraziando Dio.

*Notes * Notas * Note * Ghi chú*

*Notes * Notas * Note * Ghi chú*

Com'è possibile celebrare la vostra famiglia— un santuario di amore e di vita— dopo aver lasciato Incontro Mondiale delle Famiglie? **Iscrivetevi** per il Lectio Divina devozionale di 21 giorni e viaggiate attraverso il Vangelo di Luca con la vostra famiglia o comunità. Mentre ascoltate la Parola di Dio e meditate su storie di speranza e guarigione, lasciate che la Sacra Scrittura trasformi la vostra conoscenza dell'amore incondizionato di Dio.

MEDITAZIONI
SUL VANGELO
DI LUCA PER LA FAMIGLIA

Iscrivetevi per questo Lectio Divina devozionale di 21 giorni in uno dei seguenti modi:

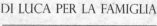 SMS: Mandate **famiglie** a 72717

Email: Visitate il nostro sito web a www.abs.us/famiglie

Applicazione web: Per scaricarlo visitate app.bible.com/wmf

Familles,
écoutez la Parole de Dieu,
méditez-la ensemble,
priez avec elle,
laissez que le Seigneur comble de miséricorde
votre vie.

Franciscus

Le blason du Pape François conserve le même protocole utilisé lorsqu'il était l'Archevêque de Buenos Aires avec l'ajout du symbole papal qui se compose de la Mitre de l'évêque, de deux clés en or et en argent attachés par un cordon rouge.

L'écu est bleu avec au centre l'emblème de l'ordre de provenance du Pape, la Compagnie de Jésus : Un soleil rayonnant chargé des lettres, en rouge, IHS, monogramme du Christ et les trois clous en noir. En bas, on trouve l'étoile et la fleur de nard. L'étoile, symbolise la Vierge Marie ; tandis que la fleur de nard indique Saint Joseph.

La devise Latine inscrite sous la crête « miserando atque eligendo », qui peut être traduit par « Choisi, parce que pardonné », ou trouver le pardon en le choisissant, est inspirée par une homélie de Saint Bède le Vénérable, docteur de l'Eglise, dans laquelle celui-ci commente la conversion de Saint-Matthieu qui est un collecteur d'impôt. En la fête de Saint-Matthieu, le pape François fit l'expérience à l'âge de 17 ans, de la présence de Dieu dans sa vie.

Archdiocese of Philadelphia
Office of the Archbishop
222 North 17th Street
Philadelphia, PA 19103-1299

Septembre 2015

Chers amis,

Le monde de Dieu est riche en rencontres grâce aux quatre Evangiles.

Mais pour beaucoup de lecteurs, Luc l'Evangile est celui qui transmet avec le plus d'émotion la miséricorde de Dieu. C'est seulement à travers Luc que nous trouvons les trois plus grandes expressions d'amour de Dieu: Les paraboles du fils prodigue, le bon Samaritain, et ses mots sur la croix pour « le bon larron ».

L'Evangile que vous avez à vos mains – Un merveilleux cadeau de l'American Bible Society – est un rappel de la tendresse de Dieu pour vous personnellement; c'est aussi une invitation pour marcher avec Jésus-Christ sur le chemin du paradis. Lisez-le. Priez avec. Prisez-le.

Que Dieu vous bénisse ainsi que ceux que vous aimerez durant la Rencontre Mondial des Familles et tous les jours qui suivront

Votre frère du Seigneur,

+ Charles J. Chaput, ofm cap.

Most Reverend Charles J. Chaput, O.F.M. Cap.
Archbishop of Philadelphia

INTRODUCTION

LA BONNE NOUVELLE *de la* MISÉRICORDE *en* FAMILLE

Chères familles,

C'est avec une grande joie que je vous présente cette édition de l'Évangile selon saint Luc, un don du Pape François aux familles du monde entier, à l'occasion de la VIIIème Rencontre mondiale de Philadelphie.

Mon souhait est que la lecture de cet Évangile accompagne l'Année Sainte de la Miséricorde que le Saint-Père a tenu à commencer dans quelques semaines : Luc est l'évangile, la Bonne Nouvelle de la miséricorde de Dieu pour la vie de chacun et de nos familles.

L'ÉVANGILE EN FAMILLE

Chaque génération chrétienne – même la nôtre – est appelée à prendre dans ses mains ce petit livret. L'Évangile est, en effet, la force de l'Église, c'est la Parole à partir de laquelle il est né et pour laquelle il vit. Le christianisme commence, en effet, quand le Verbe (la Parole) s'est faite chair dans le sein de Marie. Elle est la première parmi les croyants et elle a été immédiatement désignée comme telle par Elizabeth : « Bienheureuse celle qui a cru en l'accomplissement de ce qui lui a été dit de la part d Seigneur » (Lc 1,45). Et, après elle, vinrent les premiers disciples. Quand ils accueillirent la parole de Jésus, une nouvelle fraternité commença ; nous pourrions dire une « nouvelle famille » : celle de Jésus et de ses disciples. Après la Pentecôte, l'Évangile a commencé à se répandre à travers les maisons, les familles des chrétiens. En bref, le chemin de l'Évangile au début du premier millénaire a été marqué par l'écoute dans les familles.

Chères familles, je pense que nous aussi nous devrions parcourir à nouveau ce qui s'est déroulé au début du christianisme : reprendre l'Évangile dans nos mains, même dans nos propres familles, et retisser une nouvelle fraternité entre les personnes, une nouvelle solidarité entre les familles, afin de pouvoir donner la « bonne nouvelle » de l'amour de Dieu pour tous. Saint Jean-Paul II, en ouvrant le Grand Jubilé de l'An 2000, a exhorté les chrétiens à entrer « dans le nouveau millénaire en portant dans ses mains le livre de l'Évangile ! ». Avec cette passion qui l'a conduit comme pèlerin de l'Évangile dans le monde entier, il a ajouté : « Prenons ce Livre dans nos mains ! Recevons-le de la part du Seigneur qui nous l'offre continuellement à travers son Église (cf. Ap 10, 8). Mangeons-le (cf. Ap 10, 9), pour qu'il devienne la vie de notre vie. Goûtons-le à fond : il nous réservera des difficultés, mais il nous donnera aussi la joie car il est doux comme le miel (cf. Ap 10, 9-10). Nous serons comblés d'espérance et capables de communiquer cette espérance à tout homme et à toute femme que nous rencontrons sur notre route ».

Le Pape François nous exhorte dans cette même direction : reprenez en main l'Évangile! Il nous le dit dans la splendide Lettre intitulée « La joie de l'Évangile » (*Evangelii gaudium*). Oui, il est essentiel de reprendre en main l'Évangile et de l'écouter avec une attention renouvelée afin d'avoir un monde plus fraternel, plus solidaire, plus humain. L'insécurité et la peur qui sont en train de marquer la vie de notre monde, les injustices incroyables qui déchirent la vie de tant de peuples, la violence qui semble se répandre sans retenue même à l'intérieur de nos maisons, les conflits et les guerres qui continuent encore de faire des victimes innocentes, ne peuvent être surmontés seulement que grâce à l'Évangile. C'est pour cette raison que le Pape François a voulu offrir un million d'exemplaires de ce livre aux familles de cinq grandes villes du monde : La Havane (Cuba), Hanoi (Vietnam), Kinshasa (Congo), Marseille (France) et Sydney (Australie). Là où le contexte urbain et ses banlieues semblent rendre la coexistence humaine encore plus difficile, le Pape a souhaité que la Parole de Jésus résonne avec plus de force.

UN EXERCICE QUOTIDIEN

Lisons chaque jour un petit extrait de l'Évangile. Ainsi, nous serons comme obligés d'entrer dans le cœur et dans les jours de Jésus : nous le suivrons dans ses voyages, nous participerons à sa compassion envers tous, nous prendrons part à sa tendresse pour les petits et les faibles, nous nous laisserons émouvoir par sa compassion à être auprès des pauvres, nous pleurerons en voyant combien il nous a aimés, nous nous réjouirons de sa résurrection qui a finalement vaincu le mal. Nous le connaîtrons davantage et nous l'aimerons davantage.

Rappelons-nous de le faire réellement chaque jour. Chaque jour, nous sommes envahis de paroles, d'images, de messages, d'invitations ... Les messages ne sont pas tous positifs, et seuls quelques-uns nous aident à vivre. Et puis encore, à la maison, nous risquons même de ne pas nous parler, pour diverses raisons, et parfois, si ce ne sont pas « les assiettes qui volent », ce sont les mots, qui blessent parfois plus que les assiettes. De toute façon, nous ressentons tous le besoin de bonnes paroles qui atteignent notre cœur : l'Évangile est la parole qui atteint le cœur. Dans la prière du *Notre Père*, nous demandons à Dieu de nous donner notre « pain de ce jour ». Les paroles de Jésus sont le « pain vivant descendu du ciel », qui nous est offert tous les jours. C'est le pain le meilleur. Il nourrit le cœur et le corps.

Chères familles, lire ensemble l'Évangile en famille est une des façons les plus belles et les plus efficaces pour prier. Le Seigneur l'apprécie de façon particulière. Vous rappelez-vous l'épisode de Marthe et de Marie ? À Marthe qui s'était irritée du fait de voir Marie qui l'écoutait, Jésus souligne que Marie a choisi « la meilleure part », celle qui « est nécessaire ». Il est facile pour nous tous d'être accaparés par de multiples occupations, comme ce fut pour Marthe, par les besognes, par les questions à résoudre, par les problèmes à affronter, par les difficultés à surmonter. « Marie – c'est ce que Jésus nous dit encore aujourd'hui – a choisi la meilleure part » (Lc 10,42). Ce petit livret vous aidera à rendre l'écoute de l'Évangile la « meilleure part » de nos journées, la « meilleure part » de toutes les journées de l'année.

Nous avons besoin d'écouter. Le premier pas de la prière chrétienne est d'écouter Jésus qui nous parle. Oui, chères familles, avant de multiplier nos paroles à adresser au Seigneur, écoutons celles qu'Il nous adresse. Chaque jour. Essayons de les écouter et nous ferons la même expérience des deux disciples d'Emmaüs, qui sentirent leur cœur se réchauffer et le besoin de rester avec lui. L'écoute se transforme en prière et la rencontre avec Jésus illumine à nouveau leur vie.

Bien sûr, nous devons nous rassembler et faire un peu de silence autour de nous. Nous savons combien il est devenu difficile de trouver un moment de silence et de prière. Mais cela est essentiel. Nous pourrions dire que la prière quotidienne est notre façon de « toujours prier, sans relâche ». Oui, priez chaque jour avec l'Évangile est notre façon de prier toujours.

Il faut donc trouver un moment pour être ensemble, peut-être avant un repas ou à la fin de la journée, ou même au début. Ou en d'autres moments. Ce qui compte, c'est de choisir cinq minutes pour prier ensemble d'une façon brève mais efficace.

Après le signe de la croix et une brève invocation à l'Esprit Saint, afin qu'il descende dans nos cœurs et éclaire nos esprits, lisons un petit extrait, proposons une explication simple aux enfants, et communiquons-nous réciproquement les pensées que cette écoute suscite en nous ; ensuite, demandons-nous pour qui nous voulons prier en particulier et concluons en récitant ensemble la prière du Notre Père, et enfin remercions le Seigneur pour le don de sa Parole. N'oublions pas de décider ensemble une petite et simple proposition grâce à laquelle cette parole peut marquer nos vies.

Chères familles, tout en remerciant vivement la Société biblique américaine, qui a permis la réalisation de ce livret, je vous souhaite de tout mon cœur que le premier fruit de ces jours intenses vécus ensemble à Philadelphie soit la décision de permettre à la Parole de Dieu d'habiter vos demeures et celles de votre ville.

+ Vincenzo Paglia

Archevêque Vincenzo Paglia
Président du Conseil pontifical pour la famille

ÉVANGILE
SELON LUC

The Gospel according to Luke
French text from « La Bible en français courant »

Texte biblique tiré de la Bible en français courant, © Société biblique
française – Bibli'O, 1997
Avec autorisation.

Introduction à l'Évangile selon Luc

Les caractéristiques propres à cet évangile sont différentes de celles des autres évangiles (Matthieu, Marc et Jean) contenus dans le Nouveau Testament de la Bible. Jérusalem y tient une place privilégiée: plus que dans les autres évangiles, elle est le centre et le sommet de l'activité de Jésus. Autour de lui se déroulent les événements décisifs de «l'histoire du salut», ces interventions de Dieu qui arrachent l'humanité au mal. Maintenant arrive à son terme le long préambule que constitue l'histoire de l'ancien Israël (Ancien Testament) et s'ouvre l'époque nouvelle des croyants répandus dans le monde entier. L'attente de l'accomplissement final commence. Le salut chrétien atteint les événements concrets de l'histoire terrestre (2,1; 3,1-4) et concerne tous les hommes (3,6). Jésus s'adresse surtout aux «pauvres» – c'est-à-dire aux personnes qui ne comptent pas, aux malades, aux exclus – et c'est justement parmi eux que le message de l'évangile est le mieux écouté et que se manifestent le plus visiblement les commencements du royaume de Dieu.

Les premiers destinataires

Au moment de la rédaction de cet évangile, la génération des Apôtres est sur le point de disparaître. Il n'est désormais plus possible d'entendre de vive voix l'expérience de ceux qui ont directement connus Jésus. Eux ont entendu son enseignement et vu ses gestes, ont vécu les jours de sa passion, de sa mort et de sa résurrection. Maintenant surgissent d'autres prédicateurs, peut-être même de nouvelles doctrines se répandent. C'est pourquoi Luc prend conscience que les croyants ont besoin d'une information solide concernant les événements principaux qui regardent la foi. Il mène alors une enquête soigneuse, collecte les souvenirs écrits et oraux les plus sûrs, et les propose comme support à l'enseignement chrétien de son temps (1,1-4). Nous ne savons rien du destinataire Théophile, mais il est certainement représentatif des lecteurs pour lesquels Luc écrit.

L'AUTEUR

Quelques lettres du Nouveau Testament parlent d'un certain «Luc» (Philémon 24; Colossiens 4,14; 2 Timothée 4,11). C'est un disciple de l'Apôtre Paul, médecin de profession, de culture et de langue grecques. Est-ce le même Luc qui a écrit cet évangile et le livre des «Actes»? De très anciennes traditions l'affirment. Beaucoup de modernes sont du même avis, certains spécialistes au contraire font remarquer qu'aucune des idées caractéristiques de Paul ne ressort particulièrement dans cet évangile.

Quoi qu'il en soit, l'auteur reflète bien l'ambiance des communautés chrétiennes non palestiniennes de la fin du premier siècle. Le contenu du livre des Actes montre que l'auteur s'intéresse de près à la première diffusion missionnaire dans le monde grec. La date de composition de cet évangile se situe aux alentours de l'année 80 après J.C.

PLAN DE L'OUVRAGE

ÉVANGILE SELON LUC

Introduction

1 Cher Théophile,
Plusieurs personnes ont essayé d'écrire le récit des événements qui se sont passés parmi nous. [2] Ils ont rapporté les faits tels que nous les ont racontés ceux qui les ont vus dès le commencement et qui ont été chargés d'annoncer la parole de Dieu. [3] C'est pourquoi, à mon tour, je me suis renseigné exactement sur tout ce qui est arrivé depuis le début et il m'a semblé bon, illustre Théophile, d'en écrire pour toi le récit suivi. [4] Je le fais pour que tu puisses reconnaître la vérité des enseignements que tu as reçus.

Un ange annonce la naissance prochaine de Jean-Baptiste

[5] Au temps où Hérode était roi de Judée, il y avait un prêtre nommé Zacharie qui appartenait au groupe de prêtres d'Abia. Sa femme, une descendante d'Aaron le grand-prêtre, s'appelait Élisabeth. [6] Ils étaient tous deux justes aux yeux de Dieu et obéissaient parfaitement à toutes les lois et tous les commandements du Seigneur. [7] Mais ils n'avaient pas d'enfant, car Élisabeth ne pouvait pas en avoir et ils étaient déjà âgés tous les deux.

[8] Un jour, Zacharie exerçait ses fonctions de prêtre devant Dieu, car c'était au tour de son groupe de le faire. [9] Selon la coutume des prêtres, il fut désigné par le sort pour entrer dans le sanctuaire du Seigneur et y brûler l'encens. [10] Toute la foule des fidèles priait au-dehors à l'heure où l'on brûlait l'encens. [11] Un ange du Seigneur apparut alors à Zacharie : il se tenait à la droite de l'autel servant à l'offrande de l'encens. [12] Quand Zacharie le vit, il fut troublé et saisi de crainte. [13] Mais l'ange lui dit : « N'aie pas peur, Zacharie, car Dieu a entendu ta prière : Élisabeth, ta femme, te donnera un fils que tu nommeras Jean. [14] Tu en seras profondément heureux et beaucoup de gens se réjouiront au sujet de sa naissance. [15] Car il sera un grand serviteur du Seigneur. Il

ne boira ni vin, ni aucune autre boisson fermentée. Il sera rempli du Saint-Esprit dès avant sa naissance. ¹⁶ Il ramènera beaucoup d'Israélites au Seigneur leur Dieu. ¹⁷ Il viendra comme messager de Dieu avec l'esprit et la puissance du prophète Élie, pour réconcilier les pères avec leurs enfants et ramener les désobéissants à la sagesse des juste ; il formera un peuple prêt pour le Seigneur. » ¹⁸ Mais Zacharie dit à l'ange : « Comment saurai-je que cela est vrai ? Car je suis vieux et ma femme aussi est âgée. » ¹⁹ Et l'ange lui répondit : « Je suis Gabriel ; je me tiens devant Dieu pour le servir ; il m'a envoyé pour te parler et t'apporter cette bonne nouvelle. ²⁰ Mais tu n'as pas cru à mes paroles, qui se réaliseront pourtant au moment voulu ; c'est pourquoi tu vas devenir muet, tu seras incapable de parler jusqu'au jour où ces événements se produiront. »

²¹ Pendant ce temps, les fidèles attendaient Zacharie et s'étonnaient qu'il reste si longtemps à l'intérieur du sanctuaire. ²² Mais quand il sortit, il ne put pas leur parler et les gens comprirent qu'il avait eu une vision dans le sanctuaire. Il leur faisait des signes et restait muet.

²³ Quand Zacharie eut achevé la période où il devait servir dans le temple, il retourna chez lui. ²⁴ Quelque temps après, Élisabeth sa femme devint enceinte, et elle se tint cachée pendant cinq mois. Elle se disait : ²⁵ « Voilà ce que le Seigneur a fait pour moi : il a bien voulu me délivrer maintenant de ce qui causait ma honte devant tout le monde. »

Un ange annonce la naissance prochaine de Jésus

²⁶ Le sixième mois, Dieu envoya l'ange Gabriel dans une ville de Galilée, Nazareth, ²⁷ chez une jeune fille fiancée à un homme appelé Joseph. Celui-ci était un descendant du roi David ; le nom de la jeune fille était Marie. ²⁸ L'ange entra chez elle et lui dit : « Réjouis-toi ! Le Seigneur t'a accordé une grande faveur, il est avec toi. » ²⁹ Marie fut très troublée par ces mots ; elle se demandait ce que pouvait signifier cette salutation. ³⁰ L'ange lui dit alors : « N'aie pas peur, Marie, car tu as la faveur de Dieu. ³¹ Bientôt tu seras enceinte, puis tu mettras au monde un fils que tu nommeras Jésus. ³² Il sera grand et on l'appellera le Fils du Dieu très-haut. Le Seigneur Dieu fera de lui un roi, comme le fut David son ancêtre, ³³ et il régnera pour toujours sur le peuple d'Israël, son règne n'aura point de fin. » ³⁴ Marie dit à l'ange : « Comment cela sera-t-il possible, puisque je suis vierge ? » ³⁵ L'ange lui répondit : « Le

Saint-Esprit viendra sur toi et la puissance du Dieu très-haut te couvrira comme d'une ombre. C'est pourquoi on appellera saint et Fils de Dieu l'enfant qui doit naître. ³⁶ Élisabeth ta parente attend elle-même un fils, malgré son âge ; elle qu'on disait stérile en est maintenant à son sixième mois. ³⁷ Car rien n'est impossible à Dieu. » ³⁸ Alors Marie dit : « Je suis la servante du Seigneur ; que tout se passe pour moi comme tu l'as dit. » Et l'ange la quitta.

Marie rend visite à Élisabeth

³⁹ Dans les jours qui suivirent, Marie se mit en route et se rendit en hâte dans une localité de la région montagneus e de Judée. ⁴⁰ Elle entra dans la maison de Zacharie et salua Élisabeth. ⁴¹ Au moment où celle-ci entendit la salutation de Marie, l'enfant remua en elle. Élisabeth fut remplie du Saint-Esprit ⁴² et s'écria d'une voix forte : « Dieu t'a bénie plus que toutes les femmes et sa bénédiction repose sur l'enfant que tu auras ! ⁴³ Qui suis-je pour que la mère de mon Seigneur vienne chez moi ? ⁴⁴ Car, vois-tu, au moment où j'ai entendu ta salutation, l'enfant a remué de joie en moi. ⁴⁵ Tu es heureuse : tu as cru que le Seigneur accomplira ce qu'il t'a annoncé ! »

Le cantique de Marie

⁴⁶ Marie dit alors :

« De tout mon être je veux dire la grandeur du Seigneur,
⁴⁷ mon cœur est plein de joie
à cause de Dieu, mon Sauveur ;
⁴⁸ car il a bien voulu abaisser son regard sur moi, son humble servante.
Oui, dès maintenant et en tous les temps, les humains me diront bienheureuse,
⁴⁹ car Dieu le Tout-Puissant a fait pour moi des choses magnifiques.
Il est le Dieu saint,
⁵⁰ il est plein de bonté en tout temps
pour ceux qui le respectent.
⁵¹ Il a montré son pouvoir en déployant sa force :
il a mis en déroute les hommes au cœur orgueilleux,
⁵² il a renversé les rois de leurs trônes
et il a placé les humbles au premier rang.

⁵³ Il a comblé de biens ceux qui avaient faim,
   et il a renvoyé les riches les mains vides.
⁵⁴ Il est venu en aide au peuple d'Israël, son serviteur :
   il n'a pas oublié de manifester sa bonté
⁵⁵ envers Abraham et ses descendants, pour toujours,
   comme il l'avait promis à nos ancêtres. »

⁵⁶ Marie resta avec Élisabeth pendant environ trois mois, puis elle retourna chez elle.

La naissance de Jean-Baptiste

⁵⁷ Le moment arriva où Élisabeth devait accoucher et elle mit au monde un fils. ⁵⁸ Ses voisins et les membres de sa parenté apprirent que le Seigneur lui avait donné cette grande preuve de sa bonté et ils s'en réjouissaient avec elle. ⁵⁹ Le huitième jour après la naissance, ils vinrent pour circoncire l'enfant ; ils voulaient lui donner le nom de son père, Zacharie. ⁶⁰ Mais sa mère déclara : « Non, il s'appellera Jean. » ⁶¹ Ils lui dirent : « Mais, personne dans ta famille ne porte ce nom ! » ⁶² Alors, ils demandèrent par gestes au père comment il voulait qu'on nomme son enfant. ⁶³ Zacharie se fit apporter une tablette à écrire et il y inscrivit ces mots : « Jean est bien son nom. » Ils s'en étonnèrent tous. ⁶⁴ Aussitôt, Zacharie put de nouveau parler : il se mit à louer Dieu à haute voix. ⁶⁵ Alors, tous les voisins éprouvèrent de la crainte, et dans toute la région montagneuse de Judée l'on se racontait ces événements. ⁶⁶ Tous ceux qui en entendaient parler se mettaient à y réfléchir et se demandaient : « Que deviendra donc ce petit enfant ? » La puissance du Seigneur était en effet réellement avec lui.

Le cantique prophétique de Zacharie

⁶⁷ Zacharie, le père du petit enfant, fut rempli du Saint-Esprit ; il se mit à prophétiser en ces termes :
⁶⁸ « Loué soit le Seigneur, le Dieu du peuple d'Israël,
   parce qu'il est intervenu en faveur de son peuple et l'a délivré.
⁶⁹ Il a fait apparaître un puissant Sauveur, pour nous,
   parmi les descendants du roi David, son serviteur.
⁷⁰ C'est ce qu'il avait annoncé depuis longtemps
      par ses saints prophètes :

71 il avait promis qu'il nous délivrerait de nos ennemis
    et du pouvoir de tous ceux qui nous veulent du mal.

72 Il a manifesté sa bonté envers nos ancêtres
    et n'a pas oublié sa sainte alliance.

73 En effet, Dieu avait fait serment à Abraham, notre ancêtre,

74 de nous libérer du pouvoir des ennemis
    et de nous permettre ainsi de le servir sans peur,

75 pour que nous soyons saints et justes devant lui
    tous les jours de notre vie.

76 Et toi, mon enfant, tu seras prophète du Dieu très-haut,
    car tu marcheras devant le Seigneur pour préparer son chemin

77 et pour faire savoir à son peuple qu'il vient le sauver
    en pardonnant ses péchés.

78 Notre Dieu est plein de tendresse et de bonté :
    il fera briller sur nous une lumière d'en haut,
        semblable à celle du soleil levant,

79 pour éclairer ceux qui se trouvent dans la nuit
        et dans l'ombre de la mort,
    pour diriger nos pas sur le chemin de la paix. »

80 L'enfant grandissait et se développait spirituellement. Il demeura dans des lieux déserts jusqu'au jour où il se présenta publiquement devant le peuple d'Israël.

La naissance de Jésus

2 En ce temps-là, l'empereur Auguste donna l'ordre de recenser tous les habitants de l'empire romain. 2 Ce recensement, le premier, eut lieu alors que Quirinius était gouverneur de la province de Syrie. 3 Tout le monde allait se faire enregistrer, chacun dans sa ville d'origine. 4 Joseph lui aussi partit de Nazareth, un bourg de Galilée, pour se rendre en Judée, à Bethléem, où est né le roi David ; en effet, il était lui-même un descendant de David. 5 Il alla s'y faire enregistrer avec Marie, sa fiancée, qui était enceinte. 6 Pendant qu'ils étaient à Bethléem, le jour de la naissance arriva. 7 Elle mit au monde un fils, son premier-né. Elle l'enveloppa de langes et le coucha dans une crèche, parce qu'il n'y avait pas de place pour eux dans l'abri destiné aux voyageurs.

Un ange apparaît à des bergers

[8] Dans cette même région, il y avait des bergers qui passaient la nuit dans les champs pour garder leur troupeau. [9] Un ange du Seigneur leur apparut et la gloire du Seigneur les entoura de lumière. Ils eurent alors très peur. [10] Mais l'ange leur dit : « N'ayez pas peur, car je vous apporte une bonne nouvelle qui réjouira beaucoup tout le peuple : [11] cette nuit, dans la ville de David, est né, pour vous, un Sauveur ; c'est le Christ, le Seigneur. [12] Et voici le signe qui vous le fera reconnaître : vous trouverez un petit enfant enveloppé de langes et couché dans une crèche. »

[13] Tout à coup, il y eut avec l'ange une troupe nombreuse d'anges du ciel, qui louaient Dieu en disant :

[14] « Gloire à Dieu dans les cieux très hauts,
et paix sur la terre pour ceux qu'il aime ! »

Les bergers vont à Bethléem

[15] Lorsque les anges les eurent quittés pour retourner au ciel, les bergers se dirent les uns aux autres : « Allons donc jusqu'à Bethléem : il faut que nous voyions ce qui est arrivé, ce que le Seigneur nous a fait connaître. » [16] Ils se dépêchèrent d'y aller et ils trouvèrent Marie et Joseph, et le petit enfant couché dans la crèche. [17] Quand ils le virent, ils racontèrent ce que l'ange leur avait dit au sujet de ce petit enfant. [18] Tous ceux qui entendirent les bergers furent étonnés de ce qu'ils leur disaient. [19] Quant à Marie, elle gardait tout cela dans sa mémoire et y réfléchissait profondément. [20] Puis les bergers prirent le chemin du retour. Ils célébraient la grandeur de Dieu et le louaient pour tout ce qu'ils avaient entendu et vu, car tout s'était passé comme l'ange le leur avait annoncé.

Jésus reçoit son nom

[21] Le huitième jour après la naissance, le moment vint de circoncire l'enfant ; on lui donna le nom de Jésus, nom que l'ange avait indiqué avant que sa mère devienne enceinte.

Jésus est présenté dans le temple

[22] Puis le moment vint pour Joseph et Marie d'accomplir la cérémonie de purification qu'ordonne la loi de Moïse. Ils amenèrent alors l'enfant au temple de Jérusalem pour le présenter au Seigneur, [23] car il est

écrit dans la loi du Seigneur : « Tout garçon premier-né sera mis à part pour le Seigneur. » [24] Ils devaient offrir aussi le sacrifice que demande la même loi, « une paire de tourterelles ou deux jeunes pigeons. »

[25] Il y avait alors à Jérusalem un certain Siméon. Cet homme était droit ; il respectait Dieu et attendait celui qui devait sauver Israël. Le Saint-Esprit était avec lui [26] et lui avait appris qu'il ne mourrait pas avant d'avoir vu le Messie envoyé par le Seigneur. [27] Guidé par l'Esprit, Siméon alla dans le temple. Quand les parents de Jésus amenèrent leur petit enfant afin d'accomplir pour lui ce que demandait la loi, [28] Siméon le prit dans ses bras et remercia Dieu en disant :

[29] « Maintenant, Seigneur, tu as réalisé ta promesse :
tu peux laisser ton serviteur mourir en paix.
[30] Car j'ai vu de mes propres yeux ton salut,
[31] ce salut que tu as préparé devant tous les peuples :
[32] c'est la lumière qui te fera connaître aux nations du monde
et qui sera la gloire d'Israël, ton peuple. »

La prophétie de Siméon

[33] Le père et la mère de Jésus étaient tout étonnés de ce que Siméon disait de lui. [34] Siméon les bénit et dit à Marie, la mère de Jésus : « Dieu a destiné cet enfant à causer la chute ou le relèvement de beaucoup en Israël. Il sera un signe de Dieu auquel les gens s'opposeront, [35] et il mettra ainsi en pleine lumière les pensées cachées dans le cœur de beaucoup. Quant à toi, Marie, la douleur te transpercera l'âme comme une épée. »

Anne, la prophétesse

[36] Il y avait aussi une prophétesse, appelée Anne, qui était la fille de Penouel, de la tribu d'Asser. Elle était très âgée. Elle avait vécu sept ans avec le mari qu'elle avait épousé dans sa jeunesse, [37] puis, demeurée veuve, elle était parvenue à l'âge de quatre-vingt-quatre ans. Elle ne quittait pas le temple, mais elle servait Dieu jour et nuit : elle jeûnait et elle priait. [38] Elle arriva à ce même moment et se mit à remercier Dieu. Et elle parla de l'enfant à tous ceux qui attendaient que Dieu délivre Jérusalem.

Le retour à Nazareth

[39] Quand les parents de Jésus eurent achevé de faire tout ce que demandait la loi du Seigneur, ils retournèrent avec lui en Galilée, dans

leur ville de Nazareth. ⁴⁰ L'enfant grandissait et se fortifiait. Il était rempli de sagesse et la faveur de Dieu reposait sur lui.

Jésus à douze ans dans le temple

⁴¹ Chaque année, les parents de Jésus allaient à Jérusalem pour la fête de la Pâque. ⁴² Lorsque Jésus eut douze ans, ils l'emmenèrent avec eux selon la coutume. ⁴³ Quand la fête fut terminée, ils repartirent, mais l'enfant Jésus resta à Jérusalem et ses parents ne s'en aperçurent pas. ⁴⁴ Ils pensaient que Jésus était avec leurs compagnons de voyage et firent une journée de marche. Ils se mirent ensuite à le chercher parmi leurs parents et leurs amis, ⁴⁵ mais sans le trouver. Ils retournèrent donc à Jérusalem en continuant à le chercher. ⁴⁶ Le troisième jour, ils le découvrirent dans le temple : il était assis au milieu des maîtres de la loi, les écoutait et leur posait des questions. ⁴⁷ Tous ceux qui l'entendaient étaient surpris de son intelligence et des réponses qu'il donnait. ⁴⁸ Quand ses parents l'aperçurent, ils furent stupéfaits et sa mère lui dit : « Mon enfant, pourquoi nous as-tu fait cela ? Ton père et moi, nous étions très inquiets en te cherchant. » ⁴⁹ Il leur répondit : « Pourquoi me cherchiez-vous ? Ne saviez-vous pas que je dois être dans la maison de mon Père ? » ⁵⁰ Mais ils ne comprirent pas ce qu'il leur disait.

⁵¹ Jésus repartit avec eux à Nazareth. Il leur obéissait. Sa mère gardait en elle le souvenir de tous ces événements. ⁵² Et Jésus grandissait, il progressait en sagesse et se rendait agréable à Dieu et aux hommes.

La prédication de Jean-Baptiste

3 C'était la quinzième année du règne de l'empereur Tibère ; Ponce-Pilate était gouverneur de Judée, Hérode régnait sur la Galilée et son frère Philippe sur le territoire de l'Iturée et de la Trachonitide, Lysanias régnait sur l'Abilène, ² Hanne et Caïphe étaient grands-prêtres. La parole de Dieu se fit alors entendre à Jean, fils de Zacharie, dans le désert. ³ Jean se mit à parcourir toute la région voisine de la rivière, le Jourdain. Il lançait cet appel : « Changez de comportement, faites-vous baptiser et Dieu pardonnera vos péchés. »

⁴ Ainsi arriva ce que le prophète Ésaïe avait écrit dans son livre :

« Un homme crie dans le désert :

Préparez le chemin du Seigneur,

faites-lui des sentiers bien droits !

⁵ Toute vallée sera comblée,
toute montagne et toute colline seront abaissées ;
les courbes de la route seront redressées,
les chemins en mauvais état seront égalisés.

⁶ Et tout le monde verra le salut accordé par Dieu. »

⁷ Une foule de gens venaient à Jean pour qu'il les baptise. Il leur disait : « Bande de serpents ! Qui vous a enseigné à vouloir échapper au jugement divin, qui est proche ? ⁸ Montrez par des actes que vous avez changé de mentalité et ne vous mettez pas à dire en vous mêmes : "Abraham est notre ancêtre." Car je vous déclare que Dieu peut utiliser les pierres que voici pour en faire des descendants d'Abraham ! ⁹ La hache est déjà prête à couper les arbres à la racine : tout arbre qui ne produit pas de bons fruits va être coupé et jeté au feu. »

¹⁰ Les gens lui demandaient : « Que devons-nous donc faire ? » ¹¹ Il leur répondit : « Celui qui a deux chemises doit en donner une à celui qui n'en a pas et celui qui a de quoi manger doit partager. »

¹² Des collecteurs d'impôts vinrent aussi pour être baptisés et demandèrent à Jean : « Maître, que devons-nous faire ? » ¹³ Il leur répondit : « Ne faites pas payer plus que ce qui vous a été indiqué. »

¹⁴ Des soldats lui demandèrent également : « Et nous, que devons-nous faire ? » Il leur dit : « Ne prenez d'argent à personne par la force ou en portant de fausses accusations, mais contentez-vous de votre solde. »

¹⁵ Le peuple attendait, plein d'espoir : chacun pensait que Jean était peut-être le Messie. ¹⁶ Jean leur dit alors à tous : « Moi, je vous baptise avec de l'eau ; mais celui qui vient est plus puissant que moi : je ne suis pas même digne de délier la courroie de ses sandales. Il vous baptisera avec le Saint-Esprit et avec du feu. ¹⁷ Il tient en sa main la pelle à vanner pour séparer le grain de la paille. Il amassera le grain dans son grenier, mais il brûlera la paille dans un feu qui ne s'éteint jamais. »

¹⁸ C'est en leur adressant beaucoup d'autres appels encore que Jean annonçait la Bonne Nouvelle au peuple. ¹⁹ Cependant Jean fit des reproches à Hérode, qui régnait sur la Galilée, parce qu'il avait épousé Hérodiade, la femme de son frère, et parce qu'il avait commis beaucoup d'autres mauvaises actions. ²⁰ Alors Hérode commit une mauvaise action de plus : il fit mettre Jean en prison.

Le baptême de Jésus

²¹ Après que tout le monde eut été baptisé, Jésus fut aussi baptisé. Pendant qu'il priait, le ciel s'ouvrit ²² et le Saint-Esprit descendit sur lui sous une forme corporelle, comme une colombe. Et une voix se fit entendre du ciel : « Tu es mon Fils bien-aimé ; je mets en toi toute ma joie. »

La généalogie de Jésus

²³ Jésus avait environ trente ans lorsqu'il commença son œuvre. Il était, à ce que l'on pensait, fils de Joseph, qui était fils d'Éli, ²⁴ fils de Matthat, fils de Lévi, fils de Melchi, fils de Jannaï, fils de Joseph, ²⁵ fils de Mattatias, fils d'Amos, fils de Nahoum, fils d'Esli, fils de Naggaï, ²⁶ fils de Maath, fils de Mattatias, fils de Séméïn, fils de Josech, fils de Joda, ²⁷ fils de Yohanan, fils de Rhésa, fils de Zorobabel, fils de Chéaltiel, fils de Néri, ²⁸ fils de Melchi, fils d'Addi, fils de Kosam, fils d'Elmadam, fils d'Er, ²⁹ fils de Jésus, fils d'Éliézer, fils de Jorim, fils de Matthat, fils de Lévi, ³⁰ fils de Siméon, fils de Juda, fils de Joseph, fils de Jonam, fils d'Éliakim, ³¹ fils de Méléa, fils de Menna, fils de Mattata, fils de Natan, fils de David, ³² fils de Jessé, fils d'Obed, fils de Booz, fils de Sala, fils de Nachon, ³³ fils d'Amminadab, fils d'Admin, fils d'Arni, fils de Hesron, fils de Pérès, fils de Juda, ³⁴ fils de Jacob, fils d'Isaac, fils d'Abraham, fils de Téra, fils de Nahor, ³⁵ fils de Seroug, fils de Réou, fils de Péleg, fils d'Éber, fils de Chéla, ³⁶ fils de Quénan, fils d'Arpaxad, fils de Sem, fils de Noé, fils de Lémek, ³⁷ fils de Matusalem, fils d'Hénok, fils de Yéred, fils de Malaléel, fils de Quénan, ³⁸ fils d'Énos, fils de Seth, fils d'Adam, fils de Dieu.

La tentation de Jésus

4 Jésus, rempli de Saint-Esprit, revint du Jourdain et fut conduit par l'Esprit dans le désert. ² Il y fut tenté par le diable pendant quarante jours. Il ne mangea rien durant ces jours-là et, quand ils furent passés, il eut faim. ³ Le diable lui dit alors : « Si tu es le Fils de Dieu, ordonne à cette pierre de se changer en pain. » ⁴ Jésus lui répondit : « L'Écriture déclare : "L'homme ne vivra pas de pain seulement." »

⁵ Le diable l'emmena plus haut, lui fit voir en un instant tous les royaumes de la terre ⁶ et lui dit : « Je te donnerai toute cette puissance et la richesse de ces royaumes : tout cela m'a été remis et je peux le donner à qui je veux. ⁷ Si donc tu te mets à genoux devant moi, tout

sera à toi. » ⁸ Jésus lui répondit : « L'Écriture déclare : "Adore le Seigneur ton Dieu et ne rends de culte qu'à lui seul." »

⁹ Le diable le conduisit ensuite à Jérusalem, le plaça au sommet du temple et lui dit : « Si tu es le Fils de Dieu, jette-toi d'ici en bas ; ¹⁰ car l'Écriture déclare : "Dieu ordonnera à ses anges de te garder." ¹¹ Et encore : "Ils te porteront sur leurs mains pour éviter que ton pied ne heurte une pierre." » ¹² Jésus lui répondit : « L'Écriture déclare : "Ne mets pas à l'épreuve le Seigneur ton Dieu." » ¹³ Après avoir achevé de tenter Jésus de toutes les manières, le diable s'éloigna de lui jusqu'à une autre occasion.

Jésus commence son œuvre en Galilée

¹⁴ Jésus retourna en Galilée, plein de la puissance du Saint-Esprit. On se mit à parler de lui dans toute cette région. ¹⁵ Il y enseignait dans les synagogues et tout le monde faisait son éloge.

Jésus est rejeté à Nazareth

¹⁶ Jésus se rendit à Nazareth, où il avait été élevé. Le jour du sabbat, il entra dans la synagogue selon son habitude. Il se leva pour lire les Écritures ¹⁷ et on lui remit le rouleau du livre du prophète Ésaïe. Il le déroula et trouva le passage où il est écrit :

¹⁸ « L'Esprit du Seigneur est sur moi,
il m'a consacré pour apporter la Bonne Nouvelle aux pauvres.
Il m'a envoyé pour proclamer la délivrance aux prisonniers
et le don de la vue aux aveugles,
pour libérer les opprimés,
¹⁹ pour annoncer l'année où le Seigneur manifestera sa faveur. »

²⁰ Puis Jésus roula le livre, le rendit au serviteur et s'assit. Toutes les personnes présentes dans la synagogue fixaient les yeux sur lui. ²¹ Alors il se mit à leur dire : « Ce passage de l'Écriture est réalisé, aujourd'hui, pour vous qui m'écoutez. » ²² Tous exprimaient leur admiration à l'égard de Jésus et s'étonnaient des paroles merveilleuses qu'il prononçait. Ils disaient : « N'est-ce pas le fils de Joseph ? » ²³ Jésus leur déclara : « Vous allez certainement me citer ce proverbe : "Médecin, guéris-toi toi-même." Vous me direz aussi : "Nous avons appris tout ce que tu as fait à Capernaüm, accomplis les mêmes choses ici, dans

ta propre ville." » ²⁴ Puis il ajouta : « Je vous le déclare, c'est la vérité : aucun prophète n'est bien reçu dans sa ville natale. ²⁵ De plus, je peux vous assurer qu'il y avait beaucoup de veuves en Israël à l'époque d'Élie, lorsque la pluie ne tomba pas durant trois ans et demi et qu'une grande famine sévit dans tout le pays. ²⁶ Pourtant Dieu n'envoya Élie chez aucune d'elles, mais seulement chez une veuve qui vivait à Sarepta, dans la région de Sidon. ²⁷ Il y avait aussi beaucoup de lépreux en Israël à l'époque du prophète Élisée ; pourtant aucun d'eux ne fut guéri, mais seulement Naaman le Syrien. »

²⁸ Tous, dans la synagogue, furent remplis de colère en entendant ces mots. ²⁹ Ils se levèrent, entraînèrent Jésus hors de la ville et le menèrent au sommet de la colline sur laquelle Nazareth était bâtie, afin de le précipiter dans le vide. ³⁰ Mais il passa au milieu d'eux et s'en alla.

L'homme tourmenté par un esprit mauvais

³¹ Jésus se rendit alors à Capernaüm, ville de Galilée, et il y donnait son enseignement à tous le jour du sabbat. ³² Les gens étaient impressionnés par sa manière d'enseigner, car il parlait avec autorité. ³³ Dans la synagogue, il y avait un homme tourmenté par un esprit mauvais. Il se mit à crier avec force : ³⁴ « Ah ! que nous veux-tu, Jésus de Nazareth ? Es-tu venu pour nous détruire ? Je sais bien qui tu es : le Saint envoyé de Dieu ! » ³⁵ Jésus parla sévèrement à l'esprit mauvais et lui donna cet ordre : « Tais-toi et sors de cet homme ! » L'esprit jeta l'homme à terre devant tout le monde et sortit de lui sans lui faire aucun mal. ³⁶ Tous furent saisis d'étonnement et ils se disaient les uns aux autres : « Quel genre de parole est-ce là ? Cet homme commande avec autorité et puissance aux esprits mauvais et ils sortent ! » ³⁷ Et la renommée de Jésus se répandit partout dans cette région.

Jésus guérit beaucoup de malades

³⁸ Jésus quitta la synagogue et se rendit à la maison de Simon. La belle-mère de Simon souffrait d'une forte fièvre et l'on demanda à Jésus de faire quelque chose pour elle. ³⁹ Il se pencha sur elle et, d'un ton sévère, donna un ordre à la fièvre. La fièvre la quitta, elle se leva aussitôt et se mit à les servir.

⁴⁰ Au coucher du soleil, tous ceux qui avaient des malades atteints de divers maux les amenèrent à Jésus. Il posa les mains sur chacun

d'eux et les guérit. [41] Des esprits mauvais sortirent aussi de beaucoup de malades en criant : « Tu es le Fils de Dieu ! » Mais Jésus leur adressait des paroles sévères et les empêchait de parler, parce qu'ils savaient, eux, qu'il était le Messie.

Jésus prêche dans les synagogues

[42] Dès que le jour parut, Jésus sortit de la ville et s'en alla vers un endroit isolé. Une foule de gens se mirent à le chercher ; quand ils l'eurent rejoint, ils voulurent le retenir et l'empêcher de les quitter. [43] Mais Jésus leur dit : « Je dois annoncer la Bonne Nouvelle du Royaume de Dieu aux autres villes aussi, car c'est pour cela que Dieu m'a envoyé. » [44] Et il prêchait dans les synagogues du pays.

Jésus appelle les premiers disciples

5 Un jour, Jésus se tenait au bord du lac de Génésareth et la foule se pressait autour de lui pour écouter la parole de Dieu. [2] Il vit deux barques près de la rive : les pêcheurs en étaient descendus et lavaient leurs filets. [3] Jésus monta dans l'une des barques, qui appartenait à Simon, et pria celui-ci de s'éloigner un peu du bord. Jésus s'assit dans la barque et se mit à donner son enseignement à la foule.

[4] Quand il eut fini de parler, il dit à Simon : « Avance plus loin, là où l'eau est profonde, puis, toi et tes compagnons, jetez vos filets pour pêcher. » [5] Simon lui répondit : « Maître, nous avons peiné toute la nuit sans rien prendre. Mais puisque tu me dis de le faire, je jetterai les filets. » [6] Ils les jetèrent donc et prirent une si grande quantité de poissons que leurs filets commençaient à se déchirer. [7] Ils firent alors signe à leurs compagnons qui étaient dans l'autre barque de venir les aider. Ceux-ci vinrent et, ensemble, ils remplirent les deux barques de tant de poissons qu'elles enfonçaient dans l'eau. [8] Quand Simon Pierre vit cela, il se mit à genoux devant Jésus et dit : « Éloigne-toi de moi, Seigneur, car je suis un homme pécheur ! » [9] Simon, comme tous ceux qui étaient avec lui, était en effet saisi de crainte, à cause de la grande quantité de poissons qu'ils avaient pris. [10] Il en était de même des compagnons de Simon, Jacques et Jean, les fils de Zébédée. Mais Jésus dit à Simon : « N'aie pas peur ; désormais, ce sont des hommes que tu prendras. » [11] Ils ramenèrent alors leurs barques à terre et laissèrent tout pour suivre Jésus.

Jésus guérit un lépreux

¹² Alors que Jésus se trouvait dans une localité, survint un homme couvert de lèpre. Quand il vit Jésus, il se jeta devant lui le visage contre terre et le pria en ces termes : « Maître, si tu le veux, tu peux me rendre pur. » ¹³ Jésus étendit la main, le toucha et déclara : « Je le veux, sois pur ! » Aussitôt, la lèpre quitta cet homme. ¹⁴ Jésus lui donna cet ordre : « Ne parle de cela à personne. Mais va te faire examiner par le prêtre, puis offre le sacrifice que Moïse a ordonné, pour prouver à tous que tu es guéri. » ¹⁵ Cependant, la réputation de Jésus se répandait de plus en plus ; des foules nombreuses se rassemblaient pour l'entendre et se faire guérir de leurs maladies. ¹⁶ Mais Jésus se retirait dans des endroits isolés où il priait.

Jésus guérit un homme paralysé

¹⁷ Un jour, Jésus était en train d'enseigner. Des Pharisiens et des maîtres de la loi étaient présents ; ils étaient venus de tous les villages de Galilée et de Judée, ainsi que de Jérusalem. La puissance du Seigneur était avec Jésus et lui faisait guérir des malades. ¹⁸ Des gens arrivèrent, portant sur une civière un homme paralysé ; ils cherchaient à le faire entrer dans la maison et à le déposer devant Jésus. ¹⁹ Mais ils ne savaient par où l'introduire, à cause de la foule. Ils le montèrent alors sur le toit, firent une ouverture parmi les tuiles et le descendirent sur sa civière au milieu de l'assemblée, devant Jésus. ²⁰ Quand Jésus vit leur foi, il dit au malade : « Mon ami, tes péchés te sont pardonnés. » ²¹ Les maîtres de la loi et les Pharisiens se mirent à penser : « Qui est cet homme qui fait insulte à Dieu ? Qui peut pardonner les péchés ? Dieu seul le peut ! » ²² Jésus devina leurs pensées et leur dit : « Pourquoi avez-vous de telles pensées ? ²³ Est-il plus facile de dire : "Tes péchés te sont pardonnés", ou de dire : "Lève-toi et marche ?" ²⁴ Mais je veux que vous le sachiez : le Fils de l'homme a le pouvoir sur la terre de pardonner les péchés. » Alors il adressa ces mots au paralysé : « Je te le dis, lève-toi, prends ta civière et rentre chez toi ! » ²⁵ Aussitôt, l'homme se leva devant tout le monde, prit la civière sur laquelle il avait été couché et s'en alla chez lui en louant Dieu. ²⁶ Tous furent frappés d'étonnement. Ils louaient Dieu, remplis de crainte, et disaient : « Nous avons vu aujourd'hui des choses extraordinaires ! »

Jésus appelle Lévi

²⁷ Après cela, Jésus sortit et vit un collecteur d'impôts, nommé Lévi, assis à son bureau. Jésus lui dit : « Suis-moi ! » ²⁸ Lévi se leva, laissa tout et le suivit. ²⁹ Puis Lévi lui offrit un grand repas dans sa maison ; beaucoup de collecteurs d'impôts et d'autres personnes étaient à table avec eux. ³⁰ Les Pharisiens et les maîtres de la loi qui étaient de leur parti critiquaient cela ; ils dirent aux disciples de Jésus : « Pourquoi mangez-vous et buvez-vous avec les collecteurs d'impôts et autres gens de mauvaise réputation ? » ³¹ Jésus leur répondit : « Les personnes en bonne santé n'ont pas besoin de médecin, ce sont les malades qui en ont besoin. ³² Je ne suis pas venu appeler ceux qui s'estiment justes, mais ceux qui se savent pécheurs pour qu'ils changent de comportement. »

Jésus et le jeûne

³³ Les Pharisiens dirent à Jésus : « Les disciples de Jean, de même que les nôtres, jeûnent souvent et font des prières ; mais tes disciples, eux, mangent et boivent. » ³⁴ Jésus leur répondit : « Pensez-vous pouvoir obliger les invités d'une noce à ne pas manger pendant que le marié est avec eux ? Bien sûr que non ! ³⁵ Mais le temps viendra où le marié leur sera enlevé ; ces jours-là, ils jeûneront. »

³⁶ Jésus leur dit aussi cette parabole : « Personne ne déchire une pièce d'un vêtement neuf pour réparer un vieux vêtement ; sinon, le vêtement neuf est déchiré et la pièce d'étoffe neuve ne s'accorde pas avec le vieux. ³⁷ Et personne ne verse du vin nouveau dans de vieilles outres ; sinon, le vin nouveau fait éclater les outres : il se répand et les outres sont perdues. ³⁸ Mais non ! pour le vin nouveau, il faut des outres neuves ! ³⁹ Et personne ne veut du vin nouveau après en avoir bu du vieux. On dit en effet : "Le vieux est meilleur." »

Jésus et le sabbat

6 Un jour de sabbat, Jésus traversait des champs de blé. Ses disciples cueillaient des épis, les frottaient dans leurs mains et en mangeaient les grains. ² Quelques Pharisiens leur dirent : « Pourquoi faites-vous ce que notre loi ne permet pas le jour du sabbat ? » ³ Jésus leur répondit : « N'avez-vous pas lu ce que fit David un jour où lui-même et ses compagnons avaient faim ? ⁴ Il entra dans la maison de Dieu, prit les pains offerts à Dieu, en mangea et en donna à ses compagnons, bien que notre loi ne permette qu'aux seuls prêtres d'en manger. » [5] Jésus leur dit encore : « Le Fils de l'homme est maître du sabbat. »

L'homme à la main paralysée

[6] Un autre jour de sabbat, Jésus entra dans la synagogue et se mit à enseigner. Il y avait là un homme dont la main droite était paralysée. [7] Les maîtres de la loi et les Pharisiens observaient attentivement Jésus pour voir s'il allait guérir quelqu'un le jour du sabbat, car ils voulaient avoir une raison de l'accuser. [8] Mais Jésus connaissait leurs pensées. Il dit alors à l'homme dont la main était paralysée : « Lève-toi et tiens-toi là, devant tout le monde. » L'homme se leva et se tint là. [9] Puis Jésus leur dit : « Je vous le demande : Que permet notre loi ? de faire du bien le jour du sabbat ou de faire du mal ? de sauver la vie d'un être humain ou de la détruire ? » [10] Il les regarda tous et dit ensuite à l'homme : « Avance ta main. » Il le fit et sa main redevint saine. [11] Mais les maîtres de la loi et les Pharisiens furent remplis de fureur et se mirent à discuter entre eux sur ce qu'ils pourraient faire à Jésus.

Jésus choisit les douze apôtres

[12] En ce temps-là, Jésus monta sur une colline pour prier et y passa toute la nuit à prier Dieu. [13] Quand le jour parut, il appela ses disciples et en choisit douze qu'il nomma apôtres : [14] Simon – auquel il donna aussi le nom de Pierre – et son frère André, Jacques et Jean, Philippe et Barthélemy, [15] Matthieu et Thomas, Jacques le fils d'Alphée et Simon – dit le nationaliste –, [16] Jude le fils de Jacques et Judas Iscariote, celui qui devint un traître.

Jésus enseigne et guérit

[17] Jésus descendit de la colline avec eux et s'arrêta en un endroit plat, où se trouvait un grand nombre de ses disciples. Il y avait aussi là une foule immense : des gens de toute la Judée, de Jérusalem et des villes de la côte, Tyr et Sidon ; [18] ils étaient venus pour l'entendre et se faire guérir de leurs maladies. Ceux que tourmentaient des esprits mauvais étaient guéris. [19] Tout le monde cherchait à le toucher, parce qu'une force sortait de lui et les guérissait tous.

Le bonheur et le malheur

²⁰ Jésus regarda alors ses disciples et dit:
« Heureux, vous qui êtes pauvres,
car le Royaume de Dieu est à vous !
²¹ Heureux, vous qui avez faim maintenant,
car vous aurez de la nourriture en abondance !
Heureux, vous qui pleurez maintenant,
car vous rirez !
²² « Heureux êtes-vous si les hommes vous haïssent, s'ils vous rejettent, vous insultent et disent du mal de vous, parce que vous croyez au Fils de l'homme. ²³ Réjouissez-vous quand cela arrivera et sautez de joie, car une grande récompense vous attend dans le ciel. C'est ainsi, en effet, que leurs ancêtres maltraitaient les prophètes.
²⁴ « Mais malheur à vous qui êtes riches,
car vous avez déjà eu votre bonheur !
²⁵ Malheur à vous qui avez tout en abondance maintenant,
car vous aurez faim !
Malheur à vous qui riez maintenant,
car vous serez dans la tristesse et vous pleurerez !
²⁶ « Malheur à vous si tous les hommes disent du bien de vous, car c'est ainsi que leurs ancêtres agissaient avec les faux prophètes ! »

L'amour pour les ennemis

²⁷ « Mais je vous le dis, à vous qui m'écoutez: Aimez vos ennemis, faites du bien à ceux qui vous haïssent, ²⁸ bénissez ceux qui vous maudissent et priez pour ceux qui vous maltraitent. ²⁹ Si quelqu'un te frappe sur une joue, présente-lui aussi l'autre ; si quelqu'un te prend ton manteau, laisse-le prendre aussi ta chemise. ³⁰ Donne à quiconque te demande quelque chose, et si quelqu'un te prend ce qui t'appartient, ne le lui réclame pas. ³¹ Faites pour les autres exactement ce que vous voulez qu'ils fassent pour vous. ³² Si vous aimez seulement ceux qui vous aiment, pourquoi vous attendre à une reconnaissance particulière ? Même les pécheurs aiment ceux qui les aiment ! ³³ Et si vous faites du bien seulement à ceux qui vous font du bien, pourquoi vous attendre à une reconnaissance particulière ? Même les pécheurs en

font autant ! ³⁴ Et si vous prêtez seulement à ceux dont vous espérez qu'ils vous rendront, pourquoi vous attendre à une reconnaissance particulière ? Des pécheurs aussi prêtent à des pécheurs pour qu'ils leur rendent la même somme ! ³⁵ Au contraire, aimez vos ennemis, faites-leur du bien et prêtez sans rien espérer recevoir en retour. Vous obtiendrez une grande récompense et vous serez les fils du Dieu très-haut, car il est bon pour les ingrats et les méchants. ³⁶ Soyez pleins de bonté comme votre Père est plein de bonté. »

Ne pas juger les autres

³⁷ « Ne portez de jugement contre personne et Dieu ne vous jugera pas non plus ; ne condamnez pas les autres et Dieu ne vous condamnera pas ; pardonnez aux autres et Dieu vous pardonnera. ³⁸ Donnez aux autres et Dieu vous donnera : on versera dans la grande poche de votre vêtement une bonne mesure, bien serrée et secouée, débordante. Dieu mesurera ses dons envers vous avec la mesure même que vous employez pour les autres. »

³⁹ Jésus leur parla encore avec des images : « Un aveugle ne peut pas conduire un autre aveugle, n'est-ce pas ? Sinon, ils tomberont tous les deux dans un trou. ⁴⁰ Aucun élève n'est supérieur à son maître ; mais tout élève complètement instruit sera comme son maître. ⁴¹ Pourquoi regardes-tu le brin de paille qui est dans l'œil de ton frère, alors que tu ne remarques pas la poutre qui est dans ton œil ? ⁴² Comment peux-tu dire à ton frère : "Mon frère, laisse-moi enlever cette paille qui est dans ton œil", toi qui ne vois même pas la poutre qui est dans le tien ? Hypocrite, enlève d'abord la poutre de ton œil et alors tu verras assez clair pour enlever la paille de l'œil de ton frère. »

L'arbre et ses fruits

⁴³ « Un bon arbre ne produit pas de mauvais fruits, ni un arbre malade de bons fruits. ⁴⁴ Chaque arbre se reconnaît à ses fruits : on ne cueille pas des figues sur des buissons d'épines et l'on ne récolte pas du raisin sur des ronces. ⁴⁵ L'homme bon tire du bien du bon trésor que contient son cœur ; l'homme mauvais tire du mal de son mauvais trésor. Car la bouche de chacun exprime ce dont son cœur est plein. »

Les deux maisons

⁴⁶ « Pourquoi m'appelez-vous "Seigneur, Seigneur", et ne faites-vous pas ce que je vous dis ? ⁴⁷ Je vais vous montrer à qui ressemble quiconque vient à moi, écoute mes paroles et les met en pratique : ⁴⁸ il est comme un homme qui s'est mis à bâtir une maison ; il a creusé profondément la terre et a posé les fondations sur le roc. Quand l'inondation est venue, les eaux de la rivière se sont jetées contre cette maison, mais sans pouvoir l'ébranler, car la maison était bien bâtie. ⁴⁹ Mais quiconque écoute mes paroles et ne les met pas en pratique est comme un homme qui a bâti une maison directement sur le sol, sans fondations. Quand les eaux de la rivière se sont jetées contre cette maison, elle s'est aussitôt écroulée : elle a été complètement détruite. »

Jésus guérit le serviteur d'un officier romain

7 Quand Jésus eut fini d'adresser toutes ces paroles à la foule qui l'entourait, il se rendit à Capernaüm. ² Là, un capitaine romain avait un serviteur qui lui était très cher. Ce serviteur était malade et près de mourir. ³ Quand le capitaine entendit parler de Jésus, il lui envoya quelques anciens des Juifs pour lui demander de venir guérir son serviteur. ⁴ Ils arrivèrent auprès de Jésus et se mirent à le prier avec insistance en disant : « Cet homme mérite que tu lui accordes ton aide. ⁵ Il aime notre peuple et c'est lui qui a fait bâtir notre synagogue. » ⁶ Alors Jésus s'en alla avec eux. Il n'était pas loin de la maison, quand le capitaine envoya des amis pour lui dire : « Maître, ne te dérange pas. Je ne suis pas digne que tu entres dans ma maison ; ⁷ c'est pour cela que je ne me suis pas permis d'aller en personne vers toi. Mais dis un mot pour que mon serviteur soit guéri. ⁸ Je suis moi-même soumis à mes supérieurs et j'ai des soldats sous mes ordres. Si je dis à l'un : "Va !", il va ; si je dis à un autre : "Viens !", il vient ; et si je dis à mon serviteur : "Fais ceci !", il le fait. » ⁹ Quand Jésus entendit ces mots, il admira le capitaine. Il se retourna et dit à la foule qui le suivait : « Je vous le déclare : je n'ai jamais trouvé une telle foi, non, pas même en Israël. » ¹⁰ Les envoyés retournèrent dans la maison du capitaine et y trouvèrent le serviteur en bonne santé.

Jésus ramène à la vie le fils d'une veuve

[11] Jésus se rendit ensuite dans une localité appelée Naïn ; ses disciples et une grande foule l'accompagnaient. [12] Au moment où il approchait de la porte de cette localité, on menait un mort au cimetière : c'était le fils unique d'une veuve. Un grand nombre d'habitants de l'endroit se trouvaient avec elle. [13] Quand le Seigneur la vit, il fut rempli de pitié pour elle et lui dit : « Ne pleure pas ! » [14] Puis il s'avança et toucha le cercueil ; les porteurs s'arrêtèrent. Jésus dit : « Jeune homme, je te l'ordonne, lève-toi ! » [15] Le mort se dressa et se mit à parler. Jésus le rendit à sa mère. [16] Tous furent saisis de crainte ; ils louaient Dieu en disant : « Un grand prophète est apparu parmi nous ! » et aussi : « Dieu est venu secourir son peuple ! » [17] Et dans toute la Judée et ses environs on apprit ce que Jésus avait fait.

Les envoyés de Jean-Baptiste

[18] Les disciples de Jean racontèrent tout cela à leur maître. Jean appela deux d'entre eux [19] et les envoya au Seigneur pour lui demander : « Es-tu le Messie qui doit venir ou devons-nous attendre quelqu'un d'autre ? » [20] Quand ils arrivèrent auprès de Jésus, ils lui dirent : « Jean-Baptiste nous a envoyés pour te demander : "Es-tu le Messie qui doit venir ou devons-nous attendre quelqu'un d'autre ?" » [21] Au même moment, Jésus guérit beaucoup de personnes de leurs maladies, de leurs maux, il les délivra d'esprits mauvais et rendit la vue à de nombreux aveugles. [22] Puis il répondit aux envoyés de Jean : « Allez raconter à Jean ce que vous avez vu et entendu : les aveugles voient, les boiteux marchent, les lépreux sont guéris, les sourds entendent, les morts reviennent à la vie, la Bonne Nouvelle est annoncée aux pauvres. [23] Heureux celui qui n'abandonnera pas la foi en moi ! »

[24] Quand les envoyés de Jean furent partis, Jésus se mit à parler de Jean à la foule en disant : « Qu'êtes-vous allés voir au désert ? un roseau agité par le vent ? Non ? [25] Alors qu'êtes-vous allés voir ? un homme vêtu d'habits magnifiques ? Mais ceux qui portent de riches habits et vivent dans le luxe se trouvent dans les palais des rois. [26] Qu'êtes-vous donc allés voir ? un prophète ? Oui, vous dis-je, et même bien plus qu'un prophète. [27] Car Jean est celui dont l'Écriture déclare :

"Je vais envoyer mon messager devant toi, dit Dieu,
   pour t'ouvrir le chemin."

²⁸ « Je vous le déclare, ajouta Jésus, il n'est jamais né personne de plus grand que Jean ; pourtant, celui qui est le plus petit dans le Royaume de Dieu est plus grand que lui. ²⁹ Tout le peuple et les collecteurs d'impôts l'ont écouté, ils ont reconnu que Dieu est juste et ils se sont fait baptiser par Jean. ³⁰ Mais les Pharisiens et les maîtres de la loi ont rejeté ce que Dieu voulait pour eux et ont refusé de se faire baptiser par Jean. »

³¹ Jésus dit encore : « A qui puis-je comparer les gens d'aujourd'hui ? A qui ressemblent-ils ? ³² Ils ressemblent à des enfants assis sur la place publique, dont les uns crient aux autres : "Nous vous avons joué un air de danse sur la flûte et vous n'avez pas dansé ! Nous avons chanté des chants de deuil et vous n'avez pas pleuré !" ³³ En effet, Jean-Baptiste est venu, il ne mange pas de pain et ne boit pas de vin, et vous dites : "Il est possédé d'un esprit mauvais !" ³⁴ Le Fils de l'homme est venu, il mange et boit, et vous dites : "Voyez cet homme qui ne pense qu'à manger et à boire du vin, qui est ami des collecteurs d'impôts et autres gens de mauvaise réputation !" ³⁵ Mais la sagesse de Dieu est reconnue comme juste par tous ceux qui l'acceptent. »

Jésus dans la maison de Simon le Pharisien

³⁶ Un Pharisien invita Jésus à prendre un repas avec lui. Jésus se rendit chez cet homme et se mit à table. ³⁷ Il y avait dans cette ville une femme de mauvaise réputation. Lorsqu'elle apprit que Jésus était à table chez le Pharisien, elle apporta un flacon d'albâtre plein de parfum ³⁸ et se tint derrière Jésus, à ses pieds. Elle pleurait et se mit à mouiller de ses larmes les pieds de Jésus ; puis elle les essuya avec ses cheveux, les embrassa et répandit le parfum sur eux. ³⁹ Quand le Pharisien qui avait invité Jésus vit cela, il se dit en lui-même : « Si cet homme était vraiment un prophète, il saurait qui est cette femme qui le touche et ce qu'elle est : une femme de mauvaise réputation. » ⁴⁰ Jésus prit alors la parole et dit au Pharisien : « Simon, j'ai quelque chose à te dire. » Simon répondit : « Parle, Maître. » ⁴¹ Et Jésus dit : « Deux hommes devaient de l'argent à un prêteur. L'un lui devait cinq cents pièces d'argent et l'autre cinquante. ⁴² Comme ni l'un ni l'autre ne pouvaient le rembourser, il leur fit grâce de leur dette à tous

deux. Lequel des deux l'aimera le plus ? » ⁴³ Simon lui répondit : « Je pense que c'est celui auquel il a fait grâce de la plus grosse somme. » Jésus lui dit : « Tu as raison. »

⁴⁴ Puis il se tourna vers la femme et dit à Simon : « Tu vois cette femme ? Je suis entré chez toi et tu ne m'as pas donné d'eau pour mes pieds ; mais elle m'a lavé les pieds de ses larmes et les a essuyés avec ses cheveux. ⁴⁵ Tu ne m'as pas reçu en m'embrassant ; mais elle n'a pas cessé de m'embrasser les pieds depuis que je suis entré. ⁴⁶ Tu n'as pas répandu d'huile sur ma tête ; mais elle a répandu du parfum sur mes pieds. ⁴⁷ C'est pourquoi, je te le déclare : le grand amour qu'elle a manifesté prouve que ses nombreux péchés ont été pardonnés. Mais celui à qui l'on a peu pardonné ne manifeste que peu d'amour. » ⁴⁸ Jésus dit alors à la femme : « Tes péchés sont pardonnés. » ⁴⁹ Ceux qui étaient à table avec lui se mirent à dire en eux-mêmes : « Qui est cet homme qui ose même pardonner les péchés ? » ⁵⁰ Mais Jésus dit à la femme : « Ta foi t'a sauvée : va en paix. »

Les femmes qui accompagnaient Jésus

8 Ensuite, Jésus alla dans les villes et les villages pour y prêcher et annoncer la Bonne Nouvelle du Royaume de Dieu. Les douze disciples l'accompagnaient, ² ainsi que quelques femmes qui avaient été délivrées d'esprits mauvais et guéries de maladies : Marie – appelée Marie de Magdala –, dont sept esprits mauvais avaient été chassés ; ³ Jeanne, femme de Chuza, un administrateur d'Hérode ; Suzanne et plusieurs autres qui utilisaient leurs biens pour aider Jésus et ses disciples.

La parabole du semeur

⁴ De chaque ville, des gens venaient à Jésus. Comme une grande foule s'assemblait, il dit cette parabole : ⁵ « Un homme s'en alla dans son champ pour semer du grain. Tandis qu'il lançait la semence, une partie des grains tomba le long du chemin : on marcha dessus et les oiseaux les mangèrent. ⁶ Une autre partie tomba sur un sol pierreux : dès que les plantes poussèrent, elles se desséchèrent parce qu'elles manquaient d'humidité. ⁷ Une autre partie tomba parmi des plantes épineuses qui poussèrent en même temps que les bonnes plantes et les étouffèrent.

[8] Mais une autre partie tomba dans la bonne terre ; les plantes poussèrent et produisirent des épis : chacun portait cent grains. » Et Jésus ajouta : « Écoutez bien, si vous avez des oreilles pour entendre ! »

Pourquoi Jésus utilise des paraboles

[9] Les disciples de Jésus lui demandèrent ce que signifiait cette parabole. [10] Il leur répondit : « Vous avez reçu, vous, la connaissance des secrets du Royaume de Dieu ; mais aux autres gens, ils sont présentés sous forme de paraboles et ainsi

“Ils peuvent regarder,
mais sans voir,
ils peuvent entendre,
mais sans comprendre.” »

Jésus explique la parabole du semeur

[11] « Voici ce que signifie cette parabole : la semence, c'est la parole de Dieu. [12] Certains sont comme le bord du chemin où tombe le grain : ils entendent, mais le diable arrive et arrache la parole de leur cœur pour les empêcher de croire et d'être sauvés. [13] D'autres sont comme un sol pierreux : ils entendent la parole et la reçoivent avec joie. Mais ils ne la laissent pas s'enraciner, ils ne croient qu'un instant et ils abandonnent la foi au moment où survient l'épreuve. [14] La semence qui tombe parmi les plantes épineuses représente ceux qui entendent ; mais ils se laissent étouffer en chemin par les préoccupations, la richesse et les plaisirs de la vie, et ils ne donnent pas de fruits mûrs. [15] La semence qui tombe dans la bonne terre représente ceux qui écoutent la parole et la gardent dans un cœur bon et bien disposé, qui demeurent fidèles et portent ainsi des fruits. »

La parabole de la lampe

[16] « Personne n'allume une lampe pour la couvrir d'un pot ou pour la mettre sous un lit. Au contraire, on la place sur son support, afin que ceux qui entrent voient la lumière. [17] Tout ce qui est caché apparaîtra au grand jour, et tout ce qui est secret sera connu et mis en pleine lumière. [18] Faites attention à la manière dont vous écoutez ! Car celui qui a quelque chose recevra davantage ; mais à celui qui n'a rien on enlèvera même le peu qu'il pense avoir. »

La mère et les frères de Jésus

[19] La mère et les frères de Jésus vinrent le trouver, mais ils ne pouvaient pas arriver jusqu'à lui à cause de la foule. [20] On l'annonça à Jésus en ces termes : « Ta mère et tes frères se tiennent dehors et désirent te voir. » [21] Mais Jésus dit à tous : « Ma mère et mes frères, ce sont ceux qui écoutent la parole de Dieu et la mettent en pratique. »

Jésus apaise une tempête

[22] Un jour, Jésus monta dans une barque avec ses disciples et leur dit : « Passons de l'autre côté du lac. » Et ils partirent. [23] Pendant qu'ils naviguaient, Jésus s'endormit. Soudain, un vent violent se mit à souffler sur le lac ; la barque se remplissait d'eau et ils étaient en danger. [24] Les disciples s'approchèrent alors de Jésus et le réveillèrent en criant : « Maître, maître, nous allons mourir ! » Jésus, réveillé, menaça le vent et les grosses vagues, qui s'apaisèrent. Il y eut un grand calme. [25] Jésus dit aux disciples : « Où est votre confiance ? » Mais ils avaient peur, étaient remplis d'étonnement et se disaient les uns aux autres : « Qui est donc cet homme ? Il donne des ordres même aux vents et à l'eau, et ils lui obéissent ! »

Jésus guérit un homme possédé par des esprits mauvais

[26] Ils abordèrent dans le territoire des Géraséniens, qui est de l'autre côté du lac, en face de la Galilée. [27] Au moment où Jésus descendait à terre, un homme de la ville vint à sa rencontre. Cet homme était possédé par des esprits mauvais ; depuis longtemps il ne portait pas de vêtement et n'habitait pas dans une maison, mais vivait parmi les tombeaux. [28] Quand il vit Jésus, il poussa un cri, se jeta à ses pieds et dit avec force : « Que me veux-tu, Jésus, fils du Dieu très-haut ? Je t'en prie, ne me tourmente pas ! » [29] Jésus ordonnait en effet à l'esprit mauvais de sortir de lui. Cet esprit s'était emparé de lui bien des fois ; on attachait alors les mains et les pieds de l'homme avec des chaînes pour le garder, mais il rompait ses liens et l'esprit l'entraînait vers les lieux déserts. [30] Jésus l'interrogea : « Quel est ton nom ? » – « Mon nom est "Multitude" », répondit-il. En effet, de nombreux esprits mauvais étaient entrés en lui. [31] Et ces esprits suppliaient Jésus de ne pas les envoyer dans l'abîme.

[32] Il y avait là un grand troupeau de porcs qui cherchait sa nourriture sur la colline. Les esprits prièrent Jésus de leur permettre d'entrer

dans ces porcs. Il le leur permit. ³³ Alors les esprits mauvais sortirent de l'homme et entrèrent dans les porcs. Tout le troupeau se précipita du haut de la falaise dans le lac et s'y noya. ³⁴ Quand les hommes qui gardaient les porcs virent ce qui était arrivé, ils s'enfuirent et portèrent la nouvelle dans la ville et dans les fermes. ³⁵ Les gens sortirent pour voir ce qui s'était passé. Ils arrivèrent auprès de Jésus et trouvèrent l'homme dont les esprits mauvais étaient sortis : il était assis aux pieds de Jésus, il portait des vêtements et était dans son bon sens. Et ils prirent peur. ³⁶ Ceux qui avaient tout vu leur racontèrent comment l'homme possédé avait été guéri. ³⁷ Alors toute la population de ce territoire demanda à Jésus de s'en aller de chez eux, car ils avaient très peur. Jésus monta dans la barque pour partir. ³⁸ L'homme dont les esprits mauvais étaient sortis priait Jésus de le laisser rester avec lui. Mais Jésus le renvoya en disant : ³⁹ « Retourne chez toi et raconte tout ce que Dieu a fait pour toi. » L'homme s'en alla donc et proclama dans la ville entière tout ce que Jésus avait fait pour lui.

La fille de Jaïrus et la femme qui toucha le vêtement de Jésus

⁴⁰ Au moment où Jésus revint sur l'autre rive du lac, la foule l'accueillit, car tous l'attendaient. ⁴¹ Un homme appelé Jaïrus arriva alors. Il était chef de la synagogue locale. Il se jeta aux pieds de Jésus et le supplia de venir chez lui, ⁴² parce qu'il avait une fille unique, âgée d'environ douze ans, qui était mourante.

Pendant que Jésus s'y rendait, la foule le pressait de tous côtés. ⁴³ Il y avait là une femme qui souffrait de pertes de sang depuis douze ans. Elle avait dépensé tout ce qu'elle possédait chez les médecins, mais personne n'avait pu la guérir. ⁴⁴ Elle s'approcha de Jésus par derrière et toucha le bord de son vêtement. Aussitôt, sa perte de sang s'arrêta. ⁴⁵ Jésus demanda : « Qui m'a touché ? » Tous niaient l'avoir fait et Pierre dit : « Maître, la foule t'entoure et te presse de tous côtés. » ⁴⁶ Mais Jésus dit : « Quelqu'un m'a touché, car j'ai senti qu'une force était sortie de moi. » ⁴⁷ La femme vit qu'elle avait été découverte. Elle vint alors, toute tremblante, se jeter aux pieds de Jésus. Elle lui raconta devant tout le monde pourquoi elle l'avait touché et comment elle avait été guérie immédiatement. ⁴⁸ Jésus lui dit : « Ma fille, ta foi t'a guérie. Va en paix. »

⁴⁹ Tandis que Jésus parlait ainsi, un messager vint de la maison du chef de la synagogue et dit à celui-ci : « Ta fille est morte. Ne dérange

plus le maître. » ⁵⁰ Mais Jésus l'entendit et dit à Jaïrus : « N'aie pas peur, crois seulement, et elle guérira. » ⁵¹ Lorsqu'il fut arrivé à la maison, il ne permit à personne d'entrer avec lui, si ce n'est à Pierre, à Jean, à Jacques, et au père et à la mère de l'enfant. ⁵² Tous pleuraient et se lamentaient à cause de l'enfant. Alors Jésus dit : « Ne pleurez pas. Elle n'est pas morte, elle dort. » ⁵³ Mais ils se moquèrent de lui, car ils savaient qu'elle était morte. ⁵⁴ Cependant, Jésus la prit par la main et dit d'une voix forte : « Enfant, debout ! » ⁵⁵ Elle revint à la vie et se leva aussitôt. Jésus leur ordonna de lui donner à manger. ⁵⁶ Ses parents furent remplis d'étonnement, mais Jésus leur recommanda de ne dire à personne ce qui s'était passé.

La mission des douze disciples

9 Jésus réunit les douze disciples et leur donna le pouvoir et l'autorité de chasser tous les esprits mauvais et de guérir les maladies. ² Puis il les envoya prêcher le Royaume de Dieu et guérir les malades. ³ Il leur dit : « Ne prenez rien avec vous pour le voyage : ni bâton, ni sac, ni pain, ni argent, et n'ayez pas deux chemises chacun. ⁴ Partout où l'on vous accueillera, restez dans la même maison jusqu'à ce que vous quittiez l'endroit. ⁵ Partout où les gens refuseront de vous accueillir, quittez leur ville et secouez la poussière de vos pieds : ce sera un avertissement pour eux. » ⁶ Les disciples partirent ; ils passaient dans tous les villages, annonçaient la Bonne Nouvelle et guérissaient partout les malades.

L'inquiétude d'Hérode

⁷ Or, Hérode, qui régnait sur la Galilée, entendit parler de tout ce qui se passait. Il ne savait qu'en penser, car certains disaient : « Jean-Baptiste est revenu d'entre les morts. » ⁸ D'autres disaient : « C'est Élie qui est apparu. » D'autres encore disaient : « L'un des prophètes d'autrefois s'est relevé de la mort. » ⁹ Mais Hérode déclara : « J'ai fait couper la tête à Jean. Qui est donc cet homme dont j'entends dire toutes ces choses ? » Et il cherchait à voir Jésus.

Jésus nourrit cinq mille hommes

¹⁰ Les apôtres revinrent et racontèrent à Jésus tout ce qu'ils avaient fait. Il les emmena et se retira avec eux seuls près d'une localité appe-

lée Bethsaïda. [11] Mais les gens l'apprirent et le suivirent. Jésus les accueillit, leur parla du Royaume de Dieu et guérit ceux qui en avaient besoin. [12] Le jour commençait à baisser; alors les Douze s'approchèrent de Jésus et lui dirent: « Renvoie tous ces gens, afin qu'ils aillent dans les villages et les fermes des environs pour y trouver à se loger et à se nourrir, car nous sommes ici dans un endroit isolé. » [13] Mais Jésus leur dit: « Donnez-leur vous-mêmes à manger! » Ils répondirent: « Nous n'avons que cinq pains et deux poissons. Voudrais-tu peut-être que nous allions acheter des vivres pour tout ce monde? » [14] Il y avait là, en effet, environ cinq mille hommes. Jésus dit à ses disciples: « Faites-les asseoir par groupes de cinquante environ. » [15] Les disciples obéirent et les firent tous asseoir. [16] Jésus prit les cinq pains et les deux poissons, leva les yeux vers le ciel et remercia Dieu pour ces aliments. Il les partagea et les donna aux disciples pour qu'ils les distribuent à la foule. [17] Chacun mangea à sa faim. On emporta douze corbeilles pleines des morceaux qu'ils eurent en trop.

Pierre déclare que Jésus est le Messie

[18] Un jour, Jésus priait à l'écart et ses disciples étaient avec lui. Il leur demanda: « Que disent les foules à mon sujet? » [19] Ils répondirent: « Certains disent que tu es Jean-Baptiste, d'autres que tu es Élie, et d'autres encore que l'un des prophètes d'autrefois s'est relevé de la mort. » [20] « Et vous, leur demanda Jésus, qui dites-vous que je suis? » Pierre répondit: « Tu es le Messie de Dieu. »

Jésus annonce sa mort et sa résurrection

[21] Jésus leur ordonna sévèrement de n'en parler à personne, [22] et il ajouta: « Il faut que le Fils de l'homme souffre beaucoup; les anciens, les chefs des prêtres et les maîtres de la loi le rejetteront; il sera mis à mort et, le troisième jour, il reviendra à la vie. »

[23] Puis il dit à tous: « Si quelqu'un veut venir avec moi, qu'il cesse de penser à lui-même, qu'il porte sa croix chaque jour et me suive. [24] En effet, celui qui veut sauver sa vie la perdra; mais celui qui perdra sa vie pour moi la sauvera. [25] À quoi sert-il à un homme de gagner le monde entier, s'il se perd lui-même ou va à sa ruine? [26] Si quelqu'un a honte de moi et de mes paroles, alors le Fils de l'homme aura honte

de lui, quand il viendra dans sa gloire et dans la gloire du Père et des saints anges. ²⁷ Je vous le déclare, c'est la vérité : quelques-uns de ceux qui sont ici ne mourront pas avant d'avoir vu le Royaume de Dieu. »

La transfiguration de Jésus

²⁸ Environ une semaine après qu'il eut parlé ainsi, Jésus prit avec lui Pierre, Jean et Jacques, et il monta sur une montagne pour prier. ²⁹ Pendant qu'il priait, son visage changea d'aspect et ses vêtements devinrent d'une blancheur éblouissante. ³⁰ Soudain, il y eut là deux hommes qui s'entretenaient avec Jésus : c'étaient Moïse et Élie, ³¹ qui apparaissaient au milieu d'une gloire céleste. Ils parlaient avec Jésus de la façon dont il allait réaliser sa mission en mourant à Jérusalem. ³² Pierre et ses compagnons s'étaient profondément endormis ; mais ils se réveillèrent et virent la gloire de Jésus et les deux hommes qui se tenaient avec lui. ³³ Au moment où ces hommes quittaient Jésus, Pierre lui dit : « Maître, il est bon que nous soyons ici. Nous allons dresser trois tentes, une pour toi, une pour Moïse et une pour Élie. » – Il ne savait pas ce qu'il disait. – ³⁴ Pendant qu'il parlait ainsi, un nuage survint et les couvrit de son ombre. Les disciples eurent peur en voyant ce nuage les recouvrir. ³⁵ Du nuage une voix se fit entendre : « Celui-ci est mon Fils, que j'ai choisi. Écoutez-le ! » ³⁶ Après que la voix eut parlé, on ne vit plus que Jésus seul. Les disciples gardèrent le silence et, en ce temps-là, ne racontèrent rien à personne de ce qu'ils avaient vu.

Jésus guérit un enfant
tourmenté par un esprit mauvais

³⁷ Le jour suivant, ils descendirent de la montagne et une grande foule vint à la rencontre de Jésus. ³⁸ De la foule un homme se mit à crier : « Maître, je t'en prie, jette un regard sur mon fils, mon fils unique ! ³⁹ Un esprit le saisit, le fait crier tout à coup, le secoue avec violence et le fait écumer de la bouche ; il le maltraite et ne le quitte que difficilement. ⁴⁰ J'ai prié tes disciples de chasser cet esprit, mais ils ne l'ont pas pu. » ⁴¹ Jésus s'écria : « Gens mauvais et sans foi que vous êtes ! Combien de temps encore devrai-je rester avec vous ? Combien de temps encore devrai-je vous supporter ? Amène ton fils ici. » ⁴² Au moment où l'enfant approchait, l'esprit le jeta à terre et le secoua rudement. Mais

Jésus menaça l'esprit mauvais, guérit l'enfant et le rendit à son père. [43] Et tous étaient impressionnés par la grande puissance de Dieu.

Jésus annonce de nouveau sa mort

Comme chacun s'étonnait encore de tout ce que Jésus faisait, il dit à ses disciples : [44] « Retenez bien ce que je vous affirme maintenant : Le Fils de l'homme va être livré entre les mains des hommes. » [45] Mais ils ne comprenaient pas cette parole : son sens leur avait été caché afin qu'ils ne puissent pas le comprendre, et ils avaient peur d'interroger Jésus à ce sujet.

Qui est le plus grand ?

[46] Les disciples se mirent à discuter pour savoir lequel d'entre eux était le plus grand. [47] Jésus se rendit compte de ce qu'ils pensaient. Il prit alors un enfant, le plaça auprès de lui, [48] et leur dit : « Celui qui reçoit cet enfant par amour pour moi, me reçoit moi-même ; et celui qui me reçoit, reçoit aussi celui qui m'a envoyé. Car celui qui est le plus petit parmi vous tous, c'est lui qui est le plus grand. »

Celui qui n'est pas contre vous est pour vous

[49] Jean prit la parole : « Maître, dit-il, nous avons vu un homme qui chassait les esprits mauvais en usant de ton nom et nous avons voulu l'en empêcher, parce qu'il n'appartient pas à notre groupe. » [50] Mais Jésus lui répondit : « Ne l'en empêchez pas, car celui qui n'est pas contre vous est pour vous. »

Un village de Samarie refuse de recevoir Jésus

[51] Lorsque le moment approcha où Jésus devait être enlevé au ciel, il décida fermement de se rendre à Jérusalem. [52] Il envoya des messagers devant lui. Ceux-ci partirent et entrèrent dans un village de Samarie pour lui préparer tout le nécessaire. [53] Mais les habitants refusèrent de le recevoir parce qu'il se dirigeait vers Jérusalem. [54] Quand les disciples Jacques et Jean apprirent cela, ils dirent : « Seigneur, veux-tu que nous commandions au feu de descendre du ciel et de les exterminer ? »

[55] Jésus se tourna vers eux et leur fit des reproches. [56] Et ils allèrent dans un autre village.

Ceux qui désirent suivre Jésus

[57] Ils étaient en chemin, lorsqu'un homme dit à Jésus : « Je te suivrai partout où tu iras. » [58] Jésus lui dit : « Les renards ont des terriers et les oiseaux ont des nids, mais le Fils de l'homme n'a pas un endroit où il puisse se coucher et se reposer. »

[59] Il dit à un autre homme : « Suis-moi. » Mais l'homme dit : « Maître, permets-moi d'aller d'abord enterrer mon père. » [60] Jésus lui répondit : « Laisse les morts enterrer leurs morts ; et toi, va annoncer le Royaume de Dieu. »

[61] Un autre homme encore dit : « Je te suivrai, Maître, mais permets-moi d'aller d'abord dire adieu à ma famille. » [62] Jésus lui déclara : « Celui qui se met à labourer puis regarde en arrière n'est d'aucune utilité pour le Royaume de Dieu. »

La mission des soixante-douze disciples

10 Après cela, le Seigneur choisit soixante-douze autres hommes et les envoya deux par deux devant lui dans toutes les villes et tous les endroits où lui-même devait se rendre. [2] Il leur dit : « La moisson à faire est grande, mais il y a peu d'ouvriers pour cela. Priez donc le propriétaire de la moisson d'envoyer davantage d'ouvriers pour la faire. [3] En route ! Je vous envoie comme des agneaux au milieu des loups. [4] Ne prenez ni bourse, ni sac, ni chaussures ; ne vous arrêtez pas en chemin pour saluer quelqu'un. [5] Quand vous entrerez dans une maison, dites d'abord : "Paix à cette maison." [6] Si un homme de paix habite là, votre souhait de paix reposera sur lui ; sinon, retirez votre souhait de paix. [7] Demeurez dans cette maison-là, mangez et buvez ce que l'on vous y donnera, car l'ouvrier a droit à son salaire. Ne passez pas de cette maison dans une autre. [8] Quand vous entrerez dans une ville et que l'on vous recevra, mangez ce que l'on vous présentera ; [9] guérissez les malades de cette ville et dites à ses habitants : "Le Royaume de Dieu s'est approché de vous." [10] Mais quand vous entrerez dans une ville et que l'on ne vous recevra pas, allez dans les rues et dites à tous : [11] "Nous secouons contre vous la poussière même de votre ville qui s'est attachée à nos pieds. Pourtant, sachez bien ceci : le Royaume de Dieu s'est approché de vous." [12] Je vous le déclare : au jour du Jugement les habitants de Sodome seront traités moins sévèrement que les habitants de cette ville-là. »

Les villes qui refusent de croire

[13] « Malheur à toi, Chorazin ! Malheur à toi, Bethsaïda ! Car si les miracles qui ont été accomplis chez vous l'avaient été à Tyr et à Sidon, il y a longtemps que leurs habitants auraient pris le deuil, se seraient assis dans la cendre et auraient changé de comportement. [14] C'est pourquoi, au jour du Jugement, Tyr et Sidon seront traitées moins sévèrement que vous. [15] Et toi, Capernaüm, crois-tu que tu t'élèveras jusqu'au ciel ? Tu seras abaissée jusqu'au monde des morts. » [16] Il dit encore à ses disciples : « Celui qui vous écoute, m'écoute ; celui qui vous rejette, me rejette ; et celui qui me rejette, rejette celui qui m'a envoyé. »

Le retour des soixante-douze

[17] Les soixante-douze envoyés revinrent pleins de joie et dirent : « Seigneur, même les esprits mauvais nous obéissent quand nous leur donnons des ordres en ton nom ! » [18] Jésus leur répondit : « Je voyais Satan tomber du ciel comme un éclair. [19] Écoutez : je vous ai donné le pouvoir de marcher sur les serpents et les scorpions et d'écraser toute la puissance de l'ennemi, et rien ne pourra vous faire du mal. [20] Mais ne vous réjouissez pas de ce que les esprits mauvais vous obéissent ; réjouissez-vous plutôt de ce que vos noms sont écrits dans les cieux. »

Jésus se réjouit

[21] A ce moment même, Jésus fut rempli de joie par le Saint-Esprit et s'écria : « O Père, Seigneur du ciel et de la terre, je te remercie d'avoir révélé aux petits ce que tu as caché aux sages et aux gens instruits. Oui, Père, tu as bien voulu qu'il en soit ainsi.

[22] « Mon Père m'a remis toutes choses. Personne ne sait qui est le Fils si ce n'est le Père, et personne ne sait qui est le Père si ce n'est le Fils et ceux à qui le Fils veut bien le révéler. »

[23] Puis Jésus se tourna vers ses disciples et leur dit à eux seuls : « Heureux êtes-vous de voir ce que vous voyez ! [24] Car, je vous le déclare, beaucoup de prophètes et de rois ont désiré voir ce que vous voyez, mais ne l'ont pas vu, et entendre ce que vous entendez, mais ne l'ont pas entendu. »

La parabole du bon Samaritain

²⁵ Un maître de la loi intervint alors. Pour tendre un piège à Jésus, il lui demanda : « Maître, que dois-je faire pour recevoir la vie éternelle ? » ²⁶ Jésus lui dit : « Qu'est-il écrit dans notre loi ? Qu'est-ce que tu y lis ? » ²⁷ L'homme répondit : « "Tu dois aimer le Seigneur ton Dieu de tout ton cœur, de toute ton âme, de toute ta force et de toute ton intelligence." Et aussi : "Tu dois aimer ton prochain comme toi-même." » ²⁸ Jésus lui dit alors : « Tu as bien répondu. Fais cela et tu vivras. » ²⁹ Mais le maître de la loi voulait justifier sa question. Il demanda donc à Jésus : « Qui est mon prochain ? » ³⁰ Jésus répondit : « Un homme descendait de Jérusalem à Jéricho, lorsque des brigands l'attaquèrent, lui prirent tout ce qu'il avait, le battirent et s'en allèrent en le laissant à demi-mort. ³¹ Il se trouva qu'un prêtre descendait cette route. Quand il vit l'homme, il passa de l'autre côté de la route et s'éloigna. ³² De même, un lévite arriva à cet endroit, il vit l'homme, passa de l'autre côté de la route et s'éloigna. ³³ Mais un Samaritain, qui voyageait par là, arriva près du blessé. Quand il le vit, il en eut profondément pitié. ³⁴ Il s'en approcha encore plus, versa de l'huile et du vin sur ses blessures et les recouvrit de pansements. Puis il le plaça sur sa propre bête et le mena dans un hôtel, où il prit soin de lui. ³⁵ Le lendemain, il sortit deux pièces d'argent, les donna à l'hôtelier et lui dit : "Prends soin de cet homme ; lorsque je repasserai par ici, je te paierai moi-même ce que tu auras dépensé en plus pour lui." »

³⁶ Jésus ajouta : « Lequel de ces trois te semble avoir été le prochain de l'homme attaqué par les brigands ? » ³⁷ Le maître de la loi répondit : « Celui qui a été bon pour lui. » Jésus lui dit alors : « Va et fais de même. »

Jésus chez Marthe et Marie

³⁸ Tandis que Jésus et ses disciples étaient en chemin, il entra dans un village où une femme, appelée Marthe, le reçut chez elle. ³⁹ Elle avait une sœur, appelée Marie, qui, après s'être assise aux pieds du Seigneur, écoutait ce qu'il enseignait. ⁴⁰ Marthe était très affairée à tout préparer pour le repas. Elle survint et dit : « Seigneur, cela ne te fait-il rien que ma sœur me laisse seule pour accomplir tout le travail ? Dis-lui donc de m'aider. » ⁴¹ Le Seigneur lui répondit : « Marthe, Marthe, tu t'inquiètes et tu t'agites pour beaucoup de choses, ⁴² mais une seule est nécessaire. Marie a choisi la meilleure part, qui ne lui sera pas enlevée. »

Jésus et la prière

11 Un jour, Jésus priait en un certain lieu. Quand il eut fini, un de ses disciples lui demanda : « Seigneur, enseigne-nous à prier, comme Jean l'a appris à ses disciples. » ² Jésus leur déclara : « Quand vous priez, dites :

"Père,
que tous reconnaissent que tu es le Dieu saint ;
que ton Règne vienne.

³ Donne-nous chaque jour le pain nécessaire.

⁴ Pardonne-nous nos péchés,
car nous pardonnons nous-mêmes à tous ceux
qui nous ont fait du tort.
Et ne nous expose pas à la tentation." »

⁵ Jésus leur dit encore : « Supposons ceci : l'un d'entre vous a un ami qu'il s'en va trouver chez lui à minuit pour lui dire : "Mon ami, prête-moi trois pains. ⁶ Un de mes amis qui est en voyage vient d'arriver chez moi et je n'ai rien à lui offrir." ⁷ Et supposons que l'autre lui réponde de l'intérieur de la maison : "Laisse-moi tranquille ! La porte est déjà fermée à clé, mes enfants et moi sommes au lit ; je ne peux pas me lever pour te donner des pains." ⁸ Eh bien, je vous l'affirme, même s'il ne se lève pas par amitié pour les lui donner, il se lèvera pourtant et lui donnera tout ce dont il a besoin parce que son ami insiste sans se gêner ⁹ Et moi, je vous dis : demandez et vous recevrez, cherchez et vous trouverez ; frappez et l'on vous ouvrira la porte. ¹⁰ Car quiconque demande reçoit, qui cherche trouve et l'on ouvrira la porte à qui frappe. ¹¹ Si l'un d'entre vous est père, donnera-t-il un serpent à son fils alors que celui-ci lui demande un poisson ? ¹² Ou bien lui donnera-t-il un scorpion s'il demande un œuf ? ¹³ Tout mauvais que vous êtes, vous savez donner de bonnes choses à vos enfants. À combien plus forte raison, donc, le Père qui est au ciel donnera-t-il le Saint-Esprit à ceux qui le lui demandent ! »

Jésus répond à une accusation portée contre lui

¹⁴ Jésus était en train de chasser un esprit mauvais qui rendait un homme muet. Quand l'esprit mauvais sortit, le muet se mit à parler et, dans la foule, les gens furent remplis d'étonnement. ¹⁵ Cependant, quelques-uns dirent : « C'est Béelzébul, le chef des esprits mauvais, qui

lui donne le pouvoir de chasser ces esprits ! » ¹⁶ D'autres voulaient lui tendre un piège : ils lui demandèrent de montrer par un signe miraculeux qu'il venait de Dieu. ¹⁷ Mais Jésus connaissait leurs pensées ; il leur dit alors : « Tout royaume dont les habitants luttent les uns contre les autres finit par être détruit, ses maisons s'écroulent les unes sur les autres. ¹⁸ Si donc Satan est en lutte contre lui-même, comment son royaume pourra-t-il se maintenir ? Vous dites, en effet, que je chasse les esprits mauvais parce que Béelzébul m'en donne le pouvoir. ¹⁹ Si je les chasse de cette façon, qui donne à vos partisans le pouvoir de les chasser ? Vos partisans eux-mêmes démontrent que vous avez tort ! ²⁰ En réalité, c'est avec la puissance de Dieu que je chasse les esprits mauvais, ce qui signifie que le Royaume de Dieu est déjà venu jusqu'à vous.

²¹ « Quand un homme fort et bien armé garde sa maison, tous ses biens sont en sûreté. ²² Mais si un homme plus fort que lui arrive et s'en rend vainqueur, il lui enlève les armes dans lesquelles il mettait sa confiance et il distribue tout ce qu'il lui a pris.

²³ « Celui qui n'est pas avec moi est contre moi ; et celui qui ne m'aide pas à rassembler disperse. »

Le retour de l'esprit mauvais

²⁴ « Lorsqu'un esprit mauvais est sorti d'un homme, il va et vient dans des espaces déserts en cherchant un lieu où s'établir. S'il n'en trouve pas, il se dit alors : "Je vais retourner dans ma maison, celle que j'ai quittée." ²⁵ Il y retourne et la trouve balayée, bien arrangée. ²⁶ Alors il s'en va prendre sept autres esprits encore plus malfaisants que lui ; ils reviennent ensemble dans la maison et s'y installent. Finalement, l'état de cet homme est donc pire qu'au début. »

Le vrai bonheur

²⁷ Jésus venait de parler ainsi, quand une femme s'adressa à lui du milieu de la foule : « Heureuse est la femme qui t'a porté en elle et qui t'a allaité ! » ²⁸ Mais Jésus répondit : « Heureux plutôt ceux qui écoutent la parole de Dieu et la mettent en pratique ! »

La demande d'un signe miraculeux

²⁹ Tandis que les foules s'amassaient autour de Jésus, il se mit à dire : « Les gens d'aujourd'hui sont mauvais ; ils réclament un signe mi-

raculeux, mais aucun signe ne leur sera accordé si ce n'est celui de Jonas. [30] En effet, de même que Jonas fut un signe pour les habitants de Ninive, ainsi le Fils de l'homme sera un signe pour les gens d'aujourd'hui. [31] Au jour du Jugement, la reine du Sud se lèvera en face des gens d'aujourd'hui et les accusera, car elle est venue des régions les plus lointaines de la terre pour écouter les paroles pleines de sagesse de Salomon. Et il y a ici plus que Salomon ! [32] Au jour du Jugement, les habitants de Ninive se lèveront en face des gens d'aujourd'hui et les accuseront, car les Ninivites ont changé de comportement quand ils ont entendu prêcher Jonas. Et il y a ici plus que Jonas ! »

La lumière du corps

[33] « Personne n'allume une lampe pour la cacher ou la mettre sous un seau ; au contraire, on la place sur son support, afin que ceux qui entrent voient la lumière. [34] Tes yeux sont la lampe de ton corps : si tes yeux sont en bon état, tout ton corps est éclairé ; mais si tes yeux sont mauvais, alors ton corps est dans l'obscurité. [35] Ainsi, prends garde que la lumière qui est en toi ne soit pas obscurité. [36] Si donc tout ton corps est éclairé, sans aucune partie dans l'obscurité, il sera tout entier en pleine lumière, comme lorsque la lampe t'illumine de sa brillante clarté. »

Jésus accuse les Pharisiens et les maîtres de la loi

[37] Quand Jésus eut fini de parler, un Pharisien l'invita à prendre un repas chez lui. Jésus entra et se mit à table. [38] Le Pharisien s'étonna lorsqu'il remarqua que Jésus ne s'était pas lavé avant le repas. [39] Le Seigneur lui dit alors : « Voilà comme vous êtes, vous les Pharisiens : vous nettoyez l'extérieur de la coupe et du plat, mais à l'intérieur vous êtes pleins du désir de voler et pleins de méchanceté. [40] Insensés que vous êtes ! Dieu qui a fait l'extérieur n'a-t-il pas aussi fait l'intérieur ? [41] Donnez donc plutôt aux pauvres ce qui est dans vos coupes et vos plats, et tout sera pur pour vous.

[42] « Malheur à vous, Pharisiens ! Vous donnez à Dieu le dixième de plantes comme la menthe et la rue, ainsi que de toutes sortes de légumes, mais vous négligez la justice et l'amour pour Dieu : c'est pourtant là ce qu'il fallait pratiquer, sans négliger le reste.

⁴³ « Malheur à vous, Pharisiens ! Vous aimez les sièges les plus en vue dans les synagogues et vous aimez à recevoir des salutations respectueuses sur les places publiques. ⁴⁴ Malheur à vous ! Vous êtes comme des tombeaux qu'on ne remarque pas et sur lesquels on marche sans le savoir ! »

⁴⁵ Un des maîtres de la loi lui dit : « Maître, en parlant ainsi, tu nous insultes nous aussi ! » ⁴⁶ Jésus répondit : « Malheur à vous aussi, maîtres de la loi ! Vous mettez sur le dos des gens des fardeaux difficiles à porter, et vous ne bougez pas même un seul doigt pour les aider à porter ces fardeaux. ⁴⁷ Malheur à vous ! Vous construisez de beaux tombeaux pour les prophètes, ces prophètes que vos ancêtres ont tués ! ⁴⁸ Vous montrez ainsi que vous approuvez les actes de vos ancêtres, car ils ont tué les prophètes, et vous, vous construisez leurs tombeaux ! ⁴⁹ C'est pourquoi Dieu, dans sa sagesse, a déclaré : "Je leur enverrai des prophètes et des apôtres ; ils tueront certains d'entre eux et en persécuteront d'autres." ⁵⁰ Par conséquent, les gens d'aujourd'hui supporteront les conséquences des meurtres commis contre tous les prophètes depuis la création du monde, ⁵¹ depuis le meurtre d'Abel jusqu'à celui de Zacharie, qui fut tué entre l'autel et le sanctuaire. Oui, je vous l'affirme, les gens d'aujourd'hui supporteront les conséquences de tous ces meurtres !

⁵² « Malheur à vous, maîtres de la loi ! Vous avez pris la clé permettant d'ouvrir la porte du savoir : vous n'entrez pas vous-mêmes et vous empêchez d'entrer ceux qui le désirent. »

⁵³ Quand Jésus fut sorti de cette maison, les maîtres de la loi et les Pharisiens se mirent à lui manifester une violente fureur et à lui poser des questions sur toutes sortes de sujets : ⁵⁴ ils lui tendaient des pièges pour essayer de surprendre quelque chose de faux dans ses paroles.

Une mise en garde contre l'hypocrisie

12 Pendant ce temps, les gens s'étaient assemblés par milliers, au point qu'ils se marchaient sur les pieds les uns des autres. Jésus s'adressa d'abord à ses disciples : « Gardez-vous, leur dit-il, du levain des Pharisiens, c'est-à-dire de leur hypocrisie. ² Tout ce qui est caché sera découvert, et tout ce qui est secret sera connu. ³ C'est pourquoi tout ce que vous aurez dit dans l'obscurité sera entendu à la lumière du jour, et ce que vous aurez murmuré à l'oreille d'autrui dans une chambre fermée sera crié du haut des toits. »

Celui qu'il faut craindre

⁴ « Je vous le dis, à vous mes amis : ne craignez pas ceux qui tuent le corps mais qui, ensuite, ne peuvent rien faire de plus. ⁵ Je vais vous montrer qui vous devez craindre : craignez Dieu qui, après la mort, a le pouvoir de vous jeter en enfer. Oui, je vous le dis, c'est lui que vous devez craindre ! ⁶ Ne vend-on pas cinq moineaux pour deux sous ? Cependant, Dieu n'en oublie pas un seul. ⁷ Et même vos cheveux sont tous comptés. N'ayez donc pas peur : vous valez plus que beaucoup de moineaux ! »

Confesser ou renier Jésus-Christ

⁸ « Je vous le dis : quiconque reconnaît publiquement qu'il est mon disciple, le Fils de l'homme aussi reconnaîtra devant les anges de Dieu qu'il est à lui ; ⁹ mais si quelqu'un affirme publiquement ne pas me connaître, le Fils de l'homme aussi affirmera devant les anges de Dieu qu'il ne le connaît pas. ¹⁰ Quiconque dira une parole contre le Fils de l'homme sera pardonné ; mais celui qui aura fait insulte au Saint-Esprit ne recevra pas de pardon. ¹¹ Quand on vous conduira pour être jugés dans les synagogues, ou devant les dirigeants ou les autorités, ne vous inquiétez pas de la manière dont vous vous défendrez ou de ce que vous aurez à dire, ¹² car le Saint-Esprit vous enseignera à ce moment-là ce que vous devez exprimer. »

La parabole du riche insensé

¹³ Quelqu'un dans la foule dit à Jésus : « Maître, dis à mon frère de partager avec moi les biens que notre père nous a laissés. » ¹⁴ Jésus lui répondit : « Mon ami, qui m'a établi pour juger vos affaires ou pour partager vos biens ? » ¹⁵ Puis il dit à tous : « Attention ! Gardez-vous de tout amour des richesses, car la vie d'un homme ne dépend pas de ses biens, même s'il est très riche. »

¹⁶ Il leur raconta alors cette parabole : « Un homme riche avait des terres qui lui rapportèrent de bonnes récoltes. ¹⁷ Il réfléchissait et se demandait : "Que vais-je faire ? Je n'ai pas de place où amasser toutes

mes récoltes." [18] Puis il ajouta : "Voici ce que je vais faire : je vais démolir mes greniers, j'en construirai de plus grands, j'y amasserai tout mon blé et mes autres biens. [19] Ensuite, je me dirai à moi-même : Mon cher, tu as des biens en abondance pour de nombreuses années ; repose-toi, mange, bois et jouis de la vie." [20] Mais Dieu lui dit : "Insensé ! Cette nuit même tu cesseras de vivre. Et alors, pour qui sera tout ce que tu as accumulé ?" » [21] Jésus ajouta : « Ainsi en est-il de celui qui amasse des richesses pour lui-même, mais qui n'est pas riche aux yeux de Dieu. »

Avoir confiance en Dieu

[22] Puis Jésus dit à ses disciples : « Voilà pourquoi je vous dis : Ne vous inquiétez pas au sujet de la nourriture dont vous avez besoin pour vivre, ou au sujet des vêtements dont vous avez besoin pour votre corps. [23] Car la vie est plus importante que la nourriture et le corps plus important que les vêtements. [24] Regardez les corbeaux : ils ne sèment ni ne moissonnent, ils n'ont ni cave à provisions ni grenier, mais Dieu les nourrit ! Vous valez beaucoup plus que les oiseaux ! [25] Qui d'entre vous parvient à prolonger un peu la durée de sa vie par le souci qu'il se fait ? [26] Si donc vous ne pouvez rien pour ce qui est très peu de chose, pourquoi vous inquiétez-vous au sujet du reste ? [27] Regardez comment poussent les fleurs des champs : elles ne travaillent pas et ne tissent pas de vêtements. Pourtant, je vous le dis, même Salomon, avec toute sa richesse, n'a pas eu de vêtements aussi beaux qu'une seule de ces fleurs. [28] Dieu revêt ainsi l'herbe des champs qui est là aujourd'hui et qui demain sera jetée au feu : à combien plus forte raison vous vêtira-t-il vous-mêmes ! Comme votre confiance en lui est faible ! [29] Ne vous tourmentez donc pas à chercher continuellement ce que vous allez manger et boire. [30] Ce sont les païens de ce monde qui recherchent sans arrêt tout cela. Mais vous, vous avez un Père qui sait que vous en avez besoin. [31] Préoccupez-vous plutôt du Royaume de Dieu et Dieu vous accordera aussi le reste. »

Des richesses dans le ciel

[32] « N'aie pas peur, petit troupeau ! Car il a plu à votre Père de vous donner le Royaume. [33] Vendez vos biens et donnez l'argent aux pauvres. Munissez-vous de bourses qui ne s'usent pas, amassez-vous

des richesses dans les cieux, où elles ne disparaîtront jamais : les voleurs ne peuvent pas les y atteindre ni les vers les détruire. [34] Car votre cœur sera toujours là où sont vos richesses. »

Des serviteurs qui veillent

[35] « Soyez prêts à agir, avec la ceinture serrée autour de la taille et vos lampes allumées. [36] Soyez comme des serviteurs qui attendent leur maître au moment où il va revenir d'un mariage, afin de lui ouvrir la porte dès qu'il arrivera et frappera. [37] Heureux ces serviteurs que le maître, à son arrivée, trouvera éveillés ! Je vous le déclare, c'est la vérité : il attachera sa ceinture, les fera prendre place à table et viendra les servir. [38] S'il revient à minuit ou même plus tard encore et qu'il les trouve éveillés, heureux sont-ils ! [39] Comprenez bien ceci : si le maître de la maison savait à quelle heure le voleur doit venir, il ne le laisserait pas pénétrer dans la maison. [40] Tenez-vous prêts, vous aussi, car le Fils de l'homme viendra à l'heure que vous ne pensez pas. »

Le serviteur fidèle
et le serviteur infidèle

[41] Alors Pierre demanda : « Seigneur, dis-tu cette parabole pour nous seulement ou bien pour tout le monde ? »

[42] Le Seigneur répondit : « Quel est donc le serviteur fidèle et intelligent ? En voici un que son maître va charger de veiller sur la maison et de donner aux autres serviteurs leur part de nourriture au moment voulu. [43] Heureux ce serviteur si le maître, à son retour chez lui, le trouve occupé à ce travail ! [44] Je vous le déclare, c'est la vérité : le maître lui confiera la charge de tous ses biens. [45] Mais si le serviteur se dit : "Mon maître tarde à revenir", s'il se met alors à battre les autres serviteurs et les servantes, s'il mange, boit et s'enivre, [46] alors le maître reviendra un jour où le serviteur ne l'attend pas et à une heure qu'il ne connaît pas ; il chassera le serviteur et lui fera partager le sort des infidèles. [47] Le serviteur qui sait ce que veut son maître, mais ne se tient pas prêt à le faire, recevra de nombreux coups. [48] Par contre, le serviteur qui ne sait pas ce que veut son maître et agit de telle façon qu'il mérite d'être battu, recevra peu de coups. A qui l'on a beaucoup donné, on demandera beaucoup ; à qui l'on a confié beaucoup, on demandera encore plus. »

Jésus, cause de division

[49] « Je suis venu apporter un feu sur la terre et combien je voudrais qu'il soit déjà allumé ! [50] Je dois recevoir un baptême et quelle angoisse pour moi jusqu'à ce qu'il soit accompli ! [51] Pensez-vous que je sois venu apporter la paix sur la terre ? Non, je vous le dis, mais la division. [52] Dès maintenant, une famille de cinq personnes sera divisée, trois contre deux et deux contre trois. [53] Le père sera contre son fils et le fils contre son père, la mère contre sa fille et la fille contre sa mère, la belle-mère contre sa belle-fille et la belle-fille contre sa belle-mère. »

Comprendre le sens des temps

[54] Jésus disait aussi à la foule : « Quand vous voyez un nuage se lever à l'ouest, vous dites aussitôt : "Il va pleuvoir", et c'est ce qui arrive. [55] Et quand vous sentez souffler le vent du sud, vous dites : "Il va faire chaud", et c'est ce qui arrive. [56] Hypocrites ! Vous êtes capables de comprendre ce que signifient les aspects de la terre et du ciel ; alors, pourquoi ne comprenez-vous pas le sens du temps présent ? »

Trouver un arrangement avec son adversaire

[57] « Pourquoi ne jugez-vous pas par vous-mêmes de la juste façon d'agir ? [58] Si tu es en procès avec quelqu'un et que vous alliez ensemble au tribunal, efforce-toi de trouver un arrangement avec lui pendant que vous êtes en chemin. Tu éviteras ainsi que ton adversaire ne te traîne devant le juge, que le juge ne te livre à la police et que la police ne te jette en prison. [59] Tu ne sortiras pas de là, je te l'affirme, tant que tu n'auras pas payé ta dette jusqu'au dernier centime. »

Changer de comportement ou mourir

13 En ce temps-là, quelques personnes vinrent raconter à Jésus comment Pilate avait fait tuer des Galiléens au moment où ils offraient des sacrifices à Dieu. [2] Jésus leur répondit : « Pensez-vous que si ces Galiléens ont été ainsi massacrés, cela signifie qu'ils étaient de plus grands pécheurs que tous les autres Galiléens ? [3] Non, vous dis-je ; mais si vous ne changez pas de comportement, vous mourrez tous comme eux. [4] Et ces dix-huit personnes que la tour de Siloé a écrasées en s'écroulant, pensez-vous qu'elles étaient plus coupables que tous les autres habitants de Jérusalem ? ⁵ Non, vous dis-je ; mais si vous ne changez pas de comportement, vous mourrez tous comme eux. »

La parabole du figuier sans figues

⁶ Puis Jésus leur dit cette parabole : « Un homme avait un figuier planté dans sa vigne. Il vint y chercher des figues, mais n'en trouva pas. ⁷ Il dit alors au vigneron : "Regarde : depuis trois ans je viens chercher des figues sur ce figuier et je n'en trouve pas. Coupe-le donc ! Pourquoi occupe-t-il du terrain inutilement ?" ⁸ Mais le vigneron lui répondit : "Maître, laisse-le cette année encore ; je vais creuser la terre tout autour et j'y mettrai du fumier. ⁹ Ainsi, il donnera peut-être des figues l'année prochaine ; sinon, tu le feras couper." »

Jésus guérit une femme infirme le jour du sabbat

¹⁰ Un jour de sabbat, Jésus enseignait dans une synagogue. ¹¹ Une femme malade se trouvait là : depuis dix-huit ans, un esprit mauvais la tenait courbée et elle était totalement incapable de se redresser. ¹² Quand Jésus vit cette femme, il l'appela et lui dit : « Tu es délivrée de ta maladie. » ¹³ Il posa les mains sur elle et, aussitôt, elle se redressa et se mit à louer Dieu. ¹⁴ Mais le chef de la synagogue était indigné de ce que Jésus avait accompli une guérison le jour du sabbat. Il s'adressa alors à la foule : « Il y a six jours pendant lesquels on doit travailler ; venez donc vous faire guérir ces jours-là et non le jour du sabbat ! » ¹⁵ Le Seigneur lui répondit en ces mots : « Hypocrites que vous êtes ! Le jour du sabbat, chacun de vous détache de la crèche son bœuf ou son âne pour le mener boire, n'est-ce pas ? ¹⁶ Et cette femme, descendante d'Abraham, que Satan a tenue liée pendant dix-huit ans, ne fallait-il pas la détacher de ses liens le jour du sabbat ? » ¹⁷ Cette réponse de Jésus remplit de honte tous ses adversaires ; mais la foule entière se réjouissait de toutes les œuvres magnifiques qu'il accomplissait.

La parabole de la graine de moutarde

¹⁸ Jésus dit : « A quoi le Royaume de Dieu ressemble-t-il ? A quoi puis-je le comparer ? ¹⁹ Il ressemble à une graine de moutarde qu'un homme a prise et mise en terre dans son jardin : elle a poussé, elle est devenue un arbre et les oiseaux ont fait leurs nids dans ses branches. »

La parabole du levain

²⁰ Jésus dit encore : « A quoi puis-je comparer le Royaume de Dieu ? ²¹ Il ressemble au levain qu'une femme prend et mêle à une grande quantité de farine, si bien que toute la pâte lève. »

La porte étroite

²² Jésus traversait villes et villages et enseignait en faisant route vers Jérusalem. ²³ Quelqu'un lui demanda : « Maître, n'y a-t-il que peu de gens qui seront sauvés ? » Jésus répondit : ²⁴ « Efforcez-vous d'entrer par la porte étroite ; car, je vous l'affirme, beaucoup essaieront d'entrer et ne le pourront pas.

²⁵ « Quand le maître de maison se sera levé et aura fermé la porte à clé, vous vous trouverez dehors, vous vous mettrez à frapper à la porte et à dire : "Maître, ouvre-nous." Il vous répondra : "Je ne sais pas d'où vous êtes !" ²⁶ Alors, vous allez lui dire : "Nous avons mangé et bu avec toi, tu as enseigné dans les rues de notre ville." ²⁷ Il vous dira de nouveau : "Je ne sais pas d'où vous êtes. Écartez-vous de moi, vous tous qui commettez le mal !" ²⁸ C'est là que vous pleurerez et grincerez des dents, quand vous verrez Abraham, Isaac, Jacob et tous les prophètes dans le Royaume de Dieu et que vous serez jetés dehors ! ²⁹ Des hommes viendront de l'est et de l'ouest, du nord et du sud et prendront place à table dans le Royaume de Dieu. ³⁰ Et alors, certains de ceux qui sont maintenant les derniers seront les premiers et d'autres qui sont maintenant les premiers seront les derniers. »

Jésus et Jérusalem

³¹ A ce moment-là, quelques Pharisiens s'approchèrent de Jésus et lui dirent : « Pars d'ici, va-t'en ailleurs, car Hérode veut te faire mourir. » ³² Jésus leur répondit : « Allez dire à cette espèce de renard : "Je chasse des esprits mauvais et j'accomplis des guérisons aujourd'hui et demain, et le troisième jour j'achève mon œuvre." ³³ Mais il faut que je continue ma route aujourd'hui, demain et le jour suivant, car il ne convient pas qu'un prophète soit mis à mort ailleurs qu'à Jérusalem.

³⁴ « Jérusalem, Jérusalem, toi qui mets à mort les prophètes et tues à coups de pierres ceux que Dieu t'envoie ! Combien de fois ai-je dé-

siré rassembler tes habitants auprès de moi comme une poule rassemble ses poussins sous ses ailes, mais vous ne l'avez pas voulu ! ³⁵ Eh bien, votre maison va être abandonnée. Je vous le déclare : vous ne me verrez plus jusqu'à ce que vienne le moment où vous direz : "Que Dieu bénisse celui qui vient au nom du Seigneur !" »

Jésus guérit un malade

14 Un jour de sabbat, Jésus se rendit chez un des chefs des Pharisiens pour y prendre un repas. Ceux qui étaient là observaient attentivement Jésus. ² Un homme atteint d'hydropisie se tenait devant lui. ³ Jésus prit la parole et demanda aux maîtres de la loi et aux Pharisiens : « Notre loi permet-elle ou non de faire une guérison le jour du sabbat ? » ⁴ Mais ils ne voulurent pas répondre. Alors Jésus toucha le malade, le guérit et le renvoya. ⁵ Puis il leur dit : « Si l'un de vous a un fils ou un bœuf qui tombe dans un puits, ne va-t-il pas l'en retirer aussitôt, même le jour du sabbat ? » ⁶ Ils furent incapables de répondre à cela.

La façon de choisir une place et la façon d'inviter

⁷ Jésus remarqua comment les invités choisissaient les meilleures places. Il dit alors à tous cette parabole : ⁸ « Lorsque quelqu'un t'invite à un repas de mariage, ne va pas t'asseoir à la meilleure place. Il se pourrait en effet que quelqu'un de plus important que toi ait été invité ⁹ et que celui qui vous a invités l'un et l'autre vienne te dire : "Laisse-lui cette place." Alors tu devrais, tout honteux, te mettre à la dernière place. ¹⁰ Au contraire, lorsque tu es invité, va t'installer à la dernière place, pour qu'au moment où viendra celui qui t'a invité, il te dise : "Mon ami, viens t'asseoir à une meilleure place." Ainsi, ce sera pour toi un honneur devant tous ceux qui seront à table avec toi. ¹¹ En effet, quiconque s'élève sera abaissé, et celui qui s'abaisse sera élevé. »

¹² Puis Jésus dit à celui qui l'avait invité : « Quand tu donnes un déjeuner ou un dîner, n'invite ni tes amis, ni tes frères, ni les membres de ta parenté, ni tes riches voisins ; car ils pourraient t'inviter à leur tour et tu serais ainsi payé pour ce que tu as donné. ¹³ Mais quand tu offres un repas de fête, invite les pauvres, les infirmes, les boiteux et les aveugles. ¹⁴ Tu seras heureux, car ils ne peuvent pas te le rendre. Dieu te le rendra lorsque ceux qui ont fait le bien se relèveront de la mort. »

La parabole du grand repas

[15] Après avoir entendu ces mots, un de ceux qui étaient à table dit à Jésus : « Heureux celui qui prendra son repas dans le Royaume de Dieu ! » [16] Jésus lui raconta cette parabole : « Un homme offrit un grand repas auquel il invita beaucoup de monde. [17] A l'heure du repas, il envoya son serviteur dire aux invités : "Venez, car c'est prêt maintenant." [18] Mais tous, l'un après l'autre, se mirent à s'excuser. Le premier dit au serviteur : "J'ai acheté un champ et il faut que j'aille le voir ; je te prie de m'excuser." [19] Un autre lui dit : "J'ai acheté cinq paires de bœufs et je vais les essayer ; je te prie de m'excuser." [20] Un autre encore dit : "Je viens de me marier et c'est pourquoi je ne peux pas y aller." [21] Le serviteur retourna auprès de son maître et lui rapporta ces réponses. Le maître de la maison se mit en colère et dit à son serviteur : "Va vite sur les places et dans les rues de la ville, et amène ici les pauvres, les infirmes, les aveugles et les boiteux." [22] Après un moment, le serviteur vint dire : "Maître, tes ordres ont été exécutés, mais il y a encore de la place." [23] Le maître dit alors à son serviteur : "Va sur les chemins de campagne, le long des haies, et oblige les gens à entrer, afin que ma maison soit remplie. [24] Je vous le dis : aucun de ceux qui avaient été invités ne mangera de mon repas !" »

Les conditions nécessaires pour être disciple

[25] Une foule immense faisait route avec Jésus. Il se retourna et dit à tous : [26] « Celui qui vient à moi doit me préférer à son père, sa mère, sa femme, ses enfants, ses frères, ses sœurs, et même à sa propre personne. Sinon, il ne peut pas être mon disciple. [27] Celui qui ne porte pas sa croix pour me suivre ne peut pas être mon disciple. [28] Si l'un de vous veut construire une tour, il s'assied d'abord pour calculer la dépense et voir s'il a assez d'argent pour achever le travail. [29] Autrement, s'il pose les fondations sans pouvoir achever la tour, tous ceux qui verront cela se mettront à rire de lui [30] en disant : "Cet homme a commencé de construire mais a été incapable d'achever le travail !" [31] De même, si un roi veut partir en guerre contre un autre roi, il s'assied d'abord pour examiner s'il peut, avec dix mille hommes, affronter son adversaire qui marche contre lui avec vingt mille hommes. [32] S'il ne le peut pas, il envoie des messagers à l'autre roi, pendant qu'il est

encore loin, pour lui demander ses conditions de paix. ³³ Ainsi donc, ajouta Jésus, aucun de vous ne peut être mon disciple s'il ne renonce pas à tout ce qu'il possède. »

Le sel inutile

³⁴ « Le sel est une bonne chose. Mais s'il perd son goût, comment pourrait-on le lui rendre ? ³⁵ Il n'est alors bon ni pour la terre, ni pour le fumier ; on le jette dehors. Écoutez bien, si vous avez des oreilles pour entendre ! »

La parabole du mouton perdu et retrouvé

15 Les collecteurs d'impôts et autres gens de mauvaise réputation s'approchaient tous de Jésus pour l'écouter. ² Les Pharisiens et les maîtres de la loi critiquaient Jésus ; ils disaient : « Cet homme fait bon accueil aux gens de mauvaise réputation et mange avec eux ! » ⁴ « Si quelqu'un parmi vous possède cent moutons et qu'il perde l'un d'entre eux, ne va-t-il pas laisser les quatre-vingt-dix-neuf autres dans leur pâturage pour partir à la recherche de celui qui est perdu jusqu'à ce qu'il le retrouve ? ⁵ Et quand il l'a retrouvé, il est tout joyeux : il met le mouton sur ses épaules, ⁶ il rentre chez lui, puis appelle ses amis et ses voisins et leur dit : "Réjouissez-vous avec moi, car j'ai retrouvé mon mouton, celui qui était perdu !" ⁷ De même, je vous le dis, il y aura plus de joie dans le ciel pour un seul pécheur qui commence une vie nouvelle que pour quatre-vingt-dix-neuf justes qui n'en ont pas besoin. »

La pièce d'argent perdue et retrouvée

⁸ « Ou bien, si une femme possède dix pièces d'argent et qu'elle en perde une, ne va-t-elle pas allumer une lampe, balayer la maison et chercher avec soin jusqu'à ce qu'elle la retrouve ? ⁹ Et quand elle l'a retrouvée, elle appelle ses amies et ses voisines et leur dit : "Réjouissez-vous avec moi, car j'ai retrouvé la pièce d'argent que j'avais perdue !" ¹⁰ De même, je vous le dis, il y a de la joie parmi les anges de Dieu pour un seul pécheur qui commence une vie nouvelle. »

Le fils perdu et retrouvé

¹¹ Jésus dit encore : « Un homme avait deux fils. ¹² Le plus jeune dit à son père : "Mon père, donne-moi la part de notre fortune qui doit

me revenir." Alors le père partagea ses biens entre ses deux fils. ¹³ Peu de jours après, le plus jeune fils vendit sa part de la propriété et partit avec son argent pour un pays éloigné. Là, il vécut dans le désordre et dissipa ainsi tout ce qu'il possédait. ¹⁴ Quand il eut tout dépensé, une grande famine survint dans ce pays, et il commença à manquer du nécessaire. ¹⁵ Il alla donc se mettre au service d'un des habitants du pays, qui l'envoya dans ses champs garder les cochons. ¹⁶ Il aurait bien voulu se nourrir des fruits du caroubier que mangeaient les cochons, mais personne ne lui en donnait. ¹⁷ Alors, il se mit à réfléchir sur sa situation et se dit : "Tous les ouvriers de mon père ont plus à manger qu'ils ne leur en faut, tandis que moi, ici, je meurs de faim ! ¹⁸ Je veux repartir chez mon père et je lui dirai : Mon père, j'ai péché contre Dieu et contre toi, ¹⁹ je ne suis plus digne que tu me regardes comme ton fils. Traite-moi donc comme l'un de tes ouvriers." ²⁰ Et il repartit chez son père.

« Tandis qu'il était encore assez loin de la maison, son père le vit et en eut profondément pitié : il courut à sa rencontre, le serra contre lui et l'embrassa. ²¹ Le fils lui dit alors : "Mon père, j'ai péché contre Dieu et contre toi, je ne suis plus digne que tu me regardes comme ton fils..." ²² Mais le père dit à ses serviteurs : "Dépêchez-vous d'apporter la plus belle robe et mettez-la-lui ; passez-lui une bague au doigt et des chaussures aux pieds. ²³ Amenez le veau que nous avons engraissé et tuez-le ; nous allons faire un festin et nous réjouir, ²⁴ car mon fils que voici était mort et il est revenu à la vie, il était perdu et je l'ai retrouvé." Et ils commencèrent la fête.

²⁵ « Pendant ce temps, le fils aîné de cet homme était aux champs. A son retour, quand il approcha de la maison, il entendit un bruit de musique et de danses. ²⁶ Il appela un des serviteurs et lui demanda ce qui se passait. ²⁷ Le serviteur lui répondit : "Ton frère est revenu, et ton père a fait tuer le veau que nous avons engraissé, parce qu'il a retrouvé son fils en bonne santé." ²⁸ Le fils aîné se mit alors en colère et refusa d'entrer dans la maison. Son père sortit pour le prier d'entrer. ²⁹ Mais le fils répondit à son père : "Écoute, il y a tant d'années que je te sers sans avoir jamais désobéi à l'un de tes ordres. Pourtant, tu ne m'as jamais donné même un chevreau pour que je fasse la fête avec mes amis. ³⁰ Mais quand ton fils que voilà revient, lui qui a dépensé entièrement ta fortune avec des prostituées, pour lui tu fais tuer le

veau que nous avons engraissé !" ³¹ Le père lui dit : "Mon enfant, tu es toujours avec moi, et tout ce que je possède est aussi à toi. ³² Mais nous devions faire une fête et nous réjouir, car ton frère que voici était mort et il est revenu à la vie, il était perdu et le voilà retrouvé !" »

Le gérant habile

16 Jésus dit à ses disciples : « Un homme riche avait un gérant et l'on vint lui rapporter que ce gérant gaspillait ses biens. ² Le maître l'appela et lui dit : "Qu'est-ce que j'apprends à ton sujet ? Présente-moi les comptes de ta gestion, car tu ne pourras plus être mon gérant." ³ Le gérant se dit en lui-même : "Mon maître va me retirer ma charge. Que faire ? Je ne suis pas assez fort pour travailler la terre et j'aurais honte de mendier. ⁴ Ah ! je sais ce que je vais faire ! Et quand j'aurai perdu ma place, des gens me recevront chez eux !" ⁵ Il fit alors venir un à un tous ceux qui devaient quelque chose à son maître. Il dit au premier : "Combien dois-tu à mon maître ?" ⁶ – "Cent tonneaux d'huile d'olive", lui répondit-il. Le gérant lui dit : "Voici ton compte ; vite, assieds-toi et note cinquante." ⁷ Puis il dit à un autre : "Et toi, combien dois-tu ?" – "Cent sacs de blé", répondit-il. Le gérant lui dit : "Voici ton compte ; note quatre-vingts." ⁸ Eh bien, le maître loua le gérant malhonnête d'avoir agi si habilement. En effet, les gens de ce monde sont bien plus habiles dans leurs rapports les uns avec les autres que ceux qui appartiennent à la lumière. »

⁹ Jésus ajouta : « Et moi je vous dis : faites-vous des amis avec les richesses trompeuses de ce monde, afin qu'au moment où elles n'existeront plus pour vous on vous reçoive dans les demeures éternelles. ¹⁰ Celui qui est fidèle dans les petites choses est aussi fidèle dans les grandes ; celui qui est malhonnête dans les petites choses est aussi malhonnête dans les grandes. ¹¹ Si donc vous n'avez pas été fidèles dans votre façon d'utiliser les richesses trompeuses de ce monde, qui pourrait vous confier les vraies richesses ? ¹² Et si vous n'avez pas été fidèles en ce qui concerne le bien des autres, qui vous donnera le bien qui vous est destiné ?

¹³ « Aucun serviteur ne peut servir deux maîtres : ou bien il haïra le premier et aimera le second ; ou bien il s'attachera au premier et méprisera le second. Vous ne pouvez pas servir à la fois Dieu et l'argent. »

Diverses déclarations de Jésus

¹⁴ Les Pharisiens entendaient toutes ces paroles et se moquaient de Jésus, car ils aimaient l'argent. ¹⁵ Jésus leur dit : « Vous êtes des gens qui se font passer pour justes aux yeux des hommes, mais Dieu connaît vos cœurs. Car ce que les hommes considèrent comme grand est détestable aux yeux de Dieu.

¹⁶ « Le temps de la loi de Moïse et des livres des Prophètes a duré jusqu'à l'époque de Jean-Baptiste. Depuis cette époque, la Bonne Nouvelle du Royaume de Dieu est annoncée et chacun use de force pour y entrer. ¹⁷ Mais le ciel et la terre peuvent disparaître plus facilement que le plus petit détail de la loi.

¹⁸ « Tout homme qui renvoie sa femme et en épouse une autre commet un adultère, et celui qui épouse une femme renvoyée par son mari commet un adultère. »

L'homme riche et Lazare

¹⁹ « Il y avait une fois un homme riche qui s'habillait des vêtements les plus fins et les plus coûteux et qui, chaque jour, vivait dans le luxe en faisant de bons repas. ²⁰ Devant la porte de sa maison était couché un pauvre homme, appelé Lazare. Son corps était couvert de plaies. ²¹ Il aurait bien voulu se nourrir des morceaux qui tombaient de la table du riche. De plus, les chiens venaient lécher ses plaies. ²² Le pauvre mourut et les anges le portèrent auprès d'Abraham. Le riche mourut aussi et on l'enterra. ²³ Il souffrait beaucoup dans le monde des morts ; il leva les yeux et vit de loin Abraham et Lazare à côté de lui. ²⁴ Alors il s'écria : "Père Abraham, aie pitié de moi ; envoie donc Lazare tremper le bout de son doigt dans de l'eau pour me rafraîchir la langue, car je souffre beaucoup dans ce feu." ²⁵ Mais Abraham dit : "Mon enfant, souviens-toi que tu as reçu beaucoup de biens pendant ta vie, tandis que Lazare a eu beaucoup de malheurs. Maintenant, il reçoit ici sa consolation, tandis que toi tu souffres. ²⁶ De plus, il y a un profond abîme entre vous et nous ; ainsi, ceux qui voudraient passer d'ici vers vous ne le peuvent pas et l'on ne peut pas non plus parvenir jusqu'à nous de là où tu es." ²⁷ Le riche dit : "Je t'en prie, père, envoie donc Lazare dans la maison de mon père, ²⁸ où j'ai cinq frères. Qu'il aille les avertir, afin qu'ils ne viennent pas eux aussi dans ce lieu de souffrances." ²⁹ Abraham ré-

pondit: "Tes frères ont Moïse et les prophètes pour les avertir: qu'ils les écoutent!" [30] Le riche dit: "Cela ne suffit pas, père Abraham. Mais si quelqu'un revient de chez les morts et va les trouver, alors ils changeront de comportement." [31] Mais Abraham lui dit: "S'ils ne veulent pas écouter Moïse et les prophètes, ils ne se laisseront pas persuader même si quelqu'un se relevait d'entre les morts." »

Le péché et le pardon

17 Jésus dit à ses disciples: « Il est inévitable qu'il y ait des faits qui entraînent les hommes à pécher. Mais malheur à celui qui en est la cause! [2] Il vaudrait mieux pour lui qu'on lui attache au cou une grosse pierre et qu'on le jette dans la mer, plutôt que de faire tomber dans le péché un seul de ces petits. [3] Prenez bien garde! Si ton frère se rend coupable, parle-lui sérieusement. Et s'il regrette son acte, pardonne-lui. [4] S'il se rend coupable à ton égard sept fois en un jour et que chaque fois il revienne te dire: "Je le regrette", tu lui pardonneras. »

La foi

[5] Les apôtres dirent au Seigneur: « Augmente notre foi. » [6] Le Seigneur répondit: « Si vous aviez de la foi gros comme un grain de moutarde, vous pourriez dire à cet arbre, ce mûrier: "Déracine-toi et va te planter dans la mer", et il vous obéirait. »

Le devoir du serviteur

[7] « Supposons ceci: l'un d'entre vous a un serviteur qui laboure ou qui garde les troupeaux. Lorsqu'il le voit revenir des champs, va-t-il lui dire: "Viens vite te mettre à table?" [8] Non, il lui dira plutôt: "Prépare mon repas, puis change de vêtements pour me servir pendant que je mange et bois; après quoi, tu pourras manger et boire à ton tour." [9] Il n'a pas à remercier son serviteur d'avoir fait ce qui lui était ordonné, n'est-ce pas? [10] Il en va de même pour vous: quand vous aurez fait tout ce qui vous est ordonné, dites: "Nous sommes de simples serviteurs; nous n'avons fait que notre devoir." »

Jésus guérit dix lépreux

[11] Tandis que Jésus faisait route vers Jérusalem, il passa le long de la frontière qui sépare la Samarie et la Galilée. [12] Il entrait dans un villa-

ge quand dix lépreux vinrent à sa rencontre. Ils se tinrent à distance [13] et se mirent à crier : « Jésus, Maître, aie pitié de nous ! » [14] Jésus les vit et leur dit : « Allez vous faire examiner par les prêtres. » Pendant qu'ils y allaient, ils furent guéris. [15] L'un d'entre eux, quand il vit qu'il était guéri, revint sur ses pas en louant Dieu à haute voix. [16] Il se jeta aux pieds de Jésus, le visage contre terre, et le remercia. Cet homme était Samaritain. [17] Jésus dit alors : « Tous les dix ont été guéris, n'est-ce pas ? Où sont les neuf autres ? [18] Personne n'a-t-il pensé à revenir pour remercier Dieu, sinon cet étranger ? » [19] Puis Jésus lui dit : « Relève-toi et va ; ta foi t'a sauvé. »

La venue du Royaume

[20] Les Pharisiens demandèrent à Jésus quand viendrait le Royaume de Dieu. Il leur répondit : « Le Royaume de Dieu ne vient pas de façon spectaculaire. [21] On ne dira pas : "Voyez, il est ici !" ou bien : "Il est là !" Car, sachez-le, le Royaume de Dieu est au milieu de vous. »

[22] Puis il dit aux disciples : « Le temps viendra où vous désirerez voir le Fils de l'homme même un seul jour, mais vous ne le verrez pas. [23] On vous dira : "Regardez là !" ou : "Regardez ici !" Mais n'y allez pas, n'y courez pas. [24] Comme l'éclair brille à travers le ciel et l'illumine d'une extrémité à l'autre, ainsi sera le Fils de l'homme en son jour. [25] Mais il faut d'abord qu'il souffre beaucoup et qu'il soit rejeté par les gens d'aujourd'hui. [26] Ce qui s'est passé du temps de Noé se passera de la même façon aux jours du Fils de l'homme. [27] Les gens mangeaient et buvaient, se mariaient ou étaient donnés en mariage, jusqu'au jour où Noé entra dans l'arche : la grande inondation vint alors et les fit tous périr. [28] Ce sera comme du temps de Loth : les gens mangeaient et buvaient, achetaient et vendaient, plantaient et bâtissaient ; [29] mais le jour où Loth quitta Sodome, il tomba du ciel une pluie de soufre enflammé qui les fit tous périr. [30] Il se passera la même chose le jour où le Fils de l'homme doit apparaître.

[31] « En ce jour-là, celui qui sera sur la terrasse de sa maison et aura ses affaires à l'intérieur, ne devra pas descendre pour les prendre ; de même, celui qui sera dans les champs ne devra pas retourner dans sa maison. [32] Rappelez-vous la femme de Loth ! [33] Celui qui cherchera à préserver sa vie la perdra ; mais celui qui perdra sa vie la conserve-

ra. ³⁴ Je vous le déclare, en cette nuit-là, deux personnes seront dans un même lit : l'une sera emmenée et l'autre laissée. ³⁵ Deux femmes moudront du grain ensemble : l'une sera emmenée et l'autre laissée. » [³⁶ Deux hommes seront dans un champ : l'un sera emmené et l'autre laissé.] ³⁷ Les disciples lui demandèrent : «Où cela se passera-t-il, Seigneur ? » Et il répondit : « Où sera le cadavre, là aussi se rassembleront les vautours. »

La parabole de la veuve et du juge

18 Jésus leur dit ensuite cette parabole pour leur montrer qu'ils devaient toujours prier, sans jamais se décourager : ² « Il y avait dans une ville un juge qui ne se souciait pas de Dieu et n'avait d'égards pour personne. ³ Il y avait aussi dans cette ville une veuve qui venait fréquemment le trouver pour obtenir justice : "Rends-moi justice contre mon adversaire", disait-elle. ⁴ Pendant longtemps, le juge refusa, puis il se dit : "Bien sûr, je ne me soucie pas de Dieu et je n'ai d'égards pour personne ; ⁵ mais comme cette veuve me fatigue, je vais faire reconnaître ses droits, sinon, à force de venir, elle finira par m'exaspérer." » ⁶ Puis le Seigneur ajouta : « Écoutez ce que dit ce juge indigne ! ⁷ Et Dieu, lui, ne ferait-il pas justice aux siens quand ils crient à lui jour et nuit ? Tardera-t-il à les aider ? ⁸ Je vous le déclare : il leur fera justice rapidement. Mais quand le Fils de l'homme viendra, trouvera-t-il la foi sur la terre ? »

La parabole du Pharisien et du collecteur d'impôts

⁹ Jésus dit la parabole suivante à l'intention de ceux qui se croyaient justes aux yeux de Dieu et méprisaient les autres : ¹⁰ « Deux hommes montèrent au temple pour prier ; l'un était Pharisien, l'autre collecteur d'impôts. ¹¹ Le Pharisien, debout, priait ainsi en lui-même : "O Dieu, je te remercie de ce que je ne suis pas comme le reste des hommes, qui sont voleurs, mauvais et adultères ; je te remercie de ce que je ne suis pas comme ce collecteur d'impôts. ¹² Je jeûne deux jours par semaine et je te donne le dixième de tous mes revenus." ¹³ Le collecteur d'impôts, lui, se tenait à distance et n'osait pas même lever les yeux vers le ciel, mais il se frappait la poitrine et disait : "O Dieu, aie pitié de moi, qui suis un pécheur." ¹⁴ Je vous le dis, ajouta Jésus, cet homme était en règle avec Dieu quand il retourna chez lui, mais pas le Pharisien. En effet, quiconque s'élève sera abaissé, mais celui qui s'abaisse sera élevé. »

Jésus bénit des petits enfants

¹⁵ Des gens amenèrent à Jésus même des bébés pour qu'il pose les mains sur eux. En voyant cela, les disciples leur firent des reproches. ¹⁶ Mais Jésus fit approcher les enfants et dit : « Laissez les enfants venir à moi ! Ne les en empêchez pas, car le Royaume de Dieu appartient à ceux qui sont comme eux. ¹⁷ Je vous le déclare, c'est la vérité : celui qui ne reçoit pas le Royaume de Dieu comme un enfant ne pourra jamais y entrer. »

L'homme riche

¹⁸ Un chef juif demanda à Jésus : « Bon maître, que dois-je faire pour obtenir la vie éternelle ? » ¹⁹ Jésus lui dit : « Pourquoi m'appelles-tu bon ? Personne n'est bon si ce n'est Dieu seul. ²⁰ Tu connais les commandements : "Ne commets pas d'adultère ; ne commets pas de meurtre ; ne vole pas ; ne prononce pas de faux témoignage contre quelqu'un ; respecte ton père et ta mère." » ²¹ L'homme répondit : « J'ai obéi à tous ces commandements depuis ma jeunesse. » ²² Après avoir entendu cela, Jésus lui dit : « Il te manque encore une chose : vends tout ce que tu as et distribue l'argent aux pauvres, alors tu auras des richesses dans les cieux ; puis viens et suis-moi. » ²³ Mais quand l'homme entendit ces mots, il devint tout triste, car il était très riche. ²⁴ Jésus vit qu'il était triste et dit : « Qu'il est difficile aux riches d'entrer dans le Royaume de Dieu ! ²⁵ Il est difficile à un chameau de passer par le trou d'une aiguille, mais il est encore plus difficile à un riche d'entrer dans le Royaume de Dieu. » ²⁶ Ceux qui l'écoutaient dirent : « Mais qui donc peut être sauvé ? » ²⁷ Jésus répondit : « Ce qui est impossible aux hommes est possible à Dieu. » ²⁸ Pierre dit alors : « Écoute, nous avons quitté ce que nous avions pour te suivre. » ²⁹ Jésus leur dit : « Je vous le déclare, c'est la vérité : si quelqu'un quitte, pour le Royaume de Dieu, sa maison, ou sa femme, ses frères, ses parents, ses enfants, ³⁰ il recevra beaucoup plus dans le temps présent et dans le monde futur il recevra la vie éternelle. »

Jésus annonce une troisième fois sa mort et sa résurrection

³¹ Jésus prit les douze disciples avec lui et leur dit : « Écoutez, nous allons à Jérusalem où se réalisera tout ce que les prophètes ont écrit

au sujet du Fils de l'homme. ³² On le livrera aux païens, qui se moqueront de lui, l'insulteront et cracheront sur lui. ³³ Ils le frapperont à coups de fouet et le mettront à mort. Et le troisième jour il se relèvera de la mort. » ³⁴ Mais les disciples ne comprirent rien à cela ; le sens de ces paroles leur était caché et ils ne savaient pas de quoi Jésus parlait.

Jésus guérit un aveugle

³⁵ Jésus approchait de Jéricho. Or, un aveugle était assis au bord du chemin et mendiait. ³⁶ Il entendit la foule qui avançait et demanda ce que c'était. ³⁷ On lui apprit que Jésus de Nazareth passait par là. ³⁸ Alors il s'écria : « Jésus, Fils de David, aie pitié de moi ! » ³⁹ Ceux qui marchaient en avant lui faisaient des reproches pour qu'il se taise, mais il criait encore plus fort : « Fils de David, aie pitié de moi ! » ⁴⁰ Jésus s'arrêta et ordonna qu'on le lui amène. Quand l'aveugle se fut approché, Jésus lui demanda : ⁴¹ « Que veux-tu que je fasse pour toi ? » Il répondit : « Maître, fais que je voie de nouveau. » ⁴² Et Jésus lui dit : « Eh bien, ta foi t'a guéri. » ⁴³ Aussitôt, il put voir, et il suivait Jésus en louant Dieu. Toute la foule vit cela et se mit aussi à louer Dieu.

Jésus et Zachée

19 Après être entré dans Jéricho, Jésus traversait la ville. ² Il y avait là un homme appelé Zachée ; c'était le chef des collecteurs d'impôts et il était riche. ³ Il cherchait à voir qui était Jésus, mais comme il était de petite taille, il ne pouvait pas y parvenir à cause de la foule. ⁴ Il courut alors en avant et grimpa sur un arbre, un sycomore, pour voir Jésus qui devait passer par là. ⁵ Quand Jésus arriva à cet endroit, il leva les yeux et dit à Zachée : « Dépêche-toi de descendre, Zachée, car il faut que je loge chez toi aujourd'hui. » ⁶ Zachée se dépêcha de descendre et le reçut avec joie. ⁷ En voyant cela, tous critiquaient Jésus ; ils disaient : « Cet homme est allé loger chez un pécheur ! » ⁸ Zachée, debout devant le Seigneur, lui dit : « Écoute, Maître, je vais donner la moitié de mes biens aux pauvres, et si j'ai pris trop d'argent à quelqu'un, je vais lui rendre quatre fois autant. » ⁹ Jésus lui dit : « Aujourd'hui, le salut est entré dans cette maison, parce que tu es, toi aussi, un descendant d'Abraham. ¹⁰ Car le Fils de l'homme est venu chercher et sauver ceux qui étaient perdus. »

La parabole des pièces d'or

[11] Jésus dit encore une parabole pour ceux qui venaient d'entendre ces paroles. Il était en effet près de Jérusalem et l'on pensait que le Royaume de Dieu allait se manifester d'un instant à l'autre. [12] Voici donc ce qu'il dit : « Un homme de famille noble se rendit dans un pays éloigné pour y être nommé roi ; il devait revenir ensuite. [13] Avant de partir, il appela dix de ses serviteurs, leur remit à chacun une pièce d'or de grande valeur et leur dit : "Faites des affaires avec cet argent jusqu'à mon retour." [14] Mais les gens de son pays le haïssaient ; ils envoyèrent une délégation derrière lui pour dire : "Nous ne voulons pas de lui comme roi." [15] Il fut pourtant nommé roi et revint dans son pays. Il fit alors appeler les serviteurs auxquels il avait remis l'argent, pour savoir ce qu'ils avaient gagné. [16] Le premier se présenta et dit : "Maître, j'ai gagné dix pièces d'or avec celle que tu m'as donnée." [17] Le roi lui dit : "C'est bien, bon serviteur ; puisque tu as été fidèle dans de petites choses, je te nomme gouverneur de dix villes." [18] Le deuxième serviteur vint et dit : "Maître, j'ai gagné cinq pièces d'or avec celle que tu m'as donnée." [19] Le roi dit à celui-là : "Toi, je te nomme gouverneur de cinq villes." [20] Un autre serviteur vint et dit : "Maître, voici ta pièce d'or ; je l'ai gardée cachée dans un mouchoir. [21] J'avais peur de toi, car tu es un homme dur : tu prends ce que tu n'as pas déposé, tu moissonnes ce que tu n'as pas semé." [22] Le roi lui dit : "Mauvais serviteur, je vais te juger sur tes propres paroles. Tu savais que je suis un homme dur, que je prends ce que je n'ai pas déposé et moissonne ce que je n'ai pas semé. [23] Alors, pourquoi n'as-tu pas placé mon argent dans une banque ? A mon retour, j'aurais pu le retirer avec les intérêts." [24] Puis il dit à ceux qui étaient là : "Enlevez-lui cette pièce d'or et remettez-la à celui qui en a dix." [25] Ils lui dirent : "Maître, il a déjà dix pièces !" [26] "Je vous l'affirme, répondit-il, à celui qui a quelque chose l'on donnera davantage ; tandis qu'à celui qui n'a rien on enlèvera même le peu qui pourrait lui rester. [27] Quant à mes ennemis qui n'ont pas voulu de moi comme roi, amenez-les ici et exécutez-les devant moi." »

Jésus se rend à Jérusalem

[28] Après avoir ainsi parlé, Jésus partit en tête de la foule sur le chemin qui monte à Jérusalem. [29] Lorsqu'il approcha de Bethfagé et de Bétha-

nie, près de la colline appelée mont des Oliviers, il envoya en avant deux disciples : [30] « Allez au village qui est en face, leur dit-il. Quand vous y serez arrivés, vous trouverez un petit âne attaché, sur lequel personne ne s'est jamais assis. Détachez-le et amenez-le ici. [31] Et si quelqu'un vous demande : "Pourquoi le détachez-vous ?", dites-lui : "Le Seigneur en a besoin." »

[32] Les envoyés partirent et trouvèrent tout comme Jésus le leur avait dit. [33] Pendant qu'ils détachaient l'ânon, ses propriétaires leur dirent : « Pourquoi détachez-vous cet ânon ? » [34] Ils répondirent : « Le Seigneur en a besoin. » [35] Puis ils amenèrent l'ânon à Jésus ; ils jetèrent leurs manteaux sur l'animal et y firent monter Jésus. [36] A mesure qu'il avançait, les gens étendaient leurs manteaux sur le chemin. [37] Tandis qu'il approchait de Jérusalem, par le chemin qui descend du mont des Oliviers, toute la foule des disciples, pleine de joie, se mit à louer Dieu d'une voix forte pour tous les miracles qu'ils avaient vus. [38] Ils disaient : « Que Dieu bénisse le roi qui vient au nom du Seigneur ! Paix dans le ciel et gloire à Dieu ! »

[39] Quelques Pharisiens, qui se trouvaient dans la foule, dirent à Jésus : « Maître, ordonne à tes disciples de se taire. » [40] Jésus répondit : « Je vous le déclare, s'ils se taisent, les pierres crieront ! »

Jésus pleure sur Jérusalem

[41] Quand Jésus fut près de la ville et qu'il la vit, il pleura sur elle, [42] en disant : « Si seulement tu comprenais toi aussi, en ce jour, comment trouver la paix ! Mais maintenant, cela t'est caché, tu ne peux pas le voir ! [43] Car des jours vont venir pour toi où tes ennemis t'entoureront d'ouvrages fortifiés, t'assiégeront et te presseront de tous côtés. [44] Ils te détruiront complètement, toi et ta population ; ils ne te laisseront pas une seule pierre posée sur une autre, parce que tu n'as pas reconnu le temps où Dieu est venu te secourir ! »

Jésus dans le temple

[45] Jésus entra dans le temple et se mit à en chasser les marchands, [46] en leur disant : « Dans les Écritures, Dieu déclare : "Ma maison sera une maison de prière." Mais vous, ajouta-t-il, vous en avez fait une caverne de voleurs ! »

[47] Jésus enseignait tous les jours dans le temple. Les chefs des prêtres, les maîtres de la loi, ainsi que les notables du peuple, cherchaient à le faire mourir. [48] Mais ils ne savaient pas comment y parvenir, car tout le peuple l'écoutait avec une grande attention.

D'où vient l'autorité de Jésus ?

20 Un jour, Jésus donnait son enseignement au peuple dans le temple et annonçait la Bonne Nouvelle. Les chefs des prêtres et les maîtres de la loi survinrent alors avec les anciens [2] et lui demandèrent : « Dis-nous de quel droit tu fais ces choses, qui t'a donné autorité pour cela ? » [3] Jésus leur répondit : « Je vais vous poser une question, moi aussi. Dites-moi : [4] qui a envoyé Jean baptiser ? Est-ce Dieu ou les hommes ? » [5] Mais ils se mirent à discuter entre eux et se dirent : « Si nous répondons : "C'est Dieu qui l'a envoyé", il nous demandera : "Pourquoi n'avez-vous pas cru Jean ?" [6] Mais si nous disons : "Ce sont les hommes qui l'ont envoyé", le peuple tout entier nous jettera des pierres pour nous tuer, car il est persuadé que Jean a été un prophète. » [7] Ils répondirent alors : « Nous ne savons pas qui l'a envoyé baptiser. » [8] « Eh bien, répliqua Jésus, moi non plus, je ne vous dirai pas de quel droit je fais ces choses. »

La parabole des méchants vignerons

[9] Ensuite, Jésus se mit à dire au peuple la parabole suivante : « Un homme planta une vigne, la loua à des ouvriers vignerons et partit en voyage pour longtemps. [10] Au moment voulu, il envoya un serviteur aux ouvriers vignerons pour qu'ils lui remettent sa part de la récolte. Mais les vignerons battirent le serviteur et le renvoyèrent les mains vides. [11] Le propriétaire envoya encore un autre serviteur, mais les vignerons le battirent aussi, l'insultèrent et le renvoyèrent sans rien lui donner. [12] Il envoya encore un troisième serviteur ; celui-là, ils le blessèrent aussi et le jetèrent dehors. [13] Le propriétaire de la vigne dit alors : "Que faire ? Je vais envoyer mon fils bien-aimé ; ils auront probablement du respect pour lui." [14] Mais quand les vignerons le virent, ils se dirent les uns aux autres : "Voici le futur héritier. Tuons-le, pour que la vigne soit à nous." [15] Et ils le jetèrent hors de la vigne et le tuèrent.

« Eh bien, que leur fera le propriétaire de la vigne ? demanda Jésus.
[16] Il viendra, il mettra à mort ces vignerons et confiera la vigne à
d'autres. » Quand les gens entendirent ces mots, ils affirmèrent : « Cela n'arrivera certainement pas ! » [17] Mais Jésus les regarda et dit : « Que signifie cette parole de l'Écriture :

"La pierre que les bâtisseurs avaient rejetée
est devenue la pierre principale" ?

[18] Tout homme qui tombera sur cette pierre s'y brisera ; et si la pierre
tombe sur quelqu'un, elle le réduira en poussière. »

L'impôt payé à l'empereur

[19] Les maîtres de la loi et les chefs des prêtres cherchèrent à arrêter
Jésus à ce moment même, car ils savaient qu'il avait dit cette parabole
contre eux ; mais ils eurent peur du peuple. [20] Ils se mirent alors à sur-
veiller Jésus. A cet effet, ils lui envoyèrent des gens qui faisaient sem-
blant d'être des hommes honorables. Ces gens devaient prendre Jésus
au piège par une question, afin qu'on ait l'occasion de le livrer au
pouvoir et à l'autorité du gouverneur. [21] Ils lui posèrent cette question : « Maître, nous savons que ce que tu dis et enseignes est juste ; tu
ne juges personne sur les apparences, mais tu enseignes la vérité sur la
conduite qui plaît à Dieu. [22] Eh bien, dis-nous, notre loi permet-elle
ou non de payer des impôts à l'empereur romain ? » [23] Mais Jésus se
rendit compte de leur ruse et leur dit : [24] « Montrez-moi une pièce
d'argent. Le visage et le nom gravés sur cette pièce, de qui sont-ils ? » –
« De l'empereur », répondirent-ils. [25] Alors Jésus leur dit : « Eh bien,
payez à l'empereur ce qui lui appartient, et à Dieu ce qui lui appartient. » [26] Ils ne purent pas le prendre en faute pour ce qu'il disait devant le peuple. Au contraire, sa réponse les remplit d'étonnement et
ils gardèrent le silence.

Une question sur la résurrection des morts

[27] Quelques Sadducéens vinrent auprès de Jésus. – Ce sont eux qui
affirment qu'il n'y a pas de résurrection. – Ils l'interrogèrent [28] de la façon suivante : « Maître, Moïse nous a donné ce commandement écrit :
"Si un homme marié, qui a un frère, meurt sans avoir eu d'enfants, il
faut que son frère épouse la veuve pour donner des descendants à celui
qui est mort." [29] Or, il y avait une fois sept frères. Le premier se maria et

mourut sans laisser d'enfants. ³⁰ Le deuxième épousa la veuve, ³¹ puis le troisième. Il en fut de même pour tous les sept, qui moururent sans laisser d'enfants. ³² Finalement, la femme mourut aussi. ³³ Au jour où les morts se relèveront, de qui sera-t-elle donc la femme ? Car tous les sept l'ont eue comme épouse ! » ³⁴ Jésus leur répondit : « Les hommes et les femmes de ce monde-ci se marient ; ³⁵ mais les hommes et les femmes qui sont jugés dignes de se relever d'entre les morts et de vivre dans le monde à venir ne se marient pas. ³⁶ Ils ne peuvent plus mourir, ils sont pareils aux anges. Ils sont fils de Dieu, car ils ont passé de la mort à la vie. ³⁷ Moïse indique clairement que les morts reviendront à la vie. Dans le passage qui parle du buisson en flammes, il appelle le Seigneur "le Dieu d'Abraham, le Dieu d'Isaac et le Dieu de Jacob." ³⁸ Dieu, ajouta Jésus, est le Dieu des vivants, et non des morts, car tous sont vivants pour lui. » ³⁹ Quelques maîtres de la loi prirent alors la parole et dirent : « Tu as bien parlé, Maître. » ⁴⁰ Car ils n'osaient plus lui poser d'autres questions.

Le Messie et David

⁴¹ Jésus leur dit : « Comment peut-on affirmer que le Messie est descendant de David ? ⁴² Car David déclare lui-même dans le livre des Psaumes :

"Le Seigneur Dieu a déclaré à mon Seigneur :
Viens siéger à ma droite,
⁴³ je veux contraindre tes ennemis
à te servir de marchepied."

⁴⁴ David l'appelle donc "Seigneur" : comment le Messie peut-il être aussi le descendant de David ? »

Jésus met en garde contre les maîtres de la loi

⁴⁵ Tandis que toute l'assemblée l'écoutait, Jésus dit à ses disciples : ⁴⁶ « Gardez-vous des maîtres de la loi qui se plaisent à se promener en longues robes et qui aiment à recevoir des salutations respectueuses sur les places publiques ; ils choisissent les sièges les plus en vue dans les synagogues et les places d'honneur dans les grands repas. ⁴⁷ Ils prennent aux veuves tout ce qu'elles possèdent et, en même temps, font de longues prières pour se faire remarquer. Ils seront jugés d'autant plus sévèrement. »

Le don offert par une veuve pauvre

21 Jésus regarda autour de lui et vit des riches qui déposaient leurs dons dans les troncs à offrandes du temple. [2] Il vit aussi une veuve pauvre qui y mettait deux petites pièces de cuivre. [3] Il dit alors : « Je vous le déclare, c'est la vérité : cette veuve pauvre a mis plus que tous les autres. [4] Car tous les autres ont donné comme offrande de l'argent dont ils n'avaient pas besoin ; mais elle, dans sa pauvreté, a offert tout ce dont elle avait besoin pour vivre. »

Jésus annonce la destruction du temple

[5] Quelques personnes parlaient du temple et disaient qu'il était magnifique avec ses belles pierres et les objets offerts à Dieu. Mais Jésus déclara : [6] « Les jours viendront où il ne restera pas une seule pierre posée sur une autre de ce que vous voyez là ; tout sera renversé. »

Des malheurs et des persécutions

[7] Ils lui demandèrent alors : « Maître, quand cela se passera-t-il ? Quel sera le signe qui indiquera le moment où ces choses doivent arriver ? » [8] Jésus répondit : « Faites attention, ne vous laissez pas tromper. Car beaucoup d'hommes viendront en usant de mon nom et diront : "Je suis le Messie !" et : "Le temps est arrivé !" Mais ne les suivez pas. [9] Quand vous entendrez parler de guerres et de révolutions, ne vous effrayez pas ; il faut que cela arrive d'abord, mais ce ne sera pas tout de suite la fin de ce monde. » [10] Puis il ajouta : « Un peuple combattra contre un autre peuple, et un royaume attaquera un autre royaume ; [11] il y aura de terribles tremblements de terre et, dans différentes régions, des famines et des épidémies ; il y aura aussi des phénomènes effrayants et des signes impressionnants venant du ciel. [12] Mais avant tout cela, on vous arrêtera, on vous persécutera, on vous livrera pour être jugés dans les synagogues et l'on vous mettra en prison ; on vous fera comparaître devant des rois et des gouverneurs à cause de moi. [13] Ce sera pour vous l'occasion d'apporter votre témoignage à mon sujet. [14] Soyez donc bien décidés à ne pas vous inquiéter par avance de la manière dont vous vous défendrez. [15] Je vous donnerai moi-même des paroles et une sagesse telles qu'aucun de vos adversaires ne pourra leur résister ou les contredire. [16] Vous serez livrés même par

vos père et mère, vos frères, vos parents et vos amis ; on fera condamner à mort plusieurs d'entre vous. ¹⁷Tout le monde vous haïra à cause de moi. ¹⁸Mais pas un cheveu de votre tête ne sera perdu. ¹⁹Tenez bon : c'est ainsi que vous sauverez vos vies. »

Jésus annonce la destruction de Jérusalem

²⁰ « Quand vous verrez Jérusalem encerclée par des armées, vous saurez, à ce moment-là, qu'elle sera bientôt détruite. ²¹Alors, ceux qui seront en Judée devront s'enfuir vers les montagnes ; ceux qui seront à l'intérieur de Jérusalem devront s'éloigner, et ceux qui seront dans les campagnes ne devront pas entrer dans la ville. ²²Car ce seront les jours du Jugement, où se réalisera tout ce que déclarent les Écritures. ²³Quel malheur ce sera, en ces jours-là, pour les femmes enceintes et pour celles qui allaiteront ! Car il y aura une grande détresse dans ce pays et la colère de Dieu se manifestera contre ce peuple. ²⁴Ils seront tués par l'épée, ils seront emmenés prisonniers parmi toutes les nations, et les païens piétineront Jérusalem jusqu'à ce que le temps qui leur est accordé soit écoulé. »

La venue du Fils de l'homme

²⁵ « Il y aura des signes dans le soleil, dans la lune et dans les étoiles. Sur la terre, les nations seront dans l'angoisse, rendues inquiètes par le bruit violent de la mer et des vagues. ²⁶Des hommes mourront de frayeur en pensant à ce qui devra survenir sur toute la terre, car les puissances des cieux seront ébranlées. ²⁷Alors on verra le Fils de l'homme arriver sur un nuage, avec beaucoup de puissance et de gloire. ²⁸Quand ces événements commenceront à se produire, redressez-vous et relevez la tête, car votre délivrance sera proche. »

L'enseignement donné par le figuier

²⁹Puis Jésus leur dit cette parabole : « Regardez le figuier et tous les autres arbres : ³⁰quand vous voyez leurs feuilles commencer à pousser, vous savez que la bonne saison est proche. ³¹De même, quand vous verrez ces événements arriver, sachez que le Royaume de Dieu est proche. ³²Je vous le déclare, c'est la vérité : les gens d'aujourd'hui n'auront pas tous disparu avant que tout cela arrive. ³³Le ciel et la terre disparaîtront, tandis que mes paroles ne disparaîtront jamais. »

La nécessité de veiller

³⁴ « Prenez garde ! Ne laissez pas votre esprit s'alourdir dans les fêtes et l'ivrognerie, ainsi que dans les soucis de cette vie, sinon le jour du Jugement vous surprendra tout à coup, ³⁵ comme un piège ; car il s'abattra sur tous les habitants de la terre entière. ³⁶ Ne vous endormez pas, priez en tout temps ; ainsi vous aurez la force de surmonter tout ce qui doit arriver et vous pourrez vous présenter debout devant le Fils de l'homme. »

³⁷ Pendant le jour, Jésus enseignait dans le temple ; mais, le soir, il s'en allait passer la nuit sur la colline appelée mont des Oliviers. ³⁸ Et tout le peuple venait au temple tôt le matin pour l'écouter.

Les chefs complotent contre Jésus

22 La fête des pains sans levain, appelée la Pâque, approchait. ² Les chefs des prêtres et les maîtres de la loi cherchaient un moyen de mettre à mort Jésus, mais ils avaient peur du peuple.

Judas est prêt à livrer Jésus aux chefs

³ Alors Satan entra dans Judas, appelé Iscariote, qui était l'un des douze disciples. ⁴ Judas alla parler avec les chefs des prêtres et les chefs des gardes du temple de la façon dont il pourrait leur livrer Jésus. ⁵ Ils en furent très contents et promirent de lui donner de l'argent. ⁶ Judas accepta et se mit à chercher une occasion favorable pour leur livrer Jésus sans que la foule le sache.

Jésus fait préparer le repas de la Pâque

⁷ Le jour arriva, pendant la fête des pains sans levain, où l'on devait sacrifier les agneaux pour le repas de la Pâque. ⁸ Jésus envoya alors Pierre et Jean en avant avec l'ordre suivant : « Allez nous préparer le repas de la Pâque. » ⁹ Ils lui demandèrent : « Où veux-tu que nous le préparions ? » ¹⁰ Il leur dit : « Écoutez : au moment où vous arriverez en ville, vous rencontrerez un homme qui porte une cruche d'eau. Suivez-le dans la maison où il entrera ¹¹ et dites au propriétaire de la maison : "Le Maître te demande : Où est la pièce où je prendrai le repas de la Pâque avec mes disciples ?" ¹² Et il vous montrera, en haut de

la maison, une grande chambre avec tout ce qui est nécessaire. C'est là que vous préparerez le repas. » [13] Ils s'en allèrent, trouvèrent tout comme Jésus le leur avait dit et préparèrent le repas de la Pâque.

La sainte cène

[14] Quand l'heure fut venue, Jésus se mit à table avec les apôtres. [15] Il leur dit : « Combien j'ai désiré prendre ce repas de la Pâque avec vous avant de souffrir ! [16] Car, je vous le déclare, je ne le prendrai plus jusqu'à ce que son sens soit pleinement réalisé dans le Royaume de Dieu. » [17] Il saisit alors une coupe, remercia Dieu et dit : « Prenez cette coupe et partagez-en le contenu entre vous ; [18] car, je vous le déclare, dès maintenant je ne boirai plus de vin jusqu'à ce que vienne le Royaume de Dieu. » [19] Puis il prit du pain et, après avoir remercié Dieu, il le rompit et le leur donna en disant : « Ceci est mon corps qui est donné pour vous. Faites ceci en mémoire de moi. » [20] Il leur donna de même la coupe, après le repas, en disant : « Cette coupe est la nouvelle alliance de Dieu, garantie par mon sang qui est versé pour vous. [21] Mais regardez : celui qui me trahit est ici, à table avec moi ! [22] Certes, le Fils de l'homme va mourir suivant le plan de Dieu ; mais quel malheur pour celui qui le trahit ! » [23] Ils se mirent alors à se demander les uns aux autres qui était celui d'entre eux qui allait faire cela.

Qui est le plus important ?

[24] Les disciples se mirent à discuter vivement pour savoir lequel d'entre eux devait être considéré comme le plus important. [25] Jésus leur dit : « Les rois des nations leur commandent et ceux qui exercent le pouvoir sur elles se font appeler "Bienfaiteurs." [26] Mais il n'en va pas ainsi pour vous. Au contraire, le plus important parmi vous doit être comme le plus jeune, et celui qui commande doit être comme celui qui sert. [27] Car qui est le plus important, celui qui est à table ou celui qui sert ? Celui qui est à table, n'est-ce pas ? Eh bien, moi je suis parmi vous comme celui qui sert ! [28] Vous êtes demeurés continuellement avec moi dans mes épreuves ; [29] et de même que le Père a disposé du Royaume en ma faveur, de même j'en dispose pour vous : [30] vous mangerez et boirez à ma table dans mon Royaume, et vous siégerez sur des trônes pour juger les douze tribus d'Israël. »

Jésus annonce que Pierre le reniera

[31] « Simon, Simon ! Écoute : Satan a demandé de pouvoir vous passer tous au crible comme on le fait pour purifier le grain. [32] Mais j'ai prié pour toi, afin que la foi ne vienne pas à te manquer. Et quand tu seras revenu à moi, fortifie tes frères. » [33] Pierre lui dit : « Seigneur, je suis prêt à aller en prison avec toi et à mourir avec toi. » [34] Jésus lui répondit : « Je te le déclare, Pierre, le coq n'aura pas encore chanté aujourd'hui que tu auras déjà prétendu trois fois ne pas me connaître. »

La bourse, le sac et l'épée

[35] Puis Jésus leur dit : « Quand je vous ai envoyés en mission sans bourse, ni sac, ni chaussures, avez-vous manqué de quelque chose ? » – « De rien », répondirent-ils. [36] Alors il leur dit : « Mais maintenant, celui qui a une bourse doit la prendre, de même celui qui a un sac ; et celui qui n'a pas d'épée doit vendre son manteau pour en acheter une. [37] Car, je vous le déclare, il faut que se réalise en ma personne cette parole de l'Écriture : "Il a été placé au nombre des malfaiteurs." En effet, ce qui me concerne va se réaliser. » [38] Les disciples dirent : « Seigneur, voici deux épées. » – « Cela suffit », répondit-il.

Jésus prie au mont des Oliviers

[39] Jésus sortit et se rendit, selon son habitude, au mont des Oliviers. Ses disciples le suivirent. [40] Quand il fut arrivé à cet endroit, il leur dit : « Priez afin de ne pas tomber dans la tentation. » [41] Puis il s'éloigna d'eux à la distance d'un jet de pierre environ, se mit à genoux et pria [42] en ces termes : « Père, si tu le veux, éloigne de moi cette coupe de douleur. Toutefois, que ce ne soit pas ma volonté qui se fasse, mais la tienne. » [[43] Alors un ange du ciel lui apparut pour le fortifier. [44] Saisi d'angoisse, Jésus priait avec encore plus d'ardeur. Sa sueur devint comme des gouttes de sang qui tombaient à terre.]

[45] Après avoir prié, il se leva, revint vers les disciples et les trouva endormis, épuisés de tristesse. [46] Il leur dit : « Pourquoi dormez-vous ? Levez-vous et priez, afin que vous ne tombiez pas dans la tentation. »

L'arrestation de Jésus

[47] Il parlait encore quand une foule apparut. Judas, l'un des douze disciples, la conduisait ; il s'approcha de Jésus pour l'embrasser.

[48] Mais Jésus lui dit : « Judas, est-ce en l'embrassant que tu trahis le Fils de l'homme ? » [49] Quand les compagnons de Jésus virent ce qui allait arriver, ils lui demandèrent : « Seigneur, devons-nous frapper avec nos épées ? » [50] Et l'un d'eux frappa le serviteur du grand-prêtre et lui coupa l'oreille droite. [51] Mais Jésus dit : « Laissez, cela suffit. » Il toucha l'oreille de cet homme et le guérit. [52] Puis Jésus dit aux chefs des prêtres, aux chefs des gardes du temple et aux anciens qui étaient venus le prendre : « Deviez-vous venir armés d'épées et de bâtons, comme si j'étais un brigand ? [53] Tous les jours j'étais avec vous dans le temple et vous n'avez pas cherché à m'arrêter. Mais cette heure est à vous et à la puissance de la nuit. »

Pierre renie Jésus

[54] Ils se saisirent alors de Jésus, l'emmenèrent et le conduisirent dans la maison du grand-prêtre. Pierre suivait de loin. [55] On avait fait du feu au milieu de la cour et Pierre prit place parmi ceux qui étaient assis autour. [56] Une servante le vit assis près du feu ; elle le fixa du regard et dit : « Cet homme aussi était avec lui ! » [57] Mais Pierre le nia en lui déclarant : « Je ne le connais pas. » [58] Peu après, quelqu'un d'autre le vit et dit : « Toi aussi, tu es l'un d'eux ! » Mais Pierre répondit à cet homme : « Non, je n'en suis pas. » [59] Environ une heure plus tard, un autre encore affirma avec force : « Certainement, cet homme était avec lui, car il est de Galilée. » [60] Mais Pierre répondit : « Je ne sais pas ce que tu veux dire, toi. » Au moment même où il parlait un coq chanta. [61] Le Seigneur se retourna et regarda fixement Pierre. Alors Pierre se souvint de ce que le Seigneur lui avait dit : « Avant que le coq chante aujourd'hui, tu auras prétendu trois fois ne pas me connaître. »

Jésus insulté et battu

[63] Les hommes qui gardaient Jésus se moquaient de lui et le frappaient. [64] Ils lui couvraient le visage et lui demandaient : « Qui t'a frappé ? Devine ! » [65] Et ils lui adressaient beaucoup d'autres paroles insultantes.

Jésus devant le Conseil supérieur

[66] Quand il fit jour, les anciens du peuple juif, les chefs des prêtres et les maîtres de la loi s'assemblèrent. Ils firent amener Jésus devant

leur Conseil supérieur [67] et lui demandèrent : « Es-tu le Messie ? Dis-le-nous. » Il leur répondit : « Si je vous le dis, vous ne me croirez pas, [68] et si je vous pose une question, vous ne me répondrez pas. [69] Mais dès maintenant le Fils de l'homme siégera à la droite du Dieu puissant. » [70] Tous s'exclamèrent : « Tu es donc le Fils de Dieu ? » Il leur répondit : « Vous le dites : je le suis. » [71] Alors ils ajoutèrent : « Nous n'avons plus besoin de témoins ! Nous avons nous-mêmes entendu ses propres paroles ! »

Jésus devant Pilate

23 L'assemblée entière se leva et ils amenèrent Jésus devant Pilate. [2] Là, ils se mirent à l'accuser en disant : « Nous avons trouvé cet homme en train d'égarer notre peuple : il leur dit de ne pas payer les impôts à l'empereur et prétend qu'il est lui-même le Messie, un roi. » [3] Pilate l'interrogea en ces mots : « Es-tu le roi des Juifs ? » Jésus lui répondit : « Tu le dis. » [4] Pilate s'adressa alors aux chefs des prêtres et à la foule : « Je ne trouve aucune raison de condamner cet homme. » [5] Mais ils déclarèrent avec encore plus de force : « Il pousse le peuple à la révolte par son enseignement. Il a commencé en Galilée, a passé par toute la Judée et, maintenant, il est venu jusqu'ici. »

Jésus devant Hérode

[6] Quand Pilate entendit ces mots, il demanda : « Cet homme est-il de Galilée ? » [7] Et lorsqu'il eut appris que Jésus venait de la région gouvernée par Hérode, il l'envoya à celui-ci, car il se trouvait aussi à Jérusalem ces jours-là. [8] Hérode fut très heureux de voir Jésus. En effet, il avait entendu parler de lui et désirait le rencontrer depuis longtemps ; il espérait le voir faire un signe miraculeux. [9] Il lui posa beaucoup de questions, mais Jésus ne lui répondit rien. [10] Les chefs des prêtres et les maîtres de la loi étaient là et portaient de violentes accusations contre Jésus. [11] Hérode et ses soldats se moquèrent de lui et le traitèrent avec mépris. Ils lui mirent un vêtement magnifique et le renvoyèrent à Pilate. [12] Hérode et Pilate étaient ennemis auparavant ; ce jour-là, ils devinrent amis.

Jésus est condamné à mort

[13] Pilate réunit les chefs des prêtres, les dirigeants et le peuple, [14] et leur dit : « Vous m'avez amené cet homme en me disant qu'il égare le

peuple. Eh bien, je l'ai interrogé devant vous et je ne l'ai trouvé coupable d'aucune des mauvaises actions dont vous l'accusez. [15] Hérode ne l'a pas non plus trouvé coupable, car il nous l'a renvoyé. Ainsi, cet homme n'a commis aucune faute pour laquelle il mériterait de mourir. [16] Je vais donc le faire battre à coups de fouet, puis je le relâcherai. » [[17] A chaque fête de la Pâque, Pilate devait leur libérer un prisonnier.]

[18] Mais ils se mirent à crier tous ensemble : « Fais mourir cet homme ! Relâche-nous Barabbas ! » [19] – Barabbas avait été mis en prison pour une révolte qui avait eu lieu dans la ville et pour un meurtre.– [20] Comme Pilate désirait libérer Jésus, il leur adressa de nouveau la parole. [21] Mais ils lui criaient : « Cloue-le sur une croix ! Cloue-le sur une croix ! » [22] Pilate prit la parole une troisième fois et leur dit : « Quel mal a-t-il commis ? Je n'ai trouvé en lui aucune faute pour laquelle il mériterait de mourir. Je vais donc le faire battre à coups de fouet, puis je le relâcherai. » [23] Mais ils continuaient à réclamer à grands cris que Jésus soit cloué sur une croix. Et leurs cris l'emportèrent : [24] Pilate décida de leur accorder ce qu'ils demandaient. [25] Il libéra l'homme qu'ils réclamaient, celui qui avait été mis en prison pour révolte et meurtre, et leur livra Jésus pour qu'ils en fassent ce qu'ils voulaient.

Jésus est cloué sur la croix

[26] Tandis qu'ils emmenaient Jésus, ils rencontrèrent Simon, un homme de Cyrène, qui revenait des champs. Les soldats se saisirent de lui et le chargèrent de la croix pour qu'il la porte derrière Jésus. [27] Une grande foule de gens du peuple le suivait, ainsi que des femmes qui pleuraient et se lamentaient à cause de lui. [28] Jésus se tourna vers elles et dit : « Femmes de Jérusalem, ne pleurez pas à mon sujet ! Pleurez plutôt pour vous et pour vos enfants ! [29] Car le moment approche où l'on dira : "Heureuses celles qui ne peuvent pas avoir d'enfant, qui n'en ont jamais mis au monde et qui n'en ont jamais allaité !" [30] Alors les gens se mettront à dire aux montagnes : "Tombez sur nous !" et aux collines : "Cachez-nous !" [31] Car si l'on traite ainsi le bois vert, qu'arrivera-t-il au bois sec ? »

[32] On emmenait aussi deux autres hommes, des malfaiteurs, pour les mettre à mort avec Jésus. [33] Lorsqu'ils arrivèrent à l'endroit appelé « Le Crâne », les soldats clouèrent Jésus sur la croix à cet endroit-là et

mirent aussi les deux malfaiteurs en croix, l'un à sa droite et l'autre à sa gauche. [34] Jésus dit alors : « Père, pardonne-leur, car ils ne savent pas ce qu'ils font. » Ils partagèrent ses vêtements entre eux en les tirant au sort. [35] Le peuple se tenait là et regardait. Les chefs juifs se moquaient de lui en disant : « Il a sauvé d'autres gens ; qu'il se sauve lui-même, s'il est le Messie, celui que Dieu a choisi ! » [36] Les soldats aussi se moquèrent de lui ; ils s'approchèrent, lui présentèrent du vinaigre [37] et dirent : « Si tu es le roi des Juifs, sauve-toi toi-même ! » [38] Au-dessus de lui, il y avait cette inscription : « Celui-ci est le roi des Juifs. »

[39] L'un des malfaiteurs suspendus en croix l'insultait en disant : « N'es-tu pas le Messie ? Sauve-toi toi-même et nous avec toi ! » [40] Mais l'autre lui fit des reproches et lui dit : « Ne crains-tu pas Dieu, toi qui subis la même punition ? [41] Pour nous, cette punition est juste, car nous recevons ce que nous avons mérité par nos actes ; mais lui n'a rien fait de mal. » [42] Puis il ajouta : « Jésus, souviens-toi de moi quand tu viendras pour être roi. » [43] Jésus lui répondit : « Je te le déclare, c'est la vérité : aujourd'hui tu seras avec moi dans le paradis. »

La mort de Jésus

[44-45] Il était environ midi quand le soleil cessa de briller : l'obscurité se fit sur tout le pays et dura jusqu'à trois heures de l'après-midi. Le rideau suspendu dans le temple se déchira par le milieu. [46] Jésus s'écria d'une voix forte : « Père, je remets mon esprit entre tes mains. » Après avoir dit ces mots, il mourut. [47] Le capitaine romain vit ce qui était arrivé ; il loua Dieu et dit : « Certainement cet homme était innocent ! » [48] Tous ceux qui étaient venus, en foule, assister à ce spectacle virent ce qui était arrivé. Alors ils s'en retournèrent en se frappant la poitrine de tristesse. [49] Tous les amis de Jésus, ainsi que les femmes qui l'avaient accompagné depuis la Galilée, se tenaient à distance pour regarder ce qui se passait.

Jésus est mis dans un tombeau

[50-51] Il y avait un homme appelé Joseph, qui était de la localité juive d'Arimathée. Cet homme était bon et juste, et espérait la venue du Royaume de Dieu. Il était membre du Conseil supérieur, mais n'avait pas approuvé ce que les autres conseillers avaient décidé et fait. [52] Il

alla trouver Pilate et lui demanda le corps de Jésus. ⁵³ Puis il descendit le corps de la croix, l'enveloppa dans un drap de lin et le déposa dans un tombeau qui avait été creusé dans le roc, un tombeau dans lequel on n'avait jamais mis personne. ⁵⁴ C'était vendredi et le sabbat allait commencer. ⁵⁵ Les femmes qui avaient accompagné Jésus depuis la Galilée vinrent avec Joseph ; elles regardèrent le tombeau et virent comment le corps de Jésus y était placé. ⁵⁶ Puis elles retournèrent en ville et préparèrent les huiles et les parfums pour le corps. Le jour du sabbat, elles se reposèrent, comme la loi l'ordonnait.

La résurrection de Jésus

24 Très tôt le dimanche matin, les femmes se rendirent au tombeau, en apportant les huiles parfumées qu'elles avaient préparées. ² Elles découvrirent que la pierre fermant l'entrée du tombeau avait été roulée de côté ; ³ elles entrèrent, mais ne trouvèrent pas le corps du Seigneur Jésus. ⁴ Elles ne savaient qu'en penser, lorsque deux hommes aux vêtements brillants leur apparurent. ⁵ Comme elles étaient saisies de crainte et tenaient leur visage baissé vers la terre, ces hommes leur dirent : « Pourquoi cherchez-vous parmi les morts celui qui est vivant ? ⁶ Il n'est pas ici, mais il est revenu de la mort à la vie. Rappelez-vous ce qu'il vous a dit lorsqu'il était encore en Galilée : ⁷ "Il faut que le Fils de l'homme soit livré à des pécheurs, qu'il soit cloué sur une croix et qu'il se relève de la mort le troisième jour." »

⁸ Elles se rappelèrent alors les paroles de Jésus. ⁹ Elles quittèrent le tombeau et allèrent raconter tout cela aux onze et à tous les autres disciples. ¹⁰ C'étaient Marie de Magdala, Jeanne et Marie, mère de Jacques. Les autres femmes qui étaient avec elles firent le même récit aux apôtres. ¹¹ Mais ceux-ci pensèrent que ce qu'elles racontaient était absurde et ils ne les crurent pas. ¹² Cependant Pierre se leva et courut au tombeau ; il se baissa et ne vit que les bandes de lin. Puis il retourna chez lui, très étonné de ce qui s'était passé.

Sur le chemin d'Emmaüs

¹³ Ce même jour, deux disciples se rendaient à un village appelé Emmaüs, qui se trouvait à environ deux heures de marche de Jérusalem. ¹⁴ Ils parlaient de tout ce qui s'était passé. ¹⁵ Pendant qu'ils par-

laient et discutaient, Jésus lui-même s'approcha et fit route avec eux. [16] Ils le voyaient, mais quelque chose les empêchait de le reconnaître. [17] Jésus leur demanda : « De quoi discutez-vous en marchant ? » Et ils s'arrêtèrent, tout attristés. [18] L'un d'eux, appelé Cléopas, lui dit : « Es-tu le seul habitant de Jérusalem qui ne connaisse pas ce qui s'est passé ces derniers jours ? » [19] « Quoi donc ? » leur demanda-t-il. Ils lui répondirent : « Ce qui est arrivé à Jésus de Nazareth ! C'était un prophète puissant ; il l'a montré par ses actes et ses paroles devant Dieu et devant tout le peuple. [20] Les chefs de nos prêtres et nos dirigeants l'ont livré pour le faire condamner à mort et l'ont cloué sur une croix. [21] Nous avions l'espoir qu'il était celui qui devait délivrer Israël. Mais en plus de tout cela, c'est aujourd'hui le troisième jour depuis que ces faits se sont passés. [22] Quelques femmes de notre groupe nous ont étonnés, il est vrai. Elles se sont rendues tôt ce matin au tombeau [23] mais n'ont pas trouvé son corps. Elles sont revenues nous raconter que des anges leur sont apparus et leur ont déclaré qu'il est vivant. [24] Quelques-uns de nos compagnons sont allés au tombeau et ont trouvé tout comme les femmes l'avaient dit, mais lui, ils ne l'ont pas vu. » [25] Alors Jésus leur dit : « Gens sans intelligence, que vous êtes lents à croire tout ce qu'ont annoncé les prophètes ! [26] Ne fallait-il pas que le Messie souffre ainsi avant d'entrer dans sa gloire ? » [27] Puis il leur expliqua ce qui était dit à son sujet dans l'ensemble des Écritures, en commençant par les livres de Moïse et en continuant par tous les livres des Prophètes.

[28] Quand ils arrivèrent près du village où ils se rendaient, Jésus fit comme s'il voulait poursuivre sa route. [29] Mais ils le retinrent en disant : « Reste avec nous ; le jour baisse déjà et la nuit approche. » Il entra donc pour rester avec eux. [30] Il se mit à table avec eux, prit le pain et remercia Dieu ; puis il rompit le pain et le leur donna. [31] Alors, leurs yeux s'ouvrirent et ils le reconnurent ; mais il disparut de devant eux. [32] Ils se dirent l'un à l'autre : « N'y avait-il pas comme un feu qui brûlait au-dedans de nous quand il nous parlait en chemin et nous expliquait les Écritures ? »

[33] Ils se levèrent aussitôt et retournèrent à Jérusalem. Ils y trouvèrent les onze disciples réunis avec leurs compagnons, [34] qui disaient : « Le Seigneur est vraiment ressuscité ! Simon l'a vu ! » [35] Et eux-mêmes

leur racontèrent ce qui s'était passé en chemin et comment ils avaient reconnu Jésus au moment où il rompait le pain.

Jésus se montre à ses disciples

[36] Ils parlaient encore, quand Jésus lui-même se présenta au milieu d'eux et leur dit : « La paix soit avec vous ! » [37] Ils furent saisis de crainte, et même de terreur, car ils croyaient voir un fantôme. [38] Mais Jésus leur dit : « Pourquoi êtes-vous troublés ? Pourquoi avez-vous ces doutes dans vos cœurs ? [39] Regardez mes mains et mes pieds : c'est bien moi ! Touchez-moi et voyez, car un fantôme n'a ni chair ni os, contrairement à moi, comme vous pouvez le constater. » [40] Il dit ces mots et leur montra ses mains et ses pieds. [41] Comme ils ne pouvaient pas encore croire, tellement ils étaient remplis de joie et d'étonnement, il leur demanda : « Avez-vous ici quelque chose à manger ? » [42] Ils lui donnèrent un morceau de poisson grillé. [43] Il le prit et le mangea devant eux. [44] Puis il leur dit : « Quand j'étais encore avec vous, voici ce que je vous ai déclaré : ce qui est écrit à mon sujet dans la loi de Moïse, dans les livres des Prophètes et dans les Psaumes, tout cela devait se réaliser. » [45] Alors il leur ouvrit l'intelligence pour qu'ils comprennent les Écritures, [46] et il leur dit : « Voici ce qui est écrit : le Messie doit souffrir, puis se relever d'entre les morts le troisième jour, [47] et il faut que l'on prêche en son nom devant toutes les nations, en commençant par Jérusalem ; on appellera les humains à changer de comportement et à recevoir le pardon des péchés. [48] Vous êtes témoins de tout cela. [49] Et je vais envoyer moi-même sur vous ce que mon Père a promis. Quant à vous, restez dans la ville jusqu'à ce que vous soyez remplis de la puissance d'en haut. »

Jésus monte au ciel

[50] Puis Jésus les emmena hors de la ville, près de Béthanie, et là, il leva les mains et les bénit. [51] Pendant qu'il les bénissait, il se sépara d'eux et fut enlevé au ciel. [52] Quant à eux, ils l'adorèrent et retournèrent à Jérusalem, pleins d'une grande joie. [53] Ils se tenaient continuellement dans le temple et louaient Dieu.

*Notes * Notas * Note * Ghi chú*

*Notes * Notas * Note * Ghi chú*

*Notes * Notas * Note * Ghi chú*

Comment rendre hommage à votre famille – un sanctuaire d'amour et de vie – après avoir quitté le congrès de la Rencontre Mondial des Familles ? Inscrivez-vous pour un voyage de 21 jours dévoué au Lectio Divina et à l'approche de l'Evangile selon Luc avec votre famille ou votre communauté. Lorsque vous entendrez les Mots de Dieu, et méditerez sur des histoires liées l'espoir et la guérison, permettez à la Sainte Ecriture d'altérer votre approche sur l'amour inconditionnel de Dieu.

MEDITATION
SUR L'EVANGILE
DE LUC POUR LES FAMILLES

Trois moyens de s'inscrire pour cet évènement de 21 jours Lectio Divina.

📱 SMS: Composez **familles** au 72717

✉️ Email: Rendez-vous sur www.abs.us/familles

⊕ Application sur votre mobile à télécharger: app.bible.com/wmf

---

MISERANDO ATQUE ELIGENDO

Prezadas famílias,
Escutai a palavra de Deus,
meditai na palavra de Deus, juntos,
orai com a palavra do Senhor,
deixai que o Senhor
preencha vossas vidas com a misericórdia.

Franciscus

O brasão do Papa Francisco preserva o desenho utilizado quando ele era Arcebispo de Buenos Aires. Foram acrescentados os símbolos da dignidade pontifícia: a mitra e as chaves cruzadas, ligadas por um cordão vermelho.

O brasão é azul. No centro está o emblema da ordem religiosa do Papa, a Companhia de Jesus: um sol radiante com uma cruz, as letras vermelhas IHS (o monograma de Cristo) e três pregos pretos. Abaixo do desenho, uma estrela dourada simboliza a Virgem Maria, e um ramo de flores de nardo representa São José.

Sob a insígnia está o mote em latim: "miserando atque eligendo", que significa algo como "misericordioso porém eleito". A tradução do trecho é: "olhou para ele com sentimento de amor e o escolheu". O mote foi retirado de uma homilia de São Beda, o Venerável, que fala sobre a vocação de São Mateus – o cobrador de impostos – para ser um Apóstolo. Foi durante a festa de São Mateus, quando tinha 17 anos, que o Papa Francisco experimentou o primeiro chamado para a vida religiosa.

Setembro de 2015

Prezado(a) amigo(a),

Todos os quatro Evangelhos são encontros valiosos com a Palavra de Deus, mas, para muitos leitores, Lucas é o Apóstolo que mais lhes toca o coração, falando com a voz da misericórdia Divina. Somente em Lucas encontramos três das maiores expressões o amor de Jesus: as parábolas do Filho Pródigo e do Bom Samaritano e suas palavras sobre o "Bom Ladrão".

O Evangelho que você tem em mãos — um presente maravilhoso da Sociedade Bíblica Americana — é uma lembrança pessoal da ternura de Deus; um convite para que você trilhe com Jesus o caminho de volta ao reino dos céus. Leia-o. Reze com ele. Guarde-o com apreço.

Que Deus abençoe você e seus entes queridos durante a semana do Encontro Mundial das Famílias e em todos os dias de vossas vidas.

Seu irmão em Deus,

+ Charles J. Chaput, ofm. cap.

Reverendíssimo Charles J. Chaput, O.F.M. Cap.
Arcebispo da Filadélfia

INTRODUÇÃO

A BOA NOTÍCIA *da* MISERICÓRDIA *na* FAMÍLIA

Queridas famílias,

Com grande alegria introduzo esta edição do Evangelho de Lucas, um presente do Papa Francisco às famílias em todo o mundo por ocasião do VIII Encontro Mundial de Filadélfia.

Eu espero que a leitura deste Evangelho acompanhe o Ano Santo da Misericórdia que o Santo Padre quis começar em poucas semanas: Lucas é o Evangelho, a Boa Nova da misericórdia de Deus para a vida de cada um e de nossas famílias.

O EVANGELHO NA FAMÍLIA

Cada geração de cristãos – inclusive a nossa – é chamada a ter em mãos este pequeno livro. O Evangelho de fato é a força da Igreja, é a Palavra da qual nasceu e onde vive. O cristianismo começa, de fato, quando o Verbo (a Palavra) se fez carne no seio de Maria. Ela é a primeira entre os fiéis e logo foi indicada como tal por Isabel: «Bendita aquela que acreditou no cumprimento da palavra do Senhor» (Lc 01,45). E, depois dela, vieram os primeiros discípulos. Quando receberam a palavra de

Jesus começou uma nova fraternidade, poderíamos dizer uma "nova família": a de Jesus com os seus discípulos. Depois do Pentecostes o Evangelho começou a se difundir pelas casas, nas famílias dos cristãos. Em suma, o caminho do Evangelho no início do primeiro milênio foi marcado pela escuta nas famílias.

Queridas famílias, creio que nós devemos falar sobre o que aconteceu no início do cristianismo: levar o Evangelho em nossas mãos, também nas nossas próprias famílias, e voltar a tecer uma nova fraternidade entre as pessoas, uma nova solidariedade entre as famílias, a fim de dar a "boa notícia" do amor de Deus para todos. São João Paulo II, abrindo o Grande Jubileu do ano 2000, exortou os cristãos a entrar «no novo milênio com o livro do Evangelho!». Com essa paixão que o levou peregrino do Evangelho por todo o mundo, acrescentou: «Tenhamos este livro! Acolhemos do Senhor que oferece continuamente a nós através da sua Igreja (cfr. Ap 10,8). Vamos devorá-lo (cfr. Ap 10,9) para que se torne vida da nossa vida. Vamos saboreá-lo com profundidade: virão cansaços, mas nos dará alegria porque é doce como o mel. (cfr Ap 10,9-10.) Ficaremos cheios de esperança, e capazes de comunicá-lo a cada homem e mulher que se encontram no nosso caminho».

Papa Francisco nos exorta da mesma forma: Ter em mãos o Evangelho! Ele nos diz na bela Carta intitulada "A alegria do Evangelho" (*Evangelii gaudium*). Sim, é essencial ter em mãos o Evangelho e ouvi-lo com uma renovada atenção para ter um mundo mais fraterno, mais solidário, mais humano. A insegurança e o medo que estão marcando a vida deste mundo, as injustiças incríveis que dilacera a vida de tantas pessoas, a violência que parece expandir-se sem restrições, mesmo dentro de nossas casas, conflitos e guerras ainda continuam a reivindicar vítimas inocentes, possam ser superadas graças ao Evangelho. Por esta razão o Papa Francisco quis dar um milhão de cópias deste livro para as famílias das cinco grandes cidades do mundo: Havana (Cuba), Hanói (Vietnã), Kinshasa (Congo), Marselha (França), Sidney (Austrália). Sempre que o contexto urbano e seus subúrbios parecem torná-lo ainda mais difícil a convivência humana, o Papa desejou que a Palavra de Jesus ressoe mais fortemente.

UM EXERCÍCIO DIÁRIO

Leremos todos os dias um pequeno versículo do Evangelho. Sejamos como compelidos a entrar no coração e nos dias de Jesus, o seguiremos em suas viagens, participaremos de sua compaixão por todos, participaremos de sua ternura para com os pequenos e os fracos, nós comoveremos por sua compaixão estando com os pobres, choraremos ao ver o quanto nós o amávamos, regozijemo-nos, na sua ressurreição que finalmente derrotou o mal. O conheceremos mais e o amaremos mais.

Lembremos de fazer isso todos os dias realmente. Diariamente seremos inundados pelas palavras, pelas imagens, mensagens, convites ... E nem tudo são boas mensagens, e somente alguns ajudam a viver. Em casa então há o risco de que, por várias razões que até mesmo falamos sobre isso, ou, se não "voam os pratos", voam palavras que as vezes ferem mais que os pratos. Em todo o caso, todos nós sentimos a necessidade de boas palavras que chegam ao coração: o Evangelho é a palavra que vem ao coração. Na oração do Pai Nosso pedimos a Deus que nos dê o «pão de cada dia». As palavras de Jesus são o «pão vivo do céu» oferecido a nós diariamente. É o melhor pão. Nutre o coração e o corpo.

Queridas famílias, ler juntos o Evangelho em família é uma das mais bonitas e eficazes maneiras de orar. O Senhor gosta disso de uma maneira particular. Você se lembra do episódio de Marta e Maria? Jesus, à Marta, que estava irritada ao ver Maria que escutava Jesus, aponta que Maria escolheu «a melhor parte», a que mais «precisava». É fácil para todos nós estar sobrecarregados, como era para Marta, a partir de coisas a fazer as questões a serem resolvidas, sobre os problemas, as dificuldades a superar. «Maria – Jesus diz para nós hoje – escolheu a melhor parte» (Lc 10,42). Este pequeno livro vai ajudar a tornar-nos ouvintes do Evangelho a "melhor parte" dos nossos dias, a "melhor parte" de todos os dias do ano.

Temos necessidade de escutar. O primeiro passo da oração cristã é ouvir Jesus que nos fala. Sim, queridas famílias, antes de multiplicar as nossas palavras para pedir ao Senhor, escute o que ele faz por nós.

Todos os dias. Vamos ouvi-lo e faremos a mesma experiência dos dois discípulos de Emaús, que sentiram o seu coração aquecimento e a necessidade de ficar com Ele. A escuta torna-se oração e o encontro com Jesus ilumina suas vidas novamente.

Claro, devemos reunir-nos e fazer um pouco 'de silêncio' em torno dele. Sabemos o quanto tornou-se difícil encontrar um momento de silêncio e oração. Mas é indispensável. Poderíamos dizer que a oração diária é a nossa maneira de «orar sempre incansavelmente». Sim, rezar cada dia com o Evangelho é a nossa maneira de rezar sempre.

Então você deve encontrar um tempo para estar juntos, talvez antes de uma refeição, ou no final do dia, ou até mesmo no início. Ou, em outros momentos. O que importa é a escolha de cinco minutos para rezar juntos de uma maneira breve, mas eficaz.

Após o sinal da cruz e uma breve invocação ao Espírito Santo para que desça em nossos corações e ilumine as nossas mentes, nós leremos um pequeno versículo, ofereceremos uma explicação simples para crianças e comunicaremos qualquer pensamento que essa escuta desperta; neste momento nos perguntamos para quem queremos rezar de uma maneira particular e concluímos recitando juntos o Pai Nosso e agradecendo ao Senhor pelo dom da sua Palavra. Não nos esqueçamos de decidir em conjunto um pequeno e simples propósito pela qual esta palavra pode marcar as nossas vidas.

Queridas famílias, enquanto agradeço de coração a American Bible Society, que permitiu a criação deste livro, eu desejo com todo meu coração que o primeiro resultado destes intensos dias passados juntos, na Filadélfia, seja a decisão de permitir que a Palavra de Deus habite as suas casas e daqueles de sua cidade.

+ Vincenzo Paglia

Arcebispo Vincenzo Paglia
Presidente do Pontifício Conselho para a Família

O Evangelho
segundo Lucas

O Evangelho segundo Lucas
texto da *Tradução em Português Corrente*, primeira edição

© 1993
Sociedade Bíblica de Portugal. Usado com permissão.

O texto final desta tradução tem a aprovação das Sociedades Bíblicas Unidas
e da Conferência Episcopal Portuguesa.

O EVANGELHO SEGUNDO LUCAS

Introdução

1 [1] Prezado Teófilo,
Já muitos tentaram contar a história do que aconteceu entre nós [2] e escreveram o que nos foi transmitido por aqueles que assistiram a tudo desde o princípio e se tornaram mensageiros da Boa Nova. [3] Também eu, depois de averiguar cuidadosamente tudo o que se passou desde o começo, achei conveniente escrever isso para ti, de maneira ordenada, [4] para que fiques seguro de quanto te ensinaram.

Um anjo anuncia o nascimento de João Baptista

[5] No tempo de Herodes, rei da Judeia, havia um sacerdote chamado Zacarias, que fazia parte da turma de Abias. A mulher de Zacarias chamava-se Isabel e era descendente do sacerdote Aarão. [6] Tanto o marido como a esposa levavam uma vida que agradava a Deus, cumprindo inteiramente os mandamentos e preceitos do Senhor. [7] Mas não tinham filhos, porque Isabel não os podia ter, e nessa altura já os dois eram bastante idosos.

[8] Um dia, estava Zacarias no templo a cumprir as suas obrigações como sacerdote, porque era a sua vez. [9] Era costume entre os sacerdotes fazer-se um sorteio para ver quem devia entrar no santuário do templo e queimar incenso no altar. Dessa vez calhou a Zacarias. [10] Enquanto ele queimava o incenso, o povo orava do lado de fora. [11] Apareceu então a Zacarias um anjo do Senhor, de pé, à direita do altar do incenso. [12] Mal viu o anjo, assustou-se e ficou cheio de medo. [13] Mas o anjo disse-lhe: "Não tenhas medo, Zacarias! Deus ouviu as tuas orações: Isabel, tua mulher, vai dar-te um filho e tu vais pôr-lhe o nome de João. [14] Terás uma grande alegria e muita gente se vai alegrar também com esse nascimento. [15] O teu filho será grande diante de Deus. Não beberá vinho, nem qualquer bebida alcoólica, e quan-

do nascer já virá cheio do Espírito Santo. ¹⁶ Fará com que muitos israelitas voltem para o Senhor seu Deus. ¹⁷ Ele irá adiante do Senhor e terá um espírito forte como o do profeta Elias. Há-de pôr os pais de acordo com os filhos e ensinará os rebeldes a seguir o caminho dos bons. Assim preparará o povo para receber o Senhor."

¹⁸ Então Zacarias perguntou ao anjo: "Como posso eu ter a certeza disso, se já estou velho e a minha mulher também?" ¹⁹ O anjo respondeu-lhe: "Eu sou Gabriel. Estou ao serviço de Deus e ele mandou-me falar contigo para te dar esta boa nova. ²⁰ Mas, como não acreditaste no que te disse, vais ficar sem fala até ao dia em que isso acontecer, pois tudo se realizará no tempo devido."

²¹ O povo, que estava à espera de Zacarias, estranhava a sua demora no santuário. ²² Quando ele saiu, não conseguia falar, e eles perceberam que tinha tido uma visão. Falava-lhes por sinais e continuava mudo.

²³ Quando Zacarias acabou os dias de serviço no templo, voltou para casa. ²⁴ Algum tempo depois, Isabel ficou grávida e não saiu de casa durante cinco meses. ²⁵ E dizia para consigo: "Deus foi bom para mim. Agora já não tenho de que me envergonhar diante de ninguém."

Um anjo anuncia o nascimento de Jesus

²⁶ Quando Isabel já andava de seis meses, Deus mandou o anjo Gabriel a Nazaré, na província da Galileia, ²⁷ para falar com uma jovem chamada Maria, que estava noiva de José, descendente do rei David. ²⁸ O anjo aproximou-se dela e disse-lhe: "Eu te saúdo, ó escolhida de Deus. O Senhor está contigo." ²⁹ Maria ficou perturbada com estas palavras e perguntava a si própria o que queria dizer aquela saudação. ³⁰ Então o anjo continuou: "Não tenhas medo, Maria, pois foste abençoada por Deus. ³¹ Ficarás grávida e terás um filho, a quem vais pôr o nome de Jesus. ³² Ele será grande e será chamado o Filho do Deus altíssimo. O Senhor Deus lhe dará o trono do seu antepassado David. ³³ Governará para sempre os descendentes de Jacob e o seu reinado não terá fim."

³⁴ Maria perguntou então ao anjo: "Como é que isso pode ser, se eu sou virgem?" ³⁵ Mas o anjo respondeu-lhe: "O Espírito Santo descerá sobre ti e o poder do Deus altíssimo te cobrirá como uma nuvem. Por

isso o que vai nascer é santo e será chamado Filho de Deus. [36] Também a tua parente Isabel vai ter um filho, apesar da sua muita idade. Dizia-se que não podia ter filhos, mas já está no sexto mês. [37] É que para Deus não há nada impossível." [38] Maria disse então: "Servirei o Senhor como ele quiser. Seja como tu dizes." E o anjo retirou-se.

Maria visita Isabel

[39] Por aqueles dias, Maria apressou-se em ir a uma povoação nas montanhas da Judeia. [40] Entrou em casa de Zacarias e cumprimentou Isabel. [41] Quando Isabel ouviu a saudação de Maria, a criança mexeu-se dentro dela. Isabel ficou cheia do Espírito Santo [42] e disse em voz alta: "Abençoada és tu mais do que todas as mulheres e abençoado é o filho que de ti há-de nascer! [43] Que grande honra para mim ser visitada pela mãe do meu Senhor! [44] Mal ouvi a tua saudação, logo a criança que trago dentro de mim saltou de alegria. [45] Feliz de ti que acreditaste, pois há-de acontecer tudo o que te foi dito da parte do Senhor."

Cântico de Maria

[46] Maria disse então:

"O meu coração louva o Senhor
[47] e alegra-se em Deus, meu Salvador,
[48] porque ele olhou com amor para esta sua humilde serva!
Daqui em diante toda a gente me vai chamar ditosa,
[49] pois grandes coisas me fez o Deus poderoso.
Ele é Santo!
[50] Ele é sempre misericordioso para aqueles que o adoram,
em todas as gerações.
[51] Faz coisas grandiosas com o seu poder extraordinário.
Vence os orgulhosos e deixa-os confundidos.
[52] Derruba os poderosos
e levanta os humildes.
[53] Enche de coisas boas os que têm fome,
e manda embora os ricos de mãos vazias.
[54] Conforme tinha prometido aos nossos antepassados,
ajudou o povo de Israel, que o serve.

Lembrou-se dele, cheio de misericórdia.
⁵⁵ Foi bondoso para Abraão e seus descendentes para sempre."

⁵⁶ Maria ficou com Isabel cerca de três meses e depois voltou para sua casa.

Nascimento de João Baptista

⁵⁷ Quando acabou o tempo, Isabel teve um menino. ⁵⁸ Os vizinhos e os parentes foram dar-lhe os parabéns com muita alegria, por verem que Deus tinha sido tão bom para ela.
⁵⁹ Quando a criança tinha oito dias foram circuncidá-la, e queriam pôr-lhe o nome de Zacarias, como o pai. ⁶⁰ Mas a mãe disse: "De maneira nenhuma! Ele vai chamar-se João." ⁶¹ Responderam-lhe: "Mas não há ninguém na tua família com esse nome!" ⁶² E perguntaram por gestos ao pai do menino como é que ele queria que o filho se chamasse. ⁶³ Zacarias pediu então uma tabuinha e escreveu: "O nome dele é João." E ficaram todos muito admirados.
⁶⁴ Nesse momento, voltou a fala a Zacarias e ele pôs-se a dar louvores a Deus. ⁶⁵ Os vizinhos ficaram assustados com o que viram. E a notícia espalhou-se logo por toda a região montanhosa da Judeia. ⁶⁶ Todos os que ouviam falar do que tinha acontecido ficavam a pensar, e perguntavam: "Que virá a ser este menino?" De facto, o poder do Senhor estava com ele.

Cântico de Zacarias

⁶⁷ Zacarias, o pai do menino, ficou cheio do Espírito Santo
       e pôs-se a profetizar assim:
⁶⁸ "Louvado seja o Senhor, Deus de Israel,
       porque veio socorrer e salvar o seu povo.
⁶⁹ Ele fez nascer entre nós um poderoso Salvador,
       descendente do seu servo David.
⁷⁰ Há muito tempo que ele prometeu, por meio dos seus
       santos profetas,
⁷¹ que nos ia livrar dos nossos inimigos
       e do poder de todos aqueles que nos odeiam;
⁷² que havia de tratar com misericórdia os nossos antepassados,

e lembrar-se da santa aliança que tinha feito.
73 Deus tinha prometido com juramento ao nosso
    antepassado Abraão
74 que nos ia livrar dos nossos inimigos para podermos
    servi-lo sem receio,
75 como pessoas santas e justas todos os dias da nossa vida.
76 E tu, meu filho, serás chamado profeta do Deus altíssimo.
    Irás adiante do Senhor para lhe preparares o caminho.
77 Anunciarás ao seu povo que ele o salvará, perdoando-lhe
    os pecados,
78 porque o nosso Deus é cheio de misericórdia.
    Ele fará brilhar entre nós uma luz que vem do céu.
79 Essa luz iluminará os que se encontram na escuridão
    e na sombra da morte
    e guiará os nossos passos pelo caminho da paz."

80 O menino desenvolvia-se no corpo e no espírito e viveu no deserto até ao dia em que se apresentou ao povo de Israel.

Nascimento de Jesus

2 1 Por essa altura, o imperador Augusto deu ordem para se fazer o recenseamento de toda a população do Império Romano. 2 Este primeiro recenseamento fez-se quando Quirino era governador da Síria. 3 Todos iam inscrever-se, cada um na sua cidade. 4 Por isso, José partiu de Nazaré, na província da Galileia, e foi para Belém, na província da Judeia, onde tinha nascido o rei David. Como José era descendente de David, 5 foi lá inscrever-se com Maria, sua mulher, que estava grávida.

6 Enquanto estavam em Belém chegou o momento de Maria dar à luz. 7 Nasceu-lhe então o menino, que era o seu primeiro filho. Envolveu-o em panos e deitou-o numa manjedoura, por não conseguirem arranjar lugar em casa.

Os anjos e os pastores

8 Naquela região havia pastores que passavam a noite no campo, guardando os rebanhos. 9 Apareceu-lhes um anjo, e a luz gloriosa do

Senhor envolveu-os. Ficaram muito assustados, [10] mas o anjo disse-
-lhes: "Não tenham medo! Venho aqui trazer-vos uma boa nova, que
será motivo de grande alegria para vocês e para todo o povo. [11] Pois
nasceu hoje, na cidade de David, o vosso Salvador, que é Cristo, o
Senhor! [12] Poderão reconhecê-lo assim: encontrarão o menino en-
volvido em panos e deitado numa manjedoura."

[13] Nisto, juntaram-se ao anjo muitos outros, e louvavam a Deus,
cantando:

[14] "Glória a Deus no mais alto dos céus
    e paz na terra aôs homens
    a quem ele quer bem!"

[15] Mal os anjos partiram para o céu, os pastores disseram uns para
os outros: "Vamos a Belém para vermos o que o Senhor nos deu a conhecer." [16] Foram a toda a pressa e lá encontraram Maria e José, e o
menino, que estava deitado na manjedoura. [17] Depois de verem, puseram-se a contar a toda a gente o que lhes tinha sido dito a respeito
daquele menino. [18] Todos os que ouviram o que os pastores diziam,
ficavam muito admirados. [19] Porém Maria recordava todas estas coisas e meditava nelas atentamente. [20] Os pastores foram-se embora, e
pelo caminho cantavam louvores a Deus, por tudo o que tinham ouvido e visto, exactamente como lhes fora anunciado.

Circuncisão e apresentação de Jesus

[21] Quando o menino tinha oito dias, circuncidaram-no e puse-
ram-lhe então o nome de Jesus, tal como o anjo tinha indicado, antes
de ele ser concebido.

[22] Chegado o tempo da cerimónia da sua purificação, conforme a
Lei de Moisés, levaram o menino ao templo de Jerusalém para o
apresentarem ao Senhor. [23] É que na Lei de Deus está escrito: *Se o primeiro filho que nascer for menino, deverá ser consagrado ao Senhor.*
[24] José e Maria ofereceram também um sacrifício, como manda a lei:
um par de rolas ou dois pombinhos.

[25] Ora vivia nessa altura em Jerusalém um homem chamado Simeão. Era bom e muito piedoso e esperava que Deus mandasse a sal-

vação ao povo de Israel. O Espírito Santo estava com ele [26] e tinha-lhe assegurado que não havia de morrer sem ver o Messias enviado por Deus. [27] Simeão foi ao templo, guiado pelo Espírito Santo. E quando os pais do menino Jesus lá entravam para cumprirem o que a lei mandava a respeito dele, [28] Simeão tomou-o nos braços, deu graças a Deus e disse:

[29] "Agora, Senhor, já podes deixar-me morrer em paz,
        pois cumpriste a tua palavra!
[30] Já vi com os meus olhos o Salvador
[31] que enviaste para todos os povos.
[32] Ele é luz que iluminará os pagãos
        e glória de Israel, teu povo."

[33] Os pais de Jesus estavam admiradíssimos com o que Simeão dizia do menino. [34] Simeão abençoou-os e disse a Maria sua mãe: "Este menino é para muitos em Israel motivo de ruína ou salvação. Ele é sinal de divisão entre os homens, [35] para revelar os pensamentos escondidos de muitos. Uma grande dor, como golpe de espada, trespassará a tua alma."

[36] Vivia também em Jerusalém uma profetisa chamada Ana, filha de Fanuel, da tribo de Asser. Já tinha oitenta e quatro anos de idade e tinha-lhe morrido o marido ao fim de sete anos de casada. [37] Depois continuou sempre viúva e não saía do templo, onde adorava a Deus de dia e de noite com jejuns e orações. [38] Ana apareceu naquele momento e começou também a louvar a Deus. E falava do menino a todos os que esperavam que Deus salvasse Jerusalém.

[39] Depois de terem cumprido tudo o que a Lei de Deus manda fazer, José e Maria voltaram com Jesus para a sua terra, Nazaré da Galileia. [40] O menino crescia e tornava-se mais forte e cheio de sabedoria. E a graça de Deus estava com ele.

Jesus aos doze anos

[41] Todos os anos os pais de Jesus iam a Jerusalém à festa da Páscoa. [42] Quando o menino tinha doze anos, foram lá como de costume. [43] Passados os dias da festa, José e Maria voltaram para casa, mas

Jesus ficou em Jerusalém, sem os pais darem por isso. ⁴⁴ Julgavam que ele ia com algum grupo pelo caminho. Ao fim de um dia de viagem começaram a procurá-lo entre os parentes e os amigos, ⁴⁵ mas não o encontraram. Voltaram por isso a Jerusalém à sua procura. ⁴⁶ Ao fim de três dias descobriram-no dentro do templo, sentado entre os doutores. Escutava o que eles diziam e fazia-lhes perguntas. ⁴⁷ Todos os que o ouviam ficavam maravilhados com a sua inteligência e as suas respostas. ⁴⁸ Quando os pais o viram, ficaram muito impressionados e a mãe disse-lhe: "Filho, por que nos fizeste isso? O teu pai e eu temos andado aflitos à tua procura." ⁴⁹ Jesus respondeu-lhes: "Por que é que me procuravam? Não sabiam que eu tinha de estar na casa de meu Pai?" ⁵⁰ Mas eles não compreenderam o que lhes disse.

⁵¹ Jesus voltou então com eles para Nazaré, e continuou a ser-lhes obediente. Sua mãe guardava todas estas coisas no coração.

⁵² Jesus crescia em sabedoria e idade, agradando a Deus e aos homens.

Pregação de João Baptista

3 ¹ Foi no ano quinze do governo do imperador Tibério. Pôncio Pilatos era então governador da Judeia, Herodes governava a Galileia, seu irmão Filipe governava a Itureia e a Traconite. Lisânias governava a Abilena. ² Anás e Caifás eram os chefes dos sacerdotes. Foi nessa altura que Deus falou no deserto a João, filho de Zacarias. ³ João foi por todas as terras junto do rio Jordão e pregava assim ao povo: "Arrependam-se do mal e recebam o baptismo para Deus vos perdoar os pecados." ⁴ Isto aconteceu como o profeta Isaías tinha escrito no seu livro: *Alguém grita no deserto: Preparem o caminho do Senhor e abram-lhe estradas direitas. ⁵ Todo o vale será aterrado, todo o monte e toda a colina serão aplanados. Os caminhos tortos serão endireitados e os pedregosos serão arranjados. ⁶ E toda a humanidade verá a salvação de Deus.*

⁷ João dizia às multidões que iam ter com ele para serem baptizadas: "Que raça de víboras! Quem vos disse que podiam escapar ao castigo de Deus que se aproxima? ⁸ Mostrem pelas acções que estão verdadeiramente arrependidos, em vez de andarem a dizer: "Nós somos descendentes de Abraão." Pois eu garanto-vos que Deus até des-

tas pedras pode fazer descendentes de Abraão. [9] O machado já está pronto para cortar as árvores pela raiz. Toda a árvore que não der bons frutos será abatida e lançada no fogo."

[10] O povo perguntava a João Baptista: "Que devemos então fazer?" E ele respondia: [11] "O que tem duas camisas deve dar uma a quem não tem nenhuma, e o que tiver comida, reparta-a com os outros."

[12] Também lá foram cobradores de impostos para serem baptizados e perguntaram a João: "Mestre, que devemos nós fazer?" [13] E ele respondeu: "Não cobrem mais do que vos mandaram." [14] Houve também soldados que lhe perguntaram: "E nós, que devemos fazer?" João respondeu: "Não roubem a ninguém usando a força ou fazendo falsas acusações, mas contentem-se com o que ganham."

[15] O povo começou a suspeitar, e todos perguntavam a si próprios se João não seria o Messias. [16] Mas ele explicou a todos: "Eu baptizo-vos com água, mas está a chegar quem tem mais autoridade do que eu, e a esse eu nem sequer mereço a honra de lhe desatar as correias das sandálias. Ele há-de baptizar-vos com o Espírito Santo e com fogo. [17] Tem nas mãos a pá para separar, na eira, o trigo da palha. Guardará o trigo no seu celeiro e queimará a palha numa fogueira que não se apaga."

[18] Era com estas e outras exortações que João Baptista anunciava ao povo a Boa Nova.

[19] Também repreendia o governador Herodes, por viver com Herodias, mulher do irmão, e por muitas outras coisas em que Herodes tinha procedido mal. [20] Então Herodes acrescentou às suas culpas ainda mais esta: mandou prender João.

Baptismo de Jesus

[21] Toda a gente recebia o baptismo de João. Também Jesus foi baptizado, e estava a orar quando o céu se abriu [22] e o Espírito Santo desceu sobre ele em forma visível, como uma pomba. E uma voz do céu disse: "Tu és o meu Filho querido. Tenho em ti a maior satisfação."

Antepassados de Jesus, em linha ascendente

[23] Quando Jesus começou a sua actividade, tinha cerca de trinta anos. Era filho de José, como se pensava. Os outros ascendentes

eram: Heli, [24] Matat, Levi, Malqui, Janai, José, [25] Matatias, Amós, Naum, Esli, Nagai, [26] Maat, Matatias, Simei, Josec, Jodá, [27] Joanan, Ressa, Zorobabel, Salatiel, Neri, [28] Malqui, Adi, Cosam, Elmadam, Er, [29] Jessua, Eliézer, Jorim, Matat, Levi, [30] Simeão, Judá, José, Jonam, Eliaquim, [31] Melea, Mená, Matatá, Nachon, David, [32] Jessé, Jobed, Booz, Salá, Nachon, [33] Aminadab, Admin, Arni, Hesron, Peres, Judá, [34] Jacob, Isaac, Abraão, Tera, Naor, [35] Serug, Reú, Peleg, Éber, Chela, [36] Quenan, Arpaxad, Sem, Noé, Lamec, [37] Matusalém, Henoc, Jared, Malaliel, Quenan, [38] Enós, Set e Adão, que foi criado por Deus.

Jesus é tentado

4 [1] Jesus, cheio do Espírito Santo, voltou do rio Jordão. O Espírito conduziu-o para o deserto, [2] onde esteve durante quarenta dias e foi tentado pelo Diabo. Nesses dias, não comeu nada e quando chegou ao fim teve fome. [3] O Diabo disse-lhe então: "Se tu és o Filho de Deus, diz a esta pedra que se transforme em pão." [4] Mas Jesus respondeu: "A Sagrada Escritura diz: *Não se vive só de pão*."

[5] Então o Diabo levou-o para mais alto e mostrou-lhe num momento todos os países do mundo. [6] Depois disse-lhe: "Posso dar-te todo este poder e toda esta grandeza, porque tudo isto me foi entregue a mim e eu dou-o a quem eu quiser. [7] Tudo será teu, se me adorares." [8] Mas Jesus respondeu-lhe: "A Escritura diz: *Adorarás o Senhor teu Deus e só a ele prestarás culto*."

[9] Depois, o Diabo conduziu Jesus a Jerusalém, levou-o ao ponto mais alto do templo e disse-lhe: "Se és o Filho de Deus, atira-te daqui abaixo, [10] porque lá diz a Escritura: *Deus dará ordens aos seus anjos a teu respeito para te ampararem:* [11] *eles hão-de levar-te nas mãos para evitar que magoes os pés contra as pedras*."

[12] Jesus respondeu: "Mas a Escritura também diz: *Não tentarás o Senhor teu Deus*."

[13] Depois de ter tentado Jesus de todas as maneiras, o Diabo afastou-se dele por um determinado tempo.

Actividade de Jesus na Galileia

[14] Jesus voltou para a Galileia conduzido pelo Espírito Santo. A sua fama espalhou-se por toda aquela região. [15] Ensinava nas casas de oração e todos o elogiavam.

16 Foi depois para Nazaré, a terra onde se tinha criado. No sábado, foi à casa de oração, como era seu costume, e pôs-se de pé para ler as Escrituras. 17 Deram-lhe o livro do profeta Isaías, ele abriu-o e encontrou o lugar onde estava escrito assim:

18 *O Espírito do Senhor tomou posse de mim, por isso me escolheu para levar a Boa Nova aos pobres. Enviou-me para anunciar a libertação aos prisioneiros, para dar vista aos cegos, para pôr em liberdade os oprimidos* 19 *e para anunciar o tempo em que o Senhor quer salvar o seu povo.*

20 Depois, Jesus fechou o livro, devolveu-o ao encarregado e sentou-se. Ficaram todos com os olhos fixos nele. 21 Jesus começou então a dizer-lhes: "Esta parte da Escritura que acabaram de ouvir, cumpriu-se hoje mesmo." 22 Todos diziam bem de Jesus e estavam admiradíssimos com as suas belas palavras. E perguntavam: "Este não é o filho de José?"

23 Jesus disse-lhes ainda: "Certamente vão lembrar-me aquele provérbio que diz: *Médico, cura-te a ti mesmo.* Faz aqui na tua terra tudo o que fizeste em Cafarnaum, conforme nos contaram." 24 E acrescentou: "Digo-vos com toda a verdade que nenhum profeta é bem recebido na sua terra. 25 Com certeza que havia muitas viúvas em Israel no tempo de Elias, quando deixou de chover durante três anos e meio e houve muita fome em todo o país. 26 No entanto, Elias não foi enviado a nenhuma dessas viúvas, mas sim a uma que vivia em Sarepta, nos arredores de Sídon. 27 E havia muitas pessoas com lepra em Israel no tempo do profeta Eliseu, mas nenhuma delas foi curada, a não ser Naaman, que era da Síria."

28 Ficaram todos muito zangados na casa de oração, quando ouviram Jesus dizer aquilo. 29 Levantaram-se e puseram-no fora da cidade. Levaram-no então ao alto do monte onde a cidade estava edificada, para o atirarem dali abaixo, 30 mas Jesus passou pelo meio deles e foi-se embora.

O homem com um espírito mau

31 Jesus foi então para Cafarnaum, na Galileia, e aí ensinava aos sábados. 32 Os que o ouviam ficavam admirados com os seus ensinamentos, porque ele falava com autoridade.

³³ Num desses sábados estava na casa de oração um homem possuído dum espírito mau, que, aos gritos, disse a Jesus: ³⁴ "Que queres tu de nós, Jesus de Nazaré? Vieste aqui para dar cabo de nós? Eu bem sei que tu és o Santo que Deus mandou!" ³⁵ Jesus repreendeu-o: "Cala-te e sai desse homem." O espírito mau deitou o homem ao chão diante de todos e saiu dele sem lhe fazer mal. ³⁶ Toda a gente ficou pasmada, e diziam uns aos outros: "Que significa isto? Ele dá ordens aos espíritos maus, com autoridade e poder, e eles obedecem-lhe!" ³⁷ E a fama de Jesus espalhava-se por todos os lugares daquela região.

Jesus cura muitos doentes

³⁸ Jesus saiu da casa de oração e foi para casa de Simão Pedro. Como a sogra de Pedro estava de cama com muita febre, pediram por ela a Jesus. ³⁹ Ele inclinou-se para ela, mandou que a febre saísse e a febre passou-lhe. Ela levantou-se e começou logo a servi-los.

⁴⁰ Ao pôr-do-Sol, todos os que tinham doentes com vários padecimentos traziam-nos a Jesus. Ele punha as mãos sobre cada um deles e curava-os. ⁴¹ E também de muitas pessoas saíam espíritos maus, que diziam aos gritos: "Tu és o Filho de Deus!" Mas Jesus repreendia-os e não os deixava falar, porque eles sabiam que ele era o Messias.

Jesus anuncia a Boa Nova

⁴² Mal rompeu o dia, Jesus saiu da cidade e foi para um lugar isolado. A multidão pôs-se à procura dele. Quando o encontraram, não o queriam deixar ir embora. ⁴³ Mas Jesus disse-lhes: "É preciso que eu vá anunciar a Boa Nova do Reino de Deus também a outras povoações. Foi por isso que Deus me enviou." ⁴⁴ E pregava por todo o país nas casas de oração.

Primeiros companheiros de Jesus

5 ¹ Um dia estava Jesus à beira do lago de Genesaré e a multidão apertava-o, porque queria ouvir a mensagem de Deus. ² Ele viu dois barcos parados junto à praia. Os pescadores tinham saído e estavam a lavar as redes. ³ Jesus entrou num dos barcos, que era de Simão Pedro, e pediu-lhe que o afastasse um pouco da terra. Sentou-se e do barco ensinava a multidão.

⁴ Quando acabou de falar, disse a Simão: "Leva o barco para a parte mais funda do lago, com os teus companheiros, e lança as redes." ⁵ Simão respondeu-lhe: "Mestre, andámos toda a noite à pesca e não apanhámos nada, mas, já que tu o dizes, vou lançar as redes." ⁶ Deitaram as redes à água e apanharam tanto peixe que elas ficaram quase a rebentar. ⁷ Fizeram então sinais aos companheiros que estavam no outro barco para os irem ajudar. Eles foram e encheram os dois barcos com tanto peixe que quase se afundavam. ⁸ Quando Simão Pedro viu aquilo, ajoelhou-se aos pés de Jesus e disse: "Afasta-te de mim, Senhor, que eu sou um pecador." ⁹ Tanto Simão como os que estavam com ele ficaram pasmados com a enorme quantidade de peixe que tinham apanhado. ¹⁰ O mesmo aconteceu com os companheiros de Simão, que se chamavam Tiago e João, filhos de Zebedeu. Jesus disse a Simão: "Não tenhas medo! Daqui em diante serás pescador de homens." ¹¹ Eles puxaram então os barcos para terra, deixaram tudo e foram com Jesus.

Cura dum homem com lepra

¹² Uma vez estava Jesus numa certa povoação onde havia um homem cheio de lepra. Mal viu Jesus, inclinou-se até ao chão e pediu-lhe: "Senhor, se tu quisesses, podias curar-me." ¹³ Jesus tocou-lhe e disse: "Quero sim! Fica curado." E ao dizer isto logo o homem ficou são. ¹⁴ Mas Jesus deu-lhe ordem para não contar a ninguém o que se tinha passado e acrescentou: "Vai mostrar-te ao sacerdote e oferece a Deus pela tua cura o sacrifício que Moisés mandou. Assim ficam a saber que estás curado." ¹⁵ Entretanto, a fama de Jesus espalhava-se cada vez mais, de modo que muitas pessoas iam para o ouvir e para serem curadas das suas doenças. ¹⁶ Mas Jesus procurava lugares isolados, onde ficava em oração.

Cura dum paralítico

¹⁷ Jesus estava um dia a ensinar e entre os ouvintes estavam sentados alguns fariseus e doutores da Lei, que tinham vindo de todas as aldeias da Galileia e da Judeia, bem como de Jerusalém.

O poder de Deus estava com Jesus para curar os doentes. ¹⁸ Nisto, chegaram ali uns homens que transportavam um paralítico numa enxerga. Tentaram passar com ele e deixá-lo diante de Jesus, [19] mas não conseguiram por causa da multidão. Subiram então ao telhado e desceram a enxerga com o paralítico por entre as telhas até ficar no meio de todos, em frente de Jesus. [20] Quando ele viu a fé daqueles homens, disse ao doente: "Amigo, os teus pecados estão perdoados!" [21] Mas os doutores da Lei e os fariseus começaram a dizer para consigo: "Quem é este homem que ofende Deus desta maneira? Só Deus é que pode perdoar pecados!" [22] Porém, Jesus, percebendo o que eles estavam a pensar, disse-lhes: "Que é que estão a pensar lá no íntimo? [23] Que será mais fácil? Dizer a este paralítico: "os teus pecados estão perdoados", ou dizer-lhe: "levanta-te e anda"? [24] Pois fiquem sabendo que o Filho do Homem tem poder na terra para perdoar pecados." Voltando-se então para o paralítico disse-lhe: "Sou eu que te digo: levanta-te, pega na tua enxerga e vai para casa." [25] Ele levantou-se imediatamente, à vista de todos, levou a enxerga em que estava deitado e foi para casa dando graças a Deus. [26] Ficaram todos tão maravilhados que davam louvores a Deus e diziam cheios de admiração: "O que vimos hoje é extraordinário!"

Jesus chama Levi (Mateus)

[27] Depois disto, Jesus saiu e viu um cobrador de impostos, chamado Levi, sentado no posto de cobrança. Disse-lhe: "Vem comigo." [28] Levi deixou tudo, levantou-se e foi com Jesus. [29] Depois deu em sua casa um grande banquete em honra de Jesus e tomaram parte também muitos cobradores de impostos e outras pessoas. [30] Os fariseus e os doutores da Lei puseram-se então a criticar os discípulos de Jesus e perguntaram-lhes: "Por que é que vocês comem e bebem com os cobradores de impostos e outra gente de má fama?" [31] Jesus então respondeu-lhes: "Não são os que têm saúde que precisam de médico, mas sim os doentes. [32] Eu não vim para chamar os justos, mas sim os pecadores, para que se arrependam."

A questão do jejum

[33] Fizeram-lhe ainda outra pergunta: "Por que é que os discípulos de João Baptista e dos fariseus jejuam tantas vezes e fazem orações, e os teus discípulos comem e bebem?" [34] Jesus respondeu: "Poderão

obrigar os convidados duma boda a jejuar enquanto o noivo estiver com eles? [35] Lá virá o tempo em que hão-de jejuar, quando o noivo lhes for tirado." [36] Jesus apresentou-lhes depois esta comparação: "Ninguém corta um bocado de roupa nova para o coser em roupa velha; se fizer isso, estraga a roupa nova e o remendo não vai ficar bem na roupa velha. [37] E ninguém deita vinho novo em vasilhas velhas, porque o vinho rebenta-as, perdendo-se desse modo o vinho e as vasilhas. [38] Portanto, o vinho novo deve ser metido em vasilhas novas. [39] E ninguém deseja beber vinho novo depois de ter bebido do velho, pois acha que o velho é melhor."

Jesus e o sábado

6 [1] Num sábado, Jesus e os discípulos passavam por uma seara. Os discípulos iam arrancando espigas, que debulhavam com as mãos e comiam. [2] Então uns fariseus perguntaram: "Por que é que vocês fazem ao sábado aquilo que a lei não permite?" [3] Jesus respondeu-lhes: "Nunca leram o que David fez um dia, quando ele e os seus homens tiveram fome? [4] Entrou na casa de Deus, pegou nos pães consagrados e comeu-os com os companheiros. Ora, só os sacerdotes é que podiam comer esses pães." [5] E acrescentou: "O Filho do Homem tem autoridade sobre o próprio sábado."

Um homem com a mão paralítica

[6] Num outro sábado, Jesus entrou na casa de oração e pôs-se a ensinar. Estava lá um homem com a mão direita paralisada. [7] Então os doutores da Lei e os fariseus observavam Jesus para verem se ele o curava, sendo sábado, pois queriam achar uma razão para o acusarem. [8] Mas como Jesus sabia muito bem o que eles pensavam, disse ao homem: "Levanta-te e vem aqui para o meio." Ele levantou-se e ficou de pé. [9] Depois perguntou aos que ali estavam: "Digam-me lá: a lei permite fazer bem ao sábado ou fazer mal? Salvar a vida a uma pessoa ou deixá-la morrer?" [10] E olhando para todos à sua volta, disse ao homem: "Estende a mão." Ele estendeu-a e a mão ficou sã. [11] Eles ficaram fora de si e combinavam uns com os outros o que haviam de fazer contra Jesus.

Os doze apóstolos

[12] Por essa altura Jesus subiu a um monte para orar e passou lá a noite em oração. [13] Quando já era dia, reuniu os seus discípulos e escolheu doze, a quem chamou apóstolos. Eram eles: [14] Simão (ao qual deu o nome de Pedro), André (irmão de Pedro), Tiago, João, Filipe, Bartolomeu, [15] Mateus, Tomé, Tiago (filho de Alfeu), Simão (do partido dos Nacionalistas), [16] Judas (filho de Tiago) e Judas Iscariotes, aquele que atraiçoou Jesus.

Jesus ensina e cura

[17] Jesus desceu com eles o monte e chegou a um lugar plano com muitos dos que o seguiam. Estava ali uma grande multidão vinda de toda a Judeia e de Jerusalém, e das cidades costeiras de Tiro e Sídon. [18] Vieram para ouvir Jesus e para serem curados dos seus males. E os possuídos de espíritos maus foram curados. [19] Toda a multidão tentava tocar Jesus, porque dele saía um poder que curava os que lhe tocavam.

A verdadeira felicidade

[20] Jesus olhou para os seus discípulos e disse-lhes:

"Felizes de vocês, os pobres,
     porque vos pertence o Reino de Deus.
[21] Felizes de vocês os que têm fome,
     porque irão ser satisfeitos.
Felizes de vocês os que choram,
     porque depois hão-de rir.

[22] Felizes quando vos odiarem, rejeitarem, insultarem e disserem que são maus, por serem seguidores do Filho do Homem. [23] Alegrem-se quando isso acontecer, saltem de contentamento, porque no céu serão largamente recompensados. Foi assim que os antepassados dessa gente maltrataram também os profetas.

[24] Mas ai de vocês, os ricos,
     porque já tiveram a recompensa.

²⁵ Ai de vocês, que estão fartos de comida,
porque irão passar fome.
Ai de vocês, os que agora riem,
pois vão ter muito que lamentar e chorar.

²⁶ Ai de vocês, quando toda a gente vos elogiar, porque era assim que os vossos antepassados tratavam os falsos profetas."

Amor aos inimigos

²⁷ "Digo a todos os que me estão a ouvir: tenham amor aos inimigos e façam bem a quem vos tem ódio. ²⁸ Abençoem quem vos amaldiçoa e orem por aqueles que vos tratam mal. ²⁹ Ao que te bater num lado da cara, deixa-o bater também no outro. Ao que te tirar o casaco, não o impeças de levar a camisa. ³⁰ Dá a quem te pedir, e se alguém levar o que é teu, não tornes a pedi-lo. ³¹ Façam aos outros como desejam que os outros vos façam.

³² Se amarem apenas aqueles que vos amam, que recompensa poderão esperar de Deus? Até os maus têm amor àqueles que os amam a eles. ³³ Se fizerem bem somente aos que vos fazem bem, que recompensa poderão esperar? Até os maus procedem assim. ³⁴ Se emprestarem apenas àqueles de quem esperam tornar a receber, que recompensa poderão esperar? Até os maus emprestam uns aos outros para tornarem a receber. ³⁵ Mas pelo contrário, tenham amor aos vossos inimigos, façam-lhes bem, e emprestem sem nada esperar em troca. Assim, receberão grande recompensa e serão filhos do Deus altíssimo, porque ele é bom até para as pessoas ingratas e más. ³⁶ Sejam bondosos como o vosso Pai é bondoso."

Não julgar os outros

³⁷ "Não julguem ninguém, e Deus não vos julgará. Não condenem os outros, e Deus não vos condenará. Perdoem aos outros, e Deus vos perdoará. ³⁸ Dêem aos outros, e Deus vos dará também. Deus há-de dar-vos uma boa medida, calcada, batida e bem cheia. Deus usará convosco a mesma medida que usarem para os outros."

³⁹ Jesus apresentou-lhes depois esta comparação: "Pode um cego guiar outro cego? Não irão cair os dois nalgum buraco? ⁴⁰ Nenhum

aluno está acima do seu professor, mas todo o aluno bem ensinado será como o professor. [41] Por que é que tu reparas no cisco que está na vista do teu semelhante, e não vês a trave que está nos teus próprios olhos? [42] Como podes tu dizer ao teu semelhante: "Anda cá, deixa-me tirar-te isso", se não consegues ver aquilo que tens nos teus olhos? Fingido! Tira primeiro a trave que está nos teus olhos e depois já vês melhor para tirares o cisco da vista do teu semelhante."

A árvore e os seus frutos

[43] "Não há nenhuma árvore boa que dê frutos ruins, nem árvore ruim que dê frutos bons. [44] Qualquer árvore se reconhece pelos seus frutos. Não se colhem figos dos espinheiros nem uvas das silvas. [45] Quem é bom diz coisas boas, porque tem um tesouro de bondade no seu coração, mas quem é mau diz coisas más, porque o seu coração está cheio de maldade. Cada qual fala daquilo que tem no coração."

Cumprir a Palavra de Deus

[46] "Por que é que estão sempre a chamar-me: "Senhor! Senhor!" e não fazem o que eu digo? [47] Todo aquele que vem ter comigo para ouvir as minhas palavras e as põe em prática, sabem com quem o comparo? [48] Com um homem que construiu uma casa, escavando bem fundo para assentar os alicerces na rocha. Veio uma cheia, a água bateu com força contra a casa, mas não a abalou, porque estava assente na rocha. [49] Porém, todo aquele que ouve o que eu digo e não pratica pode comparar-se ao homem que contruiu uma casa sobre a terra, sem alicerces. Quando a corrente embateu contra ela, caiu logo e ficou completamente destruída."

Cura do empregado dum oficial romano

7 [1] Quando Jesus acabou de dizer aquelas coisas ao povo, entrou em Cafarnaum. [2] Havia ali um oficial do exército romano que tinha um empregado, a quem estimava muito, e que estava doente, quase a morrer. [3] Quando o oficial ouviu falar de Jesus, mandou ir ter com ele alguns anciãos dos judeus, para lhe pedirem que fosse curar o seu empregado. [4] Quando eles chegaram junto de Jesus pediram-lhe com insistência que lá fosse, e diziam: "Este oficial merece que lhe faças isso, [5] porque estima o nosso povo e foi ele quem mandou construir a nossa casa de oração." [6] Então Jesus foi com eles, mas quando já estava perto da casa, o oficial mandou uns amigos ao encontro de Jesus para lhe dizerem: "Senhor, não te incomodes, que eu não mereço que tu entres em minha casa. [7] Foi por isso que não me julguei digno de ir ter contigo pessoalmente. Basta que tu dês uma ordem e o meu empregado ficará curado. [8] Também eu tenho os meus superiores a quem devo obediência e os meus soldados a quem dou ordens. Digo a um que vá, e ele vai. Digo a outro que venha, e ele vem. E digo ao meu empregado: "Faz isto", e ele faz." [9] Ao ouvir aquilo, Jesus sentiu admiração por aquele homem. Voltou-se para a multidão que ia atrás dele e disse: "Fiquem sabendo que ainda não encontrei tamanha fé, nem mesmo entre o povo de Israel." [10] Quando os enviados do oficial romano chegaram a casa dele, viram que o doente já estava curado.

Jesus ressuscita o filho duma viúva

[11] Depois disto, Jesus foi a uma povoação chamada Naim. Iam com ele os seus discípulos e uma grande multidão. [12] Quando estava a entrar na povoação viu que passava um enterro. O morto era o filho único de uma viúva. Ia muita gente com ela no funeral. [13] Quando o Senhor viu a viúva, teve pena dela e disse-lhe: "Não chores." [14] E aproximando-se, tocou no caixão. Os homens que o levavam, pararam. Jesus disse então: "Rapaz, sou eu que te digo, levanta-te!" [15] Nisto, o rapaz sentou-se e pôs-se a falar. Jesus entregou-o à mãe. [16] Ficaram todos muito impressionados e louvavam a Deus dizendo: "Um grande profeta apareceu entre nós! Deus veio salvar o seu povo!" [17] E por todo o país e fora dele correu a fama do que Jesus tinha feito.

Resposta de Jesus aos discípulos de João Baptista

[18] Os discípulos de João Baptista foram contar-lhe tudo. [19] Ele chamou então dois deles e mandou-os ir ter com Jesus para lhe perguntarem: "És tu aquele que há-de vir, ou devemos esperar outro?" [20] Quando chegaram junto de Jesus, disseram-lhe: "João mandou-nos cá para te perguntarmos se tu és aquele que está para vir ou se de-

vemos esperar outro." [21] Naquele momento curou Jesus muitos doentes de vários males e enfermidades, possessos de espíritos maus e muitos cegos. [22] Então Jesus respondeu aos enviados: "Vão contar a João isto que agora viram e ouviram: que os cegos vêem, os coxos andam, os que têm lepra são curados, os surdos ouvem, os mortos são ressuscitados e aos pobres é anunciada a Boa Nova. [23] Feliz daquele que não tropeçar por causa de mim."

Jesus fala de João Baptista

[24] Quando os enviados de João se foram embora, Jesus pôs-se a falar dele ao povo: "Que é que foram ver ao deserto? Uma cana abanada pelo vento? [25] Que é que lá foram ver? Um homem bem vestido? Bem sabem que os homens que andam bem vestidos e vivem no luxo se encontram nos palácios reais. [26] Digam lá então, que é que foram ver? Um profeta? Sim, e digo-lhes ainda: ele é mais do que um profeta, [27] pois é aquele de quem as Escrituras dizem: *Enviarei o meu mensageiro à tua frente, para te preparar o caminho.*

[28] E fiquem sabendo isto: entre os homens não há ninguém maior do que João Baptista. No entanto, o mais pequeno no Reino de Deus é maior do que ele."

[29] Todas as pessoas que o ouviram, incluindo os cobradores de impostos, sabiam que cumpriram a vontade de Deus ao serem baptizados por João. [30] Mas os fariseus e os doutores da Lei desprezaram a vontade de Deus para com eles por não terem querido ser baptizados.

[31] Jesus disse ainda: "Com quem hei-de comparar as pessoas desta época? Com quem se parecem elas? [32] Com as crianças que andam a brincar na rua e dizem umas às outras:

"Tocámos música alegre e vocês não dançaram,
cantámos coisas tristes e não choraram."

[33] Realmente, aparece João, que jejua e não bebe vinho, e dizem logo que tem o Demónio com ele. [34] Depois vem o Filho do Homem, que come e bebe, e dizem dele: "Olhem para este homem! Come bem e bebe melhor, e é amigo de cobradores de impostos e outra gente de má fama."

[35] Mas a sabedoria de Deus só se mostra nos que de facto a aceitam."

Jesus em casa de um fariseu

[36] Um dia, um fariseu convidou Jesus para comer em sua casa. Jesus foi e sentou-se à mesa. [37] Então uma mulher de má vida, que havia naquela terra, ao saber que Jesus estava à mesa em casa do fariseu, foi lá com um frasco de alabastro cheio de perfume puro. [38] Pôs-se atrás de Jesus e, chorando muito, molhava-lhe os pés com as lágrimas e enxugava-os com os cabelos, beijava-os e deitava-lhes perfume. [39] Quando o fariseu viu aquilo, disse para consigo: "Se este homem fosse um profeta devia saber que espécie de mulher é esta que lhe está a tocar nos pés, pois é uma pecadora." [40] Então Jesus disse ao fariseu: "Simão, tenho uma coisa a dizer-te." Ele respondeu: "Diz lá, Mestre." [41] E Jesus falou assim: "Havia dois homens que deviam dinheiro a outro: um devia-lhe quinhentas moedas de prata, e o outro, cinquenta. [42] Nenhum dos dois tinha possibilidades de pagar a dívida, por isso ele perdoou a ambos. Qual deles ficará com mais amor ao credor?" [43] Simão respondeu: "Julgo que será aquele a quem mais perdoou." Jesus acrescentou: "Julgaste muito bem." [44] E apontando para a mulher, disse a Simão: "Vês esta mulher? Entrei em tua casa e não me deste água para os pés, mas ela lavou-mos com lágrimas e enxugou-os com os cabelos. [45] Não me recebeste com um beijo, mas ela, desde que entrou, não deixou de me beijar os pés. [46] Não me deste óleo perfumado para a cabeça, mas ela deitou-me perfume nos pés. [47] Digo-te que os seus muitos pecados lhe foram perdoados, por isso mostrou muito amor. A quem pouco se perdoa, pouco amor mostra." [48] Depois disse à mulher: "Os teus pecados estão perdoados." [49] Nisto, os outros convidados puseram-se a comentar assim: "Quem será este homem, que até perdoa pecados?"

[50] Mas Jesus disse à mulher: "A tua fé te salvou. Vai em paz."

As mulheres que ajudavam Jesus

8 [1] Depois disto, Jesus ia de terra em terra, anunciando a Boa Nova do Reino de Deus. Os doze apóstolos andavam com ele, [2] bem como algumas mulheres que ele tinha curado de espíritos maus e de doenças. Entre elas, Maria Madalena, de quem tinha expulsado sete espíritos maus, [3] Joana, mulher de Cuza, oficial da corte de Herodes, Susana e muitas outras, que com os seus bens ajudavam Jesus e os discípulos.

O semeador

⁴ Muita gente vinda de toda a parte continuava a procurar Jesus. Quando já havia uma multidão à sua volta, ele falou-lhes por meio desta comparação: ⁵ "Andava uma vez um homem a semear. Quando lançava a semente, houve alguma que caiu à beira do caminho, foi pisada e os pássaros comeram-na toda. ⁶ Outra caiu em terreno pedregoso e, quando rompeu, secou, por não haver humidade. ⁷ Outra parte caiu entre espinhos, que cresceram com as plantas e abafaram-na. ⁸ Mas houve outra parte da semente que caiu em boa terra. As plantas desenvolveram-se e produziram fruto à razão de cem grãos por semente." E por fim disse: "Quem tem ouvidos, preste atenção!"

Razão das comparações

⁹ Os discípulos perguntaram depois a Jesus o que queria ele dizer com aquela comparação. ¹⁰ Ele respondeu-lhes: "A vocês é dado conhecer os mistérios do Reino de Deus, mas aos outros serão apresentados por comparações, para que olhem mas não vejam, e oiçam mas não entendam."

Jesus explica a comparação do semeador

¹¹ "O significado da comparação é este: A semente representa a Palavra de Deus. ¹² A que caiu junto do caminho representa as pessoas que escutam, mas vem o Diabo e tira-lhes a palavra que nelas tinha sido semeada, para que não creiam e não sejam salvas. ¹³ A semente que caiu em cima de pedras representa aquelas pessoas que ouvem a palavra e a recebem com muita alegria. Mas, como não ganham raízes, crêem por algum tempo e desistem, quando chegam as tentações. ¹⁴ A que caiu entre os espinhos significa as pessoas que ouvem, mas acabam por se deixar sufocar pelas preocupações da vida, pelas riquezas e pelos prazeres, de modo que nunca chegam a dar fruto. ¹⁵ E a semente que caiu em boa terra representa as pessoas que ouvem a mensagem com um coração bom e leal e a conservam com firmeza até dar bom fruto."

A luz é para alumiar

¹⁶ "Não há ninguém que acenda um candeeiro para o tapar com uma caixa ou para o colocar debaixo da cama. Põe-se antes num lu-

gar em que alumie bem os que entram. ¹⁷ Pois não há nada que esteja escondido que não venha a descobrir-se: tudo o que é segredo virá sempre a ser conhecido e posto a claro. ¹⁸ Oiçam bem o que eu vos digo: Deus dará mais àqueles que já têm, mas aos que não têm, até o pouco que julgam ter lhes tirará."

A família de Jesus

¹⁹ A mãe e os irmãos de Jesus foram ter com ele, mas não conseguiram aproximar-se por causa da multidão. ²⁰ Houve entretanto alguém que lhe disse: "Olha que a tua mãe e os teus irmãos estão lá fora à tua procura." ²¹ Mas Jesus respondeu: "A minha mãe e os meus irmãos são aqueles que ouvem a mensagem de Deus e a praticam."

Jesus acalma a tempestade

²² Certo dia, entrou Jesus num barco com os discípulos e disse-lhes: "Vamos para a outra banda do lago." ²³ Ora, durante a travessia, Jesus adormeceu. Nisto, formou-se uma tempestade no lago e entrava tanta água no barco que já estavam em perigo de se afundar. ²⁴ Os discípulos acordaram Jesus e disseram-lhe: "Mestre, Mestre, estamos perdidos!" Ele levantou-se, deu ordem ao vento e às ondas, e o vento parou e as ondas amansaram. ²⁵ Depois disse aos discípulos: "Onde está a vossa fé?" Eles porém tremiam de medo, e diziam uns para os outros, muito admirados: "Mas quem é este homem que até o vento e as ondas lhe obedecem!"

Cura dum homem com espíritos maus

²⁶ Navegaram depois para o território de Gerasa, que fica do outro lado do lago em frente da Galileia. ²⁷ Quando Jesus saiu do barco, foi ter com ele um homem daquela terra, que estava possesso de espíritos maus. Há muito tempo que não se vestia e não vivia em casa, mas nos sepulcros. ²⁸ Quando viu Jesus, caiu por terra, gritando diante dele, e disse em alta voz: "Por que te metes comigo, Jesus, Filho do Deus altíssimo? Peço-te que não me atormentes!" ²⁹ Ele disse isto, porque Jesus dava ordens ao espírito mau para que saísse dele. Já muitas vezes o espírito mau se tinha apoderado dele. Prendiam-no com cadeias de ferro nos pés e nas mãos, mas ele rebentava tudo e era

levado pelo espírito mau para lugares desertos. ³⁰ Jesus perguntou-
-lhe: "Como te chamas?" Ele respondeu: "Chamo-me Multidão." Isto,
porque estava possuído por muitos espíritos maus. ³¹ E os espíritos
pediam a Jesus que não os mandasse para o abismo.

³² Ora andava a pastar ali no monte uma grande quantidade de
porcos. Os espíritos pediram a Jesus que os deixasse entrar neles e Jesus consentiu. ³³ Os espíritos saíram então do homem e entraram nos
porcos, que se puseram a correr pelo monte abaixo até ao lago e lá se
afogaram.

³⁴ Os guardadores dos porcos, quando viram aquilo, fugiram e
foram à cidade e aos arredores contar o que se tinha passado. ³⁵ Foi
lá muita gente para ver o que tinha acontecido. Aproximaram-se de
Jesus e encontraram o homem, de quem tinham saído os espíritos,
sentado aos pés de Jesus, vestido e em perfeito juízo. Ao verem isso, ficaram impressionados. ³⁶ Então, os que tinham presenciado tudo,
contaram aos outros como é que o homem tinha sido curado. ³⁷ Toda
a gente do território de Gerasa pediu a Jesus que se fosse embora dali, porque estavam todos cheios de medo. Jesus voltou para o barco e,
quando ia a partir, ³⁸ o homem que tinha sido curado pedia-lhe muito que o deixasse ir com ele. Mas Jesus mandou-o embora e disse-lhe:
³⁹ "Volta para tua casa e conta tudo aquilo que Deus te fez." O homem
foi então por toda a cidade contar o que Jesus lhe tinha feito.

Ressurreição da filha de Jairo e cura duma doente

⁴⁰ Quando Jesus voltou, foi recebido pela multidão que estava à sua
espera. ⁴¹ Nisto, aproximou-se dele um homem chamado Jairo, que
era dirigente da casa de oração. Ajoelhou-se aos pés de Jesus e pediu-
-lhe muito que fosse a sua casa, ⁴² porque tinha uma filha única, de
cerca de doze anos de idade, que estava à morte.

Quando iam a caminho, a multidão apertava Jesus de todos os lados. ⁴³ Ia lá também uma mulher que havia já doze anos sofria duma
doença que a fazia perder sangue. Tinha gasto com os médicos tudo
quanto possuía, mas ninguém a pôde curar. ⁴⁴ Ela foi então por detrás
de Jesus, tocou-lhe na ponta do manto e ficou logo curada da doença. ⁴⁵ Jesus então perguntou: "Quem foi que me tocou?" Todos nega-
ram. E Pedro disse: "Mestre, é a multidão que te aperta e empurra de

todos os lados!" [46] Mas Jesus repetiu: "Houve alguém que me tocou. Eu bem senti que algum poder saiu de mim." [47] Então a mulher, vendo que não podia passar despercebida, aproximou-se de Jesus, toda a tremer, ajoelhou-se aos seus pés e confessou diante de toda a gente a razão por que tinha tocado em Jesus e como tinha ficado curada imediatamente. [48] Jesus então disse-lhe: "Minha filha, a tua fé te salvou. Vai em paz."

[49] Ainda Jesus não tinha acabado de falar, quando chegou alguém da casa de Jairo a dizer: "A tua filha já morreu. Não incomodes mais o Mestre." [50] Assim que Jesus ouviu a notícia, disse a Jairo: "Não te assustes, tem fé, que a tua filha há-de viver." [51] Entrou em casa de Jairo, mas não deixou ninguém ir com ele, a não ser Pedro, Tiago e João e os pais da menina. [52] Toda a gente chorava com pena dela, mas Jesus disse: "Não chorem, que a menina não está morta, está a dormir." [53] Puseram-se todos a fazer troça dele, pois sabiam que ela estava morta. [54] Então Jesus pegou na mão da menina e ordenou: "Menina, levanta-te!" [55] Ela voltou a viver e levantou-se imediatamente. Jesus mandou então que lhe dessem de comer. [56] Os pais da menina ficaram maravilhados, mas Jesus mandou que não contassem nada a ninguém.

Jesus envia os apóstolos

9 [1] Jesus reuniu os doze apóstolos e deu-lhes poder e autoridade para expulsarem espíritos maus e curarem doenças. [2] Mandou-os também anunciar o Reino de Deus e curar doentes. [3] Mas recomendou-lhes: "Não levem nada para o caminho: nem cajado, nem saco, nem pão, nem dinheiro, nem muda de roupa. [4] Quando entrarem numa casa, fiquem lá até saírem da povoação. [5] Se nalguma terra as pessoas não vos quiserem receber, quando saírem de lá sacudam o pó dos pés, como aviso para essa gente." [6] Os discípulos então partiram e foram de terra em terra, anunciando a Boa Nova e curando doentes por toda a parte.

Herodes preocupado com Jesus

[7] Herodes, o governador da Galileia, teve conhecimento de tudo o que se estava a passar e ficou muito confuso, porque havia quem dissesse que era João Baptista, que tinha ressuscitado. [8] Outros diziam

que era Elias que tinha aparecido, e outros afirmavam que era um dos profetas antigos, que tinha ressuscitado. ⁹ Mas Herodes exclamou: "A João Baptista mandei eu cortar a cabeça. Quem será então este de quem me vêm contar estas coisas?" E procurava ver Jesus.

Jesus dá de comer a uma multidão

¹⁰ Quando os apóstolos voltaram, contaram a Jesus tudo o que tinham feito. Ele então retirou-se só com eles para uma povoação chamada Betsaida. ¹¹ Mas assim que a multidão deu por isso foi logo atrás de Jesus. Ele recebeu-a, falou do Reino de Deus e curou os doentes.

¹² Como o Sol já se estava a pôr, os apóstolos foram ter com Jesus e disseram-lhe: "Manda embora a multidão, para irem pelos campos e aldeias das redondezas arranjar onde descansar e comer, porque estamos num lugar deserto." ¹³ Jesus respondeu-lhes: "Dêem-lhes vocês de comer." Mas eles disseram: "Só aqui temos cinco pães e dois peixes. A não ser que vamos comprar comida para esta gente toda!" ¹⁴ É que estavam lá uns cinco mil homens. Jesus disse então aos discípulos: "Mandem sentar o povo em grupos de cinquenta." ¹⁵ Eles assim fizeram e acomodaram toda a gente. ¹⁶ Jesus pegou então nos cinco pães e nos dois peixes, levantou os olhos ao céu e deu graças a Deus por aqueles alimentos. Depois partiu-os e entregou-os aos discípulos para distribuírem pela multidão. ¹⁷ Todos comeram até ficarem satisfeitos e ainda se recolheram doze cestos dos pedaços que sobejaram.

Pedro declara que Jesus é o Messias

¹⁸ Um dia, quando Jesus estava a orar sozinho, os discípulos aproximaram-se dele. Então ele perguntou-lhes: "Quem sou eu, no dizer do povo?" ¹⁹ E eles responderam: "Uns dizem que és João Baptista, outros que és Elias, e outros ainda, que és um dos profetas antigos, que ressuscitou." ²⁰ Jesus acrescentou: "E para vocês, quem sou eu?" Pedro respondeu logo: "Tu és o Messias enviado por Deus."

Jesus fala da sua morte e ressurreição

²¹ Então Jesus deu-lhes ordem para não contarem aquilo a ninguém ²² e acrescentou: "É preciso que o Filho do Homem sofra mui-

to, e seja rejeitado pelos anciãos, pelos chefes dos sacerdotes e pelos doutores da Lei. Terá de ser morto, mas ao terceiro dia ressuscitará."

²³ Depois disse a todos: "Se alguém me quiser acompanhar tem de se esquecer de si próprio e carregar com a sua cruz todos os dias, para vir comigo. ²⁴ Pois todo o que quiser salvar a sua vida, perde-a, mas aquele que perder a vida por causa de mim, salva-a. ²⁵ Que aproveita a alguém ganhar o mundo inteiro, se acabar por perder-se ou destruir-se? ²⁶ Se alguém tiver vergonha de mim e do que eu ensino, também o Filho do Homem terá vergonha dessa pessoa, quando vier na sua glória e na glória de seu Pai e dos santos anjos. ²⁷ Lembrem-se do que vos digo: há aqui algumas pessoas que não hão-de morrer sem verem chegar o Reino de Deus."

Transfiguração de Jesus

²⁸ Cerca de uma semana depois de ter dito estas palavras, Jesus levou consigo Pedro, João e Tiago e subiu a um monte para orar. ²⁹ Quando estava em oração, o seu aspecto transformou-se e a sua roupa ficou de um branco muito brilhante. ³⁰ Nisto dois homens puseram-se a falar com ele. Eram Moisés e Elias, ³¹ rodeados duma luz celestial, a falar da sua morte, que ia cumprir-se em Jerusalém. ³² Pedro e os companheiros estavam a cair de sono, mas quando acordaram viram a glória de Jesus e os dois homens que estavam lá com ele. ³³ Quando aqueles homens se iam a retirar, Pedro, sem saber bem o que estava a dizer, exclamou: "Mestre, é tão bom estarmos aqui! Vamos levantar três tendas: uma para ti, outra para Moisés e outra para Elias." ³⁴ Enquanto dizia estas coisas, uma nuvem apareceu por cima deles e os discípulos ficaram cheios de medo quando a nuvem passou por eles. ³⁵ Da nuvem saiu então uma voz, que dizia: "Este é o meu Filho querido. Escutem o que ele diz." ³⁶ Quando se ouviu aquela voz, Jesus já estava sozinho. Os discípulos calaram-se e naqueles dias não contaram a ninguém nada do que tinham visto.

Jesus cura um possesso

³⁷ No dia seguinte, quando desciam do monte, veio uma grande multidão ao encontro de Jesus. ³⁸ Então um homem do meio da multidão gritou para Jesus: "Mestre, peço-te que olhes para o meu filho,

que é o único que tenho. [39] Há um espírito mau que toma posse dele e de repente o faz gritar e o sacode com violência até o fazer deitar espuma pela boca. Não o larga enquanto não o deixa completamente arrasado. [40] Pedi muito aos teus discípulos para expulsarem o espírito mau, mas eles não conseguiram." [41] Jesus disse então ao povo: "Oh que gente sem fé e desorientada! Até quando é que eu tenho de estar convosco? Até quando terei de vos aturar?" Depois disse ao pai do rapaz: "Traz-me cá o teu filho." [42] Quando o rapaz se aproximava de Jesus, o espírito mau atirou-o ao chão com um ataque. Jesus repreendeu o espírito mau, curou o rapaz e entregou-o ao pai. [43] E todos ficaram impressionados com o grande poder de Deus.

Jesus fala outra vez da sua morte

Toda a gente andava maravilhada com aquilo que Jesus fazia. Então ele disse aos discípulos: [44] "Oiçam bem o que vos vou dizer: O Filho do Homem vai ser entregue nas mãos dos homens." [45] Eles não compreendiam aquelas palavras. Eram para eles misteriosas e não as entendiam, mas tinham receio de lhe fazer perguntas.

Quem será o mais importante?

[46] Certa vez estavam os discípulos a discutir sobre qual deles seria o mais importante. [47] Jesus percebeu as ideias deles e, pegando num menino, colocou-o junto de si [48] e disse: "Todo aquele que receber esta criança em meu nome, é a mim que recebe. E quem me recebe a mim, recebe aquele que me enviou. Aquele de vocês que for o mais humilde, esse é que é o maior."

Quem não é contra nós é por nós

[49] João disse a Jesus: "Mestre, vimos um homem a expulsar espíritos maus em teu nome e proibimo-lo, porque não é dos nossos." [50] Mas Jesus disse-lhes: "Não proibam isso, porque quem não é contra nós é por nós."

Jesus é mal recebido na Samaria

[51] Como já estava a chegar a altura em que havia de ser levado deste mundo, Jesus tomou a decisão de ir a Jerusalém. [52] Mandou à fren-

te alguns mensageiros e eles foram a uma aldeia de samaritanos para prepararem a chegada de Jesus. ⁵³ Mas como os da aldeia perceberam que ele ia para Jerusalém, não o quiseram receber. ⁵⁴ Então os discípulos Tiago e João, ao verem aquilo, disseram: "Senhor, queres que mandemos descer fogo do céu para os destruir?" ⁵⁵ Mas Jesus voltou-se para eles e repreendeu-os. ⁵⁶ E foram para outra aldeia.

Convite para seguir Jesus

⁵⁷ Quando iam a caminho, houve alguém que disse a Jesus: "Irei contigo para onde quer que fores." ⁵⁸ Jesus respondeu-lhe: "As raposas têm tocas e as aves têm ninhos, mas o Filho do Homem não tem onde encostar a cabeça." ⁵⁹ Depois disse a outro: "Vem comigo." Mas ele respondeu: "Senhor, deixa-me ir primeiro fazer o enterro ao meu pai." ⁶⁰ Jesus replicou: "Deixa lá os mortos enterrar os seus mortos, mas tu vai anunciar o Reino de Deus." ⁶¹ Houve outro que lhe disse: "Senhor, eu quero ir contigo, mas primeiro deixa-me ir despedir da família." ⁶² Jesus respondeu: "Todo aquele que pega na charrua e olha para trás não serve para o Reino de Deus."

Jesus envia setenta e dois discípulos

10 ¹ Depois disto, o Senhor escolheu setenta e dois discípulos e mandou-os adiante dele, dois a dois, a todas as povoações aonde ele havia de ir. ² E disse-lhes: "Há uma colheita abundante, mas os trabalhadores são poucos. Peçam ao dono da seara que mande mais gente para fazer a colheita. ³ Vão, mas reparem que vos mando como cordeiros para o meio de lobos. ⁴ Não levem bolsa, nem saco, nem sandálias, e não parem a cumprimentar ninguém pelo caminho. ⁵ Em qualquer casa aonde entrarem, digam primeiro: "Haja paz nesta casa." ⁶ Se lá houver pessoas de paz, a saudação ficará com elas; se não houver, ficará convosco. ⁷ Não andem de casa em casa. Fiquem numa só casa e comam e bebam do que vos oferecerem, pois todo o trabalhador merece ser pago. ⁸ Quando chegarem a uma povoação que vos receba, comam do que vos servirem. ⁹ Curem todos os doentes que lá houver e digam ao povo: "Já chegou o Reino de Deus." ¹⁰ Mas em qualquer povoação onde entrarem e não vos quiserem receber, digam, ao passarem pelas ruas: [11] "Até o pó desta povoação, que se nos pegou aos pés, nós sacudimos como protesto contra vocês. Mas fiquem a saber que já chegou o Reino de Deus."

[12] Jesus disse ainda: "Afirmo-vos que, no dia do juízo, os habitantes da cidade de Sodoma serão tratados com menos dureza do que essa gente."

As cidades rebeldes

[13] "Ai de ti, Corazin! Ai de ti, Betsaida! Se os milagres que em ti se fizeram tivessem sido feitos nas cidades de Tiro e Sídon, há muito tempo que os seus habitantes se tinham arrependido dos seus pecados, vestindo-se de luto e com cinza na cabeça. [14] Portanto, no dia do juízo, os habitantes de Tiro e Sídon serão tratados com menos dureza do que vocês. [15] E tu, Cafarnaum, querias elevar-te até ao céu? Serás rebaixada até ao inferno!"

[16] Depois disse aos discípulos: "Quem vos escutar é a mim que escuta; quem vos rejeitar, rejeita-me também a mim. E quem me rejeitar, rejeitará aquele que me enviou."

Os discípulos regressam

[17] Os setenta e dois discípulos voltaram muito contentes e diziam: "Senhor, até os espíritos maus nos obedecem quando falamos em teu nome." [18] Jesus respondeu-lhes: "Eu via Satanás a cair do céu como um raio. [19] Escutem! Eu dei-vos poder para pisarem cobras e escorpiões e vencerem a força do inimigo, sem que vos aconteça mal. [20] Mas não se alegrem só porque os espíritos maus vos obedecem. Alegrem-se antes por terem os vossos nomes escritos no céu."

Deus revela-se aos humildes

[21] Naquele momento, Jesus, cheio de alegria por acção do Espírito Santo, disse: "Agradeço-te, ó Pai, Senhor do céu e da terra, porque mostraste aos simples as coisas que tinhas escondido aos sábios e entendidos. Sim, Pai, agradeço-te, por ter sido essa a tua vontade. [22] Meu Pai entregou-me tudo. Ninguém sabe quem é o Filho senão o Pai, e ninguém sabe quem é o Pai senão o Filho e aqueles a quem o Filho o quiser dar a conhecer."

²³ Depois virou-se para os discípulos e disse-lhes em particular: "Felizes de vocês, por verem as coisas que vêem. ²⁴ Digo-vos que muitos profetas e reis gostariam de ter visto o mesmo, mas não puderam, e de ter ouvido o que vocês ouvem, mas não ouviram."

O samaritano de bom coração

²⁵ Um certo doutor da Lei, que queria experimentar Jesus, levantou-se e fez-lhe esta pergunta: "Mestre, que devo eu fazer para ter direito à vida eterna?" ²⁶ Jesus respondeu: "Que diz a Escritura acerca disso e como a entendes tu?" ²⁷ E ele disse: "*Ama o Senhor teu Deus com todo o teu coração, com toda a alma, com todas as forças e com todo o entendimento. E ama o teu próximo como a ti mesmo.*" ²⁸ Jesus comentou: "Respondeste bem. Faz isso e terás direito à vida." ²⁹ Mas o doutor da Lei, querendo justificar-se, disse a Jesus: "E quem é o meu próximo?" ³⁰ Então Jesus respondeu: "Ia um homem a descer de Jerusalém para Jericó. Caíram sobre ele uns ladrões, que lhe roubaram roupa e tudo, espancaram-no e foram-se embora deixando-o quase morto. ³¹ Por casualidade, descia um sacerdote por aquele caminho. Quando viu o homem, afastou-se para o outro lado. ³² Também por lá passou igualmente um levita que, ao vê-lo, se afastou também. ³³ Entretanto, um samaritano, que ia de viagem, passou junto dele e ao vê-lo teve pena. ³⁴ Aproximou-se, tratou-lhe os ferimentos com azeite e vinho e pôs-lhe ligaduras. Depois, colocou-o em cima do seu jumento, levou-o para uma pensão e tratou dele. ³⁵ No outro dia, deu duas moedas de prata ao dono da pensão e disse-lhe: "Cuida deste homem, e quando eu voltar pago-te tudo o que gastares a mais com ele." ³⁶ Jesus perguntou então ao doutor da Lei: "Qual dos três te parece que foi o próximo do homem assaltado pelos ladrões?" ³⁷ E ele respondeu: "O que foi bom para ele." Jesus concluiu: "Então vai e faz o mesmo."

Em casa de Marta e Maria

³⁸ Jesus e os discípulos seguiam o seu caminho. Ao entrarem numa aldeia, uma mulher chamada Marta recebeu Jesus em sua casa. ³⁹ Ela tinha uma irmã chamada Maria, que se sentou aos pés do Senhor para o ouvir. ⁴⁰ Ora Marta andava muito atarefada, por ter muito que fa-

zer. Aproximou-se e disse: "Senhor, não te preocupa que a minha irmã me deixe só com todo o trabalho? Diz-lhe então que me venha
ajudar." [41] Mas Jesus respondeu: "Marta, Marta, andas preocupada e
aflita com tantas coisas, [42] quando uma só é necessária. Maria escolheu a melhor parte, que não lhe será tirada."

Jesus ensina a orar

11 [1] Uma vez estava Jesus a orar num certo lugar. Quando acabou, disse-lhe um dos seus discípulos: "Senhor, ensina-nos a
orar, como João Baptista ensinou os seus discípulos."

[2] Jesus disse-lhes então:

"Quando orarem digam assim:
Pai,
santificado seja o teu nome.
Venha o teu Reino.
[3] Dá-nos cada dia o pão que precisamos.
[4] Perdoa as nossas ofensas,
pois nós também perdoamos a todos os que nos ofendem.
E não nos deixes cair em tentação."

[5] Jesus disse-lhes ainda: "Suponham que um de vocês vai a casa de
um amigo à meia-noite e lhe diz: "Empresta-me três pães, [6] porque
me apareceu em casa um amigo que vem de viagem e eu não tenho
nada para lhe dar." [7] Ora imaginem que o outro diz lá de dentro: "Não
me incomodes! A porta já está fechada; os meus filhos e eu já estamos
na cama. Não posso levantar-me para te dar os pães."

[8] Jesus acrescentou: "Pois eu digo-vos: ainda que ele não se queira levantar para lhe dar os pães, acaba por levantar-se e dar-lhe tudo o que for preciso, não por ser seu amigo, mas para não ser
mais incomodado. [9] Por isso vos digo: Peçam, que Deus vos dará,
procurem, que hão-de encontrar, batam à porta, e ela há-de abrir-
-se, [10] pois o que pede, recebe; o que procura, encontra; e a quem
bate, a porta se abrirá. [11] Algum de vocês, que seja pai, será capaz de
dar ao filho uma cobra, se ele pedir peixe? [12] Ou um escorpião, se
pedir um ovo? [13] Ora, se vocês, que são maus, sabem dar coisas boas

aos filhos, quanto mais o Pai do céu dará o Espírito Santo àqueles que lho pedirem!"

Jesus e Satanás

[14] Jesus estava a expulsar um espírito mau que era mudo. Quando o espírito mau saiu, o mudo pôs-se a falar e o povo ficou admiradíssimo. [15] Mas alguns disseram: "É pelo poder de Satanás, príncipe dos espíritos maus, que ele os expulsa." [16] Outros, para o experimentarem, pediam-lhe que fizesse um milagre pelo poder de Deus. [17] Mas Jesus sabia o que eles estavam a pensar e disse-lhes: "Um país dividido em grupos que lutem entre si acaba por se arruinar, e as casas caem umas após outras. [18] Ora se Satanás está em luta contra si próprio, como poderá o seu reino aguentar-se? Dizem que eu expulso os espíritos maus pelo poder de Satanás. [19] Se eu os expulso por Satanás, por quem os expulsam os vossos adeptos? Por isso são eles que mostram que vocês estão enganados. [20] Mas se é pelo poder de Deus que eu expulso os espíritos maus, isto quer dizer que o Reino de Deus já aqui chegou. [21] Quando um homem forte e bem armado guarda a sua casa, todos os seus bens estão em segurança, [22] mas se aparece outro mais forte do que ele e o vence, tira-lhe as armas em que confiava e reparte o que lhe roubou. [23] Quem não está comigo está contra mim, e quem comigo não ajunta, espalha."

Regresso do espírito mau

[24] Jesus continuou: "Quando um espírito mau sai duma pessoa, vai por lugares secos à procura de repouso. Não o encontrando, diz: "Voltarei para a minha casa donde saí." [25] Ao chegar lá, encontra a casa varrida e bem arranjada. [26] Vai então buscar outros sete espíritos piores do que ele, e vão todos viver dentro dessa pessoa. E assim ela acaba por ficar pior do que antes."

Felicidade verdadeira

[27] Quando Jesus acabou de dizer estas coisas, uma mulher da multidão levantou a voz e disse: "Feliz a mulher que te deu à luz e te amamentou." [28] Mas Jesus respondeu: "Muito mais felizes são os que ouvem a Palavra de Deus e lhe obedecem."

Jesus, sinal de Deus

²⁹ Juntou-se uma multidão à volta de Jesus e ele começou a dizer: "A gente deste tempo é má. Pede-me um sinal de Deus, mas o único que lhe será dado é o do profeta Jonas. ³⁰ Pois assim como Jonas foi um sinal de Deus para os habitantes de Nínive, assim o Filho do Homem será também sinal para a gente deste tempo. ³¹ A rainha do Sul há-de levantar-se no dia do juízo contra os homens deste tempo para os condenar, porque ela veio lá do fim do mundo para ouvir a sabedoria de Salomão. ³² Também os habitantes de Nínive se hão-de levantar no dia do juízo, para condenar a gente deste tempo, porque eles arrependeram-se dos seus pecados, quando ouviram a pregação de Jonas. Ora o que está aqui é maior do que Jonas!"

Luz e escuridão

³³ Jesus continuou: "Ninguém acende um candeeiro para o colocar em sítio escondido ou debaixo dum caixote. Põe-no mas é num lugar próprio para alumiar os que entram em casa. ³⁴ A luz do teu corpo são os teus olhos: se eles forem bons, todo o teu corpo tem luz, mas se forem maus, o teu corpo fica às escuras. ³⁵ Por isso, tem cuidado, não aconteça que a tua luz seja escuridão. ³⁶ Mas se o teu corpo estiver cheio de luz, sem qualquer escuridão, tudo será claro, como quando a luz do candeeiro te alumia."

Jesus censura os fariseus e os doutores da Lei

³⁷ Quando Jesus acabou de falar, um fariseu convidou-o para almoçar com ele em sua casa. Jesus entrou e sentou-se à mesa. ³⁸ Ora, o fariseu ficou muito admirado por ver que ele não tinha cumprido a cerimónia de lavar as mãos antes de comer. ³⁹ Mas o Senhor disse-lhe: "Vocês, os fariseus, limpam os copos e os pratos por fora, mas lá por dentro vocês estão cheios de roubos e de maldade. ⁴⁰ Gente sem juízo! Então não sabem que quem fez o lado de fora também fez o de dentro? ⁴¹ Dêem antes aos pobres o que têm e assim tudo ficará puro para vocês. ⁴² Ai de vocês, fariseus! Dão a Deus a décima parte da hortelã, da arruda e de todos os vegetais. No entanto, não fazem caso nem da justiça nem do amor de Deus. Eram estas coisas que interessava praticar, sem desprezar as outras. ⁴³ Ai de vocês, fariseus! Gos-

tam muito de ter os lugares de honra nas casas de oração, e de ser cumprimentados em público. [44] Ai de vocês que são como as sepulturas que não se vêem e anda-se por cima delas sem se saber."

[45] Então um dos doutores da Lei disse a Jesus: "Mestre, ao dizeres isso também nos ofendes a nós." [46] Ele respondeu: "Ai de vocês também, doutores da Lei, que põem sobre os outros cargas insuportáveis, e vocês nem sequer com um dedo lhes tocam. [47] Ai de vocês, que constroem os sepulcros dos profetas, os mesmos que os vossos antepassados mataram. [48] Contudo vocês bem mostram que estão de acordo com os actos dos vossos antepassados, porque eles mataram os profetas e vocês levantam-lhes sepulcros. [49] Por isso é que a Sabedoria de Deus diz: "Vou mandar-lhes profetas e apóstolos, mas eles matarão uns e perseguirão os outros." [50] Deste modo, Deus vai pedir contas à gente de hoje por todos os profetas que foram assassinados, desde a criação do mundo — [51] a começar pelo assassinato de Abel até ao de Zacarias, que foi morto entre o altar e o santuário. Repito: Deus vai pedir contas disso à gente desta época. [52] Ai de vocês, doutores da Lei, que se apoderaram da chave do conhecimento religioso, mas nem entraram, nem deixaram entrar os outros."

[53] Quando Jesus saiu dali, os doutores da Lei e os fariseus puseram-se a criticá-lo com dureza e a incomodá-lo com muitas perguntas traiçoeiras, [54] para ver se o apanhavam nalguma resposta.

Aviso contra o fingimento

12 [1] Entretanto, juntaram-se ali milhares de pessoas, que até se atropelavam umas às outras. Jesus começou por dizer primeiro aos seus discípulos: "Tenham cuidado com o fermento dos fariseus, isto é, o seu fingimento. [2] Não há nada encoberto que não venha a descobrir-se, nem há nada escondido que não venha a saber-se. [3] Por isso, tudo o que vocês disserem na escuridão, será ouvido à luz do dia, e aquilo que segredarem dentro de casa será apregoado em cima dos telhados."

A quem devemos temer

[4] Jesus continuou: "Digo-vos meus amigos: não receiem os que matam o corpo e depois não podem fazer mais nada. [5] Eu vou dizer-

-vos a quem devem temer: temam a Deus, que, depois de tirar a vida, pode ainda lançar no inferno. Dele é que devem ter medo."

⁶ E disse ainda: "Não se vendem cinco pássaros por duas moedas? No entanto, Deus não se esquece de nenhum deles. ⁷ Pois bem, até os cabelos da vossa cabeça estão todos contados. Portanto, não tenham medo, porque vocês valem mais do que muitos pássaros."

Aceitar ou negar Cristo

⁸ "Digo-vos ainda que a todo aquele que se declarar a meu favor diante dos outros, o Filho do Homem fará o mesmo por ele diante dos anjos de Deus. ⁹ Mas àquele que me negar diante dos outros, o Filho do Homem também o negará diante dos anjos de Deus. ¹⁰ Deus perdoará àquele que disser alguma coisa contra o Filho do Homem, mas não perdoará ao que disser palavras ofensivas contra o Espírito Santo. ¹¹ Quando vos levarem às casas de oração, ou à presença dos chefes e das autoridades, não se preocupem como terão de se defender ou com aquilo que terão de dizer, ¹² porque o Espírito Santo vos ensinará nessa altura o que deverão dizer."

O perigo de ser rico

¹³ Alguém do meio da multidão disse a Jesus: "Mestre, diz ao meu irmão que divida a herança comigo." ¹⁴ Mas Jesus respondeu: "Amigo, quem me deu o direito de julgar ou fazer partilhas entre vocês?" ¹⁵ Depois disse à multidão: "Tenham cuidado! Não se deixem dominar pela ganância, porque a vida de qualquer pessoa não depende da abundância dos seus bens."

¹⁶ A seguir apresentou-lhes esta comparação: "A quinta dum certo rico tinha dado uma grande colheita. ¹⁷ E o rico pôs-se a pensar assim: "Que hei-de eu fazer? Não tenho onde guardar a colheita! ¹⁸ Já sei: deito abaixo os celeiros e faço outros maiores, onde guardarei o trigo e todos os meus bens. ¹⁹ Depois disso, poderei dizer para comigo: "És feliz! Tens em depósito tantos bens, que te vão dar para muitos anos. Não te rales: come, bebe e diverte-te." ²⁰ Mas Deus disse-lhe: "Louco, esta noite vais morrer, e o que tens guardado, para quem será?"

²¹ Jesus concluiu: "Assim acontecerá àqueles que só amontoam riquezas para si, mas que não são ricos aos olhos de Deus."

Deus cuida dos seus filhos

²² Jesus continuou a falar aos seus discípulos: "É por isso que eu vos digo: não andem preocupados com o que hão-de comer, nem com a roupa de que precisam para vestir. ²³ A vida vale mais do que a comida e o corpo mais do que a roupa. ²⁴ Reparem nos corvos: nem semeiam, nem colhem, nem têm despensas nem celeiros, mas Deus dá-lhes de comer. Ora vocês valem muito mais do que as aves. ²⁵ Qual é de vocês que, por mais que se preocupe, poderá prolongar um pouco o tempo da vossa vida? ²⁶ Portanto, se nem as coisas mais pequenas são capazes de fazer, por que se preocupam com as outras? ²⁷ Reparem nos lírios, que não fiam nem tecem. Contudo, digo-vos que nem o rei Salomão, que era riquíssimo, se vestiu como qualquer deles. ²⁸ Ora, se Deus veste assim as plantas que hoje estão no campo e amanhã são queimadas, quanto mais vos há-de vestir a vocês, gente sem fé? ²⁹ Portanto, não estejam preocupados nem inquietos com o que hão-de comer e beber. ³⁰ Tudo isso procuram os que só pensam neste mundo, mas vocês têm um Pai que sabe muito bem do que precisam. ³¹ Procurem primeiro o Reino de Deus que tudo isso vos será dado."

³² Jesus continuou: "Não tenham medo, pequeno rebanho! O vosso Pai achou por bem dar-vos o seu Reino. ³³ Vendam o que têm e dêem o dinheiro aos pobres. Arranjem bolsas que nunca se estraguem e depositem no céu uma riqueza que não se esgota. Ali não chegam os ladrões, nem a traça. ³⁴ Pois onde tiverem a riqueza, aí terão o coração."

Preparados para a vinda do Senhor

³⁵ Jesus disse ainda: "Estejam sempre preparados e de lanternas acesas. ³⁶ Façam como aqueles empregados que estão à espera do patrão que há-de voltar duma festa de casamento, para lhe abrirem a porta quando ele bater. ³⁷ Felizes são aqueles que o patrão encontrar acordados quando chegar. Acreditem no que vos digo: o patrão irá convidar-vos a sentarem-se à mesa e será ele próprio quem vos servirá a comida. ³⁸ Quer ele chegue à meia-noite, quer de madrugada, felizes os que se mantiverem acordados. ³⁹ Lembrem-se disto: se o dono da casa soubesse a que horas vinha o ladrão, não deixaria arrombar

a casa. ⁴⁰ Portanto, estejam também preparados, porque o Filho do Homem virá quando menos o esperam."

Deveres no trabalho

⁴¹ Então Pedro perguntou-lhe: "Senhor, esta comparação é só para nós, ou é para toda a gente?" ⁴² Jesus respondeu: "Como poderá mostrar-se fiel e prudente o empregado a quem o patrão deixou a tomar conta dos outros, para lhes dar a comida a horas? ⁴³ Feliz será aquele empregado a quem o patrão, quando vier, encontrar a proceder assim. ⁴⁴ Digo-vos que certamente o fará administrador de todos os seus bens. ⁴⁵ Mas que acontecerá se aquele empregado disser para consigo: "O meu patrão ainda se demora", e começar a maltratar os colegas, e a comer e a beber até ficar embriagado? ⁴⁶ Quando o patrão chegar, em dia e hora em que ele menos espera, irá aplicar-lhe um grande castigo, condenando-o como infiel. ⁴⁷ Este empregado, que conhecia a vontade do patrão, mas não se preparou nem fez nada de acordo com o que ele queria, será bastante castigado. ⁴⁸ Porém, o empregado que sem saber fez coisas erradas, será menos castigado. A quem muito for dado, muito se exigirá, e a quem muito for confiado, mais ainda se pedirá."

Jesus, motivo de divisão

⁴⁹ Jesus continuou: "Eu vim lançar fogo à terra, e quem me dera que já estivesse a arder! ⁵⁰ Tenho que passar por uma dura prova, e estou angustiado até que isso aconteça! ⁵¹ Julgam que vim trazer paz ao mundo?! De modo nenhum: o que eu vim trazer foi a divisão. ⁵² Pois daqui em diante, se houver cinco pessoas numa família, três estarão contra as outras duas, e as duas contra as três. ⁵³ Os pais estarão contra os filhos, e os filhos contra os pais; as mães contra as filhas, e as filhas contra as mães; as sogras contra as noras, e as noras contra as sogras."

Sinais do poder de Jesus

⁵⁴ Jesus disse também à multidão: "Quando vêem uma nuvem levantar-se no Poente dizem logo: "Vem lá chuva." E assim acontece. ⁵⁵ Quando o vento sopra do Sul, dizem: "Vai haver muito calor." E as-

sim acontece. [56] Impostores! Se sabem compreender os sinais da terra e do céu, como é que não compreendem os da época em que vivem? [57] Como é que vocês não sabem julgar devidamente as coisas?"

[58] E acrescentou: "Quando tiveres que ir com um adversário à presença das autoridades, procura fazer as pazes com ele pelo caminho, não vá ele levar-te ao juiz e o juiz te entregue ao oficial de justiça para te meter na prisão. [59] Digo-te que não sairás dali enquanto não pagares o último centavo."

Necessidade de arrependimento

13 [1] Nessa ocasião chegaram ali algumas pessoas que contaram a Jesus que Pilatos tinha mandado matar uns homens da Galileia, quando estavam a oferecer a Deus sacrifícios de animais. Deste modo se misturou o sangue deles com o dos animais sacrificados. [2] Então Jesus disse-lhes: "Julgam que esses eram mais pecadores do que os outros galileus, lá porque foram mortos dessa maneira? [3] Digo-vos que se enganam e que vocês morrerão como eles, se não se arrependerem. [4] Julgam também que aqueles dezoito que morreram quando a torre de Siloé lhes caiu em cima tinham mais culpas do que os outros habitantes de Jerusalém? [5] Pois digo-vos que se enganam e que vocês morrerão como eles, se não se arrependerem."

A figueira sem fruto

[6] Jesus apresentou-lhes esta comparação: "Havia um homem que tinha uma figueira plantada na sua vinha. Foi lá ver se tinha figos e não encontrou nenhum. [7] Disse então ao homem que lá trabalhava: "Escuta! Há três anos que venho procurar figos a esta figueira e não encontro nada. Portanto, corta-a. Por que há-de ela continuar a ocupar o terreno?" [8] Mas o trabalhador respondeu: "Deixa-a ficar ainda este ano, que eu vou cavar em volta e deitar-lhe estrume. [9] Talvez assim dê fruto. Se não der, manda-a cortar então."

Jesus cura uma doente num sábado

[10] Num certo sábado Jesus estava a ensinar numa casa de oração. [11] Havia lá uma mulher que há dezoito anos estava doente. Andava muito curvada, sem se poder endireitar, porque estava possessa dum

espírito mau. ¹² Quando Jesus a viu, chamou-a e disse: "Mulher, estás livre do teu mal." ¹³ Pôs as mãos sobre ela e nesse momento a mulher endireitou-se e começou logo a dar louvores a Deus. ¹⁴ Mas o dirigente da casa de oração ficou indignado por Jesus ter curado ao sábado e disse ao povo: "Há seis dias na semana em que se deve trabalhar. Venham cá nesses dias para serem curados, mas não ao sábado." ¹⁵ Jesus respondeu: "Mas que fingidos! Haverá alguém que ao sábado não desprenda da manjedoura o boi, ou o burro, para o levar a beber? ¹⁶ Ora, esta mulher, que também pertence ao povo de Abraão, estava presa por Satanás há dezoito anos. Por que motivo não havia ela de ficar livre da sua doença, embora seja sábado?" ¹⁷ Esta resposta de Jesus deixou envergonhados os seus inimigos. Mas o povo mostrava-se alegre com todas as maravilhas que Jesus fazia.

O grão de mostarda e o fermento

¹⁸ Jesus disse então: "A que é semelhante o Reino de Deus? Com que o hei-de comparar? ¹⁹ É semelhante a um grão de mostarda que alguém semeia na sua horta. A planta cresce até se fazer árvore, e as aves fazem ninho nos seus ramos."

²⁰ Disse também: "A que hei-de comparar ainda o Reino de Deus? ²¹ Ao fermento que uma mulher mistura em três medidas de farinha e faz levedar toda a massa."

O caminho para a vida eterna

²² Jesus dirigia-se para Jerusalém, e ensinava nas cidades e povoados por onde passava. ²³ Houve alguém que lhe perguntou: "Senhor, são poucos os que se salvam?" E ele respondeu: ²⁴ "Esforcem-se por entrar pela porta estreita, pois digo-vos que muitos hão-de procurar entrar e não vão conseguir. ²⁵ Depois de o dono da casa se levantar e fechar a porta, vocês os que ficarem de fora, hão-de bater e dizer: "Senhor, abre-nos a porta." Mas ele responderá: "Não sei donde são." ²⁶ Vocês vão então dizer: "Comemos e bebemos contigo e ensinaste nas nossas ruas." ²⁷ Mas ele responderá: "Já vos disse que não sei donde são: afastem-se de mim todos, malfeitores!" ²⁸ Irão chorar e ranger os dentes, quando virem Abraão, Isaac, Jacob e todos os profetas no

Reino de Deus, enquanto vocês são postos fora. [29] Mas virão pessoas do Oriente e do Ocidente, do Norte e do Sul, para tomar lugar no Reino de Deus. [30] Alguns dos que agora são os últimos, serão os primeiros; enquanto outros que agora são os primeiros, serão os últimos."

Jesus tem pena de Jerusalém

[31] Naquele momento, alguns fariseus foram ter com Jesus e disseram-lhe: "Vai-te embora daqui, porque Herodes quer matar-te." [32] Mas Jesus respondeu: "Vão lá dizer a essa raposa que eu expulso espíritos maus e faço curas hoje e amanhã, mas depois de amanhã termino. [33] Porém, é preciso que eu siga o meu caminho nestes três dias, porque um profeta não pode morrer fora de Jerusalém. [34] Oh Jerusalém, Jerusalém! Matas os profetas e apedrejas os mensageiros que Deus te envia! Quantas vezes eu quis juntar os teus habitantes, como uma galinha junta os pintainhos debaixo das asas, e tu não quiseste! [35] Agora, vão ficar com a casa abandonada. E digo-vos que já não me hão-de ver mais, senão quando chegar a altura em que disserem: Bendito seja aquele que vem em nome do Senhor."

Jesus cura um doente ao sábado

14 [1] Num certo sábado Jesus foi a casa dum dos chefes dos fariseus para comer com ele, e todos observavam o que Jesus fazia. [2] Mesmo em frente dele estava um homem que sofria duma doença que o trazia inchado. [3] Então Jesus perguntou aos doutores da Lei e aos fariseus: "Pode-se curar ao sábado ou não?" [4] Eles ficaram calados. Jesus tocou no homem, curou-o e mandou-o embora. [5] Depois disse-lhes: "Qual de vocês não vai tirar imediatamente do poço um filho ou um boi que lá lhe tenha caído a um sábado?" [6] Mas eles não conseguiram responder-lhe.

Prémio da humildade

[7] Ao reparar como alguns convidados escolhiam os lugares de honra à mesa, Jesus disse isto: [8] "Quando alguém te convidar para um casamento, não te sentes no lugar principal, porque pode acontecer que tenha sido convidado alguém mais importante do que tu. [9] Então, aquele que convidou os dois terá que te dizer: "Dá o lugar a

este." Ficarás depois envergonhado quando tiveres de procurar o último lugar. ¹⁰ Por isso, quando fores convidado, senta-te no último lugar, e assim quando vier o que te convidou, dirá: "Amigo, passa para um lugar mais honroso." Nessa altura, ficarás muito honrado diante de todos os que estiverem contigo à mesa. ¹¹ Pois todo aquele que se engrandece será humilhado, e todo o que se humilha será engrandecido."

Dar sem esperar recompensa

¹² Depois disse àquele que o tinha convidado: "Quando ofereceres um almoço ou um jantar, não convides os teus amigos, nem os teus irmãos, nem os teus parentes, nem os vizinhos ricos, para que eles não tenham, por sua vez, que te convidar, a fim de te compensarem. ¹³ Quando deres uma festa, convida os pobres, os inválidos, os coxos e os cegos. ¹⁴ Assim serás feliz, porque esses não têm com que te recompensar, mas serás recompensado por Deus, na ressurreição dos justos."

Convidados para o Reino de Deus

¹⁵ Ao ouvir isto, um dos que estavam sentados à mesa disse a Jesus: "Feliz aquele que se sentar à mesa no Reino de Deus!" ¹⁶ Jesus respondeu-lhe: "Um certo homem preparou um dia um grande banquete e convidou muita gente. ¹⁷ À hora da festa mandou um criado dizer aos convidados: "Venham, que está tudo pronto." ¹⁸ Mas todos eles, um por um, se foram desculpando. O primeiro disse: "Comprei um campo e tenho que ir vê-lo. Desculpa, mas não posso ir." ¹⁹ Outro disse: "Comprei cinco juntas de bois e vou experimentá-los. Desculpa, mas não posso ir." ²⁰ Outro desculpou-se assim: "Acabei de me casar e por isso não posso ir." ²¹ O criado voltou e contou isso tudo ao dono da casa. Ele então, muito zangado, deu-lhe esta ordem: "Vai depressa pelas praças e pelas ruas da cidade e traz para cá os pobres, os inválidos, os cegos e os coxos." ²² Quando o criado voltou, disse: "Já fiz como mandaste, mas ainda há lugares." ²³ Então aquele senhor acrescentou: "Vai pelos caminhos e pelos atalhos e obriga-os a vir, para que a minha casa fique cheia. ²⁴ Garanto-vos que nenhum daqueles que convidei primeiro, há-de provar da minha ceia."

Condições para ser discípulo de Cristo

²⁵ Numa ocasião em que ia muita gente com Jesus, ele voltou-se para a multidão e disse: ²⁶ "Se alguém vier ter comigo e não me tiver mais amor do que ao pai, à mãe, à mulher, aos filhos, aos irmãos e às irmãs e até a si próprio, não pode ser meu discípulo. ²⁷ E aquele que não quiser pegar na sua cruz e vir comigo, também não pode ser meu discípulo. ²⁸ Se algum de vocês quiser contruir uma torre, não começará primeiro por se sentar e fazer os cálculos do que vai gastar, para ver se tem possibilidade de a acabar? ²⁹ Isto para que não aconteça que comece a construir e não possa acabar. Não faltará então quem faça troça dele e diga: ³⁰ "Este começou a construir, mas não conseguiu chegar ao fim." ³¹ Ou, se um rei tiver que fazer guerra a outro rei, não começará por se sentar para pensar bem e ver se com dez mil homens pode fazer frente ao exército de vinte mil que vem contra ele? ³² Se vir que não, manda embaixadores a esse rei, que ainda está longe, e pergunta-lhe as condições para fazerem a paz. ³³ Da mesma maneira, qualquer de vocês, que não deixar tudo o que lhe pertence, não pode ser meu discípulo."

³⁴ E acrescentou: "O sal é realmente bom, mas se ele perder o sabor que é que se lhe pode fazer para novamente salgar? ³⁵ Nem presta para a terra, nem para o estrume: deita-se fora. Quem tem ouvidos, preste atenção!"

Alegria pela ovelha encontrada

15 ¹ Todos os cobradores de impostos e outras pessoas de má fama se chegavam a Jesus para o ouvirem. ² Por isso, os fariseus e os doutores da Lei puseram-se a criticá-lo. "Este recebe gente de má fama e come com ela." ³ Jesus apresentou-lhes então esta comparação: ⁴ "Suponham que um de vocês tem cem ovelhas e perde uma delas. Não deixará logo as noventa e nove para ir à procura da ovelha perdida até a encontrar? ⁵ Quando a encontra, põe-na aos ombros, todo satisfeito, ⁶ e, ao chegar a casa, diz aos amigos e vizinhos: "Alegrem-se comigo, porque já encontrei a minha ovelha que andava perdida." ⁷ Da mesma maneira, digo-vos que haverá mais alegria no céu por um pecador que se arrepende do que por noventa e nove pessoas boas que não precisam de se arrepender."

Alegria pela moeda achada

[8] E disse ainda: "Suponham também que uma mulher tem dez moedas de prata e perde uma delas. Que é que ela faz? Acende a lâmpada, varre a casa e procura cuidadosamente até a encontrar. [9] Quando a encontra, diz às amigas e vizinhas: "Alegrem-se comigo, porque já encontrei a moeda perdida." [10] Da mesma maneira, digo-vos que há alegria entre os anjos de Deus cada vez que um pecador se arrepende dos seus pecados."

Alegria pelo regresso do filho

[11] Jesus disse também: "Um certo homem tinha dois filhos. [12] O mais novo pediu ao pai: "Pai, dá-me a parte da herança que me pertence." E o pai repartiu os bens pelos dois filhos. [13] Poucos dias depois, o mais novo vendeu o que era dele e partiu para uma terra muito distante, onde gastou todo o dinheiro numa vida desregrada. [14] Quando já não tinha dinheiro, e como houve muita fome naquela região, começou a ter necessidade. [15] Foi pedir trabalho a um homem da região e ele mandou-o para os seus campos guardar porcos. [16] Desejava encher o estômago mesmo com as bolotas que os porcos comiam, mas ninguém lhas dava. [17] Foi então que ele caiu em si e pensou: "Tantos trabalhadores do meu pai têm quanta comida querem, e eu estou para aqui a morrer de fome! [18] Vou mas é ter com o meu pai e digo-lhe: "Pai, pequei contra Deus e contra ti. [19] Já nem mereço ser teu filho, mas aceita-me como um dos teus trabalhadores." [20] Levantou-se e voltou para o pai. Mas ainda ele vinha longe de casa e já o pai o tinha visto. Cheio de ternura, correu para ele, apertou-o nos braços e cobriu-o de beijos. [21] O filho disse-lhe então: "Pai, pequei contra Deus e contra ti. Já nem mereço ser teu filho." [22] Mas o pai disse logo aos empregados: "Tragam depressa o melhor fato e vistam-lhe. Ponham-lhe também um anel no dedo e calcem-lhe sandálias. [23] Tragam o bezerro mais gordo e matem-no. Vamos fazer um banquete, [24] porque este meu filho estava morto e voltou a viver, estava perdido e apareceu." E começaram com a festa.

[25] Ora, o filho mais velho estava no campo. Ao regressar, quando se aproximava de casa, ouviu a música e as danças. [26] Chamou um dos empregados e perguntou-lhe o que era aquilo. [27] E o empregado dis-

se-lhe: "Foi o teu irmão que voltou e o teu pai matou o bezerro mais gordo, por ele ter chegado são e salvo." [28] Ao ouvir isto, ficou zangado e nem queria entrar. O pai saiu para o convencer. [29] Mas ele respondeu: "Sirvo-te há tantos anos, sem nunca ter desobedecido às tuas ordens, e não me deste sequer um cabrito para fazer uma festa com os meus amigos. [30] Vem agora este teu filho, que desperdiçou o teu dinheiro com mulheres de má vida, e mataste logo o bezerro mais gordo." [31] O pai disse-lhe: "Meu filho, tu estás sempre comigo e tudo o que eu tenho é teu, [32] mas era preciso fazermos uma festa e alegrarmo-nos, porque o teu irmão estava morto e voltou a viver, estava perdido e apareceu."

Esperteza dum feitor desonesto

16 [1] Jesus disse aos seus discípulos: "Havia um homem rico que tinha um feitor. Foram-lhe dizer que esse feitor desperdiçava os seus bens. [2] Ele chamou-o e disse-lhe: "Que é isso que me têm dito de ti? Apresenta-me contas, porque vais deixar de trabalhar para mim." [3] O feitor disse então para consigo: "Que hei-de eu fazer, se o meu patrão me põe na rua? Cavar, não posso; de pedir esmola, tenho vergonha. [4] Já sei o que vou fazer, para quando for despedido ter quem me receba." [5] Chamou os devedores do patrão um a um e disse ao primeiro: "Quanto deves ao meu patrão?" [6] E ele respondeu: "Cem medidas de azeite." O feitor acrescentou: "Pega lá depressa nas tuas contas, senta-te e escreve só cinquenta." [7] Depois perguntou a outro: "E tu, quanto deves?" Ele respondeu: "Cem sacos de trigo." Disse-lhe o feitor: "Pega lá nas tuas contas e escreve só oitenta." [8] O patrão acabou por elogiar o feitor desonesto pela habilidade que teve. Realmente aqueles que se ocupam das coisas deste mundo são mais espertos, nos negócios uns com os outros, do que os que se ocupam das coisas de Deus."

[9] Jesus continuou: "Também vos digo: aproveitem as riquezas deste mundo para fazerem amigos, para ver se, quando as riquezas se acabarem, eles vos receberão no céu! [10] O que é honesto nas coisas sem importância, também o será nas importantes. E quem é desonesto nas pequenas coisas, também o é nas grandes. [11] Mas se não forem honestos com as riquezas deste mundo, quem vos vai confiar as

riquezas verdadeiras? [12] E se não forem fiéis com aquilo que é dos outros, como querem vocês que vos dêem aquilo que vos pertence? [13] Nenhum empregado pode servir dois patrões, porque ou não gosta dum deles e estima o outro, ou há-de ser leal para um e desprezar o outro. Não podem servir a Deus e ao dinheiro."

A Lei e o Reino de Deus

[14] Os fariseus, que eram avarentos, ouviam tudo aquilo e faziam troça de Jesus. [15] Mas ele disse-lhes: "Vocês são os tais que se fazem passar por bons diante de toda a gente, mas Deus é que vos conhece bem. Pois aquilo que para os homens tem muito valor, nada vale para Deus.

[16] Até ao tempo de João Baptista, estavam em vigor a Lei de Moisés e o ensino dos profetas. A partir daí anuncia-se a Boa Nova do Reino de Deus e todos se esforçam por entrar nele. [17] No entanto, é mais fácil acabar o céu e a terra do que cair uma só vírgula da lei."

O problema do divórcio

[18] Disse mais: "Todo o homem que se separar da sua mulher e casar com outra, comete adultério. E o que casar com a separada também comete adultério."

Lázaro e o rico

[19] Acrescentou ainda: "Havia um rico que se vestia com fatos caríssimos e todos os dias fazia grandes festas. [20] Havia também um pobre, chamado Lázaro, coberto de chagas, que costumava ir para a porta do rico, [21] para ver se ao menos comia as migalhas que caíam da sua mesa. Mas até os cães vinham lamber-lhe as chagas.

[22] O pobre morreu e foi levado pelos anjos de Deus para junto de Abraão. O rico também morreu e foi enterrado. [23] No lugar de sofrimento onde se encontrava, levantou os olhos e viu lá longe Abraão e Lázaro com ele. [24] Disse então em voz alta: "Pai Abraão! Tem pena de mim e manda Lázaro molhar na água a ponta do dedo e vir refrescar-me a língua, porque sofro horrivelmente neste fogo!" [25] Mas Abraão disse-lhe: "Lembra-te, meu filho, que em toda a tua vida só tiveste coisas boas, enquanto Lázaro só teve males. Agora ele é consolado e tu

atormentado. ²⁶ Além disso, há um grande abismo entre nós e vocês, de modo que nem os de cá podem passar para lá, nem os daí para aqui." ²⁷ E o rico exclamou: "Peço-te, pai Abraão, que mandes Lázaro a casa do meu pai. ²⁸ Tenho cinco irmãos e se Lázaro lá fosse avisá-los já não vinham para este lugar de sofrimento." ²⁹ Respondeu-lhe Abraão: "Para isso têm os ensinamentos de Moisés e dos profetas. Que lhes prestem atenção." ³⁰ Mas o rico disse: "Não, pai Abraão. É que se alguém dos que já morreram lá fosse falar-lhes, eles arrependiam-se dos pecados." ³¹ Mas Abraão respondeu: "Se não fazem caso de Moisés e dos profetas, também não acreditarão num morto que volte à vida."

Alguns avisos de Jesus

17 ¹ Jesus disse aos discípulos: "Não se pode evitar que haja ocasiões de pecado, mas ai de quem for responsável por elas! ² Seria melhor para essa pessoa ser atirada ao mar com uma pedra de moinho amarrada ao pescoço, do que ela fazer cair em pecado um destes pequeninos. ³ Tenham cuidado! Se o teu irmão te ofender, repreende-o. E se ele se arrepender, perdoa-lhe. ⁴ Se ele te ofender sete vezes no dia, e outras tantas for ter contigo para te dizer que está arrependido, deves perdoar-lhe."

⁵ Os apóstolos pediram então ao Senhor: "Aumenta a nossa fé." ⁶ E o Senhor respondeu: "Se tivessem fé do tamanho de um grão de mostarda, poderiam dizer a esta amoreira: "Arranca-te e vai plantar-te no mar", que ela obedecia-vos.

⁷ Qual de vocês, tendo um trabalhador a lavrar-lhe o campo ou a guardar-lhe o gado, lhe vai dizer, quando ele voltar, "anda, senta-te à mesa"? ⁸ Não lhe dirá antes, "faz-me o jantar e serve-me e, depois de eu ter comido, podes ir tu comer"? ⁹ Acham que ele deve ficar agradecido ao trabalhador por este ter feito o que lhe mandou? ¹⁰ Assim, também vocês, quando tiverem feito tudo o que Deus vos mandou, digam: "Somos simples trabalhadores, porque não fizemos mais do que a nossa obrigação."

Cura de dez doentes com lepra

¹¹ Quando Jesus se dirigia a Jerusalém, atravessou a Galileia e a Samaria. ¹² Ao entrar em certa aldeia, saíram-lhe ao encontro dez doen-

tes com lepra. Ficaram a uma certa distância [13] e puseram-se a gritar: "Jesus, Mestre, tem pena de nós!" [14] Jesus olhou para eles e disse: "Vão ter com os sacerdotes para que eles vos examinem." Eles foram e enquanto iam no caminho, ficaram curados. [15] Um deles, quando viu que estava curado, voltou e louvava a Deus em voz alta. [16] Ajoelhou-se aos pés de Jesus, curvando-se até ao chão em agradecimento. E este era samaritano. [17] Então Jesus perguntou: "Não eram dez os que foram curados? Onde estão os outros nove? [18] Mais nenhum voltou para dar graças a Deus, a não ser este estrangeiro?" [19] Depois disse-lhe: "Levanta-te e vai-te embora. A tua fé te salvou."

A vinda do Reino de Deus

[20] Alguns fariseus perguntaram a Jesus quando é que chegava o Reino de Deus. Jesus respondeu-lhes: "O Reino de Deus não vem como uma coisa que se possa observar. [21] Não se poderá dizer: "Está aqui", ou "está acolá". Na verdade, o Reino de Deus já está no meio de vocês."

[22] Depois disse aos discípulos: "Lá virá o tempo em que desejarão ver ao menos um só dos dias do Filho do Homem e não poderão ver. [23] Alguns hão-de dizer-vos: "Olha, está aqui", ou "está acolá". Mas não vão atrás desses boatos, [24] porque o Filho do Homem virá no seu dia próprio como um relâmpago que ilumina o céu dum extremo ao outro. [25] Mas primeiro tem ele que sofrer muito e ser rejeitado pelas pessoas deste tempo.

[26] Tal como aconteceu no tempo de Noé, assim vai ser nos dias do Filho do Homem. [27] Comiam, bebiam e casavam-se, até ao dia em que Noé entrou na arca. Depois veio o dilúvio e morreram todos. [28] Assim aconteceu também no tempo de Lot: comiam, bebiam, compravam, vendiam, plantavam e construíam. [29] Mas, no dia em que Lot saiu de Sodoma, Deus fez chover fogo e enxofre sobre a cidade e morreram todos. [30] Assim sucederá no dia em que o Filho do Homem aparecer.

[31] Nesse dia, quem estiver no terraço não desça a casa para tirar de lá seja o que for e se estiver no campo, não volte para trás. [32] Lembrem-se da mulher de Lot! [33] Aquele que quiser salvar a vida, perde-a; e o que a perder, salva-a. [34] Digo-vos que nessa noite estarão duas pes-

soas na mesma cama: uma será levada e a outra fica. [35] Duas mulheres estarão juntas a moer farinha: uma será levada e a outra fica. [36] Dois homens estarão no campo: um será levado e o outro fica." [37] Então os discípulos perguntaram-lhe: "E onde vai ser isso, Senhor?" Ele respondeu: "Onde estiver o corpo morto é que se juntam os abutres."

Insistência na oração

18 [1] Jesus fez esta comparação para lhes mostrar que deviam orar sempre, sem nunca desanimar: [2] "Havia numa certa povoação um juiz que não acreditava em Deus e não tinha respeito por ninguém. [3] Nessa mesma povoação morava uma viúva que procurava muitas vezes o juiz e lhe dizia: "Faça-me justiça contra o meu inimigo." [4] Durante muito tempo o juiz não fez caso dela, mas depois pensou: "Apesar de eu não acreditar em Deus, nem ter consideração por ninguém, [5] como esta viúva me anda a incomodar, vou fazer-lhe justiça, para que ela não me faça esgotar a paciência." [6] E o Senhor acrescentou: "Ora vejam lá o que faz o mau juiz. [7] Não fará Deus justiça aos seus escolhidos que chamam por ele dia e noite? Acham que os vai fazer esperar muito? [8] Pois eu afirmo-vos que Deus vos fará justiça sem demora. Mas quando o Filho do Homem vier, achará ele ainda fé sobre a terra?"

Humildade na oração

[9] Jesus fez também esta comparação para alguns que se julgavam pessoas muito justas e desprezavam os outros: [10] "Dois homens foram ao templo para orar. Um deles era fariseu e o outro, cobrador de impostos. [11] O fariseu altivo, orava assim: "Ó Deus, agradeço-te porque não sou como os outros, que são ladrões, injustos e adúlteros, nem como este cobrador de impostos que ali está. [12] Jejuo duas vezes na semana e dou a décima parte de tudo o que ganho." [13] Mas o cobrador de impostos ficou à distância e nem sequer se atrevia a levantar os olhos para o céu; apenas batia com a mão no peito e dizia: "Ó meu Deus, tem compaixão de mim, que sou pecador!" [14] E Jesus concluiu: "Afirmo-vos que o cobrador de impostos foi para sua casa mais justo aos olhos de Deus do que o fariseu. Pois todo aquele que se engrandece será humilhado e todo o que se humilha será engrandecido." —

As crianças e o Reino de Deus

[15] Algumas pessoas levavam também as criancinhas a Jesus para ele as abençoar, mas os discípulos, ao verem isso, repreendiam aquelas pessoas. [16] Então Jesus mandou trazer as criancinhas e disse: "Deixem-nas vir ter comigo! Não as estorvem, porque o Reino de Deus é dos que são como elas. [17] Lembrem-se disto: quem não receber o Reino de Deus como uma criancinha, não entrará nele."

Os ricos e o Reino de Deus

[18] Um judeu importante perguntou a Jesus: "Bom Mestre, que hei-de eu fazer para possuir a vida eterna?" [19] Jesus respondeu-lhe: "Por que me chamas bom? Só Deus é bom, e mais ninguém. [20] Com certeza sabes os mandamentos: *Não cometas adultério, não mates, não roubes, não dês falso testemunho e respeita o teu pai e a tua mãe.*" [21] Ele disse: "Desde rapaz que cumpro todos esses mandamentos." [22] Jesus ouviu-o e acrescentou: "Só te falta uma coisa: vai vender tudo o que tens e dá o dinheiro aos pobres. Ficarás assim com um tesouro no céu. Depois vem comigo." [23] Mas ele ficou desolado com aquelas palavras, porque era muito rico.

[24] Quando Jesus o viu assim, comentou: "Como é difícil aos ricos entrar no Reino de Deus! [25] Sim, é mais fácil um camelo passar pelo fundo duma agulha do que um rico entrar no Reino de Deus." [26] Os que ouviram isto, disseram: "Neste caso quem é que pode salvar-se?" [27] Mas Jesus respondeu: "Aquilo que é impossível aos homens, é possível a Deus."

[28] Então Pedro disse a Jesus: "Olha que nós deixámos tudo para sermos teus discípulos." [29] Jesus respondeu: "Pois eu garanto-vos que todo aquele que tenha deixado casa, mulher, irmãos, pais ou filhos por causa do Reino de Deus, [30] receberá muito mais neste mundo, e no outro possuirá a vida eterna."

Jesus fala outra vez da sua morte e ressurreição

[31] Jesus chamou à parte os doze discípulos e disse-lhes: "Escutem! Vamos para Jerusalém, onde se cumprirá tudo o que os profetas es-

creveram acerca do Filho do Homem. ³² Será entregue aos pagãos, que vão troçar dele, insultá-lo e cuspir-lhe, ³³ bater-lhe e dar-lhe a morte. Mas ao terceiro dia ele há-de ressuscitar." ³⁴ Os discípulos não perceberam nada daquilo, nem sabiam de que é que Jesus lhes estava a falar, porque eram coisas que eles não podiam compreender.

Cura dum cego

³⁵ Jesus estava quase a chegar à cidade de Jericó, e à beira do caminho encontrava-se um cego a pedir esmola. ³⁶ Ao perceber que passava muita gente, o cego perguntou o que era aquilo. ³⁷ Disseram-lhe que era Jesus, o Nazareno, que ia a passar. ³⁸ Então ele gritou dali: "Jesus, Filho de David, tem pena de mim!" ³⁹ Os que iam à frente mandavam-no calar, mas ele gritava cada vez mais: "Filho de David, tem pena de mim!" ⁴⁰ Jesus parou e mandou-o chamar. Quando ele chegou, perguntou-lhe: ⁴¹ "Que queres que eu te faça?" E ele respondeu: "Senhor, queria voltar a ver." ⁴² Jesus disse-lhe: "Pois vê! A tua fé te salvou." ⁴³ Naquele mesmo instante o cego começou a ver e seguiu também com Jesus louvando a Deus pelo caminho. E toda a gente, vendo aquilo, dava louvores a Deus.

Jesus chama Zaqueu

19 ¹ Jesus entrou em Jericó e atravessava a cidade. ² Havia lá um homem rico chamado Zaqueu, chefe de cobradores de impostos. ³ Queria ver quem era Jesus, mas como era muito baixo não conseguia, por causa da multidão. ⁴ Correu então adiante do povo, subiu a uma figueira brava e ficou à espera que Jesus por ali passasse para o ver. ⁵ Quando Jesus lá chegou, olhou para cima e disse-lhe: "Zaqueu, desce depressa, porque hoje preciso de ficar em tua casa." ⁶ Ele desceu imediatamente e recebeu Jesus com alegria. ⁷ Ao verem isto, começaram todos a criticar e a dizer que Jesus tinha ido para casa de um homem de má fama. ⁸ Então Zaqueu pôs-se de pé e falou assim: "Escuta-me, Senhor! Vou dar aos pobres metade de todos os meus bens e às pessoas a quem prejudiquei vou dar-lhes quatro vezes mais." ⁹ Jesus então declarou: "Hoje entrou a salvação nesta casa, pois este homem também é descendente de Abraão. ¹⁰ Na verdade, o Filho do Homem veio buscar e salvar os que estavam perdidos."

Rendimento dos nossos dons

[11] A multidão ouvia Jesus acerca de todas estas coisas. Como ele estava perto de Jerusalém e o povo pensava que ia chegar imediatamente o Reino de Deus, Jesus acrescentou ainda esta comparação: [12] "Havia um homem de boas famílias que partiu para outro país a fim de ser nomeado rei e em seguida voltar. [13] Antes de partir, chamou dez dos seus empregados, entregou a cada um deles uma moeda de ouro e disse-lhes: "Façam negócio com este dinheiro até que eu volte." [14] Ora o povo daquele país odiava esse homem e enviou atrás dele uma comissão com este recado: "Não queremos que ele seja o nosso rei." [15] Depois de ele ser nomeado rei, voltou. Mandou logo chamar os empregados a quem tinha deixado o dinheiro, para saber quanto tinha ganho cada um deles no negócio. [16] Chegou o primeiro e disse: "Senhor, o teu dinheiro rendeu dez vezes mais." [17] E o rei disse: "Está muito bem! És um bom empregado. Já que foste fiel numa coisa tão pequena, faço-te governador de dez cidades." [18] Depois veio o segundo empregado e disse: "Senhor, o teu dinheiro rendeu cinco vezes mais." [19] O rei disse também a este: "Tu serás governador de cinco cidades." [20] Apareceu então um a dizer: "Senhor, aqui tens a moeda de ouro. Guardei-a num lenço, [21] porque tive medo de ti, por seres muito rigoroso, pois vais buscar aonde não puseste e colhes o que não semeaste." [22] Mas o rei respondeu-lhe: "Tu és um mau empregado, e vou julgar-te pelas tuas próprias palavras. Sabias que sou um homem rigoroso, que vou buscar aonde não pus e colho o que não semeei. [23] Por que não puseste então o meu dinheiro no banco para que, quando eu voltasse, o recebesse com juros?" [24] E disse aos que estavam com ele: "Tirem-lhe a moeda de ouro e dêem-na ao que tem dez." [25] Mas eles disseram: "Senhor, esse já tem dez moedas!" [26] O rei respondeu: "Pois eu digo-vos que ao que tem dá-se-lhe mais, mas ao que não tem tira-se-lhe até o pouco que possui. [27] Quanto àqueles inimigos que não queriam que eu fosse o rei, tragam-mos cá e matem-nos na minha presença."

Entrada de Jesus em Jerusalém

[28] Depois de dizer isto, Jesus seguia à frente do povo para Jerusalém. [29] Quando estava perto de Betfagé e Betânia, junto do Monte das

Oliveiras, mandou dois discípulos [30] com este recado: "Vão à povoação que fica ali em frente. Logo que lá entrarem encontrarão um jumentinho preso, que ainda ninguém montou. Soltem-no e tragam-no cá. [31] Se alguém lhes perguntar por que é que fazem isso, digam que é o Senhor que precisa dele." [32] Eles foram e encontraram tudo como Jesus lhes tinha dito. [33] Quando estavam a soltar o jumentinho, os donos disseram: "Por que é que estão a soltar o jumento?" [34] E eles responderam: "O Senhor precisa dele." [35] Levaram-no então a Jesus e puseram as suas capas por cima do jumento. Depois ajudaram Jesus a montar. [36] À medida que Jesus avançava, as pessoas estendiam as suas capas pelo caminho. [37] Ao chegarem perto da descida do Monte das Oliveiras, todos os seus discípulos começaram a gritar de alegria e a dar louvores a Deus por todos os milagres que tinham visto. [38] E exclamavam:

> "Bendito seja o rei,
> que vem em nome do Senhor!
> Paz no céu e glória a Deus!"

[39] Então alguns fariseus que estavam entre a multidão disseram: "Mestre, repreende os teus discípulos." [40] Mas Jesus respondeu-lhes: "Olhem que se estes se calarem, até as pedras hão-de gritar." [41] Quando chegou perto de Jerusalém, ao ver a cidade, Jesus chorou por ela [42] e disse: "Se tu também compreendesses, ao menos hoje, aquilo que te pode dar a paz! Mas por agora não conseguirás entender! [43] Lá virá o tempo em que os teus inimigos farão uma muralha em volta de ti e te cercarão por todos os lados. [44] Hão-de deitar-te por terra e matar os teus habitantes e não deixarão em ti uma pedra sobre outra, porque não reconheceste o tempo em que Deus te veio salvar."

Contra os abusos no templo

[45] Jesus entrou no templo começou a pôr de lá para fora os que estavam a fazer negócio, [46] dizendo-lhes: "Deus afirma na Sagrada Escritura: *O meu templo será casa de oração.* Mas vocês transformaram-no em caverna de ladrões."

[47] Jesus ensinava todos os dias no templo. Os chefes dos sacerdotes e os doutores da Lei, bem como os chefes do povo, andavam entre-

tanto a ver como podiam matá-lo. [48] Mas não encontravam maneira, porque toda a gente andava entusiasmada em o ouvir.

A autoridade de Jesus é contestada

20 [1] Um dia estava Jesus no templo a ensinar o povo e a pregar a Boa Nova, quando chegaram uns chefes dos sacerdotes e doutores da Lei, juntamente com anciãos, [2] e lhe perguntaram: "Diz-nos lá, que autoridade tens tu para fazer o que fazes? Quem te deu esse direito?" [3] Jesus respondeu-lhes: "Também eu vos vou fazer uma pergunta. Ora, digam-me lá: [4] João baptizava com autoridade de Deus ou dos homens?" [5] Eles puseram-se então a discutir uns com os outros, e diziam: "Se respondermos que é de Deus, ele vai já perguntar-nos por que razão não acreditámos em João. [6] Mas, se dissermos que é dos homens, toda a gente nos vai atirar pedras, porque João Baptista é tido como verdadeiro profeta." [7] Responderam então que não sabiam. [8] E Jesus concluiu: "Pois também eu não vos digo com que autoridade faço estas coisas."

Rendeiros criminosos

[9] Depois Jesus apresentou ao povo esta comparação: "Certo homem plantou uma vinha, arrendou-a a uns camponeses e ausentou-se para fora da terra por muito tempo. [10] Quando chegou a época das vindimas, mandou um criado aos camponeses para eles pagarem a sua parte do fruto. Mas eles agarraram o criado, espancaram-no e mandaram-no embora de mãos vazias. [11] Então o dono da vinha mandou outro e eles espancaram também este, insultaram-no e mandaram-no embora de mãos vazias. [12] Mandou-lhes um terceiro criado, mas eles feriram-no também e mandaram-no embora. [13] Então o dono da vinha disse para consigo: "Que hei-de eu fazer? Vou lá mandar o meu querido filho. Certamente que a ele o vão respeitar." [14] Mas quando os camponeses o viram, disseram logo uns para os outros: "Este é que é o herdeiro! Vamos matá-lo e a herança dele fica para nós." [15] Levaram-no então para fora da vinha e mataram-no. Em face disto, que lhes fará o dono da vinha? [16] Irá matar aqueles homens e arrendará a vinha a outros."

Quando o povo ouviu isto, disse:"Deus queira que tal não aconteça!" [17] Mas Jesus olhou para o povo e perguntou: "Qual será então o significado desta frase da Escritura: *A pedra que os construtores rejeitaram veio a tornar-se a pedra principal*"?

[18] E acrescentou:"Todo aquele que cair em cima dessa pedra ficará feito em pedaços, e aquele em cima de quem ela cair, ficará reduzido a pó."

Jesus confunde os inimigos

[19] Os doutores da Lei e os chefes dos sacerdotes procuravam maneira de prender Jesus naquela altura, porque perceberam muito bem que aquela história se referia a eles, mas tinham medo do povo. [20] Puseram-se então a vigiá-lo e mandaram ter com Jesus uns espiões que se fingiam muito religiosos, para ver se o apanhavam em falso naquilo que dizia e o entregarem depois à autoridade e ao poder do governador. [21] Estes apresentaram a Jesus o seguinte problema:"Mestre, sabemos que tudo o que dizes e ensinas está certo, e que não julgas as pessoas pela aparência, pois ensinas com fidelidade a vontade de Deus. [22] Diz-nos uma coisa: Devemos ou não pagar imposto ao Imperador romano?"[23] Jesus percebeu a malícia deles e disse: [24] "Deixem cá ver uma moeda. De quem é esta figura, e esta inscrição?" Eles responderam: "Do Imperador". [25] Jesus disse-lhes: "Pois bem, dêem então ao Imperador o que é do Imperador e a Deus o que é de Deus." [26] E não conseguiram apanhá-lo em nada do que disse diante de toda a gente. Mas, admirados com a sua resposta, calaram-se.

O assunto da ressurreição

[27] Uns saduceus foram ter com Jesus. Ora eles dizem que não há ressurreição e por isso perguntaram-lhe: [28] "Mestre, Moisés deixou-nos escrito na lei que *se um homem morrer e deixar a mulher sem nenhum filho, o irmão a seguir deve casar com a viúva, para assim dar descendência ao irmão falecido*. [29] Acontece que havia sete irmãos. O mais velho casou-se e morreu sem deixar filhos. [30] Ora, o segundo, [31] depois o terceiro e os outros, até ao sétimo, todos casaram com ela e todos morreram sem deixar filhos. [32] Por último, morreu a mulher.

[33] Ora bem, no dia da ressurreição, de qual deles será a mulher, visto que os sete casaram com ela?"

[34] Jesus respondeu-lhes: "Neste mundo é que as pessoas se casam. [35] Mas os que merecerem chegar ao outro mundo e ressuscitar dos mortos, esses não se casam. [36] São como os anjos e já não podem morrer: são filhos de Deus porque são herdeiros da ressurreição. [37] Até o próprio Moisés, naquele trecho acerca do arbusto nos deu a entender que os mortos ressuscitam, quando chama ao Senhor *o Deus de Abraão, de Isaac e de Jacob*. [38] Ele não é Deus de mortos, mas de vivos; por isso, para ele todos estão vivos." [39] Houve então alguns doutores da Lei que lhe disseram: "Muito bem, Mestre!" [40] Depois disto, ninguém mais tinha coragem de lhe fazer perguntas.

O Messias e David

[41] Jesus então perguntou-lhes: "Como pode dizer-se que o Messias é descendente de David? [42] Vejam que o próprio David disse no livro dos Salmos: *Deus disse ao meu Senhor: Senta-te à minha direita,* [43] *até que eu ponha os teus inimigos debaixo dos teus pés.*

[44] Ora, se David chama Senhor, como pode o Messias ser seu descendente?"

Vaidade e exploração

[45] Estando toda a gente a ouvi-lo, Jesus disse aos discípulos: [46] "Cuidado com os doutores da Lei! Gostam de andar a passear bem trajados e de serem cumprimentados com todas as atenções nas praças públicas. Escolhem os lugares de destaque tanto nas casas de oração como nos banquetes. [47] Devoram os bens das viúvas e desculpam-se fazendo longas orações. Mas Deus há-de castigá-los ainda mais por causa disso."

A oferta da viúva pobre

21 [1] Jesus observava os ricos a deitarem dinheiro na caixa das ofertas do templo. [2] Viu também uma viúva muito pobre, que lá deitou duas moedas com pouco valor. [3] Então Jesus disse: "Garanto-vos que esta pobre viúva deitou na caixa mais do que todos os outros. [4] É que eles deram do que lhes sobejava, mas ela, na sua pobreza, deu tudo o que tinha para viver."

Jesus fala da destruição do templo

[5] Estavam ali alguns a dizer que o templo era muito belo, com as suas pedras formosas, bem trabalhadas, e com as ofertas que o adornavam. Então Jesus disse: [6] "Lá virá o dia em que tudo isto que aqui vêem será deitado abaixo. Nem uma só destas pedras ficará no lugar."

Sofrimento e perseguição

[7] Perguntaram então a Jesus: "Mestre, quando será isso e qual vai ser o sinal de que todas essas coisas estão para acontecer?" [8] Ele respondeu: "Tenham cuidado e não se deixem enganar por ninguém! Hão-de aparecer muitos a fingir que vêm em meu nome e a dizer: "Sou eu o Messias, chegou a hora!" Não vão atrás deles! [9] E quando ouvirem dizer que há guerras e revoluções, não tenham medo. Estas coisas têm de acontecer primeiro, mas não quer dizer que já seja o fim." [10] Jesus continuou: "As nações hão-de entrar em luta umas com as outras, e os países vão atacar-se uns aos outros. [11] Haverá grandes terramotos, fomes e pestes em muitos lugares, hão-de ver-se coisas espantosas e do céu virão grandes sinais. [12] Mas antes de tudo isso, vocês serão presos e perseguidos, serão levados a julgamento nas casas de oração e lançados na prisão. Vão ter que comparecer diante de reis e governadores, por minha causa, [13] e terão assim oportunidade de lhes falar de mim. [14] Mas convençam-se que não é preciso preocuparem-se com a própria defesa, [15] porque eu vos darei palavras e sabedoria a que nenhum dos vossos inimigos poderá resistir, nem será capaz de contradizer. [16] Vocês serão atraiçoados pelos próprios pais, irmãos, parentes e amigos. E alguns serão mesmo levados à morte. [17] Vão ser odiados por toda a gente por minha causa, [18] mas nem um só cabelo das vossas cabeças se irá perder. [19] Mantenham-se firmes até ao fim e serão salvos."

Julgamento de Jerusalém

[20] "Quando virem Jerusalém cercada por exércitos, ficarão a saber que não tardará a ser destruída. [21] Nessa altura, aqueles que estiverem na Judeia devem fugir para os montes. Os que estiverem dentro da cidade devem sair dela, e os que estiverem nos campos não devem en-

trar na cidade, [22] porque serão esses os dias de castigo, em que se há-
-de cumprir tudo o que diz a Escritura. [23] Ai das mulheres que estiverem grávidas nessa altura e das que andarem a amamentar crianças,
pois haverá grande miséria no país e este povo será muito castigado.
[24] Muitos serão mortos à espada e outros serão levados prisioneiros
para todos os países. E Jerusalém será calcada aos pés pelos estran-
geiros até que eles terminem o seu tempo."

Vinda do Filho do Homem

[25] E disse também: "Haverá sinais no Sol, na Lua e nas estrelas, e
todas as nações da terra ficarão aflitas e assustadas com o terrível
bramido do mar agitado. [26] Haverá quem desfaleça com medo do
que vai acontecer em toda a terra, porque as forças do espaço serão
abaladas. [27] Verão então o Filho do Homem chegar numa nuvem
com grande poder e glória. [28] Quando estas coisas começarem a
acontecer, animem-se e levantem a cabeça, porque já estará próxima
a vossa salvação."

[29] Jesus apresentou-lhes depois esta comparação: "Reparem na figueira e em todas as outras árvores. [30] Quando as suas folhas come-
çam a aparecer, vocês vêem logo que o Verão se aproxima. [31] Do mesmo modo, quando virem acontecer estas coisas, fiquem sabendo que
o Reino de Deus está perto. [32] Garanto-vos que tudo isso há-de acontecer antes de desaparecer a gente deste tempo. [33] Desaparecerão os
céus e a terra, mas as minhas palavras não desaparecem!"

Necessidade de estar atento

[34] E acrescentou: "Tenham muito cuidado! Não se deixem cair nos
exageros do comer e do beber, nem se deixem absorver pelos muitos
cuidados desta vida! Não vá acontecer que aquele dia vos apanhe de
surpresa, [35] pois ele virá como uma armadilha, sobre todos os habitantes da terra. [36] Estejam bem atentos, e peçam sempre a Deus para
que possam escapar a todas estas coisas que vão acontecer e para que
possam apresentar-se firmes diante do Filho do Homem."

[37] Jesus passava os dias a ensinar no templo e ao cair da noite saía
para ir descansar no Monte das Oliveiras. [38] Toda a gente ia ter com
ele ao templo logo de manhã para o ouvir.

Planos para matar Jesus

22 ¹ Estava já próxima a festa em que se comem os pães sem fermento, ou seja a festa da Páscoa. ² Os chefes dos sacerdotes e os doutores da Lei procuravam a maneira de matar Jesus, mas tinham medo do povo. ³ Então Satanás entrou em Judas, que tinha o sobrenome de Iscariotes e que pertencia ao número dos doze apóstolos. ⁴ Judas foi ter com os chefes dos sacerdotes e com os oficiais do templo e combinou com eles a maneira de lhes entregar Jesus. ⁵ Eles ficaram muito contentes com isso e prometeram dar-lhe dinheiro. ⁶ Judas concordou e começou a procurar a melhor ocasião de o entregar sem que o povo desse por isso.

Preparação da ceia da Páscoa

⁷ Chegou o dia da festa dos pães sem fermento em que deviam matar-se os cordeiros para a Páscoa. ⁸ Jesus mandou Pedro e João à cidade e recomendou-lhes isto: "Vão preparar o necessário para comermos a ceia da Páscoa." ⁹ Eles perguntaram-lhe: "Aonde queres que a vamos preparar?" ¹⁰ Jesus respondeu: "Quando entrarem na cidade, hão-de encontrar um homem que leva um cântaro de água. Vão atrás dele até à casa em que ele entrar. ¹¹ Uma vez lá, dirão ao dono da casa: "O Mestre manda perguntar: onde é que fica a sala para eu comer a ceia da Páscoa com os meus discípulos?" ¹² Ele há-de mostrar-vos uma grande sala no andar de cima, com tudo o que é preciso. Preparem lá a nossa Páscoa." ¹³ Eles partiram, encontraram tudo como Jesus lhes tinha dito e prepararam a ceia da Páscoa.

Última ceia de Jesus

¹⁴ Quando chegou a altura, Jesus sentou-se à mesa com os apóstolos ¹⁵ e disse-lhes: "Desejei ardentemente comer convosco esta Páscoa antes de morrer. ¹⁶ Pois afirmo-vos que não voltarei a comê-la até que ela receba o seu significado completo no Reino de Deus." ¹⁷ Pegou então no cálice, deu graças a Deus e disse: "Tomem, repartam-no entre todos, ¹⁸ pois afirmo-vos que não voltarei a beber vinho até que chegue o Reino de Deus." ¹⁹ Depois pegou no pão, deu graças a Deus, partiu-o, deu-o aos discípulos e disse: "Isto é o meu corpo entregue à

morte para vosso benefício. Façam isto em memória de mim." [20] Do mesmo modo pegou no cálice depois da ceia e disse: "Este cálice é a nova aliança de Deus confirmada com o meu sangue, derramado para vosso benefício."

[21] E disse ainda: "Mas reparem que aquele que me vai atraiçoar está aqui comigo à mesa. [22] Na realidade, o Filho do Homem vai seguir o caminho que lhe foi traçado por Deus, mas ai daquele homem que o vai trair!" [23] Eles então começaram a perguntar uns aos outros qual deles é que iria fazer uma coisa daquelas.

Quem é o mais importante no Reino de Deus

[24] Os discípulos tiveram uma discussão sobre qual deles seria o mais importante. [25] Mas Jesus disse-lhes: "Os reis do mundo consideram-se senhores dos povos e os que têm poder passam por benfeitores públicos. [26] Mas entre vocês não pode ser assim. Pelo contrário, aquele que for o maior, proceda como se fosse o mais pequeno, e o que governar proceda como quem serve os outros. [27] Qual será mais importante? O que está sentado à mesa a comer, ou o que está a servir? Claro que é o que está sentado à mesa! Pois bem, aqui entre todos eu sou como aquele que serve."

[28] E acrescentou: "Vocês são aqueles que têm estado sempre comigo em todas as minhas aflições. [29] Por isso ponho à vossa disposição o Reino, como meu Pai o pôs à minha disposição, [30] para que comam e bebam à minha mesa no meu reino e se sentem em tronos para julgarem as doze tribos de Israel."

Jesus avisa Pedro

[31] O Senhor disse ainda: "Simão! Simão! Olha que Satanás pediu para vos experimentar a todos, como quem passa o trigo por um crivo, [32] mas eu roguei a Deus por ti para que a tua fé não falhe. E tu, quando voltares para mim, encoraja os teus irmãos." [33] Pedro respondeu: "Senhor, estou disposto a ir contigo até à prisão e até à morte." [34] Mas Jesus avisou-o: "Olha, Pedro, não cantará hoje o galo sem que tu me tenhas negado três vezes."

Considerado como um criminoso

³⁵ Jesus perguntou aos discípulos: "Quando vos mandei sem bolsa, nem saco, nem calçado, faltou-vos por acaso alguma coisa?" Eles responderam: "Não!" ³⁶ Jesus disse: "Pois agora, aquele que tiver bolsa, leve-a consigo, bem como o saco. E o que não tiver espada venda a capa e compre uma. ³⁷ Afirmo-vos que irá cumprir-se em mim aquela frase da Escritura: *Foi considerado como um criminoso*. Realmente, tudo o que está escrito a meu respeito vai-se cumprir." ³⁸ Eles então disseram-lhe: "Senhor, temos aqui duas espadas." E Jesus respondeu: "Chegam."

Oração no Monte das Oliveiras

³⁹ Jesus saiu para o Monte das Oliveiras, como era seu costume. Os discípulos foram com ele. ⁴⁰ Quando lá chegou, disse-lhes: "Peçam a Deus para não caírem em tentação." ⁴¹ Afastou-se deles cerca de trinta metros e pondo-se de joelhos, orava assim: ⁴² "Pai, se for do teu agrado, livra-me deste cálice de amargura. No entanto, não se faça a minha vontade, mas sim a tua." ⁴³ Nisto apareceu-lhe um anjo do céu que veio dar-lhe forças. ⁴⁴ Jesus estava muito angustiado e orava ainda com mais fervor, enquanto o suor lhe caía no chão, como grandes gotas de sangue.

⁴⁵ Depois da oração, levantou-se e foi ter com os discípulos, mas encontrou-os abatidos pela tristeza. ⁴⁶ Disse-lhes então: "Estão a dormir? Levantem-se e orem, para não caírem em tentação."

Prisão de Jesus

⁴⁷ Ainda Jesus estava a falar, quando chegou uma multidão. À frente vinha Judas, que era um dos doze discípulos. Aproximou-se de Jesus para lhe dar um beijo ⁴⁸ e Jesus disse-lhe: "Judas, é com um beijo que atraiçoas o Filho do Homem?" ⁴⁹ Quando os discípulos que estavam com Jesus viram o que ia acontecer, perguntaram: "Senhor, queres que ataquemos à espada?" ⁵⁰ E um deles atacou logo o criado do chefe dos sacerdotes, cortando-lhe a orelha direita. ⁵¹ Mas Jesus respondeu: "Basta! Deixem lá." E, tocando com a mão na orelha do homem, curou-o.

⁵² Jesus disse então aos chefes dos sacerdotes, aos oficiais do templo e aos anciãos que foram para o prender: "Vieram aqui com espadas e paus para me prenderem, como se eu fosse um ladrão?... ⁵³ Estava convosco todos os dias no templo e não me prenderam! Mas esta é a vossa hora, é o poder das trevas!"

Pedro diz que não conhece Jesus

⁵⁴ Eles prenderam Jesus e levaram-no à casa do chefe dos sacerdotes. Pedro seguia-o à distância. ⁵⁵ Alguns acenderam uma fogueira no meio do pátio e estavam sentados à volta dela para se aquecerem. Pedro sentou-se também entre eles. ⁵⁶ Nisto, uma criada que o viu sentado junto da fogueira pôs-se a olhar para ele e disse: "Este também lá estava com ele!" ⁵⁷ Mas Pedro negou, dizendo: "Eu nem o conheço, mulher!" ⁵⁸ Pouco depois, outro criado viu-o e disse: "Tu também és um deles!" Porém Pedro respondeu: "Ó homem, não sou!" ⁵⁹ Daí por cerca de uma hora apareceu outro que insistiu: "Não há dúvida de que este estava com ele, porque também é da Galileia!" ⁶⁰ E Pedro respondeu de novo: "Ó homem, não sei de que estás a falar!" Ainda ele estava a dizer estas palavras, quando um galo cantou. ⁶¹ O Senhor então voltou-se, olhou para Pedro e ele lembrou-se do que lhe tinha dito: "Não cantará hoje o galo sem que me tenhas negado três vezes." ⁶² Então Pedro saiu dali e chorou amargamente.

Os guardas fazem troça de Jesus

⁶³ Os homens que estavam a guardar Jesus faziam troça dele. ⁶⁴ Tapavam-lhe os olhos, batiam-lhe e perguntavam: "Se és profeta, adivinha quem te bateu!" ⁶⁵ E diziam muitas outras coisas para o insultarem.

Jesus no tribunal judaico

⁶⁶ Quando se fez dia, reuniu-se o conselho dos anciãos do povo, chefes dos sacerdotes e doutores da Lei e levaram Jesus à presença do tribunal judaico. ⁶⁷ Perguntaram então a Jesus: "Diz-nos lá, és tu o Messias?" E ele respondeu: "Se vos disser que sim, não acreditam, ⁶⁸ e se vos fizer uma pergunta não me respondem. ⁶⁹ Mas a partir de agora o Filho do Homem estará sentado à direita de Deus todo-poderoso."

[70] Eles disseram à uma: "Então és o Filho de Deus?" Ao que Jesus respondeu: "Vocês dizem que sou!" [71] Assim eles concluíram: "Já não precisamos de mais provas! Nós próprios ouvimos o que ele afirmou!"

Jesus acusado de subversivo

23 [1] Todos eles se levantaram e levaram Jesus a Pilatos. [2] Então começaram a acusá-lo: "Apanhámos este homem a revoltar o nosso povo, dizendo que não se deviam pagar impostos ao Imperador e fazendo-se passar pelo Messias-Rei." [3] Pilatos perguntou-lhe: "És tu o rei dos judeus?" Jesus respondeu: "Tu o dizes." [4] Então Pilatos falou assim aos chefes dos sacerdotes e à multidão: "Não acho razão para condenar este homem." [5] Mas eles insistiram cada vez mais: "Olha que ele tem andado a agitar o povo com aquilo que ensina por todo o país, desde a Galileia até aqui."

De Herodes para Pilatos

[6] Quando Pilatos ouviu isto, perguntou se aquele homem era da Galileia. [7] Sendo informado que Jesus pertencia à região governada por Herodes, mandou-lho, pois Herodes estava naquela altura em Jerusalém. [8] Herodes ficou muito contente por ver Jesus. Com efeito desde há bastante tempo que desejava conhecê-lo, pois ouvia falar muito dele. Esperava mesmo que Jesus fizesse algum milagre na sua presença. [9] Perguntou-lhe muitas coisas, mas Jesus não respondeu a nenhuma. [10] Os chefes dos sacerdotes e os doutores da Lei levantaram-se, acusando Jesus com grande insistência. [11] Então Herodes, juntamente com os seus soldados, tratou-o com desprezo. Mandou-o vestir com um manto vistoso e enviou-o a Pilatos. [12] Nesse mesmo dia Pilatos e Herodes ficaram amigos, pois antes disso andavam de relações cortadas.

Jesus condenado à morte

[13] Pilatos reuniu então os chefes dos sacerdotes, as autoridades e o povo, e falou-lhes assim: [14] "Trouxeram-me este homem e disseram-me que ele tem andado a revoltar o povo. Mas interroguei-o aqui na presença de todos e não lhe encontro crime nenhum daqueles de que vocês o acusam. [15] Nem mesmo Herodes o achou culpado, pois co-

mo estão a ver ele mandou-o outra vez para nós. Olhem que ele não fez nada que mereça a pena de morte. [16] Portanto, vou pô-lo em liberdade, depois de o ter castigado." [17] Durante a festa da Páscoa, Pilatos tinha sempre que lhes soltar um preso. [18] Mas todos começaram a gritar ao mesmo tempo: "Fora daqui com ele! Solta-nos mas é Barrabás!" [19] Este Barrabás tinha sido preso por causa duma revolta na cidade e por ter assassinado uma pessoa. [20] Então Pilatos, querendo soltar Jesus, falou outra vez ao povo. [21] Mas aquela multidão gritava cada vez mais: "Crucifica-o! Crucifica-o!" [22] Pilatos falou-lhes pela terceira vez: "Mas que mal fez ele? Não lhe encontro nenhum crime que mereça a pena de morte. Por isso, vou pô-lo em liberdade, depois de o castigar." [23] Mas eles insistiam aos gritos que ele fosse crucificado. E tanto gritaram [24] que Pilatos acabou por lhes fazer a vontade: [25] soltou-lhes, como eles queriam, o homem que tinha sido preso como revoltoso e assassino, e entregou Jesus para que o povo fizesse dele o que quisesse.

Jesus crucificado

[26] Quando o levavam, obrigaram um homem de Cirene chamado Simão, que vinha do campo, a levar a cruz de Jesus às costas e a seguir atrás dele. [27] Ia também uma grande multidão em que se viam algumas mulheres que choravam e se lamentavam por causa dele. [28] Jesus voltou-se então para elas e disse: "Mulheres de Jerusalém, não chorem por mim, chorem antes por vocês e pelos vossos filhos. [29] Há-de vir o tempo em que se dirá: "Felizes as mulheres que não podem ter filhos, e que nunca os tiveram, e que nunca os amamentaram!" [30] Nessa altura as pessoas começarão a dizer às montanhas: "Caiam em cima de nós!" e às colinas: "Escondam-nos!" [31] Pois, se tratam desta maneira a árvore verde, que será da que estiver seca?"

[32] Também levavam dois criminosos para os matarem juntamente com Jesus. [33] Chegaram ao lugar chamado Caveira e ali o pregaram numa cruz, bem como aos dois criminosos: um à sua direita e o outro à sua esquerda. [34] Jesus porém dizia: "Pai, perdoa-lhes, que não sabem o que fazem!" Eles dividiram entre si a roupa de Jesus, depois de terem deitado sortes. [35] O povo olhava para aquilo tudo, enquanto as autoridades judaicas faziam troça dele e diziam: "Salvou os outros,

que se salve a si mesmo, se é o Messias a quem Deus escolheu!" [36] Também os soldados escarneciam dele: aproximavam-se, ofereciam-lhe vinagre [37] e diziam: "Salva-te a ti mesmo, se és o rei dos judeus." [38] Por cima de Jesus estava um letreiro com estes dizeres: "ESTE É O REI DOS JUDEUS."

[39] Um dos criminosos crucificados insultava-o assim: "Então não és o Messias? Salva-te a ti mesmo e a nós!" [40] Mas o outro repreendia-o com estas palavras: "Não tens temor a Deus, tu que estás a sofrer a mesma condenação? [41] Nós estamos aqui a pagar o justo castigo pelos actos que temos praticado, mas este não fez nada de mal." [42] E disse: "Jesus, lembra-te de mim quando chegares ao teu reino." [43] Jesus respondeu-lhe: "Podes ter a certeza que hoje mesmo estarás comigo no Paraíso."

Morte de Jesus

[44] Era quase meio-dia quando o Sol deixou de brilhar e toda a terra ficou às escuras até às três horas da tarde. [45] A cortina do templo rasgou-se ao meio. [46] Então Jesus deu um grande grito e disse: "Pai, nas tuas mãos entrego o meu espírito." Mal acabou de pronunciar estas palavras, morreu. [47] Ao ver isto, o oficial romano que ali estava louvou a Deus exclamando: "Este homem era realmente bom!" [48] As pessoas que lá se juntaram para presenciar o que acontecia, depois do que viram, voltaram para casa a bater no peito. [49] Todos os que conheciam Jesus pessoalmente, incluindo as mulheres que o tinham acompanhado desde a Galileia, ficaram a uma certa distância a ver o que se passava.

Sepultura de Jesus

[50] Havia um homem chamado José, da cidade de Arimateia, na região da Judeia, que era pessoa de bem, muito religioso e que esperava também a vinda do Reino de Deus. [51] Fazia parte do tribunal judaico, mas não tinha concordado com o que se fez. [52] Foi ter com Pilatos e pediu-lhe o corpo de Jesus. [53] Depois tirou-o da cruz, envolveu-o num lençol e foi sepultá-lo num túmulo aberto na rocha, onde ainda ninguém tinha sido sepultado. [54] Era sexta-feira e estava quase a começar o sábado.

⁵⁵ As mulheres que tinham vindo com Jesus desde a Galileia foram atrás de José. Viram o túmulo e como o corpo de Jesus lá foi sepultado. ⁵⁶ Quando voltaram para casa prepararam perfumes e unguentos para o corpo de Jesus. Mas no sábado descansaram, como manda a lei.

Ressurreição de Jesus

24 ¹ No domingo de manhãzinha, as mulheres levaram os perfumes que tinham preparado e foram ao túmulo. ² Nisto, viram que a pedra que tapava a entrada do sepulcro tinha sido rodada para o lado. ³ Entraram, mas não encontraram o corpo de Jesus. ⁴ Estavam ainda sem saber o que haviam de fazer, quando viram dois homens de pé junto delas, vestidos com roupas brilhantes. ⁵ Elas baixaram os olhos para o chão, cheias de medo, mas eles disseram-lhes: "Por que procuram entre os mortos aquele que está vivo? ⁶ Não está aqui, mas ressuscitou. Não se lembram do que ele vos disse, quando ainda estava na Galileia, ⁷ que é preciso que o Filho do Homem seja entregue ao poder dos maus, que seja pregado numa cruz e que ao terceiro dia ressuscite?" ⁸ Elas então lembraram-se daquelas palavras. ⁹ Saíram do túmulo e foram dizer tudo isto aos onze apóstolos e a todos os demais. ¹⁰ Essas mulheres eram Maria Madalena, Joana e Maria, mãe de Tiago, e ainda outras que também confirmavam isso. ¹¹ Mas os apóstolos acharam que aquelas coisas que as mulheres contaram não faziam sentido e não acreditaram nelas. ¹² No entanto, Pedro levantou-se e correu até ao sepulcro. Inclinou-se, viu apenas as ligaduras e voltou para casa admirado com o que tinha acontecido.

A caminho de Emaús

¹³ Nesse mesmo dia iam dois dos discípulos para uma aldeia chamada Emaús, a cerca de onze quilómetros de Jerusalém. ¹⁴ Pelo caminho iam a falar um com o outro a respeito de tudo o que tinha acontecido. ¹⁵ No meio da conversa, Jesus aproximou-se e pôs-se a caminho com eles. ¹⁶ Mas eles embora o vissem, não o reconheceram. ¹⁷ Jesus então perguntou-lhes: "Que é que vocês vão a discutir pelo caminho?" Eles pararam, com ar muito triste. ¹⁸ Um deles, que

se chamava Cleófas, respondeu: "Serás tu o único visitante que não sabe o que se passou em Jerusalém nestes últimos dias?" ¹⁹ E ele perguntou: "Mas que aconteceu?" Eles responderam: "O que se passou com Jesus de Nazaré, que era um profeta poderoso em obras e palavras, diante de Deus e de toda a gente. ²⁰ Os nossos chefes dos sacerdotes e as nossas autoridades entregaram-no para ser condenado à morte e pregaram-no numa cruz. ²¹ E nós que esperávamos que fosse ele quem viria libertar Israel! Mas, com todas estas coisas, já lá vão três dias desde que isto aconteceu. ²² É verdade que algumas mulheres do nosso grupo nos deixaram em sobressalto porque foram de madrugada ao sepulcro ²³ e não encontraram lá o corpo. Depois vieram dizer-nos que tinham tido uma visão de anjos a anunciar-lhes que ele estava vivo. ²⁴ Alguns dos nossos companheiros foram logo ao sepulcro e encontraram tudo como as mulheres tinham dito, mas a Jesus não o viram."

²⁵ Jesus então disse-lhes: "Mas que faltos de entendimento vocês são, e que lentos para acreditarem em tudo o que os profetas disseram! ²⁶ Então o Messias não tinha que sofrer tudo isso antes de ser glorificado?" ²⁷ E pôs-se a explicar-lhes o que acerca dele se dizia em todas as Escrituras, começando pelos livros de Moisés e seguindo por todos os livros dos profetas.

²⁸ Quando chegaram à aldeia para onde iam, Jesus fez como quem ia para mais longe. ²⁹ Mas eles convenceram-no a ficar e disseram-lhe: "Fica connosco, porque já se está a fazer tarde, já é quase noite." Jesus entrou e ficou com eles. ³⁰ Quando estavam à mesa, pegou no pão, deu graças a Deus, partiu-o e dividiu-o com eles. ³¹ Foi então que se lhes abriu o entendimento e o reconheceram, mas nisto ele desapareceu. ³² Disseram então um para o outro: "Não é verdade que o coração nos ardia no peito, quando ele nos vinha a falar pelo caminho e nos explicava as Escrituras?"

³³ Levantaram-se imediatamente e voltaram para Jerusalém, onde encontraram os onze apóstolos reunidos com outros companheiros, ³⁴ que lhes disseram: "É verdade que o Senhor ressuscitou! Simão já o viu!" ³⁵ Os dois que vieram de Emaús contaram-lhes então o que lhes tinha acontecido pelo caminho, e como o tinham reconhecido ao partir do pão.

Jesus aparece aos discípulos

[36] Estavam a contar estas coisas, quando Jesus apareceu no meio deles e disse: "A paz esteja convosco." [37] Assustaram-se e ficaram cheios de medo, porque pensavam que era um fantasma. [38] Mas Jesus disse-lhes: "Por que é que se assustam, e por que têm tantas dúvidas a meu respeito? [39] Olhem para as minhas mãos e para os meus pés. Sou eu mesmo. Toquem-me e vejam, porque um espírito não tem carne nem ossos, como vêem que eu tenho." [40] Ao dizer isto, mostrou-lhes as mãos e os pés. [41] Mas até lhes custava a acreditar, tão cheios de alegria e de admiração eles estavam! Então Jesus perguntou-lhes: "Têm aqui alguma coisa para comer?" [42] E eles deram-lhe uma posta de peixe assado, [43] que comeu à vista deles.

[44] Jesus acrescentou ainda: "O que eu vos tinha dito, quando andávamos juntos, é que tudo o que estava escrito a meu respeito na Lei de Moisés, nos livros dos profetas e nos Salmos, tinha de se cumprir." [45] Depois abriu-lhes o entendimento para compreenderem as Escrituras [46] e disse-lhes: "É assim que está escrito: que o Messias tinha de morrer, e que ao terceiro dia havia de ressuscitar dos mortos, [47] e que em seu nome se havia de pregar a mensagem sobre o arrependimento e o perdão dos pecados a todas as nações, começando em Jerusalém. [48] São vocês as testemunhas destas coisas. [49] Vou enviar-vos eu próprio o que meu Pai prometeu. Devem esperar aqui em Jerusalém, até que recebam o poder que vos há-de vir do céu."

Jesus sobe ao céu

[50] Jesus levou-os depois para fora da cidade, para os lados de Betânia. Ali levantou as mãos e abençoou-os. [51] Enquanto os abençoava, afastou-se deles e foi elevado ao céu. [52] Eles adoraram-no e voltaram para Jerusalém muito contentes, [53] e estavam constantemente no templo dando graças a Deus.

*Notes * Notas * Note * Ghi chú*

De que maneira você pode celebrar sua família — um santuário de amor e vida — após deixar o Encontro Mundial das Famílias? Inscreva-se para uma jornada devocional de 21 dias de Lectio Divina do Evangelho Segundo Lucas com sua família e comunidade. Ao ouvir a palavra de Deus e meditar sobre as histórias de esperança e cura, permita que a Escritura Sagrada transforme sua compreensão do amor incondicional de Deus.

MEDITAÇÕES
SOBRE O EVANGELHO
SEGUNDO LUCAS PARA A FAMÍLIA

Inscreva-se para essa jornada devocional de 21 dias de Lectio Divina de uma de três maneiras.

- Mensagens de texto: Envie **familias** para 72717

- Email: Visite www.abs.us/familias

- Aplicativo móvel: Visite app.bible.com wmf para baixar

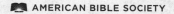

MISERANDO ATQUE ELIGENDO

Thưa các gia đình,
Hãy lắng nghe Lời Chúa Trời,
cùng nhau tĩnh tâm về Lời Chúa,
cầu nguyện với Lời Chúa,
hãy để Chúa lấp đầy cuộc sống của bạn
bằng lòng khoan dung.

Franciscus

Huy hiệu của Giáo Hoàng Francis giữ nguyên thiết kế được dùng khi ngài còn là Tổng Giám Mục Buenos Aires, có thêm các biểu tượng giáo hoàng là một góc vuông của giám mục và hai chìa khóa bắt chéo với sợi dây đỏ vắt ngang.

Tấm lá chắn có phông nền xanh dương. Ở chính giữa là biểu tượng của trật tự tôn giáo của Giáo Hoàng, Hội Thánh của Chúa Jesus: một mặt trời rực rỡ với một cây thập giá ba chữ cái IHS (ký hiệu của Chúa Jesus) màu đỏ, và ba cây đinh màu đen. Phía dưới là một ngôi sao vàng kim, biểu trưng cho Đức Mẹ Đồng Trinh, và một chùm hoa hương cam tùng, tượng trưng cho thánh Joseph.

Câu châm ngôn Latin bên dưới tấm chắn là "miserando atque eligendo," tạm dịch là "thấp kém nhưng được chọn." Dịch sát nghĩa đen thì nó là, "bởi có lòng thương xót, bởi chọn ngài." Nó được lấy từ một bài giảng bình dân của Đức Bede về lời kêu gọi làm Tông Đồ của Thánh Matthew người thu thuế. Giáo Hoàng Francis được kêu gọi vào đời sống tôn giáo ở tuổi 17 trong buổi lễ Bổn Mạng của Thánh Matthew.

Archdiocese of Philadelphia
Office of the Archbishop
222 North 17th Street
Philadelphia, PA 19103-1299

Tháng 9 năm 2015

Tất cả bốn sách Phúc Âm đều là những cuộc trải nghiệm phong phú với Lời Chúa. Nhưng đối với nhiều độc giả, Luke là Nhà Truyền Giáo, người nói chuyện truyền cảm nhất khi có tiếng nói của lòng khoan dung từ Thiên Chúa. Chỉ có ở Luke chúng ta mới tìm thấy ba sự diễn đạt tuyệt vời nhất của chúa Jesus về tình yêu: dụ ngôn Đứa Con Phóng Đãng và Người Samari, và lời ngài trên thánh giá về "Kẻ Trộm Lành".

Phúc Âm mà bạn có trong tay – một món quà tuyệt vời từ American Bible Society (Hội Thánh Kinh Mỹ) - là lời nhắc nhở về sự nhẹ nhàng của Chúa cho riêng cá nhân bạn; một lời mời dạo bước cùng đức Jesus trên đường trở về trời. Hãy đọc nó. Hãy trân trọng nó.

Xin Thiên Chúa ban phước lành cho bạn và những người thân yêu trong đợt Họp Mặt Gia Đình Thế Giới, và mỗi ngày tiếp theo nữa.

Người anh em trong Chúa của bạn,

+ Charles J. Chaput, ofm. ap.

Đức Tổng Giám Mục Charles J. Chaput, Dòng Tiểu Đệ
Tổng Giám Mục Philadelphia

GIỚI THIỆU

TIN MỪNG VỀ LÒNG KHOAN DUNG TRONG GIA ĐÌNH

Các gia đình thân mến,

Tôi rất vui mừng được giới thiệu phiên bản này của sách Phúc Âm của Luke, một món quà từ đức Giáo Hoàng Francis dành cho mọi gia đình khắp thế giới nhân dịp Đại Hội Thế Giới VIII ở Philadelphia.

Chúng tôi hy vọng rằng sách Phúc Âm này sẽ đồng hành cùng Năm Khoan Dung Đại Xá mà, theo ước muốn của Đức Thánh Cha, sẽ bắt đầu sau vài tuần nữa: Luke là Phúc Âm, là Tin Mừng, của lòng khoan dung Thiên Chúa cho đời sống từng người và cho các gia đình chúng ta.

PHÚC ÂM TRONG GIA ĐÌNH

Mỗi thế hệ người Kitô Giáo—kể cả chúng ta—đều được kêu gọi giữ cuốn sách nhỏ này trong tay. Vì Phúc Âm là sức mạnh của Giáo Hội; từ lời Phúc Âm mà Giáo Hội ra đời và Giáo Hội sống vì nó. Trên thực tế, Ki Tô Giáo bắt đầu khi ngôi Lời trở thành thịt trong bụng đức mẹ Mary. Mẹ là người đầu tiên có đức tin, và mẹ đã được Elizabeth tức thì chỉ định như vậy: "phước cho người đã tin, vì lời Chúa truyền cho sẽ được ứng nghiệm" (Luke 1:45). Sau đó, kế mẹ Mary là đến các tông đồ đầu tiên. Khi họ tiếp nhận lời chúa Jesus, một tình bằng hữu mới bắt đầu—có thể nói một "gia đình mới," giữa chúa Jesus và các tông đồ của ngài. Sau lễ Ngũ Tuần, Phúc Âm bắt đầu lan tỏa khắp nhà của các gia đình Kitô Giáo. Tóm lại, vào đầu thiên nhiên kỷ thứ nhất, con đường của Phúc Âm được đánh dấu bởi việc lắng nghe trong các gia đình.

Các gia đình thân mến, tôi nghĩ chúng ta cũng nên làm điều mà đã được làm vào buổi đầu Kitô Giáo: giữ sách Phúc Âm trong tay, trong chính gia đình của mình, và tái tạo một tình huynh đệ mới giữa con người, tình đoàn kết mới giữa các gia đình, nhằm truyền tải "Tin Mừng" của tình yêu Thiên Chúa đến mọi người. Vào đầu năm Đại Xá 2000, Thánh John Paul II hô hào người Kitô Giáo bước vào "thiên niên kỷ mới bằng Phúc Âm!" Với cùng niềm đam mê đã dẫn dắt ngài làm lữ khách của Phúc Âm trên khắp thế giới, ngài nói thêm: "Hãy đi, lấy cuốn sách nhỏ mở ra trong tay vị thiên sứ đương đứng trên biển và đất (Khải Huyền 10:8). Ngươi hãy lấy và nuốt đi (Khải Huyền 10:9) để nó có thể trở thành đời sống của đời sống ta. Hãy hít sâu hương thơm nó: nó sẽ đắng trong bụng ngươi, nhưng trong miệng ngươi nó sẽ ngọt như mật (Khải Huyền 10:9–10). Khi tràn đầy hy vọng, chúng ta sẽ có thể chia sẻ nó cùng mỗi người nam và nữ ta gặp trên đường."

Giáo Hoàng Francis kêu gọi chúng ta đi theo hướng đó: Hãy cầm Phúc Âm trong tay! Ngài bảo chúng ta như vậy trong bức thư nhan đề "Niềm Vui của Phúc Âm" *(Evangelii Gaudium)*. Vâng, rất cần cầm sách Phúc Âm lên và lắng nghe với sự chú ý mới, nếu chúng ta muốn có một thế giới đầy tình huynh đệ và nhân văn, và đoàn kết hơn. Sự bất an và nỗi sợ mà đang tạo nên đời sống thế giới chúng ta, những sự bất công đến khó tin đang hủy diệt mạng sống của bao người, bạo lực dường như lan tràn ngoài tầm kiểm soát ngay cả trong nhà chúng ta, những cuộc xung đột và chiến tranh liên tục lấy đi mạng sống của người vô tội, chỉ có thể được chế ngự qua Phúc Âm. Vì vậy, Giáo Hoàng Francis muốn trao một triệu cuốn sách này cho các gia đình thuộc năm thành phố chính của thế giới: Havana (Cuba), Hà Nội (Việt Nam), Kinshasa (Congo), Marseille (Pháp), và Sydney (Úc). Ở những nơi mà bối cảnh đô thị và ngoại ô của nó dường như khiến cho sự tồn tại đồng thời của con người còn khó khăn hơn, Giáo Hoàng muốn Lời chúa Jesus được cộng hưởng mạnh mẽ thêm.

THỰC HÀNH HÀNG NGÀY

Chúng ta hãy đọc một đoạn ngắn Phúc Âm mỗi ngày. Chúng ta sẽ buộc phải nhập tâm và bước vào cuộc sống hàng ngày của chúa Jesus, theo ngài trên bước đường; chúng ta sẽ chia sẻ tình thương của ngài cho tất cả, và sát cánh cùng ngài trong lòng trắc ẩn đối với kẻ nhỏ bé yếu hèn; chúng ta sẽ động lòng trước lòng nhân từ của ngài khi ngài đồng hành với người nghèo; và chúng ta sẽ khóc khi thấy ngài yêu chúng ta đến nhường nào; cuối cùng, chúng ta sẽ hân hoan trong sự phục sinh của ngài, mà chắc hẳn đã đánh bại cái xấu. Chúng ta sẽ hiểu và yêu ngài hơn.

Hãy nhớ làm điều này thực tâm hàng ngày. Chúng ta hàng ngày bị ngập tràn bởi từ ngữ, hình ảnh, thông điệp, lời mời... Và không phải mọi thông điệp đều tốt; chỉ một số ít giúp chúng ta sống. Rồi, ở nhà, lại có nguy cơ mà vì nhiều lý do, chúng ta ngưng nói chuyện với nhau hoặc, ngay cả khi không có "bát đĩa bay," thì có những lời bay, đôi khi gây hại hơn cả bát đĩa. Trong mọi trường hợp, chúng ta đều cảm thấy nhu cầu có những lời tốt đẹp chạm đến trái tim. Giờ đây, Phúc Âm chính là lời nói đến được trái tim. Trong Lời Nguyện Cầu của Chúa, chúng ta xin Thiên Chúa ban cho ta "bánh hàng ngày." Những lời của chúa Jesus là "bánh hằng sống từ trời," được ban cho chúng ta hàng ngày. Đây là bánh tốt nhất. Nó nuôi dưỡng con tim và cơ thể.

Các gia đình thân mến, việc cùng đọc sách Phúc Âm trong gia đình là một trong những cách hay và hữu hiệu nhất để cầu nguyện. Chúa đặc biệt thích điều đó. Các bạn có nhớ đoạn về Martha và Mary không? Khi Martha khó chịu khi thấy Mary lắng nghe chúa Jesus, ngài chỉ ra rằng Mary đã "chọn phần hay hơn," "thứ duy nhất cần thiết." Thật dễ cho tất cả chúng ta đều choáng ngợp, như Martha, bởi tất cả những thứ cần phải làm, các vấn đề cần được giải quyết, và những khó khăn cần được vượt qua. Ngày nay cũng vậy, chúa Jesus bảo chúng ta, "Mary đã lựa phần tốt" (Luke 10:42). Cuốn sách nhỏ này sẽ giúp việc lắng nghe Phúc Âm trở thành "phần hay nhất" trong ngày, "phần hay nhất" của tất cả các ngày trong năm.

Chúng ta cần lắng nghe. Bước đầu tiên trong việc cầu nguyện Kitô Giáo là lắng nghe chúa Jesus nói chuyện với chúng ta. Vâng, thưa các gia đình, trước khi nhân rộng lời nói của chúng ta khi cầu nguyện với

Chúa, chúng ta hãy lắng nghe những lời Ngài nói với chúng ta. Mỗi ngày. Chúng ta hãy lắng nghe họ, và ta sẽ có cùng những trải nghiệm như hai tông đồ của Emmaus, những người cảm thấy tim mình ấm áp và nhu cầu ở lại cùng ngài. Việc lắng nghe biến thành lời cầu nguyện, và cuộc gặp gỡ chúa Jesus thắp sáng lại đời sống chúng ta.

Tất nhiên, chúng ta phải tập hợp cùng nhau và giữ yên lặng một lúc khi ngài có mặt. Chúng ta biết việc tìm ra một khoảnh khắc yên lặng và cầu nguyện đã trở nên khó khăn như thế nào. Tuy nhiên, điều đó rất thiết yếu. Có thể nói rằng cầu nguyện hàng ngày là cách chúng ta "cầu nguyện không mệt mỏi." Vâng, cầu nguyện hàng ngày với Phúc Âm là cách chúng ta luôn luôn cầu nguyện.

Vì vậy, chúng ta cần tìm ra một khoảnh khắc để ở bên nhau—có thể trước một bữa ăn, hoặc vào cuối ngày, hay thậm chí đầu ngày, hoặc trong những giây phút khác. Điều quan trọng là chọn ra năm phút để cùng cầu nguyện ngắn nhưng hữu hiệu.

Sau khi làm dấu thánh giá và một lời thỉnh nguyện với Thánh Thần, hãy xin ngài bước vào trong tim và thắp sáng tâm hồn chúng ta, chúng ta đọc một đoạn ngắn, chúng ta đưa ra một lời giải thích đơn giản cho con cái, và chia sẻ những suy nghĩ rằng việc lắng nghe đoạn văn này sẽ tạo cảm hứng; vào lúc này, chúng ta bảo nhau, những người ta muốn cầu nguyện, một cách đặc biệt, và chúng ta kết luận bằng cách trích dẫn Lời Kinh của Chúa cùng nhau và tạ ơn Chúa vì món quà Lời người. Sau đó, chúng ta đừng quên cùng nhau quyết tâm một cách đơn giản và ngắn gọn trong đó lời nói này có thể đánh dấu đời sống chúng ta.

Các gia đình thân mến, trong khi nồng nhiệt cảm tạ Hội Thánh Kinh Mỹ đã cho phép soạn cuốn sách này, tôi thành tâm ước nguyện cho các bạn rằng kết quả đầu tiên của những ngày này khi chúng ta ở bên nhau tại Philadelphia có thể là quyết định để đón nhận Lời Chúa vào sống trong nhà các bạn và những người cùng thành phố với bạn.

+ Vincenzo Paglia

Tổng Giám Mục Vincenzo Paglia
Chủ Tịch Hội Đồng Giám Mục dành cho Gia Đình

TIN-LÀNH
THEO
LU-CA

TIN-LÀNH THEO LU-CA

Tiểu-dẫn

1 ¹ Hỡi Thê-ô-phi-lơ quí-nhân, vì có nhiều kẻ dốc lòng chép sử về những sự đã làm nên trong chúng ta, ² theo như các người chứng-kiến từ lúc ban đầu và trở nên người giảng đạoᵃ đã truyền lại cho chúng ta, ³ vậy, sau khi đã xét kỹ-càng từ đầu mọi sự ấy, tôi cũng tưởng nên theo thứ-tự viết mà tỏ ra cho ông, ⁴ để ông biết những điều mình đã học là chắc-chắn.

Sự giáng-sanh Đức Chúa Jêsus và thuở Ngài còn nhỏ
(Từ 1:5 đến đoạn 2)

Lời tiên-tri về sự sanh Giăng Báp-tít

⁵ Trong đời Hê-rốt, vua nước Giu-đê, có một thầy tế-lễ, về ban A-bi-a, tên là Xa-cha-ri; vợ người là Ê-li-sa-bét, thuộc về chi-phái A-rôn. ⁶ Cả hai đều là công-bình trước mặt Đức Chúa Trời, vâng-giữ mọi điều-răn và lễ-nghi của Chúa một cách không chỗ trách được. ⁷ Hai người không có con, vì Ê-li-sa-bét son-sẻ, và cả hai đều cao tuổi.

⁸ Vả, Xa-cha-ri cứ theo thứ-tự trong ban mình mà làm chức tế-lễ trước mặt Đức Chúa Trời. ⁹ Khi đã bắt thăm theo lệ các thầy cả lập ra rồi, thì người được gọi vào nơi thánhᵇ của Chúa để dâng hương. ¹⁰ Đương giờ dâng hương, cả đoàn dân đông đều ở ngoài cầu-nguyện. ¹¹ Bấy giờ có một thiên-sứ của Chúa hiện ra cùng Xa-cha-ri, đứng bên hữu bàn-thờ xông hương. ¹² Xa-cha-ri thấy, thì bối-rối sợ-hãi. ¹³ Nhưng thiên-sứ nói cùng người rằng: Hỡi Xa-cha-ri, đừng sợ, vì lời cầu-nguyện ngươi đã được nhậm rồi. Ê-li-sa-bét, vợ ngươi, sẽ sanh một con trai, ngươi khá đặt tên là Giăng. ¹⁴ Con trai đó sẽ làm cho ngươi vui-mừng hớn-hở, và nhiều kẻ sẽ mừng-rỡ về sự sanh người

---

a **1:2** Ctd: *cung ứng lời Chúa*
b **1:9** Là nơi ở trong đền-thờ, để riêng cho các thầy tế-lễ.

ra. ¹⁵ Vì người sẽ nên tôn-trọng trước mặt Chúa; không uống rượu hay là giống gì làm cho say, và sẽ được đầy-dẫy Đức Thánh-Linh từ khi còn trong lòng mẹ. ¹⁶ Người sẽ làm cho nhiều con trai Y-sơ-ra-ên trở lại cùng Chúa, là Đức Chúa Trời của họ; ¹⁷ chính người lại sẽ lấy tâm-thần quyền-phép Ê-li mà đi trước mặt Chúa, để đem lòng cha trở về con-cái, kẻ loạn-nghịch đến sự khôn-ngoan của người công-bình, đặng sửa-soạn cho Chúa một dân sẵn lòng. ¹⁸ Xa-cha-ri thưa rằng: Bởi sao tôi biết được điều đó? Vì tôi đã già, vợ tôi đã cao tuổi rồi. ¹⁹ Thiên-sứ trả lời rằng: Ta là Gáp-ri-ên, đứng trước mặt Đức Chúa Trời; Ngài đã sai ta đến truyền cho ngươi và báo tin mừng nầy. ²⁰ Nầy, ngươi sẽ câm, không nói được cho đến ngày nào các điều ấy xảy ra, vì ngươi không tin lời ta, là lời đến kỳ sẽ ứng-nghiệm.

²¹ Bấy giờ, dân-chúng đợi Xa-cha-ri, và lấy làm lạ, vì người ở lâu trong nơi thánh. ²² Khi Xa-cha-ri ra, không nói với chúng được, thì họ mới hiểu rằng người đã thấy sự hiện-thấy gì trong đền-thánh; người ra dấu cho họ, mà vẫn còn câm. ²³ Khi những ngày về phần việc mình đã trọn, người trở về nhà. ²⁴ Khỏi ít lâu, vợ người là Ê-li-sa-bét chịu thai, ẩn mình đi trong năm tháng, mà nói rằng: ²⁵ Ấy là ơn Chúa đã làm cho tôi, khi Ngài đã đoái đến tôi, để cất sự xấu-hổ tôi giữa mọi người.

Thiên-sứ báo tin Đức Chúa Jêsus giáng-sanh

²⁶ Đến tháng thứ sáu, Đức Chúa Trời sai thiên-sứ Gáp-ri-ên đến thành Na-xa-rét, xứ Ga-li-lê, ²⁷ tới cùng một người nữ đồng-trinh tên là Ma-ri, đã hứa gả cho một người nam tên là Giô-sép, về dòng vua Đa-vít. ²⁸ Thiên-sứ vào chỗ người nữ ở, nói rằng: Hỡi người được ơn, mừng cho ngươi; Chúa ở cùng ngươi. ²⁹ Ma-ri nghe nói thì bối-rối, tự hỏi rằng lời chào ấy có nghĩa gì. ³⁰ Thiên-sứ bèn nói rằng: Hỡi Ma-ri, đừng sợ, vì ngươi đã được ơn trước mặt Đức Chúa Trời. ³¹ Nầy, ngươi sẽ chịu thai và sanh một con trai mà đặt tên là Jêsus. ³² Con trai ấy sẽ nên tôn-trọng, được xưng là Con của Đấng Rất-Cao; và Chúa, là Đức Chúa Trời, sẽ ban cho Ngài ngôi Đa-vít là tổ-phụ Ngài. ³³ Ngài sẽ trị-vì đời đời nhà Gia-cốp, nước Ngài vô-cùng. ³⁴ Ma-ri bèn thưa rằng: Tôi chẳng hề nhận-biết người nam nào, thì làm sao có được sự đó? ³⁵ Thiên-sứ truyền rằng: Đức Thánh-Linh sẽ đến trên

ngươi, và quyền-phép Đấng Rất-Cao sẽ che-phủ ngươi dưới bóng mình, cho nên con thánh sanh ra, phải xưng là Con Đức Chúa Trời. [36] Kìa, Ê-li-sa-bét, bà-con ngươi, cũng đã chịu thai một trai trong lúc già-nua; người ấy vốn có tiếng là son, mà nay cưu-mang được sáu tháng rồi. [37] Bởi vì không việc chi Đức Chúa Trời chẳng làm được. [38] Ma-ri thưa rằng: Tôi đây là tôi-tớ Chúa; xin sự ấy xảy ra cho tôi như lời người truyền! Đoạn thiên-sứ lìa khỏi Ma-ri.

Ma-ri thăm Ê-li-sa-bét. – Bài ca-tụng của Ma-ri

[39] Trong những ngày đó, Ma-ri chờ dậy, lật-đật đi trong miền núi, đến một thành về xứ Giu-đa, [40] vào nhà Xa-cha-ri mà chào Ê-li-sa-bét. [41] Vả, Ê-li-sa-bét vừa nghe tiếng Ma-ri chào, con nhỏ ở trong lòng liền nhảy-nhót; và Ê-li-sa-bét được đầy Đức Thánh-Linh, [42] bèn cất tiếng kêu rằng: Ngươi có phước trong đám đàn-bà, thai trong lòng ngươi cũng được phước. [43] Nhân đâu ta được sự vẻ-vang nầy, là mẹ Chúa ta đến thăm ta? [44] Bởi vì tai ta mới nghe tiếng ngươi chào, thì con nhỏ ở trong lòng ta liền nhảy mừng. [45] Phước cho người đã tin, vì lời Chúa truyền cho sẽ được ứng-nghiệm! [46] Ma-ri bèn nói rằng:

Linh-hồn tôi ngợi-khen Chúa,
[47] Tâm-thần tôi mừng-rỡ trong Đức Chúa Trời, là Cứu-Chúa tôi,
[48] Vì Ngài đã đoái đến sự hèn-hạ của tôi-tớ Ngài.
Nầy, từ rày về sau, muôn đời sẽ khen tôi là kẻ có phước;
[49] Bởi Đấng Toàn-năng đã làm các việc lớn cho tôi.
Danh Ngài là thánh,
[50] Và Ngài thương-xót kẻ kính-sợ Ngài từ đời nầy sang đời kia.
[51] Ngài đã dùng cánh tay mình để tỏ ra quyền-phép;
Và phá tan mưu của kẻ kiêu-ngạo toan trong lòng.
[52] Ngài đã cách người có quyền khỏi ngôi họ,
Và nhắc kẻ khiêm-nhượng lên
[53] Ngài đã làm cho kẻ đói được đầy thức ngon,
Và đuổi kẻ giàu về tay không.
[54] Ngài đã vùa-giúp Y-sơ-ra-ên, tôi-tớ Ngài,
Và nhớ lại sự thương-xót mình
Đối với Áp-ra-ham cùng con cháu người luôn luôn,

⁵⁵ Như Ngài đã phán cùng tổ-phụ chúng ta vậy.

⁵⁶ Ma-ri ở với Ê-li-sa-bét chừng ba tháng, rồi trở về nhà mình.

Giăng Báp-tít sanh ra

⁵⁷ Bấy giờ, đến ngày mãn-nguyệt, Ê-li-sa-bét sanh được một trai. ⁵⁸ Xóm-giềng bà-con nghe Chúa tỏ ra sự thương-xót cả thể cho Ê-li-sa-bét, thì chia vui cùng người. ⁵⁹ Qua ngày thứ tám, họ đều đến để làm lễ cắt-bì cho con trẻ; và đặt tên là Xa-cha-ri theo tên của cha. ⁶⁰ Nhưng mẹ nói rằng: Không! Phải đặt tên con là Giăng. ⁶¹ Họ nói: Trong bà-con ngươi không ai có tên đó. ⁶² Họ bèn ra dấu hỏi cha muốn đặt tên gì cho con. ⁶³ Xa-cha-ri biểu lấy bảng nhỏ, và viết rằng: Giăng là tên nó. Ai nấy đều lấy làm lạ. ⁶⁴ Tức thì miệng người mở ra, lưỡi được thong-thả, nói và ngợi-khen Đức Chúa Trời. ⁶⁵ Hết thảy xóm-giềng đều kinh-sợ, và người ta nói chuyện với nhau về mọi sự ấy khắp miền núi xứ Giu-đê. ⁶⁶ Ai nghe cũng ghi vào lòng mà nói rằng: Ấy vậy, con trẻ đó sẽ ra thể nào? Vì tay Chúa ở cùng con trẻ ấy.

Bài ca-tụng của Xa-cha-ri

⁶⁷ Bấy giờ, Xa-cha-ri, cha con trẻ ấy, được đầy-dẫy Đức Thánh-Linh, thì nói tiên-tri rằng:

⁶⁸ Ngợi-khen Chúa, là Đức Chúa Trời của Y-sơ-ra-ên,

Vì đã thăm-viếng và chuộc dân Ngài,

⁶⁹ Cùng sanh ra cho chúng tôi trong nhà Đa-vít, tôi-tớ Ngài,

Một Đấng Cứu-thế[c] có quyền-phép!

⁷⁰ Như lời Ngài đã dùng miệng các thánh tiên-tri phán từ thuở trước,

⁷¹ Ngài cứu chúng tôi khỏi kẻ thù và tay mọi người ghen-ghét chúng tôi;

⁷² Ngài tỏ lòng thương-xót đến tổ-tông chúng tôi,

Và nhớ lại lời giao-ước thánh của Ngài,

⁷³ Theo như Ngài đã thề với Áp-ra-ham là tổ-phụ chúng tôi,

⁷⁴ Mà hứa rằng khi chúng tôi đã được cứu khỏi tay kẻ nghịch-thù,

Ngài sẽ ban ơn lành cho chúng tôi, trước mặt Ngài,

---

c **1:69** Nt: *sừng cứu rỗi*

⁷⁵ Lấy sự thánh-khiết và công-bình mà hầu việc Ngài, trọn đời
mình không sợ-hãi gì hết.

⁷⁶ Hỡi con trẻ, người ta sẽ kêu con là tiên-tri của Đấng Rất-Cao;
Con sẽ đi trước mặt Chúa, dọn đường Ngài,

⁷⁷ Để cho dân Ngài bởi sự tha tội họ mà biết sự rỗi.

⁷⁸ Vì Đức Chúa Trời chúng tôi động lòng thương-xót,
Và mặt trời mọc lên từ nơi cao thăm-viếng chúng tôi,

⁷⁹ Để soi những kẻ ngồi chỗ tối-tăm và trong bóng sự chết,
Cùng đưa chân chúng tôi đi đường bình an.

⁸⁰ Và, con trẻ ấy lớn lên, tâm-thần mạnh-mẽ, ở nơi đồng vắng cho
đến ngày tỏ mình ra cùng dân Y-sơ-ra-ên.

Đức Chúa Jêsus giáng-sanh

2 ¹ Lúc ấy, Sê-sa Au-gút-tơ ra chiếu-chỉ phải lập sổ dân trọng cả
thiên-hạ. ² Việc lập sổ dân nầy là trước hết, và nhằm khi Qui-ri-
ni-u làm quan tổng-đốc xứ Sy-ri. ³ Ai nấy đều đến thành mình khai
tên vào sổ.

⁴ Vì Giô-sép là dòng-dõi nhà Đa-vít, cho nên cũng từ thành Na-
xa-rét, xứ Ga-li-lê, lên thành Đa-vít, gọi là Bết-lê-hem, xứ Giu-đê,
⁵ để khai vào sổ tên mình và tên Ma-ri, là người đã hứa gả cho mình,
đương có thai. ⁶ Đang khi hai người ở nơi đó, thì ngày sanh đẻ của
Ma-ri đã đến. ⁷ Người sanh con trai đầu lòng, lấy khăn bọc con mình,
đặt nằm trong máng cỏ, vì nhà quán không có đủ chỗ ở.

⁸ Và, cũng trong miền đó, có mấy kẻ chăn chiên trú ngoài đồng,
thức đêm canh-giữ bầy chiên. ⁹ Một thiên-sứ của Chúa đến gần họ, và
sự vinh-hiển của Chúa chói-lòa xung-quanh họ, rất sợ-hãi. ¹⁰ Thiên-
sứ bèn phán rằng: Đừng sợ chi; vì nầy, ta báo cho các ngươi một tin
lành, sẽ là một sự vui-mừng lớn cho muôn dân; ¹¹ ấy là hôm nay tại
thành Đa-vít đã sanh cho các ngươi một Đấng Cứu-thế, là Christ,
là Chúa. ¹² Nầy là dấu cho các ngươi nhìn-nhận Ngài: Các ngươi sẽ
gặp một con trẻ bọc bằng khăn, nằm trong máng cỏ. ¹³ Bỗng-chúc
có muôn-vàn thiên-binh với thiên-sứ đó ngợi-khen Đức Chúa Trời
rằng:

¹⁴ Sáng danh Chúa trên các từng trời rất cao,
Bình-an dưới đất, ân-trạch cho loài người!

¹⁵ Sau khi các thiên-sứ lìa họ lên trời rồi, bọn chăn chiên nói với nhau rằng: Chúng ta hãy tới thành Bết-lê-hem, xem việc đã xảy đến mà Chúa cho chúng ta hay. ¹⁶ Vậy, họ vội-vàng đi đến đó, thấy Ma-ri, Giô-sép, và thấy con trẻ đang nằm trong máng cỏ. ¹⁷ Đã thấy vậy, họ bèn thuật lại những lời thiên-sứ nói về con trẻ đó. ¹⁸ Ai nấy nghe chuyện bọn chăn chiên nói, đều lấy làm lạ. ¹⁹ Còn Ma-ri thì ghi-nhớ mọi lời ấy và suy-nghĩ trong lòng. ²⁰ Bọn chăn chiên trở về, làm sáng danh và ngợi-khen Đức Chúa Trời về mọi điều mình đã nghe và thấy y như lời đã bảo trước cùng mình.

²¹ Đến ngày thứ tám, là ngày phải làm phép cắt-bì cho con trẻ, thì họ đặt tên là Jêsus, là tên thiên-sứ đã đặt cho, trước khi chịu cưu-mang trong lòng mẹ.

Làm lễ dâng nơi đền-thờ

²² Khi đã hết những ngày tinh-sạch rồi, theo luật-pháp Môi-se, Giô-sép và Ma-ri đem con trẻ lên thành Giê-ru-sa-lem để dâng cho Chúa, ²³ như đã chép trong luật-pháp Chúa rằng: Hễ con trai đầu lòng, phải dâng cho Chúa, ²⁴ lại dâng một cặp chim cu, hoặc chim bồ-câu con, như luật-pháp Chúa đã truyền.

Bài ca-tụng của Si-mê-ôn. – Bà tiên-tri An-ne

²⁵ Và, trong thành Giê-ru-sa-lem có một người công-bình đạo-đức, tên là Si-mê-ôn, trông-đợi sự yên-ủi dân Y-sơ-ra-ên, và Đức Thánh-Linh ngự trên người. ²⁶ Đức Thánh-Linh đã bảo trước cho người biết mình sẽ không chết trước khi thấy Đấng Christ của Chúa. ²⁷ Vậy người cảm bởi Đức Thánh-Linh vào đền-thờ, lúc có cha mẹ đem con trẻ là Jêsus đến, để làm trọn cho Ngài các thường-lệ mà luật-pháp đã định, ²⁸ thì người bồng-ẩm con trẻ, mà ngợi-khen Đức Chúa Trời rằng:

²⁹ Lạy Chúa, bây giờ xin Chúa cho tôi-tớ Chúa được qua đời
      bình-an, theo như lời Ngài;
³⁰ Vì con mắt tôi đã thấy sự cứu-vớt của Ngài,
³¹ Mà Ngài đã sắm-sửa đặng làm ánh-sáng trước mặt muôn dân,
³² Soi khắp thiên-hạ,
Và làm vinh-hiển cho dân Y-sơ-ra-ên là dân Ngài.

³³ Cha mẹ con trẻ lấy làm lạ về mấy lời người ta nói về con. ³⁴ Si-mê-ôn bèn chúc phước cho hai vợ chồng, nói với Ma-ri, mẹ con trẻ rằng: Đây, con trẻ nầy đã định làm một cớ cho nhiều người trong Y-sơ-ra-ên vấp-ngã hoặc dấy lên, và định làm một dấu gây nên sự cãi-trả; ³⁵ còn phần ngươi, có một thanh gươm sẽ đâm thấu qua lòng ngươi. Ấy vậy tư-tưởng trong lòng nhiều người sẽ được bày-tỏ.

³⁶ Lại có bà tiên-tri An-ne, con gái của Pha-nu-ên, về chi-phái A-se, đã cao tuổi lắm. Từ lúc còn đồng-trinh đã ở với chồng được bảy năm; ³⁷ rồi thì ở góa. Bấy giờ đã tám mươi bốn tuổi, chẳng hề ra khỏi đền-thờ, cứ đêm ngày hầu việc Đức Chúa Trời, kiêng ăn và cầu-nguyện. ³⁸ Một lúc ấy, người cũng thình-lình đến đó, ngợi-khen Đức Chúa Trời, và nói chuyện về con trẻ với mọi người trông-đợi sự giải-cứu của thành Giê-ru-sa-lem.

³⁹ Khi Giô-sép và Ma-ri đã làm trọn mọi việc theo luật-pháp Chúa rồi, thì trở về thành của mình là Na-xa-rét trong xứ Ga-li-lê. ⁴⁰ Con trẻ lớn lên, và mạnh-mẽ, được đầy-dẫy sự khôn-ngoan, và ơn[d] Đức Chúa Trời ngự trên Ngài.

Đức Chúa Jêsus lúc mười hai tuổi

⁴¹ Vả, hằng năm đến ngày lễ Vượt-qua, cha mẹ Đức Chúa Jêsus thường đến thành Giê-ru-sa-lem. ⁴² Khi Ngài lên mười hai tuổi, theo lệ thường ngày lễ, cùng lên thành Giê-ru-sa-lem. ⁴³ Các ngày lễ qua rồi, cha mẹ trở về, con trẻ là Jêsus ở lại thành Giê-ru-sa-lem, mà cha mẹ không hay chi hết. ⁴⁴ Hai người tưởng rằng Ngài cũng đồng đi với bạn đi đường, đi trót một ngày, rồi mới tìm hỏi trong đám bà-con quen-biết; ⁴⁵ nhưng không thấy Ngài, bèn trở lại thành Giê-ru-sa-lem mà tìm. ⁴⁶ Khỏi ba ngày, gặp Ngài tại trong đền-thờ đang ngồi giữa mấy thầy thông-thái, vừa nghe vừa hỏi. ⁴⁷ Ai nấy nghe, đều lạ khen về sự khôn-ngoan và lời đối-đáp của Ngài. ⁴⁸ Khi cha mẹ thấy Ngài, thì lấy làm lạ, và mẹ hỏi rằng: Hỡi con, sao con làm cho hai ta thể nầy? Nầy, cha và mẹ đã khó-nhọc lắm mà tìm con. ⁴⁹ Ngài thưa rằng: Cha mẹ kiếm tôi làm chi? Há chẳng biết tôi phải lo việc Cha tôi sao?[e] ⁵⁰ Nhưng hai người không hiểu lời Ngài nói chi hết.

---

d **2:40** Ctd: *ân điển, ân sủng*

e **2:49** Ctd: *con phải ở trong nhà Cha con sao?*

⁵¹ Đoạn, Ngài theo về thành Na-xa-rét và chịu lụy cha mẹ. Mẹ Ngài ghi các lời ấy vào lòng.

⁵² Đức Chúa Jêsus khôn-ngoan càng thêm, thân-hình càng lớn, càng được đẹp lòng Đức Chúa Trời và người ta.

Sự sửa-soạn về chức-vụ Đức Chúa Jêsus

(Từ đoạn 3 đến 4:13)

Chức-vụ giảng đạo của Giăng Báp-tít

3 ¹ Năm thứ mười lăm đời Sê-sa Ti-be-rơ, — khi Bôn-xơ Phi-lát làm quan tổng-đốc xứ Giu-đê, Hê-rốt làm vua chư-hầu xứ Ga-li-lê, Phi-líp em vua ấy làm vua chư-hầu xứ Y-tu-rê và tỉnh Tra-cô-nít, Ly-sa-ni-a làm vua chư-hầu xứ A-by-len, ² An-ne và Cai-phe làm thầy cả thượng-phẩm, — thì có lời Đức Chúa Trời truyền cho Giăng, con Xa-cha-ri, ở nơi đồng vắng. ³ Giăng bèn dạo qua hết thảy miền lân-cận sông Giô-đanh, giảng-dạy phép báp-têm về sự ăn-năn để được tha tội, ⁴ như lời đã chép trong sách đấng tiên-tri Ê-sai rằng:

Có tiếng kêu-la trong đồng vắng:
Hãy dọn đường Chúa, ban bằng các nẻo Ngài.
⁵ Mọi nơi sũng-thấp sẽ lấp cho đầy,
Các núi các gò thì bị hạ xuống;
Đường quanh-quẹo thì làm cho ngay,
Đường gập-ghềnh thì làm cho bằng;
⁶ Và mọi loài xác-thịt sẽ thấy sự cứu của Đức Chúa Trời.

⁷ Vậy, Giăng nói cùng đoàn dân đến để chịu mình làm phép báp-têm rằng: Hỡi dòng-dõi rắn lục, ai đã dạy các ngươi tránh khỏi cơn thạnh-nộ ngày sau? ⁸ Thế thì, hãy kết-quả xứng-đáng với sự ăn-năn; và đừng tự nói rằng: Áp-ra-ham là tổ-phụ chúng ta; vì ta nói cùng các ngươi, Đức Chúa Trời có thể khiến từ những đá nầy sanh ra con-cái cho Áp-ra-ham được. ⁹ Cái búa đã để kề gốc cây; hễ cây nào không sanh trái tốt thì sẽ bị đốn và chụm.

¹⁰ Chúng bèn hỏi Giăng rằng: Vậy thì chúng tôi phải làm gì? ¹¹ Người đáp rằng: Ai có hai áo, hãy lấy một cái cho người không có; và ai có đồ-ăn cũng nên làm như vậy. ¹² Cũng có những người

thâu thuế đến để chịu phép báp-têm; họ hỏi rằng: Thưa thầy, chúng tôi phải làm gì? ¹³ Người nói rằng: Đừng đòi chi ngoài số luật định. ¹⁴ Quân-lính cũng hỏi rằng: Còn chúng tôi phải làm gì? Người nói rằng: Đừng hà-hiếp, đừng phỉnh-gạt ai hết, nhưng hãy bằng lòng về lương-hướng mình.

¹⁵ Bởi dân-chúng vẫn trông-đợi, và ai nấy đều tự hỏi trong lòng nếu Giăng phải là Đấng Christ chăng, ¹⁶ nên Giăng cất tiếng nói cùng mọi người rằng: Phần ta làm phép báp-têm cho các ngươi bằng nước; song có một Đấng quyền-phép hơn ta sẽ đến, ta không đáng mở dây giày Ngài. Chính Ngài sẽ làm phép báp-têm cho các ngươi bằng Đức Thánh-Linh và bằng lửa. ¹⁷ Tay Ngài sẽ cầm nia mà giê thật sạch sân lúa mình, và thâu lúa mì vào kho; nhưng đốt trấu trong lửa chẳng hề tắt.

¹⁸ Trong khi Giăng rao-truyền tin lành, thì cũng khuyên-bảo dân-chúng nhiều điều nữa. ¹⁹ Song Hê-rốt, vua chư-hầu, đã bị Giăng can-gián về việc Hê-rô-đia vợ của em mình, cùng về các điều ác vua đã làm, ²⁰ thì lại thêm một điều ác nữa, là bắt Giăng bỏ tù.

Đức Chúa Jêsus chịu phép báp-têm

²¹ Vả, khi hết thảy dân-chúng đều chịu phép báp-têm, Đức Chúa Jêsus cũng chịu phép báp-têm. Ngài đương cầu-nguyện thì trời mở ra, ²² Đức Thánh-Linh lấy hình chim bồ-câu ngự xuống trên Ngài; lại có tiếng từ trên trời phán rằng: Ngươi là Con yêu-dấu của ta, đẹp lòng ta mọi đường.

Gia-phổ Đức Chúa Jêsus

²³ Khi Đức Chúa Jêsus khởi-sự làm chức-vụ mình thì Ngài có độ ba mươi tuổi. Theo ý người ta tin, thì Ngài là con Giô-sép, Giô-sép con Hê-li, ²⁴ Hê-li con Mát-tát, Mát-tát con Lê-vi, Lê-vi con Mên-chi, Mên-chi con Gia-nê, Gia-nê con Giô-sép, ²⁵ Giô-sép con Ma-ta-thia, Ma-ta-thia con A-mốt, A-mốt con Na-hum, Na-hum con Ếch-li, Ếch-li con Na-ghê, ²⁶ Na-ghê con Ma-át, Ma-át con Ma-ta-thia, Ma-ta-thia con Sê-mê-in, Sê-mê-in con Giô-sếch, Giô-sếch con Giô-đa, ²⁷ Giô-đa con Giô-a-nan, Giô-a-nan con Rê-sa, Rê-sa con Xô-rô-ba-bên, Xô-rô-ba-bên con Sa-la-thi-ên, Sa-la-thi-ên con Nê-ri, ²⁸ Nê-ri

con Mên-chi, Mên-chi con A-đi, A-đi con Cô-sam, Cô sam con Ên-ma-đan, Ên-ma-đan con Ê-rơ, ²⁹ Ê-rơ con Giê-su, Giê-su con Ê-li-ê-se, Ê-li-ê-se con Giô-rim, Giô-rim con Mát-thát, Mát-thát con Lê-vi, ³⁰ Lê-vi con Si-mê-ôn, Si-mê-ôn con Giu-đa, Giu-đa con Giô-sép, Giô-sép con Giô-nam, Giô-nam con Ê-li-a-kim, Ê-li-a-kim con Mê-lê-a, ³¹ Mê-lê-a con Men-na, Men-na con Mát-ta-tha, Mát-ta-tha con Na-than, Na-than con Đa-vít, ³² Đa-vít con Gie-sê, Gie-sê con Giô-bết, Giô-bết con Bô-ô, Bô-ô con Sa-la, Sa-la con Na-ách-son, Na-ách-son con A-mi-na-đáp, ³³ A-mi-na-đáp con Át-min, Át-min con A-rơ-ni, A-rơ-ni con Ếch-rôm, Ếch-rôm con Pha-rê, Pha-rê con Giu-đa, ³⁴ Giu-đa con Gia-cốp, Gia-cốp con Y-sác, Y-sác con Áp-ra-ham, Áp-ra-ham con Tha-rê, Tha-rê con Na-cô, ³⁵ Na-cô con Sê-rúc, Sê-rúc con Ra-gao, Ra-gao con Pha-léc, Pha-léc con Hê-be, Hê-be con Sa-la, ³⁶ Sa-la con Cai-nam, Cai-nam con A-bác-sát, A-bác-sát con Sem, Sem con Nô-ê, Nô-ê con La-méc, ³⁷ La-méc con Ma-tu-sê-la, Ma-tu-sê-la con Hê-nóc, Hê-nóc con Gia-rết, Gia-rết con Mê-lê-lê-ên, Mê-lê-lê-ên con Cai-nam, ³⁸ Cai-nam con Ê-nót, Ê-nót con Sết, Sết con A-đam, A-đam con Đức Chúa Trời.

Sự cám-dỗ

4 ¹ Đức Chúa Jêsus đầy-dẫy Đức Thánh-Linh, ở bờ sông Giô-đanh về, thì được Đức Thánh-Linh đưa đến trong đồng vắng, ² tại đó, Ngài bị ma-quỉ cám-dỗ trong bốn mươi ngày. Trong những ngày ấy, Ngài không ăn chi hết, kỳ đã mãn thì Ngài đói. ³ Ma-quỉ bèn nói với Ngài rằng: Nếu ngươi là Con Đức Chúa Trời, thì hãy khiến đá nầy trở nên bánh đi. ⁴ Đức Chúa Jêsus đáp: Có chép rằng: Loài người được sống chẳng phải chỉ nhờ bánh mà thôi. ⁵ Ma-quỉ đem Ngài lên, cho xem mọi nước thế-gian trong giây phút; ⁶ và nói rằng: Ta sẽ cho ngươi hết thảy quyền-phép và sự vinh-hiển của các nước đó; vì đã giao cho ta hết, ta muốn cho ai tùy ý ta. ⁷ Vậy, nếu ngươi sấp mình xuống trước mặt ta, mọi sự đó sẽ thuộc về ngươi cả. ⁸ Đức Chúa Jêsus đáp: Có chép rằng: Ngươi phải thờ-phượng Chúa, là Đức Chúa Trời ngươi, và chỉ hầu việc một mình Ngài mà thôi. ⁹ Ma-quỉ cũng đem Ngài đến thành Giê-ru-sa-lem, để Ngài trên nóc đền-thờ, mà nói rằng: Nếu ngươi là Con Đức Chúa Trời, hãy gieo mình xuống đi; ¹⁰ vì có chép rằng:

Chúa sẽ truyền cho thiên-sứ gìn-giữ ngươi,

¹¹ Các đấng ấy sẽ nâng ngươi trong tay,

Kẻo ngươi vấp chân nhằm đá nào chăng.

¹² Đức Chúa Jêsus đáp: Có phán rằng: Ngươi đừng thử Chúa, là Đức Chúa Trời ngươi. ¹³ Ma-quỉ dùng hết cách cám-dỗ Ngài rồi, bèn tạm lìa Ngài.

Chức-vụ Đức Chúa Jêsus tại xứ Ga-li-lê

(Từ 4:14 đến 9:50)

Lời giảng tại thành Na-xa-rét

¹⁴ Đức Chúa Jêsus được quyền-phép Đức Thánh-Linh, trở về xứ Ga-li-lê, và danh-tiếng Ngài đồn khắp các xứ chung-quanh. ¹⁵ Ngài dạy-dỗ trong các nhà hội, ai nấy đều khen-ngợi Ngài.

¹⁶ Đức Chúa Jêsus đến thành Na-xa-rét, là nơi dưỡng-dục Ngài. Theo thói quen, nhằm ngày Sa-bát, Ngài vào nhà hội, đứng dậy và đọc. ¹⁷ Có người trao sách tiên-tri Ê-sai cho Ngài, Ngài dở ra, gặp chỗ có chép rằng:

¹⁸ Thần của Chúa ngự trên ta;

Vì Ngài đã xức dầu cho ta đặng truyền tin lành cho kẻ nghèo;

¹⁹ Ngài đã sai ta để rao cho kẻ bị cầm được tha,

Kẻ mù được sáng,

Kẻ bị hà-hiếp được tự-do;

Và để đồn ra năm lành của Chúa.

²⁰ Đoạn, Ngài xếp sách, trả lại cho kẻ giúp việc, rồi ngồi xuống; mọi người trong nhà hội đều chăm-chỉ ngó Ngài. ²¹ Ngài bèn phán rằng: Hôm nay đã được ứng-nghiệm lời Kinh-thánh mà các ngươi mới vừa nghe đó.

²² Ai nấy đều làm chứng về Ngài, lấy làm lạ về các lời đầy ơn lành từ miệng Ngài ra, và nói rằng: Có phải con Giô-sép chăng? ²³ Ngài phán rằng: Chắc các ngươi lấy lời tục-ngữ nầy mà nói cùng ta rằng: Hỡi thầy thuốc, hãy tự chữa lấy mình; mọi điều chúng ta nghe ngươi đã

làm tại Ca-bê-na-um, thì cũng hãy làm tại đây, là quê-hương ngươi. ²⁴ Ngài lại phán rằng: Quả thật, ta nói cùng các ngươi, không có một đấng tiên-tri nào được trọng-đãi trong quê-hương mình. ²⁵ Ta nói thật cùng các ngươi, về đời Ê-li, khi trời đóng chặt trong ba năm sáu tháng, cả xứ bị đói-kém, trong dân Y-sơ-ra-ên có nhiều đàn-bà góa; ²⁶ dầu vậy, Ê-li chẳng được sai đến cùng một người nào trong đám họ, nhưng được sai đến cùng một đàn-bà góa ở Sa-rép-ta, xứ Si-đôn. ²⁷ Trong đời đấng tiên tri Ê-li-sê, dân Y-sơ-ra-ên cũng có nhiều kẻ mắc tật phung; song không có ai lành sạch được, chỉ Na-a-man, người xứ Sy-ri mà thôi.

²⁸ Ai nấy ở trong nhà hội nghe những điều đó, thì tức giận lắm. ²⁹ Họ đứng dậy kéo Ngài ra ngoài thành, đưa Ngài lên đến chót núi, là nơi họ xây thành ở trên, để quăng Ngài xuống; ³⁰ song Ngài qua giữa bọn họ và đi khỏi.

Sự chữa người bị quỉ ám

³¹ Ngài xuống thành Ca-bê-na-um, thuộc xứ Ga-li-lê, dạy-dỗ trong ngày Sa-bát. ³² Mọi người đều cảm-động về sự dạy-dỗ của Ngài; vì Ngài dùng quyền-phép mà phán.

³³ Vả, trong nhà hội có một người bị tà-ma ám, cất tiếng kêu lớn lên rằng: Hỡi Jêsus Na-xa-rét! ³⁴ Chúng tôi với Ngài có sự gì chăng? Ngài đến để diệt chúng tôi sao? Tôi biết Ngài là ai: Là Đấng Thánh của Đức Chúa Trời! ³⁵ Song Đức Chúa Jêsus quở nặng nó, mà rằng: Hãy nín đi, và ra khỏi người nầy. Quỉ bèn vật ngã người giữa đám đông, rồi ra khỏi, không làm hại chi đến người. ³⁶ Mọi người đều sững-sờ, nói cùng nhau rằng: Ấy là đạo gì đó? Người lấy phép và quyền đuổi tà-ma, và chúng nó liền ra! ³⁷ Vậy, danh-tiếng Ngài đồn khắp các nơi xung-quanh.

Bà gia Phi-e-rơ

³⁸ Đức Chúa Jêsus ra khỏi nhà hội, vào nhà Si-môn. Bà gia Si-môn đang đau rét nặng lắm. Người ta xin Ngài chữa cho, ³⁹ Ngài bèn nghiêng mình trên người, truyền cho cơn rét, rét liền lìa khỏi. Tức thì người chờ dậy hầu việc.

Các thứ phép lạ khác

⁴⁰ Khi mặt trời lặn rồi, ai nấy có người đau, bất-kỳ bịnh gì, đều đem đến cùng Ngài; Ngài đặt tay lên từng người mà chữa cho họ. ⁴¹ Cũng có các quỉ ra khỏi nhiều kẻ, mà kêu lên rằng: Ngài là Đấng Christ, Con Đức Chúa Trời! Nhưng Ngài quở nặng chúng nó, cấm không cho nói mình biết Ngài là Đấng Christ.

⁴² Vừa rạng ngày, Ngài ra đi đến nơi vắng-vẻ, một đoàn dân đông kéo đi tìm Ngài. Họ theo kịp, giữ Ngài ở lại, không muốn để Ngài đi. ⁴³ Nhưng Ngài phán cùng họ rằng: Ta cũng phải rao Tin-lành của nước Đức Chúa Trời nơi các thành khác; vì cốt tại việc đó mà ta được sai đến. ⁴⁴ Vậy Ngài giảng-dạy trong các nhà hội xứ Ga-li-lê.

Sự đánh cá lạ-lùng

5 ¹ Khi Đức Chúa Jêsus ở trên bờ hồ Ghê-nê-xa-rết, đoàn dân đông chen-lấn nhau xung-quanh Ngài đặng nghe đạo Đức Chúa Trời. ² Ngài thấy hai chiếc thuyền đậu gần bờ, người đánh cá đã xuống khỏi thuyền giặt lưới, ³ thì Ngài lên một chiếc thuyền trong hai chiếc, là chiếc của Si-môn, biểu người đem ra khỏi bờ một chút; rồi Ngài ngồi mà dạy-dỗ dân-chúng.

⁴ Khi Ngài phán xong thì biểu Si-môn rằng: Hãy chèo ra ngoài sâu, thả lưới mà đánh cá. ⁵ Si-môn thưa rằng: Thưa thầy, chúng tôi đã làm suốt đêm không bắt được chi hết; dầu vậy, tôi cũng theo lời thầy mà thả lưới. ⁶ Họ thả lưới xuống, được nhiều cá lắm, đến nỗi lưới phải đứt ra. ⁷ Họ bèn ra vọi gọi đồng-bạn mình ở thuyền khác đến giúp; bạn kia đến chở cá đầy hai chiếc thuyền, đến nỗi gần chìm. ⁸ Si-môn Phi-e-rơ thấy vậy, liền sấp mình xuống ngang đầu gối Đức Chúa Jêsus, mà thưa rằng: Lạy Chúa, xin ra khỏi tôi, vì tôi là người có tội. ⁹ Số là, vì đánh cá dường ấy, nên Si-môn cùng mọi người ở với mình đều thất-kinh; Gia-cơ và Giăng con Xê-bê-đê, là những kẻ đồng-bạn với Si-môn cũng đồng một thể ấy. ¹⁰ Đức Chúa Jêsus bèn phán cùng Si-môn rằng: Đừng sợ chi, từ nay trở đi, ngươi sẽ nên tay đánh lưới người. ¹¹ Đoạn, họ đem thuyền vào bờ, bỏ hết thảy mà theo Ngài.

Sự chữa bịnh phung

¹² Đức Chúa Jêsus đương ở trong thành kia, có một người mắc bịnh phung đầy mình, thấy Ngài thì sấp mặt xuống đất, mà nài-xin rằng: Lạy Chúa, nếu Chúa khứng, chắc có thể làm cho tôi được sạch! ¹³ Đức Chúa Jêsus giơ tay rờ đến người ấy, mà phán rằng: Ta khứng, hãy sạch đi. Tức thì, bịnh phung liền hết. ¹⁴ Đức Chúa Jêsus cấm người đó học chuyện lại với ai; nhưng dặn rằng: Hãy đi tỏ mình cùng thầy tế-lễ; và dâng của-lễ về sự ngươi được sạch, theo như Môi-se dạy, để điều đó làm chứng cho họ.

¹⁵ Danh-tiếng Ngài càng ngày càng vang ra, và một đoàn dân đông nhóm-họp để nghe Ngài và để được chữa lành bịnh. ¹⁶ Song Ngài lánh đi nơi đồng vắng mà cầu-nguyện.

Sự chữa bịnh bại

¹⁷ Một ngày kia, Đức Chúa Jêsus đang dạy-dỗ, có người Pha-ri-si^f và mấy thầy dạy luật từ các làng xứ Ga-li-lê, xứ Giu-đê, và thành Giê-ru-sa-lem đều đến, ngồi tại đó, quyền-phép Chúa ở trong Ngài để chữa lành các bịnh. ¹⁸ Bấy giờ, có mấy người khiêng một kẻ đau bại trên giường, kiếm cách đem vào để trước mặt Đức Chúa Jêsus. ¹⁹ Nhân vì người ta đông lắm, không biết bởi đâu mà qua, họ bèn trèo lên mái nhà, dỡ ngói ra, dòng người và giường nhỏ xuống trước mặt Ngài, giữa đám đô-hội. ²⁰ Đức Chúa Jêsus thấy đức-tin của họ, bèn phán rằng: Hỡi người, tội-lỗi ngươi đã được tha. ²¹ Các thầy thông-giáo và người Pha-ri-si bèn nghị-luận rằng: Người nầy là ai mà nói phạm-thượng vậy? Ngoài Đức Chúa Trời, há có ai tha tội được sao? ²² Nhưng Đức Chúa Jêsus biết ý-tưởng họ, cất tiếng phán rằng: Các ngươi nghị-luận gì trong lòng? ²³ Nay nói rằng: Tội ngươi đã được tha, hoặc rằng: Ngươi hãy đứng dậy mà đi, thì bên nào dễ hơn? ²⁴ Và, hầu cho các ngươi biết Con người ở thế-gian có quyền tha tội: Ngài phán cùng kẻ bại rằng: Ta biểu ngươi đứng dậy, vác giường trở về nhà. ²⁵ Tức thì kẻ bại đứng dậy trước mặt chúng, vác giường mình đã nằm, và đi về nhà, ngợi-khen Đức Chúa Trời. ²⁶ Ai nấy đều sững-sờ, ngợi-khen Đức Chúa Trời; và sợ-sệt lắm mà nói rằng: Hôm nay chúng ta đã thấy những việc dị-thường.

---

f **5:17** Xem chú thích ở Mat 3:7

Chúa gọi Lê-vi. – Sự kiêng ăn

²⁷ Kế đó, Đức Chúa Jêsus ra ngoài, thấy một người thâu thuế, tên là Lê-vi, đương ngồi tại sở thâu thuế. Ngài phán cùng người rằng: Hãy theo ta! ²⁸ Lê-vi bỏ hết mọi sự, đứng dậy đi theo Ngài.

²⁹ Lê-vi dọn tiệc trọng-thể đãi Ngài tại nhà mình, có nhiều người thâu thuế và kẻ khác cùng ngồi ăn đồng bàn. ³⁰ Các người Pha-ri-si và các thầy thông-giáo họ lằm-bằm, nói cùng môn-đồ Ngài rằng: Sao các ngươi ăn uống với người thâu thuế và kẻ phạm tội? ³¹ Đức Chúa Jêsus phán cùng họ rằng: Không phải người khỏe mạnh cần thầy thuốc, song là người đau ốm. ³² Ta không phải đến gọi kẻ công-bình hối-cải, song gọi kẻ có tội.

³³ Họ thưa Ngài rằng: Môn-đồ của Giăng thường kiêng ăn cầu-nguyện, cũng như môn-đồ của người Pha-ri-si, chẳng như môn-đồ của thầy ăn và uống. ³⁴ Ngài đáp rằng: Trong khi chàng rể còn ở cùng bạn mừng cưới mình,ᵍ các ngươi dễ bắt họ phải kiêng ăn được sao? ³⁵ Song đến ngày nào chàng rể phải đem đi khỏi họ, thì trong những ngày ấy họ mới kiêng ăn vậy.

³⁶ Ngài lại lấy thí-dụ mà phán cùng họ rằng: Không ai xé một miếng áo mới mà vá áo cũ. Nếu vậy, áo mới phải rách, và miếng giẻ mới cũng không xứng với áo cũ. ³⁷ Cũng không ai đổ rượu mới vào bầu da cũ, nếu vậy, rượu mới làm nứt bầu ra; rượu chảy mất và bầu cũng phải hư đi. ³⁸ Song rượu mới phải đổ vào bầu mới. ³⁹ Lại cũng không ai uống rượu cũ lại đòi rượu mới; vì người nói rằng: Rượu cũ ngon hơn.

Bứt bông lúa mì

6 ¹ Nhằm ngày Sa-bát, Đức Chúa Jêsus đi qua giữa đồng lúa mì, môn-đồ bứt bông lúa, lấy tay vò đi và ăn. ² Có mấy người Pha-ri-si nói rằng: Sao các ngươi làm điều không nên làm trong ngày Sa-bát? ³ Đức Chúa Jêsus phán rằng: Vậy các ngươi chưa đọc chuyện vua Đa-vít làm trong khi vua cùng kẻ đi theo bị đói sao? ⁴ Thể nào vua vào đến Đức Chúa Trời, lấy bánh bày ra mà ăn, và cho kẻ đi theo

---

ᵍ 5:34 Nt: *các con trai của phòng tiệc cưới*

ăn nữa, dầu là bánh chỉ các thầy tế-lễ mới được phép ăn thôi? [5] Ngài lại phán rằng: Con người cũng là Chúa ngày Sa-bát.

Người teo tay

[6] Một ngày Sa-bát khác, Đức Chúa Jêsus vào nhà hội dạy-dỗ. Tại đó, có một người bàn tay hữu bị teo. [7] Và, các thầy thông-giáo và người Pha-ri-si chăm-chỉ xem Ngài, coi thử Ngài có chữa bịnh trong ngày Sa-bát chăng, để tìm dịp mà cáo Ngài. [8] Nhưng Ngài biết ý-tưởng họ, nên phán cùng người teo tay rằng: Hãy chờ dậy, đứng giữa chúng ta. Người ấy chờ dậy, và đứng lên. [9] Đức Chúa Jêsus liền phán cùng họ rằng: Ta hỏi các ngươi: Trong ngày Sa-bát, nên làm điều lành hay là làm điều dữ, nên cứu người hay là giết người? [10] Đoạn, Ngài lấy mắt liếc khắp mọi người xung-quanh mình, rồi phán cùng người bịnh rằng: Hãy giơ tay ra. Người giơ ra, thì tay được lành. [11] Nhưng họ giận lắm, bèn bàn cùng nhau về việc mình có thể xử với Đức Chúa Jêsus cách nào.

Sự chọn mười hai sứ-đồ

[12] Trong lúc đó, Đức Chúa Jêsus đi lên núi để cầu-nguyện; và thức thâu đêm cầu-nguyện Đức Chúa Trời. [13] Đến sáng ngày, Ngài đòi môn-đồ đến, chọn mười hai người gọi là sứ-đồ: [14] Si-môn, Ngài đặt tên là Phi-e-rơ, Anh-rê em ruột của Phi-e-rơ, Gia-cơ và Giăng, Phi-líp và Ba-thê-lê-my, [15] Ma-thi-ơ, và Thô-ma, Gia-cơ con của A-phê, Si-môn gọi là Xê-lốt, [16] Giu-đe con của Gia-cơ, và Giu-đa Ích-ca-ri-ốt là kẻ phản Ngài.

Các sự dạy-bảo khác

[17] Kế đó, Ngài cùng môn-đồ xuống, dừng lại nơi đồng bằng. Ở đó, có nhiều môn-đồ Ngài cùng đoàn dân rất đông từ khắp xứ Giu-đê, thành Giê-ru-sa-lem, và miền biển Ty-rơ, Si-đôn mà đến, để nghe Ngài dạy và cho được chữa lành bịnh mình. [18] Những kẻ mắc tà-ma khuấy-hại cũng đều được lành. [19] Cả đoàn dân đến kiếm cách rờ Ngài, vì từ Ngài có quyền-phép ra, chữa lành hết mọi người.

²⁰ Đức Chúa Jêsus bèn ngước mắt ngó môn-đồ, mà phán rằng: Phước cho các ngươi nghèo-khó, vì nước Đức Chúa Trời thuộc về các ngươi! ²¹ Phước cho các ngươi hiện đương đói, vì sẽ được no-đủ! Phước cho các ngươi hiện đương khóc-lóc, vì sẽ được vui-mừng! ²² Phước cho các ngươi khi vì cớ Con người, thiên-hạ sẽ ghét, đuổi, mắng-nhiếc các ngươi, bỏ tên các ngươi như đồ ô-uế! ²³ Ngày đó, hãy vui-vẻ, nhảy-nhót và mừng-rỡ, vì phần thưởng các ngươi trên trời sẽ lớn lắm: Bởi tổ-phụ họ cũng đối-đãi các đấng tiên-tri dường ấy.

²⁴ Song, khốn cho các ngươi là người giàu-có, vì đã được sự yên-ủi của mình rồi! ²⁵ Khốn cho các ngươi là kẻ hiện đương no, vì sẽ đói! Khốn cho các ngươi là kẻ hiện đương cười, vì sẽ để tang và khóc-lóc! ²⁶ Khốn cho các ngươi, khi mọi người sẽ khen các ngươi, vì tổ-phụ họ cũng xử với các tiên-tri giả như vậy!

²⁷ Nhưng ta phán cùng các ngươi, là người nghe ta: Hãy yêu kẻ thù mình, làm ơn cho kẻ ghét mình, ²⁸ chúc phước cho kẻ rủa mình, và cầu-nguyện cho kẻ sỉ-nhục mình. ²⁹ Ai vả ngươi má bên nầy, hãy đưa luôn má bên kia cho họ; còn nếu ai giựt áo ngoài của ngươi, thì cũng đừng ngăn họ lấy luôn áo trong. ³⁰ Hễ ai xin, hãy cho, và nếu có ai đoạt lấy của các ngươi, thì đừng đòi lại. ³¹ Các ngươi muốn người ta làm cho mình thể nào, hãy làm cho người ta thể ấy.

³² Nếu các ngươi yêu kẻ yêu mình, thì có ơn chi? Người có tội cũng yêu kẻ yêu mình. ³³ Nếu các ngươi làm ơn cho kẻ làm ơn mình, thì có ơn chi? Người có tội cũng làm như vậy. ³⁴ Nếu các ngươi cho ai mượn mà mong họ trả, thì có ơn chi? Người có tội cũng cho người có tội mượn, để được thâu lại y số. ³⁵ Song các ngươi hãy yêu kẻ thù mình; hãy làm ơn, hãy cho mượn, mà đừng ngã lòng. Vậy, phần thưởng của các ngươi sẽ lớn, và các ngươi sẽ làm con của Đấng Rất-Cao, vì Ngài lấy nhân-từ đối-đãi kẻ bạc và kẻ dữ.

³⁶ Hãy thương-xót như Cha các ngươi hay thương-xót. ³⁷ Đừng đoán-xét ai, thì các ngươi khỏi bị đoán-xét; đừng lên án ai, thì các ngươi khỏi bị lên án; hãy tha-thứ, người sẽ tha-thứ mình. ³⁸ Hãy cho, người sẽ cho mình; họ sẽ lấy đấu lớn, nhận, lắc cho đầy tràn, mà nộp trong lòng các ngươi; vì các ngươi lường mực nào, thì họ cũng lường lại cho các ngươi mực ấy.

³⁹ Ngài cũng phán cùng họ một thí-dụ rằng: Kẻ mù có thể dắt kẻ mù được chăng? Cả hai há chẳng cùng té xuống hố sao?

⁴⁰ Môn-đồ không hơn thầy; nhưng hễ môn-đồ được trọn-vẹn thì sẽ bằng thầy mình. ⁴¹ Sao ngươi nhìn thấy cái rác trong mắt anh em mình, mà không thấy cây đà trong mắt ngươi? ⁴² Sao ngươi nói được với anh em rằng: Anh ơi, để tôi lấy cái rác trong mắt anh ra, còn ngươi, thì không thấy cây đà trong mắt mình? Hỡi kẻ giả-hình, hãy lấy cây đà ra khỏi mắt mình trước đã, rồi mới thấy rõ mà lấy cái rác ra khỏi mắt anh em.

⁴³ Cây sanh trái xấu không phải là cây tốt, cây sanh trái tốt không phải là cây xấu; ⁴⁴ vì hễ xem trái thì biết cây. Người ta không hái được trái vả nơi bụi gai, hay là hái trái nho nơi chòm kinh-cước. ⁴⁵ Người lành bởi lòng chứa điều thiện mà phát ra điều thiện, kẻ dữ bởi lòng chứa điều ác mà phát ra điều ác; vì do sự đầy-dẫy trong lòng mà miệng nói ra.

⁴⁶ Sao các ngươi gọi ta: Chúa, Chúa, mà không làm theo lời ta phán? ⁴⁷ Ta sẽ chỉ cho các ngươi biết kẻ nào đến cùng ta, nghe lời ta, và làm theo, thì giống ai. ⁴⁸ Kẻ ấy giống như một người kia cất nhà, đào đất cho sâu, xây nền trên vầng đá: Nước tràn-lan, dòng nước chảy mạnh xô vào nhà đó, nhưng không xô-động được, vì đã cất chắc-chắn. ⁴⁹ Song kẻ nào nghe lời ta mà không làm theo, thì giống như một người kia cất nhà trên đất không xây nền: Dòng nước chảy mạnh xô vào nhà đó, tức thì nhà sụp xuống, và sự hư-hại lớn-lao.

Thầy đội ở thành Ca-bê-na-um

7 ¹ Khi Đức Chúa Jêsus rao-giảng xong mọi lời ấy trước mặt dân-chúng nghe rồi, thì Ngài vào thành Ca-bê-na-um.

² Vả, một thầy đội kia có đứa đầy-tớ rất thiết-nghĩa đau gần chết, ³ nghe nói Đức Chúa Jêsus, bèn sai mấy trưởng-lão trong dân Giu-đa xin Ngài đến chữa cho đầy-tớ mình. ⁴ Mấy người đó đến cùng Đức Chúa Jêsus, mà nài-xin rằng: Thầy đội thật đáng cho thầy nhậm điều nầy; ⁵ vì người yêu dân ta, và đã cất nhà hội cho chúng tôi. ⁶ Đức Chúa Jêsus bèn đi với họ. Khi Ngài gần tới nhà, thầy đội sai bạn-hữu mình đi thưa Ngài rằng: Lạy Chúa, xin đừng tự phiền đến thế, vì tôi không đáng rước Chúa vào nhà tôi. ⁷ Tôi cũng nghĩ mình không đáng đến cùng Chúa; song xin phán một lời, thì đầy-tớ tôi sẽ được lành. ⁸ Vì chính mình tôi là người thuộc dưới quyền kẻ khác, tôi cũng

có quân-lính dưới quyền tôi; tôi biểu tên nầy rằng: Hãy đi! Thì nó đi; biểu tên khác rằng: Hãy đến! Thì nó đến; và biểu đầy-tớ tôi rằng: Hãy làm việc nầy! Thì nó làm. ⁹ Đức Chúa Jêsus nghe những lời ấy, lấy làm lạ cho thầy đội, bèn xây lại cùng đoàn dân theo mình, mà phán rằng: Ta nói cùng các ngươi, dầu trong dân Y-sơ-ra-ên, ta cũng chưa thấy một đức-tin lớn dường ấy. ¹⁰ Những kẻ sai đến trở về nhà, thấy đầy-tớ lành-mạnh.

Người trai-trẻ ở Na-in

¹¹ Bữa sau, Đức Chúa Jêsus đi đến một thành, gọi là Na-in, có nhiều môn-đồ và một đoàn dân đông cùng đi với Ngài. ¹² Khi Ngài đến gần cửa thành, họ vừa khiêng ra một người chết, là con trai một của mẹ góa kia; có nhiều người ở thành đó đi đưa với bà góa ấy. ¹³ Chúa thấy, động lòng thương-xót người, mà phán rằng: Đừng khóc! ¹⁴ Đoạn, Ngài lại gần, rờ quan-tài, thì kẻ khiêng dừng lại. Ngài bèn phán rằng: Hỡi người trẻ kia, ta biểu ngươi chờ dậy. ¹⁵ Người chết vùng ngồi dậy và khởi-sự nói. Đức Chúa Jêsus giao người lại cho mẹ. ¹⁶ Ai nấy đều sợ-hãi, và ngợi-khen Đức Chúa Trời rằng: Có đấng tiên-tri lớn đã dấy lên giữa chúng tôi, và Đức Chúa Trời đã thăm-viếng dân Ngài. ¹⁷ Tin nầy đồn ra khắp xứ Giu-đê, và khắp xứ xung-quanh nơi đó nữa.

Sự thăm-hỏi của Giăng Báp-tít

¹⁸ Môn-đồ của Giăng trình lại hết cả chuyện đó với người. ¹⁹ Người bèn gọi hai môn-đồ mình, sai đến thưa cùng Chúa rằng: Thầy có phải là Đấng phải đến, hay chúng tôi còn phải đợi Đấng khác? ²⁰ Hai người đã đến cùng Đức Chúa Jêsus, thưa rằng: Giăng Báp-tít sai chúng tôi đến hỏi thầy: Thầy có phải là Đấng phải đến, hay chúng tôi còn phải đợi Đấng khác? ²¹ Vả, chính giờ đó, Đức Chúa Jêsus chữa lành nhiều kẻ bịnh, kẻ tàn-tật, kẻ mắc quỉ dữ, và làm cho nhiều người đui được sáng. ²² Đoạn, Ngài đáp rằng: Hãy về báo cho Giăng sự các ngươi đã thấy và đã nghe: Kẻ đui được sáng, kẻ què được đi, kẻ phung được sạch, kẻ điếc được nghe, kẻ chết được sống lại, Tin-lành đã rao-giảng cho kẻ nghèo. ²³ Phước cho kẻ không vấp-phạm vì cớ ta!

²⁴ Hai người của Giăng sai đến đã đi rồi, Đức Chúa Jêsus mới phán cùng đoàn dân về việc Giăng rằng: Các ngươi đã đi xem chi nơi đồng vắng? Xem cây sậy bị gió rung chăng?… ²⁵ Lại các ngươi còn đi xem gì? Xem người ăn mặc tốt-đẹp chăng? Kìa, những người mặc áo sang-trọng, và ăn-ở sung-sướng, thì ở trong đền-đài các vua! ²⁶ Song, rốt lại, các ngươi đi xem gì? Xem một đấng tiên-tri ư? Phải, ta nói, một đấng trọng hơn tiên-tri nữa. ²⁷ Ấy về đấng đó mà có lời chép rằng:

Nầy, ta sẽ sai sứ ta đến trước mặt ngươi,

Người sẽ dọn đường trước ngươi.

²⁸ Ta nói cùng các ngươi, trong những người bởi đàn-bà sanh ra, không có ai lớn hơn Giăng Báp-tít đâu; nhưng trong nước Đức Chúa Trời, kẻ rất nhỏ còn lớn hơn Giăng vậy. ²⁹ Cả dân-chúng cùng kẻ thâu thuế chịu Giăng làm phép báp-têm, đều xưng Đức Chúa Trời là công-bình. ³⁰ Song người Pha-ri-si cùng các thầy dạy luật không chịu Giăng làm phép báp-têm, nên chê-bỏ ý Đức Chúa Trời định về mình.

³¹ Vậy, ta sẽ sánh người đời nầy với gì, họ giống như ai? ³² Họ giống như con trẻ ngồi ngoài chợ, nói cùng nhau rằng: Ta đã thổi sáo, mà bay không nhảy-múa; ta đã than-vãn, mà bay không khóc. ³³ Và, Giăng Báp-tít đã đến, không ăn bánh, không uống rượu; thì các ngươi nói rằng: Người mắc quỉ dữ. ³⁴ Con người đến, ăn và uống, thì các ngươi nói rằng: Ấy đó là người ham ăn mê uống, bạn với người thâu thuế và kẻ có tội. ³⁵ Song sự khôn-ngoan được xưng công-bình nhờ những việc làmʰ của nó.

Người đàn-bà có tội được tha-thứ

³⁶ Có một người Pha-ri-si mời Đức Chúa Jêsus ăn tại nhà mình. Vậy, khi đã vào nhà người Pha-ri-si thì Ngài ngồi bàn. ³⁷ Và, có một người đàn-bà xấu nết ở thành đó, nghe nói Đức Chúa Jêsus đương ngồi bàn tại nhà người Pha-ri-si, bèn đem đến một bình ngọc trắng đựng đầy dầu thơm. ³⁸ Người đứng đẳng sau, nơi chân Đức Chúa Jêsus, khóc, sa nước mắt trên chân Ngài, rồi lấy tóc mình mà chùi; lại hôn chân Ngài, và xức dầu thơm cho. ³⁹ Người Pha-ri-si đã mời

---

h 7:35 Nt: *nhờ con cái*

Ngài, thấy vậy, tự nghĩ rằng: Nếu người nầy là đấng tiên-tri, chắc biết người đàn-bà rờ đến mình đó là ai, cùng biết ấy là người đàn-bà xấu nết. ⁴⁰ Đức Chúa Jêsus bèn cất tiếng phán cùng người rằng: Hỡi Si-môn, ta có vài lời nói cùng ngươi. Người thưa rằng: Thưa thầy, xin cứ nói.

⁴¹ Một chủ nợ có hai người mắc nợ: Một người mắc năm trăm đơ-ni-ê,ⁱ một người mắc năm chục. ⁴² Vì hai người đều không có chi mà trả, nên chủ nợ tha cả hai. Trong hai người đó, ai yêu chủ nợ hơn? ⁴³ Si-môn thưa rằng: Tôi tưởng là người mà chủ nợ đã tha nhiều nợ hơn. Đức Chúa Jêsus phán rằng: Ngươi đoán phải lắm. ⁴⁴ Đoạn, Ngài xây lại người đàn-bà mà phán cùng Si-môn rằng: Ngươi thấy đàn-bà nầy không? Ta vào nhà ngươi, ngươi không cho nước rửa chân; nhưng người đã lấy nước mắt thấm ướt chân ta, rồi lấy tóc mình mà chùi. ⁴⁵ Ngươi không hôn ta, nhưng người từ khi vào nhà ngươi, thì hôn chân ta hoài. ⁴⁶ Ngươi không xức dầu đầu ta; nhưng người lấy dầu thơm xức chân ta. ⁴⁷ Vậy nên ta nói cùng ngươi, tội-lỗi đàn-bà nầy nhiều lắm, đã được tha hết, vì người đã yêu-mến nhiều; song kẻ được tha ít thì yêu-mến ít. ⁴⁸ Ngài bèn phán cùng người đàn-bà rằng: Tội-lỗi ngươi đã được tha rồi. ⁴⁹ Các người ngồi bàn với Ngài nghĩ thầm rằng: Người nầy là ai, mà cũng tha tội? ⁵⁰ Nhưng Ngài phán cùng người đàn-bà rằng: Đức-tin của ngươi đã cứu ngươi; hãy đi cho bình-an.

Ví-dụ về người gieo giống

8 ¹ Kế đó, Đức Chúa Jêsus đi thành nầy đến thành kia, làng nầy đến làng khác, giảng-dạy và rao-truyền tin lành của nước Đức Chúa Trời. Có mười hai sứ-đồ ở với Ngài. ² Cũng có mấy người đàn-bà đi theo Ngài, là những người đã được cứu khỏi quỉ dữ và chữa khỏi bịnh: Ma-ri, gọi là Ma-đơ-len, từ người bảy quỉ dữ đã ra, ³ Gian-nơ vợ Chu-xa, là quan nội-vụ của vua Hê-rốt, Su-xan-nơ và nhiều người khác nữa giúp của-cải cho Ngài.

⁴ Khi có đoàn dân đông nhóm lại, và người hết thảy các thành đều đến cùng Ngài, thì Ngài lấy thí-dụ mà phán cùng họ rằng: ⁵ Người gieo đi ra để gieo giống mình. Khi vãi giống, một phần giống rơi ra

---

i 7:41 Xem chú thích ở Mat 18:28

dọc đường, bị giày-đạp và chim trời xuống ăn hết. ⁶ Một phần khác rơi ra nơi đất đá-sỏi, khi mới mọc lên, liền héo đi, vì không có hơi ẩm. ⁷ Một phần khác rơi vào bụi gai, gai mọc lên với hột giống, làm cho nghẹt-ngòi. ⁸ Lại có một phần khác rơi xuống nơi đất tốt, thì mọc lên, và kết-quả, một thành trăm. Đương phán mấy lời đó, Ngài kêu lên rằng: Ai có tai mà nghe, hãy nghe!

⁹ Môn-đồ hỏi Ngài thí-dụ ấy có nghĩa gì. ¹⁰ Ngài đáp rằng: Đã ban cho các ngươi được biết những sự mầu-nhiệm nước Đức Chúa Trời; song, với kẻ khác thì dùng thí-dụ mà nói, để họ xem mà không thấy, nghe mà không hiểu. ¹¹ Nầy, lời thí-dụ đó nghĩa như vầy: Hột giống là đạo Đức Chúa Trời. ¹² Phần rơi ra dọc đường, là những kẻ đã nghe đạo; nhưng về sau ma-quỉ đến, cướp lấy đạo từ trong lòng họ, e rằng họ tin mà được cứu chăng. ¹³ Phần rơi ra đất đá-sỏi là kẻ nghe đạo, bèn vui-mừng chịu lấy; nhưng họ không có rễ, chỉ tin tạm mà thôi; nên khi sự thử-thách xảy đến, thì họ tháo lui. ¹⁴ Phần rơi vào bụi gai, là những kẻ đã nghe đạo, nhưng rồi đi, để cho sự lo-lắng, giàu-sang, sung-sướng đời nầy làm cho đạo phải nghẹt-ngòi, đến nỗi không sanh trái nào được chín. ¹⁵ Song phần rơi vào nơi đất tốt, là kẻ có lấy lòng thật-thà tử-tế nghe đạo, gìn-giữ, và kết-quả một cách bền lòng.

¹⁶ Không ai đã thắp đèn lại lấy thùng úp lại, hay là để dưới giường; nhưng để trên chân đèn, hầu cho ai vào nhà đều thấy sáng. ¹⁷ Thật không có điều gì kín mà không phải lộ ra, không có điều gì giấu mà chẳng bị biết và tỏ ra. ¹⁸ Vậy, hãy coi chừng về cách các ngươi nghe; vì kẻ đã có, sẽ cho thêm; kẻ không có, sẽ cất lấy sự họ tưởng mình có.

Mẹ và anh em Đức Chúa Jêsus

¹⁹ Mẹ và anh em Đức Chúa Jêsus đến tìm Ngài; song vì người ta đông lắm, nên không đến gần Ngài được. ²⁰ Vậy có kẻ báo cho Ngài biết rằng: Mẹ và anh em thầy ở ngoài, muốn thấy thầy. ²¹ Nhưng Ngài đáp rằng: Mẹ ta và anh em ta là kẻ nghe đạo Đức Chúa Trời và làm theo đạo ấy.

Cơn bão

²² Một ngày kia, Ngài xuống thuyền với môn-đồ, mà phán rằng: Hãy qua bên kia hồ; rồi đi. ²³ Khi thuyền đương chạy, thì Ngài ngủ.

Có cơn bão nổi lên trong hồ, nước vào đầy thuyền, đương nguy-hiểm lắm. ²⁴ Môn-đồ bèn đến thức Ngài dậy, rằng: Thầy ôi, Thầy ôi, chúng ta chết! Nhưng Ngài, vừa thức dậy, khiến gió và sóng phải bình-tịnh, thì liền bình-tịnh và yên-lặng như tờ. ²⁵ Ngài bèn phán cùng môn-đồ rằng: Đức-tin các ngươi ở đâu? Môn-đồ sợ-hãi và bỡ-ngỡ, nói với nhau rằng: Người nầy là ai, khiến đến gió và nước, mà cũng phải vâng lời người?

Người Giê-ra-sê bị quỉ ám

²⁶ Kế đó, ghé vào đất của dân Giê-ra-sê, ngang xứ Ga-li-lê. ²⁷ Khi Đức Chúa Jêsus lên bờ, có một người ở thành ấy bị nhiều quỉ ám đi gặp Ngài. Đã lâu nay, người không mặc áo, không ở nhà, song ở nơi mồ-mả. ²⁸ Người ấy vừa thấy Đức Chúa Jêsus, thì la lên inh-ỏi, và đến gieo mình nơi chân Ngài, nói lớn tiếng rằng: Lạy Đức Chúa Jêsus, Con Đức Chúa Trời Rất-Cao, tôi với Ngài có sự chi chăng? Tôi cầu-xin Ngài đừng làm khổ tôi. ²⁹ Vì Đức Chúa Jêsus đương truyền cho tà-ma phải ra khỏi người đó mà nó ám đã lâu; dầu họ giữ người, xiềng và còng chân lại, người cứ bẻ xiềng tháo còng, và bị quỉ dữ đem vào nơi đồng vắng. ³⁰ Đức Chúa Jêsus hỏi người rằng: Mầy tên gì? Người thưa rằng: Quân-đội;ʲ vì nhiều quỉ đã ám vào người. ³¹ Chúng nó bèn cầu-xin Đức Chúa Jêsus đừng khiến mình xuống vực sâu.

³² Vả, ở đó có một bầy heo đông đương ăn trên núi. Các quỉ xin Đức Chúa Jêsus cho chúng nó nhập vào những heo ấy, Ngài bèn cho phép. ³³ Vậy, các quỉ ra khỏi người đó, nhập vào bầy heo, bầy heo từ trên bực cao đâm đầu xuống hồ và chết chìm. ³⁴ Các kẻ chăn heo thấy vậy, chạy trốn, đồn tin ấy ra trong thành và trong nhà-quê.

³⁵ Thiên-hạ bèn đổ ra xem việc mới xảy ra; khi họ đến cùng Đức Chúa Jêsus, thấy người mà các quỉ mới ra khỏi ngồi dưới chân Đức Chúa Jêsus, mặc áo-quần, bộ tỉnh-táo, thì sợ-hãi lắm. ³⁶ Những người đã xem thấy sự lạ đó, thuật lại cho thiên-hạ biết người bị quỉ ám được cứu khỏi thế nào.

³⁷ Hết thảy dân ở miền người Giê-ra-sê xin Đức Chúa Jêsus lìa khỏi xứ họ, vì họ sợ-hãi lắm. Ngài bèn xuống thuyền trở về. ³⁸ Người đã khỏi những quỉ ám xin phép ở với Ngài, nhưng Đức Chúa Jêsus

biểu về, mà rằng: ³⁹ Hãy về nhà ngươi, thuật lại mọi điều Đức Chúa Trời đã làm cho ngươi. Vậy người ấy đi, đồn khắp cả thành mọi điều Đức Chúa Jêsus đã làm cho mình.

Con gái Giai-ru và người đàn-bà đau huyết

⁴⁰ Khi trở về, có đoàn dân đông rước Ngài; vì ai nấy cũng trông-đợi Ngài. ⁴¹ Có người cai nhà hội tên là Giai-ru đến sấp mình xuống nơi chân Đức Chúa Jêsus, xin Ngài vào nhà mình. ⁴² Vì người có con gái một mười hai tuổi gần chết.

Khi Đức Chúa Jêsus đương đi, dân-chúng lấn-ép Ngài tứ phía. ⁴³ Bấy giờ, có một người đàn-bà đau bịnh mất huyết mười hai năm rồi, cũng đã tốn hết tiền-của về thầy thuốc, không ai chữa lành được, ⁴⁴ đến đằng sau Ngài rờ trôn áo; tức thì huyết cầm lại. ⁴⁵ Đức Chúa Jêsus bèn phán rằng: Ai rờ đến ta? Ai nấy đều chối; Phi-e-rơ và những người đồng bạn thưa rằng: Thưa thầy, đoàn dân vây lấy và ép thầy. ⁴⁶ Đức Chúa Jêsus phán rằng: Có người đã rờ đến ta, vì ta nhận-biết có quyền-phép từ ta mà ra. ⁴⁷ Người đàn-bà thấy mình không thể giấu được nữa, thì run-sợ, đến sấp mình xuống nơi chân Ngài, tỏ thật trước mặt dân-chúng vì cớ nào mình đã rờ đến, và liền được lành làm sao. ⁴⁸ Nhưng Đức Chúa Jêsus phán rằng: Hỡi con gái ta, đức-tin ngươi đã chữa lành ngươi; hãy đi cho bình-an.

⁴⁹ Ngài còn đương phán, có kẻ ở nhà người cai nhà hội đến nói với người rằng: Con gái ông chết rồi; đừng làm phiền thầy chi nữa. ⁵⁰ Song Đức Chúa Jêsus nghe vậy, phán cùng Giai-ru rằng: Đừng sợ, hãy tin mà thôi, thì con ngươi sẽ được cứu. ⁵¹ Khi đến nhà, Ngài chỉ cho Phi-e-rơ, Gia-cơ, Giăng, và cha mẹ con ấy vào cùng Ngài. ⁵² Ai nấy đều khóc-lóc than-vãn về con đó. Nhưng Ngài phán rằng: Đừng khóc, con nầy không phải chết, song nó ngủ. ⁵³ Họ biết nó thật chết rồi, bèn nhạo-báng Ngài. ⁵⁴ Nhưng Đức Chúa Jêsus cầm lấy tay con ấy, gọi lớn tiếng lên rằng: Con ơi, hãy chờ dậy! ⁵⁵ Thần-linh bèn hoàn lại, con ấy chờ dậy liền; rồi Ngài truyền cho nó ăn. ⁵⁶ Cha mẹ nó lấy làm lạ; nhưng Ngài cấm nói lại sự xảy ra đó với ai.

Mười hai sứ-đồ được sai đi

9 ¹ Đức Chúa Jêsus nhóm-họp mười hai sứ-đồ, ban quyền-năng phép-tắc để trị quỉ chữa bịnh. ² Rồi Ngài sai đi rao-giảng về nước Đức Chúa Trời cùng chữa lành kẻ có bịnh. ³ Ngài dạy rằng: Đi đường chớ đem gì theo hết, hoặc gậy, hoặc bao, hoặc bánh, hoặc tiền-bạc; cũng đừng đem hai áo. ⁴ Hễ các ngươi vào nhà nào, hãy ở đó cho đến khi đi. ⁵ Còn ai không tiếp-rước các ngươi, hãy ra khỏi thành họ, và phủi bụi chân mình để làm chứng nghịch cùng họ. ⁶ Vậy, các sứ đồ ra đi, từ làng nầy tới làng kia, rao-giảng Tin-lành khắp nơi và chữa lành người có bịnh.

Sự lo-sợ của vua Hê-rốt

⁷ Bấy giờ, Hê-rốt là vua chư-hầu, nghe nói về các việc xảy ra, thì không biết nghĩ làm sao; vì kẻ nầy nói rằng: Giăng đã từ kẻ chết sống lại; ⁸ kẻ khác nói rằng: Ê-li đã hiện ra; và kẻ khác nữa thì rằng: Một trong các đấng tiên-tri đời xưa đã sống lại. ⁹ Song Hê-rốt thì nói: Ta đã truyền chém Giăng rồi: Vậy người nầy là ai, mà ta nghe làm những việc dường ấy? Vua bèn tìm cách thấy Đức Chúa Jêsus.

Sự hóa bánh ra nhiều

¹⁰ Các sứ-đồ trở về trình cùng Đức Chúa Jêsus mọi việc mình đã làm. Ngài bèn đem các sứ-đồ đi tẻ ra với mình đến gần thành kia gọi là Bết-sai-đa. ¹¹ Nhưng dân-chúng nghe vậy, thì đi theo Ngài. Đức Chúa Jêsus tiếp-đãi dân-chúng, giảng cho họ về nước Đức Chúa Trời, và chữa cho những kẻ cần được lành bịnh. ¹² Khi gần tối, mười hai sứ-đồ đến gần Ngài mà thưa rằng: Xin truyền cho dân-chúng về, để họ đến các làng các ấp xung-quanh mà trọ và kiếm chi ăn; vì chúng ta ở đây là nơi vắng-vẻ. ¹³ Song Ngài phán rằng: Chính các ngươi hãy cho họ ăn. Các sứ-đồ thưa rằng: Ví thử chính mình chúng tôi không đi mua đồ-ăn cho hết thảy dân nầy, thì chỉ có năm cái bánh và hai con cá mà thôi. ¹⁴ Vả, bấy giờ có độ năm ngàn người nam ở đó. Ngài bèn phán cùng môn-đồ rằng: Hãy biểu chúng ngồi từng hàng năm mươi người. ¹⁵ Môn-đồ làm theo lời; chúng ngồi xuống hết thảy. ¹⁶ Đoạn, Đức Chúa Jêsus lấy năm cái bánh và hai con cá,

ngước mắt lên trời, chúc-tạ, rồi bẻ ra trao cho môn-đồ, đặng phát cho đoàn dân. ¹⁷ Ai nấy ăn no rồi, người ta thâu được mười hai giỏ đầy những miếng thừa.

Phi-e-rơ xưng Đức Chúa Jêsus là Đấng Christ

¹⁸ Một ngày kia, Đức Chúa Jêsus đang cầu-nguyện riêng, môn-đồ nhóm lại xung-quanh Ngài, Ngài hỏi rằng: Trong dân-chúng, họ nói ta là ai? ¹⁹ Thưa rằng: Người nầy nói là Giăng Báp-tít, người kia nói là Ê-li; kẻ khác nói là một trong các đấng tiên-tri đời xưa sống lại. ²⁰ Ngài lại hỏi rằng: Còn về phần các ngươi thì nói ta là ai? Phi-e-rơ thưa rằng: Thầy là Đấng Christ của Đức Chúa Trời. ²¹ Đức Chúa Jêsus nghiêm-cấm môn-đồ nói sự ấy với ai, ²² và phán thêm rằng: Con người phải chịu nhiều điều khốn-khổ, phải bị các trưởng-lão, các thầy tế-lễ cả, và các thầy thông-giáo bỏ ra, phải bị giết, ngày thứ ba phải sống lại.

²³ Đoạn, Ngài phán cùng mọi người rằng: Nếu ai muốn theo ta, phải tự bỏ mình đi, mỗi ngày vác thập-tự-giá mình mà theo ta. ²⁴ Vì ai muốn cứu sự sống mình thì sẽ mất, còn ai vì cớ ta mất sự sống, thì sẽ cứu. ²⁵ Nếu ai được cả thiên-hạ, mà chính mình phải mất hoặc hư đi, thì có ích gì? ²⁶ Vì nếu ai hổ-thẹn về ta và lời ta, thì Con người sẽ hổ-thẹn về họ, khi Ngài ngự trong sự vinh-hiển của mình, của Cha, và của thiên-sứ thánh mà đến. ²⁷ Quả thật, ta nói cùng các ngươi, một vài người trong các ngươi đương đứng đây sẽ không chết trước khi chưa thấy nước Đức Chúa Trời.

Sự hóa-hình

²⁸ Độ tám ngày sau khi phán các lời đó, Đức Chúa Jêsus đem Phi-e-rơ, Giăng và Gia-cơ đi với mình lên trên núi để cầu-nguyện. ²⁹ Đương khi cầu-nguyện, diện-mạo Ngài khác thường, áo Ngài trở nên sắc trắng chói-lòa. ³⁰ Và nầy, có hai người nói chuyện cùng Ngài; ấy là Môi-se và Ê-li, ³¹ hiện ra trong sự vinh-hiển, và nói về sự Ngài qua đời, là sự sẽ phải ứng-nghiệm tại thành Giê-ru-sa-lem. ³² Phi-e-rơ cùng đồng-bạn mình buồn ngủ lắm, nhưng vừa tỉnh-thức ra, thấy vinh-hiển của Đức Chúa Jêsus và hai đấng ấy đứng gần Ngài. ³³ Lúc hai đấng ấy lìa khỏi Đức Chúa Jêsus, Phi-e-rơ thưa Ngài rằng: Thưa

thấy, chúng ta ở đây tốt lắm, hãy đóng ba trại, một cái cho thấy, một cái cho Môi-se, và một cái cho Ê-li. Vì Phi-e-rơ không biết mình nói chi. [34] Khi người còn đương nói, có một đám mây kéo đến, bao-phủ lấy; và khi vào trong đám mây, các môn-đồ đều sợ-hãi. [35] Bấy giờ, nghe có tiếng từ trong đám mây phán ra rằng: Nầy là Con ta, Người được lựa-chọn của ta, hãy nghe Người. [36] Khi tiếng ấy phát ra, thì Đức Chúa Jêsus ở một mình. Các môn-đồ nín-lặng, không nói cùng ai về sự mình đã thấy.

Người bị qui ám

[37] Bữa sau, khi Chúa cùng môn-đồ từ núi xuống, có đoàn dân đông đến đón-rước Ngài. [38] Một người trong đám đông kêu lên rằng: Lạy thầy, xin thầy đoái đến con trai tôi, vì là con một tôi. [39] Một quỉ ám nó, thình-lình kêu-la; quỉ vật-vã nó dữ-tợn, làm cho sôi bọt miếng, mình-mẩy nát hết, rồi mới ra khỏi. [40] Tôi đã xin môn-đồ thầy đuổi quỉ đó, nhưng họ đuổi không được. [41] Đức Chúa Jêsus đáp rằng: Hỡi dòng-dõi không tin và bội-nghịch kia, ta ở với các ngươi và nhịn các ngươi cho đến chừng nào? Hãy đem con của ngươi lại đây. [42] Đứa con trai vừa lại gần, quỉ xô nó nhào xuống đất, và vật-vã dữ-tợn. Song Đức Chúa Jêsus quở nặng tà-ma, chữa lành con trẻ ấy, và giao lại cho cha nó.

Đức Chúa Jêsus phán trước về sự chết mình

[43] Ai nấy đều lấy làm lạ về quyền-phép cao-trọng của Đức Chúa Trời. Khi mọi người đang khen-lạ các việc Đức Chúa Jêsus làm, Ngài phán cùng môn-đồ rằng: [44] Về phần các ngươi, hãy nghe kỹ điều ta sẽ nói cùng: Con người sẽ bị nộp trong tay người ta. [45] Nhưng các môn-đồ không hiểu lời ấy, vì đã che-khuất cho mình để chẳng rõ nghĩa làm sao; và sợ không dám hỏi Ngài về lời ấy.

Sự cao-trọng thật

[46] Các môn-đồ biện-luận cùng nhau cho biết ai là lớn hơn hết trong hàng mình. [47] Nhưng Đức Chúa Jêsus biết ý-tưởng trong lòng môn-đồ, thì lấy một đứa con trẻ để gần mình, [48] mà phán rằng: Hễ ai

vì danh ta mà tiếp con trẻ nầy, tức là tiếp ta; còn ai tiếp ta, tức là tiếp Đấng đã sai ta. Vì kẻ nào hèn-mọn hơn hết trong vòng các ngươi, ấy chính người đó là kẻ cao-trọng.

⁴⁹ Giăng cất tiếng nói rằng: Thưa thầy, chúng tôi từng thấy có kẻ nhân danh thầy mà trừ quỉ; chúng tôi đã cấm họ, vì không cùng chúng tôi theo thầy. ⁵⁰ Nhưng Đức Chúa Jêsus phán rằng: Đừng cấm họ, vì ai không nghịch cùng các ngươi, là thuận với các ngươi.

Sự Đức Chúa Jêsus đi lên thành Giê-ru-sa-lem

(Từ 9:51 đến 19:28)

Đức Chúa Jêsus tại Sa-ma-ri

⁵¹ Khi gần đến kỳ Đức Chúa Jêsus được đem lên khỏi thế-gian, Ngài quyết-định đi thành Giê-ru-sa-lem. ⁵² Ngài sai kẻ đem tin đi trước mình. Họ ra đi, vào một làng của người Sa-ma-ri để sửa-soạn nhà trọ cho Ngài; ⁵³ song người Sa-ma-ri không tiếp-rước Ngài, vì Ngài đi thẳng lên thành Giê-ru-sa-lem. ⁵⁴ Gia-cơ và Giăng là môn-đồ Ngài, thấy vậy, nói rằng: Thưa Chúa, Chúa có muốn chúng tôi khiến lửa từ trên trời xuống thiêu họ chăng? ⁵⁵ Nhưng Đức Chúa Jêsus xây lại quở hai người, [mà rằng: Các ngươi không biết tâm-thần nào xui-giục mình.]ᵏᵏ ⁵⁶ Rồi Ngài cùng môn-đồ đi qua làng khác.

Cần phải thể nào đặng theo Chúa

⁵⁷ Đang khi đi đường, có kẻ thưa Ngài rằng: Chúa đi đâu tôi sẽ theo đó. ⁵⁸ Đức Chúa Jêsus đáp rằng: Con cáo có hang, chim trời có ổ; song Con người không có chỗ mà gối đầu.

⁵⁹ Ngài phán cùng kẻ khác rằng: Ngươi hãy theo ta. Kẻ ấy thưa rằng: Xin cho phép tôi đi chôn cha tôi trước đã. ⁶⁰ Nhưng Đức Chúa Jêsus phán rằng: Hãy để kẻ chết chôn kẻ chết; còn ngươi, hãy đi rao-giảng nước Đức Chúa Trời.

⁶¹ Có kẻ khác nữa thưa rằng: Lạy Chúa, tôi sẽ theo Chúa, song xin cho phép tôi trước về từ-giã người trong nhà tôi. ⁶² Đức Chúa Jêsus

---

k ᵏ**9:55** Câu trong hai móc nầy có mấy bản không có. Có bản lại thêm cả câu nầy: *Con người đã đến không phải để diệt các linh-hồn, song để cứu cho.*

phán rằng: Ai đã tra tay cầm cày, còn ngó lại đằng sau, thì không xứng-đáng với nước Đức Chúa Trời.

Sự sai bảy mươi môn-đồ đi

10 ¹ Kế đó, Chúa chọn bảy mươi môn-đồ khác,ˡ sai từng đôi đi trước Ngài, đến các thành các chỗ mà chính Ngài sẽ đi. ² Ngài phán cùng môn-đồ rằng: Mùa gặt thì trúng, song con gặt thì ít. Vậy, hãy xin Chủ mùa gặt sai con gặt đến trong mùa của mình. ³ Hãy đi; nầy, ta sai các ngươi đi, khác nào như chiên con ở giữa bầy muông-sói. ⁴ Đừng đem túi, bao, giày, và đừng chào ai dọc đường. ⁵ Hễ các ngươi vào nhà nào, trước hết hãy nói rằng: Cầu sự bình-an cho nhà nầy! ⁶ Nếu nhà đó có người nào đáng được bình-an, sự bình-an của các ngươi sẽ giáng cho họ; bằng không, sẽ trở về các ngươi. ⁷ Hãy ở nhà đó, ăn uống đồ người ta sẽ cho các ngươi, vì người làm công đáng được tiền lương mình. Đừng đi nhà nầy sang nhà khác. ⁸ Hễ các ngươi vào thành nào, mà người ta tiếp-rước, hãy ăn đồ họ sẽ dọn cho. ⁹ Hãy chữa kẻ bịnh ở đó, và nói với họ rằng: Nước Đức Chúa Trời đến gần các ngươi. ¹⁰ Song hễ các ngươi vào thành nào, họ không tiếp-rước, hãy đi ra ngoài chợ, mà nói rằng: ¹¹ Đối với các ngươi, chúng ta cũng phủi bụi của thành các ngươi đã dính chân chúng ta; nhưng phải biết nước Đức Chúa Trời đã đến gần các ngươi rồi. ¹⁰ Ta phán cùng các ngươi, đến ngày cuối-cùng, thành Sô-đôm sẽ chịu nhẹ hơn thành nầy.

¹³ Khốn cho mầy, thành Cô-ra-xin! Khốn cho mầy, thành Bết-sai-đa! Vì nếu các phép lạ đã làm giữa bay, đem làm trong thành Ty-rơ và thành Si-đôn, thì hai thành ấy đã mặc áo gai và đội tro mà ăn-năn từ lâu rồi. ¹⁴ Vậy, đến ngày phán-xét, thành Ty-rơ và thành Si-đôn sẽ chịu nhẹ hơn bay. ¹⁵ Còn mầy, thành Ca-bê-na-um, mầy sẽ được nhắc lên tận trời sao? Không, sẽ bị hạ xuống tới dưới Âm-phủ!ᵐ ¹⁶ Ai nghe các ngươi, ấy là nghe ta; ai bỏ các ngươi, ấy là bỏ ta; còn ai bỏ ta, ấy là bỏ Đấng đã sai ta.

¹⁷ Bảy mươi môn-đồ trở về cách vui-vẻ, thưa rằng: Lạy Chúa, vì danh Chúa các quỉ cũng phục chúng tôi. ¹⁸ Đức Chúa Jêsus bèn phán

rằng: Ta đã thấy quỉ Sa-tan từ trời sa xuống như chớp. ¹⁹ Nầy, ta đã ban quyền cho các ngươi giày-đạp rắn, bò-cạp, và mọi quyền của kẻ nghịch dưới chân; không gì làm hại các ngươi được. ²⁰ Dầu vậy, chớ mừng vì các quỉ phục các ngươi; nhưng hãy mừng vì tên các ngươi đã ghi trên thiên-đàng.

Tin-lành tỏ ra cho trẻ con

²¹ Cũng giờ đó, Đức Chúa Jêsus nức lòng bởi Đức Thánh-Linh, bèn nói rằng: Lạy Cha, là Chúa trời đất, tôi ngợi-khen Cha, vì Cha đã giấu những sự nầy với kẻ khôn-ngoan, người sáng dạ, mà tỏ ra cho trẻ nhỏ hay! Thưa Cha, phải, thật như vậy, vì Cha đã thấy điều đó là tốt-lành. ²² Cha ta đã giao mọi sự cho ta; ngoài Cha không ai biết Con là ai; ngoài Con, và người nào mà Con muốn tỏ ra cùng, thì cũng không có ai biết Cha là ai.

²³ Đoạn, Ngài xây lại cùng môn-đồ mà phán riêng rằng: Phước cho mắt nào được thấy điều các ngươi thấy! ²⁴ Vì ta nói cùng các ngươi, có nhiều đấng tiên-tri và vua-chúa ước-ao thấy điều các ngươi thấy, mà chẳng từng thấy, ước-ao nghe điều các ngươi nghe, mà chẳng từng nghe.

Thí-dụ về người Sa-ma-ri nhân-lành

²⁵ Bấy giờ, một thầy dạy luật đứng dậy hỏi đặng thử Đức Chúa Jêsus rằng: Thưa thầy, tôi phải làm gì để được hưởng sự sống đời đời? ²⁶ Ngài phán rằng: Trong luật-pháp có chép điều gì? Ngươi đọc gì trong đó? ²⁷ Thưa rằng: Ngươi phải hết lòng, hết linh-hồn, hết sức, hết trí mà kính-mến Chúa là Đức Chúa Trời ngươi; và yêu người lân-cận như mình. ²⁸ Đức Chúa Jêsus phán rằng: Ngươi đáp phải lắm; hãy làm điều đó, thì được sống.

²⁹ Song thầy ấy muốn xưng mình là công-bình, nên thưa cùng Đức Chúa Jêsus rằng: Ai là người lân-cận tôi? ³⁰ Đức Chúa Jêsus lại cất tiếng phán rằng: Có một người từ thành Giê-ru-sa-lem xuống thành Giê-ri-cô, lầm vào tay kẻ cướp, nó giụt-lột hết, đánh cho mình-mẩy bị thương rồi đi, để người đó nửa sống nửa chết. ³¹ Và, gặp một thầy tế-lễ đi xuống đường đó, thấy người ấy, thì đi qua khỏi. ³² Lại có một người Lê-vi cũng đến nơi, lại gần, thấy, rồi đi qua khỏi. ³³ Song có

một người Sa-ma-ri đi đường, đến gần người đó, ngó thấy thì động lòng thương; [34] bèn áp lại, lấy dầu và rượu xức chỗ bị thương, rồi rịt lại; đoạn, cho cỡi con vật mình đem đến nhà quán, mà săn-sóc cho. [35] Đến bữa sau, lấy hai đơ-ni-ê đưa cho chủ quán, dặn rằng: Hãy săn-sóc người nầy, nếu tốn hơn nữa, khi tôi trở về sẽ trả. [36] Trong ba người đó, ngươi tưởng ai là lân-cận với kẻ bị cướp? [37] Thầy dạy luật thưa rằng: Ấy là người đã lấy lòng thương-xót đãi người. Đức Chúa Jêsus phán rằng: Hãy đi, làm theo như vậy.

Ma-thê và Ma-ri

[38] Khi Đức Chúa Jêsus cùng môn-đồ đi đường, đến một làng kia, có người đàn-bà, tên là Ma-thê, rước Ngài vào nhà mình. [39] Người có một em gái, tên là Ma-ri, ngồi dưới chân Chúa mà nghe lời Ngài. [40] Vả, Ma-thê mảng lo về việc vặt, đến thưa Đức Chúa Jêsus rằng: Lạy Chúa, em tôi để một mình tôi hầu việc, Chúa há không nghĩ đến sao? Xin biểu nó giúp tôi. [41] Chúa đáp rằng: Hỡi Ma-thê, Ma-thê, ngươi chịu khó và bối-rối về nhiều việc; [42] nhưng có một việc cần mà thôi. Ma-ri đã lựa phần tốt, là phần không có ai cất lấy được.

Sự cầu-nguyện

11 [1] Có một ngày, Đức Chúa Jêsus cầu nguyện, ở nơi kia. Khi cầu-nguyện xong, một môn-đồ thưa Ngài rằng: Lạy Chúa, xin dạy chúng tôi cầu-nguyện, cũng như Giăng đã dạy môn-đồ mình. [2] Ngài phán rằng: Khi các ngươi cầu-nguyện, hãy nói: Lạy Cha! Danh Cha được thánh; nước Cha được đến; [3] xin cho chúng tôi ngày nào đủ bánh ngày ấy; [4] xin tha tội chúng tôi, vì chúng tôi cũng tha kẻ mích lòng[n] mình; và xin chớ đem chúng tôi vào sự cám-dỗ!

[5] Đoạn, Ngài phán cùng môn-đồ rằng: Nếu một người trong các ngươi có bạn-hữu, nửa đêm đến nói rằng: Bạn ơi, cho tôi mượn ba cái bánh, [6] vì người bạn tôi đi đường mới tới, tôi không có chi đãi người. [7] Nếu người kia ở trong nhà trả lời rằng: Đừng khuấy-rối tôi, cửa đóng rồi, con-cái và tôi đã đi ngủ, không dậy được mà lấy bánh cho anh; — [8] ta nói cùng các ngươi, dầu người ấy không chịu dậy cho

---

n 11:4 Nt *mắc nợ*

bánh vì là bạn mình, nhưng vì cớ người kia làm rộn, sẽ dậy và cho người đủ sự cần-dùng. [9] Ta lại nói cùng các ngươi: Hãy xin, sẽ ban cho; hãy tìm, sẽ gặp; hãy gõ cửa, sẽ mở cho. [10] Vì hễ ai xin thì được, ai tìm thì gặp, và sẽ mở cửa cho ai gõ.

[11] Trong các ngươi có ai làm cha, khi con mình xin bánh mà cho đá chăng? Hay là xin cá, mà cho rắn thay vì cá chăng? [12] Hay là xin trứng, mà cho bò-cạp chăng? [13] Vậy nếu các ngươi là người xấu, còn biết cho con-cái mình vật tốt thay, huống chi Cha các ngươi ở trên trời lại chẳng ban Đức Thánh-Linh cho người xin Ngài!

Chúa chữa lành người bị quỉ ám; binh-vực chức-vụ mình và từ-chối làm phép lạ

[14] Đức Chúa Jêsus đuổi một quỉ câm; khi quỉ ra khỏi, người câm liền nói được. Dân-chúng đều lấy làm lạ; [15] song có mấy kẻ nói rằng: Người nầy nhờ Bê-ên-xê-bun là chúa quỉ mà trừ quỉ. [16] Kẻ khác muốn thử Ngài, thì xin Ngài một dấu lạ từ trời xuống.

[17] Đức Chúa Jêsus biết ý-tưởng họ, bèn phán rằng: Nước nào tự chia-rẽ nhau thì tan-hoang, nhà nào tự chia-rẽ nhau thì đổ xuống. [18] Vậy, nếu quỉ Sa-tan tự chia-rẽ nhau, thì nước nó còn sao được, vì các ngươi nói ta nhờ Bê-ên-xê-bun mà trừ quỉ? [19] Nếu ta nhờ Bê-ên-xê-bun mà trừ quỉ, thì con các ngươi nhờ ai mà trừ quỉ? Bởi vậy, chính con các ngươi sẽ làm quan án các ngươi. [20] Nhưng nếu ta cậy ngón tay Đức Chúa Trời mà trừ quỉ, thì nước Đức Chúa Trời đã đến nơi các ngươi rồi. [21] Khi một người mạnh sức cầm khí-giới giữ cửa nhà mình, thì của-cải nó vững-vàng. [22] Nhưng có người khác mạnh hơn đến thắng được, thì cướp lấy khí-giới người kia đã nhờ-cậy, và phân-phát sạch của-cải.

[23] Phàm ai không theo ta, thì nghịch cùng ta, ai không thâu-hiệp với ta, thì tan-lạc. [24] Khi tà-ma đã ra khỏi một người, thì đi dông-dài các nơi khô-khan để kiếm chỗ nghỉ. Kiếm không được, thì nó nói rằng: Ta sẽ trở về nhà ta là nơi ta mới ra khỏi. [25] Nó trở về, thấy nhà quét sạch và dọn-dẹp tử-tế, [26] bèn đi rủ bảy quỉ khác dữ hơn mình vào nhà mà ở; vậy, số-phận người nầy lại khốn-khổ hơn phen trước.

[27] Đức Chúa Jêsus đương phán những điều ấy, có một người đàn-bà ở giữa dân-chúng cất tiếng thưa rằng: Phước cho dạ đã mang

Ngài và vú đã cho Ngài bú! ²⁸ Đức Chúa Jêsus đáp rằng: Những kẻ nghe và giữ lời Đức Chúa Trời còn có phước hơn!

²⁹ Khi dân-chúng nhóm lại đông lắm, Đức Chúa Jêsus phán rằng: Dòng-dõi nầy là dòng-dõi độc-ác; họ xin một dấu lạ, song sẽ không cho dấu lạ nào khác hơn dấu lạ của Giô-na. ³⁰ Vì Giô-na là dấu lạ cho dân thành Ni-ni-ve, thì cũng một thể ấy, Con người sẽ là dấu lạ cho dòng-dõi nầy. ³¹ Đến ngày phán-xét, nữ-hoàng Nam-phương sẽ đứng dậy với người của dòng-dõi nầy và lên án họ, vì người từ nơi đầu-cùng đất đến nghe lời khôn-ngoan vua Sa-lô-môn, mà nầy, ở đây có Đấng hơn Sa-lô-môn! ³² Đến ngày phán-xét, dân thành Ni-ni-ve sẽ đứng dậy với người của dòng-dõi nầy và lên án họ, vì dân ấy đã nghe lời Giô-na giảng-dạy và ăn-năn; mà nầy, ở đây có Đấng hơn Giô-na!

³³ Không ai thắp đèn mà để chỗ khuất hay là dưới thùng, nhưng để trên chân đèn, hầu cho kẻ vào được thấy sáng. ³⁴ Mắt là đèn của thân-thể; nếu mắt ngươi sõi-sàng, cả thân-thể ngươi được sáng-láng; song nếu mắt ngươi xấu, thân-thể ngươi phải tối-tăm. ³⁵ Ấy vậy, hãy coi chừng kẻo sự sáng trong mình ngươi hóa ra sự tối chăng. ³⁶ Nếu cả thân-thể ngươi sáng-láng, không có phần nào tối-tăm, thì sẽ được sáng hết thảy, cũng như khi có cái đèn soi sáng cho ngươi vậy.

Lời giảng cho người Pha-ri-si

³⁷ Đức Chúa Jêsus đương phán, có một người Pha-ri-si mời Ngài về nhà dùng bữa. Ngài vào ngồi bàn. ³⁸ Người Pha-ri-si thấy Ngài không rửa trước bữa ăn, thì lấy làm lạ. ³⁹ Nhưng Chúa phán rằng: Hỡi các ngươi là người Pha-ri-si, các ngươi rửa sạch bề ngoài chén và mâm, song bề trong đầy sự trộm-cướp và điều dữ. ⁴⁰ Hỡi kẻ dại-dột! Đấng đã làm nên bề ngoài, há không làm nên bề trong nữa sao? ⁴¹ Thà các ngươi lấy của mình có mà bố-thí, thì mọi điều sẽ sạch cho các ngươi. ⁴² Song khốn cho các ngươi, người Pha-ri-si, vì các ngươi, nộp một phần mười về bạc-hà, hồi-hương, cùng mọi thứ rau, còn sự công-bình và sự kính-mến Đức Chúa Trời, thì các ngươi bỏ qua! Ấy là các việc phải làm, mà cũng không nên bỏ qua các việc khác. ⁴³ Khốn cho các ngươi, người Pha-ri-si, vì các ngươi ưa ngôi cao nhứt trong nhà hội, và thích người ta chào mình giữa chợ! ⁴⁴ Khốn cho các

ngươi, vì các ngươi giống như mả loạn, người ta bước lên trên mà không biết!

⁴⁵ Một thầy dạy luật bèn cất tiếng nói rằng: Thưa thầy, thầy nói vậy cũng làm sỉ-nhục chúng tôi. ⁴⁶ Đức Chúa Jêsus đáp rằng: Khốn cho các ngươi nữa, là thầy dạy luật, vì các ngươi chất cho người ta gánh nặng khó mang, mà tự mình thì không động ngón tay đến! ⁴⁷ Khốn cho các ngươi, vì các ngươi xây mồ-mả các đấng tiên-tri mà tổ-phụ mình đã giết! ⁴⁸ Như vậy, các ngươi làm chứng và ưng-thuận việc tổ-phụ mình đã làm; vì họ đã giết các đấng tiên-tri, còn các ngươi lại xây mồ cho. ⁴⁹ Vậy nên, sự khôn-ngoan của Đức Chúa Trời đã phán rằng: Ta sẽ sai đấng tiên-tri và sứ-đồ đến cùng chúng nó; chúng nó sẽ giết kẻ nầy, bắt-bớ kẻ kia, ⁵⁰ hầu cho huyết mọi đấng tiên-tri đổ ra từ khi sáng-thế, cứ dòng-dõi nầy mà đòi, ⁵¹ là từ huyết A-bên cho đến huyết Xa-cha-ri đã bị giết giữa khoảng bàn-thờ và đền-thờ; phải, ta nói cùng các ngươi, sẽ cứ dòng-dõi nầy mà đòi huyết ấy. ⁵² Khốn cho các ngươi, là thầy dạy luật, vì các ngươi đã đoạt lấy chìa khóa của sự biết, chính mình không vào, mà người khác muốn vào, lại ngăn-cấm không cho!

⁵³ Khi Đức Chúa Jêsus ra khỏi đó rồi, các thầy thông-giáo và người Pha-ri-si bèn ra sức ép Ngài dữ-tợn, lấy nhiều câu hỏi khêu-chọc Ngài, ⁵⁴ và lập mưu để bắt-bẻ lời nào từ miệng Ngài nói ra.

Lời răn-dạy các môn-đồ

12 ¹ Khi ấy, dân-chúng nhóm lại kể hàng ngàn người, đến nỗi giày-đạp nhau, Đức Chúa Jêsus mới trước hết phán cùng môn-đồ rằng: Hãy giữ mình về men của người Pha-ri-si, là sự giả-hình. ² Chẳng có sự gì giấu mà không phải lộ ra, chẳng có sự gì kín mà không được biết. ³ Vậy nên mọi điều mà các ngươi đã nói nơi tối, sẽ nghe ra nơi sáng; mọi điều mà các ngươi đã nói vào lỗ tai trong buồng kín, sẽ giảng ra trên mái nhà. ⁴ Ta nói cùng các ngươi, là bạn-hữu ta: Đừng sợ kẻ giết xác rồi sau không làm gì được nữa. ⁵ Song ta chỉ cho các ngươi biết phải sợ ai: Phải sợ Đấng khi đã giết rồi, có quyền bỏ xuống địa-ngục; phải, ta nói cùng các ngươi, ấy là Đấng các ngươi phải sợ! ⁶ Người ta há chẳng bán năm con chim sẻ giá hai đồng tiền sao? Nhưng Đức Chúa Trời không quên một con nào hết.

⁷ Dầu đến tóc trên đầu các ngươi cũng đã đếm cả rồi. Đừng sợ chi, vì các ngươi trọng hơn nhiều chim sẻ.

⁸ Ta nói cùng các ngươi, ai sẽ xưng ta trước mặt thiên-hạ, thì Con người cũng sẽ xưng họ trước mặt thiên-sứ của Đức Chúa Trời. ⁹ Nhưng ai chối ta trước mặt thiên-hạ, thì họ sẽ bị chối trước mặt thiên-sứ của Đức Chúa Trời. ¹⁰ Ai nói nghịch cùng Con người, thì sẽ được tha; song kẻ nói lộng-ngôn phạm đến Đức Thánh-Linh, thì không được tha đâu. ¹¹ Khi người ta đem các ngươi đến nhà hội, trước mặt quan án và quan cai-trị, thì chớ lo về nói cách nào để binh-vực mình, hoặc nói lời gì; ¹² bởi vì chính giờ đó Đức Thánh-Linh sẽ dạy các ngươi những lời phải nói.

Sự hà-tiện

¹³ Bấy giờ, một người giữa dân-chúng thưa rằng: Thưa thầy, xin biểu anh tôi chia gia-tài cho tôi. ¹⁴ Nhưng Đức Chúa Jêsus đáp rằng: Hỡi người kia, ai đặt ta làm quan xử kiện hay là chia của cho các ngươi? ¹⁵ Đoạn, Ngài phán cùng chúng rằng: Hãy giữ cẩn-thận chớ hà-tiện gì hết; vì sự sống của người ta không phải cốt tại của-cải mình dư-dật đâu.

¹⁶ Ngài lại phán cùng chúng lời ví-dụ nầy: Ruộng của một người giàu kia sinh lợi nhiều lắm, ¹⁷ người bèn tự nghĩ rằng: Ta phải làm thể nào? Vì không có đủ chỗ chứa hết sản-vật ¹⁸ Lại nói: Nầy, việc ta sẽ làm: Ta phá cả kho tàng và cất cái khác lớn hơn, thâu-trữ sản-vật và gia-tài vào đó; ¹⁹ rồi sẽ nói với linh-hồn ta rằng: Linh-hồn ơi, mầy đã được nhiều của để dành dùng lâu năm; thôi, hãy nghỉ, ăn uống, và vui-vẻ. ²⁰ Song Đức Chúa Trời phán cùng người rằng: Hỡi kẻ dại! Chính đêm nay linh-hồn ngươi sẽ bị đòi lại; vậy những của-cải ngươi đã sắm-sẵn sẽ thuộc về ai? ²¹ Hễ ai thâu-trữ của cho mình mà không giàu-có nơi Đức Chúa Trời thì cũng như vậy.

Sự lo-lắng

²² Đức Chúa Jêsus bèn phán cùng môn-đồ rằng: Ấy vậy, ta nói cùng các ngươi, đừng vì sự sống mà lo đồ mình ăn, cũng đừng vì thân-thể mà lo đồ mình mặc. ²³ Sự sống trọng hơn đồ-ăn, thân-thể trọng hơn đồ-mặc. ²⁴ Hãy xem con quạ: Nó không gieo, không gặt, cũng không

có hầm-vựa kho-tàng chi, mà Đức Chúa Trời còn nuôi nó; hướng chi các ngươi quí hơn chim-chóc là dường nào! ²⁵ Có ai trong các ngươi lo-lắng mà làm cho đời mình dài thêm một khắc không? ²⁶ Vậy nếu đến việc rất nhỏ các ngươi cũng không có thể được, sao các ngươi lo việc khác? ²⁷ Hãy xem hoa huệ mọc lên thể nào: Nó chẳng làm khó-nhọc, cũng không kéo chỉ; song ta phán cùng các ngươi, dẫu vua Sa-lô-môn sang-trọng đến đâu, cũng không được mặc áo như một hoa nào trong giống ấy. ²⁸ Hỡi kẻ ít đức-tin, nếu loài cỏ ngoài đồng là loài nay sống mai bỏ vào lò, mà Đức Chúa Trời còn cho mặc thể ấy, hướng chi là các ngươi! ²⁹ Vậy các ngươi đừng kiếm đồ-ăn đồ-uống, cũng đừng có lòng lo-lắng. ³⁰ Vì mọi sự đó, các dân ngoại ở thế-gian vẫn thường tìm, và Cha các ngươi biết các ngươi cần dùng mọi sự đó rồi. ³¹ Nhưng thà các ngươi hãy tìm-kiếm nước Đức Chúa Trời, rồi mọi sự đó sẽ được cho thêm.

³² Hỡi bầy nhỏ, đừng sợ chi; vì Cha các ngươi đã bằng lòng cho các ngươi nước thiên-đàng. ³³ Hãy bán gia-tài mình mà bố-thí. Hãy sắm cho mình túi không hư, và của báu không hề hao-kém ở trên trời, là nơi kẻ trộm không đến gần, sâu mọt không làm hư-nát. ³⁴ Vì của báu các ngươi ở đâu, thì lòng cũng ở đó.

Khuyên về sự tỉnh-thức

³⁵ Lưng các ngươi phải thắt lại, đèn các ngươi phải thắp lên. ³⁶ Hãy làm như người chờ-đợi chủ mình ở tiệc cưới về, để lúc chủ đến gõ cửa thì liền mở. ³⁷ Phước cho những đầy-tớ ấy, khi chủ về thấy họ thức canh! Quả thật, ta nói cùng các ngươi, chủ sẽ thắt lưng mình, cho đầy-tớ ngồi bàn mình, và đến hầu việc họ. ³⁸ Hoặc canh hai, canh ba, chủ trở về, nếu thấy đầy-tớ như vậy thì phước cho họ! ³⁹ Hãy biết rõ, nếu chủ nhà hay kẻ trộm đến giờ nào, thì sẽ tỉnh-thức, chẳng để cho nó đào ngạch nhà đâu. ⁴⁰ Các ngươi cũng vậy, hãy chực cho sẵn-sàng, vì Con người sẽ đến trong giờ các ngươi không ngờ.

⁴¹ Phi-e-rơ bèn thưa Ngài rằng: Lạy Chúa, thí-dụ nẩy Chúa phán cho chúng tôi, hay là cũng cho mọi người? ⁴² Chúa đáp rằng: Ai là người quản-gia ngay-thật khôn-ngoan, chủ nhà đặt coi cả người nhà mình, để đến dịp-tiện, phát lương-phạn cho họ? ⁴³ Phước cho đầy-tớ ấy khi chủ nhà về, thấy làm như vậy! ⁴⁴ Quả thật, ta nói cùng các

ngươi, chủ sẽ cho nó quản-lý cả gia-tài mình. ⁴⁵ Nhưng nếu đầy-tớ ấy tự nghĩ rằng: Chủ ta chậm đến; rồi cứ đánh-đập đầy-tớ trai và gái, ăn uống say-sưa, ⁴⁶ thì chủ nó sẽ đến trong ngày nó không dè, và giờ nó không biết; lấy roi đánh xé da nó,ᵒ và để cho nó đồng số-phận với kẻ bất-trung. ⁴⁷ Đầy-tớ nầy đã biết ý chủ mình, mà không sửa-soạn sẵn và không theo ý ấy, thì sẽ bị đòn nhiều. ⁴⁸ Song đầy-tớ không biết ý chủ, mà làm việc đáng phạt, thì bị đòn ít. Vì ai đã được ban cho nhiều, thì sẽ bị đòi lại nhiều; và ai đã được giao cho nhiều, thì sẽ bị đòi lại nhiều hơn.

Những lời răn-dạy khác

⁴⁹ Ta đã đến quăng lửa xuống đất; nếu cháy lên rồi, ta còn ước-ao chi nữa! ⁵⁰ Có một phép báp-têm mà ta phải chịu, ta đau-đớn biết bao cho đến chừng nào phép ấy được hoàn-thành! ⁵¹ Các ngươi tưởng ta đến đem sự bình-an cho thế-gian sao? Ta nói cùng các ngươi, không, nhưng thà đem sự phân-rẽ. ⁵² Vì từ nay về sau, nếu năm người ở chung một nhà, thì sẽ phân-ly nhau, ba người nghịch cùng hai, hai người nghịch cùng ba; ⁵³ cha nghịch cùng con trai, con trai nghịch cùng cha; mẹ nghịch cùng con gái, con gái nghịch cùng mẹ; bà gia nghịch cùng dâu, dâu nghịch cùng bà gia.

⁵⁴ Ngài lại phán cùng đoàn dân rằng: Khi các ngươi thấy đám mây nổi lên phương tây, liền nói rằng: Sẽ có mưa; thì quả có vậy. ⁵⁵ Lại khi gió nam thổi, các ngươi nói rằng: Sẽ nóng-nực; thì quả có vậy. ⁵⁶ Hỡi kẻ giả-hình! Các ngươi biết phân-biệt khí-sắc của trời đất; vậy sao không biết phân-biệt thời nầy? ⁵⁷ Lại sao các ngươi cũng không tự mình xét-đoán điều gì là công-bình?

⁵⁸ Vậy, khi ngươi đi với kẻ kiện mình đến trước mặt quan tòa, dọc đường hãy gắng sức giải-hòa cùng họ, e họ kéo ngươi đến trước mặt quan án, quan án giao cho thầy đội, rồi bỏ tù ngươi chăng. ⁵⁹ Ta nói cùng ngươi, ngươi trả còn thiếu một đồng tiền, thì không ra khỏi tù được.

Những người Ga-li-lê bị giết. – Cây vả đưng

13 ¹Cũng lúc ấy, có mấy người ở đó thuật cho Đức Chúa Jêsus nghe về việc Phi-lát giết mấy người Ga-li-lê, lấy huyết trộn lộn với của-lễ họ. ²Đức Chúa Jêsus cất tiếng đáp rằng: Các ngươi tưởng mấy người đó vì chịu khốn-nạn dường ấy, có tội-lỗi trọng hơn mọi người Ga-li-lê khác sao? ³Ta nói cùng các ngươi, không phải; song nếu các ngươi chẳng ăn-năn, thì hết thảy sẽ bị hư-mất như vậy. ⁴Hay là mười tám người bị tháp Si-lô-ê ngã xuống đè chết kia, các ngươi tưởng họ có tội-lỗi trọng hơn mọi kẻ khác ở thành Giê-ru-sa-lem sao? ⁵Ta nói cùng các ngươi, không phải; nhưng nếu các ngươi chẳng ăn-năn, thì hết thảy cũng sẽ bị hư-mất như vậy.

⁶Ngài lại phán thí-dụ nầy: Người kia có một cây vả trồng trong vườn nho mình, đến hái trái mà không thấy; ⁷bèn nói cùng kẻ trồng nho rằng: Kìa đã ba năm nay ta đến hái trái nơi cây vả nầy mà không thấy: Hãy đốn nó đi; cớ sao nó choán đất vô-ích? ⁸Kẻ trồng nho rằng: Thưa chúa, xin để lại năm nầy nữa, tôi sẽ đào đất xung-quanh nó rồi đổ phân vào. ⁹Có lẽ về sau nó sẽ ra trái; bằng không, chúa sẽ đốn.

Sự chữa bịnh trong ngày Sa-bát

¹⁰Một ngày Sa-bát, Đức Chúa Jêsus giảng-dạy trong nhà hội kia. ¹¹Và, tại đó, có người đàn-bà mắc quỉ ám, phải đau liệt đã mười tám năm; cong lưng chẳng đứng thẳng được. ¹²Đức Chúa Jêsus vừa thấy, gọi mà phán rằng: Hỡi đàn-bà kia, ngươi đã được cứu khỏi bịnh; ¹³Ngài bèn đặt tay trên mình người. Tức thì, người đứng thẳng lên được, và ngợi-khen Đức Chúa Trời. ¹⁴Bấy giờ người cai nhà hội nhân Đức Chúa Jêsus đã chữa bịnh trong ngày Sa-bát, thì giận mà cất tiếng nói cùng đoàn dân rằng: Có sáu ngày phải làm việc, vậy hãy đến trong những ngày ấy để được chữa cho, đừng đến trong ngày Sa-bát. ¹⁵Nhưng Chúa đáp rằng: Hỡi kẻ giả-hình, mỗi người trong các ngươi đang ngày Sa-bát, há không mở bò hoặc lừa mình ra khỏi máng cỏ, dắt đi uống nước hay sao? ¹⁶Con gái của Áp-ra-ham nầy, quỉ Sa-tan đã cầm-buộc mười tám năm, há chẳng nên mở trói cho nó trong ngày Sa-bát sao? ¹⁷Ngài phán như vậy, thì các kẻ thù-

nghịch cùng Ngài đều hổ-thẹn, và cả dân-chúng vui-mừng về mọi việc vinh-hiển Ngài đã làm.

Hột cải và men

¹⁸ Vậy, Đức Chúa Jêsus phán rằng: Nước Đức Chúa Trời giống như gì, ta lấy chi mà sánh với? ¹⁹ Nước ấy giống như một hột cải, người kia lấy gieo trong vườn; nó mọc lên trở nên cây-cối, và chim trời làm ổ trên nhành.

²⁰ Ngài lại phán rằng: Ta sẽ sánh nước Đức Chúa Trời với gì? ²¹ Nước ấy giống như men, người đàn-bà kia lấy trộn vào ba đấu bột, cho đến chừng bột dậy cả lên.

Cửa hẹp

²² Đức Chúa Jêsus trải qua các thành các làng, vừa dạy-dỗ vừa đi thẳng tới thành Giê-ru-sa-lem. ²³ Có người thưa Ngài rằng: Lạy Chúa, có phải chỉ ít kẻ được cứu chăng? ²⁴ Ngài đáp rằng: Hãy gắng sức vào cửa hẹp, vì, ta nói cùng các ngươi, nhiều người sẽ tìm cách vào mà không vào được. ²⁵ Khi chủ nhà chờ dậy, đóng cửa lại rồi, các ngươi ở ngoài gõ cửa kêu rằng: Lạy Chúa, xin mở cho chúng tôi! Chủ sẽ trả lời rằng: Ta không biết các ngươi đến từ đâu. ²⁶ Bấy giờ các ngươi sẽ thưa rằng: Chúng tôi đã ăn uống trước mặt Chúa, và Chúa đã dạy-dỗ trong các chợ chúng tôi. ²⁷ Chủ lại sẽ trả lời rằng: Ta nói cùng các ngươi, không biết các ngươi đến từ đâu; hết thảy những kẻ làm dữ kia, hãy lui ra khỏi ta! ²⁸ Khi ấy, các ngươi thấy Áp-ra-ham, Y-sác và Gia-cốp, cùng hết thảy các đấng tiên-tri đều ở trong nước Đức Chúa Trời, còn các ngươi sẽ bị quăng ra ngoài, là nơi có khóc-lóc và nghiến răng. ²⁹ Lại từ Đông Tây Nam Bắc, người ta sẽ đến mà ngồi bàn ở trong nước Đức Chúa Trời. ³⁰ Nầy, khi ấy có kẻ rốt sẽ nên đầu, kẻ đầu sẽ là rốt.

Vua Hê-rốt muốn giết Đức Chúa Jêsus

³¹ Cũng trong lúc đó, có mấy người Pha-ri-si đến thưa Ngài rằng: Thầy nên bỏ chỗ nầy mà đi, vì vua Hê-rốt muốn giết thầy. ³² Ngài đáp rằng: Hãy đi nói với con chồn-cáo ấy rằng: Ngày nay, ngày mai, ta

đuổi quỉ chữa bịnh, đến ngày thứ ba, thì đời ta sẽ xong rồi. [33] Nhưng ngày nay, ngày mai, và ngày kia ta phải đi, vì không có lẽ một đấng tiên-tri phải chết ngoài thành Giê-ru-sa-lem.

[34] Hỡi Giê-ru-sa-lem, Giê-ru-sa-lem, ngươi giết các tiên-tri, và quăng đá các đấng chịu sai đến cùng ngươi, ghe phen ta muốn nhóm-họp con-cái ngươi, như gà mái túc và ấp con mình dưới cánh, mà các ngươi chẳng muốn! [35] Nầy, nhà các ngươi sẽ bỏ hoang. Ta nói cùng các ngươi, các ngươi không còn thấy ta nữa cho đến chừng nào sẽ nói rằng: Phước cho Đấng nhân danh Chúa mà đến!

Bữa ăn tại nhà người Pha-ri-si. – Dạy về sự khiêm-nhường và nhân-đức

14 [1] Một ngày Sa-bát, Đức Chúa Jêsus vào nhà một người kẻ cả dòng Pha-ri-si để dùng bữa, những người ở đó dòm-hành Ngài. [2] Số là có một người mắc bịnh thủy-thũng ở trước mặt Ngài. [3] Đức Chúa Jêsus cất tiếng hỏi thầy dạy luật và người Pha-ri-si rằng: Trong ngày Sa-bát, có nên chữa bịnh hay không? [4] Họ đều làm thinh. Ngài bèn đem người bịnh chữa lành, rồi cho về. [5] Đoạn, Ngài phán cùng họ rằng: Nào có ai trong các ngươi, đương ngày Sa-bát, nếu có con trai hay là bò mình té xuống giếng mà không kéo liền lên sao? [6] Họ không đối-đáp gì về điều đó được.

[7] Ngài thấy những kẻ được mời đều lựa chỗ ngồi trên, nên phán cùng họ thí-dụ nầy: [8] Khi người ta mời ngươi dự tiệc cưới, chớ ngồi chỗ cao nhứt, vì e rằng trong những khách mời có ai tôn-trọng hơn ngươi, [9] người đứng mời sẽ đến nói cùng ngươi rằng: Hãy nhường chỗ cho người nầy ngồi, mà ngươi xấu-hổ vì phải xuống chỗ chót chăng. [10] Nhưng khi ngươi được mời, hãy ngồi chỗ chót, người đứng mời sẽ đến nói cùng ngươi rằng: Hỡi bạn, xin ngồi lên cao hơn. Vậy thì điều đó sẽ làm cho ngươi được kính-trọng trước mặt những người đồng-bàn với mình. [11] Bởi vì ai tự nhắc mình lên, sẽ phải hạ xuống, còn ai tự hạ mình xuống, sẽ được nhắc lên.

[12] Ngài cũng phán với người mời Ngài rằng: Khi ngươi đãi bữa trưa hoặc bữa tối, đừng mời bạn-hữu, anh em, bà-con và láng-giềng giàu, e rằng họ cũng mời lại mà trả cho ngươi chăng. [13] Song khi ngươi đãi tiệc, hãy mời những kẻ nghèo-khó, tàn-tật, què, đui, [14] thì ngươi sẽ

được phước, vì họ không có thể trả lại cho ngươi; đến kỳ kẻ công-bình sống lại, ngươi sẽ được trả.

Ví-dụ về tiệc yến lớn

¹⁵ Một người đồng-tiệc nghe lời đó, thì thưa Ngài rằng: Phước cho kẻ sẽ được ăn bánh trong nước Đức Chúa Trời! ¹⁶ Nhưng Đức Chúa Jêsus đáp rằng: Có người kia dọn tiệc lớn, mời nhiều người ăn. ¹⁷ Khi đến giờ ăn, sai đầy-tớ mình đi nói với những kẻ được mời rằng: Hãy đến, mọi sự đã sẵn rồi. ¹⁸ Song họ đồng-tình xin kiếu hết. Người thứ nhứt nói rằng: Tôi có mua một đám ruộng, cần phải đi coi; xin cho tôi kiếu. ¹⁹ Kẻ khác rằng: Tôi có mua năm cặp bò, phải đi xem thử; xin cho tôi kiếu. ²⁰ Kẻ khác nữa rằng: Tôi mới cưới vợ, vậy tôi đi không được. ²¹ Đầy-tớ trở về, trình việc đó cho chủ mình. Chủ bèn nổi giận, biểu đầy-tớ rằng: Hãy đi mau ra ngoài chợ, và các đường phố, đem những kẻ nghèo-khó, tàn-tật, đui, què vào đây. ²² Sau lại đầy-tớ trình rằng: Thưa chủ, điều chủ dạy, đã làm rồi, mà hãy còn thừa chỗ. ²³ Chủ nhà lại biểu rằng: Hãy ra ngoài đường và dọc hàng rào, gặp ai thì ép mời vào, cho được đầy nhà ta. ²⁴ Vì, ta nói cùng các ngươi, trong những kẻ đã mời trước, không có ai được nếm bữa tiệc của ta đâu.

Các điều yếu-cần để làm môn-đồ Đức Chúa Jêsus

²⁵ Có đoàn dân đông cùng đi với Đức Chúa Jêsus; Ngài xây lại cùng họ mà phán rằng: ²⁶ Nếu có ai đến theo ta mà không ghét cha mẹ, vợ con, anh em, chị em mình, và chính sự sống mình nữa, thì không được làm môn-đồ ta. ²⁷ Còn ai không vác thập-tự-giá mình mà theo ta, cũng không được làm môn-đồ ta.

²⁸ Và, trong các ngươi có ai là người muốn xây một cái tháp, mà trước không ngồi tính phí-tổn cho biết mình có đủ của đặng làm xong việc cùng chăng sao? ²⁹ E khi đã xây nền rồi, không làm xong được, thì mọi người thấy liền chê-cười, ³⁰ và rằng: Người nầy khởi-công xây, mà không thể làm xong được! ³¹ Hay là có vua nào đi đánh trận cùng vua khác, mà trước không ngồi bàn-luận xem mình đem đi một muôn lính có thể địch nổi vua kia đem hai muôn cùng chăng sao? ³² Bằng chẳng nổi, khi vua kia còn ở xa, sai sứ đi xin hòa. ³³ Như

vậy, nếu ai trong các ngươi không bỏ mọi sự mình có, thì không được làm môn-đồ ta.

³⁴ Muối là giống tốt, nhưng nếu muối mất mặn, thì lấy chi làm cho nó mặn lại được? ³⁵ Không dùng chi được cho ruộng hoặc cho phân; người ta phải bỏ nó ra ngoài. Ai có tai mà nghe, hãy nghe!

Ví-dụ về chiên lạc mất, về đồng bạc mất, về con trai phá của

15 ¹ Hết thảy các người thâu thuế và người có tội đến gần Đức Chúa Jêsus đặng nghe Ngài giảng. ² Các người Pha-ri-si và các thầy thông-giáo lằm-bằm mà nói rằng: Người nầy tiếp những kẻ tội-lỗi, và cùng ăn với họ!

³ Ngài bèn phán cho họ lời thí-dụ nầy: ⁴ Trong các ngươi ai là người có một trăm con chiên, nếu mất một con, mà không để chín mươi chín con nơi đồng vắng, đặng đi tìm con đã mất cho kỳ được sao? ⁵ Khi đã kiếm được, thì vui-mừng vác nó lên vai; ⁶ đoạn, về đến nhà, kêu bạn-hữu và kẻ lân-cận, mà rằng: Hãy chung vui với ta, vì ta đã tìm được con chiên bị mất. ⁷ Ta nói cùng các ngươi, trên trời cũng như vậy, sẽ vui-mừng cho một kẻ có tội ăn-năn hơn là chín mươi chín kẻ công-bình không cần phải ăn-năn.

⁸ Hay là, có người đàn-bà nào có mười đồng bạc, mất một đồng, mà không thắp đèn, quét nhà, kiếm kỹ-càng cho kỳ được sao? ⁹ Khi tìm được rồi, gọi bầu-bạn và người lân-cận mình, mà rằng: Hãy chung vui với ta, vì ta đã tìm được đồng bạc bị mất. ¹⁰ Ta nói cùng các ngươi, trước mặt thiên-sứ của Đức Chúa Trời cũng như vậy, sẽ mừng-rỡ cho một kẻ có tội ăn-năn.

¹¹ Ngài lại phán rằng: Một người kia có hai con trai. ¹² Người em nói với cha rằng: Thưa cha, xin chia cho tôi phần của mà tôi sẽ được. Người cha liền chia của mình cho hai con. ¹³ Cách ít ngày, người em tóm thâu hết, đi phương xa, ở đó, ăn chơi hoang-đàng, tiêu sạch gia-tài mình. ¹⁴ Khi đã xài hết của rồi, trong xứ xảy có cơn đói lớn; nó mới bị nghèo thiếu, ¹⁵ bèn đi làm mướn cho một người bổn-xứ, thì họ sai ra đồng chăn heo. ¹⁶ Nó muốn lấy vỏ đậu của heo ăn mà ăn cho no, nhưng chẳng ai cho.

¹⁷ Vậy nó mới tỉnh-ngộ, mà rằng: Tại nhà cha ta, biết bao người làm mướn được bánh ăn dư-dật, mà ta đây phải chết đói! ¹⁸ Ta sẽ

đứng dậy trở về cùng cha, mà rằng: Thưa cha, tôi đã đặng tội với trời và với cha, ¹⁹không đáng gọi là con của cha nữa; xin cha đãi tôi như đứa làm mướn của cha vậy.

²⁰Nó bèn đứng dậy mà về cùng cha mình. Khi còn ở đàng xa, cha nó thấy thì động lòng thương-xót, chạy ra ôm lấy cổ mà hôn. ²¹Con thưa cùng cha rằng: Cha ơi, tôi đã đặng tội với trời và với cha, chẳng còn đáng gọi là con của cha nữa. ²²Nhưng người cha bảo đầy-tớ rằng: Hãy mau mau lấy áo tốt nhứt mặc cho nó; đeo nhẫn vào ngón tay, mang giày vào chân. ²³Hãy bắt bò con mập làm thịt đi. Chúng ta hãy ăn mừng, ²⁴vì con ta đây đã chết mà bây giờ lại sống, đã mất mà bây giờ lại thấy được. Đoạn, họ khởi-sự vui-mừng.

²⁵Và, con trai cả đương ở ngoài đồng. Khi trở về gần đến nhà, nghe tiếng đàn ca nhảy múa, ²⁶bèn gọi một đầy-tớ mà hỏi cớ gì. ²⁷Đầy-tớ thưa rằng: Em cậu bây giờ trở về, nên cha cậu đã làm thịt bò con mập, vì thấy em về được mạnh-khoẻ. ²⁸Con cả liền nổi giận, không muốn vào nhà. Vậy cha nó ra khuyên nó vào. ²⁹Nhưng nó thưa cha rằng: Nầy, tôi giúp việc cha đã bấy nhiêu năm, chưa từng trái phép, mà cha chẳng hề cho tôi một con dê con đặng ăn chơi với bạn-hữu tôi. ³⁰Nhưng nay con của cha kia, là đứa đã ăn hết gia-tài cha với phường điếm-đĩ rồi trở về, thì cha vì nó làm thịt bò con mập! ³¹Người cha nói rằng: Con ơi, con ở cùng cha luôn, hết thảy của cha là của con. ³²Nhưng thật nên dọn tiệc và vui-mừng, vì em con đây đã chết mà lại sống, đã mất mà lại thấy được.

Ví-dụ về người quản-gia bất-trung. – Các lời khuyên-bảo khác

16 ¹Đức Chúa Jêsus lại phán cùng môn-đồ rằng: Người giàu kia có một quản-gia, bị cáo với chủ rằng người tiêu phá của chủ. ²Vậy, chủ đòi người đó mà nói rằng: Ta nghe nói về ngươi nỗi chi? Hãy khai ra việc quản-trị của ngươi, vì từ nay ngươi không được cai-quản gia-tài ta nữa. ³Người quản-gia tự nghĩ rằng: Chủ cách chức ta, ta sẽ làm gì? Làm ruộng thì ta không có sức làm nổi, còn đi ăn-mày thì hổ-ngươi. ⁴Ta biết điều ta sẽ làm, để khi bị cách chức, có kẻ tiếp-rước ta về nhà. ⁵Người ấy bèn gọi riêng từng người mắc nợ chủ mình đến, và hỏi người thứ nhứt rằng: Ngươi mắc nợ chủ ta bao nhiêu? ⁶Trả lời rằng: Một trăm thùng dầu. Quản-gia nói rằng: Hãy cầm lấy tờ khế, ngồi xuống đó, viết mau: Năm chục. [7] Rồi hỏi người kia rằng: Còn ngươi, mắc bao nhiêu? Trả lời rằng: Một trăm hộc lúa mì. Quản-gia rằng: Hãy cầm lấy tờ khế và viết: Tám chục. [8] Chủ bèn khen quản-gia bất-nghĩa ấy về việc người đã làm khôn-khéo như vậy. Vì con đời nầy trong việc thông-công với người đồng-đời mình thì khôn-khéo hơn con sáng-láng. [9] Còn ta nói cho các ngươi: Hãy dùng của bất-nghĩa mà kết bạn, để khi của ấy hết đi, họ tiếp các ngươi vào nhà đời đời.

[10] Ai trung-tín trong việc rất nhỏ, cũng trung-tín trong việc lớn; ai bất-nghĩa trong việc rất nhỏ, cũng bất-nghĩa trong việc lớn. [11] Vậy nếu các ngươi không trung-tín về của bất-nghĩa, có ai đem của thật giao cho các ngươi? [12] Nếu các ngươi không trung-tín về của người khác, ai sẽ cho các ngươi được của riêng mình? [13] Không có đầy-tớ nào làm tôi hai chủ được; vì sẽ ghét chủ nầy mà yêu chủ kia, hay là hiệp với chủ nầy mà khinh-dể chủ kia. Các ngươi không có thể đã làm tôi Đức Chúa Trời, lại làm tôi Ma-môn[p] nữa.

[14] Người Pha-ri-si là kẻ ham tiền-tài, nghe mọi điều đó, bèn chê-cười Ngài. [15] Ngài phán cùng họ rằng: Các ngươi làm bộ công-bình qua mặt người ta, song Đức Chúa Trời biết lòng các ngươi; vì sự người ta tôn-trọng là sự gớm-ghiếc trước mặt Đức Chúa Trời. [16] Luật-pháp và các lời tiên-tri có đến đời Giăng mà thôi; từ đó, tin lành của nước Đức Chúa Trời được truyền ra, và ai nấy dùng sức-mạnh mà vào đó. [17] Trời đất qua đi còn dễ hơn một nét chữ[q] trong luật-pháp phải bỏ đi. [18] Ai bỏ vợ mình mà cưới vợ khác, thì phạm tội tà-dâm, ai cưới đàn-bà bị chồng để, thì cũng phạm tội tà-dâm.

Người giàu xấu nết và La-xa-rơ

[19] Có một người giàu mặc áo tía và áo bằng vải gai mịn, hằng ngày ăn-ở rất là sung-sướng. [20] Lại có một người nghèo, tên là La-xa-rơ, nằm ngoài cửa người giàu đó, mình đầy những ghẻ. [21] Người ước-ao được ăn những đồ ở trên bàn người giàu rớt xuống; cũng có chó đến liếm ghẻ người.

[22] Và, người nghèo chết, thiên-sứ đem để vào lòng Áp-ra-ham; người giàu cũng chết, người ta đem chôn. [23] Người giàu ở nơi Âm-

phủʳ đang bị đau-đớn, ngước mắt lên, xa thấy Áp-ra-ham, và La-xa-rơ trong lòng người; [24] bèn kêu lên rằng: Hỡi Áp-ra-ham tổ tôi, xin thương lấy tôi, sai La-xa-rơ nhúng đầu ngón tay vào nước đặng làm cho mát lưỡi tôi; vì tôi bị khổ trong lửa nầy quá đỗi. [25] Nhưng Áp-ra-ham trả lời rằng: Con ơi, hãy nhớ lại lúc ngươi còn sống đã được hưởng những sự lành của mình rồi, còn La-xa-rơ phải những sự dữ; bây giờ, nó ở đây được yên-ủi, còn ngươi phải bị khổ-hình. [26] Vả lại, có một vực sâu ở giữa chúng ta với ngươi, đến nỗi ai muốn từ đây qua đó không được, mà ai muốn từ đó qua đây cũng không được. [27] Người giàu nói rằng: Tổ tôi ơi! Vậy thì xin sai La-xa-rơ đến nhà cha tôi, — [28] vì tôi có năm anh em, — đặng người làm chứng cho họ về những điều nầy, kẻo họ cũng xuống nơi đau-đớn nầy chăng. [29] Áp-ra-ham trả lời rằng: Chúng nó đã có Môi-se và các đấng tiên-tri; chúng nó phải nghe lời các đấng ấy! [30] Người giàu nói rằng: Thưa Áp-ra-ham tổ tôi, không phải vậy đâu; nhưng nếu có kẻ chết sống lại đến cùng họ, thì họ sẽ ăn-năn. [31] Song Áp-ra-ham rằng: Nếu không nghe Môi-se và các đấng tiên-tri, thì dầu có ai từ kẻ chết sống lại, chúng nó cũng chẳng tin vậy.

Các lời khuyên-bảo khác

17 [1] Đức Chúa Jêsus lại phán cùng môn-đồ rằng: Không có thể khỏi xảy đến sự gây nên phạm tội được; song khốn thay cho ai là kẻ làm ra sự ấy! [2] Nếu ai gây cho chỉ một kẻ nhỏ nầy phạm tội, thì thà rằng buộc cối đá vào cổ nó mà quăng xuống biển còn hơn. [3] Các ngươi hãy giữ lấy mình. Nếu anh em ngươi đã phạm tội hãy quở-trách họ; và nếu họ ăn-năn, thì hãy tha-thứ. [4] Dầu trong một ngày, họ phạm tội cùng ngươi bảy lần, và bảy lần trở lại cùng ngươi mà nói rằng: Tôi ăn-năn, thì hãy tha tội cho họ.

[5] Các sứ-đồ thưa Chúa rằng: Xin thêm đức-tin cho chúng tôi! [6] Chúa đáp rằng: Nếu các ngươi có đức-tin trộng bằng hột cải, các ngươi khiến cây dâu nầy rằng: Hãy nhổ đi mà trồng dưới biển, thì nó sẽ vâng lời.

[7] Ai trong các ngươi có đầy-tớ đi cày hoặc đi chăn, khi ở ngoài đồng về, biểu nó rằng: Hãy đến ngay mà ngồi ăn, hay sao? [8] Trái lại,

---

r **16:23** Nguyên-văn là *Hadès*, theo ý người Gờ-réc là *nơi người chết ở.*

há không biểu nó rằng: Hãy dọn cho ta ăn, thắt lưng hầu ta, cho đến chừng nào ta ăn uống xong, rồi sau ngươi sẽ ăn uống sao? [9] Đầy-tớ vâng lịnh mà làm, thì chủ có biết ơn gì nó chăng? [10] Các ngươi cũng vậy, khi làm xong việc truyền phải làm, thì hãy nói rằng: Chúng tôi là đầy-tớ vô-ích; điều chúng tôi đã làm là điều chắc phải làm.

Mười người phung

[11] Đức Chúa Jêsus đương lên thành Giê-ru-sa-lem, trải qua bờ-cõi xứ Sa-ma-ri và Ga-li-lê. [12] Nhằm khi vào làng kia, có mười người phung đến đón-rước Ngài, đứng đằng xa, [13] lên tiếng rằng: Lạy Jêsus, lạy Thầy, xin thương-xót chúng tôi cùng! [14] Khi Ngài thấy họ, liền phán rằng: Hãy đi, tỏ mình cùng thầy tế-lễ. Họ đương đi thì phung lành hết thảy. [15] Có một người trong bọn họ thấy mình đã được sạch, bèn trở lại, lớn tiếng khen-ngợi Đức Chúa Trời; [16] lại đến sấp mặt xuống đất, nơi chân Đức Chúa Jêsus, mà tạ ơn Ngài. Và, người đó là người Sa-ma-ri. [17] Đức Chúa Jêsus bèn cất tiếng phán rằng: Không phải mười người đều được sạch cả sao? Còn chín người kia ở đâu? [18] Chỉ có người ngoại-quốc nầy trở lại ngợi-khen Đức Chúa Trời ư! [19] Ngài lại phán rằng: Đứng dậy, đi; đức-tin ngươi đã cứu ngươi.

Sự đến của nước Đức Chúa Trời

[20] Người Pha-ri-si hỏi Đức Chúa Jêsus nước Đức Chúa Trời chừng nào đến, thì Ngài đáp rằng: Nước Đức Chúa Trời không đến cách rõ-ràng, [21] và người ta sẽ không nói: Ở đây, hay là: Ở đó; vì nầy, nước Đức Chúa Trời ở trong[ss] các ngươi.

[22] Ngài lại phán cùng môn-đồ rằng: Sẽ có kỳ các ngươi ước-ao thấy chỉ một ngày của Con người, mà không thấy được. [23] Người ta sẽ nói cùng các ngươi rằng: Ngài ở đây, hay là: Ngài ở đó; nhưng đừng đi, đừng theo họ. [24] Vì như chớp nháng lòe từ dưới phương trời nầy đến dưới phương trời kia, thì Con người trong ngày Ngài cũng như vậy. [25] Nhưng Ngài trước phải chịu đau-đớn nhiều, và bị dòng-dõi nầy bỏ ra. [26] Việc đã xảy đến trong đời Nô-ê, thì cũng sẽ xảy đến trong ngày Con người: [27] Người ta ăn, uống, cưới, gả, cho đến ngày Nô-ê vào tàu, và nước lụt đến hủy-diệt thiên-hạ hết. [28] Việc đã xảy ra trong

---

s '17:21 Ctd: *ở giữa hoặc trong tầm tay*

đời Lót cũng vậy, người ta ăn, uống, mua, bán, trồng-tỉa, cất-dựng; [29] đến ngày Lót ra khỏi thành Sô-đôm, thì trời mưa lửa và diêm-sinh, giết hết dân thành ấy. [30] Ngày Con người hiện ra cũng một thể nầy. [31] Trong ngày đó, ai ở trên mái nhà, có của để trong nhà, đừng xuống mà chuyên đi; ai ở ngoài đồng, cũng đừng trở về nữa. [32] Hãy nhớ lại vợ của Lót. [33] Ai kiếm cách cứu sự sống mình, thì sẽ mất; ai mất sự sống mình, thì sẽ được lại. [34] Ta phán cùng các ngươi, trong đêm đó, hai người nằm chung giường, một người sẽ được rước đi, còn một bị để lại. [35] Hai người đàn-bà xay chung cối, một người được rước đi, còn một bị để lại.[t] [37] Các môn-đồ bèn thưa Ngài rằng: Thưa Chúa, sự ấy sẽ ở tại đâu? Ngài đáp rằng: Xác chết ở đâu, chim ó nhóm tại đó.

Ví-dụ về quan án không công-bình

18 [1] Đức Chúa Jêsus phán cùng môn-đồ một thí-dụ, để tỏ ra rằng phải cầu-nguyện luôn, chớ hề mỏi-mệt: [2] Trong thành kia, có một quan án không kính-sợ Đức Chúa Trời, không vị-nể ai hết. [3] Trong thành đó cũng có một người đàn-bà góa, đến thưa quan rằng: Xin xét lẽ công-bình cho tôi về kẻ nghịch cùng tôi. [4] Quan ấy từ-chối đã lâu. Nhưng kế đó, người tự nghĩ rằng: Dầu ta không kính-sợ Đức Chúa Trời, không vị-nể ai hết, [5] song vì đàn-bà góa nầy khuấy-rầy ta, ta sẽ xét lẽ công-bình cho nó, để nó không tới luôn làm nhức đầu ta. [6] Đoạn, Chúa phán thêm rằng: Các ngươi có nghe lời quan án không công-bình đó đã nói chăng? [7] Vậy, có lẽ nào Đức Chúa Trời chẳng xét lẽ công-bình cho những người đã được chọn, là kẻ đêm ngày kêu xin Ngài, mà lại chậm-chạp đến cứu họ sao! [8] Ta nói cùng các ngươi, Ngài sẽ vội-vàng xét lẽ công-bình cho họ. Song khi Con người đến, há sẽ thấy đức-tin trên mặt đất chăng?

Ví-dụ về người Pha-ri-si và người thâu thuế

[9] Ngài lại phán thí-dụ nầy về kẻ cậy mình là người công-bình và khinh-dể kẻ khác: [10] Có hai người lên đền-thờ cầu-nguyện: một người Pha-ri-si và một người thâu thuế. [11] Người Pha-ri-si đứng cầu-nguyện thầm như vậy: Lạy Đức Chúa Trời, tôi tạ ơn Ngài, vì tôi

---

t **17:35** Có mấy bản thêm câu 36 rằng: *Hai người ở ngoài đồng, một người được rước đi, còn một bị để lại.*

không phải như người khác, tham-lam, bất-nghĩa, gian-dâm, cũng không phải như người thâu thuế nầy. ¹²Tôi kiêng ăn một tuần-lễ hai lần, và nộp một phần mười về mọi món lợi của tôi. ¹³Người thâu thuế đứng xa xa, không dám ngước mắt lên trời, đấm ngực mà rằng: Lạy Đức Chúa Trời, xin thương-xót lấy tôi, vì tôi là kẻ có tội! ¹⁴Ta nói cùng các ngươi, người nầy trở về nhà mình, được xưng công-bình hơn người kia; vì ai tự nhắc mình lên sẽ phải hạ xuống, ai tự hạ mình xuống sẽ được nhắc lên.

Những con trẻ

¹⁵Người ta cũng đem con trẻ đến cùng Đức Chúa Jêsus, cho được Ngài rờ đến chúng nó. Môn-đồ thấy vậy, trách những người đem đến. ¹⁶Nhưng Đức Chúa Jêsus gọi họ mà phán rằng: Hãy để con trẻ đến cùng ta, đừng ngăn-cấm; vì nước Đức Chúa Trời thuộc về những người giống như con trẻ ấy. ¹⁷Quả thật, ta nói cùng các ngươi, ai không nhận-lãnh nước Đức Chúa Trời như một đứa trẻ, thì sẽ không được vào đó.

Người trai-trẻ giàu-có

¹⁸Bấy giờ có một quan hỏi Đức Chúa Jêsus rằng: Thưa thầy nhân-lành, tôi phải làm gì cho được hưởng sự sống đời đời? ¹⁹Đức Chúa Jêsus phán rằng: Sao ngươi gọi ta là nhân-lành? Chỉ có một Đấng nhân-lành, là Đức Chúa Trời. ²⁰Ngươi đã biết các điều-răn nầy: Ngươi chớ phạm tội tà-dâm; chớ giết người; chớ trộm-cướp; chớ nói chứng dối; hãy hiếu-kính cha mẹ. ²¹Người ấy thưa rằng: Tôi đã giữ các điều ấy từ thuở nhỏ. ²²Đức Chúa Jêsus nghe vậy, bèn phán rằng: Còn thiếu cho ngươi một điều; hãy bán hết gia-tài mình, phân-phát cho kẻ nghèo, thì ngươi sẽ có của-cải ở trên trời; bấy giờ hãy đến mà theo ta. ²³Nhưng người ấy nghe mấy lời thì trở nên buồn-rầu, vì giàu-có lắm. ²⁴Đức Chúa Jêsus thấy người buồn-rầu, bèn phán rằng: Kẻ giàu vào nước Đức Chúa Trời là khó biết dường nào! ²⁵Lạc-đà chui qua lỗ kim còn dễ hơn người giàu vào nước Đức Chúa Trời! ²⁶Những người nghe điều đó, nói rằng: Vậy thì ai được cứu? ²⁷Ngài đáp rằng: Sự chi người ta không làm được, thì Đức Chúa Trời làm được.

²⁸ Phi-e-rơ bèn thưa rằng: Nầy, chúng tôi đã bỏ sự mình có mà theo thầy. ²⁹ Đức Chúa Jêsus phán rằng: Quả thật, ta nói cùng các ngươi, người nào vì cớ nước Đức Chúa Trời mà bỏ nhà-cửa, cha mẹ, anh em, vợ con, ³⁰ thì trong đời nầy được lãnh nhiều hơn, và đời sau được sự sống đời đời.

Đức Chúa Jêsus phán trước về sự thương-khó của Ngài

³¹ Kế đó, Đức Chúa Jêsus đem mười hai sứ-đồ riêng ra mà phán rằng: Nầy, chúng ta lên thành Giê-ru-sa-lem, mọi điều mà các đấng tiên-tri đã chép về Con người sẽ ứng-nghiệm. ³² Vì Ngài sẽ bị nộp cho dân ngoại; họ sẽ nhạo-báng Ngài, mắng-nhiếc Ngài, nhổ trên Ngài, ³³ sau khi đánh đòn rồi, thì giết Ngài đi; đến ngày thứ ba, Ngài sẽ sống lại. ³⁴ Song các môn-đồ không hiểu chi hết; vì nghĩa những lời đó kín-giấu cho môn-đồ, nên không rõ ý Đức Chúa Jêsus nói là gì.

Người mù ở thành Giê-ri-cô

³⁵ Đức Chúa Jêsus đến gần thành Giê-ri-cô, có một người đui ngồi xin ở bên đường, ³⁶ nghe đoàn dân đi qua, bèn hỏi việc gì đó. ³⁷ Người ta trả lời rằng: Ấy là Jêsus, người Na-xa-rét đi qua. ³⁸ Người đui bèn kêu lên rằng: Lạy Jêsus, con vua Đa-vít, xin thương-xót tôi cùng! ³⁹ Những kẻ đi trước rầy người cho nín đi; song người càng kêu lớn hơn nữa rằng: Lạy con vua Đa-vít, xin thương-xót tôi cùng! ⁴⁰ Đức Chúa Jêsus dừng lại, truyền đem người đến. Khi người đui lại gần, thì Ngài hỏi rằng: ⁴¹ Ngươi muốn ta làm gì cho? Thưa rằng: Lạy Chúa, xin cho tôi được sáng mắt lại. ⁴² Đức Chúa Jêsus phán rằng: Hãy sáng mắt lại; đức-tin của ngươi đã chữa lành ngươi. ⁴³ Tức thì, người sáng mắt, đi theo Đức Chúa Jêsus, ngợi-khen Đức Chúa Trời. Hết thảy dân-chúng thấy vậy, đều ngợi-khen Đức Chúa Trời.

Đức Chúa Jêsus vào nhà Xa-chê

19 ¹ Đức Chúa Jêsus vào thành Giê-ri-cô, đi ngang qua phố. ² Tại đó, có một người tên là Xa-chê, làm đầu bọn thâu thuế, và giàu-có. ³ Người đó tìm xem Đức Chúa Jêsus là ai, nhưng không thấy được, vì đoàn dân đông lắm, mà mình lại thấp. ⁴ Vậy, Xa-chê chạy trước, trèo lên cây sung, để ngó thấy Đức Chúa Jêsus, vì Ngài phải đi qua đó. ⁵ Đức Chúa Jêsus đến chỗ ấy, ngước mắt lên mà phán rằng: Hỡi Xa-chê, hãy xuống cho mau, vì hôm nay ta phải ở nhà ngươi. ⁶ Xa-chê vội-vàng xuống và mừng rước Ngài. ⁷ Ai nấy thấy vậy, đều lằm-bằm rằng: Người nầy vào nhà kẻ có tội mà trọ! ⁸ Song Xa-chê đứng trước mặt Chúa, thưa rằng: Lạy Chúa, nầy, tôi lấy nửa gia-tài mình mà cho kẻ nghèo, và nếu có làm thiệt-hại ai, bất-kỳ việc gì, tôi sẽ đền gấp tư. ⁹ Đức Chúa Jêsus bèn phán rằng: Hôm nay sự cứu đã vào nhà nầy, vì người nầy cũng là con cháu Áp-ra-ham. ¹⁰ Bởi Con người đã đến tìm và cứu kẻ bị mất.

Lời ví-dụ về những nén bạc

¹¹ Họ nghe những lời ấy, thì Đức Chúa Jêsus thêm một thí-dụ nữa, vì Ngài gần đến thành Giê-ru-sa-lem, và người ta tưởng rằng nước Đức Chúa Trời sẽ hiện ra ngay. ¹² Vậy, Ngài phán rằng: Có một vị thế-tử đi phương xa, đặng chịu phong chức làm vua rồi trở về; ¹³ bèn gọi mười người trong đám đầy-tớ mình, giao cho mười nén bạc, và dạy rằng: Hãy dùng bạc nầy sanh lợi cho đến khi ta trở về. ¹⁴ Song dân xứ ấy ghét người, thì sai sứ theo đặng nói rằng: Chúng tôi không muốn người nầy cai-trị chúng tôi!

¹⁵ Khi người đã chịu phong chức làm vua rồi, trở về, đòi các đầy-tớ đã lãnh bạc đến, đặng cho biết mỗi người làm lợi được bao nhiêu. ¹⁶ Đầy-tớ thứ nhứt đến trình rằng: Lạy chúa, nén bạc của chúa sanh lợi ra được mười nén. ¹⁷ Chủ rằng: Hỡi đầy-tớ ngay-lành kia, được lắm; vì ngươi trung-tín trong sự nhỏ-mọn, ngươi sẽ được cai-trị mười thành. ¹⁸ Người thứ hai đến thưa rằng: Lạy chúa, nén bạc của chúa sanh lợi ra được năm nén. ¹⁹ Chủ rằng: Ngươi được cai-trị năm thành. ²⁰ Người khác đến thưa rằng: Lạy chúa, đây nầy, nén bạc của chúa tôi đã gói giữ trong khăn; ²¹ bởi tôi sợ chúa, vì chúa là người nghiêm-nhặt, hay lấy trong nơi không để, gặt trong chỗ không gieo. ²² Chủ rằng: Hỡi đầy-tớ ngoan-ác kia, ta cứ lời ngươi nói ra mà xét ngươi. Ngươi đã biết ta là người nghiêm-nhặt, hay lấy trong nơi không để, gặt trong chỗ không gieo; ²³ cớ sao ngươi không giao bạc ta cho hàng bạc? Khi ta về, sẽ lấy lại vốn và lời. ²⁴ Chủ lại nói cùng các người đứng đó rằng: Hãy lấy nén bạc nó đi, cho người có mười

nén. [25] Họ bèn thưa rằng: Lạy chúa, người ấy có mười nén rồi. [26] Ta nói cùng các ngươi, ai có, thì sẽ cho thêm; song ai không có, thì sẽ cất luôn của họ đã có nữa. [27] Còn như những kẻ nghịch cùng ta, không muốn ta cai-trị họ, hãy kéo họ đến đây, và chém đi trước mặt ta.

[28] Sau khi Đức Chúa Jêsus phán điều đó, thì đi trước mặt dân-chúng lên thành Giê-ru-sa-lem.

Chức-vụ Đức Chúa Jêsus tại thành Giê-ru-sa-lem
(Từ 19:29 đến đoạn 21)

Sự vào thành Giê-ru-sa-lem

[29] Đức Chúa Jêsus gần đến thành Bê-pha-giê và Bê-tha-ni, ngang núi gọi là Ô-li-ve, sai hai môn-đồ đi, [30] và dặn rằng: Hãy đi đến làng trước mặt các ngươi; khi vào làng, sẽ thấy một lừa con buộc đó, chưa hề có ai cỡi; hãy mở và dắt về cho ta. [31] Hoặc có ai hỏi sao các ngươi mở nó ra, hãy trả lời rằng: Chúa cần dùng lừa nầy. [32] Hai người được sai ra đi, quả gặp mọi điều y như Đức Chúa Jêsus đã phán. [33] Đang mở lừa con, các chủ lừa hỏi rằng: Sao mở lừa con nầy ra? [34] Hai người trả lời rằng: Chúa cần dùng nó. [35] Hai người bèn dắt lừa về cho Đức Chúa Jêsus; rồi lấy áo mình trải trên con lừa, nâng Ngài lên cỡi. [36] Khi Đức Chúa Jêsus đang đi tới, có nhiều kẻ trải áo trên đường. [37] Lúc đến gần dốc núi Ô-li-ve, cả đám môn-đồ lấy làm mừng-rỡ, và cả tiếng ngợi-khen Đức Chúa Trời về những phép lạ mình đã thấy, [38] mà nói rằng: Đáng ngợi-khen Vua nhân danh Chúa mà đến! Bình-an ở trên trời, và vinh-hiển trên các nơi rất cao! [39] Bấy giờ, có mấy người Pha-ri-si ở trong đám dân đông nói cùng Ngài rằng: Thưa thầy, xin quở-trách môn-đồ thầy! [40] Ngài đáp rằng: Ta phán cùng các ngươi, nếu họ nín-lặng thì đá sẽ kêu lên.

[41] Khi Đức Chúa Jêsus gần đến thành, thấy thì khóc về thành, và phán rằng: [42] Ước gì, ít nữa là ngày nay, mầy đã hiểu biết sự làm cho mầy được bình-an! Song hiện nay những sự ấy kín-giấu nơi mắt mầy. [43] Vì sẽ có ngày xảy đến cho mầy, khi quân nghịch đào hố xung-quanh mầy, vây mầy chặt bốn bề. [44] Họ sẽ hủy hết thảy, mầy và con-

cái ở giữa mấy nữa. Không để cho mấy hòn đá nầy trên hòn đá kia, vì mấy không biết lúc mình đã được thăm-viếng.

Sự dẹp sạch trong đền-thờ

⁴⁵ Đức Chúa Jêsus vào đền-thờ rồi, bèn đuổi những kẻ bán ở đó ra, ⁴⁶ mà phán rằng: Có lời chép rằng: Nhà ta sẽ là nhà cầu-nguyện; song các ngươi làm thành ra một cái hang trộm-cướp.

⁴⁷ Hằng ngày Ngài giảng-dạy trong đền-thờ. Các thầy tế-lễ cả, các thầy thông-giáo, cùng người tôn-trưởng trong dân tìm phương giết Ngài; ⁴⁸ nhưng họ không biết dùng chước chi, vì dân-sự đều chăm-chỉ mà nghe Ngài nói.

Câu hỏi về quyền-phép

20 ¹ Một ngày trong những ngày đó, Đức Chúa Jêsus đương dạy-dỗ dân-chúng trong đền-thờ và rao-truyền Tin-lành, thì các thầy tế-lễ cả, các thầy thông-giáo, và các trưởng-lão đến thình-lình, ² hỏi Ngài như vầy: Hãy nói cho chúng tôi, bởi quyền-phép nào mà thầy làm những điều nầy, hay là ai đã ban cho thầy quyền-phép ấy? ³ Ngài đáp rằng: Ta cũng hỏi các ngươi một câu. Hãy nói cho ta: ⁴ Phép báp-têm của Giăng đến bởi trên trời, hay là bởi người ta? ⁵ Và, những người ấy bàn cùng nhau rằng: Nếu chúng ta nói: Bởi trời, thì người sẽ nói với ta rằng: Vậy sao các ngươi không tin lời người? ⁶ Lại nếu chúng ta nói: Bởi người ta, thì cả dân-sự sẽ ném đá chúng ta; vì họ đã tin chắc Giăng là một đấng tiên-tri. ⁷ Vậy nên họ trả lời rằng không biết phép ấy bởi đâu mà đến. ⁸ Đức Chúa Jêsus bèn phán rằng: Ta cũng không nói cho các ngươi bởi quyền-phép nào ta làm những điều nầy.

Ví-dụ về người trồng nho

⁹ Đức Chúa Jêsus phán cùng dân-chúng lời thí-dụ nầy: Người kia trồng một vườn nho, đã cho kẻ trồng nho mướn, rồi bỏ xứ đi lâu ngày. ¹⁰ Đến mùa nho, chủ sai một đầy-tớ tới cùng những kẻ trồng nho đặng nhận một phần hoa-lợi; song bọn trồng nho đánh đầy-tớ, đuổi về tay không. ¹¹ Chủ lại sai một đầy-tớ khác nữa; song họ cũng

đánh, chưởi, và đuổi về tay không. ¹²Chủ lại sai đầy-tớ thứ ba; song họ cũng đánh cho bị thương và đuổi đi. ¹³Chủ vườn nho bèn nói rằng: Ta làm thể nào? Ta sẽ sai con trai yêu-dấu ta đến; có lẽ chúng nó sẽ kính-nể! ¹⁴Song khi bọn trồng nho thấy con trai ấy, thì bàn với nhau như vầy: Kìa, ấy là con kế-tự; hãy giết nó, hầu cho gia-tài nó sẽ về chúng ta. ¹⁵Họ bèn liệng con trai ấy ra ngoài vườn nho, và giết đi. Vậy chủ vườn sẽ xử họ làm sao? ¹⁶Chủ ấy chắc sẽ đến diệt những kẻ trồng nho nầy, rồi lấy vườn giao cho người khác.

Ai nấy nghe những lời đó, thì nói rằng: Đức Chúa Trời nào nỡ vậy! ¹⁷Đức Chúa Jêsus bèn ngó họ mà rằng: Vậy thì lời chép:

Hòn đá thợ xây nhà bỏ ra,

Trở nên đá góc nhà,

nghĩa là gì? ¹⁸Hễ ai ngã nhằm đá nầy, thì sẽ bị giập-nát, còn đá nầy ngã nhằm ai, thì sẽ giập người ấy. ¹⁹Chính giờ đó, các thầy tế-lễ cả và các thầy thông-giáo tìm cách giết Ngài, vì hiểu Ngài phán thí-dụ ấy chỉ về mình; nhưng lại sợ dân-chúng.

Đức Chúa Trời và Sê-sa

²⁰Họ bèn dòm-hành Ngài, sai mấy kẻ do-thám giả làm người hiền-lành, để bắt-bẻ Ngài trong lời nói, hầu để nộp Ngài cho kẻ cầm quyền và trong tay quan tổng-đốc. ²¹Những người đó hỏi Đức Chúa Jêsus câu nầy: Thưa thầy, chúng tôi biết thầy nói và dạy-dỗ theo lẽ ngay-thẳng, không tư-vị ai, lấy lẽ thật mà dạy đạo Đức Chúa Trời. ²²Chúng tôi có nên nộp thuế cho Sê-sa hay không? ²³Song Đức Chúa Jêsus biết mưu họ, thì đáp rằng: ²⁴Hãy cho ta xem một đơ-ni-ê. Đơ-ni-ê nầy mang hình và hiệu của ai? Họ thưa rằng: Của Sê-sa. ²⁵Ngài bèn phán rằng: Vậy thì của Sê-sa hãy trả lại cho Sê-sa, của Đức Chúa Trời hãy trả lại cho Đức Chúa Trời. ²⁶Trước mặt dân-chúng, họ không bắt lỗi lời Ngài phán chi được; và lấy lời đáp của Ngài làm lạ, thì nín-lặng.

Sự sống lại

²⁷Có mấy người Sa-đu-sê,ᵘ là người vẫn quyết rằng không có sự sống lại, đến gần Đức Chúa Jêsus, mà hỏi rằng: ²⁸Thưa thầy, Môi-se

---

u **20:27** Xem chú thích ở Mat 3:7

đã truyền lại luật nầy cho chúng tôi: Nếu người kia có anh, cưới vợ rồi chết, không con, thì người phải cưới lấy vợ góa đó để nối dòng cho anh mình. ²⁹ Vậy, có bảy anh em. Người thứ nhứt cưới vợ, rồi chết, không con. ³⁰ Người thứ hai cũng lấy vợ đó, ³¹ rồi đến người thứ ba; hết thảy bảy người cũng vậy, đều chết đi không có con. ³² Rốt lại, người đàn-bà cũng chết. ³³ Vậy thì đến ngày sống lại, đàn-bà đó sẽ là vợ ai? Vì bảy người đều đã lấy làm vợ. ³⁴ Đức Chúa Jêsus phán rằng: Con-cái của đời nầy lấy vợ gả chồng; ³⁵ song những kẻ đã được kể đáng dự phần đời sau và đáng từ kẻ chết sống lại, thì không lấy vợ gả chồng. ³⁶ Bởi họ sẽ không chết được nữa, vì giống như các thiên-sứ, và là con của Đức Chúa Trời, tức là con của sự sống lại. ³⁷ Còn về sự kẻ chết sống lại, Môi-se đã cho biết trong câu chuyện về Bụi gai, khi người gọi Chúa là Đức Chúa Trời của Áp-ra-ham, Đức Chúa Trời của Y-sác, và Đức Chúa Trời của Gia-cốp. ³⁸ Vậy, Đức Chúa Trời không phải là Đức Chúa Trời của kẻ chết, nhưng của kẻ sống; vì ai nấy đều sống cho Ngài. ³⁹ Có mấy thầy thông-giáo cất tiếng thưa Ngài rằng: Lạy thầy, thầy nói phải lắm. ⁴⁰ Họ không dám hỏi Ngài câu nào nữa.

Đấng Christ con vua Đa-vít

⁴¹ Đức Chúa Jêsus hỏi họ rằng: Làm sao người ta nói được rằng Đấng Christ là con vua Đa-vít? ⁴² vì chính vua Đa-vít đã nói trong sách Thi-thiên rằng:

Chúa phán cùng Chúa tôi rằng:

Hãy ngồi bên hữu ta,

⁴³ Cho đến khi ta bắt kẻ nghịch ngươi làm bệ-chân ngươi.

⁴⁴ Vậy, vua Đa-vít gọi Ngài bằng Chúa; có lẽ nào Ngài là con vua ấy được?

Lời trách các thầy thông-giáo

⁴⁵ Khi dân-chúng đương nghe, thì Ngài phán cùng môn-đồ rằng: ⁴⁶ Hãy giữ mình về các thầy thông-giáo, là người ưa mặc áo dài đi dạo, và thích những sự chào-hỏi giữa chợ, muốn ngồi cao trong nhà hội, ngồi đầu trong tiệc lớn, ⁴⁷ làm bộ đọc lời cầu-nguyện dài, mà nuốt gia-tài của đàn-bà góa. Họ sẽ bị đoán-phạt nặng hơn.

Đàn-bà góa dâng của

21 ¹ Đức Chúa Jêsus vừa ngó lên, thấy những kẻ giàu bỏ tiền lễ vào rương, ² lại thấy một mụ góa nghèo bỏ vào hai đồng tiền. ³ Ngài phán rằng: Quả thật, ta nói cùng các ngươi, mụ góa nghèo nầy đã bỏ vào nhiều hơn hết mọi người khác. ⁴ Vì mọi người kia đều lấy của dư mình mà làm của dâng; nhưng mụ nầy thiếu-thốn, mà đã dâng hết của mình có để nuôi mình.

Đức Chúa Jêsus phán về thành Giê-ru-sa-lem tàn-phá và sự Chúa đến

⁵ Có mấy người nói về đền-thờ, về đá đẹp và đồ dâng làm rực-rỡ trong đền-thờ. Đức Chúa Jêsus phán rằng: ⁶ Những ngày sẽ đến, mọi điều các ngươi ngó thấy đây, sẽ không còn một hòn đá nào chồng trên hòn khác mà không đổ xuống. ⁷ Họ bèn hỏi Ngài rằng: Lạy thầy, vậy việc đó chừng nào sẽ xảy đến, và có điềm gì cho người ta biết rằng việc gần xảy đến không? ⁸ Ngài đáp rằng: Các ngươi hãy giữ, kẻo bị cám-dỗ; vì có nhiều người sẽ mạo danh ta mà đến, và nói rằng: Ấy chính ta là Đấng Christ, thì-giờ đã đến gần. Các ngươi đừng theo họ. ⁹ Lại khi các ngươi nghe nói về giặc-giã loạn-lạc, thì đừng kinh-khiếp, vì các điều đó phải đến trước; nhưng chưa phải cuối-cùng liền đâu.

¹⁰ Ngài cũng phán cùng họ rằng: Dân nầy sẽ dấy lên nghịch cùng dân khác, nước nọ nghịch cùng nước kia; ¹¹ sẽ có sự động đất lớn, có đói-kém và dịch-lệ trong nhiều nơi, có những điềm lạ kinh-khiếp và dấu lớn ở trên trời. ¹² Song trước những điều đó, thiên-hạ sẽ vì cớ danh ta mà tra tay bắt-bớ các ngươi, nộp tại các nhà hội, bỏ vào ngục, kéo đến trước mặt các vua và các quan tổng-đốc. ¹³ Điều ấy xảy ra cho các ngươi để làm chứng-cớ ¹⁴ Vậy các ngươi hãy nhớ kỹ trong trí, đừng lo trước về sự binh-vực mình thể nào. ¹⁵ Vì ta sẽ ban cho các ngươi lời-lẽ và sự khôn-ngoan, mà kẻ nghịch không chống-cự và bẻ-bác được. ¹⁶ Các ngươi cũng sẽ bị cha, mẹ, anh, em, bà-con, bạn-hữu mình nộp mình; và họ sẽ làm cho nhiều người trong các ngươi phải chết. ¹⁷ Các ngươi sẽ vì cớ danh ta bị mọi người ghen-ghét. ¹⁸ Nhưng

một sợi tóc trên đầu các ngươi cũng không mất đâu. ¹⁹ Nhờ sự nhịn-nhục của các ngươi mà giữ được linh-hồn mình.

²⁰ Vả, khi các ngươi sẽ thấy quân-lính vây thành Giê-ru-sa-lem, hãy biết sự tàn-phá thành ấy gần đến. ²¹ Lúc đó, ai ở trong xứ Giu-đê hãy trốn lên núi; ai ở trong thành phải đi ra ngoài, ai ở ngoài đồng đừng trở vào thành. ²² Vì những ngày đó là ngày báo thù, hầu cho mọi lời đã chép được ứng-nghiệm. ²³ Trong những ngày ấy, khốn cho đàn-bà có thai, và đàn-bà cho con bú! Vì sẽ có tai-nạn lớn trong xứ, và cơn thạnh-nộ nghịch cùng dân nầy. ²⁴ Họ sẽ bị ngã dưới lưỡi gươm, sẽ bị đem đi làm phu-tù giữa các dân ngoại, thành Giê-ru-sa-lem sẽ bị dân ngoại giày-đạp, cho đến chừng nào các kỳ dân ngoại được trọn. ²⁵ Sẽ có các điềm lạ trong mặt trời, mặt trăng, cùng các ngôi sao; còn dưới đất, dân các nước sầu-não rối-loạn vì biển nổi tiếng om-sòm và sóng-đào. ²⁶ Người ta nhân trong khi đợi việc hung-dữ xảy ra cho thế-gian, thì thất-kinh mất vía, vì các thế-lực trên trời sẽ rúng-động. ²⁷ Bấy giờ thiên-hạ sẽ thấy Con người dùng đại-quyền đại-vinh mà ngự đến trên đám mây.

²⁸ Chừng nào các việc đó khởi xảy đến, hãy đứng thẳng lên, ngước đầu lên, vì sự giải-cứu của các ngươi gần tới. ²⁹ Đoạn, Ngài phán cùng họ một lời ví-dụ rằng: Hãy xem cây vả và các cây khác; ³⁰ khi nó mới nứt lộc, các ngươi thấy thì tự biết rằng mùa hạ đã gần đến. ³¹ Cũng vậy, khi các ngươi thấy những điều ấy xảy ra, hãy biết nước Đức Chúa Trời gần đến. ³² Quả thật, ta nói cùng các ngươi, dòng-dõi nầy chẳng qua trước khi mọi sự kia chưa xảy đến. ³³ Trời đất sẽ qua, song lời ta nói sẽ không qua đâu.

³⁴ Vậy, hãy tự giữ lấy mình, e rằng vì sự ăn uống quá-độ, sự say-sưa và sự lo-lắng đời nầy làm cho lòng các ngươi mê-mẩn chăng, và e ngày ấy đến thình-lình trên các ngươi như lưới bủa; ³⁵ vì ngày đó sẽ đến cho mọi người ở khắp trên mặt đất cũng vậy. ³⁶ Vậy, hãy tỉnh-thức luôn và cầu-nguyện, để các ngươi được tránh khỏi các tai-nạn sẽ xảy ra, và đứng trước mặt Con người.

³⁷ Và, ban ngày, Đức Chúa Jêsus dạy-dỗ trong đền-thờ; còn đến chiều, Ngài đi lên núi, gọi là núi Ô-li-ve, mà ở đêm tại đó. ³⁸ Vừa tảng sáng, cả dân-sự đến cùng Ngài trong đền-thờ, đặng nghe Ngài dạy.

Sự đau-đớn, sự chết, và sự sống lại của Đức Chúa Jêsus

(Từ đoạn 22 đến đoạn 24)

Sự lập-mưu của các thầy tế-lễ

22 ¹ Ngày lễ ăn bánh không men tức là lễ Vượt-qua đến gần. ² Các thầy tế-lễ cả cùng các thầy thông-giáo tìm phương đặng giết Đức Chúa Jêsus; vì họ sợ dân.

Dứa phản Chúa

³ Và, quỉ Sa-tan ám vào Giu-đa, gọi là Ích-ca-ri-ốt, là người trong số mười hai sứ-đồ, ⁴ nó đi kiếm các thầy tế-lễ cả và các thầy đội, để đồng mưu dùng cách nào nộp Ngài cho họ. ⁵ Các người kia mừng lắm, hứa sẽ cho nó tiền bạc. ⁶ Nó đã ưng-thuận với họ, bèn kiếm dịp-tiện đặng nộp Đức Chúa Jêsus trong khi dân-chúng không biết.

Lễ Tiệc-thánh lập ra

⁷ Đến ngày lễ ăn bánh không men, là ngày người ta phải giết con sinh làm lễ Vượt-qua, ⁸ Đức Chúa Jêsus sai Phi-e-rơ và Giăng đi, mà phán rằng: Hãy đi dọn lễ Vượt-qua cho chúng ta ăn. ⁹ Hai người thưa rằng: Thầy muốn chúng tôi dọn lễ ấy tại đâu? ¹⁰ Ngài đáp rằng: Khi các ngươi vào thành, sẽ gặp một người mang vò nước; hãy theo người vào nhà, ¹¹ và nói cùng chủ nhà rằng: Thầy phán cùng ngươi rằng: Phòng khách là chỗ ta sẽ ăn lễ Vượt-qua với môn-đồ ta ở đâu? ¹² Chủ nhà sẽ chỉ cho một cái phòng rộng và cao, đồ-đạc sẵn-sàng; các ngươi hãy dọn ở đó. ¹³ Hai môn-đồ đi, quả gặp những điều như Ngài đã phán, bèn dọn lễ Vượt-qua.

¹⁴ Đến giờ, Ngài ngồi bàn ăn, các sứ-đồ cùng ngồi với Ngài. ¹⁵ Ngài phán rằng: Ta rất muốn ăn lễ Vượt-qua nầy với các ngươi trước khi ta chịu đau-đớn. ¹⁶ Vì, ta nói cùng các ngươi, ta sẽ không ăn lễ nầy nữa cho đến khi lễ ấy được trọn trong nước Đức Chúa Trời. ¹⁷ Ngài bèn cầm chén, tạ ơn, rồi phán rằng: Hãy lấy cái nầy phân-phát cho nhau. ¹⁸ Vì, ta nói cùng các ngươi, từ nay ta sẽ không uống trái nho nữa, cho tới khi nước Đức Chúa Trời đến rồi. ¹⁹ Đoạn, Ngài cầm

lấy bánh, tạ ơn xong, bẻ ra phân-phát cho môn-đồ, mà phán rằng: Nầy là thân-thể ta, đã vì các ngươi mà phó cho; hãy làm sự nầy để nhớ đến ta. [20] Khi ăn xong, Ngài cũng làm như vậy, lấy chén đưa cho môn-đồ, mà phán rằng: Chén nầy là giao-ước mới trong huyết ta vì các ngươi mà đổ ra... [21] Vả lại, nầy, bàn tay kẻ phản ta ở gần ta, nơi bàn nầy. [22] Con người đi, theo như điều đã chỉ-định; nhưng khốn cho người nầy phản Ngài! [23] Môn-đồ bèn hỏi nhau trong bọn mình ai là người sẽ làm điều đó.

Sự biện-luận trong môn-đồ

[24] Môn-đồ lại cãi-lẫy nhau, cho biết ai sẽ được tôn là lớn hơn hết trong đám mình. [25] Nhưng Ngài phán cùng môn-đồ rằng: Các vua của các dân ngoại lấy phép riêng mình mà cai-trị, những người cầm quyền cai-trị được xưng là người làm ơn. [26] Về phần các ngươi, đừng làm như vậy; song ai lớn hơn trong các ngươi phải như kẻ rất nhỏ, và ai cai-trị phải như kẻ hầu việc. [27] Vì một người ngồi ăn với một người hầu việc, ai là lớn hơn? Có phải là kẻ ngồi ăn không? Nhưng ta ở giữa các ngươi như kẻ hầu việc vậy. [28] Còn như các ngươi đã bền lòng theo ta trong mọi sự thử-thách ta, [29] nên ta ban nước cho các ngươi, cũng như Cha ta đã ban cho ta vậy, [30] để các ngươi được ăn uống chung bàn trong nước ta, và được ngồi ngai để xét-đoán mười hai chi-phái Y-sơ-ra-ên.

Lời bảo trước cho Phi-e-rơ

[31] Hỡi Si-môn, Si-môn, nầy, quỉ Sa-tan đã đòi sàng-sảy ngươi như lúa mì. [32] Song ta đã cầu-nguyện cho ngươi, hầu cho đức-tin ngươi không thiếu-thốn. Vậy, đến khi ngươi đã hối-cải, hãy làm cho vững chí anh em mình. [33] Phi-e-rơ thưa rằng: Thưa Chúa, tôi sẵn lòng đi theo Chúa, đồng tù đồng chết. [34] Đức Chúa Jêsus đáp rằng: Hỡi Phi-e-rơ, ta nói cùng ngươi, hôm nay khi gà chưa gáy, ngươi sẽ ba lần chối không biết ta.

[35] Đoạn, Ngài lại phán rằng: Khi ta đã sai các ngươi đi, không đem túi, bao, giày chi hết, các ngươi có thiếu gì không? Môn-đồ thưa rằng: Không thiếu chi hết. [36] Ngài phán rằng: Nhưng bây giờ, ai có túi bạc, hãy lấy đi, ai có bao, cũng vậy; ai không có gươm, hãy bán áo

ngoài đi mà mua. ³⁷ Vì ta rao cho các ngươi, có lời chép rằng: Ngài đã bị kể vào hàng kẻ dữ. Lời ấy phải ứng-nghiệm về chính mình ta. Thật vậy, sự đã chỉ về ta hầu được trọn. ³⁸ Các sứ-đồ thưa rằng: Thưa Chúa, có hai thanh gươm đây. Ngài phán rằng: Ấy là đủ.

Vườn Ghết-sê-ma-nê. – Sự bắt Đức Chúa Jêsus

³⁹ Đoạn, Đức Chúa Jêsus ra đi, lên núi Ô-li-ve theo như thói quen; các môn-đồ cùng đi theo Ngài. ⁴⁰ Khi đã đến nơi đó, Ngài phán cùng môn-đồ rằng: Hãy cầu-nguyện, hầu cho các ngươi khỏi sa vào sự cám-dỗ. ⁴¹ Ngài bèn đi khỏi các môn-đồ, cách chừng liệng một cục đá, quì xuống mà cầu-nguyện ⁴² rằng: Lạy Cha, nếu Cha muốn, xin cất chén nầy khỏi tôi! Dầu vậy, xin ý Cha được nên, chớ không theo ý tôi!… ⁴³ Có một thiên-sứ từ trên trời hiện xuống cùng Ngài, mà thêm sức cho Ngài. ⁴⁴ Trong cơn rất đau-thương, Ngài cầu-nguyện càng thiết, mồ-hôi trở nên như giọt máu lớn rơi xuống đất.ᵛ ⁴⁵ Cầu-nguyện xong, Ngài đứng dậy trở lại cùng các môn-đồ, thấy đương ngủ mê vì buồn-rầu. ⁴⁶ Ngài phán rằng: Sao các ngươi ngủ? Hãy đứng dậy cầu-nguyện, để cho khỏi sa vào sự cám-dỗ.

⁴⁷ Khi Ngài còn đương phán, một lũ đông kéo đến. Tên Giu-đa, một trong mười hai sứ-đồ, đi trước hết, lại gần Đức Chúa Jêsus đặng hôn Ngài. ⁴⁸ Đức Chúa Jêsus hỏi rằng: Hỡi Giu-đa, ngươi lấy cái hôn để phản Con người sao? ⁴⁹ Những người ở với Ngài thấy sự sắp xảy đến, bèn nói rằng: Thưa Chúa, chúng tôi nên dùng gươm đánh chăng? ⁵⁰ Một người trong các sứ-đồ đánh đầy-tớ của thầy cả thượng-phẩm và chém đứt tai bên hữu. ⁵¹ Nhưng Đức Chúa Jêsus cất tiếng phán rằng: Hãy để cho họ đến thế! Ngài bèn rờ tai đầy-tớ ấy, làm cho nó được lành. ⁵² Đoạn, Đức Chúa Jêsus phán cùng các thầy tế-lễ cả, các thầy đội coi đền thờ, và các trưởng lão đã đến bắt Ngài, rằng: Các ngươi cầm gươm và gậy đến bắt ta, như bắt kẻ trộm-cướp. ⁵³ Hằng ngày ta ở trong đền-thờ với các ngươi, mà các ngươi không ra tay bắt ta. Nhưng nầy là giờ của các ngươi, và quyền của sự tối-tăm vậy.

---

v 22:44 Một vài bản không có các câu 43-44

Đức Chúa Jêsus trước mặt Cai-phe. – Sự chối của Phi-e-rơ

⁵⁴ Bấy giờ họ bắt Đức Chúa Jêsus đem đi, giải Ngài đến nhà thầy cả thượng-phẩm. Phi-e-rơ đi theo Ngài xa xa. ⁵⁵ Họ nhúm lửa giữa sân, rồi ngồi với nhau; Phi-e-rơ cũng ngồi giữa đám họ. ⁵⁶ Một con đòi kia thấy Phi-e-rơ ngồi gần lửa, thì ngó chăm-chỉ, mà nói rằng: Người nầy vốn cũng ở với người ấy. ⁵⁷ Song Phi-e-rơ chối Đức Chúa Jêsus, nói rằng: Hỡi đàn-bà kia, ta không biết người đó. ⁵⁸ Một lát, có người khác thấy Phi-e-rơ, nói rằng: Ngươi cũng thuộc về bọn đó! Phi-e-rơ đáp rằng: Hỡi người, ta không phải thuộc về bọn đó đâu. ⁵⁹ Độ cách một giờ, có kẻ khác để quyết như vậy mà rằng: Thật người nầy cũng ở với Jêsus, vì người là dân Ga-li-lê. ⁶⁰ Nhưng Phi-e-rơ cãi rằng: Hỡi người, ta không biết ngươi nói chi! Đương lúc Phi-e-rơ còn nói, thì gà liền gáy; ⁶¹ Chúa xây mặt lại ngó Phi-e-rơ. Phi-e-rơ nhớ lại lời Chúa đã phán cùng mình rằng: Hôm nay trước khi gà chưa gáy, ngươi sẽ chối ta ba lần; ⁶² rồi đi ra ngoài, khóc-lóc thảm-thiết.

⁶³ Vả, những kẻ canh Đức Chúa Jêsus nhạo-báng và đánh Ngài; ⁶⁴ che mặt Ngài lại, rồi nói rằng: Hãy nói tiên-tri đi, hãy đoán xem ai đánh ngươi! ⁶⁵ Họ lại nhiếc-móc Ngài nhiều lời khác nữa.

⁶⁶ Đến sáng ngày, các trưởng-lão trong dân, các thầy tế-lễ cả, và các thầy thông-giáo nhóm lại, rồi sai đem Đức Chúa Jêsus đến nơi tòa công-luận. ⁶⁷ Họ hỏi Ngài rằng: Nếu ngươi phải là Đấng Christ, hãy xưng ra cho chúng ta. Ngài đáp rằng: Nếu ta nói, thì các ngươi không tin; ⁶⁸ nếu ta tra-gạn các ngươi, thì các ngươi không trả lời. ⁶⁹ Nhưng từ nay về sau, Con người sẽ ngồi bên hữu quyền-phép Đức Chúa Trời. ⁷⁰ Ai nấy đều hỏi rằng: Vậy, ngươi là Con Đức Chúa Trời sao? Ngài đáp rằng: Chính các ngươi nói ta là Con Ngài. ⁷¹ Họ bèn nói rằng: Chúng ta nào có cần chứng-cớ nữa làm chi? Chính chúng ta đã nghe từ miệng nó nói ra rồi.

Đức Chúa Jêsus trước mặt Phi-lát và Hê-rốt

23 ¹ Đoạn, cả hội-đồng đứng dậy điệu Ngài đến trước mặt Phi-lát. ² Họ bèn khởi cáo Ngài rằng: Chúng tôi đã thấy người nầy xui dân ta làm loạn, cấm nộp thuế cho Sê-sa, và xưng mình là Đấng Christ, là Vua. ³ Phi-lát gạn Ngài rằng: Chính ngươi là Vua dân Giu-đa phải không? Đức Chúa Jêsus đáp rằng: Thật như lời. ⁴ Phi-lát bèn nói với các thầy tế-lễ cả và dân-chúng rằng: Ta không thấy người nầy có tội gì. ⁵ Nhưng họ cố nài rằng: Người nầy xui-giục dân-sự, truyền-giáo khắp đất Giu-đê, bắt đầu từ xứ Ga-li-lê rồi đến đây. ⁶ Khi Phi-lát nghe điều đó, thì hỏi nếu người nầy thật là dân Ga-li-lê chăng. ⁷ Biết Ngài thuộc quyền cai-trị của vua Hê-rốt, bèn giải đến cho vua Hê-rốt, vua ấy ở tại thành Giê-ru-sa-lem trong mấy ngày đó.

⁸ Vua Hê-rốt thấy Đức Chúa Jêsus thì mừng lắm; vì lâu nay vua muốn gặp Ngài, nhân đã nghe nói về chuyện Ngài, và mong xem Ngài làm phép lạ. ⁹ Vậy, vua hỏi Ngài nhiều câu, song Ngài không trả lời gì hết. ¹⁰ Các thầy tế-lễ cả và các thầy thông-giáo ở đó, cáo Ngài dữ lắm. ¹¹ Bấy giờ vua Hê-rốt và quân-lính hầu vua đều đãi Ngài cách khinh-dể và nhạo-báng Ngài; đoạn, họ mặc áo hoa-hòe cho Ngài, rồi giao Ngài về cho Phi-lát. ¹² Trước kia Phi-lát với vua Hê-rốt thù-hiềm nhau, nhưng nội ngày ấy trở nên bạn-hữu.

¹³ Phi-lát hiệp các thầy tế-lễ cả, các quan đề-hình và dân-chúng lại, mà nói rằng: ¹⁴ Các ngươi đã đem nộp người nầy cho ta, về việc xui dân làm loạn; nhưng đã tra-hỏi trước mặt các ngươi đây, thì ta không thấy người mắc một tội nào mà các ngươi đã cáo; ¹⁵ vua Hê-rốt cũng vậy, vì đã giao người về cho ta. Vậy người nầy đã không làm điều gì đáng chết, ¹⁶ nên ta sẽ đánh đòn rồi tha đi.ʷ ¹⁸ Chúng bèn đồng-thanh kêu lên rằng: Hãy giết người nầy đi, mà tha Ba-ra-ba cho chúng tôi! ¹⁹ Vả, tên nầy bị tù vì dấy loạn trong thành, và vì tội giết người. ²⁰ Phi-lát có ý muốn tha Đức Chúa Jêsus, nên lại nói cùng dân-chúng nữa. ²¹ Song chúng kêu lên rằng: Đóng đinh nó trên cây thập-tự đi! Đóng đinh nó trên cây thập-tự đi! ²² Phi-lát lại nói đến lần thứ ba, rằng: Vậy người nầy đã làm điều ác gì? Ta không tìm thấy người có sự gì đáng chết. Vậy, đánh đòn xong, ta sẽ tha. ²³ Nhưng chúng cố nài, kêu lớn tiếng rằng phải đóng đinh Ngài trên cây thập-tự; tiếng kêu của họ được thắng. ²⁴ Phi-lát truyền làm y như lời chúng xin. ²⁵ Bèn tha tên tù vì tội dấy loạn và giết người, là người chúng đã xin tha; rồi phó Đức Chúa Jêsus cho mặc ý họ.

---

w **23:16** Có mấy bản thêm câu 17 rằng: *Số là, đến ngày lễ, quan phải tha một tên tù cho dân.*

Đức Chúa Jêsus bị đóng đinh trên cây thập-tự

²⁶ Khi chúng điệu Đức Chúa Jêsus đi, bắt một người xứ Sy-ren, tên là Si-môn, từ ngoài đồng về, buộc phải vác cây thập-tự theo sau Ngài. ²⁷ Có đoàn dân đông lắm đi theo Đức Chúa Jêsus, và có mấy người đàn-bà đấm ngực khóc về Ngài. ²⁸ Nhưng Đức Chúa Jêsus xây mặt lại với họ mà phán rằng: Hỡi con gái thành Giê-ru-sa-lem, đừng khóc về ta, song khóc về chính mình các ngươi và về con-cái các ngươi. ²⁹ Vì nầy, ngày hầu đến, người ta sẽ nói rằng: Phước cho đàn-bà son, phước cho dạ không sanh-đẻ và vú không cho con bú! ³⁰ Bấy giờ, người ta sẽ nói với núi rằng: Hãy đổ xuống trên chúng ta! Với gò rằng: Hãy che chúng ta! ³¹ Vì nếu người ta làm những sự ấy cho cây xanh, thì cây khô sẽ xảy ra sao?

³² Chúng cũng đem hai người đi nữa, là kẻ trộm-cướp, để giết cùng với Ngài.

³³ Khi đến một chỗ gọi là chỗ Sọ, họ đóng đinh Ngài trên cây thập-tự tại đó, cùng hai tên trộm-cướp, một tên bên hữu Ngài, một tên bên tả. ³⁴ Song Đức Chúa Jêsus cầu rằng: Lạy Cha, xin tha cho họ, vì họ không biết mình làm điều gì. Đoạn, họ bắt thăm chia nhau áo-xống của Ngài. ³⁵ Dân-chúng đứng đó mà ngó. Các người coi việc nhạo-cười Ngài, rằng: Nó đã cứu kẻ khác; nếu nó là Đấng Christ, Đấng Đức Chúa Trời đã lựa, thì hãy cứu mình đi! ³⁶ Quân-lính cũng giỡn-cợt Ngài, lại gần đưa giấm cho Ngài uống, ³⁷ mà rằng: Nếu ngươi là Vua dân Giu-đa, hãy tự cứu lấy mình đi! ³⁸ Phía trên đầu Ngài, có để rằng: <u>Người nầy là Vua dân Giu-đa.</u>

³⁹ Vả, một tên trộm-cướp bị đóng đinh cũng mắng-nhiếc Ngài rằng: Ngươi không phải là Đấng Christ sao? Hãy tự cứu lấy mình ngươi cùng chúng ta nữa! ⁴⁰ Nhưng tên kia trách nó rằng: Ngươi cũng chịu một hình-phạt ấy, còn chẳng sợ Đức Chúa Trời sao? ⁴¹ Về phần chúng ta, chỉ là sự công-bình, vì hình ta chịu xứng với việc ta làm; nhưng người nầy không hề làm một điều gì ác. ⁴² Đoạn lại nói rằng: Hỡi Jêsus, khi Ngài đến trong nước mình rồi, xin nhớ lấy tôi! ⁴³ Đức Chúa Jêsus đáp rằng: Quả thật, ta nói cùng ngươi, hôm nay ngươi sẽ được ở với ta trong nơi Ba-ra-đi.ˣ

---

x **23:43** *Ba-ra-đi (Paradis)* hoặc dịch là *vườn vui-vẻ*, hoặc dịch là *thiên-đàng*.

⁴⁴ Khi đó, ước giờ thứ sáu, khắp xứ đều tối-tăm cho đến giờ thứ chín.ʸ ⁴⁵ Mặt trời trở nên tối, và màn trong đền-thờ xé chính giữa ra làm hai. ⁴⁶ Đức Chúa Jêsus bèn kêu lớn rằng: Hỡi Cha, tôi giao linh-hồn lại trong tay Cha! Ngài vừa nói xong thì tắt hơi.

⁴⁷ Thấy đội thấy sự đã xảy ra, ngợi-khen Đức Chúa Trời rằng: Thật người nầy là người công-bình. ⁴⁸ Cả dân-chúng đi xem, thấy nông-nổi làm vậy, đấm ngực mà trở về. ⁴⁹ Song những kẻ quen-biết Đức Chúa Jêsus và các người đàn-bà theo Ngài từ xứ Ga-li-lê, đều đứng đằng xa mà ngó.

Sự chôn Chúa

⁵⁰ Có một người, tên là Giô-sép, làm nghị-viên tòa công-luận, là người chánh-trực công-bình, ⁵¹ không đồng ý và cũng không dự việc các người kia đã làm. Người ở A-ri-ma-thê, là thành thuộc về xứ Giu-đê, vẫn trông-đợi nước Đức Chúa Trời. ⁵² Người bèn đi đến Phi-lát mà xin xác Đức Chúa Jêsus. ⁵³ Khi đã đem xác Ngài xuống khỏi cây thập-tự, người lấy vải liệm mà bọc, rồi chôn trong huyệt đã đục nơi hòn đá, là huyệt chưa chôn ai hết. ⁵⁴ Bấy giờ là ngày sắm-sửa, và ngày Sa-bát gần tới. ⁵⁵ Các người đàn-bà đã từ xứ Ga-li-lê đến với Đức Chúa Jêsus, theo Giô-sép, xem mả và cũng xem xác Ngài đặt thể nào. Khi trở về, họ sắm-sửa những thuốc thơm và sáp thơm. ⁵⁶ Ngày Sa-bát, họ nghỉ-ngơi theo luật-lệ.

Sự Chúa sống lại

24 ¹ Ngày thứ nhứt trong tuần-lễ, khi mờ sáng, các người đàn-bà ấy lấy thuốc thơm đã sửa-soạn đem đến mồ Ngài. ² Họ thấy hòn đá đã lăn ra khỏi cửa mồ; ³ nhưng, bước vào, không thấy xác Đức Chúa Jêsus. ⁴ Đương khi không biết nghĩ làm sao, xảy có hai người nam mặc áo sáng như chớp, hiện ra trước mặt họ. ⁵ Họ đương thất-kinh, úp mặt xuống đất; thì hai người ấy nói rằng: Sao các ngươi tìm người sống trong vòng kẻ chết? ⁶ Ngài không ở đây đâu, song Ngài đã sống lại. Hãy nhớ khi Ngài còn ở xứ Ga-li-lê, phán cùng các ngươi thể nào, ⁷ Ngài đã phán rằng: Con người phải bị nộp trong tay

---

y **23:44** Giờ thứ sáu đến giờ thứ chín: tức khoảng giữa trưa đến ba giờ chiều

kẻ có tội, phải đóng đinh trên cây thập-tự, và ngày thứ ba phải sống lại. ⁸ Họ bèn nhớ lại những lời Đức Chúa Jêsus đã phán.

⁹ Họ ở mổ trở về, rao-truyền mọi sự ấy cho mười một sứ-đồ và những người khác. ¹⁰ Ấy là Ma-ri Ma-đơ-len, Gian-nơ, và Ma-ri mẹ của Gia-cơ, cùng các đàn-bà khác đi với họ đã rao-truyền như vậy cho các sứ-đồ. ¹¹ Song các sứ-đồ không tin, cho lời ấy như là hư-không. ¹² Dẫu vậy, Phi-e-rơ đứng dậy, chạy đến mổ, cúi xuống mà dòm, chỉ thấy vải liệm ở trên đất, đoạn về nhà, lạ-lùng cho việc đã xảy ra.

Hai môn-đồ tại làng Em-ma-út

¹³ Cũng trong ngày ấy, có hai môn-đồ đi đến làng kia, gọi là Em-ma-út, cách thành Giê-ru-sa-lem sáu mươi ếch-ta-đơ;ᶻ ¹⁴ họ đàm-luận về những sự đã xảy ra. ¹⁵ Đang khi nói và cãi lẽ nhau, chính Đức Chúa Jêsus đến gần, cùng đi đường với họ. ¹⁶ Nhưng mắt hai người ấy bị che khuất không nhìn biết Ngài được. ¹⁷ Ngài phán cùng họ rằng: Các ngươi đương đi đường, nói chuyện gì cùng nhau vậy? Họ dừng lại, buồn-bực lắm. ¹⁸ Một trong hai người tên là Cơ-lê-ô-ba, trả lời rằng: Có phải chỉ ngươi là khách lạ ở thành Giê-ru-sa-lem, không hay việc đã xảy đến tại đó cách mấy bữa rày sao? ¹⁹ Ngài hỏi rằng: Việc gì vậy? Họ trả lời rằng: Ấy là việc đã xảy ra cho Jêsus Na-xa-rét, một đấng tiên-tri, có quyền-phép trong việc làm và trong lời nói, trước mặt Đức Chúa Trời và cả chúng dân; ²⁰ làm sao mà các thầy tế-lễ cả cùng các quan đề-hình ta đã nộp Ngài để xử-tử, và đã đóng đinh trên cây thập-tự. ²¹ Chúng tôi trông-mong Ngài sẽ cứu lấy dân Y-sơ-ra-ên; dẫu thể ấy, việc xảy ra đã được ba ngày rồi. ²² Thật có mấy người đàn-bà trong vòng chúng tôi đã làm cho chúng tôi lấy làm lạ lắm: Khi mờ sáng, họ đến mổ, ²³ không thấy xác Ngài, thì về báo rằng có thiên-sứ hiện đến, nói Ngài đương sống. ²⁴ Có mấy người trong vòng chúng tôi cũng đi thăm mổ, thấy mọi điều y như lời họ nói; còn Ngài thì không thấy. ²⁵ Đức Chúa Jêsus bèn phán rằng: Hỡi những kẻ dại-dột, có lòng chậm tin lời các đấng tiên-tri nói! ²⁶ Há chẳng phải Đấng Christ chịu thương-khó thể ấy, mới được vào sự vinh-hiển mình sao? ²⁷ Đoạn, Ngài bắt đầu từ Môi-se rồi kế đến mọi đấng

---

z **24:13** Sáu mươi **ếch-ta-đơ** độ bằng *mười hai ki-lô-mét.*

tiên-tri mà cắt nghĩa cho hai người đó những lời chỉ về Ngài trong cả Kinh-thánh. ²⁸ Khi hai người đi gần đến làng mình định đi, thì Đức Chúa Jêsus dường như muốn đi xa hơn nữa. ²⁹ Nhưng họ ép Ngài dừng lại, mà thưa rằng: Xin ở lại với chúng tôi; vì trời đã xế chiều hầu tối. Vậy, Ngài vào ở lại cùng họ. ³⁰ Đương khi Ngài ngồi ăn cùng hai người, thì lấy bánh, chúc-tạ, đoạn, bẻ ra cho họ. ³¹ Mắt họ bèn mở ra, mà nhìn biết Ngài; song Ngài thoạt biến đi không thấy. ³² Hai người nói cùng nhau rằng: Khi nãy đi đường, Ngài nói cùng chúng ta và cắt nghĩa Kinh-thánh, lòng chúng ta há chẳng nóng-nảy sao?

³³ Nội giờ đó, họ liền đứng dậy, trở về thành Giê-ru-sa-lem, gặp mười một sứ-đồ cùng các môn-đồ khác đương nhóm lại, ³⁴ nói với họ rằng: Chúa thật đã sống lại, và hiện ra với Si-môn. ³⁵ Rồi hai người thuật lại sự đã xảy đến khi đi đường, và nhìn biết Ngài lúc bẻ bánh ra là thể nào.

Sự hiện đến cùng mười một sứ-đồ

³⁶ Môn-đồ đương nói với nhau như vậy, chính Đức Chúa Jêsus hiện ra giữa đó mà phán rằng: Bình-an cho các ngươi! ³⁷ Nhưng môn-đồ đều sửng-sốt rụng-rời, tưởng thấy thần. ³⁸ Ngài phán rằng: Sao các ngươi bối-rối, và sao trong lòng các ngươi nghi làm vậy? ³⁹ Hãy xem tay chân ta: Thật chính ta. Hãy rờ đến ta, và hãy xem; thần thì không có thịt xương, mà các ngươi thấy ta có. ⁴⁰ Đương phán vậy, Ngài giơ tay và chân ra cho xem. ⁴¹ Nhưng vì cớ môn-đồ vui-mừng, nên chưa tin chắc, và lấy làm lạ, thì Ngài phán rằng: Ở đây các ngươi có gì ăn không? ⁴² Môn-đồ dâng cho Ngài một miếng cá nướng. ⁴³ Ngài nhận lấy mà ăn trước mặt môn-đồ.

⁴⁴ Đoạn, Ngài phán rằng: Ấy đó là điều mà khi ta còn ở với các ngươi, ta bảo các ngươi rằng mọi sự đã chép về ta trong luật-pháp Môi-se, các sách tiên-tri, cùng các thi-thiên phải được ứng-nghiệm. ⁴⁵ Bấy giờ Ngài mở trí cho môn-đồ được hiểu Kinh-thánh. ⁴⁶ Ngài phán: Có lời chép rằng Đấng Christ phải chịu đau-đớn dường ấy, ngày thứ ba sẽ từ kẻ chết sống lại, ⁴⁷ và người ta sẽ nhân danh Ngài mà rao-giảng cho dân các nước sự ăn-năn để được tha tội, bắt đầu từ thành Giê-ru-sa-lem. ⁴⁸ Các ngươi làm chứng về mọi việc đó; ta đây, sẽ ban cho các ngươi điều Cha ta đã hứa, ⁴⁹ còn về phần các ngươi,

hãy đợi trong thành[aa] cho đến khi được mặc lấy quyền-phép từ trên cao.

Sự ngự lên trời

⁵⁰ Kế đó, Ngài đem môn-đồ đi đến nơi xung-quanh làng Bê-tha-ni, giơ tay lên mà ban phước cho. ⁵¹ Đương khi ban phước, Ngài lìa môn-đồ mà được đem lên trời. ⁵² Môn-đồ thờ-lạy Ngài rồi trở về thành Giê-ru-sa-lem, mừng-rỡ lắm. ⁵³ Môn-đồ cứ ở trong đền-thờ luôn, ngợi-khen Đức Chúa Trời.

---

aa **24:49** Tức là *thành Giê-ru-sa-lem.*

*Notes * Notas * Note * Ghi chú*

Quý vị ăn mừng cùng gia đình mình—một tổ ấm của tình yêu và cuộc sống—ra sao sau khi quý vị rời khỏi Hội Ngộ Gia Đình Thế Giới? Hãy ghi danh cho một hành trình đọc kinh cống hiến Lectio Divina dài 21 ngày qua sách Phúc Âm Luke cùng gia đình hoặc cộng đồng quý vị. Khi quý vị lắng nghe Lời Chúa, và tĩnh tâm về những câu chuyện về hy vọng và hàn gắn, hãy để cho lời Thánh Kinh Thiêng Liêng chuyển đổi sự hiểu biết của quý vị về tình yêu vô điều kiện của Chúa Trời.

TĨNH TÂM
VỀ SÁCH PHÚC ÂM
LUKE CHO GIA ĐÌNH

Hãy ghi danh cho lần đọc kinh cống hiến Lectio Divina dài 21 ngày bằng một trong ba cách.

📱 Tin nhắn: Gởi tin nhắn **giadinh** đến 72717

✉️ Email: Vào trang www.abs.us/giadinh

⊕ Ứng dụng di động: Vào trang app.bible.com/wmf để tải xuống